Essential Papers on Judaism and Christianity in Conflict

ESSENTIAL PAPERS ON JEWISH STUDIES
General Editor: Robert M. Seltzer

Essential Papers on Judaism and Christianity in Conflict:
From Late Antiquity to the Reformation
Edited by Jeremy Cohen

Essential Papers on Hasidism: Origins to Present
Edited by Gershon David Hundert

Essential Papers on Jewish-Christian Relations in the United States:
Imagery and Reality
Edited by Naomi W. Cohen

Essential Papers on Israel and the Ancient Near East
Edited by Frederick E. Greenspahn

ESSENTIAL PAPERS ON JUDAISM AND CHRISTIANITY IN CONFLICT

From Late Antiquity to the Reformation

Edited by Jeremy Cohen

New York University Press
New York and London

Library of Congress Cataloging-in-Publication Data
Essential papers on Judaism and Christianity in conflict : from late
   antiquity to the Reformation / edited by Jeremy Cohen.
      p.   cm.—(Essential papers on Jewish studies)
   Includes bibliographical references.
      ISBN 0–8147–1442–0 (alk. paper)—ISBN 0–8147–1443–9
   (pbk. : alk. paper)
      1. Judaism—Relations—Christianity—History. 2. Christianity and
   other religions—Judism—History. 3. Judaism (Christian theology)—
   —History of doctrines. 4. Christianity and antisemitism.
   I. Cohen, Jeremy, 1953–   . II. Series.
   BM535.E86 1990
   261.2'6'09—dc20   90–5991
                             CIP

New York University Press books are printed on acid-free paper
and their binding materials are chosen for strength and durability.

Book design by Ken Venezio

Contents

III The Reformation

IV The Jewish Response

Acknowledgments

Grateful acknowledgment is due the College of Humanities and the Center for Medieval and Renaissance Studies at The Ohio State University, the Shalom Hartman Institute, and the State of Israel's Ministry of Absorption for grants which facilitated my research during the preparation of this volume. The Melton Center for Jewish Studies at The Ohio State University generously subsidized the cost of the index. My colleague Marc Lee Raphael offered valuable reactions to an earlier draft of the introduction. And, as always, my wife and children supported me and this project with their unfailing interest and encouragement.

Abbreviations

AHR	*American Historical Review*
ANRW	*Aufsteig und Niederhang der römischen Welt*
Ant.	Josephus, *Antiquities*
ʿAv. Zara	*ʿAvodah Zarah*
A.Z.	*ʿAvodah Zarah*
b,B	Babylonian Talmud
Barn.	Epistle of Barnabas
B.C.	*The Beginnings of Christianity,* ed. F. J. Foakes-Jackson and Kirsopp Lake, 5 vols., London, 1928.
BCH	*Bulletin de correspondance héllenistique*
Ber	*Bᵉrakhot*
BEvT	Beiträge zur evangelische Theologie
BJ	Josephus, *Jewish War*
B.J.R.L.	*Bulletin of the John Rylands Library*
Bul.	R. Bultmann, *Theologie des Neuen Testaments,* 2nd ed., Tübingen, 1954.
B.T.	Babylonian Talmud
C.A.H.	*Cambridge Ancient History*
CBQ	*Catholic Biblical Quarterly*
CCCM	Corpus Christianorum, Continuatio mediaevalis
CCSL	Corpus Christianorum, Series latina
CDC	Damascus Document
Civ. Dei	Augustine, *On the City of God*
C&J	Solomon Grayzel, *The Church and the Jews in the XIIIth Century*
I Clem.	First Epistle of Clement

COD	*Conciliorum oecumenicorum decreta*, ed. G. Alberigo *et al.*, Basel, 1962.
CR	*Corpus reformatorum*, Halle/Saale, 1835–60; 1905–.
CSEL	Corpus scriptorum ecclesiasticorum latinorum
DAC	*Dictionnaire d'archéologie chrétienne et de liturgie*
DSD	Manual of Discipline (1QS)
DSH	Commentary on Habakkuk (4QHab.)
DSS	Dead Sea Scrolls
DST	Thanksgiving Psalms (1QH)
DSW	War of the Sons of Light and the Sons of Darkness (1QM)
EJ	*Encyclopedia Judaica*, 16 vols., Jerusalem 1971–72.
E.R.E.	*Encyclopedia of Religion and Ethics*, ed. J. Hastings, 12 vols. and index vol., Edinburgh, 1908–26.
E.T.	English Translation
Gitt	*Giṭṭin*
G.J.V.	*Geschichte des jüdischen Volkes im Zeitalter Jesu Christi*, 3 vols., Leipzig, 1898–1901.
H.	Hilkhot
H.D.B.[2]	*Dictionary of the Bible*, ed. J. Hastings, 2nd ed., Edinburgh, 1963.
HE	*Historia ecclesiastica*
Herm.	*Shepherd of Hermas*
HF	*Recueil des historiens des Gaules et de la France*, 24 vols., Paris, 1738–1904.
HJ	*Historia judaica*
Hor	*Horayot*
HR	*History of Religions*
HTR	*Harvard Theological Review*
HUCA	*Hebrew Union College Annual*
Hull	*Ḥullin*
IEJ	*Israel Exploration Journal*
ILR	*Israel Law Review*
Interp	*Interpretation*
JBL	*Journal of Biblical Literature*
JBLMS	Journal of Biblical Literature Monograph Series
JJS	*Journal of Jewish Studies*
JQR	*Jewish Quarterly Review*
JTS	*Journal of Theological Studies*

KJ	King James Version
Krot.	Krotoszyn
LPV	*The Letters of Peter the Venerable*, ed. G. Constable, 2 vols., Harvard Historical Studies 78, Cambridge, Mass., 1967
LXX	Septuagint
m	Mishnah
Mag	To the Magnesians
Maim.	Maimonides
Mand.	Mandates
Meg	*M^egillah*
MGH	*Monumenta Germaniae historica*
MGWJ	*Monatsschrift für die Geschichte und Wissenschaft des Judentums*
MP	Matthew Paris, *Chronica majora*, ed. H. R. Luard, 7 vols., Rolls Series 57, London, 1872–84.
NTS	*New Testament Studies*
N.V.	*Nizzaḥon Vetus*
p	Palestinian Talmud
PAAJR	*Proceedings of the American Academy for Jewish Research*
PG	*Patrologia graeca*
Philadel	To the Philadelphians
PIBA	*Proceedings of the Irish Biblical Association*
PL	*Patrologia latina*
QI	D. Barthélemy and J. T. Milik, *Qumran Cave I*, Discovery in the Judaean Desert 1, Oxford, 1955.
R.A.C.	*Reallexikon für Antike und Christentum*, ed. T. Klauser, vols. I–VI (continuing), Stuttgart, 1950–66.
RB	*Revue biblique*
RE	*Real-Encyclopädie der klassischen Altertumswissenschaft* (Pauly-Wissowa)
REJ	*Revue des études juives*
RQH	*Revue des questions historiques*
RSh	*Rosh ha-Shanah*
RSV	Revised Standard Version
Sanh	*Sanhedrin*
SBL	Society for Biblical Literature

SBLDS	Society for Biblical Literature Dissertations Series
SBLSBS	Society for Biblical Literature Sources for Biblical Study
Shab.	*Shabbat*
Shek	*Sheqalim*
SJLA	Studies in Judaism in Late Antiquity
SNTSMS	Society for New Testament Studies Monograph Series
SPCK	Society for the Promotion of Christian Knowledge
SR	*Studies in Religion/Sciences religieuses*
SRH	S. W. Baron, *A Social and Religious History of the Jews*
t	Tosefta
Test. Judah	Testament of Judah
Test. Levi	Testament of Levi
TK	*Tosefta ki-Fshutah*, ed. Saul Lieberman, 9 vols., New York, 1955–73.
TNA	E. Martène and U. Durand, *Thesaurus novus anecdotorum*, vol. 5, Paris, 1717.
VC	*Vigiliae christianae*
Vit.	Josephus, *Life*
WA	D. Martin Luthers Werke: *Kritische Gesamtausgabe*, 58 vols. Weimar, 1883–.
WABr	D. Martin Luthers Werke: *Briefwechsel*, 15 vols., Weimar, 1930–.
WATR	D. Martin Luthers Werke: *Tischreden*, 6 vols., Weimar, 1912–21.
Yad.	*Yadayim*
Yer.	Palestinian Talmud
ZAW	*Zeitschrift für alttestamentliche Wissenschaft*
ZNTW	*Zeitschrift für neutestamentliche Wissenschaft*
ZNW	*Zeitschrift für neutestamentliche Wissenschaft*
1QSa,b	Manual of Discipline fragments

Editor's Note

Some chapters in this volume have abbreviated and slightly altered references. The reader is urged to consult the original sources for complete bibliographical citations.

Introduction

Jeremy Cohen

For the student of Jewish history, the topic of this book bears upon the very foundations of Jewish experience in Mediterranean and Western societies during the last two thousand years. For the generalist, too, it offers both a framework and material for discussion. The modern, critical study of the history of religions has yielded a more dispassionate approach to the phenomenon of conflict between religious communities, as well as to the polemical literature such conflict has produced. In the case of Christianity, an understanding of its origins within and its departure from the Jewish community necessarily informs an appreciation of its subsequent impact on Western social, political, and cultural history. Although we do not classify the Jews as "a minority" in contemporary American life, for centuries they were the only religious minority to be tolerated consistently in Christendom; their past relations with the Gentile majority continue to illuminate the dynamic of minority-majority interaction in a universal sense.

Perhaps most significant of all, the systematic extermination of one third of the world's Jews during World War II has awakened Jewish and Christian communities to the long history of their mutual hostility. As if to overcome the tragedy of the Holocaust by studying its etiology, a flurry of scholarly investigations has searched for the roots of modern anti-Semitism in pagan and Christian antiquity. Not only have such efforts developed in the academy, but they have facilitated a continuous series of ecumenical encounters between Christians and Jews—in books, in journals dedicated to this exchange of ideas, and at conferences. Lecturing at one such interfaith gathering several years ago, I learned that thousands of Americans regularly convene "to dialogue" in this ecumenical sense of a distinctive activity with objectives, techniques, and rules of etiquette all its own. Many Jews have welcomed this opportunity as a trail-blazing gesture of reconciliation and openmindedness among their Christian neighbors. For Christians, however, the incentive for dialogue has also reflected a nagging doctrinal and historical problem of paramount importance. As John Gager has eloquently observed, "the experience of the Holocaust reintroduced with unprecedented urgency the question of Christianity's responsibility for anti-Semitism: not simply whether individual Christians had added fuel to modern European anti-Semitism, but whether Christianity itself was, in its essence and from its beginnings, the primary source of anti-Semitism in Western culture."[1]

These modern concerns have generated an abundance of scholarly writing, which has constituted the subject of several valuable historiographical essays.[2] Yet the interest of theologians and other intellectuals in the antagonism between Judaism and Christianity extends back to antiquity, and the vast literature expressing that interest is as old as the conflict itself. Indeed, one often has difficulty distinguishing literary reflection *about* the conflict from active engagement *in* it, adding complexity to the task of the historian who seeks to survey and to classify the pertinent sources. In the face of these considerations, any selection of readings demands an explanation of its criteria; for even an anthology of modern scholarly interpretations, like this book, must be eclectic and, at times, perhaps arbitrary as well.

Above all else, I have endeavored to compile an anthology that will prove helpful in the classroom, in graduate and advanced undergraduate courses. In my own colloquium on "Judaism and Christianity in Conflict," I attempt to expose a broad spectrum of students, not merely the specialists in the history of one religion or the other, to the key issues of method and interpretation this subject entails. And I have assembled this volume with an eye to both student and teacher, presenting an array of readings that themselves suggest an agenda for such a course, even if an instructor should not assign them all. This introduction will therefore not undertake a comprehensive review of the field; nor will it serve as an exhaustive bibliographical guide.[3] But, highlighting the questions and the historiographical perspectives that have profitably afforded my courses their direction, it will explain the logic of my selections. These have been limited to publications in English and of sufficient brevity. Proceeding in the chronological order of their topics (and not that of their composition), they focus primarily on the history of ideas—that is, on the doctrinal substance of the Jewish-Christian dispute—and touch only secondarily on matters of political, socioeconomic, and literary history. Subjects like these are no less worthy of consideration; they neither figured insignificantly in the relations between Christians and Jews, nor failed to have an impact upon theology. Weighing on the nexus between religion and society, however, they lead the historian along a different path, they evoke different questions, and they warrant a separate volume. In weighing the respective merits of specific essays, I have sought to balance the stature of their authors, their historiographical influence, and their representation of the state of the field today. The deans of prior decades of scholarship shaped the very contours of the field, and the pioneering efforts of writers like Cecil Roth, Solomon Grayzel, Marcel Simon, and Bernhard Blumenkranz still have much to teach. Interspersed with the contributions of these sages, other entries in the table of contents exemplify landmark developments of historiography: S. G. F. Brandon's analysis of New Testament accounts of the crucifixion, for example; Jacob Katz's use of medieval legal texts to reconstruct the history of the rabbinic ethos; and Rosemary Ruether's conviction that anti-Judaism pervades the doctrinal core of classical Christianity. Finally, essays of the current decade reveal new directions and concerns to which the field has progressed—as in Ivan Marcus' employment of paradigm theory to analyze the Hebrew chronicles of the First Crusade or in Mark Edwards' even-handed approach to an evaluation of Martin Luther's anti-Jewish polemic.

This survey will focus first on the origins of conflict between Judaism and Christianity in late antiquity. It will next consider the character and evolution of Christian anti-Judaism within the purview of the medieval Roman Church. And then it will turn to developments of the sixteenth century and the reformation of Western Christianity—developments that at once marked the culmination of the Middle Ages and the emergence of a new, distinctively modern, era. For reasons elaborated below, discussion of Jewish anti-Christian polemic will await a final section all its own.

LATE ANTIQUITY

Christianity's birth within the Jewish community and its gradual with-drawal from that community are both fascinating and complex topics. The crucifixion of Jesus occurred between two centuries that saw the capitulation of an independent, Hasmonean Judea to the legions of Pompey the Great, the reign of Herod, the destruction of the Second Temple, the institutional foundation of rabbinic leadership, the canonization of the Hebrew Bible, and the failure of the Bar Kokhba rebellion. The conflict between the biblical ethos of Jerusalem and the classical civilization of Athens and Rome, an opposition that had already produced civil war and changed the configuration of Jewish society, continued to demand resolution. In the eyes of many Jews, the very survival of their biblical covenant with God was now at stake. This was a critical period in their history, an age of intense cultural ferment, of creative religious experimentation, and of desperate attempts to close the gap between the realities of the present and the glorified status that properly accompanied divine election.

For centuries, Christian writers consistently perceived Judaism of the late Second Temple period as theologically decadent and morally bankrupt. Such a characterization directly served the needs of their perspective, justifying the replacement of a stagnant *Spätjudentum,* or "late Judaism," by the new, upright, and vital faith of Christianity. Typical in this regard, the French Jesuit scholar Joseph Bonsirven thus concluded his study of *Palestinian Judaism in the Time of Christ:*

How shall we judge the Judaism we have described, that intermediate space, the bridge between the two Testaments? We cannot determine to what degree it benefits from the divine assistance reserved to the true religion, guardian and instrument of the unique revelation. In the eyes of a Christian, after the economy of the Law had been replaced by the economy of Faith, ancient Judaism had become more and more Pharisaic, and could not lay claim to divine assistance which would save it from error and deviation, sustain it with grace, and assure it of constant progress.[4]

The Pharisees, argued Bonsirven, brought Judaism to its unfortunate demise. They above all bore responsibility for its numerous "deficiencies":

the strict and hostile particularism, the rejection of mysticism and of supernatural concepts or operations, an anthropocentrism which leads to the exaggeration of the dignity of man and of the inviolability of his essence in relation to divine grace, a preference for the material and the sensible in religion, and finally, the tendency to make ethics a department of law.[5]

Responding to these developments, runs the argument, God transferred his election from a Pharisaic Israel of the flesh to a Christian Israel of the spirit.

One cannot but surmise that Bonsirven's characterization of "late" Judaism is in fact caricature: Christianity lacks all that which Judaism has, and *vice versa*. Bonsirven's work testifies to the difficulty of distinguishing scholarly treatment of the conflict between Judaism and Christianity from active participation in it, even in our own day and age. Yet, in recent decades, several factors have led both Jewish and Christian scholars to realize the numerous, substantive similarities between Judaism of the intertestamental period and primitive Christianity. First, some investigators have grown increasingly sensitive to the cultural heterogeneity of the Jewish community at the time of Jesus: A Jew might choose from a spectrum of sectarian ideologies and associations, or, like the majority of his coreligionists, he might remain "unaffiliated." One ought certainly to avoid depicting this Judaism as monolithic or stagnant, and one ought to use terms like "normative Judaism" only with caution and qualification. Similar tendencies have appeared in New Testament scholarship, allowing more for the notion of continuum—rather than polar opposition—in our appreciation of the earliest Jewish-Christian relations. Second, other scholars have illustrated the methodological flaws in an argument like Bonsirven's. For he used the surviving documents of classical rabbinic literature, none of which antedate the third century C.E., to generalize concerning Jewish life and belief some two hundred years earlier. (Many Jewish historians have committed the same error, although with resulting interpretations of rabbinic literature much more favorable to their forebears.)[6] At the same time, Bonsirven wrote too early to appreciate the significance of the Dead Sea Scrolls,[7] texts that were written by a Jewish community before the destruction of the Temple and that reveal a religious lifestyle closely related to that of the early Church. And third, the growth of an ecumenically concerned historiography in the wake of the Second Vatican Council has led to an increasingly sensitive demand for dispassionate, nonpartisan scholarly method. The flowering of classical rabbinic Judaism, only after the crucifixion of Jesus and the destruction of the Temple, can no longer evade recognition; it too derived from the same Jewish cultural milieu that gave birth to Christianity.

In "The Dead Sea Sect and Pre-Pauline Christianity," David Flusser presents from among the first fruits of this recent, more critical orientation. Reviewing the distinctive beliefs of the community at Qumran, Flusser notes a striking disparity between its theology and that of Jesus and his disciples reflected in the Synoptic Gospels. This proves, according to Flusser, that "Jesus and his followers were nearer to Pharisaic Judaism than to the Qumran sect"—a conclusion forcefully echoed by other recent investigators.[8] Nevertheless, Flusser does find considerable correspondence between the doctrine of the Dead Sea Scrolls and the Epistles and Johannine texts of the New Testament; he thereby lends support to the thesis of Rudolf Bultmann that a second theological stratum, that of "Hellenistic Christianity," existed alongside that of Palestinian Christianity in the earliest history of the Church. Practically all that was essential to the Qumran sectarians they bequeathed to this Christian outlook:

The world is divided into the realms of good and evil; mankind consists of two large camps: the Sons of Light—actually the community itself—and those who are of the Devil. The division is preordained by the sovereign will of God (double predestination). The Sons of Light are the Elect of Divine grace and were granted the Spirit which frees them from the sins of the flesh. Baptism functions as a means of atonement. The company of the Elect is a kind of spiritual temple; this company is constituted by a new covenant with God; this covenant is eschatological and additional to the old covenant made with Israel.

On the one hand, the consistent appearance of these motifs in most of the New Testament works mentioned suggests that their Christian authors did not draw directly on the Dead Sea Scrolls but on an intervening Christian source that influenced them all. On the other hand, the Qumran sectarians did not anticipate the early Church in every respect—particularly not in its Christology—nor did the Church use these ideas to erect so exclusive a social barrier around itself. In Flusser's words, old stones were used to erect a new house: "The material was not only collected, but fused, refashioned and enriched by the impact of the personality and teaching of Jesus and the tremendous creative forces unleashed by the new faith."

Given the ideological kinship between the first Christians and religious associations that remained within the fold of Judaism, how ought one to understand the manner whereby Christianity gradually departed from it? So much of the New Testament addresses this question in one respect or another, that it would be impossible here to summarize and classify the plethora of resulting scholarly viewpoints. Rather, we point to one particularly instructive framework for discussion, proposed by Peter Richardson some twenty years ago. Richardson established that the use of the term "Israel" to denote the Christian Church (as opposed to the Jewish community) first occurred in Justin Martyr's *Dialogue with Trypho*, composed around 160 C.E., and he proceeded to schematize the process of separation and distinction that culminated in that formulation. Richardson discerned historical, theological, and sociological dimensions to the problem, which arose in the aftermath of the crucifixion.

The most searching difficulties, after Jesus had come and revealed himself as Son of Man and Messiah, were posed by the twin questions of the status of unbelieving pious Jews and of Jews who had followed Jesus in the new Way of salvation. The original Jewish constitution of the Church depended upon certain simple facts: Jesus was himself a Jew; all his early disciples were Jews; his whole mission was centred upon Israel. To a very large extent, the function of these followers was to engage in a mission to Israel: to call all Israel to repentance before the Son of Man should come again. This Israelitic concern embraced an expectation for the gathering of the Gentiles as well, in fulfillment of the prophets' hope, but the mission was not Gentile-centred, becoming so only at a later date. As an initially Jewish protest movement, problems of the self-designation, life, and organization of the early community were all set by an *apologia* to the rest of the Jewish people.[9]

Most Jews, however, refused to accept the announcement of the heavenly kingdom, isolating its heralds from the mainstream, and the failure of the second coming to materialize rapidly further complicated their self-perceptions. The key in overcoming these difficulties was, of course, the theology of Paul, who opened the doors of the Church to the Gentiles. Just as important, Paul redirected the missionary priorities of the Church outside of the Jewish community, and at the same time he offered Gentile converts all that Scripture had promised Israel, without demanding that they keep the Law as Jews. Paul thus proffered the first, tentative distinction between the true Israel and the Jews. As Gentiles flowed into the Church, as the destruction of the Temple intensified resistance and hostility among the Jews, and as the evangelists all aired the belief that the divine covenant no longer resided within the Jewish community, that distinction grew progressively more pronounced in the Christian consciousness.

The sort of interpretation proposed by Richardson reflects much of the direction taken by New Testament scholarship until the mid-1960s, and it also enables one to appreciate developments that have transpired since. More recent investigators have sought to nuance, to modify, and, at times, to revise the substance of Richardson's thesis. Collectively, perhaps they have questioned the nearly teleological thrust of the argument: Richardson appears to suggest that the Church's departure from the Synagogue was inevitable and appropriate and that most of the documents of the New Testament derived from and contributed to the process. Granted, the Church did ultimately appropriate the title "Israel" for itself. Yet some scholars have explored the diverse mechanisms at work at each step along the way from the crucifixion to Justin; sociological and psychological factors not only joined theological issues in forging the character of Christianity, but may even have generated those issues. Some writers have challenged the clarity of the distinction between Christian and Jew implied by Justin's terminology. Although theologians like Justin may have advocated complete separation from the Jewish community, evidence from Justin's age and succeeding generations reveals more of a socioreligious continuum between Christians and Jews than a polar opposition. Such proximity may actually have motivated the *Adversus Judaeos* polemic of Justin, John Chrysostom, Cyril of Alexandria, and others in the first place.

Other investigators, like Wayne Meeks in "Breaking Away: Three Separate Pictures of Christianity's Separation from the Jewish Communities," have challenged the coherence of the New Testament's reaction to the Jews. Meeks demonstrates considerable diversity in the perspectives of New Testament writers on the Jews and their way of life—writers whose theological expressions may only be understood as products of their respective—and markedly different—social contexts. Meeks envisions John's Gospel as originating within a (probably Palestinian) matrix of interaction between Judeans ("the Jews" in most biblical translations), Galileans, and Samaritans—readily distinguishable groups with defining characteristics and tendencies. John and his Church perceive the Judeans as organized into synagogues, the Christians' recent exclusion from which results in animus toward the Judeans, just as it bolsters the singular identity of the Christians. Paul's constituencies, however, reside in the Greek *poleis* of the Eastern Empire, having little regular interaction with an organized Jewish community. The Pauline Epistles contain strikingly few references to the Jews, and Judaism—or, more precisely, the status of the Torah—constitutes a doctrinal issue internal to the Church, bearing only indirectly on actual relations to the Synagogue. The uniquely Matthean diatribe against the Pharisees and scribes, argues Meeks, strikes a middle ground. Matthew converses in the language and frame of reference of an early rabbinic community; yet his Christian audience already feels alienated from that world, having evolved in a way that perhaps parallels Jesus' own dramatic development as a character in the First Gospel.

Surely the indictment of the Jews as collectively responsible for the death of Jesus marked one milestone in the divergence of Jewish and Christian communities. Matthew's Gospel (27:24–25 RSV) depicts the Jews as acknowledging their own culpability in this regard:

So when Pilate saw that he was gaining nothing, but rather that a riot was beginning, he took water and washed his hands before the crowd, saying, "I am innocent of this man's blood, see to it yourselves." And all the people answered, "His blood be on us and on our children!"

As early as the second century, the stereotypical identification of the Jew as Christ-killer fueled actual discussion between Christians and Jews; in his poem *On Pascha,* Bishop Melito of Sardis condemned the Jews for their crime despite their protestations.

> What have you done, Israel? Or is it not written for you,
> "You shall not shed innocent blood,"
>   so that you may not die an evil death?"
> "I did," says Israel, "kill the Lord.
>   Why? Because he had to die."
> You are mistaken, Israel, to use such subtle evasions
>   about the slaying of the Lord.
> He had to suffer, but not by you;
> he had to be dishonoured, but not by you;
> he had to be judged, but not by you;
> he had to be hung up, but not by you
>   and your right hand.[10]

Although Melito's *On Pascha* was written for the liturgical celebration of Easter and was not the transcript of a debate, the poem clearly reflects

actual discussion between Christians and Jews, as well as what comprised a typical Jewish response to the Christian accusation: According
to Christian belief, if Jesus were the divine messiah, he had to suffer and
die to fulfill his salvific role; the Jews who killed him deserve praise for
their assistance, not reproach and condemnation. Curiously, even the
Jews accepted the essential veracity of the Gospels' Passion narrative.
Only at the Second Vatican Council, in its ecumenically minded decree
of *Nostra aetate,* did the Church repudiate its long established tradition:
"True, authorities of the Jews and those who followed their lead pressed
for the death of Christ; still, what happened in His passion cannot be
blamed upon all the Jews then living, without distinction, nor upon the
Jews of today."[11]

The Vatican decree is striking in that it confronts the stereotype of the
Jew as Christ-killer merely as a problem of evangelistic hyperbole: Some
Jews, but not all, shared in the responsibility for the crucifixion. One
immediately wants to ask, how many? A few? A large number? Most?
Yet such a line of inquiry overlooks the theological origins of the Christ-
killer motif—that it developed and flourished as a typological expression of (real and/or perceived) Jewish hostility after the crucifixion of
Jesus much more than it reflected the actual events of his life. Twentieth-
century scholars have wisely begun to treat the problem as historiographical rather than historical. In "History or Theology? The Basic
Problems of the Evidence of the Trial of Jesus," S. G. F. Brandon
elucidates the theological character of New Testament reflection on the
crucifixion. Brandon postulates the existence of an earlier Passion narrative maintained by the disciples of Jesus in Jerusalem, from which the
evangelists drew the core of their accounts but from which their Pauline
and Gentile orientation caused them to differ. While Paul and the evangelists regarded the death of Jesus "as the vicarious sacrifice of the Son
of God for the salvation of mankind," the earliest Jewish Christians had
little to profit from casting blame on the Jewish community at large.

They, on the contrary, were essentially concerned with the life of the historical
Jesus, whom they recognised as the Messiah of their people. Their desire to win
their countrymen to their own faith in the Messiahship of Jesus caused them
both to formulate accounts of Jesus' sayings and deeds which attested his Messianic character, and to compose an apologia concerning his trial which defended
him against an accusation of hostility towards the Temple.

Many have argued strenuously against Brandon's own reconstruction of the events of Jesus' last days,[12] but his underlying methodological premises deserve recognition: Traditions concerning Jewish guilt for the crucifixion ultimately derive from the history of Christian theology more than they originate in the biography of Jesus.

The question of the sources of early Christian anti-Judaism also received the attention of Marcel Simon, whose *Verus Israel: A Study of the Relations Between Christians and Jews in the Roman Empire (135–425)* has only recently appeared in English translation. More than most of his Christian predecessors, Simon endeavored to present a balanced picture of competition between Christianity and Judaism during the first three centuries of the patristic era. He deviated from a partisan, ideologically motivated posture in casting late antique Judaism as the faith of a thriving, vital religious community, the destruction of the Temple and the defeat of the Bar Kokhba rebellion notwithstanding. And in the chapter on "Christian Anti-Semitism" (reprinted in this collection), Simon acknowledges the prominence of anti-Jewish sentiments among Christian clergy and laity alike, particularly after the conversion of Constantine early in the fourth century. Noting the virulent animosity of Church fathers like Gregory of Nyssa and John Chrysostom, Simon explains how they and others systematically incorporated their prejudices into the heart of their Christian theology. Yet Simon still criticizes Jewish historians like Jean Juster for underestimating the pagan roots of Christian anti-Judaism, and thus for exaggerating the hatred which Christological doctrine itself had spawned. Rooted in the peculiarity and separatism of Jewish religious life, "the anti-Semitic attitudes of the pagan world were, on any showing, the foundation on which Christian anti-Semitism was built." To be sure, patristic writers transformed social prejudice and resentment into moral and doctrinal categories of condemnation; they accorded their hatred of Jews theological sanction and authority; and they added to the existing (i.e., pagan) catalogue of anti-Jewish calumnies. But in so doing, they perpetuated the general sentiments of a classical civilization. "The old accusations, which sprang originally from pagan malevolence, gain a new lease of life under the pens of Christians. They also gain a new virulence. They thus continue, in a revived form, the traditional animosity of the Greco-Roman world, lately Christianized."

No modern study of the Jewish-Christian conflict can properly bypass the monumental contribution of Catholic theologian Rosemary Ruether, whose *Faith and Fratricide: The Theological Roots of Anti-Semitism* laid the blame for modern anti-Semitism squarely upon Christianity. More forcefully than any non-Jewish scholar before her, Ruether argued that Christian theology is quintessentially anti-Jewish, that the rejection and degradation of Judaism were central to the messages of Paul, the evangelists, and other New Testament writers. Understandably, Ruether has elicited both acclaim and opposition in contemporary Christian circles. But whatever one's reaction to her thesis, one must acknowledge that she has enunciated her position without reticence or qualification, compelling her readers to review and refine—if not to revise—their own respective interpretations.

Ruether opened her book with an essay on Jews and Judaism in the first-century Greco-Roman world, in which she minimized the influence of pagan hostility toward the Jews in the evolution of Christian anti-Judaism. Hotly contesting the interpretation of Simon, J. N. Sevenster, and others, she acknowledged that

pagan anti-Semitism provided a certain seed bed of cultural antipathy to the Jews in Greco-Roman society, which Christianity inherited in inheriting that world. But this antipathy had been kept in check and balanced by Roman practicality and Hellenistic Jewish cultural apologetics. It was only when Christianity, with its distinctively religious type of anti-Semitism, based on profound theological cleavage within the fraternity of biblical religion, entered the picture that we begin to have that special translation of religious hatred into social hatred that is to become characteristic of Christendom.[13]

Proceeding next to an analysis of Christian Scripture, Ruether then turned to the patristic era, her treatment of which, in abridged form, reappeared in "The *Adversus Judaeos* Tradition in the Church Fathers: The Exegesis of Christian Anti-Judaism." As the Church emerged from the apostolic age with a need systematically to define its ideology and its institutional character, patristic authors combed through the "Old Testament" to amass additional evidence for the Christology of the New.

This anti-Judaic "left hand" of Christological interpretation was designed to show why the Jewish religious community, from which Christianity got both its Scripture and its messianic hope (which it believed fulfilled in Jesus), did not accept this "fulfillment" of its own tradition. In effect, the Church sought to discredit the rival rabbinic exegesis of this same Scripture and to build up a case against the Jewish religious community and its teachers in order to confirm its own faith as the authentic culmination of the Jewish religious tradition.

The fathers amassed biblical testimony to substantiate the divine rejection of the Jews and election of the Christians, the replacement of the old covenant, and the essentially inferior and reprobate character of Judaism: The refusal to accept Christianity culminated a lengthy series of crimes that comprised the substance of Jewish history. God had always foreseen his convenant with a spiritually defined, Gentile "Israel," of which the Hebrew Bible itself offers ample prefiguration. Simply put, *Adversus Judaeos* polemic amounted to an assertion of Christianity through the negation of Judaism. Directed almost exclusively to Christians, it allowed the Church fathers to convince their constituency that the fundamental principles of their theology—not those of the more ancient Jewish community—were indeed authentic. As John Chrysostom instructed his parishioners in late fourth-century Antioch:

Where Christ-killers gather, the cross is ridiculed, God blasphemed, the father unacknowledged, the son insulted, the grace of the Spirit rejected. . . . If the Jewish rites are holy and venerable, our way of life must be false. But if our way is true, as indeed it is, theirs is fraudulent. I am not speaking of the Scriptures. Far from it! For they lead one to Christ. I am speaking of their present impiety and madness.[14]

Ruether's exposition of patristic anti-Judaism is probably the most compelling component of her thesis; one is hard pressed to discount the hatred that permeates the sermons and writings of the most illustrious fathers. Nevertheless, perhaps her most vulnerable contention is that anti-Judaism resulted inevitably and necessarily from Christianity. Ruether's critics have argued vehemently that Christian theology could conceivably have developed otherwise, without compromising the Christological integrity of the faith.[15] Indeed, the Judaizing among the Christians of Antioch that precipitated Chrysostom's sermons suggests that, unlike the preacher, many refused to see Judaism and Christianity as mutually exclusive.

MEDIEVAL LATIN CHRISTENDOM

Adversus Judaeos emerged from late antiquity as a cornerstone of Christian doctrine, but, paradoxically, it facilitated the survival and protection of the Jews during much of the European Middle Ages. This paradox received its most influential expression in Augustine of Hippo's *On the City of God*. Reviewing the Jews' rejection of Christianity and their responsibility for the crucifixion of Jesus, Augustine questioned why God permitted them to survive in a world now predominantly Christian.

But the Jews who killed him and refused to believe in him, to believe that he had to die and rise again, suffered a more wretched devastation at the hands of the Romans and were utterly uprooted from their kingdom, where they had already been under the dominion of foreigners. They were dispersed all over the world —for indeed there is no part of the earth where they are not to be found—and thus by the evidence of their own Scriptures they bear witness for us that we have not fabricated the prophecies about Christ. . . . We recognize that it is in order to give this testimony, which, in spite of themselves, they supply for our benefit by their possession and preservation of those books, that they themselves are dispersed among all nations, in whatever direction the Christian Church spreads. . . . This is the reason for his [God's] forbearing to slay them—that is for not putting an end to their existence as Jews, although they have been conquered and oppressed by the Romans; it is for fear that they should not forget the Law of God and thus fail to bear convincing witness.[16]

Christian society required the presence of Jews, whose Scripture and whose blind adherence to its carnal, strictly literal meaning established that while Christians had inherited the election of God, Jews remained "stationary in useless antiquity."[17] As one medieval writer later observed, "Even today the Jews are to be allowed to live, because they are our enslaved book-bearers, as they carry around the prophets and the law of Moses for the assertion of our faith. Not only in their books but also in their faces do we read of the passion of Christ."[18]

More than anyone else, Bernhard Blumenkranz has investigated the complexities and impact of the Augustinian position *vis-à-vis* the Jews. Summarizing the insights of his groundbreaking books on the subject,[19] Blumenkranz's "The Roman Church and the Jews" maintains that throughout the early Middle Ages, the theological climate of European Christendom usually facilitated the security and prosperity of the Jewish community.

In the history of relations between the Church and the Jews, the High Middle Ages in the West is an exceptional period. Generally speaking, at no other time were relations between the two communities so relatively smooth—and this without the Jews having to renounce any of their beliefs and practices, even the right to conduct missionary activities.

Violence against the Jews was prohibited. The assertion that Christians everywhere required a Jewish presence in their midst effectively eliminated any theological incentive for missionizing among the Jews or for expelling them. The function performed by the Jews depended upon their observance of Mosaic law. And while churchmen consistently interpreted the Jews' purpose as demanding their subjugation and inferiority to Christians, conciliar decrees and royal edicts seeking to implement such discrimination regularly remained unenforced. Albeit small in number, early medieval European Jewry thrived and actually competed with the Christian majority, perhaps winning more converts to Judaism than losing Jews to Christianity. To be sure, political and economic considerations induced princes and prelates alike to accord the Jews favorable treatment. Yet the very nature of the Augustinian argument also militated against a tendency to observe and to police the *realia* of Jewish life with care. Church fathers like Augustine simply presumed that the Jews and their Judaism, having resisted the teleological imperatives of the Old Testament in its replacement by the New, were relics of a moribund past. In making this assumption, however, the fathers themselves were blind to the efflorescence of a postbiblical, rabbinic Judaism precisely in the centuries after the crucifixion of Jesus. Christian theology demanded otherwise! Beryl Smalley has rightly noted that "Philo's 'wise architect' [of allegorical exegesis] had built a prison for the Jewish people."[20] Having derived from historically inaccurate premises, such typological internment may have predisposed Christendom to remain aloof to historical reality. Allowing European Jews to "do their own thing," the medieval Church unwittingly became their foremost protector.

In "The Papal Bull *Sicut Judeis*," Solomon Grayzel traces the history of the law with which nearly two dozen medieval popes sought to guarantee the toleration of European Jews. The bull drew its title from an edict of Pope Gregory the Great adjudicating a grievance lodged by Jews in 598. Just as the Jews ought not to be permitted to exceed their privileges in Christian society, so they ought not to be denied what is rightfully permitted them. Gregory thus responded to Jewish complaints of Christian violence and persecution, and, beginning in the twelfth century, Gregory's high and late medieval successors regularly followed suit. In the wake of the anti-Jewish violence that accompanied the early Crusades, European rulers commonly recognized the Jews' need for special protection; and once it was issued by Pope Calixtus II around 1120, the Jews of Rome and the Holy Roman Empire deemed the bull an armament to use in their defense. Several popes of the high Middle Ages expanded the general formula of restriction *cum* toleration in noteworthy fashion. The most powerful of all medieval popes, Innocent III (1198–1216) prefaced his rendition of *Sicut Judeis* with a theological rationale, explaining the bull's dependence on *Adversus Judaeos* doctrine of an Augustinian variety.

Although the Jewish distortion of the faith is deserving of thorough condemnation, nevertheless, because the truth of our own faith is proved through them, they must not be severely oppressed by the faithful. So the prophet says, "Thou shalt not kill them, lest in time they forget Thy Law"; or, more clearly put: Thou shalt not destroy the Jews completely so that the Christians may not possibly forget Thy Law which, though they themselves fail to understand it, they display in their books for those who do understand.

Popes Innocent IV and Gregory X added clauses to their *Sicut Judeis* bulls protecting the Jewish community from ritual murder accusations, and Pope Martin IV appended a warning against undue harassment by inquisitors. But as the Middle Ages wore on, *Sicut Judeis* grew less effective in its ability to protect Jews from actual violence. Perhaps its text had become too commonplace and formulaic; perhaps the climate of opinion in Christendom had changed as well. Grayzel therefore concludes that "it is an exaggeration to speak of the Bull *Sicut Judeis* as the papal pronouncement that protected the Jews during the Middle Ages." Its significance was at least as symbolic as it was practical. For it proclaimed the obverse of patristic *Adversus Judaeos* theology: The Jews have a rightful place in a properly ordered Christian society. "Probably the greatest protection offered by the Church was its constant reminder of human decencies and its reference to the Jewish people as an integral part of the Divine Plan. Christianity's unwillingness to surrender completely to its Greek heritage and its retention of its heritage from Judaism thus contributed to the survival of the Jewish people."

The relative tranquility of Jewish-Christian relations during the early medieval period contrasts sharply with their decline several centuries later. Between 1290 and 1541, the Jews were expelled from England, France, Spain, Sicily, Portugal, the Kingdom of Naples, and much of

Germany. Where they remained in Western Europe—in the papal states, northern Italy, and portions of Germany—they were increasingly confined to ghettoes and subject to other forms of discrimination. Jewish books were burned and censored; Jews were barred from numerous forms of economic activity; and Jewish synagogues were open to visits from hostile Christian preachers. Modern historians have debated the extent to which considerations of Christian religious ideology contributed to the worsening station of medieval European Jewry, and some have discounted theological factors completely; political and socioeconomic developments, they maintain, hold the key to the puzzle.[21] Yet others have continued to search for changes in ideological climate that bear on the problem as well: If the Church stood by its commitment to the tenets of *Adversus Judaeos* theology, how could it have countenanced—and even fueled—the expulsion of the Jews from Christendom?

Many investigators have looked to the anti-Jewish violence that accompanied the Crusades as a decisive turning point in medieval Jewish history, after which the plight of the Jew grew steadily worse. The massacres of Franco-German Jewish communities in the name of Catholic piety revealed the inadequacy of existing legal safeguards for the person and property of the Jew. The need for greater protection enhanced his dependence on Christian princes, without whose good will he remained at the mercy of an increasingly hostile European society. The physical persecution of the Jews, although technically illegal, simultaneously awakened Latin Christendom to their anomalous situation. Why were the enemies of Christ permitted to thrive within the borders of Christian Europe, which was depleting its resources in holy wars against the infidels abroad? Haim Hillel Ben-Sasson has thus concluded: "Christian religious fervour had kindled a fire in the tents of Jacob and had led to slaughter in his habitations. The blood of the Jews had, as it were, been made free for the Christian masses. In respect to legal formulations, security, and possibilities of livlihood, the First Crusade inaugurated a new and harsh epoch for Jews in Christian lands."[22]

Among the more nuanced expositions of this interpretation, Hans Liebeschütz's "The Crusading Movement in Its Bearing on the Christian Attitude towards Jewry" stresses the "interplay of ideas and actions" in the Crusades' negative impact on the Jewish community. The mobilization of European society in the service of God, fueled by the classic reverence for religious pilgrimage and by rising messianic expectation, transformed the Church and its flock into a zealous "fighting force in the most literal sense of the word." And such a trend understandably boded ill for the Jews.

The most lasting result of this development was a stronger feeling of Christian solidarity, which could be mobilised against any whose attitude characterised them, in particular circumstances, as outsiders. This possibility would necessarily increase sensitivity towards any group who, of their own will, stood out as permanent antagonists of Christianity. For this attitude Jewry was the classical example in the midst of a world now deeply penetrated in its everyday life by ecclesiastical doctrine.

Although the crusading movement subsided by the end of the thirteenth century, its negative impact on the image of the Jews lived on, and the perception of the Jew as outsider served as a catalyst for political, social, and economic processes to take their toll.

In his chapter on the Jews in *Religious Poverty and the Profit Economy in Medieval Europe,* Lester K. Little also highlights the crusading era as a turning point in the medieval Jewish experience, yet for strikingly different reasons. As Christian Europe underwent a transition from a "gift economy" to a "profit economy," Little argues, it projected onto the Jews its own theologically derived guilt for numerous shortcomings. Just as Christian guilt for anti-Jewish violence underlay charges that Jews committed ritual murder and Christian doubts concerning transubstantiation yielded accusations that Jews desecrated the host, numerous associations of the Jews with filth, feces, and the devil betrayed the misgivings of Christians for their own financial enterprise. "Christians hated Jews because they saw in Jews the same calculating for profit in which they themselves were deeply and, in their own view, unjustifiably involved. It was above all the guilt for this involvement that they projected onto the Jews. The Jews functioned as a scapegoat for Christian failure to adapt successfully to the profit economy." According to Little, anti-Jewish violence continued in medieval Europe until new urban expressions of Christian spiritually could neutralize the guilt that the marketplace generated. At that point, Jews neither provided economic services otherwise unavailable, nor were they needed as scapegoats, and the rulers of Europe conveniently expelled them.

Like Bernhard Blumenkranz, Cecil Roth has noted the decline of European Jewry after 1096, but he has looked elsewhere than to the

Crusades in order to explain the animus and persecution which the Jews encountered in late medieval Christendom. In "The Medieval Conception of the Jew," one of his early and seldom quoted essays, Roth ponders "the amazing mentality which contemporary [i.e., medieval] literature, records, and chronicles appear to ascribe to the Jew." The Jew behaves like no other humans, he defies the blatant rationality of Christianity, and he clings to his perversity even when publicly ridiculed. How could medieval churchmen find proof for Christianity in the Bible, Talmud, and Midrash, and the Jews still refuse to believe? Roth responds to this question by delineating a medieval conception of the Jew as "a deliberate unbeliever"—not one who was blind to the truth, but one who knew the truth and spurned it nonetheless. Only such a Jewish mentality could explain the betrayal and crucifixion of Jesus, and such was the mentality bequeathed to posterity by the Jews of the first century. "Their medieval descendants, had they been present at the time, would *ex hypothesi* have acted in a precisely similar manner, for the attitude was one inherent in the Jewish nature in all ages." On this basis, Roth concludes, Christian society accused the Jews of inhuman, utterly demonic behavior—in a word, all that undermined the foundations of nature and civilization. Accusations that Jews engaged in desecration of the host, well-poisoning, treason, and ritual murder, along with the outlandish blood libel, flourished during the high and later Middle Ages, because the Jews were deemed the "constitutional antagonists of Jesus Christ." And "individuals whose whole life was a perpetual conflict against Jesus and his followers were capable of any crime, imaginable or unimaginable."

Convinced that Roth's interpretation has much to commend it and that the contribution of his essay has not been sufficiently appreciated, I have endeavored to investigate the causes and impact of changing theological evaluations of Judaism in the Middle Ages. In a series of recent studies, I have argued that the conception of the Jew as heretic or deliberate unbeliever emerged primarily in the anti-Jewish polemic and activities of Dominican and Franciscan friars.[23] Established by the papacy early in the thirteenth century in order to combat heresy, the two new mendicant orders provided the Church with the most effective means for realizing its vision of an ideally ordered Christian society. The friars served Christendom as university professors, inquisitors, missionaries, itinerant preachers, royal confessors, and exemplars of apostolic piety, as they sought to regulate all aspects of thought and action in European society in accordance with a grand design. It is no wonder that they moved to the forefront of interaction between the Church and the Jews and that they quickly perceived that medieval Jews were not in fact the relics of "useless antiquity" whose preservation in Christendom Augustine had sanctioned. In the first extensive Christian encounter with the Talmud, thirteenth-century friars realized that medieval Judaism was a vital, evolving, postbiblical religion, whose adherents thereby challenged the fundamental premise of Christian theology—that the sole fulfillment of the Old Testament lay in the New. Obsessed with the medieval concern for order, however, the friars did not simply update and correct the misguided patristic understanding of Judaism. Rather, they concluded that contemporary Jews were not the biblical Jews properly included in Christendom; they were heretics vis-à-vis their own Judaism! The rabbis of late antiquity had indeed recognized the truth of Christianity, but for reasons of spite and self-aggrandizement, they had fabricated a new, nonbiblical, talmudic religion instead.

Such a reconstruction of Jewish history, I believe, underlay the medieval condemnations of the Talmud and rabbinic literature, which began in the thirteenth century. It moved mendicant inquisitors and missionaries to harass medieval Jews, to engage them in disputation, and to proselytize actively among them. It was reflected in a new appreciation of the Jewish role in Jesus' crucifixion: If, until the twelfth century, most Christian writers had believed that the Jews crucified Jesus in ignorance of his divine character, mendicant professors of theology at the University of Paris now argued that the Jews recognized Jesus as their messiah, perhaps even as the son of God, and killed him nonetheless. Although they proceeded from the same theoretical premise, that a real Jew was a petrified, biblical Jew,[24] the friars effectively reversed the practical applications of patristic Adversus Judaeos theology; in their view, the books and adherents of contemporary Judaism no longer had a rightful place in Western Christendom.

My "Scholarship and Intolerance in the Medieval Academy" attempts to set these developments against the background of the great cultural and intellectual awakening of Europe in the twelfth and thirteenth centuries. In particular, the shift of the focus of medieval scholarship from rural monastery to urban school and then to metropolitan university infused new vitality and awareness into the study of Scripture and theology. During the twelfth century, a growing critical spirit in biblical exegesis drove Christian commentators on the Old Testament to consult with rabbis and even to study Hebrew in search of its literal sense. At first, the Christian scholar continued to assume that in talking to a medieval rabbi, "he was telephoning to the Old Testament." But gradually churchmen came to sense the chronological and substantive distance between medieval rabbinic Judaism and biblical antiquity. And as the thirteenth-century university curriculum glorified theology as the queen of the sciences, builders of the Scholastic synthesis, most of them friars, grew sensitive to the interplay of their use of Judaic traditions with the logical demands of *Adversus Judaeos* polemic. While biblical exegetes continued to place greater emphasis on the literal sense of Scripture, recognizing the value of the *hebraica veritas,* increased Christian knowledge of Hebrew also allowed for the "liberation" of Old Testament study from rabbinic interpretation. The thirteenth century saw a new polemical rejection of the contemporary Jew as no longer valuable in facilitating a Christian encounter with the Old Testament. At the same time, familiarity with Hebraic sources also fueled a more direct and aggressive anti-Jewish polemic, which, alongside various political and socioeconomic factors, undermined the security and presence of the Jew in European Christendom.

PROTESTANT REFORMATION AND CATHOLIC RESTORATION

The sixteenth century marked a critical period of transition for European Jews and Christians alike. In the wake of the flurry of medieval expulsions, Jewish life in Western Europe came to a virtual standstill. By midcentury, Jews could reside only in portions of Germany, in the papal states, and in the Northern Italian cities, areas where most Jewish communities encountered increasingly harsh forms of discrimination. In Eastern Europe, however, Ashkenazic Jewry had discovered refuge and opportunity. Several generations of marked material prosperity and intense cultural creativity now awaited the Jews of Poland and Lithuania, prior to the Chmielnitzki massacres and the socioreligious decay that would ensue in their aftermath.

While Jews still struggled to cope with the alienation and political subjugation that life in the Diaspora had entailed for over a thousand years and more, for the Christian society of Western Europe the Middle

Ages had ended. The mold of the mystical body of Christ, conformity to whose design the Roman Church repeatedly demanded of European Christendom, had suffered a series of permanent dismemberments. The Scholastic synthesis succumbed before the critique of the nominalists and the vitality of Renaissance humanism. Catholic discipline could not restrain the free spirit of popular heresy which threatened the very credibility and survival of holy mother Church. The throne of St. Peter had fallen prey to schism, opportunism, and abuse. The conciliar movement that attempted to mend these wounds awakened new debate over the propriety of papal rule in the community of God's faithful. National states and independent principalities now replaced the feudal organization of medieval polities. Concisely put, the foundations of medieval civilization were giving way to those of modernity.

With the early phases of the Reformation, this volume reaches the final extent of its chronological purview—not because the conflict between Judaism and Christianity has ended, but because, in theological terms, it too then reached an outer limit in its development. Having arisen within the Jewish community of late antiquity, Christianity departed from that community, triumphed over the Greco-Roman world, and contributed to the forging of a Western Europe virtually *Judenrein*. The centuries following the sixteenth witnessed the gradual return of Jews to the West on a qualitatively different basis; previously aliens on the periphery of medieval society, Jews have since secured civil emancipation throughout the Western world. While Hitler's Final Solution for the Jews unquestionably capitalized upon traditions and myths of Christian anti-Judaism deeply rooted in European culture, and while these traditions and myths may well have expedited the ignoble results of the Holocaust, Nazi anti-Semitism hardly constitutes development within Christian theology.

What of the Reformation itself? In his important monograph on *The Roots of Anti-Semitism in the Age of Renaissance and Reformation,* Heiko Oberman has insightfully observed that the issues of the conflict between Christianity and Judaism were central to much of that which distinguishes the Reformation in the cultural history of Europe.

In the sixteenth century, the Jewish question in the [German] empire was as virulent and pressing as ever, even after the great wave of the earlier expulsions had ebbed away. It is true that violent measures such as mass expulsions or forced conversions occurred for the most part before the turn of the century. But humanism and Reformation carried on the struggle against the Jews with their own weapons. These movements could not realize their hopes for a reconstruction of church and society without first settling their spiritual score with the Jews and with Judaism. The intensification and deepening of the ideological conflict was in fact a characteristic feature of the incipient new era. Both humanism and Reformation, soon completely allied in several ways, together diagnosed the affliction of the age as symptomatic of its deepest disorders: reform demanded the absolute renunciation of a "Judaism" that had infiltrated into all aspects of life—the church and the monastery, the schools and the universities, the imperial free city and the episcopal see.[25]

For many key players in the drama of sixteenth century—for Johannes Reuchlin, for Erasmus of Rotterdam, above all for Martin Luther, and for others as well—Christian antagonism toward Judaism epitomized the urgent priorities of the moment. Was the result an essentially new breed of Christian anti-Judaism, or did it simply extend the medieval ethos into early modern times?

Noting the five-hundredth anniversary of Martin Luther's birth in 1483, many scholars in the present decade have turned to the anti-Judaism of his later years, which helped to fuel Nazi propaganda earlier in this century. In 1523, Luther's *That Jesus Christ Was Born a Jew* had addressed the Jews in a rather conciliatory fashion, condemning Catholic maltreatment of Jews as the cause of their unwillingness to approach the baptismal font. But between 1536 and 1543, Luther's tone turned increasingly more hostile. *Against the Sabbatarians* (1538) responded to reports of Jewish proselytizing in Bohemia, condemning the Jews for their observance of a now invalid law and for their stubborn refusal to acknowledge Jesus as messiah. *On the Jews and Their Lies* (1543) denounced the Jews' self-aggrandizing interpretation of Scripture and their slanders against Jesus, the Virgin, and Christians. There, Luther urged Christian princes

to set fire to their synagogues or schools . . . , that their houses also be razed and destroyed . . .—instead they might be lodged under a roof or in a barn . . .— that all their prayer books and talmudic writings, in which idolatry, lies, cursing, and blasphemy are taught, be taken from them . . . , that their rabbis be forbidden to teach henceforth on a pain of loss of life and limb . . . , that safe-conduct on the highways be abolished completely for the Jews . . . , that usury be prohibited to them, and that all cash and treasure of silver and gold be taken from them. . . . But if we are afraid that they might harm us . . . , then eject them forever from the country.[26]

And in *Vom Shem Hamphoras* (*On the Ineffable Name*), written in the same year—that is, only three years before his death—Luther ridiculed the Jews and their rabbinic doctrine with frequently scatalogical vulgarity.

In his book on *Luther's Last Battles,* Mark Edwards reviews the development of Luther's polemic "Against the Jews" and the manner in which twentieth-century theologians have attempted to explain its offensive tone and program. On the one hand, some have asserted that "Luther's attitude toward the Jews can be understood *exclusively* from the presuppositions of his theology," that these principles remained unchanged throughout his career, and that what varied were simply "the practical and legal conclusions Luther drew from them." Although such an approach permits modern readers to uphold Lutheran theology and simultaneously to dissociate themselves from the specific anti-Semitic conclusions Luther—and others—eventually drew from them, Edwards correctly notes the flaw in its reasoning. Luther himself would never have differentiated so between theory and practice but saw a clear, logical relationship between them. "For the historian the distinction between 'essential theology' and 'medieval remnants' [of anti-Jewish prejudice] tells more about the twentieth than about the sixteenth century." On the other hand, Edwards insists, those who wisely choose to explain Luther's anti-Judaism as deriving from a particular constellation of external factors must subject even the more pleasant statements of Luther's theology to the same contextual analysis. "It is not intellectually honest to pick and choose."

Unlike Luther's pronouncements concerning the Jews, those of John Calvin have received much less scholarly attention. In "John Calvin and the Jews," Salo W. Baron demonstrates how Judaism was truly an issue for Christian leaders of the Reformation period. Calvin had few contacts with Jews but was influenced by the anti-Judaism of other reformers, particularly Martin Bucer. Calvin accused some of his contemporaries of excessive respect for Jewish lore and exegesis, and, defending himself against such charges from others, he marshaled an array of standard anti-Jewish arguments to substantiate his Christian loyalties. Yet Calvin's polemic lacked the vulgarity and extremism of Luther's, even when he may have encountered a Jewish opponent in actual debate. Ironically, Baron concludes, Calvin may offer "a classical example of heroes making history in a way unknown to, and unintended by them." His tyrannical rule in Geneva stimulated others to argue for freedom of conscience and religious toleration. His legalist temperament generated sympathy for—and considerable agreement with—rabbinic exegesis of biblical law, ultimately contributing to Christian interest in Hebraic scholarship. Controversy over "the sweeping theses by Max Weber and Werner Sombart concerning the far-reaching relationships between the Protestant ethic or the Jewish spirit and the rise and evolution of modern capitalism" notwithstanding, "the historic fact that both Protestants and Jews contributed much more than their share to the rise of capitalist institutions . . . has remained unimpaired." Calvin's noninvolvement in European nationalism similarly underlay a movement toward separation of church and state, as it gave credence to the motives of religious minorities that refused to acquiesce and conform to the way of the majority. In all, Calvin's anti-Judaism resembled the biblical prophecies of Balaam. As Baron puts it, "The Geneva reformer, too, set out to curse the Jews, but in the end turned out to have blessed them."

When the Catholic Church responded to the Protestant Reformation with an extensive program for restoring spiritual vitality and discipline to its ranks, it, too, took a deliberate stance with regard to the Jews. Although the Jews were consistently permitted to remain in the papal states, the popes of the mid–sixteenth century imposed a variety of harsh measures on them. Jews were segregated in ghettoes and restricted to the most demeaning sorts of economic activity. Jewish books were burned and censored. The Holy Office of the Inquisition opened in Rome to coordinate the exposure and prosecution of heresy, including the Judaizing of the Marranos. And Jewish funds were appropriated to finance a hostel for converts to Christianity. In "The Burning of the Talmud in 1553," Kenneth R. Stow establishes the avowedly conversionist motivation for the Church's renewed persecution of rabbinic literature. Some sixteenth-century Christians argued for the eradication of the Talmud, while others clamored for its exploitation—and even translation—to promote conversion; still others combined both arguments. But in every case, the desire to induce Jews to enter the Church provided the motivation, and it explains how popes and other prominent clerics might differ so openly in their respective policies toward the Talmud.

Stow attributes this apparent ambivalence to a reconciliation of conflicting medieval traditions. Several medieval popes had already condemned the entire Talmud for reasons of heresy and doctrinal error. Yet others had adopted the approach of thirteenth-century Friar Raymond Martini's *Pugio fidei* (*The Dagger of the Faith*) that, properly used, the Talmud could prove the truth of Christianity to the Jews. What facilitated the novel synthesis of these attitudes, alongside all the other anti-Jewish policies of the sixteenth-century Church, was an unprecedented drive to undermine the Jewish presence in Christendom through conversion. While medieval churchmen had generally advocated toleration of the Jews irrespective of the possibility of their conversion, the Counter-Reformation papacy "did reverse the stand of all previous popes on the issue of the link between toleration and conversion. Henceforth Jews would be tolerated so that they could be constantly and actively pressed to convert." [27]

I believe that in the activity and polemic of thirteenth-century friars one can indeed find medieval precedent for a Christian policy of eliminating a Jewish presence in Christendom; and if such is the case, Stow's thesis is questionable in certain respects. Nevertheless, Stow has shown conclusively that the Counter-Reformation Church did move beyond the anti-Judaism of the Middle Ages. In prior centuries, even when some sought to reverse the traditional ecclesiastical policy of toleration, they did so on the grounds that medieval Jews no longer performed the functions that justified their toleration and preservation in Christian society. As a result, zealous churchmen called for the persecution of Jewish books, harassment of Jewish communities, and concerted missionary efforts to the Jews. But in the sixteenth century, the papacy now implied that the sole basis for tolerating the Jews was their progress toward conversion. Just as Heiko Oberman has attributed Luther's anti-Judaism to rising apocalyptic expectation,[28] so, too, Stow has linked sixteenth-century papal Jewry policy to eschatological speculation. If the end was near, the *Adversus Judaeos* rationale for toleration was outlived. To the contrary, conversion became an imperative. Protestants and Catholics of the Reformation period hardly overhauled the theological framework for evaluating the Jewish presence in Christendom, nor did they invent any untried policies for dealing with the Jews. Their ideas do suggest, however, that the conflict between Christianity and Judaism had reached a logical conclusion: In both theory and practice, Western Christendom was largely devoid of any meaningful Jewish presence.

ANCIENT AND MEDIEVAL JEWS ON CHRISTIANITY

Several considerations have motivated reserving discussion of Jewish anti-Christian polemic for the concluding sections of this introduction and this volume. First, the quantity—although not the hostility—of Christian anti-Jewish literature greatly exceeds that of Jewish attacks on Christianity, and the same relation characterizes modern scholarly treatment of these textual genres. Interspersing occasional essays on this final subject throughout the book would have obscured its significance and the noteworthy features of its development. Second, in the history of religious ideas, Jewish anti-Christian polemic is simply not as interesting as Christian anti-Judaism. Owing to its Jewish origins and its claim on the biblical covenant, Christianity has always treated Judaism as a theological issue of the utmost importance. That most Jews never followed the path from Old to New Testaments constantly troubled Christian theologians, but interest in Judaism—along with anti-Jewish polemic— has regularly characterized Christian society even in the absence of Jews. Were Jewish life to come to an end, Christians would still scrutinize Judaism; at some point, they might even feel obliged to invent its Jewish adherents! But the reverse is hardly the case. The Jewish worldview rests on the fundamental distinction between Jew and Gentile. Within such an outlook, one assumes *a priori* that the Jews comprise a minority; even the ultimate eschatological fulfillment need not entail the conversion of the Gentiles to Judaism. As soon as there was clear separation between Christian and Jewish communities, the existence of Christianity therefore ceased to constitute a theological issue for the Jew. Here was just one among many Gentile religions. While scores of Christian authors wrote *Adversus Judaeos* treatises throughout late antiquity and the early Middle Ages, the first Jewish works dedicated to anti-Christian polemic date from the twelfth century. Third, and perhaps most important, failure to treat the Jewish attack on Christianity as an independent unit might have obviated recognition of its real motivation. Jews typically responded to Christian polemic in kind, so as to allow Jews to survive, resolutely *as Jews,* among a hostile Christian majority. The essays in the final unit of this book explore different facets of this process of responding defensively to facilitate survival.

As noted above, recent scholarship has recognized the length and complexity of the developments that resulted in the separation of Jewish and
Christian communities, and in "At the Crossroads: Tannaitic Perspectives on the Jewish-Christian Schism," Lawrence H. Schiffman approaches the problem as reflected in early rabbinic literature. Schiffman
questions why Judaism consistently tolerated sectarian diversity and
pluralism in the final generations of the Second Temple period but then
came to view Christians as Gentiles. Identifying both doctrinal and
sociohistorical roots of the Jewish-Christian schism, Schiffman directs
his inquiry to the legal criteria and rituals of membership and initiation
in the Jewish community, which reflect instructively on its perceptions
of self and outsider. While rabbinic Judaism accords Jewish status to
those born of a Jewish mother and to those who properly convert, it has
no prescribed mechanism of exclusion. No sin however grave, not even
the crime of heresy, can disqualify the offender as a Jew; even the
traditional liturgical curse of sectarians, informers, and apostates *(Birkat
ha-Minim)*, which sought to prevent Jewish Christians from officiating
in synagogues,[29] did not signify the excommunication of those individuals from the community. When and how was Christianity transformed
into a non-Jewish religion? As the Pharisees assumed leadership of the
Jewish community following the destruction of the Temple, the vast
majority of those flocking to Christianity were not Jews, nor did they
become Jews through the rites of conversion. Yet as late as the Bar-
Kokhba uprising against Rome (132–135 C.E.), when Christians refused
to join forces with the Jewish rebellion, the Christian community in
Palestine still included many Jews. Only after the Romans quashed the
rebellion, transformed Jerusalem into Aelia Capitolina, and prohibited
Jewish entrance into the City, did the final break occur, according to
Schiffman. The Jerusalem church now had to be a Gentile community,
and Jewish Christians receded into the background.

Schiffman's essay suggests that Jewish polemic against Christianity as
an alien religion could not have begun until the second century, and
most rabbinic invective against Christianity postdates the tannaitic period altogether. As Christianity gained adherents, claimed possession of
the biblical covenant, and eventually won the allegiance of the emperors
of Rome, Jews did begin to vent their hostility toward the new religion.
Curiously, however, while rabbis hurled virulent—and often vulgar—
insults at Jesus, his family, and his disciples, and while they bemoaned

Jacob's subjection to the rule of a Christian Esau, those who facilitated the "Gentilization" of Christianity were generally not the objects of Jewish attack. Collections of rabbinic tales about Jesus, commonly dubbed the *Tol*e*dot Yeshu,* depict the teacher of Nazareth in a most uncomplimentary fashion, but they cast Peter and Paul in a positive light, precisely because they spurred the departure of Christianity from the Jewish community, effectively eliminating an internal problem of heresy. Christianity confronted the rabbis with doctrinal difficulty only when they perceived it as within the province of Judaism.

Links between *Halakhah* (rabbinic law) and Jewish responses to Christianity, as well as the underlying defensive motivations of these responses, are also evidenced in "Social and Religious Segregation," a chapter in Jacob Katz's seminal work *Exclusiveness and Tolerance: Studies in Jewish-Gentile Relations in Medieval and Modern Times.* The scenario in Katz's study is remarkably different from that of first- and second-century Palestine. Jews lived dispersed throughout Christian Europe of the high Middle Ages, in communities often numbering no more than a handful of families, hard pressed to survive economically and, simultaneously, to withstand the social and cultural lures of assimilation into the Christian majority. Survival depended on extensive economic intercourse with Christians—engaging them in trade, employing them in Jewish homes, and utilizing their help in the preparation of food. Yet such forms of interaction contravened talmudic injunctions against contact with adherents of an idolatrous, "alien religion." Medieval rabbinic authorities, writes Katz, "understood quite clearly the incongruity between circumstances as they were and the law which had to be applied to them." They recognized that such law might entail financial ruin but that it also allowed for ethnic distinctiveness and independence. They therefore worked extensively to relax existing regulations that impeded economic intercourse, excluding the Christian from the category of idolater so as to allow for trading with him (even in Christian wine) and for employing him (even in the preparation of food), at the same time as they enforced the same rules to maintain social and cultural isolation (e.g., to ban drinking Christian wine or consuming Christian food). While pursuing this policy, they maintained the formal sanctity and integrity of their legal system, which served as the primary foundation of medieval Jewish life in the first place.

According to Katz, the seemingly casuistic distinctions that permitted medieval rabbis to achieve these goals testify to the truly sociocultural function of *Halakhah* in enunciating a Jewish response to Christianity.

Its function was that of holding the balance between two driving forces, namely the necessary adjustment to new conditions and the preservation of Jewish identity. That the Halakhah followed in the wake of social change has been observed very often by historians. Again and again we have had occasion to refer to instances of this. But the other function, that of safeguarding Jewish identity by means of rationalization, is no less conspicuous a task. It was the achievement of the Halakhah that it prevented the community and the individual from being engulfed by the social and religious life of the Christian environment, by setting a limit to what might be conceded to the force of circumstances.

Jewish law thus responded to the cultural threat of Christianity as well as to the economic necessities of survival in European Christendom. Just as the *Adversus Judaeos* theology of late antiquity and the early Middle Ages addressed the subject of Judaism as a predominantly "in-house" concern of the Church, with little concern for the realia of Jewish life, so medieval Jewish halakhists depicted Christianity so as to service their constituency—to situate Jews within a Christian world and to insulate them from it.

As the Middle Ages wore on, however, Christians did begin to interfere in the daily life of European Jewry, often to undermine its security and its welfare, and Jews responded accordingly. When Christians attacked Jewish communities in the Rhineland during the First Crusade, they did so to avenge the martyrdom of Jesus, hoping thereby to demonstrate their piety and insure salvation for themselves. Both Latin and Hebrew sources attest to the decision of numerous Jews to slaughter themselves, rather than to submit to baptism or to the violence of the angry mob. Employing theories of shifting cultural paradigms developed by Thomas Kuhn and Victor Turner, Ivan Marcus has proposed not only that martyrdom constituted a polemical statement on the part of Rhenish Jewry but also that the famous Hebrew "Crusade chronicles" recounting the massacres developed this polemic considerably further. In "From Politics to Martyrdom: Shifting Paradigms in the Hebrew Narratives of the 1096 Crusade Riots," Marcus challenges the traditional scholarly approach to these texts as accurate records of recent events. Subjecting the documents to an insightful literary analysis, Marcus regrets their classification as chronicles.

That term usually denotes texts which contain documentary historical data which are embedded in a theological narrative framework. But ... such texts cannot be treated as though the "facts" are preserved in narrative like fossils in amber. Most medieval narrators were not interested in what happened for its own sake. Instead, a monk or royal biographer or a hagiographer usually made use of what he considered to be facts—especially miracles—in order to demonstrate the wonders of God or his royal or ecclesiastical servant. . . . The events actually reported qualify for inclusion only when they fit the narrator's preconceived religious-literary schema. Medieval chronicles are, in this sense, fictions: imaginative reorderings of experience within a cultural framework and system of symbols.

Marcus' careful analysis demonstrates the methodological importance of treating the experience and statements of medieval Jews within a framework broader than that of strictly Jewish religious and literary history. Moreover, his reading of the Crusade chronicles reveals their essentially polemical message and the intricacy of its expression. The narratives in question repeatedly shift their focus from political to theological arenas, from terrestrial to supernal paradigms; Christians may have vanquished the Jews in the former context, but Jews took control of their situation by transforming their deaths into ritual acts of self-sacrifice, and they emerged victorious in the latter context. If these stories teach us about what actually transpired in 1096, Marcus concludes, it is entirely "a coincidence." The meaning of the narrative truly lies

in the way it demonstrates the truth of Judaism and the falsehood of Christianity. The narrative shows that the Crusaders, who had set out to restore Christian hegemony over Jerusalem, never got there; the Jews, whom the Crusaders tried to destroy en route, were even capable of rebuilding the Temple in Mainz—their own Jerusalem.

Again one might suggest that medieval Jews responded to the attack of Christians in kind: The Crusaders sought to slaughter Rhenish Jewry in the name of Jesus, in avenging whose passion—the perfect martyrdom and sacrifice—they beheld salvation for themselves. As the Hebrew narratives depicted them, the Jews chose to slaughter themselves in "the sanctification of the divine name"; true martyrdom, they contended, was theirs alone, as was the ultimate spiritual reward.

The regularity and intensity of debate between Christians and Jews increased during the centuries which followed 1096, and the final two selections in this volume consider Jewish involvement in such disputation. Nearly a century ago, the Anglo-Jewish theologian Solomon Schechter bemoaned the rancor, the frustration, and the bias that pervade the texts of medieval religious polemic; he doubted "that there is in the whole domain of literature less profitable reading." [30] But scholars of the past two decades have successfully demonstrated the value of polemical literature in the reconstruction of social as well as intellectual history. In his nuanced introduction to *The Jewish-Christian Debate in the High Middle Ages,* an exhaustively annotated edition of the Hebrew polemic *Sefer Nizzahon Yashan (Nizzahon Vetus),* David Berger offers an overview of the context, issues, and strategems of religious disputation between medieval Jews and Christians. Although, as he noted, "Jewish-Christian polemic begins at the very dawn of Christianity," Jews did not compose works expressly for the purpose of debating with Christians until the twelfth century. Polemics were thus products of the medieval European reality in which they emerged, and Berger touches upon both static and changing elements in this genre of literature: for instance, doctrinal principles and presuppositions of biblical exegesis, on the one hand; "economic exploitation, usury, the expansion of monasticism, martyrdom, the blood libel, Christian heresy, the failure of the Crusades, wider familiarity with the New Testament and the Talmud," and the like, on the other. Correcting the plaint of Solomon Schechter, Berger provides ample explanation why polemical literature is, indeed, "one of the liveliest manifestations of Jewish-Christian relations in the Middle Ages."

The World of a Renaissance Jew, David Ruderman's biography of Abraham ben Mordecai Farissol (1452–ca. 1528), reveals both continuity and change in Jewish anti-Christian polemic as the Middle Ages gave way to the Renaissance. Born in the papal city of Avignon, Farissol spent most of his life near the center of the Italian Renaissance—in Ferrara, Mantua, Florence, and elsewhere—and his scholarly opus can serve as a window to the cultural history of the age. Farissol debated personally with distinguished Christian theologians at the court of the Duke of Ferrara, and in the early years of the sixteenth century, he compiled a lengthy polemical treatise, *Magen 'Avraham (Protector of Abraham),* to instruct his fellow Jews in responding to Christian argument. Apart from involvement in the ongoing Renaissance controversy over the reliability of Jerome's Vulgate, *Magen 'Avraham* added relatively little that was new to the theological issues of the Jewish-Christian dispute. But in its

rejoinder to Christian attacks on Jewish money-lending, Farissol's polemic did mark an advance on earlier rabbinic arguments. In Farissol's
day, Catholic preachers traveled throughout Italy in a vigorous campaign against usury, challenging the very basis for toleration of the Jews
in numerous Italian cities, and Scholastic thinkers were refining their
theoretical, philosophically grounded denunciation of lending money at
interest. As Ruderman shows, Farissol understood the complexity and
foundations of their arguments, and he turned their own logic against
them in his response. Farissol drew on Christian ideas of natural law to
contend that in the present age the social order would disintegrate
without private property, rents, and fees for services; Christian society
itself permits numerous exceptions to the anti-usury rule. Challenging
the Scholastic distinction between money and fungible goods, he noted
the inconsistency between the Scholastic affirmation of the just price and
the critique of usury. And arguing that the demands of the marketplace
justified the taking of interest, Farissol relied on criteria of economic
utility strikingly similar to those proffered by Bernadino of Siena himself!

Abraham Farissol's *Magen ʾAvraham* continues the pattern that typified previous Jewish polemics against Christianity. Following the separation of the Christian church from the Jewish community, Christian
doctrine mattered but little to Jewish theologians; Christianity, in Rosemary Ruether's term, became "a buried footnote" in the history of
Judaism.[31] When medieval Jews did take a stance *vis-à-vis* Christianity,
their posture was invariably a defensive one, intent upon reaffirming the
validity of Judaism for Jews and upon safeguarding the status of the
Jewish minority in Christendom. Nevertheless, at virtually every stage,
Jews responded to Christian attacks upon Judaism in kind. Not only the
specific arguments but also the tactics and overall character of their
response therefore provide insight into the history of Christian anti-
Judaism. During the early Middle Ages, when churchmen prescribed a
mold and function for the Jew which served the purposes of the *Adversus Judaeos* theology but which ignored the realities of Jewish life,
rabbinic jurists determined the status of Christianity largely on the basis
of Jewish social and cultural needs. Neither side felt impelled actively to
engage the other in debate. When Christians attacked Jews during the
Crusades to avenge the martyrdom of Jesus, Hebrew chroniclers proclaimed the superiority of Jewish martyrdom. In the century of the first

Christian condemnations of the Talmud, Jewish polemicists began to read, to cite, and to criticize the New Testament. And as late medieval and Renaissance scholars enunciated sophisticated economic theories to defend current practice in the Christian marketplace and to indict Jews for their usury, rabbis immersed themselves in the same realm of scholarly discourse to respond accordingly.

The conflict between Christianity and Judaism represents more than a chapter in the history of ideological and theological mudslinging. It illuminates the similarities and differences between the two major Western religious traditions, the extent of their interdependence, and the impact of their interaction.

NOTES

1. John G. Gager, *The Origins of Anti-Semitism: Attitudes toward Judaism in Pagan and Christian Antiquity* (New York, 1983), p. 13.
2. Among others, see George Foot Moore, "Christian Writers on Judaism," *Harvard Theological Review* 14 (1921), 197–254; Charlotte Klein, *Anti-Judaism in Christian Theology,* tr. Edward Quinn (Philadelphia, 1978); Gager, loc. cit., chs. 1–2; and selected essays in Helen Fein, ed., *The Persisting Question: Sociological Perspectives and Social Contexts of Modern Antisemitism,* Current Research on Antisemitism 1 (Berlin, 1987).
3. I have therefore kept notes to a minimum and, with only several exceptions, have restricted citations to English-language publications.
4. Joseph Bonsirven, *Palestinian Judaism in the Time of Christ,* tr. William Wolf (1964; repr., New York, 1965), p. 252.
5. Ibid., p. 254.
6. See the illuminating historiographical essay in Jacob Neusner, *The Rabbinic Traditions about the Pharisees before 70,* 3 vols. (Leiden, 1971), 3:320–68.
7. The original French version of his book appeared in 1950.
8. See, for example, Morton Smith, *Tannaitic Parallels to the Gospels, Journal of Biblical Literature* Monograph Series 6 (Philadelphia, 1951); Flusser's own *Jesus,* tr. Ronald Walls (New York, 1969); and Asher Finkel, *The Pharisees and the Teacher of Nazareth: A Study of Their Background, Their Halachic and Midrashic Teachings, the Similarities and Differences,* Arbeiten zur Geschichte des Spatjüdentums and Urchristentums 4, corr. ed. (Leiden, 1974).
9. Peter Richardson, *Israel in the Apostolic Church* (Cambridge, Eng., 1969), pp. 195–96.

10. Melito of Sardis, *On Pascha and Fragments,* ed. and tr. Stuart George Hall (Oxford, 1979), p. 41.
11. Walter M. Abbott, ed., *The Documents of Vatican II* (New York, 1966), pp. 665–66.
12. See the helpful and instructive array of scholarly viewpoints assembled in Robert Gordis, ed., "The Trial of Jesus in the Light of History," *Judaism* 20 (1971), 6–74.
13. Rosemary Ruether, *Faith and Fratricide: The Theological Roots of Anti-Semitism* (New York, 1974), p. 30.
14. John Chrysostom, *Against the Jews,* Homily 1, in Wayne A. Meeks and Robert L. Wilken, *Jews and Christians in Antioch in the First Four Centuries of the Common Era,* Society for Biblical Literature Sources for Biblical Study, vol. 13 (Missoula, Mont., 1978), p. 97.
15. Among others, see Gager, *Origins;* and the reactions assembled in Alan T. Davies, ed., *Antisemitism and the Foundations of Christianity* (New York, 1979).
16. Augustine of Hippo, *Concerning the City of God against the Pagans,* tr. Henry Bettenson, ed. David Knowles (Harmondsworth, Eng., 1972), pp. 827–28.
17. Augustine of Hippo, *In Answer to the Jews* 6.8, in *Treatises on Marriage and Other Subjects,* ed. Roy J. Deferrari, The Fathers of the Church: A New Translation, vol. 27 (New York, 1955), p. 400.
18. Peter of Blois, *Contra perfidiam Judaeorum, Patrologia latina* 207:825.
19. Bernhard Blumenkranz, *Die Judenpredigt Augustins* (Basel, 1946); *Juifs et Chrétiens dans le monde occidentale, 430–1096,* Etudes juives 2 (Paris, 1960); and *Les auteurs chrétiens latins du Moyen Age sur les Juifs et le Judaisme* (Paris, 1963).
20. Beryl Smalley, *The Study of the Bible in the Middle Ages,* 3rd ed. (Oxford, 1983), pp. 25–26.
21. See my survey of "Recent Historiography on the Medieval Church and the Decline of European Jewry," in *Popes, Teachers, and Canon Law in the Middle Ages: Studies in Honor of Brian Tierney,* ed. James Ross Sweeney and Stanley Chodorow (Ithaca, 1989), pp. 251–62.
22. Haim Hillel Ben-Sasson et al., *A History of the Jewish People,* tr. George Weidenfeld (Cambridge, Mass., 1976), p. 414.
23. In addition to the essay reprinted below, see *The Friars and the Jews: The Evolution of Medieval Anti-Judaism* (Ithaca, 1982), and "The Jews as the Killers of Christ in the Latin Tradition, from Augustine to the Friars," *Traditio* 39 (1983), 1–27.
24. See the observation of Dominican Master-General Raymond de Penaforte, in his *Summa de poenitentia et matrimonio,* tr. in Robert Chazan, ed., *Church, State, and Jew in the Middle Ages* (New York, 1980), p. 38: "Those people are designated Jews who observe the Mosaic law literally."
25. Heiko A. Oberman, *The Roots of Anti-Semitism in the Age of Renaissance and Reformation,* tr. James I. Porter (Philadelphia, 1984), pp. 49–50.

26. Martin Luther, *On the Jews and Their Lies,* tr. Martin H. Bertram, in *Luther's Works,* ed. Jaroslav Pelikan and Helmut T. Lehmann, vol. 47 (Philadelphia, 1971), pp. 268–72.

27. Kenneth R. Stow, *Catholic Thought and Papal Jewry Policy, 1555–1593,* Moreshet: Studies in Jewish History, Literature and Thought 5 (New York, 1977), p. xxiv.

28. See, however, the critique in Ken Schurb, "Luther and the Jews: A Reconsideration," *Concordia Journal* 13 (1987), 307–30.

29. Cf., however, the contrary opinion of Reuven Kimmelman, *"Birkat ha-Minim* and the Lack of Evidence for an Anti-Christian Jewish Prayer in Late Antiquity," in *Jewish and Christian Self-Definition,* ed. E. P. Sanders, vol. 2 (Philadelphia, 1981), pp. 226–44.

30. Solomon Schechter, *Studies in Judaism* (New York, 1896), p. 104.

31. Ruether, *Faith and Fratricide,* p. 59.

I

LATE ANTIQUITY

1

The Dead Sea Sect and
Pre-Pauline Christianity

David Flusser

I.

The relevance of the Dead Sea Scrolls for the study of the New Testament is nowadays generally acknowledged. Several scholars have called our attention to numerous and varied points of contact between the two groups of documents. It is therefore permissible to ask: are we dealing merely with unconnected similar features or with more or less complete identifiable doctrines? We must also ask which currents of early Christianity (as represented by different NT authors) are particularly close to the Sectarian teaching.

The second question has been partially answered by the numerous scholars who pointed out that the writings of John the Evangelist markedly resemble the Sectarian literature[1]; others have found many relevant parallels in the Pauline epistles. W. F. Albright[2], in summing up the situation, actually advanced our understanding of the problem: "There are many parallels between the new scrolls and the Synoptic Gospels, the Pauline letters and the remaining books of the NT, but these parallels are most numerous in the areas where the New Testament books in question parallel the Gospel of John most closely. The parallels between the new scrolls and the Pauline corpus are almost as important for our purposes as the others, since there has been a century-old tendency to

Reprinted by permission of the Magnes Press from *Aspects of the Dead Sea Scrolls*, ed. Chaim Rabin and Yigael Yadin, Scripta hierosolymitana 4, Jerusalem, 1958, 215–66.

put the Gospel of John as far as possible from the letters of St. Paul . . .
The same ethical dualism appears throughout the New Testament, but
again it is most strongly expressed by John and Paul".

A closer examination of the nature and occurence of the parallels to
the Scrolls in various NT writings yields, to my mind, the following
results: 1) In contrast to the Gospel of John, the synoptic Gospels show
few and comparatively unimportant parallels to the Sectarian writings.
This seems to indicate that the Scrolls will not contribute much to the
understanding of the personality of Jesus and of the religious world of
his disciples.[3] Talmudic literature remains our principal source for the
interpretation of the synoptic Gospels—which proves, to my mind, that
Jesus and his followers were nearer to Pharisaic Judaism than to the
Qumran Sect.

2) There is a marked resemblance to the Scrolls in the NT Epistles[4]
and the writings of John the Evangelist. In this group Paul[5], John the
Evangelist and the author of the Epistle to the Hebrews[6] are the outstanding personalities.

3) Most of the parallels to the Scrolls occur in material which is
common to all or at least to several authors of the above-mentioned
group. Features peculiar to any one of these authors are not, as a rule,
akin to Sectarian thought.

Our last observation—namely, that no doctrine of central importance
resembling Qumran theology (such as election or dualism) is restricted
to any single NT book—seems to indicate that no single NT author
(e.g., Paul) introduced such doctrines into Christian thought. Therefore
a common source of influence is to be postulated. It is highly improbable
that each of the New Testament authors under consideration was directly and independently influenced by the Qumran sectarians (or by
Jewish circles close to them). If this had been the case, we should expect
marked differences in the manner in which these ideas were worked into
Christianity by the different authors. But no such differences exist.
Therefore we must suppose that there existed a stratum of Christian
thought which was especially influenced by Sectarian ideas, and that
John the Evangelist, Paul and the authors of most other NT Epistles
based themselves on the theological achievements of this stratum.

The results of our analysis tally with the results obtained by Bultmann[7],
who distinguishes between two theological strata in the early Church: a)
The doctrine of the Mother-Church in Jerusalem; b) "The *Kerygma* of

the Hellenistic Community". The latter is, according to Bultmann, the common basis of Pauline and Johannine theology and of the doctrine of other New Testament writings as well as some Apostolic Fathers.[8] The present paper suggests that this second stratum of Bultmann's is the one which shows, in some of its doctrines at any rate, a marked affinity to the Dead Sea Scrolls.

It is not the purpose of this paper to deal with all the theological motifs of this assumed stratum of Christianity, but only to describe the features which are common to it and to the Dead Sea Sect. Neither do we propose to discuss here the meaning of these features in their new Christian context, or their specific function in Pauline and Johannine theology. We shall endeavour merely to reconstruct point by point the Sectarian doctrine as it was taken over by Christianity. Therefore this paper will not offer exhaustive interpretations of the NT passages quoted, but only deal with aspects relevant to the present task. Full use will be made of Bultmann's results[9], which enable us to do without extensive documentation of *theologoumena* included by Bultmann in his "Hellenistic Kerygma"; in such cases the reader is advised to look for detailed proof under the reference given to Bultmann's *Theology of the New Testament*. The present writer will, however, undertake to demonstrate (by extensive quotation) that some additional notions should be included in the stratum under consideration.

In the following survey of doctrines common to the New Testament and Qumran literature the individual *theologoumena* will be arranged according to their structural function in the Qumran theology, not according to their context in Christian thought.

II. DUALISM OF GOOD AND EVIL

A well-known feature of Qumran doctrine is its dualism: "In the source of Light are the origins of Truth and from the spring of Darkness the origins of Evil. And in the hand of the Prince of Lights is the rule of all the Sons of Righteousness and in the ways of Light they do walk, and in the hand of the Angel of Darkness is all the rule of the Sons of Evil, and in the ways of Darkness they do walk." (DSD III, 19–22). A similar dualistic terminology using the images of Light and Darkness occurs in the New Testament (*Bul.* p. 173). Compare, e.g., Paul's words: "Be ye not unequally yoked together with unbelievers: for what fellowship hath righteousness with unrighteousness? and what common hath light with darkness? And what concord hath Christ with Belial? or what part hath he that believeth with an infidel? And what agreement hath the temple of God[10] with idols?" (II Cor. vi, 14–16). In this passage Paul stresses the absolute incompatability of the two principles. He might thus be enlarging on the pronouncement of DSD (IV, 18) that "they (the two divisions of men) do not walk together."

For the antithesis Angel of Darkness–Prince of Lights, Paul has, in the passage quoted above, Belial-Christ.[11] He uses, however, the term "angel of light"[12] elsewhere, when he says that Satan himself masquerades as an angel of light (II Cor. xi, 14). The name "Belial" for the devil does not occur elsewhere in the NT, but is the common appellation of the devil in the Qumran literature. The DSD passage quoted above calls him the Angel of Darkness, because the rule of Darkness (Col. i, 13; Luke xxii, 53) is his (the name Belial is combined with the notion of the devil's rule of darkness in DSW XIII, 11). He is also the Ruler of this World according to the NT (*Bul.* pp. 172–3), a notion corresponding to the term "the days of Belial's rule" which designates the present in Qumran literature (DSD II, 19; cf. DSD I, 17–8, 23–4; IV, 19; CDC IV, 12–13; VI, 14; XII. 23; DSH V, 7; DSW XIV, 9).

In the Sectarian teaching this basic dualistic outlook leads to a fundamental division of all mankind into two camps. The sect deems itself to be identical with the righteous part of humanity and calls itself the "Sons of Light." The same appellation is used for Christians by Paul and John.[13] The corresponding Sectarian term "Sons of Darkness" for the wicked is not found in the NT[14], but the idea which underlies it, namely that the wicked belong to the Evil Principle, is expressed clearly enough by John when he says that the wicked are "from the devil" (*Bul.* pp. 173–4).

The sect expects its individual member to take part emotionally in the struggle between good and evil and commands him "to love all that (God) has chosen and to hate all that He has despised, to keep far away from all that is evil, to cleave to every good deed . . . and to love all the Sons of Light, every man according to his lot in divine counsel, and to hate all the Sons of Darkness, every man according to his guilt in divine vengeance" (DSD I, 3–11). Similarly Paul advises "to abhor[15] that which is evil, to cleave to that which is good, to be kindly affectioned one to another with brotherly love" (Rom. xii, 9–10). See also I Thess.

v, 21–2: "Hold fast that which is good, abstain from all appearance of evil."

The principle "to love all that He has chosen and to hate all that He has despised" recurs with slight variations in the Sectarian writings.[16] One of these variations could have influenced the Epistle of St. Polycarp to the Philippians ii, 2: ". . . if we shall do His will and walk in His commandments and love that which He did love, abstaining from all wrongdoing . . ."

What has been said about that the Qumran covenanter's loves and hates[17], indicates that although love among members of the sect is strongly recommended, it appears to be basically an expression of the sect's dualistic concept of the world. It seems to me that some traces of this dualistic motivation can be demonstrated in some Pauline and Johannine pronouncements on brotherly love[18] among Christians. For Paul, see the dualistic formulation of his words corresponding to the DSD passage, as quoted above; for John[19] compare, e.g., "He that saith he is in the light, and hateth his brother, is in darkness even until now. He that loveth his brother abideth in the light, and there is none occasion of stumbling in him. But he that hateth his brother, etc." (I John ii, 9–11); "Whatsoever doeth not righteousness is not of God, neither he that loveth not his brother" (ibid. iii, 10). Christian love, of course, is *not* linked with hatred for one's enemies, since Jesus expressly commanded his followers to love their enemies.[20]

III. PREDESTINATION

The Qumran sect believed that "from the God of knowledge [comes] all that is and shall be, and before their being He established all their designs, and when they become whatever they had been destined to become according to His glorious design, they fulfil their task and nothing can be changed" (DSD III, 15–6). This belief in divine predestination is linked with the belief in the division of mankind into the two lots of the wicked and the righteous (as discussed, e.g., in DSD immediately after the passage quoted). It is significant, therefore, when the author of DST addresses God: "For Thou hast created the righteous and the wicked" (IV, 38; see also XV, 14–21). Evidently, the sect believed in Double Predestination.

The significance of the doctrine of predestination in the NT has been hotly debated by Christian theologians since Augustine; we shall nevertheless have the temerity to offer a few remarks on the subject as illuminated by the Dead Sea Scrolls. For the present it will be sufficient to recall that well-known predestinational pronouncements do occur in Pauline (see *Bul.* pp. 325–6) and Johannine (*Bul.* pp. 368–370) writings. Therefore the stratum which both represent inclined, to say the least, to predestinational ideas.

Some connection or affinity between early Christianity and the community of Qumran in this matter is indicated by the circumstance that in Pauline and Johannine theology the predestinational ideas are linked with dualistic motifs: "He that is from God heareth God's words; ye therefore hear them not, because ye are not from God" (John viii, 47, cf. also, inter alia, ibid. xvii, 2–12). Similarly predestination and dualism are combined into one argument in chapter ix of the Epistle to the Romans. Paul says there amongst other things: "What if God, willing to show His wrath and make His power known, endured with much long-suffering the vessels of wrath fitted to destruction; and that he might make known the riches of his glory on the vessels of mercy, which He had afore prepared unto glory" (Rom. ix, 22–3). Thus the Divine will "to show His wrath and to make His power known"—the manifestation of His might and glory—is the reason for double predestination. It follows that the same manifestation is the real purpose of election: ". . . being predestinated according to the purpose of Him who worketh all things after the counsel of His own will, that we should be to the praise of His glory." (Eph. i, 11–12; cf. also ibid. ii, 7). The author of DST, too, is convinced that he has been granted many wondrous gifts because God has willed to show His glory through him, "so that all His creatures shall know about the power of His might and the multitude of His mercies towards all the sons of His will" (IV, 32–3), or: "and in Thy wondrous secret hast Thou shown Thy might[21] through me, showing wonders before many because of Thy glory and to make known Thy might to all those living" (ibid. IV, 28–9). The wicked, on the other hand, are predestined for a punishment which will also demonstrate Divine might: "For according to the mysteries of Thy understanding Thou didst ordain them, to smite them with great judgments[22] in the eyes of all Thy creatures, that they might be a sign and a wonder to times eternal, that all might know Thy glory and Thy great might" (ibid. XV, 17–21). Thus the fundamental division of mankind into the wicked and the righteous, with all its consequences, has no other purpose than to proclaim the glory of God.[23] The same idea is expressed, as we have already seen, in Rom. ix, 22–3.

IV. ELECTION OF GRACE

As we have seen, the sect believed that, ˄ ، a result of Divine predestination, it in itself constituted the "Lot of Light", while the rest of mankind belonged to the "Lot of Darkness". The same belief can also be expressed thus: God has elected the members of the sect to belong to His lot and rejected the "Sons of Darkness". This explains the importance of the concept of election in the teachings of the sect. The sect calls its members "the Elect" or the "Elect of God" ($b^{e}hire$ 'El, DSH X, 13; see also DSD IX, 14). The same terms (see Rom. viii, 33; Coloss. iii, 12; Tit. i, 1) are common in early Christianity (see *Bul.* p. 98).[24] Another Christian term which expresses the same notion has its parallel in the Sectarian terms $q^{e}ri$'e ha-shem (those called by name), $q^{e}ru$'e mo'ed (called to an appointed time, or to assembly), $q^{e}ru$'e 'El (called by God).[25] These common terms indicate that there is some connection between the Christian and Sectarian concepts of election and warrant a closer examination of these concepts.

The relation between the idea of the divided world and the doctrine of election can best be seen in the words of the Epistle to the Colossians: "Who has qualified us for a share of the lot of the Saints in the Light, rescuing us from the power of the Darkness and transferring us to the realm of His beloved Son" (i, 12–13). A similar passage in DSD (XI, 7) says: ". . . from out of the company of flesh, those whom God has elected He has given to an eternal inheritance and made them share in the lot of the Saints, and with the Sons of Heaven He has joined their company to a common council."[26] The dualistic concept, which corresponds exactly to the general Sectarian doctrine, happens to be worked out more clearly in the passage of the NT. The passage from DSD makes it clear that the "Holy ones" are angels in both cases. Therefore election means amongst other things that one belongs to one company with the heavenly spirits, and is thus based on the concept of cosmic dualism, in which the two camps consist not only of men but also of spirits[27], or, in the words of St. Augustine, the Elect are "societas sanctorum, non solum hominum, verum etiam angelorum" (*Civ. Dei* IV, 28).

The dualistic basis of the concept of election appears even more clearly in the Epistle to the Ephesians ii, 1–8: "You were . . . under the sway of the prince of the power of the air—the spirit which is at present active within the sons of disobedience among whom all of us lived, we as well as you, when we obeyed the passions of our flesh, carrying out the dictates of the flesh and its impulses and were by nature the children of wrath like the rest of men. But . . . He . . . seated us within the heavenly sphere in Christ Jesus . . ."[28]

The last passage, in isolation, appears to say that Christians were elected during their lifetime.[29] Strictly speaking the coming-over from the realm of Wickedness to the realm of Light, though actually happening now, has been preordained "before the foundation of the world", as the same Epistle says elsewhere (i, 4–5). Rom. viii, 29–30 is more explicit: "For whom He did foreknow, He also did predestine . . . whom He did predestine, them He also called; and whom He called, them He also justified: and whom He justified, them He also glorified." Paul shows here admirable ability in analyzing the concept of preordained election. The author of DST, whose manner is poetical rather than speculative, says simply: "Only Thou hast [cre]ated the righteous man and from the womb ordained him for the time of goodwill [i.e., for a time in which Thy goodwill to him will become manifest] to be kept in Thy covenant[30]" (XV, 14–5). As he sees it, predestination functions from the womb.[31] Paul also claims: "God who separated me from my mother's womb and called me by His grace" (Gal. i, 15). In DST the same claim is poetically elaborated: "For Thou hast known me since my father [scil. begot me] and from the womb [. . . and from the belly of] my mother Thou didst deal bountifully with me, and from the breasts of my mother Thy mercies hast Thou bestowed upon me" (IX, 29–31).[32]

In Eph. i, 11, the doctrine of preordained election is expressed thus: "In whom also we have obtained an inheritance, being predestined according to the purpose of Him who worked all things after the counsel of His own will." Here predestination is stated to be the outcome or manifestation of the sovereign and autonomous Divine will.[33] Of course, in so far as this will is benevolent towards the Elect, it may be also called Divine goodwill.[34] In Hebrew raṣon means both "benevolence" and "will". When therefore the author of DST says that through Divine will a man's inheritance has been increased (XVI, 4), he means mainly "goodwill", but the notion of Divine sovereignty is nevertheless unmistakable in his words (incidentally, the two passages last quoted have another characteristic concept in common, namely that of "inheritance").[35] The specific concept of "goodwill" or "benevolence" is equally important in Christian thought; see, e.g., Eph. i, 5. Both words correspond to Hebrew *raṣon*.[36] Those who enjoy Divine benevolence are "sanctified by His will" (Hebr. x, 10); they are therefore called the "Sons of His goodwill' (DST IV, 33; XI, 9). Yet another aspect of the same idea appears in the Gospel of John i, 13: "Which were born not of blood, nor of the will of the flesh, nor of the will of man, but of God."

Man is therefore dependent on the sovereign Divine will. This sentiment is expressed in the prayer DSD XI, 16–7: "Establish in righteousness all his [Thy servant's] works and vouchsafe unto the son of Thine handmaid [or: of Thy Truth] whatever Thou hast granted [lit. willed] to those chosen among men to stand before Thee for ever. For without Thee no way can be perfect and without Thy will nothing is done." To God's omnipotence corresponds human frailty[37], making man doubly dependent on God's decree: "And I, dust and ashes, what shall I design without Thy wishing it, what shall I plan[38] without Thy will, how shall I be strong without Thy making me stand and how shall I understand without Thy creating for me spirit" (DST X, 5–7).

This sentiment of the member of the sect induces the author of DST in another passage (XVI, 12: cf. ibid. XIV, 13) to pray that spiritual gifts be granted to him "to purify me by Thy holy Spirit and to make me approach by Thy good will according the greatness of Thy graces." In this prayer the expression "grace" is used to amplify the notion of Divine benevolence. Actually we are dealing with two aspects of a single phenomenon: what God has willed concerning his Elect is seen by the Elect as a manifestation of Divine grace. The covenanters are thus called both "Sons of His will" and "Sons of grace" (DST VII, 20). Their covenant is called the "Covenant of grace" (DSD I, 8; DST frg. 7; cf. DSW XIV, 4; also Deut. vii, 9; Neh. i, 5; ix, 32; Dan. ix, 4; II Chr. vi, 14). In the same vein Paul mentions the "election of grace" (Rom. xi, 5).[39]

The notion of grace or mercy expresses a particular aspect of Divine election, namely the idea that election is granted without any connection with human nature or deeds, without being earned, gratuitously: "For there is no difference, for all have sinned, and come short of the glory of God, being justified for nothing by His grace . . ." (Rom. iii, 22–4; cf. Eph. ii, 8; II Tim. i, 9). DST says on the same subject: "Only by Thy goodness is man righteous [justified] and by the multitude of [Thy] mer[cy] . . . and by Thy magnificence hast Thou glorified him" (XIII, 17). Deep gratitude to God is felt throughout DST: "And all the sons of Thy Truth Thou bringest forgivingly before Thee to [purify them] from their sins by the plenty of Thy goodness and the multitude of Thy mercies to make them stand before Thee for ever . . ." (VII, 30–1; cf. ibid. IV, 33; XI, 9).

Man is thus saved from the consequences of his baseness (or sin) by Divine grace, "for by grace are ye saved through faith[40] and that is not of ourselves [but] the gift of God" (Eph. ii, 8). Salvation in this context is also mentioned in DST II, 23: "By Thy grace Thou didst save my soul, for from Thee is my step." In Christian thought the concept of salvation is particularly important; it can be used to summarize all the constituent notions of the doctrine of election by grace as analyzed in the preceding pages: "Who hath saved us and called us with an holy calling, not according to our works, but according to His own purpose and grace, which was given us in Christ Jesus before the world began" (II Tim. i, 9).

Christian salvation, being *per definitionem* salvation through Christ, cannot fully resemble any Sectarian notion. In the passages noted above, the sacrifice of Christ is linked several times with the doctrine of election through grace, the similarity of which to Sectarian doctrines has been demonstrated. We can understand this linking of two basically different concepts if we suppose that the doctrine of election through grace has been used to underpin theologically, or to explain, the signficance of Jesus' sacrifice on behalf of sinful man. The speculative concepts described above supplied the why and wherefore of the plain message: "Jesus has died for us." Since Christianity accepted the doctrine of election, it could not easily do without the concepts on which that doctrine was based, such as predestination and dualism.

In the NT, the statements about election of grace are concentrated in the writings of Paul[41], who seems to have conserved and developed the particular concepts which his predecessors (as we see it) took over from Sectarian thought. Paul's special interest in this line of thinking can best be explained by his attitude towards the Law. A possible consequence of the view that man is "justified for nothing by His grace" (Rom. iii, 24, see above), not by his efforts, is the conviction that the works required by Judaism, the commandments of the Law, are useless. This conclusion was not drawn by the Qumran covenanters, who were very strict in their interpretation of the Law. It is Paul who came to the conclusion that the Christian is freed from the Law since he entered the realm of grace (see, e.g., *Bul*.pp. 258–266).[42]

V. CIVITAS DEI

A consequence of the dualistic attitude is, as we have already seen, that the sect identified itself with the "Lot of God." The community, closely knit together by its peculiar way of life and strict observance of the Law, is the actual realization of God's decision to separate for Himself those whom He had predestined to be righteous. Thus the dualistic-predestinational theology functions as an explanation for the social phenomenon of a separate, self-contained community, or, as we might call it, a Church.

It may be supposed that Jesus already intended to found a community of his followers, at least on the practical and organizational level.[43] The early Church in Jerusalem was evidently organized as a separate Jewish sect, but the ideological basis for the concept of the Church was laid down, as far as we can see, in the later stratum of Christianity which we call Pre-Pauline, under the influence of ideas which led to similar consequences amongst the Qumran covenanters.[44] The same sectarian, separatist trend which created evident tension between the Qumran covenanters and other Jews, contributed to the final severance of Christianity from Judaism.

We have already mentioned the significant designations "Elect of God", "The Called Ones", which are common to the sect and to early Christianity. The special position of both communities in the world is also expressed by the term "the Holy Ones".[45] Both communities also called themselves "Perfect".[46] The last two terms are often combined in the writings of the sect, e.g.: "the men of holiness who walk in perfection" (DSD IX, 8), or "men of holy perfection" (DSD VIII, 20; CDC XX, 2, 5, 7; cf. ibid. VII, 4–5). To this corresponds the contention of Eph. i, 4 (cf. v, 27) that "He had chosen us in Him (i.e., Jesus) ere the world was founded, to be holy and unblemished before Him." But what interests us specially at this point is the term "holy" as applied not only to the members of the sect, but also to the community as a whole, which is called *'adat qodesh* ("the community of holiness")[47] corresponding to the "Holy Church" of the Christians.[48]

The early Christians saw in their Church a true "body politic", an organic unit. The *raison d'être* of this body is the holiness contained in it. To express this concept, they used a number of metaphors comparing the Church to a spiritual house or to a temple (*Bul.* p. 99). The same tendency is expressed by similar metaphors in Sectarian writings, such as "holy edifice" (DSD XI, 8).[49] The single idea underlying all such metaphors has been recognized by St. Augustine: "Sive autem domus Dei dicatur, sive templum Dei, sive civitas Dei, idipsum est" (*Civ. Dei* XV, 19).

The Qumran literature offers not only some interesting parallels to the Christian concept of the Church as a spiritual temple, but also enables us to trace, at least partially, the gradual crystallization of this concept among Jews preceding its Christian form.

In DSW the hope is expressed that in the future the Sons of Light will take over the Temple service, so that their priests, levites and laymen "shall attend the burnt-offerings and sacrifices to set out the incense of 'pleasant savour' for God's acceptance [lit. benevolence] to atone for all His community" (II, 4–5). In its expectation of the future, the sect accepted wholeheartedly the traditional Jewish view that sacrifices are essential for atonement. But for the present, they were unable to act in accordance with this view, since the Temple service as conducted in their time by their adversaries was entirely wrong, or, as they put it, defiled.[50] Their insistence on their own strict concepts of ritual purity (and their separatist tendencies) thus conflicted with their belief in the necessity of sacrifices. This conflict was resolved by the doctrine that the rites and purification could serve as substitute for the sacrificial service[51], or as Josephus says (speaking of the Essenes)[52]: ["Although] they are sending gifts to the sanctuary, they accomplish sacrifices by [observance of] different purities[53], which they deem to be lawful, and because of this, shutting themselves out[54] from the common temple precinct, they accomplish sacrifices by themselves" (Ant. XVIII, 19). The purifications, which can be understood as the whole communal way of life with its insistence on purity at every step, are equivalent to the actual Temple service. This is the notion which underlies and explains the assertion of DSD that the sect by its very existence functions as an agency of atonement: "When these shall be in Israel according to all these regulations for a foundation of Holy Spirit for eternal truth to atone for the guilt of transgression and the iniquity of sin and to [attain Divine] goodwill for the land more than the flesh of burnt-offerings and the fat of sacrifices; and the oblation of the lips[55] for the law is like right pleasant savour and the perfection of way like the gift of an acceptable offering" (IX, 3– 5). A comparison of the sect with the Temple follows immediately: "At this time the men of the Community shall separate a House of Holiness for Aaron to unite themselves as a Holy of Holies, and a House of community for Israel who walk in perfection" (IX, 5–6; see also V, 6; VIII, 4–11; XI, 8; cf. CDC III, 19–IV, 4). Both the context and the insistence that the "House" shall be formed by "separation"[56] clearly show that no material temple is intended; this passage (as the other similar passages) deals not with the future sacrificial service, but with the present function of the sect. The passage is a full poetical and symbolical elaboration of the idea that "perfection of way" is equivalent to the "gift of an acceptable offering", or that the Sectarian life is comparable to the Temple service.

The allegory Sect-Temple recurs a number of times in DSD; a constant set of motifs is used in several combinations and variations. Prominent among these motifs is the twofold description of the sect: it is always called: ... for Aaron and ... for Israel.[57] This distinction indicates the special position of the priests in the community (which is also known from direct statements about its organization). This shows another aspect of the comparison between the sect and the Temple: The sect resembles the Temple not only because its rites are equivalent to the Temple service, but also because priests are as prominent in the sect as in the Temple. Thus the concept of a spiritual temple served, to some extent, to justify the social domination of the priests in the sect although they could not function in their main traditional task.[58]

This gradual, reluctant transformation of a religiosity based on Temple service can be observed in the development of the concept of "spiritual sacrifices". In the fullest elaboration of the allegory Sect-Temple in col. VIII of DSD (which will be quoted in full later), the priests of the sect are said to "offer pleasant savour". This being a part of the analogy between the actual sect and the ideal Temple, it would be wrong to interpret the "pleasant savour" as referring to the service in the future material Temple (in contrast to DSW II, 4–5, which uses a similar expression; see above).[59] In this context the "offering of pleasant savour" is best understood as an imagery for the rites of the sect, the "different purities" of the Essenes (as quoted above). This symbolic use of the term is quite evident from the combination "atonement of pleasant savour" (DSD III, 11), which refers to rites of purification.[60] The kind of service which the priests of the sect are supposed to perform can be better understood with the aid of a passage in the Testament of Levi (a work which shows many affinities to the Dead Sea Scrolls) which describes the fourth heaven: "The angels of the presence of the Lord . . . offer to the Lord a pleasant savour, a spiritual[61] and bloodless offering" (iii, 5–6).[62] Of course we are here concerned with earthly service, while the Testament of Levi describes a heavenly service; but the difference is not so great as may seem, because the sect enjoyed in any case the companionship of the angels (see above). They are expressly stated to be in one company with the Angels of the Presence (DST VI, 13).[63] The same statement is made in another document especially on behalf of the priests (QI p. 126; cf. Jubilees xxxi, 14). As the sect regarded the two services as parallel, the explanation given by Test. Levi for the "pleasant savour" offered by the angels, namely that "spiritual and bloodless sacrifices" are meant, seems also to be valid for the "pleasant savour" offered by the Sectarian priests on earth. We are thus entitled to ask whether "to offer sweet-smelling [sacrifices]" did not acquire the sense of "sacrifices of the spirit" with the help of the facile Hebrew play on words reaḥ-ruaḥ.[64]

The spiritual sacrifices are also expressly mentioned in I Pet. ii, 5. In the Epistle this concept forms part of an idealizing description of the Church as a spiritual temple. There is a close affinity between this description and the Temple-Sect allegory discussed above, especially with its fully elaborated version where the phrase "to offer pleasant savour" occurs. Thus the meaning which is implicit (to our mind) in this phrase occurs in a closely parallel text explicitly. The Manual of Discipline (VIII, 4–10) has: "When these things come to pass in Israel, the council of the community will be truly established for an eternal planting,[65] a holy house for Israel and a foundation of holy of holies for Aaron, true witnesses for justice and the elect of [God's] will, to make atonement for the land and to render to the wicked their recompense. This is the tested wall, a precious cornerstone; its foundations will not tremble or move from their place; a dwelling of holy of holies for Aaron in the knowledge of all for a covenant of justice and to offer a pleasant

savour, and house of perfection and truth in Israel to establish a covenant for eternal statutes. And they shall be acceptable to atone for the
land . . ." The passage in I Pet. ii, 5–6 . . . demonstrates, to my mind, a
literary connection between the Epistle and the Manual. The whole
complex of ideas and phrases (which, as we have seen, existed in many
variations) was transposed into a new language and a new *milieu*. Naturally it underwent some changes in the process, but these changes were
not extensive and can be defined with some exactitude. The typical
image of the sect as two linked houses, e.g. "a holy house for Israel *and*
a foundation of Holy of Holies for Aaron" has been resolved in the
Christian passage into two independent images, which can be combined
but need not be, according to the textual reading which we prefer: "a
spiritual house, a holy priesthood" or "a spiritual house for a holy
priesthood." The Epistle refers, according to both readings, to an undi-
vided Church which is described by the two terms. In the Sectarian
prototype the two terms are necessary because they refer to two parts of
the sect: the priests and the laity. This is so because the sect tried to
achieve a resemblance to the Temple in its life. In the Christian *milieu*
the concept acquired a wholly symbolical meaning. We have already
observed an analogous development of the concept "spiritual sacrifices."
The Hebrew text is bound by its positive attitude towards the real
Temple service (in the future), it therefore prefers to use the traditional
ritualistic language[66] to describe the "spiritual sacrifices" which are
actually meant.[67] As the symbols of the Hebrew sacrifice had no direct
emotional value for the Greek reader, the author of the Epistle (or his
predecessor) preferred in this case to give the meaning rather than the
full symbolism of the Hebrew.

In both texts the quotation from Isa. xxviii, 16, figures largely, with
its image of the firm cornerstone. In the Hebrew text this symbol of the
firmness of the Sectarian organization is loosely connected with other
poetical symbols, mainly with images taken from the Temple service.
The sect is thus described from various aspects, but there is no necessary
organic link between the verse with its imagery of firmness and the
ritualistic symbols. As a matter of fact both notions occur independently
elsewhere in the scroll.[68] The same combination of the biblical image of
the cornerstone with symbols taken from the ritual occurs in the Greek
Epistle, but there is no evident reason for this immediate connection.
The cornerstone fits only into the larger context of the passage (I Pet. ii,

4–8) which is a series of variations on the theme "stone".[69] This incidental combination of the Isaiah verse with the images of "holy priesthood"
and "spiritual sacrifices" in *both* texts indicates, to my mind, some
literary dependence of the Greek Epistle on a Hebrew prototype which
resembled the passage quoted from DST VIII, 4–11. The Epistle did not
translate the verse as quoted in the Hebrew source, but used the Septuagint version.

To sum up: As the Qumran covenanters thought that the Jerusalem
Temple was polluted, they could not take part in the Temple service of
their time. This inability to offer real sacrifices engendered an ambivalent
attitude to the sacrificial rites: On the one hand the sect hoped to offer
sacrifices according to its own rites and by its own priests in a purified
future Temple; on the other they believed that their non-sacrificial rites
(lustrations, prayers, strict observance of the Law) could serve as a full
substitute for Temple service. This belief led them to speculation about
the equality of the two services, to the use of symbols taken from the
Temple ritual when describing Sectarian rites, and, finally, to the view
that the sect itself was a kind of spiritual Temple. We have shown that
one of the NT passages which express this concept is directly dependent
on a Sectarian prototype; we have reason to believe that the concept
itself came from Sectarian circles. This view, that the Church is a spiritual Temple, did not only mean for the Christians that the Church was a
united body which contained holiness, but also that, being a spiritual
temple, it was superior to the material Temple of the Jews. The concept
thus helped in the separation of Christianity from Judaism, in a way
analogous (though not equal) to its influence on the estrangement between the sect and the rest of Judaism for whom the actual sanctuary of
Jerusalem was a symbol of religious unity.

VI. THE NEW COVENANT

Christianity distinguishes itself formally from Judaism by the New Covenant, which in its view was given to replace or fulfil the old one. The
fact that the term New Covenant was also used by the Qumran Sect
(CDC VI, 19; VIII, 21; XX, 12; DSH II, 3) is generally recognised as
remarkable.[70] We are now confronted with the question: Do both documents mean the same thing when using this term, or, if not, what is the
difference between the two evidently similar concepts?

The term New Covenant has its origin in the prophecy of Jeremiah (xxxi, 30–1): "Behold, the days come, saith the Lord, that I will make a new covenant with the house of Israel and with the house of Judah, not according to the covenant that I made with their fathers in the day that I took them by the hand to bring them out of the land of Egypt; which my covenant they brake." Evidently both communities were attracted by the eschatological content of the biblical expression "New Covenant", especially as the prophet says that the New Covenant will be different from the old broken one. Of course both communities did not interpret literally the part of the prophecy which says that the New Covenant will be made "with the house of Israel and with the house of Judah." In their opinion this expression could not mean the whole Jewish people; they saw in it a designation of the "true Israel": these are "Israel who walk in perfection" according to the Qumran covenanters (DSD IX, 6) or according to Paul "Israel of God" (Gal. vi, 16).

It so happens that most of our information about this concept in the sect is concentrated in the so-called *Damascus Document*. This is also the one Sectarian writing which explicitly uses the term New Covenant.[71]

The concept of a New Covenant is only significant when combined with, or opposed to, the idea of an Old Covenant. This is what CDC has to say on this subject: "Remembering the Covenant of the ancestors (lit. first ones—*berit rishonim*), He caused a remnant to remain of Israel" (I, 4–5); "God remembered the Covenant of the ancestors and He raised from Aaron wise men and from Israel sages" (VI, 2–3). These are allusions to the biblical verse: "But I will for their sakes remember the covenant of their ancestors *(berit rishonim); whom I brought forth out of the land of Egypt in the sight of the heathen" (Lev. xxvi, 45). By taking his cue from this eschatological verse, the author of CDC makes it clear that the covenant of the ancestors—or, to be exact, of the first ones—is the covenant made with all Israel on Sinai. This is called in Hebr. ix, 15 "the first covenant". The rendering "first covenant" for "covenant of the first ones" already appears in the LXX of Lev. xxvi, 45. We may therefore suppose that Hebr. and CDC are actually using the same biblical term, *berit rishonim*. This covenant has been broken by those who entered it, called (CDC III, 10) *ba'e berit rishonim*[72] (those who came into the covenant of the first ones—or the first covenant). To my mind this expression corresponds to "those who were told the Gospel for the first time" in Hebr. iv, 6. The generation of the wilderness is meant by both expressions, with the difference that the Epistle means only this generation, while CDC includes this and subsequent sinful generations of Israel in the concept. Both documents describe the disobedience and punishment of this particular generation.[73] I would suggest that the Greek expression is a free rendering of the Hebrew one. The Christian view, that the New Covenant is in fact identical with the Gospel, was transferred to the Old Covenant on Sinai, which appears as a kind of gospel, the first one (Hebr. iv, 2).

The doctrine of the two covenants is an expression of the general Sectarian view of Israel's history. This view is expressed with admirable fullness and clarity in three interconnected passages of CDC (I, 1–11; II, 14–III, 21; V, 20–VI, 3) which describe the course and interpret the sense of Israel's history (as mentioned before, CDC furnishes most of our information about the concept of the covenant). We read in col. III that the sons of Noah went astray and were cut off; that Abraham kept the commandments of God and "handed [this tradition] to Isaac and Jacob and they kept [it] and were written down as those who love God and partners of the covenant forever" (III, 2–4). There follows a list of all subsequent generations; we are told that they all sinned and were punished. The conclusion is that "through it[74] became culpable those who came into the covenant of the first ones[75] [or: the first covenant] and were given to the sword because they forsook the covenant of God . . . But with them that hold fast to the commandments of God—who were left over of them[76]—God established (i.e., re-established) His covenant with Israel until eternity" (III, 10–13). Or, in a shorter version: "For because they sinned in that they forsook Him, He hid His face from Israel and from His sanctuary and gave them to the sword; but remembering the covenant of the first ones [or: the first covenant] He caused a remnant to remain of Israel" (I, 3–5).[77]

This remnant has been saved because (as we have seen in the preceding quotation) it kept God's commandments, i.e., remained faithful to the original covenant. This idea is in the background of the definition of the sect given in 1QSa: "The sons of Zadok the priests and the men of their covenant, who turned aside from walking in the way of the people, they are the men of His counsel who kept His covenant in [the] wickedness" (QI p. 109, I, 2–3). The characteristic expression *saru* (they turned away)[78], which indicates separatist tendencies, recurs in another combination with the notion of the covenant in CDC VIII, 16–18: ". . . the penitent of Israel who turned from the way of the people. Because of God's love for the first ones[79]. . . , He loved those who came after them, for theirs is the covenant of the fathers". The expression "covenant of the fathers" is significant for the Sectarian view quoted above. In this view only the fathers (Abraham, Isaac, Jacob) are regarded as having been faithful to the covenant. Therefore those entering into the new covenant see themselves as heirs to the covenant of the fathers.[80] This spiritual descendance from Abraham (and not from Israel generally) is also characteristic of early Christianity (see Hebr. xi; *Bul.* p. 96).

Not only the notion of the covenant of the forefathers, but the whole Sectarian concept of sacred history resembles the Christian view of the Old and New Covenants. Both concepts are connected with the notion that the new community (the Sectarians or the Christians) represent the remnant of Israel, as foretold by the prophets.[81] Both communities distinguished the first covenant made with the whole of Israel from the new covenant which was given only to the new community. As the sect saw it, the new covenant was made necessary because the old one had been broken. This view, explained at some length in the Sectarian writings, is not explicitly stated in the NT. Nevertheless it is to my mind implicit in the exposition of Psalm xcv in Hebr. iii, 7 sqq., about the generation of the wilderness: this generation, "those who were told the gospel first", did not enter the Land of Promise, which in this exposition stands for the "rest" (eschatological bliss), because of their disobedience (iv, 6). But those to whom the Gospel is preached now, as it was to the first ones (iv, 2), are offered "today" the opportunity to reach the "rest" (iv, 7), on condition that "they do not harden their hearts". This means practically that the generation of the wilderness did not enjoy the blessing of the first covenant ("gospel" in the new setting) because of their disobedience: the new community is offered for a second time a covenant with its blessings. The old covenant, which was broken, shall be fulfilled in the new one. The sins which hindered the fulfilment of the old covenant shall not weigh upon the new one. The Epistle says so explicitly, adding a truly Christian motivation: "He mediates a New Covenant for this reason that those who have been called[82] may obtain the eternal inheritance[83] which redeems them from transgressions [committed] under the first covenant" (ix, 15).

To learn of the connection between the concept of the two covenants in early Christianity and the sect, we had to rely on a single NT document, the Epistle to the Hebrews, which happens to be the one NT writing to mention the theme without being influenced by the Pauline concept of the New Covenant "not of the letter but of the spirit" (II Cor. iii, 6). Paul found a new meaning in the contrast between the two covenants: "For these are the two covenants, the one from Mount Sinai which gendereth to bondage . . ." In the lengthy discussion, Paul evidently wants to say that the other covenant brings freedom (Gal. iv, 24–31). Paul combines the notion of the two covenants with his general view of the Law and Christian freedom which we have already mentioned.

The Christian and Sectarian ideas about the two covenants were, as we have seen, very similar, especially before Paul, but not identical. The one relevant difference is in the social significance of the covenant in the Qumran Sect. The ideal concept discussed above had its counterpart and realization in the actual life of the sect. Each new member entered the covenant formally, moreover the covenant of the sect as a whole was yearly renewed in an obligatory ceremony. Significantly, this ceremony was performed in the third month, i.e., in connection with Pentecost, regarded traditionally as the date of the covenant on Mount Sinai.[84] Thus, for the sect the covenant has a practical and ceremonial as well as a theological aspect. In Christianity the social aspect is weaker and the theological aspect is intensified by its ties with Christology: Christ is the sacrifice which institutes the New Covenant (*Bul.* p. 97).

In addition to the fundamental difference between the Christian and Sectarian concepts of the two covenants, there is a difference of degree. The sect says about itself: "And He built them a sure house [cf. Hebr. iii, 1–6] in Israel, the like of which has not stood from ancient times even until now" (CDC III, 19–20). As a divine institution, the sect is superior to all similar institutions which preceded it during the course of Jewish history. It regards itself as something new and better than traditional Judaism, but it does not go so far as the Epistle to the Hebrews, which argues: "By saying 'a new covenant' he antiquates the first. And whatever is antiquated and aged is on the verge of vanishing" (Hebr. viii, 13; see also II Cor. iii, 14). This extreme view of the Christians is, of course, a part of their opposition to the letter of the Law. The sect had no occasion to renounce the Old Covenant, because it never intended to give up the Law of Judaism (see especially CDC XV, 8–12).

The separatism of the sect led, on the contrary, to an increase (or modification) in the strictness of *halakhah*, to the revelation of special laws: "But with them that held fast to the commandments of God who were left over of them, God established His covenant with Israel even until eternity, by revealing to them hidden things concerning which all Israel erred, His holy sabbaths and His glorious appointed times, His righteous testimonies and His true ways and the requirements of His will, which a man shall do and live thereby" (CDC III, 12–16). Practically, this meant divergent religious practices in everyday life (especially in calendar reckoning)[85] and resulted in effective separation from the rest of Jewry, while (in contrast to Christianity) the connection with the Law of Judaism was maintained. But the insistence on the validity of the laws of the New Covenant leads to a rejection of other Jews who do not interpret the Law according to the New Covenant: "For vain are all those who do not know His covenant, and all those who despise His word He will destroy from the world" (DSD V, 19–20). The appellation "vain" is applied by DSW to the gentiles (*goye hevel*, nations of vanity).[86] Thus the sect tends to adopt the same attitude to those who rejected the covenant of the sect and to those who have no covenant at all.

This attitude is somewhat complicated by the hope of the sect to embrace all Israel in the future or, strictly speaking, to become in the future not only the true Israel, but the only Israel. Possibly some sectarians imagined that the rest of Jewry would simply be destroyed in the End-time, while others hoped for a mass-conversion to their point of view. We have a fairly explicit statement of this second attitude in 1QSa (*QI*, p. 109, I, 1–5), while the view that all Israel which does not belong to the sect shall be destroyed is implicit in such passages as the one quoted above: "For vain etc.", or the declaration in CDC that at a fixed time "there shall be no further joining to the House of Judah", because "the wall is built" (CDC IV, 10–12). The problem derives basically from the attempt to apply the concept of dualism and grace to the relations of the sect with the rest of Judaism and the notion of Israel's salvation in the future. We may suppose that the sect imagined that the utterly wicked would be destroyed, but that the majority of the people would somehow in the last minute escape damnation and enter the New Covenant. This problem, so incompletely solved by the sect, became even more complicated and pressing when confronted by Paul, who was forced to clarify the relationship between the historical Israel and his new universal community as well as the function of Divine grace towards both bodies. Hence his profound discussion of the problem in the whole of chapter xi of the Epistle to the Romans. The solution is offered mainly in vss. 28–9: "As far as the gospel goes, they are enemies of God— which is to your advantage; but as far as election goes, they are beloved for their fathers' sake."

VII. BAPTISM

The Covenant brought to the members of the sect amongst other things deliverance from sin: it is "the covenant which God established for the first ones[87] to atone for their transgressions" (CDC IV, 9–10), or, in a more explicit statement, "God in His wondrous mysteries atoned for their transgressions and took away their iniquity" (CDC III, 18). This practically means that one of the important functions of the sect as an institution is "to atone for the guilt of transgression and iniquity of sin" (DSD IX, 4). The Christian Church has a similar function, which is, however, based on a different theological claim: it is the death of the Saviour which atones for the sins of the Christian (*Bul.* pp. 85, 100).[88] This belief is often combined in Christianity with the institution of baptism, which also results in the deliverance from sin. In some NT passages (see I Pet. iii, 21; Eph. v, 25) there is a direct link between baptism and the death of Jesus, but originally the two notions were separate. This also emerges from the traditions about John the Baptist, who preached "a baptism of repentance for the remission of sins" (Mark i, 4; Luke iii, 3). The meaning of this religious concept becomes evident from Josephus' description of John's baptism: "For thus, it seemed to him, would baptismal ablution be acceptable, if it were not to beg off from sins committed, but for the purification of the body, when the soul had previously been cleansed by righteous conduct" (Ant. XVIII, 117).[89] By "purification of the body" Josephus means ritual purity, which was a concept of great importance in the Judaism of the Second Commonwealth generally. This purity, according to John the Baptist, is not obtainable without the previous "cleansing of the soul", i.e., repentance. This idea, that moral purity is a necessary condition for ritual purity, is emphatically preached in DSD, which says about the man whose repentance is not complete: "Unclean, unclean he will be all the days that he rejects the ordinances of God . . . But by the spirit of true counsel for the ways of man all his iniquities shall be atoned, so that he shall look at the light of life, and by the spirit of holiness which will unite him in his truth he shall be cleansed from all his iniquities; and by the spirit of upright-ness and meekness his sin will be atoned, and by the submission of his soul to all the statutes of God his flesh will be cleansed, that he may be sprinkled with water for impurity and sanctify himself[90] with water of cleanness" (DSD III, 5–9).[91] This doctrine leads to the rule: "Let him not enter the water to touch the purity of the men of Holiness, for they will not be cleansed unless they have repented from their wickedness" (DSD V, 13–4; cf. ibid. VIII, 17–18). The regular ablutions of the sect, which enabled its members to touch their pure food[92], were forbidden to outsiders (and to members of doubtful behaviour) because these ablutions were not considered valid unless preceded by full repentance.

That baptism leads to the remission of sins was accepted by Christian-ity generally (*Bul.* pp. 135–6), but the idea that the atonement is really caused by the repentance which precedes the actual immersion[93] gradu-ally weakened in the new *milieu*. When the early Church of Jerusalem introduced baptism, the connection between repentance and baptism was still clear (Acts ii, 38). There still is an indirect connection between moral purity and the significance of baptism[94] in Heb. x, 22: "Let us draw near with a true heart in full assurance of faith, having our hearts sprinkled from an evil conscience and our bodies washed with pure water." The similarity of this language to Josephus' description has already been recognized[95]; now we must also compare the language used by DSD III, 8–9: "By the submission of his soul to all the statutes of God his flesh will be cleansed, that he may be sprinkled with water for impurity and sanctify himself[96] with water of cleanness." The lan-guage, not the meaning, is similar in this case, since the author of the Epistle does not really want to say that repentance is necessary for effective baptism, but only makes use of a traditional phrase. Elsewhere in the NT Epistles and Johannine writings the connection between bap-tism and repentance is entirely lacking, in spite of the great importance which repentance had in Christianity from its very beginning in the teaching of Jesus (*Bul.* 73–4). In my opinion[97] this loss of the element of repentance in Christian baptism can be explained by the increasing importance given to its sacramental aspect, which makes it an *opus operatum*. It is interesting to note that the Apostolic Fathers, when speaking about repentance and baptism (Barn. xvi, 8–9; Herm. IV Mand. iii, 1–2), seem to regard repentance as a result of baptism, not as a condition for it.[98]

As we have seen, baptism as practised by John the Baptist and the sect had a double significance, ritual purity and atonement, or deliverance from sin. The ritual aspect naturally lost all importance in Christian baptism. Nevertheless Christian writers continued to use the language of ritual purity as a kind of poetical imagery taken over from their predecessors. Paul, e.g., addresses the gentile Christians: "But ye are washed, but ye are sanctified but ye are justified in the name of the Lord Jesus and by the Spirit . . ." (I Cor. vi, 11; cf. i, 30; see *Bul.* p. 135). He uses the terms occuring also in DSD (about the backslider): "He shall not be justified . . . he shall not be purified by atonement and he shall not be cleansed by the water for impurity: he shall not sanctify himself in seas and rivers or be made clean with any water for washing" (DSD III, 3–5). Especially interesting, in this context, is the word "to sanctify" which is used by the Jewish sect (DSD III, 4, 9; DST xi, 10) in the specific Hebrew (biblical[99] and talmudic[100]) sense "to purify." We may suppose that the early Christians also used baptismal *formulae* in which the word occurred in its original sense. In NT passages connected with baptism (I Cor. i, 30; vi, 11; Eph. v, 26), however, the word seems to be used only in the non-ritualistic sense of spiritual sanctity. Nevertheless, a palpably ritualistic formula is used, as we have seen, by Hebr. x, 22: "Let us draw near with a true heart in full assurance of faith, having our hearts sprinkled from an evil conscience and our bodies washed with pure water." The author of the Epistle made use of this formula because it was traditional, although he was consciously opposed to the "diverse ablutions" (Hebr. ix, 9–10) of the Jews, which, according to him, belong to the category of "carnal ordinances" and "cannot make the worshipper perfect as to his conscience" (ibid.). It is therefore not surprising that I Peter (iii, 21), when speaking of baptism in terms similar to Hebr. x, 22, accepts the notion of a cleared conscience, but rejects most emphatically the notion of a purified body: the baptism is "not the putting away of the filth of the flesh, but the answer of a good conscience toward God."[101]

Two elements in the baptism of John the Baptist and the sect were weakened in Christian baptism: ritual purity and the notion that repentance is a condition for valid baptism. A third element of Sectarian baptism was developed and emphasized by Christianity: the notion that baptism brings remission of sins. A fourth element common to both types of baptism, with which we have not dealt so far, is the function of the Holy Spirit at this act. It is the Spirit which according to DSD III, 6–8, effects the purification from sin. In Christian baptism the Holy Spirit is the dominant element; it is baptism by Spirit, an act which ensures the granting of the Holy Spirit (*Bul.* p. 137–8).[102] The whole development leads from a baptism that could hardly be called a sacrament to the eminently sacramental act of Christian baptism.

VIII. SPIRIT

The dualistic doctrine of the Qumran Sect is expressed, as we have seen, in terms of "the two spirits". God "created the spirits of Light and Darkness and established upon them every deed" (DSD III, 25). The righteous, the Sons of Light, are those who belong to the Spirit of Truth, while the wicked belong to the Spirit of Evil. The same juxtaposition occurs in 1 John iv, 6, the Spirits being those of Truth and Error.[103] John also identifies this Spirit of Truth with the biblical "Holy Spirit" (John xiv, 17; 26); so does the sect (DSD IV, 21; III, 6–7).[104] Only the Elect, i.e., the members of the *Yaḥad* or of the Church, have the Spirit of Truth or the Holy Spirit bestowed upon them; it is this spirit which makes them different from others: "Now we have received not the spirit of the world, but the spirit which is from God" (I Cor. ii, 12).[105]

The Holy Spirit was bestowed upon all the Elect, but not to the same degree. The individual members of the chosen community differ in the grade and quality of their spiritual perfection (*Bul.* pp. 157–8). They were granted "various powers and distributions of the Holy Spirit according to His will" (Hebr. ii, 4). DSD is even more explicit on the subject: it declares that all men inherit in the distributions of the two Spirits, of Truth and Evil, "and every action of their deeds is [determined] by their distributions, according to a man's portion, whether much or little for all times eternal" (DSD IV, 15–16).[106] The significance of "each man's portion" is clearly brought out by Paul: "Each received his manifestation of the Spirit for the common good. One man is granted words of wisdom by the Spirit, another words of knowledge by the same Spirit; one man in the same Spirit has the gift of faith, another in the one Spirit has gifts of healing; one has miraculous powers, another the gift of interpreting tongues. But all these effects are produced by one and the same Spirit, apportioning them severally to each individual as he pleases" (I Cor. xii, 7–11, cf. ibid. 12–31; Rom. xii, 3–8, Eph. iv, 3–16). Or, as the author of DST says more simply: "According to their understanding Thou madest them approach and according to their ability they shall serve Thee, according to their distributi[on]" (DST XII, 23). All the abilities (literally: powers) are various ways of serving God, as Paul also says in his introduction (I Cor. xii, 4–6) to the passage quoted above.

The personal differences in the gifts of the Spirit have their practical importance in communal life. They determine the social rank of each member and the kind of worship expected of him. Therefore the Qum-ran community was obliged officially to determine the spiritual grade— or "understanding"—of each member: "They shall be registered in order, each before his neighbour, according to his understanding and his deeds, so that every one of them shall obey his neighbour, the lesser obeying the greater; and so that they shall have an investigation of their spirits and their deeds year by year, so as to elevate each one according to his understanding and the perfection of his way or put him back according to his perversion" (DSD V, 23–4). Among the duties of the "enlightened" member of the sect was the duty "to differentiate and to weigh all the sons of Zadok according to their spirit . . . to judge each man according to his spirit and to let each man approach according to the cleanness of his hands and accept him according to his understand-ing" (DSD IX, 14, 15–16, 18). We have no information about similar social techniques among the Christians; though Paul does include the "distinguishing of spirits" among the spiritual gifts (I Cor. xii, 10).[107]

The recurring examination of the spiritual grade of each member of the sect (DSD V, 24) indicates that this grade was not considered to be constant. This explains why the author of DST asks for the spirit (XVI, 6; see XVI, 11–12), although the spirit was given to him when he entered the sect (XIV, 13)—he can never be quite sure that the more coveted kind of spirit will always be at work within him. A parallel situation exists in Christianity: the Christian has been given the spirit at his conversion, but is nevertheless exhorted to desire spiritual gifts (I Cor. xiv, 1, see *Bul.* p. 158).[108]

The usage of the term "spirit" varies both in the NT and in the Qumran writings. Sometimes the "spirit" in general is mentioned; the same spirit is occasionally called the "Holy Spirit." In other passages the word "spirit" is used with different qualifications. It seems that these specific spirits are not always aspects or even poetic descriptions of the one spirit, but also occasionally individual divine gifts to the Elect. The connection between the general and the specialized concepts of "spirit" is discussed by Paul in the passage quoted above: "Each man receives his manifestation of the Spirit for the common good . . . but all these effects are produced by one and the same spirit, apportioning them severally to each individual as he pleases" (I Cor. xii, 7-11).[109] This explanation seems to presuppose that the several spiritual gifts are distributed by the general spirit, itself beyond humanity. But it can also be said, as we have seen, that God grants the one Holy Spirit, or Spirit of Truth, to each of his Elect. Thus the list of spiritual gifts in the fourth column of DSD is summed up in the words: "These are the foundations[110] of the Spirit for the Sons of Truth of the world" (IV, 6). The list includes amongst other individual gifts the "Spirit of Meekness" (IV, 3) and the "Spirit of Knowledge" (IV, 4). Both these spirits also occur in the NT. The "Spirit of Meekness" (see also DSD III, 8) is mentioned twice by Paul (I Cor. iv, 21; Gal. vi, 1); meekness (not "Spirit of Meekness") is placed in the Jewish *Treatise of the Two Ways* in a passage parallel to the list of DST just mentioned.[111] Meekness also occurs in another list of this kind, that of the "fruits of the spirit" in Gal. v, 22-3.[112]

To the "Spirit of Knowledge" in the Manual corresponds the "Spirit of Wisdom and Revelation" in Eph. i, 17. Knowledge is also included in the list of spiritual manifestations in I Cor. xii, 8 (cf. xiv, 6) from which we have already quoted extensively. Now we must ask what kind of knowledge is meant.[113] What does the Elect one know, since heavenly wisdom has been granted to him? For John the Evangelist this knowledge is concentrated in Christology (*Bul.* p. 419-21); in the non-Johannine Epistles the concept of knowledge seems to be broader and to resemble the kind of knowledge which is characteristic for Sectarian doctrine. Thus Paul in I Cor. xiii, 2 speaks about prophecy and understanding of mysteries and knowledge[114] as being all gifts of one kind. Thus we learn indirectly that Paul meant thereby the lore of divine mysteries. The Epistle to the Ephesians (i, 17-19) offers a broader and more explicit definition: "That the God of our Lord Jesus Christ, the Father of glory[115], may give unto you the spirit of wisdom and revelation in the knowledge of him. The eyes of your heart being enlightened[116]; that ye may know what is the hope of his calling[117], and what the riches of the glory of his inheritance in the saints[118], and what is the exceeding greatness of his power to us-ward[119] who believe, according to the working of his mighty power."[120] By the gift of knowledge the Christian is made to understand the working of the divine calling or the true meaning of his election. His knowledge is the intellectual basis for his experience of being elected. This function of knowledge is not described with the same clarity in the Dead Sea Scrolls. It is nevertheless evident that the Qumran covenanters learned from their writings about the nature of their election by the sovereign power of God, so that their knowledge had practically the same function as the knowledge described in Eph. i, 17–19.

The knowledge is by its very nature restricted to the Elect, or, as John the Evangelist says, to the believers.[121] Paul's view on the subject is similar; see I Cor ii. In the Sectarian writings we find the imagery of DST: Only the trees which were hidden and planted by God are watered by the hidden perennial stream of truth; other trees, even large ones, do not send their roots to the stream (col. VIII). The Elect "were shown what [all the f]lesh of ancient [times] did not [see]" (DST XIII, 11; cf. Mt. xiii, 17; Luke x, 24; Rom. xvi, 25–6; Eph. iii, 5; Col. i, 26).[122] This means that the knowledge of the Qumran covenanters and early Christianity is esoteric; this is also the one *theologoumenon* common to the Qumran Sect and to the personal teaching of Jesus (Mark iv, 10–12; Mt. xiii, 10–15; Luke viii, 9–10). Even so, a fundamental difference between the two systems must not be forgotten: both teach that nonbelievers cannot acquire true knowledge, but only the Sect draws the practical consequence of actually forbidding the publication of the secret teaching. According to DSD IX, 17, the member of the Sect is commanded "to hide the counsel of the Law among the men of wickedness" (see DSD X, 24; DST V, 24–6; CDC XV, 10–11).

The last gift of the Spirit to be dealt with here is the ability of prayer "with the spirit" (I Cor. xiv, 14–15; see *Bul.* p. 153). The author of DST says: "And Thou didst give into my mouth thanksgiving and on my tongue [prai]se and didst circumcise my lips by the establishment of jubilation, and I shall sing about Thy mercy and about Thy might I shall converse all the day, always I shall praise Thy name and tell Thy glory among the sons of men and in the bounty of Thy goodness my soul will be delighted" (XI, 5–7). The praise is an expression of the spirit: "Be filled with the Spirit, converse with one another in the music of psalms, in hymns, and in spiritual songs, praise the Lord heartily, with words and music" (Eph. v, 18–20, cf. Col. iii, 16). Accordingly, DST mentions a "spirit in the tongue"[123]: "Thou hast created the spirit in the tongue and known its words and prepared the fruit of lips[124] before they came into being, and Thou didst put the words in a line (i.e., due sequence) and (didst order) the expression of lips' spirit in measure . . ." (I, 27–31). This passage clearly states the praise uttered by the Elect to be a direct gift of Divine grace, granted as a consequence of preordination.

Of course, the combination "spirit of x" need not always mean a spiritual quality granted by God: Thus "spirit of mercy" does not mean that the Elect are made merciful by the spirit, but expresses several times (DST XVI, 9; Hebr. x, 29; I Clem. xlvi, 6; Test. Judah xxiv, 3) a concept practically identical with the Holy Spirit, i.e., the Divine spirit which is given to men by Divine mercy. The expression "spirit of holiness" is even more difficult to define. In DSD III, *ruaḥ qᵉdushah* seems to mean the quality of holiness granted to man, and somehow resembles the "holy thought" of DSD IV, 4–5; it seems at any rate to be different from the Holy Spirit described above. In Greek we find *pneuma hagiosynes* used in somewhat different contexts: in Test. Levi xviii, 7 it is a perfection characteristic of the future Messiah[125]; in Rom. i, 4 it seems to define the Divine quality of Jesus.

IX. FLESH AND SPIRIT

The contrast between the flesh and the spirit as presented by the New Testament had been the subject of lively discussion by scholars even before the discovery of the Dead Sea Scrolls.[126] Three corpuses of thought had to be compared with the NT in this respect: a) the Bible and its understanding of man; b) trends of Greek thought which contrasted matter and spirit and emphasized that the human body belongs to matter (e.g., Plato); c) the Gnosis, which also finds that the body, being material, is opposed to the spirit. The question discussed was: is the position of the NT in these matters an outgrowth of one or several of these systems or an independent creation? One point was clear: the NT usage of the expression "'flesh" is certainly influenced by the OT; but this need not mean that the dualistic concept was developed entirely on the OT basis. There remained the possibility of a "pseudomorphosis" of OT anthropology and of dominant Greek influence in thought, if not in language. The last possibility was emphatically rejected by P. Bénoît[127], who asserted that Paul's anthropology was essentially identical with the OT position.

The discussion has been newly reopened since the Dead Sea Scrolls supplied us with a fourth corpus of thought to be compared with the New Testament doctrine about the flesh and the spirit. This is so because the contrast between the flesh and the spirit is also known to the Qumran authors, although they do not dwell on it with an emphasis comparable to the statements of Paul. The evaluation of this new fact has already led to a controversy between two scholars.[128] We have to re-examine the matter because it certainly comes under the heading of possible connections between the Dead Sea Scrolls and early Christian thought. Paul is not the only NT author who dealt with the contrast between the flesh and the spirit; John the Evangelist also says that "that which is born of the flesh is flesh, and that which is born of the spirit is spirit" (John iii, 6). This agreement between Paul and John makes it probable that we are dealing with a *theologoumenon* belonging to the stratum described in the title of this paper as "Pre-Pauline Christianity." Since the same *theologoumenon* also occurs in the Dead Sea Scrolls, it is quite possible that the "flesh-spirit" dualism is another point common to the two doctrines and part of the system described in this paper. The problem in this case is the occurrence of very similar doctrines in Greek (and Gnostic) thought; this makes it necessary for us to prove or disprove the possibility of an alternative (or concurrent) Greek influence on the Scrolls and the NT.

It is interesting and important to notice that the term "flesh" in its specific meaning, with the whole complex of connected notions, does not occur in Qumran literature outside DST and the concluding psalm of DSD.[129] W. D. Davies[130], who rightly emphasizes this fact, explains it by the theory that the greater part of the Qumran writings reflects "an earlier 'uncontaminated' stage in the history of the sect before Hellenistic influences had deeply coloured its thought, while the psalms reflect a later stage, when this had taken place." The present writer[131] came, some years ago, also to the conclusion that DST and the DSD psalm represent a later stage of Sectarian thought, partly because of their special anthropology, partly for other reasons. But the difference between the stages of Sectarian thought seemed to me perfectly amenable to explanation by inner development without the necessity of supposed outside influence.

There is indeed a basic difference between the contrast of flesh and spirit as understood by DST and the spirit-matter dualism of some Greeks. For Pythagorean, Platonic, Gnostic and similar trends, matter in itself was heavy, base and generally contemptible; their attitude to the human body was only a consequence of their general view of the universe. None of the Qumran writings, even those which do express some contempt of the flesh, shows this negative attitude towards the material world. Matter is morally neutral. The material world is regarded only as a wonderful Divine creation, worthy of admiration. The constant laws which govern this world, the "mysteries of wonder" of its creation, are contemplated as a proof of Divine might and preordainment, contrasted with human insignificance (DST I, 7–27). DSD (III, 17–18; cf. DST I, 15 and the text QI, p. 154, line 3) says that "He created man for the government of the world", thus betraying an almost positive attitude towards the enjoyment of material creation.[132] Of course, at the present time the world is under the rule of Belial, as we have seen, and thus, as a consequence of the *moral* dualism, it can be said that "the world is polluted by the ways of wickedness in the rule of Evil until the time of decisive judgment" (DSD IV, 19–20). The NT attitude to the world is not as positive as the doctrines of the Scrolls so far published (although it is quite possible that some Qumran covenanters reached a more pessimistic position). Nevertheless, it is easier to explain the NT view as deriving not from a negative attitude to the material world in itself, but rather as a broadening of the opposition to this world which is under the rule of Satan.

Not only the world, but man, too, is polluted, according to DSD IV, 20–22, by the ways of wickedness or the "spirit of impurity." This view could possibly serve as a partial admission of the doctrine that man is impure and sinful by his very nature, a doctrine rather prominent in DST and the psalm at the end of DSD. Among ascetics who undertook, among other things, "to circumcise together the foreskin of impulse and stiff neck" (DSD V, 5), some disgust with ordinary human nature was inevitable. Thus the view is reached that man is not merely polluted by the rule of Evil, but that "human impurity" (DSD XI, 14–15) and the "sin of flesh" (ibid. 12) are innate to those born of woman. Man is "a

creature of clay, kneaded with water, a fundament of shame and a
source of pollution, a cauldron of iniquity and a fabric of sin, a spirit
errant and wayward" (DST I, 21–3). DST and the psalm in DSD use the
term "flesh" to describe "the human nature at its basest, whatever is
contemptible in man."[133] They also think that "to man belongs wickedness and to the fundament of flesh evil" (DSD XI, 9). Man is naturally
enslaved by his criminal impulse. For Paul, too, "flesh" means baseness
of human nature. He chastises his followers with the words: "For ye are
yet carnal: for whereas there is among you envying and strife and
divisions, are ye not carnal and walk as men?" (I Cor. iii, 3). The
expression "sin of the flesh" (DSD XI, 12) recalls Rom. viii, 3. The use
of the term "flesh" in this specific connotation is not restricted to Paul,
but occurs elsewhere in the NT (see *Bul.* pp. 152, 103); beside John iii,
6, already quoted, there are common Christian expressions which correspond to *yezer basar* in DST X, 23.

The origin of the concept "flesh" with its full theological connotation
cannot be sufficiently explained by reference to some superficially similar
uses of the word in the OT, nor by describing it as rationalization of
some sort of sexual disgust with human nature, which might be characteristic of a community exhibiting ascetic tendencies. "Flesh" as a theological term could be coined only in the general context of the doctrine
of election-by-grace accepted by both communities. As used by our
sources, "flesh" means, to be precise, "humanity without the ennobling
gift of Divine grace."[134] Therefore they can say that God "raised from
flesh the glory" of the Elect (DST XV, 17), or: "From the company of
flesh He has given those whom He has elected to an eternal inheritance"
(DSD XI, 7). The Epistle to the Ephesians (ii, 3–7) states this explicitly:
". . . among whom (i.e., the sons of disobedience) all of us lived, we as
well as you, when we obeyed the passions of our flesh, carrying out the
dictates of the flesh and its impulses and were by nature the children of
wrath like the rest of men. But . . . it is by grace you have been saved [cf.
Rom. vii, 5] . . . to display throughout ages the exceeding riches of His
grace[135] in goodness towards us in Christ Jesus." A similar concept of
election is expressed by DST: "For Thy glory Thou hast purified man
from sin to make him sanctify himself[136] for Thee from all abominations
of impurity and guilt of iniquity" (XI, 10–11).

The election-of-grace, or raising from the iniquity of the flesh, functions through the Spirit granted to the Elect. Therefore it can be said

that the Elect one is purified by the Spirit from his innate carnal pollution. This is another aspect of the "spirit of holiness" which, as we have seen (DSD III, 6–8), is connected with baptism. The specific purifying action of the Spirit is emphasized in the description of the final and absolute cleansing of man from sin in DSD IV, 20–22: "And then God will select the deeds of man [137], and will purify for Himself the frame of man, consuming every spirit of evil from the tissues of his flesh, and cleansing him with the holy Spirit from all wicked deeds. And He will sprinkle upon him the Spirit of truth, like water for impurity, from all abominations of falsehood and wallowing in the spirit of impurity." [138] But the purifying action of the Spirit is by no means confined to the future (or to baptism), since the author of DST knows that God "sprinkled His Holy [Spirit]" upon the Elect "to atone for guilt" (frg. 2, 13; cf. VII, 7); he also requests God "to purify him by His Holy Spirit" (XVI, 12). [139]

By the Spirit, the Elect one is not only cleansed from the pollution of the flesh, he is altogether freed from his human imperfections and made righteous, as DST says in a passage (IV, 29–33) which sums up the whole doctrine: "Who that is flesh could do aught like this, what thing formed of clay could do such great wonders? He is in iniquity from the womb, and in faithless guilt to old age. I know that righteousness does not belong to man, nor to a son of man perfection of way; to the Most High God belong all works of righteousness. A man's way is not established save by the spirit which God created for him, to make perfect the way for the sons of man, that all his creatures may know the might of His power and the multitude of His mercy to all the sons of His good pleasure."

Thus God raises whomsoever He chooses from his base carnal nature by granting the spirit. Both in the NT and in DST, there is a contrast between the presence and absence of the Holy Spirit in man who is of the flesh; it is this contrast which lies at the root of the "flesh-spirit" dualism. "So then they that are in the flesh cannot please God; but ye are not in the flesh, but in the Spirit—if so be that the Spirit of God dwell in you. Now if any man have not the Spirit of Christ, he does not belong to Him" (Rom. viii, 8–9; cf. ib. 4; I Cor. iii, 1–3). The flesh is unredeemed human nature, steeped in sin, the spirit is the Holy Spirit which brings redemption. Thus the Holy Spirit makes carnal man into spiritual man: this view of the Thanksgiving Scroll and the NT differs basically from the Greek and Gnostic view which regards both spirit and matter as elements inherent in the world in general and man in particular. Thus, from the theological point of view, the "flesh-spirit" dualism of the NT and some of the Scrolls should be regarded as self-sufficient and independent of Greek (or Gnostic) influence.

It cannot be denied, of course, that both views are very similar, and almost identical in their practical moral consequences. A man in contact with both Greek and Jewish thought must easily have combined these two doctrines. An instance of such combination or contamination is offered by Wisdom ix, 13−18 [140]: "For what man shall know the counsel of God? Or who shall conceive what the Lord willeth? For the thoughts of a mortal are timorous, and our devices are prone to fail. For a corruptible body bears down on the soul, and the earthly frame [141] burdens on the mind that is full of cares. And hardly do we divine the things that are on earth, and the things that are close at hand we find with labour, but the things that are in the heavens who ever yet traced out? And who ever gained knowledge of Thy counsel, except Thou gavest wisdom, and sentest Thy Holy Spirit from on high? And it was thus that the ways of them which are on earth were made perfect, and men were taught the things that are pleasant unto Thee."

The main idea of the passage, that man cannot know the counsel of God, is Jewish. Here it is specifically motivated by a double argument: a) "For a corruptible body", etc. b) "And who ever gained knowledge of Thy counsel, except Thou gavest wisdom", etc. The first assertion (verse 15) has been recognized by scholars [142] as Greek: the second recalls Qumran theology. The first assertion is not only Greek in general but a direct verbal allusion to a well-known passage of Plato's *Phaedo* (81c): "and this bodily element, my friend, must be considered burdensome and heavy, and earthy and visible; and such a soul is borne down by it . . ." Plato's insistence on the earthiness of the human body recalled to our author's mind the Biblical story of man's creation from clay with its theological connotation. This theological significance of man's creation from clay is fully utilized on several occasions in DST, where it represents an organic part of the broader concept of human baseness and Divine grace, e.g.: "What then is man, earth is he, made from dust and to dust is his return, that Thou madest me understand such wonders and the secret of Thy truth didst Thou make known to me. And I, dust and ashes, what shall I design without Thy wishing it, what shall I plan [143] without Thy will, how shall I be strong without Thy making me stand and how shall I understand without Thy creating for me [spirit]" (X, 3–7; see also XV, 21–2; XII, 11–13, 32–4). In the passage from Wisdom, we have not only an allusion to the general Jewish concept of man's creation from dust, but also the typically Sectarian combination of this concept with the idea that wisdom is unattainable by man, unless given by God, and that this granting of wisdom is a function of the Holy Spirit: "And who ever gained knowledge of Thy counsel, except Thou gavest wisdom, and sentest the Holy Spirit from on high?" What is more, the author of Wisdom adds at this point an idea which, strictly speaking, is beside the point of his argument, but which belongs to the corresponding doctrine of DST: "And it was thus [i.e., by the Holy Spirit] that the ways of them which are on earth were made perfect." The expression sounds like a translation of the Hebrew phrase in the above-quoted passage: "A man's way is not established except by the spirit which God created for him to make perfect the way for the sons of man" (DST IV, 31–2).[144]

The concept of divinely granted knowledge, which the author of Wisdom used for his own purpose[145], figures largely in the system of DST. The author of this scroll not only mentions knowledge as one of the gifts of the Spirit (see above), but declares again and again that all he knows and tells is part of the God-granted knowledge[146] which can be grasped only by those freed of their base human nature and granted the Spirit (see, e.g., DST XII, 11–13). The Holy Spirit is the only mediator of true knowledge, which is inaccessible to carnal man (DST XIII, 14–6; X, 3–7; XV, 21–2). The idea of knowledge by the spirit is thus also linked with the "spirit-flesh" dualism: "It is not [possible] for the spirit of flesh to understand all these" (XIII, 13–14). This means that the flesh has a kind of spirit of its own, which is a hindrance in the attainment of knowledge. The author of DST declares that he *does not possess* this spirit of the flesh (XVII, 25)[147], but attains true knowledge by the spirit given to him by God: "And I, Thy servant, have known by the spirit which Thou hast given me" (XIII, 18–19).

In DST we have only scattered remarks on the subject, while Paul offers a systematic exposition of the concept of wisdom granted by divine spirit (I Cor. ii, 10–iii, 4). His exposition is useful for the understanding of Sectarian noetics, even if it differs in some important points from all Sectarian writings known to us. According both to Paul and to the Sectarians, knowledge is a preordained gift; it is "hidden (wisdom) which God preordained before the world unto our glory" and "prepared for them that love him" (I Cor. ii, 7–9). Therefore it is wisdom spoken in mystery (ibid. 7), which the Elect can grasp only with the help of the Spirit given from God: "But God had revealed them unto us by his spirit: for the spirit searcheth all things, yea, the deep things of God. For what man knoweth the things of a man, save the spirit is in him? Even so the things of God knoweth no man, but the Spirit of God.[148] Now we have received not the spirit of the world, but the spirit which is of God; that we might know the things that are freely given to us by God" (I Cor. ii, 10–12). The Elect were not only given the Spirit from God but they are also lacking the "spirit of the world", just as the author of DST says that "the spirit of the flesh" is not his (XVII, 25; see above). The difference between the Sectarian term "spirit of the flesh" and the Pauline term "spirit of the world" can be understood as a result of the Christian opposition to the "world" which, as we have seen, has no exact Sectarian parallel. This comparision will also make clearer another Pauline term *psychikos anthropos* ("man of soul", e.g., I Cor. ii, 14), which designates those who are not spiritual *pneumatikoi,* and cannot grasp spiritual wisdom. This means that *psychikos* is practically identical with *sarkikos,* the carnal man, mentioned later on in the exposition (I Cor. iii, 1).[149] Thus the "soul" of the "man of soul" seems to correspond in Pauline anthropology to the "spirit of the world", and to the "spirit of the flesh" in DST.[150]

The Elect one has been redeemed from the realm of the flesh, but nevertheless counts on God's forgiveness should he "stumble by the iniquity of the flesh" (DSD XI, 12). He even knows that, being human, he is sinful and that "evil belongs to the fundament of flesh" (ibid. 9). Thus he is both freed from the flesh and threatened by its influence, a paradox which corresponds to the one observed above, that he has the spirit and still asks for it. This apparent inconsistency is resolved when we remember that the Elect one, though raised from the realm of the flesh by the spirit, remains in fact a carnal creature. The same dialectic attitude is reflected in Pauline anthropology; he says on the one hand, "when we *were* in flesh . . ." (Rom. vii, 5), and on the other hand exhorts, "Walk in the Spirit and ye shall not fulfil the lust of the flesh. For the flesh lusteth against the Spirit and the Spirit against the flesh: and these are contrary the one to the other" (Gal. v, 16–17). Thus the

Elect one wrestles all his life with his carnal nature, but is helped in his fight by the spirit given to him. He relies on the spirit and not on the flesh, as Paul (Phil. iii, 3) and the author of DST (VII, 17–18) both declare.

The contrast between the flesh and the spirit can be combined with the opposition of the Sons of Light to the Sons of Darkness, and thus produce additional aspects of the dualistic doctrine: the Sons of Light are the Elect, and it is they that were given the spirit, while those who belong to darkness remain carnal. This is the opinion of Paul: "For they that are after the flesh do mind the things of the flesh; but they that are after the Spirit the things of the Spirit" (Rom. viii, 5), "for as many as are led by the Spirit of God, they are the sons of God" (ibid. 14; cf. Gal. iv, 6). John has an even sharper formulation of the idea: "That which is born of the flesh is flesh; and that which is born of the Spirit is spirit (iii, 6). Therefore the opposition of the "fruit of light" and "deeds of darkness" in Eph. v, 8–11 [151] corresponds to the "fruit of the spirit" and "deeds of the flesh" in Gal. v, 19–23. Both pairs of expressions mean the same thing. The "deeds of the flesh" and the "fruit of the spirit" are also enumerated in two lists of good and bad characteristics, which resemble the lists in DSD IV, 2–14. The one which deals with the fruit of the spirit shows even literary affinity.[152] Nevertheless it must be pointed out that only the NT identifies the realms of righteousness and wickedness with the domains of the spirit and the flesh. In Qumran literature we may infer that there was some tendency towards such an identification, but no direct statement of it can be found. It is thus possible that the early Christian community went a step further in this matter; but it is equally possible that the signs of such a step could be found in some Jewish document as yet undiscovered.

As we have seen, the "spirit-flesh" dualism of the NT and of some Qumran writings is based on the idea that man's base nature can be ennobled by the divine gift of the Spirit. This view is near enough to the Greek (and Gnostic) view that there are two principles in the nature of man, base matter and noble spirit. The two views could be combined by some thinkers in antiquity, but must not be confused by us. There is indeed some danger to a monotheistic system in the idea that matter is base: Did not the one wise and benevolent God create all, including matter? This reflection enables us to understand why the idea that the body, being material, belongs to the devil, is dramatically denied by

Assumptio Mosis, a book which shows some dualistic and predestinational[153] tendencies. According to this book[154], there was a dispute about Moses' body between the archangel Michael[155] and the Devil. The Devil argued: "This body is mine, because I rule over matter." Michael replies that we were all created by the Holy Spirit of God and that God is Lord of the spirits and of all flesh.[156] *Assumptio Mosis* was written approximately at the time of Paul and Simon Magus, who was an early Gnostic. The view rejected in the passage is not the Greek dualistic view, but rather the gnostic standpoint, because only the Gnosis taught that matter is not merely burdensome but also the realm of satanic powers.[157] Again we must ask whether the Gnostic view as opposed to the Christian-Qumranic view was purely Greek in origin, or whether it might best be explained as a final and consistent fusion of the Greek contempt for matter with doctrines about the rule of Evil in this world, the flesh and the spirit, such as were taught among the Qumran covenanters and some early Christians.

X. CONCLUSION

The number and importance of the notions we have shown to be common to the Dead Sea Scrolls and Pre-Pauline Christianity mean that these points of contact cannot be explained away as incidental. Therefore the question of their historical significance has to the discussed.[158]

The terms dealt with in this paper were evidently coined in the Hebrew language and passed in a Hebrew literary medium into Christianity.[159] They passed as true meaningful theological terms, not as empty or vague locutions.[160] Neither were these terms unrelated: they combine easily into a complete religious system, which can be summed up thus:

the world is divided into the realms of good and evil; mankind consists of the two camps: the Sons of Light—actually the community itself—and those who are of the Devil.[161] The division is preordained by the sovereign will of God (double predestination). The Sons of Light are the Elect of Divine grace and were granted the Spirit which frees them from the sins of the flesh. Baptism functions as a means of atonement. The company of the Elect is a kind of spiritual temple; this company is constituted by a new covenant with God; this covenant is eschatological and additional to the old covenant made with Israel.

This summary contains practically all that is important in the teaching of the Qumran covenanters. It is quite possible that some—or even the majority—of the ideas taught by the Sect did not originate in the Sect, but all of them were developed in the Sect and given their characteristic formulation and full meaning; the Sect combined them into the system discussed above. This system cannot by any means be described as reflecting notions accepted by Judaism generally; at some points it even contradicts Rabbinic Judaism; for instance, the idea that immersion has anything to do with the forgiveness of sins is quite foreign to the latter. We have also seen that the theological system of the Sect functioned as a kind of ideology or theoretical justification for a socially separatist movement: the Sect regards itself as the company of the "Sons of Light" and separates from the "people of wickedness" by going into the desert (DSD VIII, 13) and by living a strict communal life. The doctrine of election gives them the certainty that the separation is necessary and willed by God; their teaching, which compares their organization to the Temple, frees them from dependence on the Jerusalem Temple service and severs all ritualistic links with the rest of Jewry. All this means practically that the whole body of ideas described above could have come into Christianity only from the Qumran Sect[162]: it is not sufficient to presume that we are dealing with ideas that were generally diffused among Jews. Of course, it is not our intention to argue that the body of ideas passed into Christianity directly from the Sect; it is quite probable that it passed through several groups and movements[163] (which were more or less influenced by Sectarian thought) before arriving at the points where it can be observed through some writings of the New Testament.

The doctrine of the Qumran covenanters did not retain its original function when assimilated by Christianity. The practical social consequences, the organization of a close-knit community, is the most conspicuous item *not* taken over. Christians used whatever they learned from the Qumran doctrine mainly to establish their own anthropology and their own ideal about the Church as Civitas Dei. A simile equally familiar to our writings and among historians will help to describe the process: the theological structure of the Sect was taken apart and the stones re-used by early Christian thinkers to build a new and different house. Much other material also went into the construction of this new and larger edifice: both stones taken from other ancient houses (Greek and Jewish) and stones hewn out of truly original unprecedented Christian religious experience. Our image indeed ceases to be adequate at this point. The material was not only collected, but fused, refashioned and enriched by the impact of the personality and teaching of Jesus and the tremendous creative forces unleashed by the new faith. The one important instance is the Christology of the new religion, which has no true parallel. Therefore research on the Dead Sea Scrolls will never replace the study of Christian origins, but it will help us to understand some important aspects of early Christianity.

NOTES

1. See especially F. M. Braun, "L'arrière-fond judaïque du quatrième évangile et la Communauté de l'Alliance", *RB* 62 (1955), pp. 5–44; R. E. Brown, "The Qumran Scrolls and the Johannine Gospel and Epistles", in *The Scrolls and the New Testament*, ed. K. Stendahl, N.Y. 1957, pp. 183–207.
2. "Recent Discoveries in Palestine and the Gospel of St. John", in *Studies in Honour of C. H. Dodd*, Cambridge 1956, p. 167.
3. On Jesus and the Scrolls see especially: K. Schubert, "The Sermon on the Mount and the Qumran Texts", in Stendahl, op. cit. (see note 1), pp. 118–128. D. Flusser, "The Dead Sea Sect and Christianity", in *Studies in the DSS*, Jerusalem 1957, pp. 85–89 (Hebrew).
4. The exception of the Epistle of James is not accidental.
5. The detailed question of Paul's authorship of some NT Epistles is irrelevant to this inquiry. In my opinion the first Epistle of Peter is independent of Pauline influence.
6. See Y. Yadin, "The Dead Sea Scrolls and the Epistle to the Hebrews", in *Aspects of the Dead Sea Scrolls*, ed. C. Rabin and Y. Yadin, Scripta hierosolymitana IV, Jerusalem, 1958, pp. 36–55.
7. R. Bultmann, *Theologie des Neuen Testaments*, 2nd ed., Tübingen 1954. All references are to this German edition (hereafter *Bul.*).
8. Op. cit., pp. 64–66; for a discussion of this stratum, see ibid., pp. 66–182.
9. In the field of *analysis;* Bultmann's synthesis and his theological consequences are not relevant to the purpose of this inquiry.
10. The Temple symbolism will be discussed in the following pages.
11. According to Yadin, op. cit., (pp. 45–8), the Epistle to the Hebrews argues that Christ is superior even to the Angel of Light, the protagonist of the Elect according to the Sect.
12. See Y. Yadin, *The Scroll of the War of the Sons of Light against the Sons of Darkness,* Jerusalem 1955, pp. 214–5 (Hebrew).
13. John xii, 36; Eph. v, 8; I Thess. v, 5; in Luke xvi, 8 the reference to the Sons of Light is not altogether flattering.
14. There are, however, similar terms (Eph. ii, 2; v, 6).

15. On the use of participles in the Greek texts, see F. Blass and A. Debrunner, *Grammatik des neutestamentlichen Griechisch*, 1949, § 468.

16. DST XIV, 10: CDC II, 15; DST XV, 19; DST XVII, 24. The language seems to be influenced by Isa. vii, 16. See J. Licht, *The Thanksgiving Scroll*, 1957, p. 188 (Hebrew).

17. Cf. DSD IX, 14–21, and see Licht, loc. cit. The oath of the Essenes (*BJ* II, 139) "to hate the unjust and fight the battle of the just" alludes to a kindred concept. Josephus (ibid., 119) also says that the Essenes "show a greater attachment to each other than do the other sects."

18. See W. Bauer, *Griechisch-deutsches Wörterbuch zu den Schriften des Neuen Testaments*, Berlin 1952.

19. On brotherly love among the Sectarians and according to John, see R. E. Brown, in K. Stendahl, op. cit. (note 1), pp. 197–9.

20. See Schubert, op. cit. (note 3).

21. "A special term has been coined in DST to express this rather complicated idea; it is the verb *lᵉ-hagbir*, used frequently in the phrase "Thy showing Thy might in me". J. Licht, "The Doctrine of the Thanksgiving Scroll", *IEJ* 6 (1956), 100.

22. An allusion to Ex. vii, 4: "But Pharaoh shall not hearken unto you, that I may lay my hand upon Egypt and bring forth . . . the children of Israel, out of the land of Egypt, by great judgements" (cf. Ex. vi, 6). Another allusion to this biblical story occurs in DST II, 23–4; cf. Ex. xiv, 4. See also DSW XI, 8–10. The same Exodus story is used in Rom. ix, 17–22 as a proof for Paul's doctrine concerning the destiny of the wicked; but Paul bases himself on another verse, Ex. ix, 16. See Licht, op. cit. (note 16), p. 69.

23. See Licht, *IEJ* 6 (1956), pp. 9–10.

24. Bultmann thinks (op. cit., note 7, p. 39) that these designations were already used by the first Christians in Jerusalem.

25. See Yadin, op. cit. (note 12), pp. 268, 272. The term *kletoi hagioi* (Rom. i, 7; I Cor. i, 2) is to be retranslated into Hebrew as *qᵉru'e qodesh*.

26. The alternative translation, which makes the object of "given" gifts mentioned in the previous line (see Burrows, *The Dead Sea Scrolls*, 1955, p. 388), provides a less perfect parallel to Col. i, 12–13, but does not detract, to my mind, from the validity of the argument.

27. See Yadin, op. cit. (note 12), pp. 219–220, and add to the list 1QSb IV, 26 (*QI*, p. 126).

28. Though very similar, the dualistic doctrine of the Sect and the Epistle to the Ephesians differ on two important points: a) the contrast "life-death" is (as yet) absent from the Scrolls, Dt. xxx, 19–20 notwithstanding; b) the Scrolls (as known to us) do not say, in so many words, that the Elect belonged to the Realm of Evil before their election, as written in Eph. ii, 1–8 (cf. Col. i, 13; I Pet. ii, 9; Acts xxvi, 18; see also En. cviii, 11).

29. The Sect was also confronted by this problem, but its writings do not offer a solution as consistent as the Christian view (see preceding note). Though

clear definitions are (until now) lacking from the Dead Sea Scrolls, the Sect evidently believed that election took place a) before the creation of the world; b) at the birth of the elect person; c) at his entry into the Sect, when it started to function actually. See also Licht, op. cit. (note 16), p. 142.

30. In my opinion this resembles the Christian idea of "donum perseverantiae"; cf. also DST IX, 30–34.

31. See note 29.

32. The biblical verses which correspond to these passages do not mention grace.

33. Cf. the terms for God's hidden intentions in Eph. i, 9 and in DST frg. 3, 7.

34. See Licht, op. cit. (note 21), p. 89.

35. The term *kleronomia* belongs to the Pre-Pauline stratum, since it occurs in the writings of Paul and also in Hebr. ix, 15, xi, 8 and I Pet. i, 4. The term is also used by the DSS; see below.

36. See T. K. Abbot, *Ephesians and Colossians* (I.C.C.), ad loc., and cf. CDC III, 15.

37. See the discussion of the term "flesh" below.

38. See Licht, op. cit. (note 16), ad loc.

39. The doctrine of Election-of-Grace occurs in the NT only in the Epistles which bear the name of Paul. *Eleos* is not used by John; *charis* occurs in the Prologue, where there is a possible influence of Pauline doctrines. The non-Pauline Epistles emphasize the notion of God's mercy towards the believers (e.g., I Pet. i, 10; i, 13; iii, 7; Hebr. xiii, 9), but do not expressly state the full doctrine of Election-of-Grace.

40. We are not here concerned with the Christian concept of faith. In my opinion this notion is characteristically Christian and not derived from Sectarian thought.

41. See note 39.

42. It is not my intention to say that Paul's position in the matter of Law and Grace is only a personal conclusion drawn from a doctrine of election-of-grace resembling the Qumran Covenanters' teaching. Like any other independent thinker, Paul created a speculative system the inner validity and logic of which is independent of the historical circumstances of its birth. I argue merely that Paul's main theological basis was the doctrine of grace, which is also known from the Scrolls.

43. A. Hyatt, "The Dead Sea Discoveries", *JBL* 76 (1956), p. 8.

44. According to W. Kohler (*Dogmengeschichte* I, 1951, pp. 232, 234), the Book of Enoch is to be regarded as one of the originators of the idea of a Church. That book belongs to the broader trend from which the Qumran Sect crystallized. It mentions the "Elect of Righteousness" (see note 25), the "Plant of Righteousness and Truth" (see note 65), and even the "congregation of the righteous" (xxxviii, 1) or "the congregation of the elect and holy" (lxii, 8; this might be retranslated as *'adat bᵉḥire qodesh*. This congregation is certainly not to be identified with Israel "according to the flesh."

45. See *Bul.* 98, who is of the opinion that the designation was used by the Mother-Church of Jerusalem (p. 39). On the term *qᵉdoshim,* see also Licht, op. cit. (note 16), p. 113. The member of the Sect is called "man of holiness" in DSD V, 18; there are many similar expressions in the Scrolls; see also note 25 above.

46. See the glossaries of Habermann's *'Edah wᵉ-'eduth,* Jerusalem 1952 (Hebrew), and Licht's *Thanksgiving Scroll;* Yadin, op. cit. (note 12), pp. 301, 342. The term "perfect" occurs in Paul's Epistles and also in Hebr. and Jac. and even in the Gospel of Matthew. It should be noticed that both passages in Matthew in which the word "perfect" occurs show some affinity with Sectarian thought. Mt. v, 48 polemicizes (according to Schubert, see note 3 above) with our Sect; Mt. xix, 21 states: "If thou wilt be perfect, go and sell all that thou hast, and give it to the poor."

47. See *QI,* p. 113; on *'azat qodesh* see Yadin, op. cit. (note 12), pp. 237–8, 273. According to *Bul.* 39, *ekklesia* is a translation of Hebrew *qahal;* but H. Kosmala's remarks on the subject, *Hebräer-Essener-Christen: Studien zur Vorgeschichte der frühchristlichen Verkündigung,* Studia post-biblica I, Leiden, 1959, should be taken into account. On *ekklesia* in the Pre-Pauline stratum, see *Bul.* 93. On the talmudic *'edah qᵉdoshah* and *qahala qadisha* see C. Rabin, *Qumran Studies,* Oxford 1957, pp. 37–52; see also Bentz's article (note 49), p. 57.

48. An expression which does not occur in the New Testament itself, but which is accepted by Bultmann (p. 93) as a part of the Pre-Pauline stratum of Christianity.

49. In the Scrolls published so far, the Sect is nowhere compared with the human body. On the comparison with the Temple see O. Bentz, "Felsenmann und Felsengemeinde", ZNW 48 (1957), pp. 49–77.

50. See especially DSH XII, 8–9; CDC VI, 11–13; and cf. ibid. IV, 15–18; V, 6–7.

51. The religious mind finds no contradiction between the view that a non-sacrificial worship is a substitute for sacrifices and the expectation of future sacrifices. Both views are actually prevalent in Rabbinic Judaism, which offers a striking example in the prayer: "May our praise be agreeable before Thee like burnt offering and sacrifice! O Compassionate One, by Thy many mercies bring Thy *shekinah* back to Zion and the Order of the (sacrificial) service to Jerusalem, and there we shall serve Thee . . ." See Singer's *Authorised Daily Prayer Book,* p. 238a. Cf. also Ps. li, 17–21. See also note 66.

52. See also Philo's statement about the Essenes, *Quod omn. prob. lib.* 1, 75.

53. *BJ* II, 159 (cf. Hebr. ix, 10). Scholars who overlooked this simple connection translated "for the difference of sacrifices" (and indulged in speculations about "Essene sacrifices"). The reading *ouk epitelousin* is absent from all ancient manuscripts; only the Latin translation (of the 6th century) and the "Epitome" (probably 10th–11th century) have it. The nega-

tion was wrongly inserted by the authors of the two adaptations, in an attempt to make the wording clearer (oral communication of the late Professor Isaak Heinemann). See also W. H. Brownlee, "John the Baptist" in K. Stendahl, op. cit. (note 1 above), p. 38.

54. To be taken medially.
55. Cf. Hebr. xiii, 15–6: "By Him therefore let us offer the sacrifice of praise to God, continually, that is, the fruit of lips, giving thanks to His name. But to do good and to communicate forget not: for with such sacrifices God is well pleased." For "fruit of the lips" DST I, 28, and the LXX of Hos. xiv, 3. Cf. also the similar expressions in DSD X.
56. A technical term used to describe the separation of the Sect from the surrounding world; see DSD V, 1–2; VIII, 12, et al.
57. See DSDV, 6; VIII, 5–6; DSD VIII, 8–9: and DSD IX, 6.
58. Thus one of these metaphors is followed by the sentence: "Only the Sons of Aaron shall rule in (matters of) Law and wealth" (DSD IX, 7).
59. The expression "to offer pleasant savour" seems to be derived from the sacrificial language of the priests of the Second Temple. It is not biblical, but similar language is used in Sir. xiv, 29; cf. DSW II, 5; see also Test. Levi iii, 6, to be quoted presently; and the correspondence between DSD IX, 5 and Sir. vii, 33.
60. The passage quoted shows also the considerable changes of meaning or emphasis in the usage of *niḥoaḥ*. We can observe a rather subtle use of the emotional value of the old sacrificial term, which would repay a detailed investigation (see also preceding note).
61. Cf. Rom. xii, 1. *Logikas* means here "spiritual", see Bauer, op. cit. (note 18), who also quotes heathen sources for this usage; see also *Bul.* 114.
62. Charles mentions the Essenes in his commentary (*Apocrypha and Pseudepigrapha* II, 306) ad loc.
63. See Licht (op. cit. note 16) ad loc. The hymn continues "There is no mediator to Thy saints" and seems thus to ascribe to the righteous a grade higher than that given to them in Test. Levi, which says that the Angels of Presence "make propitiation to the Lord for all the sins of ignorance of the righteous."
64. A comparable explanation (but without the spiritual tendency) is possibly in B. T. Zeb. 46b; but see *Siphra* Lev. i, 9. See also. Z. Frankel, *Ueber den Einfluss der pal. Exegese*, 1851, p. 130 note.
65. On this symbol in Sectarian and Apocryphal literature, see D. Flusser, "The Apocryphal book of Ascensio Isaiae", *IEJ* 3 (1953), p. 38, note 23.
66. The expression *reaḥ niḥoaḥ* is also used by mediaeval Jewish poets as a symbol for the synagogue service, e.g. by the Paytan Mordecai bar Sabbethai, see *Service of the Synagogue*, London 1944, Day of Atonement, II, 224. See also note 51 above.
67. In accordance with general NT usage, "belonging to the Spirit"—not "spiritual" as opposed to "material", I Peter ii, 5; cf. especially Phil. iv, 18, and possibly II Cor. ii, 14–16.

68. The Sectarian exposition of Isa. xxviii, 16, had a life of its own in the Qumran writings; see DST VI, 25–7 (referring to the Sect); ibid. VII, 7–9 (referring to the individual member). The passages agree in additional points.

69. Both images, house and stone, are, of course, connected by the general idea of a building.

70. See the interesting comments of L. Goppelt, *Christentum und Judentum,* 1954, p. 26.

71. In DSH II, 3, the reading is based upon a restoration.

72. This reading is preferable to *ba'e ha-b^erit ha-rishonim,* an invention of the mediaeval scribe.

73. CDC III, 6–9: "And their males were cut off in the desert . . . and they hearkened not to the voice of their Maker . . . and they murmured in their tents. And the anger of God was kindled against their congregation." Hebr. iv, 6: "Those who were told the Gospel for the first time failed to enter, owing to their disobedience."

74. It is not possible to know to what the word refers; the text is not quite in order.

75. See note 72 above.

76. I.e. the remnant of Israel.

77. See on p. 38 of my paper (quoted above, note 65) an interpretation of the whole passage.

78. See Milik's note ad loc., *QI,* p. 111–2.

79. *Ha-rishonim* (the first ones), here the founders of the Sect, not ancient Israel; cf. CDC IV, 8–9.

80. The view seems to underlie the enigmatic expression in DSD II, 9.

81. See J. Munck, "Christus und Israel", *Acta Jutlandica* 7, (1956), p. 85.

82. See note 25 above.

83. See note 35 above.

84. J. T. Milik, *Dix ans de découvertes,* 1957, p. 77.

85. See S. Talmon "The Calendar Reckoning of the Sect from the Judaean Desert," in Rabin and Yadin, op. cit. (see note 6), pp. 162–99.

86. See Yadin, op. cit. (note 12), p. 283.

87. See note 79 above.

88. Of course, already the first disciples of Jesus were of the view that his death brought atonement, but in the second Christian stratum the belief that the death of Christ atones for those who believe in him is typical.

89. The first to interpret the NT correctly on the basis of Josephus's words was E. Meyer (*Ursprung und Anfänge des Christentums* I, Berlin 1924, p. 88). His view is confirmed by the Scrolls.

90. See below.

91. W. H. Burrows, "John the Baptist" in *The Scrolls* (see note 1 above), pp. 39–41. See also S. E. Johnson, "The Dead Sea Manual", *ZAW* 66 (1954), pp. 107–8.

92. See C. Rabin, *Qumran Studies,* Oxford 1957, pp. 7–8.

93. The outward expression of this view in the baptism of John is the notice that "They were baptised of him . . . confessing their sins" (Mark i, 5; cf. Mt. iii, 6). Cf. also Sibyll. iv, 165–170.

94. The notion that penitence precedes baptism is possibly alluded to in the obscure passage Hebr. vi, 1–6.

95. See A. Oepke in Kittel, *Theologisches Wörterbuch zum NT*, s.v.

96. See below.

97. I hope that I shall be able to substantiate this claim in a future study.

98. On this point I remain unconvinced by A. Bénoît, *Le baptême chrétien au second siècle*, Paris 1953. The notion that penitence precedes baptism reappears in Justinus, I Ap., cap. 61.

99. Some of the Septuagint translators understood "to purify oneself". See LXX Num. xi, 18; Jos. iii, 5; Isa. lxvi, 17; Chron. passim.

100. E.g. *qiddush yadayim wᵉ-raglayim* in Mishnah Yoma iii, 2. I have not found the root *qdš* for purification of the whole body in Talmudic sources.

101. The repetition of the originally Greek *synedeisis* (Hebr. ix, 9; x, 22; I Peter iii, 21) shows that the Jewish baptismal formula was formulated anew by Greek-speaking Christians.

102. The relation of the Spirit to baptism will be dealt with elsewhere.

103. *Pneuma planes* corresponds to a supposed *ruaḥ taʿut* (as yet not found in the texts), but cf. DSD III, 21–2.

104. It should be also noticed that both DSD IV, 21, and the Gospel of John speak about the granting of the holy Spirit to the Elect at the End-Time. Professor M. Buber called my attention to a possible connection between the Sectarian and Christian Holy Spirit = Spirit of Truth and the Holy Spirit in the dualistic Persian religion.

105. These words of Paul will be discussed later in this paper.

106. This means that grades of spirit—of the evil spirit of course—exist also among the Sons of Darkness. This concept of distribution belongs to the Sectarian doctrine of predestination (see DST I, 15–20). According to J. T. Milik, op. cit. (note 84), pp. 78–9, fragments of an astrological composition were found in Qumran giving mathematical proportions of the participation of men in the spirits of Light and Darkness, according to the dates of their births.

107. The phrase can be also understood as referring to the examination of the utterances of spirits, i.e., prophecies; cf. I Thess. v, 19; I Cor. xiv, 29; I John iv, 1. It should be also noticed that the NT passages quoted seem to speak about distinguishing the good spirit from the spirit of error.

108. The author of DST prays to God: vouchsafe(?) for the spirit of Thy servant (DST XVI, 14). This could mean that God is asked to vouchsafe for the good spirit in the Elect, to ensure that the worshipper shall be steadfast in his good ways. If this interpretation (there are others) be accepted, the phrase from DST would form an interesting parallel to II Cor. i, 22: "Who hath also sealed us and given the pledge of the Spirit in our hearts" (cf. ibid. v, 5; Eph. i, 14). The Hebrew word for pledge is used in these Greek

passages. The spirit is, so to speak, given as a pledge from God to the Elect one to ensure that his share in the election will not be lost (Eph. i, 14). See, however, Abbot, op. cit. (note 36), etc.

109. Paul's words could be construed to mean that everybody receives one single spiritual gift; but evidently this is not the Apostle's intention.

110. *sode*, i.e., *y*ᵉ*sode*.

111. Didache iii, 7–8. See J. P. Audet, "Affinités littéraires et doctrinales du Manuel de Discipline", *RB* 1952, pp. 219–38.

112. On the list, see note 152. There is a connection between "spirit of meekness" and "the meek of spirit", a description of the Sect identical with "the poor of spirit". Cf. Mt. v, 3–5: "Blessed are the poor by spirit, for theirs is the kingdom of heaven ... Blessed are the meek, for they shall inherit the earth." See D. Flusser, op. cit. (note 3), pp. 88–9.

113. The best discussion of the Christian concept of knowledge is L. Bouyer, "Gnosis, le sens orthodoxe de l'expression jusqu'aux pères Alexandrins", *JTS* 4 (1953), pp. 188–203. For the Sectarian material, see W. D. Davies, "Knowledge in the DSS", *HTR* 1953, pp. 113–139; Licht, op. cit. (note 21), pp. 97–9; Fr. Nötscher, *Zur theologischen Terminologie der Qumran-Texte*, 1956, pp. 15–18.

114. As evident from the context, the definition is not Paul's, but was taken over by him.

115. ʾIsh kavod (DSW XII, 9) might possibly be compared, see Yadin, op. cit. (note 12) ad loc., and *melekh ha-kavod* (ibid. XII, 7; cf. Psalms xxiv, 7–10).

116. The expression is to be interpreted with the aid of DSD II, 3. The phrase is an elaboration of the priestly blessings prescribed in Num. vi, 25. The biblical verse is made to refer to divine enlightenment by knowledge. See DSD IV, 2, also op. cit. note 140, pp. 135–6, and see Test. Gad v, 7.

117. Cf. DST IX, 14: "I know that there is hope in Thy mercies and confidence in Thine abundant power."

118. Cf. DST XVI, 4: "I know that in Thy benevolence toward man Thou hast increased his inheritance." See also note 35 above.

119. Cf. DST IV, 27–9: "Thou madest me know Thy wondrous mysteries, and in Thy wondrous secret has Thou shown Thy might through me showing wonders before many because of Thy glory and to make known to all living Thy might."

120. Cf. DST IV, 32–3: "so that all creatures shall know about the power of His might and the multitude of His mercy towards all Sons of His will."

121. See C. H. Dodd, *The Interpretation of the Fourth Gospel*, Cambridge 1954, pp. 154–169.

122. See Licht, op. cit. (note 16) ad loc.

123. See Licht, "The Doctrine" etc. (note 21), pp. 99–100.

124. See note 55 above.

125. Dependent on Isa. xi, 2, which however does not include the words *ruaḥ qᵉdushah*.

126. On this chapter see also my Hebrew article in *Tarbiz* 27 (1957–8), pp. 158–165.
127. P. Bénoît, "Corps, tête et plérôme dans les Epitres de la captivité", *RB* 53 (1956), 8; for literature see ibid., note 2.
128. G. Kuhn, "Temptation, Sin and Flesh" in Stendahl (op. cit., note 1), pp. 101–8; W. D. Davies, "Paul and the Dead Sea Scrolls, Flesh and Spirit", ibid., pp. 157–182. See also Licht op. cit. (note 21), pp. 10–11, 92. Cf. Max Weber, *Religionssoziologie* III, 1921, p. 426.
129. See also CDC III, 17, where the adversaries are described.
130. Op. cit. (note 128), p. 165. See also E. Schweitzer, "Die hellenistische Komponente im neutestamentlichen σάρξ-Begriff", *ZNW* 48 (1957), pp. 237–253.
131. "The Sect of the Judean Desert and its opinions", *Zion* 19 (1954), pp. 100–3 (Hebrew). It may be significant that the script of DST is the latest stage of development amongst the Scrolls from Qumran, see N. Avigad, supra, pp. 76–7.
132. Ibid., pp. 101–2.
133. Licht, "The Doctrine" etc. (op. cit., note 21), p. 11.
134. Ibid., p. 11.
135. The Hebrew *hamon raḥamaw* is a common expression in DST, where it has the same theological significance. It also appears in the Jewish Prayer Book (Singer, p. 237). This Hebrew expression is derived from the biblical "the sounding of Thy bowels and of Thy mercies" (Isa. lxiii, 15), which was shortened. In the original phrase *hamon* meant approximately "sounding", but as used in DST, it means multitude; cf. the parallel expressions in DST VI, 9; cf. IX, 34; see the glossary in Licht, op. cit. (note 16) for these terms. Hence the Greek translation in Eph; and also in LXX Isa. lxiii, 15; see further LXX Isa. xiv, 11.
136. See notes 99 and 100 above.
137. An expression which occurs also En. xlv, 3 (on the future deeds of the Messiah).
138. The connection with John's words about the eschatological baptism by the spirit (Mark i, 8; Acts i, 5; xi, 16; Mt. iii, 11; Luke iii, 16) is sufficiently known. The DSD passage seems to imply the idea of bodily resurrection of a "spiritual body"; cf. I Cor. xv, and perhaps Mishnah Sotah at end.
139. "May Thy Holy Spirit come upon us and purify us". Evidently this version of the prayer was quite widespread among Hellenistic Christian communities. It can refer to the present (as in DST XVI, 12) or to the eschatological future (as in DSD IV, 20–22).
140. Professor I. L. Seeligmann called my attention to this passage; see his discussion in *Tarbiz* 27 (1957–8), pp. 137–141. About the DSS and Sap. Sal. see also A. M. Dubarle, "Une source du livre de la Sagesse?", *Revue des sciences philos. et theol.* 1953, pp. 425–443.
141. Cf. Job iv, 19 and II Cor. v, 1 sqq., where Paul comes very near to the

Hellenistic-gnostic type of dualism (according to *Bul.* 198–9)—a passage not quite typical of Paul's doctrine.

142. See the commentaries on Wisdom ad loc., especially J. Fichtner, *Weisheit Salomos,* (in *Handbuch zum AT*) Tübingen 1938, pp. 36–9; K. Holmes in R. H. Charles, *The Apocrypha and Pseudepigrapha of the OT,* 1913, I, 532, 550. The connection between Wisdom and DST must *not* be understood as indication of Sectarian origin of the former, which is a typically Jewish Hellenistic composition. But the problem of a possible relationship between the Scrolls and Wisdom requires further study.

143. See note 38 above.

144. Cf. DSD XI, 10–11.

145. It enabled him to combine his own idea of the excellence of wisdom with notions taken over from other systems of thought. Another identification of wisdom and spirit occurs in Wisd. vii, 22, but there is an evident influence of the Stoic *pneuma;* see also Wisd. i, 5–7.

146. The idea is expressed in the recurring formula "these I know from Thy understanding" (DST I, 21; XIV, 12; XV, 12; DSW X, 16).

147. According to Licht's reliable restoration (because fitting the context).

148. Paul's reasoning (a minori ad maius) recalls Wisd. ix, 16–7 (quoted above): "And hardly do we divine the things that are on earth, and the things that are close at hand we find with labour; but . . . who ever gained knowledge of Thy counsel, except Thou . . . sendest Thy Holy Spirit from on high?"

149. See A. Robertson, *The First Epistle of St. Paul to the Corinthians,* (I.C.C.) Edinburgh 1914, p. 49.

150. The whole complex demands further discussion, in which we cannot engage here. The division of mankind into three grades is Gnostic and later than Paul.

151. In Eph. v, 8, Christians are called "children of Light."

152. For a list of Hebrew equivalents to Greek terms for the "fruits of the spirit," see the first edition of Flusser's article.—ED.

153. See especially Assumptio Mosis xii, 4–5.

154. See *The Assumption of Moses,* ed. R. H. Charles, London 1897. My attention was called to this matter by S. E. Loewenstamm, to whom my thanks are due. See his paper on the subject in *Tarbiz* 27 (1957–8), pp. 155–7.

155. He is the "Prince of Lights" of the Scrolls, see Yadin, op. cit. (note 12), pp. 214–5.

156. Cf. Num xvi, 22; xxvii, 16 (in the LXX version). The formula "Lord of Spirits" is frequent in Enoch; cf. also in DST X, 8 and Licht's note ad loc. See A. Deissmann, *Licht vom Osten,* 1923, p. 355.

157. See H. Jonas, *Gnosis und spätantiker Geist* I, 1934, pp. 146–156.

158. The Epistle to the Ephesians shows particularly numerous points of contact with the Scrolls. This observation is relevant to the question of its date; it

makes the assumption of a late date highly improbable, as the strong links with Qumran theology would then be hard to explain.

159. For a list of Greek and Hebrew equivalents, see the first edition of Flusser's article — ED.

160. See the interesting observation of Fridolin Stier, "Die Urkunden aus den Höhlen", *Hochland* 48, (1956), pp. 425–6: "So beginnt der Sektenkanon, in feierlichen, von der Fracht theologischer Termini überladenen Perioden. Im Alten Testament ohne Vorbild, gemahnt diese Sprache an manche Partien paulinischer Episteln [Röm., Eph.]. S. Zeitlin charakterisiert diese Sätze verächtlich als blosses 'Wortgehäuf'. Es wäre besser, stilpsychologisch und formgeschichtlich zu fragen, welche Geistesverfassung hier wie bei Paulus solche Sätze prägte."

161. This summary lists only notions which actually occur in the NT; therefore the facile formulation "The Sons of Darkness" must be avoided.

162. This would be a highly improbable assumption if we were dealing with an obscure and unknown little sect without means of influencing Israel or the world. But the numerous points of contact with what had been known hitherto about the Essenes are a sufficient answer to this objection. The evidence of the influence of the Qumran covenanters on other men is another sign of their Essene identity: the Essenes were, of course, the well known and influential.

163. Only John the Baptist is known to us, who has been recognized by numerous scholars as being close to the Sect, but not quite identical with it. Other "fellow travellers" are the author of *Duo Viae* (see note 107 above) and the author of the *Testaments of the Patriarchs;* both have a watered-down version of the Sectarian doctrine of double predestination.

2

Breaking Away: Three New Testament Pictures of Christianity's Separation from the Jewish Communities

Wayne A. Meeks

We have now become accustomed to say that earliest Christianity was a sect of Judaism. This is useful language: it helps us avoid some kinds of anachronism, and it may assist Christians to approach the painful history of Jewish-Christian relations with appropriate humility. Moreover, there is ancient support for this terminology. It was Josephus who depicted the "Jewish philosophy" as made up of three or four "sects" (*haireseis, Ant.* 13.171; *Vit.* 10–12; *B.J.* 2.162; their members *hairetistai, B.J.* 22.119, 124; cf. *Ant.* 18.11 *philosophiai*). And the book of Acts, which like Josephus speaks of Pharisees and Sadducees as *haireseis,* also has outsiders occasionally speak of Christians as a *hairesis* (Acts 24:5, 14; 28:22).

However, there are some problems with the phrase. After all, in writing as he did, Josephus had an apologetic purpose for which we have to make allowance. We should not fall into the trap of thinking that all, or even the majority, of Jews in Josephus' time belonged to one of the "sects" he named, any more than a majority of non-Jews were Stoics, Platonists, or Epicureans. Further, while it may be appropriate to translate his *hairesis* as "sect," what he and Acts called by this term is not necessarily the same as what a modern sociologist means by "sect."

Reprinted by permission of Scholars Press from *"To See Ourselves as Others See Us"*: *Christians, Jews, "Others" in Late Antiquity,* ed. Jacob Neusner and Ernest S. Frerichs, Chico, Calif., 1985, 93–115.

To make matters more difficult, the sociologists have not had an easy time agreeing on a definition of the latter category. Finally, the book of Acts, too, had apologetic aims, and the picture its author drew of early Christianity may be distorted, or, at best, may not represent the whole movement.

For all these reasons, a fresh look at the evidence may be timely. In order to take account of some of the diversity of viewpoint present in the early Christian literature while still keeping the inquiry within reasonable bounds, I propose to examine three sets of documents: the Fourth Gospel, the letters of Paul and his disciples, and the Gospel of Matthew. All these are most likely earlier than Acts, and, of the Christian writings of the first century, they are the ones most intensively concerned with the question of Christianity's relationship to Israel. Each of them gives some reason for affirming that Christianity indeed *had* been a sect of Judaism, but we shall find that each looks back at that connection from a point just *after* a decisive break has occurred. The following questions may help to focus our inquiry: (1) With what kind of Judaism was each of these writers or groups of writers concerned? (2) What was the relation between the author's Christian community and that variety of Judaism? (3) In what social context was this interaction taking place?

THE JOHANNINE GROUPS AND "THE JEWS"

Although the Fourth Gospel is certainly not the earliest of our sources, it is a convenient place to begin, because despite the occasional obscurity of its symbolic language, it portrays the Jewish-Christian issue starkly and with peculiar intensity. The rupture between the followers of Jesus and "the Jews" is at the center of attention; it has manifestly shaped the Johannine groups' language and their perception of the world. These features of the Johannine universe have become so widely recognized in recent scholarship that there is no need for me to rehearse the evidence.[1]

Even in the synoptic gospels there are predictions that Jewish authorities, among others, will persecute Jesus' followers (for example, Mark 13:9–13 and parallels). .The comparable prediction in John 16:2, however, is rather different. On the one hand, the expected hostility is intensified—"the hour is coming when everyone who kills you will think he is offering a service to God." On the other, instead of general chastisement by "councils" *(synedria)* and "synagogues," Jesus here tells the disciples that "they will make you *aposynagōgoi.*" This peculiar expression occurs also in 9:22, where we are told that "the Jews had already decreed that if anyone confessed him [sc. Jesus] as Messiah, he would become *aposynagōgos,*" and 12:42, where the "many" leaders *[archontes]* who believed in Jesus did not confess that belief "on account of the Pharisees, lest they become *aposynagōgoi.*" Those fearful leaders are exemplified in this gospel by Nicodemus (3:1–21; 7:48–52; 19:39). The positive countertype is the blind beggar healed by Jesus in chap. 9; he boldly refutes "the Jews" (not otherwise identified) who interrogate him about Jesus, whereupon they "put him out" (9:34).

Louis Martyn's ingenious "two-level reading" of John 9 and other conflict stories in this gospel has been widely accepted in its general outline if not in all its details.[2] There is a broad consensus today that many aspects of the confrontation between Jesus and the Jewish authorities are projections into the narrative from the experience of the Johannine community. The evangelist has not only made Jesus prophesy such experiences, he or she has also adapted the stories circulating among these Christian groups into vignettes that provide *exempla* of good and bad faith. Consequently, we can use the dialogues and stories in John to learn something about the separation sometime in the last quarter of the first century between these particular Christian groups and the Jewish communities. It would help if we knew exactly where this took place, but unfortunately we have no direct evidence. Further below I shall make a tentative suggestion about the Johannine locale.

The Fourth Gospel has a great deal to say—much but by no means all of it negative—about *hoi ioudaioi,* which modern translations ordinarily render as "the Jews." A fair amount has been written about this usage, for it is puzzling in several respects.[3] There are places, like John 7:1, when *hoi ioudaioi* is primarily a geographical term, and there is a strong contrast, which apparently carries some symbolic weight, between "the Galileans" and "the Judaeans." It will not do, however, to treat the term as always merely geographical.[4] Phrases like "the festival of the *ioudaioi,*" referring to festivals in which "Greeks" from the Diaspora and Galileans (including Jesus) participate, require us to think of the term as designating something like a religious community. Anachronism may trip us up, however; it is important to remember that our concept "a religion" can hardly be expressed in Greek or Latin, for the religious pluralism that was characteristic of the Roman empire was structured in a quite different way from our kind of pluralism. Cults traveled principally by the migration of people,[5] and they tended to be identified by their place of origin: "the Syrian goddess" and the like.[6] It may help to remind us that neither of our categories "religion" and "race" had been invented in antiquity if we translate *ioudaioi* as "Judaeans," keeping in mind that "Judaeans" may refer either to people residing in Judaea or to a diaspora city's community of resident aliens whose origin was in Judaea, and who preserved their identity by means of characteristic religious customs. In either case, the term is one more likely to be used by an outsider looking in than by a member of the community speaking within the group.

These considerations do not yet solve the problem of people like the blind man in John 9 who is indubitably both a "Jew" and a resident of Judaea, but who is, along with his parents, distinguished from the *ioudaioi*. Von Wahlde argues that in such passages "the Judaeans" are to be understood as "the [Jewish] authorities," and that all of the hostile references to "the Judaeans" in John *may* be so understood.[7] With what would this usage correspond in the real world? It is hard to imagine a situation in which someone resident in Judaea would say, "The Judaeans put me out of the synagogue." In a diaspora city, say Ephesus or Antioch, it is somewhat more plausible, since we may think of a Jew speaking to non-Jews.

Von Wahlde's survey focuses narrowly on the use of the term "the Judaeans," so that he does not help us much to understand the dialectic between those so designated in John and other groups, especially "the Galileans" and "the Samaritans." It is that dialectic, however, which determines the meaning of these terms in the structure of the Johannine narrative. Jouette Bassler has made that particularly clear in her analysis.[8] Correcting earlier work (including my own) which observed these symbolic oppositions but concentrated one-sidedly on the places so represented, Bassler points out that it is groups more than places in which the fourth evangelist is interested. "Galileans [and on one occasion Samaritans] symbolize those who receive the Word, Judeans symbolize those who reject it."[9] Bassler also points out the inconsistency in the reconstructions of Johannine community history by R. E. Brown and J. L. Martyn who "have exhaustively combed the Gospel (and letters) for allusions to groups that figured [negatively] in the community's history," but who nonetheless reject suggestions that "the Galileans" or "Samaritans" in the narrative prefigure real groups in the church's experience. Any reconstruction of the setting and history of the Johannine Christians must offer some explanation for the special and positive place accorded both the Galileans and the Samaritans in this Gospel.

There are a few more peculiarities of John's story which we should keep in mind before we try to deduce its geographical and social setting. First, the boundaries of the story are the boundaries of Israel. While *ioudaioi* is frequently used in a hostile sense, *Israel* is always used positively in this Gospel, which can describe Jesus' mission as to "gather into one the children of God who are scattered" (11:52). Now because the context makes it clear that these children include more than the *ethnos* of the Judaeans, the reader may jump to the conclusion that gentiles are included. Yet in fact there is hardly a hint of a specifically gentile mission in John. We do hear of "Greeks," but it is the *"diaspora* of the Greeks" (7:35) and "certain Greeks of the pilgrims who came to worship at the festival" (12:20). That is, it is Greek-speaking Jews who are meant.[10]

Second, the imagery and structure of the Johannine argument are, despite contrary appearances, profoundly Jewish. The author of the Gospel, the community traditions he employed, and presumably his audience, if they understood what was being said, were intimately familiar with scripture and with a variety of interpretive traditions. To be sure, the evangelist uses the Jewish traditions in a way that Jews would regard as perverse, but his transformation of them presupposes familiarity.[11]

Preliminary answers to our first two questions emerge from the clues we have recalled so far. What kind of Judaism is represented by the hostile "Judaeans" of the Fourth Gospel? We cannot identify these Judaeans with any of the various "sects" of Israel that we hear about in ancient sources. The Pharisees, for example, do have a leading role in the opposition to Jesus, but they seem a conventional group here, without distinguishing characteristics—in contrast to the situation in Matthew. This counts against an assumption that the Johannine communities took shape primarily vis-à-vis the formative rabbinic movement at Yavneh. Also against that assumption is the fact that the controversies in John do not turn centrally on practice, but on beliefs. Christian beliefs about Jesus seemed blasphemous to the Judaeans of John's gospel. This emphasis on beliefs does not mean that the traditions used in John do not retain a memory of controversy about practice. For example, the story of Jesus healing a paralytic (5:1–8) has at some point been converted into a controversy story by adding the note, "It was the sabbath that day" (5:9c–16). The controversy, however, does not lead to a pronouncement about what is the proper way to observe the sabbath, as for example the stories of Matthew 12:1–14 do. Instead, it leads to the much more severe accusation that Jesus "made himself equal to God" (5:17) and to a discourse on Jesus' relationship to "the Father." This observation does not help us much to discover just which group of Jews may have been in mind, however, for probably most Jews would have agreed that it was blasphemy for any human being to be called "God" in the sense the Johannine Christians meant when speaking of Jesus (10:33).[12]

If there are no grounds for identifying the opposing "Judaeans" of John with "normative Judaism" or its "formative" predecessors at Yavneh, nevertheless we must recognize that, in the eyes of the Johannine community, the "Judaeans" and their *archontes* were people who exercised power. The locus of their power, moreover, was in the synagogues, and it was sufficient to expel persons from membership, even to threaten their lives.

The relationship of the Johannine Christians to "Judaism," then, was a relationship with organized Jewish communities centered in synagogues. By the time the Fourth Gospel was written, these Christians were no longer connected with those communities. By the time when the three Johannine letters were written, there was no sign of any direct interaction with the synagogues, nor even of any interest in the issue of separation.[13] Yet when the Gospel was written, the rupture with the synagogue remained in the sect's memory as the all-important crisis which had shaped the groups' identity and helped to shape their christology. One might say that "the world" of the Fourth Gospel, in more than one sense, is the world of Judaism. It would be more accurate, however, to say that it is a world in which groups identified as "Judaeans," "Samaritans," and "Galileans" interact. If we assume, for reasons mentioned above, that the Gospel's world is not a purely artful creation but reflects in some measure the real context in which the Johannine groups took their distinctive shape, then it is worth asking whether we can think of a place or at least a kind of place where the Johannine fictions would correspond with reality.

External evidence does not take us very far. By late in the second century, some traditions connected the Fourth Gospel's author with Ephesus, but most recent students of John have been skeptical of these traditions. Even if we take them quite seriously, they do not answer the question of where the formative break between the Johannine communities and the "Judaean" synagogues took place. We are left with the internal evidence, that is, the peculiarities of the Johannine narrative. Is it more plausible to think of it as having been produced in an urban, diaspora environment, or somewhere in the Land of Israel? Attempts to argue for a Palestinian or other bilingual provenance on the basis of a putative Aramaic *Vorlage,* which were popular a generation ago, have not been successful.[14] The language of the evangelist and of the tradition upon which he immediately depended was Greek, and there is no reason to believe that Greek had not been the language of the Johannine groups for some time. Hence the chances are stong that we should look to some *polis* for the origin of this work. Martyn takes this for granted when he speaks of the events mirrored in the Gospel's stories as taking place in "the Jewish Quarter of John's city."[15]

Would controversies among "Judaeans," "Samaritans," and "Galileans" have an immediate meaning to residents of a polis like Ephesus or Antioch? The more we learn from archaeology of the immigrant communities' organization in the Graeco-Roman cities, the more plausible such scenes appear. Especially, the existence of a substantial Samaritan Diaspora side by side with the Jews seems more and more certain. Tombstones found in Thessalonica have shown that there was a Samaritan community in that city as late as the second century C. E., and we know that there was a large Jewish community there.[16] Just recently, inscriptions from the island of Delos dated to the second century B.C.E. have revealed a community who called themselves "Israelites of Delos, who offer first fruits at sacred Har Garizim."[17] Their community center, if Philippe Bruneau is right, was less than one hundred meters from the Judaean synagogue.[18] The question whether "in this mountain" or "in Jerusalem" was the place to honor God (John 4:20) was evidently a question that could be argued on Delos as well as in Palestine, and presumably in any city where there was an organized Jewish as well as a Samaritan community.[19]

The "Galileans," however, pose more of a problem in such a setting. To be sure, it is possible that "Galileans" had already become a nickname for Christians, as it would be for the emperor Julian three centuries later and perhaps already in Epictetus (*Diss.* 4.7.6). Yet the "Galileans" in John are not simply identified with those who become Jesus' disciples. They are rather those who are receptive to the signs and word of Jesus. It is possible that the evangelist hit upon the symbolic use of the term by an ingenious blending of such an outsiders' nickname with reflection on the geographical setting of Jesus' career, but his work in that case would seem extraordinarily artificial. It is more straightforward to assume that "Galileans" as well as "Judaeans" and "Samaritans" were known entities in the formative milieu of the Johannine community. It is not impossible that an association of immigrants from Galilee might have existed and been called "the Galileans" in one or another Mediterranean city in the Roman age, but I am aware of no evidence for such. A setting somewhere in Palestine thus seems more plausible.

There is one further aspect of the Gospel's imagery that speaks in favor of a Palestinian setting. If the primary Johannine milieu had been a large, cosmopolitan city, then it is strange that we hear no whisper in the Fourth Gospel about a dominant, pagan society. There is only the Roman governor who plays his necessary role. For those who picture the "Jewish Quarter of [a Graeco-Roman] city" after the model of the mediaeval ghetto, that may not seem surprising, but in fact Jewish life in Alexandria, Antioch, Sardis, Miletus, and Aphrodisias was nothing like that.[20] Yet for the Johannine Christians, as late as when the Gospel was written, "the world" into which they were sent, but to which they belonged no more (John 17:14–18), was a world dominated by the "Judaeans."

The symbolic importance of Galilee and Samaria and the presence of what seem to be old local traditions from these areas in John some years ago prompted me to posit a Galilean provenance for the Gospel.[21] My argument was simplistic in some respects, yet there are still good reasons for considering whether the Johannine groups took shape in Galilee even though we shall probably never be certain. The recent explorations by Eric Meyers and others show that some areas of Lower Galilee in particular might well provide just the socio-cultural mix which my analysis of the symbolism in John requires: the towns were both urbanized and hellenized; the community could relate closely with Samaria, Judaea, and "the Diaspora of the Greeks"; strong Jewish communities were prepared to exercise firm discipline; and there was, of course, a quite positive sense for "the Galileans."[22]

An alternative localization is that proposed by Klaus Wengst.[23] His analysis, though more detailed than mine can be here, parallels mine in most respects. There are two weaknesses. First, he does not pay adequate attention to the symbolism of the interaction among "Galileans," "Samaritans," and "Judaeans" in the Johannine narrative which I have stressed above. However it would only strengthen the conclusions he reaches. Second, and more troublesome, he assumes that a "uniform, pharisaically defined Judaism" became normative in Palestine instantly after 70 C.E., and that it was that kind of Judaism the Johannine Christians confronted (Wengst, 42). Jacob Neusner's research argues persuasively that it was not until the Bar Kochba crisis that the thoroughgoing reinstitutionalization of life in the land of Israel began,[24] and I have argued above that the Johannine controversies do not seem essentially "halakhic."[25] Further, Wengst assumes a village rather than an urban setting, and one sufficiently uniform that exclusion from the synagogues would mean effective exclusion from social and economic life. There is nothing in the Fourth Gospel, however, which speaks directly of economic pressures. The Johannine Christians evidently were able to sustain their independent and increasingly sectarian existence. A *polis,* though not a very cosmopolitan one, as explained above, seems more plausible than a circle of villages. Finally, Wengst has assumed too quickly, with many students of John, that the expulsion from synagogues is explained by the imposition of the *birkat ha-minim* (Wengst, 52–57). It is time to recognize that the *birkat ha-minim* has been a red herring in Johannine research. Not only do questions remain about its date and the earliest form of its wording—not to mention questions of where and when it would have been effective after it was promulgated[26]—the more fundamental issue for interpreting John 16:2 and John 9's depiction of the healed blind man's expulsion is whether these scenes have anything to do with the way the *birkat ha-minim* would have worked in practice. John does not speak of people who do not go to synagogue services because they cannot conscientiously say the prayers. It speaks of being put out of the synagogue. All we have to assume is that the *archontes* of the Jewish community in John's location had simply made up their minds to get rid of these trouble-making followers of a false Messiah.

Nevertheless, Wengst's proposal for the geographical setting of the formative (perhaps not the final) stage of the Fourth Gospel is attractive. He proposes the southern part of the kingdom of Agrippa II, especially the western portion around Bathyra in Batanaea. The factors present in the larger towns of Lower Galilee would be present there as well.

Whichever of these three possibilities we prefer—Galilee, Batanaea, or some small *polis* elsewhere with a relatively large presence of Judaean, Galilean, and Samaritan immigrants—the Johannine Christians had formed their lives in a society dominated by the Jewish community. In response, they had taken on the characteristics of a *sect* in the modern sociological sense.[27] Significantly, the social formation which they developed by the time the Johannine letters were written depended upon that institution so characteristic of Christianity in its early spread through the cities of the Mediterranean basin, as of other migratory cults: the Graeco-Roman household.[28] Traumatically divorced from the synagogues, Johannine Christians made a new life for themselves within private houses, starting anew just as Jewish or Samaritan immigrants in Diaspora cities had often done when they first arrived.

PAULINE CHRISTIANITY AND THE JEWS

In contrast with the Fourth Gospel, the Pauline letters provide us with a wealth of specific information about the places and social settings where existed the Christian groups founded by Paul and his co-workers.[29] I have called the setting "urban" for convenience, but that adjective may tempt us to commit anachronisms. It is important to distinguish the village and rural setting presupposed by most of the gospel stories about Jesus from the culture of the Graeco-Roman towns, but we must not confuse the latter with our post-industrial notion of a city. I mean by the term "urban" that Pauline Christianity was at home in the Greek *poleis* of the eastern Roman provinces.

One characteristic of that setting was "pluralism," if I may be permitted yet another deliberate anachronism. There was no officially sanctioned "religion" of the empire.[30] Both the hellenistic and the Roman cultures tended to be quite tolerant of different kinds of religious practices—so long as they did not endanger public order or infringe upon common decency, and so long as they seemed to have some ancient pedigrees. Specifically, the national cult of the resident aliens was ordinarily not only tolerated but even protected—even if it was a little bizarre in Roman eyes, as was the case with Judaeans. But a new superstition without any national basis, like the Christians', was something else again, and likely to attract suspicion or disdain.[31]

This pluralist context which is so strikingly absent from the Fourth Gospel is always lurking at the edges of the Pauline letters. Take, for example, the characterization of the converts in 1 Thessalonians 1:9 as those who "turned from idols to serve the living and true God," or Paul's concern about interaction between the Christian community and pagan culture as he answers questions about eating "meat offered to idols" in 1 Corinthians 8–10, or his warning not to let charismatic phenomena get out of hand, lest outsiders think the Christians were indulging in a Dionysiac orgy (1 Cor 14:23). Paul not only recognizes, as does the fourth evangelist, that it is not possible to "go out of the world" (1 Cor 5:10); he also is concerned that "the outsiders" should think well of the Christians' behavior (e.g. 1 Thess 4:11f.).

In further contrast to the Fourth Gospel, we hear very little about "the Jews" or "the Judaeans." The only place where Paul sounds like John is in 1 Thessalonians 2:14–16, and a number of commentators have suggested that all or part of that passage is an interpolation.[32] There is otherwise remarkably little in the Pauline letters to suggest any continuing contact between the Christian groups and the organized Jewish communities in their cities. Paul himself ran into conflict with Jewish authorities from time to time (2 Cor 11:24f.), but the real and potential conflicts he treats and anticipates in the congregations he addresses are either internal or between the Christian groups and the pagan society of the city.

This state of affairs is surprising on two counts. First, the book of Acts would have us believe that Paul always began his mission in the synagogue. That, however, is clearly a later idealization, although it cannot be entirely false in view of Paul's reported conflict with synagogue authorities, just mentioned, and his statement in 1 Corinthians 9:20. Nevertheless, his retrospective accounts of his missionary career assert that he saw himself commissioned entirely as "apostle of the gentiles" (Gal 1–2; Rom 15:15–21; cf.11:13f.). Accordingly, we have to set aside the Acts picture of the earliest mission in order to understand the separation of Pauline Christianity from the synagogues.

The second reason why the rarity of allusions to the Jewish commu-

nities in Pauline letters is surprising, however, has to do with a central
element in Paul's theology. The question of the continuing validity in the
Christian groups of such *miṣvot* as circumcision and *kashrut,* and the
broader issue of the relation between Israel's hopes and traditions and
Christianity (between "Jew and Greek") were vigorously debated in the
Pauline circles. Paul and some of his disciples made them the touchstone
for understanding the radical innovation entailed in accepting the gospel
of the crucified Messiah. Furthermore, there are several indications in
Paul's letters that his relationship to his own past and to "Israel according to the flesh" continued to exercise his deepest feelings (e.g. Rom
9:1–5). Nevertheless, the locus of these conflicts is altogether different
from that reflected in the Fourth Gospel.

The main difference is this: the great issue in Pauline Christianity is
not between "the synagogue" and the sect of the Christians, but within
the Christian movement. The social context of Pauline groups is the
private household provided by various patrons in each city. That form
of organization does not become visible in the Johannine communities
until the later phase marked by the Johannine letters. The household
may have served as the location of those Christian cells, too, by the time
the Fourth Gospel was written, but the Gospel provides no evidence for
it. Instead, the identity of the groups is largely determined by their
reaction to the synagogues and the synagogues' attitudes toward them.
For Pauline Christians the case is quite different. Like the fourth evangelist, Paul wants to claim the name and hopes of Israel for the followers
of Messiah Jesus.[33] *Theologically* it is correct to say that the scriptures
and traditions of Judaism are a central and ineffaceable part of the
Pauline Christians' identity. *Socially,* however, the Pauline groups were
never a sect of Judaism. They organized their lives independently from
the Jewish associations of the cities where they were founded, and
apparently, so far as the evidence reveals, they had little or no interaction
with the Jews.

Paul's own reflection on Israel's "disbelief" and destiny in God's plan
is unique in early Christian literature (Rom 9–11). Even this discussion,
however, does not arise from any active engagement between either the
Pauline groups or the various Christian groups in Rome and the Jewish
communities. This homily by Paul is the climax of the entire letter, as
commentators in the past few years have belatedly recognized.[34] It belongs to Paul's reflection on the purpose and meaning of his own mis-

sion, and that, in turn, is an integral part of his protreptic discourse on the nature of the Christian life by which he introduces himself to the Roman Christians.[35] It is thus, again, the Christian community's internal dynamics and beliefs, rather than real interaction with Jews, that evokes this discussion.

At least some of Paul's disciples understood the significance of his preoccupation with unity of Jew and gentile in "the Israel of God." The encyclical letter we know as Ephesians develops the grand idea of one "household of God" uniting Jew and gentile (2:11–22). This can be regarded as a kind of cosmic projection of an idealized Pauline house church.[36] Yet in this letter there is no hint of any relation a Christian might have with the majority of the Jews meeting in the synagogue down the street. Ephesians' sublime disregard of that issue is testimony that Pauline Christians in Asia Minor had gone their own way without much contact with the strong, well placed Jewish communities which existed in the cities of that region. The pseudonymous but more particular epistle to the Colossians points in the same direction, despite the fact that it attacks a syncretistic movement among the Christians which seems to involve a Jewish festival calendar, sabbath observance, some dietary rules (2:16), and perhaps Jewish mystical practice of some kind (2:18).[37] Even here the author does not say anything about contact between the Christians and the Jewish community of Colossae.

There is thus a certain paradox about Pauline Christianity. The apostle himself was deeply concerned about the relation between Christianity and "the Israel of God." Yet he and his associates had created an organized movement that was entirely independent of the Jewish communities in the cities of the northeastern Mediterranean basin. The scriptures and traditions from Judaism played a major part in the beliefs and practices of Pauline Christianity, yet the identity of the Pauline groups was not shaped by having once been within a Jewish context. However much Paul's own identity may have been formed by the trauma of what we call his conversion, there was no comparable trauma for the communities which he founded. Unlike the Johannine groups, the Pauline congregations were not composed of people who had become *aposynagōgoi*.

MATTHEW AGAINST THE SCRIBES AND PHARISEES

The combination of strong Jewish traditions with rejection of Jewish institutions is as fiercely ambivalent in Matthew as in John. The terms of the argument, however, are quite different. It is not always easy to determine exactly what is at issue in Matthew, and scholarly opinions have diverged widely on the question of the Matthean community's relationship to Judaism. Only in rather recent years have scholars recognized the full import of the question of precisely what kind of Judaism confronted the Matthean Christians and in what way. The recent comment by Graham Stanton is accurate: "Scholarly interest in many aspects of first-century Judaism is considerable and significant advances are being made, especially by J. Neusner and his pupils. Few Matthean specialists have yet taken these advances sufficiently seriously."[38] What would it mean for our three questions if we did take those advances seriously? First, it would mean keeping constantly in mind the diversity of both the forms of Judaism and the forms of Christianity in the first century. That point, however, is now generally conceded, at least in principle. Second, we would have to try more rigorously than has usually been the case to avoid anachronisms when comparing first-century documents with those produced by the rabbinic schools of the second century and later. Third, we would have to acknowledge that the means by which groups of Jews and Christians established their own cohesion, identity, and boundaries were not always the same. Christian scholars tend to think of group identity in terms of theological systems or "confessions," and in spite of our best intentions, we almost inevitably ask Christian theological questions of Jewish documents.[39] As a corrective, when we look through Matthew's eyes at the Jewish groups he opposed, it will be well to begin with clues to more external aspects of the groups' life, which do not imply a systematic theology.

The opponents in Matthew are preeminently "the scribes and the Pharisees," and Pharisees are particularly odious to the writer. There are other groups, too, which are mentioned as Jesus' opponents, but for the most part they seem to be relics of the remembered tradition and no longer to have sharp contours.[40] Matthew can, for example, simply merge the Sadducees with the Pharisees, even though he knows from Mark, if nowhere else, that they were distinct sects (Matt 3:7; 16:1,6,11,12 and Mark 12:13, 18). The Pharisees and scribes of Matthew's acquaintance "like . . . to be called 'Rabbi' " (23:6f.), and the prohibition of this and other titles in the Christian community identifies "rabbi" with "teacher" (23:8–10). All of this fits admirably Neusner's reconstruction of the institutionalization that occurred at Yavneh, in which leaders from the sect of the Pharisees joined with members of the professional guild of scribes to create a new thing: the rabbinic academy and, eventually, the rabbinic court.[41] It has long been recognized that the issues at stake in the Matthean controversy stories have more similarity in both form and substance with parallels in rabbinic literature than do pre-Matthean forms. W. D. Davies especially, in his pioneering work on the Sermon on the Mount, argued eloquently for seeing the work of the Christian scribes in Matthew's community as "a parallel task" to that of the rabbis at Yavneh.[42] Neusner's work requires revision of Davies' at many points, but it tends to reinforce this fundamental insight.

Even if we accept the proposition that Matthew's "scribes and Pharisees" refer to the emerging rabbinate of Yavneh, however, a number of puzzles remain. Where and in what form did the Christian community encounter Yavneh's rabbis? From the typical setting of the controversy stories, we may gather that the main location was in "their [i.e., the Jews'] synagogues." There the rabbis have or want to have "the first seats" (23:6). That they also are said to like wide phylacteries and long "hems" (presumably ṣiṣit 23:5) does not help us to be more specific, but the whole passage implies that the rabbis enjoy considerable prestige in public (in the *agorai*, at banquets) as well as in the synagogues. The problem is the more difficult because we know so little about the extent of the Yavneh academy's power and prestige outside its immediate circle. Because the majority of Matthean scholars think, though without absolutely convincing evidence, that Matthew was written in Antioch on the Orontes, we would like very much to know whether representatives of the Yavneh school, or a diaspora equivalent similarly constituted, could have exercised power in that metropolis at so early a date. Unfortunately, the prospects are slim for answering these questions definitively.

We turn then to our second question. What connections were there between the Christian groups out of which and for which Matthew was written, and the emerging new form of rabbi-led Judaism? Scholars who have pursued this question in recent years have come to dismayingly opposite conclusions. Either Matthew's Christians were a "Jewish-Christian" sect which, however alienated from the rabbinic leadership, still belonged to the "union of synagogues" (as Hummel puts it),[43] or they had no connections at all and existed in a purely pagan environment (Van Tilborg, for example). What leads serious scholars to such incompatible conclusions is a real ambivalence in the evidence in the First Gospel itself. We must decide how the "Jewish" elements in Matthew are to be reconciled with the "anti-Jewish" elements, a problem similar to that in the Fourth Gospel. The "redaction-historical" method that has come to prevail in such studies, despite the discouraging lack of agreement in results, does give promise of a solution along lines similar to those found in recent Johannine scholarship. A consensus is emerging that the Matthean community went through several stages of interaction with the Jewish communities close to it, and that these stages have left fossils in the strata of tradition and redaction.[44] A quick summary of the evidence will show the direction in which an answer to our question must be sought.

There is much in Matthew that sounds like intra-Jewish, sectarian debate. To begin with, there are the learned arguments from scripture which have led Von Dobschütz and others to identify the evangelist with the "scribe discipled to the Kingdom of Heaven" of 13:52. Then there is the concern with "commandments" that crops up throughout Matthew, culminating in the "Great Commission" of 28:20. The Sermon on the Mount reads like the ethic of a Jewish sect. Jesus speaks here as the authoritative teacher of Israel. The crowds are astonished at his teaching for he has authority, unlike *their* scribes (Matthew has added the pronoun to the Marcan phrase; 7:29). Here and elsewhere in this gospel we could say that Jesus is the authoritative interpreter of *halakha* (for example, in the Sabbath controversies of chapter 12). Yet only rarely does the form of these controversies approximate the forms typical of the debates transmitted in rabbinic tradition's early strata.[45] The Matthean debates are much broader and less stylized, and they question more fundamental issues of Jewish identity.

Jesus' authority in Matthew is that of the Messiah of Israel, the son of David, who has come to "save his people" (1.21). In illustration of this, the crowds repeatedly bring their sick to Jesus for healing, for, as Messiah, he "bears away" the diseases of Israel (8:17; citing Isa 53:4). Matthew inserts one of his summaries to this effect into the Temple Cleansing pericope: "They brought him blind and lame *in the Temple,* and he healed them" (21:14). In these passages and elsewhere, Jesus is

well received by the "crowds" *(ochloi),* but rejected by the formal leaders of Israel.[46] In Mark it was the leaders of Israel—there identified as
the high priests and scribes and elders (Mark 11:27)—who "recognized
that it was against them that he spoke the parable" of the vineyard;
Matthew connects this remark with the parable of the two sons also,
and changes the leaders to "the high priests and the Pharisees" (Matt
21:45).

From such texts we get the impression that the Matthean prophets
and disciples were an integral part of one or more of the Jewish communities in Matthew's environment, challenging the leaders on their
own ground. In support of such a reading, one could observe that 23:2f.
seems to accord some authority to the teaching of the scribes and Pharisees, even while sharply challenging their integrity and sincerity (contrast
16:5–12!). This sounds indeed like a sectarian dispute between two
schools, both of which construe the faithful life in similar terms, but
which disagree about the locus of authority and the form of internal
community life. So also, Matthew retains the Q-saying that the disciples
will "sit on twelve thrones judging the twelve tribes of Israel" (19:28). It
is easy to imagine a time when Christian missionaries actually believed
that they could win over the allegiance of masses of Jews from their
constituted leaders. Perhaps, adopting part of W. D. Davies' suggestions
in *The Background of the Sermon on the Mount,* we could even think of
an active competition between representatives of the new "rabbinic"
academy at Yavneh and missionaries of the Jesus movement.

Yet there are many indications in the First Gospel that the connections with organized Jewish communities cannot have been so close
when the gospel was written. If the Matthean Christians once held such
an optimistic view of their mission to the organized Jews in their town,
they have long since become disillusioned. In a remark that betrays a
distance quite as complete as that in John, they can speak of a story
about the disciples' faking the Resurrection, a story "spread among the
Jews until this day" (28:15). This gospel contains a rising theme, climax-
ing in the trial and passion narrative, of the alienation of "the whole
people" from Jesus, their appointed Messiah. The theme is clearly sounded
in the healing of the centurion, for "in no one in Israel" has Jesus found
such faith (8:10), and he adds that "many will come from East and West
and recline at dinner with Abraham and Isaac and Jacob, but the sons of
the Kingdom will be cast into outer darkness." The implication of this

dark saying works its way through the rest of the gospel: through the judgment pronounced in 10:14f. on towns of Israel which did not receive the apostles (emphasized by Matthew's placement of the judgment pericope from Q in 11:20–24 and the saying that no one can know the Father but the Son in 11:27); through the parables of Two Sons, the Vineyard, and the Banquet. Despite the modified Marcan statement in 21:45f. (quoted above), these parables speak not merely of judgment on Israel's leaders, but of replacing Israel by another *ethnos* (21:41, 43). Looking back, we see that this replacement is foreshadowed by the curious story of the "Canaanite" woman of 15:21–28, for Jesus' disclaimer that he is sent only to "the lost sheep of the house of Israel" is but the counterpoint to his receiving the faith of this gentile, just as the identical phrase in the sending of the twelve (10:6) is prelude for judgment on those who reject their message.[47] Thus not only is "the whole sanhedrin" responsible for Jesus' condemnation (26:59), but "all the people" confirms it by the saying which would have such terrible and unforeseeable consequences: "His blood be on us and on our children" (27:25).

Like the Johannine community, then, the Matthean was shaped to a very large extent by the attempt to define the Christian groups' relation to Jewish traditions, Jewish expectations, and the organized Jewish communities. Unlike John, but rather like Paul, Matthew sees the Jewish self-definition primarily in terms of law and commandments and, more broadly, in the question of what it means to "do the will of God." Like Paul personally, but unlike the Pauline churches, Matthew's community has had to wrestle with that issue in a way central to its own development. However, all three are alike, finally, in seeing the ultimate issue and crisis to be defined by christology. Although the christologies of John, Paul, and Matthew are different from one another in many respects, the breaking point for each is in the question of Jesus' role as Messiah vis-à-vis Israel (and the world).

The Judaism from which Matthew has separated looks much more like that taking shape in the academy of Yavneh around the same time than does the Judaism from which the Johannine Christians were expelled. The "rabbis" who represented the Yavnean (or some analogous but otherwise unknown) merging of scribal profession with Pharisaic piety were important and prestigious people in Matthew's environment. Unfortunately there are few clues that would enable us to describe that environment with any specificity. "Their synagogues" and "banquets" and *agorai* sound like an urban setting, and Matthew's Greek and the knowledge of the LXX he presupposes speak for that as well. The early mission to "the lost sheep of the house of Israel" described in chap. 10, however, sounds like itinerancy among villages on Palestinian soil[48] (though some of Matthew's redactional touches make the scenery less rural; e.g. addition of *polis* in vss. 11,14,15). Did the Christian groups for which Matthew wrote, or some significant number of their members, originate as a sect of Galilean Jews before the war, later to join the already existing Christian household communities of Antioch? It is probably not possible to advance beyond conjecture. It is not even possible to say very much about the internal organization of the Christian groups, even though such passages as 16:18–20 and 18:15–20 imply a high degree of sectarian self-consciousness and self-discipline.

CONCLUDING OBSERVATIONS

The three major witnesses from early Christian literature which we have considered show us three quite different circles of the movement, each profoundly shaped by its Jewish heritage and by the trauma of separation from Judaism experienced either by the sect as a whole or by some of its leaders. The path of separation, then, was not single or uniform. Taking these three paths as representative, it may yet be useful to ask, now, where were they leading for the future of Christianity and of Judaism? On the one hand, they were leading to a Christianity that could not allow itself to forget its origins in Judaism. That meant, preeminently, that in order to define itself, Christianity would always in some way turn to the Jewish scriptures. Moreover, it inherited some of the Jewish ways of interpreting them. If Marcion's movement had endured, Christianity would have become a very different thing.

Nevertheless, by the end of the first century, and much earlier than that in the Pauline groups, the Christian movement was socially independent of the Jewish communities in the cities of the empire. That had little or nothing to do with formal measures like the *birkat ha-minim,* but much to do with the internal dynamics illustrated by the three corpora of documents we have surveyed and with the social setting of Jews and Christians in the Greek cities. There would continue to be interactions between Jews and Christians in various places; there would continue to be followers of Jesus who remained within synagogues here and there, down through at least the fifth century, despite disapproval by leaders on both sides; there would be Christians of pagan origin who continued to be attracted to the synagogue until at least the same period. These, however, were the exceptions. By and large the separation was complete by the beginning of the second century. For example in Antioch, the first bishop, Ignatius, betrays hostility toward "Judaism" but little evidence of any knowledge of the Jews. A later successor, Theophilus, could simply take for granted that the scriptures and central traditions of Israel now belonged to the Christians.[49]

To Jews, claims like those of Theophilus must have seemed so preposterous and the Christian movement so remote or so minuscule that, save for a few local exceptions, they could ignore it altogether. That accounts for the sparse evidence about Christianity in Mishnah, Talmuds, and early midrashim. Too late, the Jewish leaders would be forced to recognize how dangerous the Christian movement was. Not even the post-Constantinian changes of the fourth century seem to have alerted them, portentous as those changes seem in retrospect. In places like Antioch, Sardis, and Aphrodisias, the Jewish communities remained secure and powerful, hardly troubled even as the legal and political mechanisms of Christian dominance were put into place. Yet what survives from those communities' glory is only what has lately been uncovered by the archaeologist's spade. In time, the Christians would dominate the cities and, in ways partly obvious and partly obscure, would choke off the growth of those Jewish communities. The living Judaism that survived, which we see taking shape as a "utopian" vision in the Mishnah and more practically in the two talmuds,[50] seems rather to have been a rural and small-town phenomenon. Thus the massive confrontation between "apostolic Christianity" and "normative Judaism," which even now haunts the imagination of students of Christian origins, never happened.

NOTES

1. See Wayne A. Meeks, " 'Am I a Jew?'—Johannine Christianity and Judaism," in Jacob Neusner, ed., *Christianity, Judaism, and Other Greco-Roman Cults: Studies for Morton Smith at Sixty* (Leiden: Brill, 1975) 1:164–

185; for more recent literature, see F. F. Segovia, "The Love and Hatred of Jesus and Johannine Sectarianism," *CBQ* 43 (1981) 258–272.

2. J. Louis Martyn, *History and Theology in the Fourth Gospel* (2nd ed.; Nashville: Abingdon, 1979).

3. Most recently, see U. C. von Wahlde, "The Johannine 'Jews': A Critical Survey," *NTS* 28 (1982) 33–60; cf. my "Am I a Jew?" cited above, n.l.

4. Against C. J. Cuming, "The Jews in the Fourth Gospel," *ExpT* 60 (1948–49) 290–292; M. Lowe, "Who were the IOUDAIOI?" *NovT* 18 (1976) 101–30; see criticism by Klaus Wengst, *Bedrängte Gemeinde und verherrlichter Christus: Der historische Ort des Johannesevangeliums als Schlüssel zu seiner Interpretation* (Biblisch Theologische Studien 5; Neukirchen: Neukirchener Verlag, 1981) 40.

5. See Ramsay MacMullen, *Paganism in the Roman Empire* (New Haven and London: Yale, 1982) 113–115.

6. Cf. my remarks in "Am I a Jew?" 182, and note the comments by Alf Thomas Kraabel, "Judaism in Western Asia Minor under the Roman Empire" (unpublished Th. D. dissertation, Harvard: 1968) 30f. An inscription of benefactors of Smyrna, ca. 125 C.E., includes a group called *hoi pote Ioudaioi;* Kraabel argues this refers to recent immigrants from Judaea, recalling Dio Cassius 37.16.5–17.1.

7. Von Wahlde, "The Johannine 'Jews'," passim.

8. Jouette M. Bassler, "The Galileans: A Neglected Factor in Johannine Community Research," *CBQ* 43 (1981) 243–257.

9. Ibid. 253.

10. These "Greeks" may of course have been Jewish proselytes or *theosebeis,* as most of the commentaries suggest, but that requires that John observed a rigorous distinction between *hellēnes* and *hellēnistai,* of which we cannot be sure. Hans Windisch observes that *hellēnes* can sometimes refer to "Hellenized Orientals" but insists that it cannot refer to Greek-speaking Jews (*TDNT* 2:509f.). Were the latter not "Hellenized Orientals"? In any case, if the *hellēnes* in John were meant to refer to a mission to gentiles, the passages in question are a strangely muted way to do so.

11. See "Am I a Jew?" and the literature referred to there.

12. See W. A. Meeks, "The Divine Agent and His Counterfeit in Philo and the Fourth Gospel," in Elisabeth Schüssler Fiorenza, ed., *Aspects of Religious Progaganda in Judaism and Early Christianity* (Notre Dame and London: University of Notre Dame Press, 1976) 43–67.

13. Pace J. A. T. Robinson, "The Destination and Purpose of the Johannine Epistles," *NTS* 7 (1960–61) 56–65.

14. See the literature discussed in "Am I a Jew?" and note the remarks by Klaus Beyer, *Semitische Syntax im Neuen Testament* (Göttingen: Vandenhoeck & Ruprecht, 1962) 1:17f.

15. Martyn, *History and Theology in the Fourth Gospel* (rev. ed.; Nashville: Abingdon, 1979) 30.

16. B. Lifshitz and J. Schiby, "Une synagogue samaritaine à Thessalonique," *RB* 75 (1968) 368–378.

17. Philippe Bruneau, " 'Les Israélites de Délos' et la Juiverie délienne," *BCH* 106 (1982) 465–504.

18. Ibid., 488; some caution is necessary, for the Jewish inscriptions discovered so far are dated to the first century C.E. The Samaritan and Jewish evidence does not therefore overlap in time, and it is a conjecture, though a reasonable one, that both communities were continuous over a long period. See Bruneau's careful discussion, 495–499.

19. Whether the temple on Gerizim destroyed by John Hyrcanus in 128 B.C.E. (Josephus, *Ant.* 13.256; the parallel in *B. J.* 1.63 mentions Hyrcanus' defeat of the "Cuthaeans," but not the destruction of the temple) was subsequently rebuilt, ancient sources do not reveal. That Mt. Gerizim remained a cultic center for the Samaritans, however, is clear.

20. This point has now been repeatedly made; Kraabel's observations are exemplary. See, besides his dissertation cited above, A. T. Kraabel, "Paganism and Judaism: The Sardis Evidence," in André Benoit et al., eds., *Paganisme, Judaïsme, Christianisme . . . Melanges offerts à Marcel Simon* (Paris: Boccard, 1978) 13–33; "The Diaspora Synagogue: Archaeological and Epigraphic Evidence since Sukenik," *ANRW* II.19.1 (1979) 477–510; "Social Systems of Six Diaspora Synagogues," in Joseph Gutmann, ed., *Ancient Synagogues: The State of Research* (Brown Judaic Studies 22; Chico, CA: Scholars, 1981) 79–91.

21. On local traditions in John, see the recent article by C.H.H. Scobie, "Johannine Geography," *SR* 11/1 (1982) 77–84.

22. E. M. Meyers, J. F. Strange, and Dennis E. Groh, "The Meiron Excavation Project: Archaeological Survey in Galilee and Golan, 1976," *BASOR* 230 (1978) 1–24; Eric M. Meyers and James F. Strange, *Archaeology, the Rabbis, and Early Christianity* (Nashville: Abingdon, 1981). See also the impressive collection of literary evidence in Sean Freyne, *Galilee from Alexander the Great to Hadrian; 323 B.C.E. to 135 C.E.* (Wilmington and Notre Dame: Michael Glazier and Univ. of Notre Dame, 1980) and Freyne's observations in "Galilean Religion of the First Century C.E. against its Social Background," *PIBA* 5 (1981) 98–114. Freyne gives very short shrift to archaeological evidence, ignores the Meyers-Strange thesis of Galilee's two cultural regions, and asserts that "the overall Galilean ethos was rural and peasant," with no significant hellenistic influence, "despite the circle of the cities" (1981, 107f.). The statement seems a priori rather than a conclusion from evidence.

23. See above, n. 4.

24. The foundations of Jacob Neusner's position were laid in his studies of traditions associated with particular named sages, especially *Eliezer ben Hyrcanus: The Tradition and the Man* (SJLA 3,4; Leiden: Brill, 1973), built up through the long series of historical and redactional studies of Mishnaic traditions by Neusner and his students (most of them published in the Brill

SJLA series), and confirmed in his *Judaism: The Evidence of the Mishnah* (Chicago and London: Univ. of Chicago, 1981).

25. Against Wengst's analysis on p. 63, which is not altogether self-consistent. Wengst cites Severino Pancaro's observations about "Law" as center of controversy (*The Law in the Fourth Gospel: The Torah and the Gospel, Moses and Jesus, Judaism and Christianity according to John* [NovTSup 42; Leiden: Brill, 1975]). However, Pancaro may have misled Wengst, for *nomos* in John usually refers to the books of Moses or scripture in general, i.e., "Torah," not *halakha*. See further my review of Pancaro in *JBL* 96 (1977) 311–314.

26. Reuven Kimelman, "*Birkat Ha-Minim* and the Lack of Evidence for an Anti-Christian Jewish Prayer in Late Antiquity," in E. P. Sanders, ed., *Jewish and Christian Self-Definition*, vol.2: *Aspects of Judaism in the Graeco-Roman Period* (Philadelphia: Fortress and London: SCM, 1981) 226–244.

27. I proposed this interpretation in "The Man from Heaven in Johannine Sectarianism," *JBL* 91 (1972) 44–72, and it is now widely accepted. See, e.g., the recent article by F. F. Segovia (above, n.1).

28. See A. J. Malherbe, "The Inhospitality of Diotrephes," in Jacob Jervell and Wayne A. Meeks, eds., *God's Christ and His People: Studies in Honour of Nils Alstrup Dahl* (Oslo: Universitetsforlaget, 1977) 222–232; reprinted with an addendum in *Social Aspects of Early Christianity* (2nd ed.; Philadelphia: Fortress, 1983) 92–112. See also W. A. Meeks, *The First Urban Christians: The Social World of the Apostle Paul* (New Haven and London: Yale, 1983), esp. chap. 3. For a massive collection of evidence on the use of households in the establishment of Jewish, Christian, and other Graeco-Roman cults, see L. Michael White, "Domus Ecclesiae, Domus Dei" (Ph.D. Diss. Yale Univ., 1982).

29. I have analyzed the sociographic information of the Pauline letters in *The First Urban Christians* (see previous note). For the evidence underlying the following summary, I refer the reader to that work, and to the large literature cited there.

30. MacMullen, *Paganism;* emphasized by also Nikolaus Walter, "Christusglaube und heidnische Religiosität in paulinischen Gemeinden," *NTS* 25 (1979) 422–442, and Gerd Theissen, *Psychologische Aspekte paulinischer Theologie* (Göttingen: Vandenhoeck & Ruprecht, 1983) 46.

31. Cf. the comments by E. A. Judge, "Christian Innovation and its Contemporary Observers," in Brian Croke and Alanna M. Emmett, eds., *History and Historians in Late Antiquity* (Sydney et al.: Pergamon, 1983) 13–15, and Robert L. Wilken, *The Christians as the Romans Saw Them* (New Haven and London: Yale University Press, 1984).

32. Birger A. Pearson, "1 Thessalonians 2:13–16: A Deutero-Pauline Interpolation," *HTR* 64 (1971) 79–94; Daryl Schmidt; "1 Thess 2:13–16: Linguistic Evidence for an Interpolation," *JBL* 102 (1983) 269–279; other literature cited by both. The case for interpolation has been rebutted, most recently by Karl Paul Donfried, "Paul and Judaism: 1 Thessalonians 2:13–

16 as a Test Case," *Interp* 38 (1984) 242–253, though I find his construal of the text strained. If commentators would stop to ask whether *hypo tōn ioudaiōn* in 2:14 should be translated "by the Jews" or not rather "by the Judaeans," I believe it would be obvious that vss. 13–14 fit quite well into the pattern of the letter and of Paul's thought elsewhere. Vss. 15–16, on the other hand, require the word to refer to "the Jews" in a global sense and import into the letter the kind of anti-Jewish polemic found in later Christian literature, especially in interpretations of the fall of Jerusalem. Donfried would make these verses an older tradition quoted by Paul; it seems to me more likely they were added later by a reader whose conception of Paul's mission was rather like that of the author of Acts. Cf. *First Urban Christians* 227, n. 117.

33. Much has been written about the phrase, "The Israel of God," in Gal 6:16. I think myself that Paul uses it here with deliberate ambiguity. It certainly includes the addressees, the Christian groups of Galatia, and it certainly is not limited to "Jewish Christians." Yet, in the light of Paul's fuller exposition of his thinking about Israel not too many years later in Rom 9–11, we are justified in thinking that "Israel" here includes not only the "remnant" who follow Messiah Jesus (Rom 11:5), but also the entire people, "all Israel," which would be reconciled in Paul's eschatological vision (Rom 11:26).

34. See especially Nils A. Dahl, *Studies in Paul* (Minneapolis: Augsburg, 1977) 137–158. Also Krister Stendahl, *Paul among Jews and Gentiles and Other Essays* (Philadelphia: Fortress, 1976) 4.

35. Stanley K. Stowers, *The Diatribe and Paul's Letter to the Romans* (SBLDS 57; Chico, CA: Scholars, 1981).

36. On Ephesians' idealization of the church, see N. A. Dahl, "Cosmic Dimensions and Religious Knowledge (Eph 3:18)," in E. Earle Ellis and Erich Grässer, eds., *Jesus und Paulus; Festschrift für Werner Georg Kümmel zum 70. Geburtstag* (Göttingen: Vandenhoeck & Ruprecht, 1975) 72f.

37. See the various proposals represented in Fred O. Francis and Wayne A. Meeks, eds., *Conflict at Colossae: A Problem in the Interpretation of Early Christianity Illustrated by Selected Modern Studies* (rev.ed., SBLSBS 4; Missoula, MT: Scholars, 1975).

38. Graham Stanton, *The Interpretation of Matthew* (Issues in Religion and Theology 3; Philadelphia: Fortress and London: SPCK, 1983) 17.

39. Jacob Neusner's criticism of E. P. Sanders, *Paul and Palestinian Judaism*, *HR* 18 (1978) 177–191, is valid at precisely this point, though I think that on the whole he treats Sanders' important contribution rather too severely.

40. Sjef van Tilborg, *The Jewish Leaders in Matthew* (Leiden: Brill, 1972) has sorted out the evidence conveniently, although his analysis is not particularly illuminating.

41. Elaborated in many places, Jacob Neusner's reconstruction is conveniently summarized in "The Formation of Rabbinic Judaism: Yavneh (Jamnia)

from A.D. 70 to 100," *ANRW* II/19.2 (1979) 3–42; cf. " 'Pharisaic-Rabbinic' Judaism: a Clarification," *HR* 12 (1973) 250–270.

42. *The Background of the Sermon on the Mount* (Cambridge: Cambridge University Press, 1964) 315.

43. Reinhart Hummel, *Die Auseinandersetzung zwischen Kirche und Judentum im Matthäusevangelium* (BEvT33, 2nd ed; Munich: Kaiser, 1966).

44. For example, W. G. Thompson, *Matthew's Advice to a Divided Community* (Analecta Biblica 44; Rome: Pontifical Biblical Institute, 1971); summarized in "An Historical Perspective in the Gospel of Matthew," *JBL* 93 (1974) 243–262; Douglas R. A. Hare, *The Theme of Jewish Persecution in the Gospel According to St. Matthew* (SNTSMS 6; Cambridge: Cambridge University Press, 1967); John P. Meier, *The Vision of Matthew: Christ, Church and Morality in the First Gospel* (Theological Inquires; New York, Ramsey, Toronto: Paulist, 1979).

45. A number of important points are still to be found in Morton Smith, *Tannaitic Parallels to the Gospels* (JBLMS 6; Philadelphia: SBL, 1951); for more extended analysis of the early rabbinic forms, see Jacob Neusner, *The Rabbinic Traditions about the Pharisees before 70* (Leiden: Brill, 1971).

46. See Van Tilborg 142–165.

47. Cf. Meier 104.

48. For a wide-ranging and suggestive discussion of the "ecology" of the early mission, see Gerd Theissen, "Wanderradikalismus: Literatursoziologische Aspekte der Überlieferung von Worten Jesu im Urchristentum," and "Legitimation und Lebensunterhalt: Ein Beitrag zur Soziologie urchristlicher Missionare," both reprinted in *Studien zur Soziologie des Urchristentums* (2d. ed., Tübingen: Mohr [Siebeck], 1983) 79–105, 201–230.

49. Ignatius, Mag 8:1-9:2; 10:3; Philad 6:1, 8:2; see also William R. Schoedel, "Ignatius and the Archives," *HTR* 71 (1978) 97–106, and Paul J. Donahue, "Jewish Christianity in the Letters of Ignatius of Antioch," *VC* 32 (1978) 81–93; Theophilus, *Ad Autol.* 2.33 et passim.

50. Jacob Neusner, *Judaism: The Evidence of the Mishnah* (Chicago and London: University of Chicago Press, 1981; *Judaism in Society: The Evidence of the Yerushalmi* (Chicago: University of Chicago Press, 1983).

3

History or Theology? The Basic Problems of the Evidence of the Trial of Jesus

S. G. F. Brandon

It can be claimed, without fear of serious contradiction, that the trial of Jesus of Nazareth is the most notable in the history of mankind. More people know of it, if only vaguely, than of the trial of any other person; its effect on human history has been incalculable. From its fatal outcome stemmed a religion that has become the faith of a large part of mankind and inspired the culture of the Western world; from it, too, has flowed terrible consequences for the Jewish people, held guilty by generations of Christians of the murder of Christ.[1]

History records other trials, equally tragic, in which religious issues have been involved. In 399 BC Socrates was tried and condemned in Athens for introducing strange gods and corrupting the Athenian youth. The case was presented by Plato and Xenophon as a travesty of justice, with Socrates as a martyr to truth against superstition and prejudice.[2] Mani, the founder of Manichaeism, a religion once of great influence in both the East and West, died in AD 276, after trial for his teaching, condemned by the Sassanian king Bahrām I.[3] The judges of Joan of Arc in 1431 sentenced her to be burnt for her belief that God had entrusted her with a special mission for her people.[4] Each of these trials is memorable for the moral heroism of the condemned, which inspired the veneration of their disciples and followers. But none of these trials, nor any

Originally published by Stein & Day, Inc., reprinted by permission of Scarborough House Publishers and Batsford, U.K., from *The Trial of Jesus of Nazareth*, by S. G. F. Brandon, New York, 1968, 13–24. Copyright © 1968 by S. G. F. Brandon.

other that might be cited, ever acquired a religious significance comparable to that attributed to the trial and execution of Jesus.

The religious significance of the death of Jesus is dramatically presented in the four Gospels which constitute the foundational documents of Christianity. The nature of this significance is difficult to define with exactitude, since the Gospels are narratives, not theological treatises; but it may fairly be described as residing in the evaluation of the death of Jesus as the vicarious sacrifice of the Son of God for mankind.

Such an evaluation of a historical event, for such is the crucifixion of Jesus, implies the use of criteria of a very peculiar kind and wholly different from those employed in historical judgment. This consideration faces the historian, who seeks to study the trial and death of Jesus as historical events, with a problem of peculiar gravity. For the Gospels constitute both the earliest and the only extant accounts of the events that resulted in the crucifixion of Jesus outside the walls of Jerusalem, probably in the year AD 30. And, since they are also Christian documents and thus may be suspect as *ex parte* accounts of the events they describe, these facts alone are sufficient to make the assessment of their testimony a task of extreme difficulty as well as one of basic importance. But the Gospels are also the work of men who believed that they were recording the earthly life of a divine being, whose death was the culminating episode in a divine plan designed to accomplish the salvation of mankind. Consequently, the historian must find himself asking whether the Gospels, although appearing to be narrative accounts of the career of Jesus, are really concerned with history or with theology.

Faced with this problem, one solution which at once suggests itself is that the Gospels may perhaps represent a later theological presentation of an original historical tradition about the career of Jesus. The fact that the Gospel narratives refer to historical persons such as Pontius Pilate and Caiaphas, the Jewish high priest, of whom we have independent information, indeed seems to indicate that a theological evaluation has been imposed on a primitive factual record. The problem, however, is more involved than this. The earliest of the Gospels, the Gospel of Mark, appears to have been written shortly after AD 70;[5] but some twenty years before its composition there is evidence that already the death of Jesus was being interpreted in a wholly esoteric manner, without any reference to its historical context. This interpretation occurs in a letter written about the year 55 by Saint Paul to his Christian converts in the

Greek city of Corinth.[6] The passage concerned must be quoted, in order to show the extraordinary nature of the problem with which we are concerned. From what Paul says here it is evident that he assumes that his readers will understand his meaning without further explanation:

among the mature we do impart wisdom, although it is not a wisdom of this age or of the rulers of this age, who are doomed to pass away. But we impart a secret and hidden mystery of God, which God decreed before the ages for our glorification. None of the rulers of this age understood this; for if they had, they would not have crucified the Lord of glory.[7]

The passage is quoted here in the American Revised Standard Version of the Bible, which certainly conveys something of the esoteric character of Paul's statement; but reference must be made to the original Greek text to bring out its full significance. The key thereto lies in the words, 'rulers of this age'. Translated thus, these words naturally seem to refer to the Roman and Jewish authorities who were responsible for the crucifixion of Jesus, according to the Gospel record. But, in their Greek form *(archontes tou aiōnes toutou),* the words have a very different meaning. They denote the demonic powers that were believed to govern this present world-order, and their use in this passage reveals that Paul was thinking in terms of current Graeco-Roman astralism. This was a very esoteric system, based upon an ancient tradition of belief that the stars, particularly the planets, ruled the destinies of men. The planets were identified with, or were regarded as inhabited by, elemental spirits, whom Paul refers to elsewhere as the *stoicheia tou kosmou* ('elemental spirits of the universe').[8]

When the astral context of Paul's thought in this passage is thus realised, what he says about the Crucifixion assumes a strange significance. For, according to him, the Crucifixion was the work of these demonic rulers of the lower planetary world, which is the abode of mankind. But that is not all: the one crucified by the *archontes* is designated the 'Lord of glory', and is clearly regarded as a supernatural being. Moreover, Paul presents this curious transaction as due to the 'secret and hidden wisdom of God', and 'decreed [by God] before the ages for our glorification'. Further, this divine plan was evidently intended to involve the deception of the *archontes* about the real significance of their crucifixion of the 'Lord of glory'.[9]

In this truly amazing statement Paul is obviously referring to the crucifixion of the historical Jesus of Nazareth. But he has, in effect, lifted the event completely out of its historical setting and assigned to it a transcendental significance. Jesus is identified with a supernatural being described as the 'Lord of glory', and his crucifixion is really the work of the demonic *archontes*. And these *archontes* had been deceived by God into perpetrating the crime, evidently to their own detriment.

That such an esoteric interpretation of the death of Jesus should have been expounded, within twenty years of its happening, by one who appears to have been the leading exponent of Christianity is indeed surprising. The fact puts the Gospels in a new light. They would seem to follow, or be in agreement with, Paul in regarding Jesus as a divine being and attributing to his death a soteriological significance; but they differ strikingly from him in their evident concern to describe the career of Jesus in its contemporary historical setting. Whereas Paul makes the demonic *archontes*, without qualification, directly responsible for the Crucifixion, the event is presented by the Evangelists as the work of the Roman and Jewish authorities ruling in Judaea at the time, without the slightest suggestion that they were only agents of supernatural beings. Now, since the Gospels were written some two or more decades after Paul's statement, we must inevitably ask what was the source of the narrative tradition which they embody; for it implies a preoccupation with the historical context of the life of Jesus which is entirely lacking in Paul's interpretation.

The answer, or at least an important part of it, is to be found in a complicated situation which must be appreciated, if we are to be in a position properly to evaluate the Gospel accounts of the trial and death of Jesus. A prerequisite to this is to understand Paul's place in the development of primitive Christianity.

A casual perusal of the New Testament suggests that Paul was the Apostle *par excellence* of Christianity. His writings far exceed those of any other Apostle, and the Acts of the Apostles clearly presents him as the most important figure in the missionary activity of the infant Church.[10] Paul's subsequent reputation in the Church, and the enormous influence which his writings have had in the formation of Christian doctrine, naturally tend to confirm the impression created by the New Testament that Paul was, from the time of his conversion, the most influential figure in the Church and the recognised exponent of its doctrine. Closer examination of Paul's writings, however, reveals a very different situation; this situation can also be discerned by careful analysis beneath the idealised picture of Christian Origins presented in the Acts.[11]

In his letters to his converts in Galatia and Corinth, Paul shows himself to be profoundly concerned about the activities of other Christians who are both presenting a different version of the faith from his own and denying his right to be an apostle. He even accuses these persons of teaching 'another Gospel' and preaching 'another Jesus'.[12] The agitation, which he shows about their activities, indicates that they were seriously threatening his authority among his converts. Paul, curiously, never identifies these opponents; however, the fact that they can challenge his authority in his own churches, while he never questions theirs, suggests that their status, or that of the persons whom they represented, was too high for Paul to repudiate. Their identity, though it is a matter of inference, cannot be seriously doubted. They were the leaders of the Church of Jerusalem, which comprised the original apostles and other disciples of Jesus.[13] We know, from Paul's own evidence, that these leaders were actually James, the 'Lord's brother', Peter and John.[14]

That such men, or their emissaries, repudiated Paul's claim to be an apostle, and that they taught a version of Christianity so essentially different from Paul's that he denigrates it as 'another gospel' about 'another Jesus', is a fact of immense significance for our understanding of the beginnings of Christianity, and, in turn, for our evaluation of the Gospel evidence concerning the trial and death of Jesus. But, to appreciate this significance fully, it is necessary to know in what manner these rival interpretations of Jesus did differ from each other.

In seeking an answer, we encounter what is undoubtedly one of the greatest obstacles in the study of Christian Origins. It is the fact that the original Christian community at Jerusalem disappeared with the destruction of the city by the Romans in AD 70, and with it perished all its records and monuments.[15] Consequently, we have no direct, self-attested evidence of the teaching of the Mother Church of Christianity. What we know of it has to be deduced from the writings of Paul, from the Acts of the Apostles, which is a document dating from towards the end of the first century,[16] and from certain early traditions that have been incorporated in amended form in the later Gospels.[17] Some information may also be gleaned from the second-century Christian writer Hegesippus, from the so-called Clementine literature, and from the Jewish historian Josephus; but what is obtained from these sources is very meagre and problematic.[18]

Difficult though this situation is, it is not completely hopeless: and, for our particular purpose here, enough can be deduced from these secondary sources to indicate the real nature of the difference between Paul's version of Christianity and that of the Mother Church of Jerusalem. We will begin with Paul's version. This has to be reconstructed from his letters, since nowhere in them does he give a systematic exposition of his doctrine; but some very distinctive aspects of it can be discerned, as we have already noticed. Paul has fortunately left us a brief biographical sketch of his past, in which he recognises the distinctive nature of his teaching and endeavours to account for it in terms of the divine purpose. It occurs, significantly, in his letter to the Galatian Christians when he is seeking to defend his 'gospel' against that of his opponents, as we have previously seen. After admonishing his converts for their disloyalty, he writes:

I would have you know, brethren, that the gospel which was preached by me is not according to man. For I did not receive it from man, nor was I taught it, but it came through a revelation of Jesus Christ. For you have heard of my former life in Judaism, how I persecuted the church of God violently and tried to destroy it; and I advanced in Judaism beyond many of my own age among my people, so extremely zealous was I for the traditions of my fathers. But when he who had set me apart before I was born, and had called me through his grace, was pleased to reveal his Son in me, in order that I might preach him among the Gentiles, I did not confer with flesh and blood, nor did I go up to Jerusalem to those who were apostles before me, but I went away into Arabia; and again I returned to Damascus.[19]

This statement is very illuminating. It was designed to show the Galatian Christians, impressed by the authority of the 'gospel' of the Jerusalem Church, that his (Paul's) gospel was of divine origin and absolutely independent of the original apostles now resident at Jerusalem. In claiming that his interpretation of the faith 'came through a revelation of Jesus Christ', Paul also explains that God's purpose in making this revelation to him was that he (Paul) 'might preach [Jesus] among the Gentiles'. The explanation is of the greatest consequence. By implication, it shows that Paul believed that his presentation of Jesus was one specially designed to be intelligible to non-Jews. The implied comparison here with the 'gospel' of the Jerusalem Church is explicitly confirmed later on in the Galatian Epistle, when Paul designates his 'gospel' as 'the gospel of the uncircumcised', in contradistinction to the other which he describes as 'the gospel to the circumcised'.[20] This essay in differentiation also helps to explain Paul's strange accusation when writing to the Christians of Corinth, that his opponents there preach 'another Jesus':[21] his meaning must surely be that they presented Jesus in a manner intelligible to Jews, and not to Gentiles.

We reach, then, an important point in our inquiry. Paul witnesses to the currency of two different interpretations of Jesus within two decades of the Crucifixion. One of these, which Paul believed had been mediated to him directly by God, was conceived in a manner such as to make it intelligible or attractive to the Gentiles. The other interpretation, which presumably would not have been to Gentile taste, was that which the original Jewish disciples of Jesus had composed, evidently in Jewish concepts and terminology.[22] Now, since Paul's agitation over the propagation of the Jerusalem 'gospel' among his converts was so great, it must surely follow that there was some difference between these interpretations more radical than that of language or imagery. Can we discern in what this lay?

Paul seems to provide a clue in his *Second Epistle to the Corinthians,* in a passage where he appears to be defending himself against criticism that insinuated that he was not mentally sound:

For if we are beside ourselves, it is for God; if we are in our right mind, it is for you. For the love of Christ controls us, because we are convinced that one has died for all; therefore, all have died. And he died for all, that those who live no longer live for themselves but for him who for their sake died and was raised. From now on, therefore, we regard no one from a human point of view; even though we once regarded Christ from a human point of view, we regard him thus no longer. Therefore, if any one is in Christ, he is a new creation; the old has passed away, behold the new has come.[23]

Paul's diction here is admittedly obscure, but his general meaning is clear. He was evidently rebutting the charge that his ideas were fantastic. The points at issue seem to be his belief that Christ's death was in some way universally vicarious—he had 'died for all'; that, because of the vicarious nature of his death, in some way all men had also died and become, or could become, incorporated in Christ; and that such incorporation made them 'a new creation'.[24] This mysterious transaction, although it was apparently related to the historical death of Jesus by crucifixion, is regarded by Paul as being so essentially mystical that he repudiates its connection with the actual historical event—'even though we once regarded [*oidamen*] Christ from a human point of view, we regard [*ginoskomen*] him thus no longer'. The expression 'Christ from a human point of view' means, in the original Greek *(kata sarka Christon)*, 'Christ according to the flesh', and it surely designates Christ as a person of flesh and blood, or, in our modern terminology, the 'historical Jesus' who lived in first-century Palestine.[25]

This repudiation of knowledge of the historical Jesus, and the consequent assertion that 'the old has passed away, behold, the new has come', are of great significance when we recall Paul's relations with the Jerusalem Christians. Paul was a late-comer to the faith, not having been an original disciple of Jesus. He maintained that he had not learnt his Christianity from 'those who were apostles before me', but through a special revelation that God had made to him. It is understandable, therefore, that in defending his authority as an apostle against the authority of the Jerusalem leaders, who had been the original disciples of Jesus and 'eye-witnesses' of his life, Paul devalued knowledge of the historical Jesus in favour of mystical communion with the Risen Christ.[26]

This attitude found doctrinal expression, as we have already seen, in Paul's evaluation of the Crucifixion as a mystic event, wholly unrelated to its historical setting, which God had so contrived that the demonic *archontes*, unwittingly, had carried it out to their own detriment. Their victim was a divine being, designated 'the Lord of glory': no reference is made to him as a historical person, for that aspect of his being was temporary and irrelevant compared with his eternal nature.

Such an esoteric doctrine was not only un-Jewish, but it contradicted the basic principles of Judaism. It envisaged the whole of mankind, both Jews and Gentiles, as being in a state of spiritual perdition, enslaved to the demonic rulers of the universe. Deliverance from this condition had been arranged by God through the vicarious death of another divine being, the 'Lord of glory', and this deliverance was available to all men, irrespective of their race. Thus the doctrine violated the two most cherished beliefs of the Jews. For, by envisaging all mankind as needing salvation from a common doom, the fundamental distinction drawn by the Jews between themselves, as the Elect People of God, and the Gentiles was ignored, thus negating the basic premise of Judaism.[27] Then, the very idea of the existence of another divine being, called the 'Lord of glory', violated the principle of monotheism, which was also basic to Jewish religion.[28] Equally alien and offensive was the identification of a human person, Jesus, with this 'second god', the Lord of glory.[29]

It is understandable, therefore, that the Jerusalem Christians were shocked when they came to realise the full implications of Paul's 'gospel', and that they repudiated it, seeking to suppress it among the Gentile converts by rejecting Paul's claim to be an apostle and perhaps suggesting that he was insane. Their attacks seriously undermined Paul's position; for they had the advantage of him in that he could not challenge their authority as the original apostles of Jesus, while they could dismiss his as a late-comer to a faith which he had once persecuted.[30]

So far as the history of the conflict can be traced out from the extant evidence, Paul finally endeavoured to reach some *modus vivendi* with the Jerusalem Christians by going personally to the city. The result was disastrous. James, the brother of Jesus, being then leader of the Jerusalem Church, compelled Paul to prove his Jewish orthodoxy by performing certain rites in the Temple. Recognised there and attacked by other Jews, who regarded him as a renegade, he was saved from death by the intervention of the Roman garrison of the nearby fortress of the Antonia.[31] To avoid trial in Judaea, Paul appealed, as a Roman citizen, to have his case judged by the Emperor; the result of the Roman trial is unknown, and Paul disappears from history.[32] The memory of his teaching would doubtless have disappeared also, and the Jerusalem 'gospel' would surely have prevailed but for the Jewish revolt against Rome in AD 66.[33] After four years of disastrous war, the Jewish nation was overthrown and its holy city destroyed: in that catastrophe, as we have already noted, the Mother Church of Jerusalem also perished.

The consequences of the Jewish disaster of AD 70 for Christianity were immense, and we shall be concerned later in assessing them in relation to our subject; but now we must turn back to our immediate task of seeking to discover what was the teaching of the Jerusalem Church, from which Paul's teaching so profoundly differed. As we noted earlier, this can only be inferred from Paul's writings and the Acts of the Apostles, and from other minor sources; for the archives of the Jerusalem Church perished with it in the holocaust of AD 70. However, some deductions can safely be made of great importance for our purpose. The first and most crucial is that the original Jewish disciples, who came to form the Church of Jerusalem, did not regard their allegiance to Jesus as requiring the abandonment of their ancestral faith. Indeed, all the evidence points to their being exceedingly zealous in the practice of Judaism: they worshipped regularly in the Temple at Jerusalem, taking part in the sacrificial ritual, they kept the Jewish festivals, and observed the Jewish Law, even in matters of peculiar ritual custom such as the Nazarite vow.[34] Many priests and Pharisees joined their community,[35] and their leader James, the 'Lord's brother', was held in high repute for his piety among his fellow-countrymen.[36] The chief point on which they differed from other Jews was in their recognition of Jesus as the Messiah of Israel.

During this period there were many claimants to Messiahship,[37] and it is important to remember that, according to contemporary Jewish belief, the Messiah was not conceived as a divine being: the fundamental monotheism of Judaism rendered such a conception impossible.[38] The Jewish Christians' interpretation of the Messiahship of Jesus did not, however, deify him; it differed in another way. According to current Messianic expectation, the Messiah would be God's appointed agent to drive out the Romans and restore sovereign power to Israel.[39] Defeat and death automatically negatived the claims of any person to be the Messiah.[40] The Jewish Christians had surmounted the shock which Jesus' execution by the Romans had constituted to their faith in him as the Messiah, through their conviction that God had raised him from death. His resurrection they interpreted as divine endorsement of his Messiahship,[41] and they believed that he would soon return with supernatural power to complete his Messianic role—to 'restore the kingdom to Israel', as it is significantly described in the Acts of the Apostles.[42]

The Jewish Christians were primarily concerned to persuade their compatriots to accept Jesus as the Messiah.[43] To this end it was necessary that they should formulate a case which demonstrated his Messianic character according to contemporary expectation. This meant the recounting of actions, particularly of a miraculous kind, which proved that Jesus had the supernatural power expected of the Messiah.[44] The Jewish historian Josephus, incidentally, tells how miracles were attributed to other Messianic claimants.[45] Another need which the Jewish Christians had to meet is of special importance for our purpose. The Roman execution of Jesus, in which the Jewish national leaders had been involved, obviously demanded explanation, if their fellow Jews were to be persuaded that it had confirmed, not contradicted, his Messianic character.

The Gospels devote considerable space to describing the trial and execution of Jesus.[46] These events naturally have an intrinsic interest which accounts for the attention devoted to them. However, in view of the fact that the Evangelists regard the death of Jesus as the vicarious sacrifice of the Son of God for the salvation of mankind, it is difficult to see how their descriptions of the historical circumstances of the event serve their theological purpose. Indeed, to the contrary, the attention of the reader becomes so focused upon the human drama that its supernatural significance tends to be forgotten. It is the actions and motives of the Jewish leaders, of Judas Iscariot, and Pontius Pilate, and the sufferings of Jesus that dominate; only the laboured exegesis of later theologians and preachers has sought to explain how this essentially human tragedy, described with so much realistic detail, had a supernatural relevance.[47]

These considerations, together with the obvious need of the Jewish Christians to explain how the execution of Jesus had endorsed, not contradicted, his Messiahship, consequently suggest that the Gospel accounts of the transaction derive from the records of the Jerusalem Church. It will be our task later to estimate how far this original tradition has been preserved in the Gospels or the reasons for its alteration. For our immediate purpose there is, however, one feature of the account of the trial in the Markan Gospel which now requires our attention, since it concerns the evaluation of the 'gospel' of the Jerusalem Church.

The Gospel of Mark, as the other Gospels, records what seem to be two trials of Jesus: the first by the Sanhedrin, the highest Jewish court,[48] and the second by Pontius Pilate, the Roman governor of Judaea.[49] Now, in the accounts of these trials only once is an attempt made to disprove a charge brought against Jesus. It occurs in the statement that at the Sanhedrin trial Jesus was accused by those who 'bore false witness' *(epseudomarturoun)* that he had threatened to destroy the Temple.[50] This accusation failed, it is asserted, because the witnesses contradicted each other.[51] The account goes on to describe how Jesus was condemned to death for blasphemy, because he had acknowledged himself to be the Messiah when questioned by the high priest.[52] In the subsequent trial before Pilate, where Jesus is accused of sedition against the Roman government, no argument is offered in the Markan account to disprove the charge;[53] the claim only is made that Pilate perceived the innocence of Jesus and sought to release him.[54]

The only charge that is specifically mentioned and refuted in the Markan account of the trials is that of Jesus' hostility to the Temple. This remarkable fact appears the more remarkable, when we note that Mark elsewhere in his Gospel believed that Jesus did foretell the destruction of the Temple, and there also existed a tradition to that effect.[55]

Since it is unlikely, therefore, that Mark would have invented an incident disproving that Jesus had spoken against the Temple, when he earlier describes him as prophesying its destruction, the trial account must surely go back to the Jerusalem Christians. That it should so do is also consistent with what we otherwise know of the veneration of the Jerusalem Christians for the Temple.[56] For it is understandable that they should have been at pains to refute a charge that their Master, whom they claimed to be the Messiah of Israel, had threatened the chosen sanctuary of the God of Israel.

We may, accordingly, discern something of an original Jewish Christian apologia concerning the trial and crucifixion of Jesus. The indications are that the first disciples formulated a record of the Sanhedrin trial which was designed to refute what they considered to be the most serious charge brought there against his Messiahship, namely, that he had spoken against the Temple. This apologia also recorded the condemnation of Jesus for acknowledging himself to be the Messiah. The fact that he was condemned for blasphemy on this admission by the high priest, who, as we shall see, collaborated with the Roman government of his country, would also have had its significance. Further, it is at least worthy of note, even if it be regarded as an *argumentum a silentio*, that Mark and the other Evangelists apparently found in this original Jewish Christian apologia no similar refutation of the charge of sedition brought against Jesus at the Roman trial. In other words, it looks as though the original Jewish Christian account of the trial of Jesus was concerned to rebut an accusation that could be used as an objection to his being the Messiah; but it showed no interest in disproving that Jesus was guilty of sedition against Rome.

It is not our purpose now to continue further with this analysis of the original Jewish Christian account of the trial. We have, instead, to turn back to our main theme, namely, the significance of the theological factor in the earliest traditions about Jesus. Our investigation of the 'gospel' of the Mother Church of Jerusalem has shown that Paul's transcendental interpretation of the death of Jesus, which completely ignored its historical context, was Paul's own view; although it was being taught by him within two decades of the Crucifixion, it did not represent the teaching of the original disciples of Jesus, resident at Jerusalem. They, on the contrary, were essentially concerned with the life of the historical Jesus, whom they recognised as the Messiah of their people. Their desire to win their countrymen to their own faith in the Messiahship of Jesus caused them both to formulate accounts of Jesus' sayings and deeds which attested his Messianic character, and to compose an apologia concerning his trial which defended him against an accusation of hostility towards the Temple.

This evidence of an original tradition of the historical Jesus which presented him as the Messiah of Israel, while establishing a point of fundamental importance for our investigation of the trial of Jesus, inevitably faces us with a problem of exceeding complexity in evaluating the evidence of the Gospels, which provide the only accounts we have of the trial. We have seen that the Gospels evidently embody the original Jewish Christian tradition; but they also conceive of Jesus as the divine Saviour of mankind. In this conception they are decisively in the tradition of Paul's teaching, which was rejected by the Jerusalem Christians; yet, in their preoccupation with the historical Jesus, they seem to appreciate an evaluation which Paul considered irrelevant, if not actually mistaken.

NOTES

1. It was only during a session (1965) of the Second Vatican Council that the Roman Catholic Church formally exonerated subsequent generations of Jews from responsibility for the murder of Christ; even then the decree met with certain opposition.
2. See Plato's *Apology*, also his *Phaedo*, and Xenophon's *Apology*. Cf. J. B. Bury in *C.A.H.*, V, pp.382ff.; A. B. Drachmann, *Atheism in Pagan Antiquity* (1922), pp. 64ff.
3. Cf. Geo. Widengren, *Mani and Manichaeism*, E.T., pp. 38–40; L. J. R. Ort, *Mani*, pp. 223–4.
4. Cf. J. Quickerat, *Procès de Condemnation et de Réhabilitation de Jeanne d'Arc* (Paris, 1861, r. ed., 1921).

5. Cf. S. G. F. Brandon, 'The Date of the Markan Gospel', *N.T.S.*, VII (1960–1); *Jesus and the Zealots,* chap.5; see pp. 68ff.
6. Cf. *R.A.C.* 3, IV, 19; *H.D.B.*², p. 180.
7. I *Cor.* ii:6–8. Cf. ed. Meyer, *Ursprung und Anfänge des Christentums,* III, pp. 350–1.
8. *Gal.* iv:3; *Col.* ii:8,20. On the *archontes* cf. M. Dibelius, 'Archonten', *R.A.C.*, I, 631–3; W. Grundel, 'Astrologie', *op. cit.,* 817–30; H. Lietzmann, *An die Korinther, I–II,* pp. 11–13; A.-J. Festugière, *La Révélation d'Hermès Trismégiste,* I, pp. 89–96; J. Seznec, *La survivance des dieux antiques,* pp. 35–46; R. Bultmann, *Das Urchristentum im Rahmen der antiken Religionen,* pp. 211–12; S. G. F. Brandon, *History, Time and Deity,* pp. 166–9.
9. Bultmann, pp. 211–12, 219; M. Werner, *Die Entstehung des christlichen Dogmas,* p.238 (E.T., p.95); A. Grillmeier, *Christ in Christian Tradition from the Apostolic Age to Chalcedon,* p. 15; Brandon, *Man and his Destiny in the Great Religions,* pp. 213–15.
10. Paul becomes the chief figure of *Acts* from chap. xiii to its end (chap. xxviii); Manson, *Studies in the Gospels and the Epistles,* p. 170, n.1.
11. *Acts* is concerned to describe the progress of Christianity, under divine guidance, from its beginnings in Jerusalem to its propagation by Paul in Rome, the capital of the Ancient World. Cf. *B.C.*,II, pp. 177–86; F. F. Bruce, *The Acts of the Apostles,* pp. 29–34; Brandon, *The Fall of Jerusalem and the Christian Church,* pp. 126–36, 208–10.
12. *Gal.* 1:6–8; II *Cor.* xi:3-4: on the significance of Paul's terms here cf. *Man and his Destiny,* p. 196, and the documentation there cited.
13. Cf. A. D. Nock, *St Paul,* pp. 110–11, 168-9; H. Lietzmann, *Gesch. d. alt. Kirche,* I, pp. 108–9; W. L. Knox, *St Paul and the Church of Jerusalem,* p. 365; M. Simon, *Les premiers Chrétiens,* pp.79–81; M. Goguel, *La naissance du Christianisme,* pp. 173–6, 320–49; ed. Meyer, *Ursprung u. Anfänge des Christentums,* III, pp. 432–45, 453–9; H. J. Schoeps, *Theologie u. Geschichte des Judenchristentums,* pp. 128ff., 157, 257, 381–4, 420–34, 448–50; T. W. Manson, *Studies in the Gospels and the Epistles,* pp. 170, 216; Brandon, *Jesus and the Zealots,* pp. 152ff.
14. *Gal.* i:19; ii:9. Cf. H. Schlier, *Der Brief an die Galater,* pp. 78–9. On James, see pp. 21, 22, 49ff.
15. This subject is discussed at length, together with a detailed examination of the late legend that the Christian community of Jerusalem fled *en masse* to Pella before the fall of the city, in *Jesus and the Zealots,* pp. 208ff.
16. *H.D.B.*², pp. 600ff.
17. Cf. *Fall of Jerusalem,* pp. 74ff.
18. Cf. *Jesus and the Zealots,* pp. 115ff., 188ff.; see pp. 55–6, 39, 151–2.
19. *Gal.* i:11–17. Cf. Schlier, pp. 43–59; H. G. Wood in *N.T.S.*, I (1954–5), pp. 278–9.
20. *Gal.* ii:7–9. The distinction which Paul draws here between these two 'gospels' seems to be theoretical rather than actual, since it did not prevent him from evangelising Diaspora Jews, nor Peter and other Jerusalem Chris-

tians from operating among Paul's Gentile converts. Cf. *Jesus and the Zealots*, pp. 154, n.i, 163–5.

21. II *Cor.* xi:4. Cf. A. Menzies, *The Second Epistle to the Corinthians*, p. 78; H.-J. Schoeps, *Paulus,* p. 74 (E.T. p. 76); F. F. Bruce in *B.J.R.L.,* 45 (1963), pp. 331–4.

22. The presentation of Jesus as the Messiah of Israel, who would punish the Gentile oppressors of Israel and 'restore the kingdom to Israel' (*Acts* i:6) was not calculated to attract Gentiles. Cf. *Man and his Destiny,* pp. 212ff.

23. II *Cor.* v:13–17. Cf. H. Lietzmann, *An die Korinther, I–II,* pp. 124–5; Nock, *St Paul,* p. 243; J. Klausner, *From Jesus to Paul,* pp. 313–15; A. Loisy, *Les mystères païens et le mystère chrétien,* pp. 242–3; Goguel, *La naissance du Christianisme,* pp. 254, 270–2; A. Schweitzer, *Paul and his Interpreters,* pp. 245–6; Schoeps, *Theologie u. Geschichte des Judenchristentums,* pp. 425–6.

24. Cf. Goguel, pp. 252–9; Bultmann, *Das Urchristentum im Rahmen der antiken Religionen,* pp. 219–22, in *N.T.S.,* I (1955), pp. 13,16; A. Schweitzer, *The Mysticism of Paul,* pp. 109–30.

25. 'Christus nach seiner natürlichen Seite', W. Bauer, *Griechisch-Deutsches Wörterbuch z. d. Schriften d. N.T.²,* 1194; H. Windisch, *Der zweite Korintherbrief,* pp. 186–8; Bultmann, *Theology of the New Test.,* I, pp. 236–8; Manson, *Studies,* pp. 224; W. Schmithals, in *Z.N.T.W.,* 53 (1962) pp. 156–8.

26. Cf. Brandon, *History, Time and Deity,* pp. 159ff.

27. See *Rom.*iii:9,23–5. Cf. W. Sanday-A. C. Headlam, *The Epistle to the Romans,* pp. 76, 84–6; H. H. Rowley, *The Biblical Doctrine of Election,* pp. 144–6; H. Wildberger, *Jahwes Eigentumsvolk,* pp. 74ff.

28. Cf. Klausner, *From Jesus to Paul,* pp. 444, 467–70.

29. Cf. *E.R.E.,* VII, pp. 199b–200a. It is significant that in the second-century *Dialogue* of Justin Martyr with the Jew Trypho, the latter objects to 'your trust in a mere crucified man' (*op. cit.,* 10), and 'you undertake to prove a thing incredible and almost impossible, that God condescended to be born, and to be made man' (*ibid.,* 68).

30. Cf. *Jesus and the Zealots,* pp. 182ff.

31. *Acts* xxi:27ff.

32. Cf. H. J. Cadbury in *B.C.,* V, p. 338, also *B.C.,* IV, pp. 349–50; Bruce, *Acts of the Apostles,* pp. 480–1, in *B.J.R.L.,* 46 (1964), pp. 342–5; Manson, *Studies,* pp. 6–7; Brandon, *Jesus and the Zealots,* pp. 186ff.

33. *Fall of Jerusalem,* pp. 152ff., 213ff.

34. *Acts* i:46, iii:1; v:12, 42; xxi:26, 42; x:14; xi:2, 3; xv:1; xxi:21–4; *Gal.* ii:11ff.

35. *Acts* vi:7; xv:5. Cf. Simon, *Les premiers Chrétiens,* pp. 39–41; Brandon, *Jesus and the Zealots,* pp. 118ff.

36. Hegesippus *apud* Eusebius, *Ecclesiastical History,* II, i.2–5, xxiii. Cf. Epiphanius, *Haer,* xxix, lxxviii.6–7; *Fall of Jerusalem,* pp. 52–3; *Jesus and the Zealots,* pp. 122ff.

37. Reference is made to them in *Mk.* xiii:21–22.
38. Cf. Schürer, *G.J.V.*, II, pp. 526–30; S. Mowinckel, *He That Cometh*, pp. 4ff., 280ff.
39. Cf. Schürer, *G.J.V.*, II, pp. 533–44; Mowinckel, pp. 284ff., 340ff.; Klausner, *From Jesus to Paul*, pp. 526–7; M. Black, *The Scrolls and Christian Origins*, pp. 145–63.
40. As Paul eloquently shows in I *Cor.* i:22–3, the idea of a 'crucified Messiah' was a *skandalon* to the Jews. Cf. Klausner, *Jesus of Nazareth*, pp. 301–2, *From Jesus to Paul*, p. 437; Schürer, *G.J.V.*, II, pp. 553–6; Mowinckel, p. 327.
41. *Acts* ii: 22–36; v: 30-1. The Jewish Christians found prophetic warranty for a suffering Messiah particularly in the figure of the Suffering Servant of Yahweh; e.g. *Acts* viii: 26–38; cf. *Acts* iii:18, *Lk.* xxiv: 17–27. Cf. *Fall of Jerusalem*, pp. 76ff.
42. *Acts* i:6. Cf. *Jesus and the Zealots*, pp. 180–1.
43. E.g. *Acts* ii:22–36.
44. *Matt.* xi:2–6; *Lk.* vii:18–23; *John* xi:47. Cf. Bultmann, *Gesch. d. syn. Trad.*, pp. 22, 54; E. Klostermann, *Matthäusevangelium*, p. 94; V. Taylor, *St Mark*, p. 362.
45. Cf. *Jesus and the Zealots*, pp. 108–11.
46. Cf. Goguel, *The Life of Jesus*, p. 463; V. Taylor, *The Formation of the Gospel Tradition*, pp. 44ff.; Manson, *Studies*, pp. 20–2.
47. The first concern of Jewish Christian exegesis was to show how the death of Jesus did not negate his claim to be the Messiah (see n. 40). So far as the early speeches in the *Acts* (e.g. ii:22–36; iii:13–26) may be regarded as reflecting an authentic tradition, the death of Jesus was interpreted as a martyrdom which had won God's favour so that he had made him both 'Lord and Christ (Messiah), this Jesus whom ye crucified' (ii:36). 'In Acts the Passion of Jesus is identified with the suffering of the Servant, but nowhere is described as giving salvation to men. In the speeches of Peter and Stephen the death of Jesus is regarded as the wicked act of the Jews, parallel to their fathers' persecution of the prophets. If men desire salvation let them repent, and be baptized'—F. J. Foakes Jackson and K. Lake, *B.C.*, I, pp. 391–2. Cf. Bultmann, *Theology of the New Test.*, I, pp. 33–7.
48. See pp. 85ff.
49. See Chapter IV.
50. *Mk.* xiv:57-8. Cf. Taylor, *St Mark*, pp. 565–6.
51. xiv:59.
52. xiv:61–4. See pp. 89ff.
53. xv:1–3. The use of the plural *polla*, 'many things' in describing the chief priests' accusation suggests that they specified more than one instance of sedition. Cf. Taylor, *St Mark*, p. 579. See pp. 92ff.
54. xv:10, 14. See pp. 96ff.
55. xiii:2. Mark, doubtless aware of the tradition of the Sanhedrin trial, is careful not to suggest here that Jesus would himself destroy the Temple and

uses a curious impersonal form of statement: 'There shall not be left one stone upon another that shall not be thrown down.' The distinction is not merely academic, because *Jn.* ii:18–19 and *Acts* vi:14 witness to the currency of a tradition in Christian circles that Jesus would destroy the Temple. Cf. Kloster-mann, *Markusevangelium*, p. 155; Bultmann, *Gesch. d. syn. Trad.*, pp. 126–7, *Ergänzungsheft*, pp. 17–18; M. Simon, *Recherches d'histoire judéo-chrétienne*, pp. 11–12; Brandon, in *N.T.S.*, VII (1961), pp. 134–6, *Jesus and the Zealots*, pp. 234ff.

56. To the Jewish Christians the Temple was the 'house of God'; cf. *Mk.* xi:17; *Matt.* xxiii:21. Taylor (*St Mark*, p. 566), recognises the difficulty here: 'It is not clear why Mark represents the testimony as false. . . . It is more probable that Mark reflects the uneasiness of primitive Christianity regarding the saying on the part of those who continued to observe the Temple worship.' See pp. 42–5.

4

Christian Anti-Semitism

Marcel Simon

I

The phenomenon of anti-Semitism was a familiar one to the ancient world long before the advent of Christianity. It was a product of friction between Jewish colonies and the surrounding pagan communities, and we may suppose therefore that it is practically as old as the Hellenistic diaspora itself.[1] In this respect there is no discontinuity between the pagan and Christian periods. Christian anti-Semitism, nevertheless, took on characteristics that were quite new and peculiar to itself. It can be detected even before the Church's triumph under Constantine, and took more definite shape during the fourth century. In order to appreciate the distinctive marks of Christian anti-Semitism, it is necessary first to set out the characteristics of the pagan anti-Semitism it replaced. If the two sorts of anti-Semitism have anything in common, in respect, for example, of their motivation, of the kinds of complaints that are made about their victims, or of their methods, it is only to the extent that anti-Semitism anywhere, in any age, displays the same features. These common features may be found just as readily in the resurgent anti-Semitism of certain modern ideologies.

The basic cause of Greco-Roman anti-Semitism[2] lay in Jewish separatism. This means, in the last analysis, that it lay in their religion, since the religion produced the separatism. Any racist element was entirely lacking.

In any case, the notion of "race," in the modern, pseudoscientific popular understanding of the word (I am thinking especially here of the distinction between Jews and "Aryans") is quite foreign to the ancient way of thinking. Naturally the Western peoples, the Romans in particular, were conscious of differences between themselves and the Jews. But as far as the differences were, either on the physical or psychological level, innate and not acquired—i.e., insofar as they were not ones deliberately adopted, like the religious differences—the Romans seem to have attached little significance to them. Or at least, they were no more aware of differences between themselves and the Jews than of those between themselves and other Semites or other Eastern peoples in general. In the eyes of the ancient authors the Jews were, ethnically speaking, simply a variety of Syrians, just as, geographically, Palestine was merely a subdivision or prolongation of Syria. In current usage the term "Syrian" often included the Jews. They were then not primarily thought of as a religious body, i.e., as sectarians who devoted themselves to the worship of Yahweh, but rather as a cultural one, as agents of the many-faceted Eastern culture. Ovid, for example, speaks of the "Syrians of Palestine."[3] The Jews, like their neighbors, were Levantines. They were distinguished only by their religion.

Even in Egypt, where, in view of the proximity of Palestine and the large Jewish colonies within its borders, we might expect common opinion to be better informed, the finer distinctions are not always clearly appreciated. According to the biographer of Alexander Severus, the Alexandrian crowd greeted him as a young emperor with the sarcastic title of "the Syrian archisynagogos." They thus showed that they knew both of his Syrian antecedents and his active sympathy for the Jews.[4] Similarly, Apion, who informs us not only about anti-Semitism but about Alexandrian nationalism and the ancient rivalry between Egypt and Syria, taunts the Jews with having come originally from Syria.[5] In this form the objection expresses a general xenophobia rather than specifically anti-Jewish sentiments.

Thus, ancient anti-Semitism had no racist background. Nor had it an economic basis. There is never any imputation of a Jewish stranglehold on commercial or industrial activity. Jews are not generally accused of an immoderate lust for money, of any special eagerness for gain, of passion or genius for business, of a lack of commercial morality or of any of the oddities of this kind that figure invariably in the mythology of modern anti-Semitism.

Such complaints are not completely absent from ancient literature, but they are aimed at people other than the Jews. They are the common coin of international jealousy. The Romans launched such accusations against the Carthaginians and the Greeks, who had a firmly established reputation throughout the West as traffickers in dubious merchandise and as commercial parasites.[6] The same reputation extended to all East-erners, without distinction of country or race.[7] There is only one pagan text in which the Jews are clearly accused of being overfond of money. This is in a letter from Hadrian to Servianus. It is preserved by Vopiscus and its authenticity is suspect. The letter contains a diatribe against various national and religious groups, of whom Israel is one. Egypt is "light, inconstant, changing at the slightest sound"; in the cosmopolitan society of Alexandria charlatans and astrologers flourish amongst all social classes: "their only god is money; the one who is worshipped by Christians, Jews and everybody else."[8]

Neither does it seem that the Jews were specially noted as preferring particular vocations. They did not all gravitate to the same social class; far from it.[9] It seems that they were not often very prominent in society. Some of them appear in Egypt, taking out leases of tax rights, or of royal domains. In Alexandria there were Jewish shipowners, bankers, and millionaires.[10] But looking at the empire as a whole, the Jewish popula-tion were mostly not high up the social scale. Jewish slaves are fairly numerous. At Rome, none of the Jewish quarters, Trastevere, Porta Capena, or Suburra, possessed much distinction. The remark most often made about the Jews was not that they were rolling in money but that they were ragged and filthy. If we are to believe Martial and Juvenal, the Jewish beggar, "trained to beg by his mother," "whose entire property was a basket and some hay,"[11] was a characteristic sight in the lower quarters of the capital. We may presume that the Jews were not alto-gether strangers to commerce, but for the most part they were concerned in it in fairly humble capacities. They were peddlers or door-to-door salesmen, offering oriental knickknacks for sale. Here again, there was nothing to differentiate them from the mass of "Syrians"; nothing to encourage any specifically anti-Jewish feelings.[12]

All that distinguished the Jews, therefore, was their religion, and, up to a point, the peculiarities of their political situation. The two are so closely related that it is difficult to distinguish one from the other. It was in their capacity as a religious community that the Jews had been repeatedly involved in political difficulties with Rome, and they continued to give trouble in this way until the destruction of the holy city, when they were finally deprived of their national independence. In Palestine the virulent anti-Roman Messianism of the masses certainly increased the animosity of the gentiles toward the Jews. And even in the diaspora there were some elements among the Jews which from time to time were infected by the same unrest and gained the Jews a reputation as a turbulent people, difficult to live with. Nevertheless, the importance of these Messianic outbursts ought not to be exaggerated. They were occasional, and usually of local significance. They never had more than a limited effect on the diaspora.[13] After A.D. 70, and all the more after A.D. 135, the political problem ceased to be a pressing one. It is very doubtful whether Jewish Messianism and Jewish political aspirations ever impressed themselves much on Roman opinion, apart from that of the Roman leaders. For the pagan authors the Jews are the people who worship without images, the people of the law. They are not primarily the people of the Messiah. The same is true for the generality of Romans, who knew little of Palestinian history and were badly informed about the details of Jewish belief.[14] It was these features which bound the Jews throughout the Mediterranean lands into a unity, and which aroused the amazement, the distrust, and the hatred of their neighbors. A Jew who apostatized no longer aroused these feelings, and a proselyte exposed himself to them unavoidably.

When the pagan polemists characterize Jewish monotheistic beliefs as "atheism," the charge is hardly more than an academic one. What really excited public distaste was not Jewish beliefs, however odd they might appear, but Jewish behavior. What was objectionable was the law and its power to isolate its devotees. The law, by enclosing the Jews' daily life in a web of rules and regulations, placed them beyond the bounds of society, outside the ordinary rules and the ordinary pattern of life. It turned them into a tightly knit group, in spite of the fact that they were individually scattered—a group that was unassimilable, exclusive, and therefore an enemy of the human race.[15]

This was the really basic complaint, and from it sprang others. Because they kept themselves apart and had no relations, except at a superficial level, with the pagans among whom they lived, and because they were united by the observance of rules and rites whose meaning was often difficult for outsiders to comprehend, they left themselves exposed to all the accusations that the malice of the mob could invent, and that it delights to invent about closed societies. The Freemasons in our own day, and the early Christian communities in the Roman Empire, have both been the object of just the same kind of suspicions and slanders. We may note in particular the similarity of the ancient reactions to Judaism on the one hand and to the nascent Christianity on the other. In both cases the accusations of a sinister exclusiveness lead to those of "misanthropy," and then to accusations of immoral practices, of perversion, and of ritual murder.[16] These accusations were worse in the case of the Christians because they maintained a closer silence about some of their ritual practices. In its beginnings Christianity was often attacked as a variety of Judaism. The anti-Christian attitudes of the pagan world were at first merely a form of anti-Semitism.

Basically, this anti-Semitism was a spontaneous reaction, an elementary and instinctive social reflex rather than a considered attempt to defend pagan religious convictions. Jews were suspected and slandered and occasionally persecuted, just as Christians were, because they were members of a foreign group who would not assimilate. Religion was not an issue except insofar as it was the agent that isolated and marked out the members of the group, and pointed the contrast between them and the surrounding world. The examples that have come down to us of pagan polemical literature against the Jews are in general hardly more than learned and systematized transcriptions of popular opinion.[17] Real anti-Semitism was popular in its roots. It reflected the general animosity against those who did not live as the rest of the world. It reflected feeling, not thought. To recognize its basic character is to be aware immediately of its limitations.

Anti-Semitism, as we might expect, flourished only in those regions or cities where there was a large Jewish population. It flourished in Rome, Antioch, and Alexandria especially. Its intensity was always proportionate to the numerical strength of the Jewish community. Two factors tended to restrain it, though without anywhere limiting it entirely. First, there was Judaism's legal standing. Judaism was officially recognized by imperial authority and everywhere given a measure of protection as a *religio licita*. Second, there was the lively influence of the synagogues of the diaspora. The beliefs, the precepts, and even the ritual practices of Judaism exercised a considerable attraction for much of the pagan populace.

Balancing the anti-Semites among the pagan population were the proselytes, the *metuentes,* and those who, though not proselytes, were nevertheless impressed by the antiquity of the biblical tradition, by Judaism's high ethic, and by the purity of its teaching. There was thus, at one extreme, virulent hatred, and at the other, sympathy and admiration. These were the two extremes between which pagan opinion concerning Judaism oscillated.

From the moment when Christianity appeared on the scene, it attracted more and more attention. Sometimes it was sympathetic attention, productive of converts; sometimes it was outright hostility.[18] Up till then, and for some time afterwards, Judaism's attractions had to some extent acted as counterweight to anti-Semitic feeling. The accommodating Judaism of a Philo was able, in presenting Judaism as a philosophy, to dampen some of the misgivings that intellectuals might feel regarding Mosaic practice and teaching. By becoming receptive to influences from outside and by increasing its apologetic effort, such Judaism had rid itself of some of its strangeness. The gentiles who associated themselves with Israel doubtless exposed themselves, in many instances, to the same mistrust and hostility as Israel had to endure, but sometimes their example helped to repel, in their own immediate circle at least, gentile malevolence. Around the synagogues, therefore, there grew up an atmosphere in which a better understanding was possible. This is a fact that ought to be considered, along with Juvenal's sarcastic comments and the diatribes of Apion.[19]

None of this was sufficient to wipe out the hatred completely. Even while they continued in their liberalism and universalism, the Jews intransigently maintained their firm monotheistic convictions and their staunch belief in their own prerogatives. In any case, strict legal observance in practice was the indispensable counterpart of liberalism in doctrine. Now, it was this very legal observance, whose rigor was relaxed only by one or two dissident Jewish bodies, which was the essential precondition of anti-Semitism. And anti-Semitism was able to vary in its extent and intensity from period to period and from region to region. It must neither be exaggerated nor minimized. The anti-Semitic attitudes of the pagan world were, on any showing, the foundation on which Christian anti-Semitism was built. And even though many of the characteristics of Christian anti-Semitism were native to itself, some of them were not, but were inherited from the pagan past.

II

When did this hostile attitude to the Jews first appear in the history of the growing Church? To find out the answer to this question, it is necessary to go back to quite an early period. It dates, it would appear, from the time when Christianity turned away from Israel, where its mission had had more setbacks than successes, and found among the gentiles the compensation for its initial disappointments. Anti-Semitism became more widespread when the later expansion of Christianity was accomplished by preachers born in paganism. By this time Judaism's initial repulse of Christianity had hardened into a permanent rejection, and the Church was no longer simply a small sectarian body on its edge, but embodied in herself the redeemed gentile world. There is no shadow of anti-Semitism in St. Paul. He was disappointed in his countrymen but incapable of hating them.[20] Anti-Jewish feeling is manifest in the Fourth Gospel, where the word *Jew* takes on a pejorative sense.[21] Christian anti-Semitism is in the first instance an expression of the resentment aroused by Israel's resistance to the gospel. It is a concomitant of the new church's claim to have taken over the privilege of election. In addition, it arises from the need to explain the outright rejection with which the Jews greeted the message meant for them.

This is to say that the basis of Christian anti-Semitism was neither social nor in the proper sense religious. At least, it was not religiously based in the sense in which this could be said of the pagan variety. The Christians could not accuse the Jews of an exclusivism they themselves also practiced. They approved of Jewish beliefs and customs, as they were codified in the Old Testament, since they were equally the foundation of the Christian faith. By the same token, they even approved of the Jewish attitude to the gentiles. But Christians approved all these things, as it were, retrospectively. The religious institutions they considered legitimate for the past they repudiated for the present. And whereas they displayed the same intransigence to the pagan world as the Jews did, they condemned that intransigence when it opposed their own message.[22]

Though Christian anti-Semitism, thus described, existed, at least in rudimentary form, at the very beginning of Christianity, it only unfolded fully in the fourth century. At that point it appears in all its complexity. On the one hand, in spite of the conversion of Constantine, it may be regarded as the continuation of the pagan world's hostility toward the Jews. The pagan world had been Christianized. It retained, nevertheless, the pagan attitude to the Jews. It took over the arguments and the complaints that public opinion had always advanced against Jewish religious and social nonconformity. On the other hand, and this is Christianity's essential contribution, the new anti-Semitism expressed the opposition that the Church felt toward the Jews as obdurate dissidents. It expressed the condemnation uttered by Christian teaching of those who crucified Christ and rebuffed his call. Although clearly different, these two aspects of the phenomenon were intimately mingled. One was secular and popular, the other was ecclesiastical and learned, and was nourished by the Bible itself. From the Bible it drew the material to support its assertions and its condemnations. This was where the genuinely Christian element was rooted. And this true Christian anti-Semitism was theological through and through.

The chief complaint, which formed the theoretical foundation for the whole case, finds expression as early as the Gospels, especially in the fourth. The Jews are worthy of hatred because they killed Christ, persecuted his disciples, and rejected his teaching. "Pilate was anxious to set him free, but the Jews shouted . . . 'Take him away, take him away! Crucify him!' "[23] The responsibility for the crime therefore falls on the whole people, and it is a crime that the Christian authors characterize as deicide.[24]

For some of these authors the death of Christ is the cause of Israel's rejection. For others it is not a cause but an indication. Many signs have demonstrated that the people have long been unworthy of their ancient election. But his sign shows more clearly than all the others how deep-rooted their perversion had become.[25] The Jews had therefore killed their savior, not by the exercise of their own free will, but because God, seeing their incurable wickedness, had condemned them to perdition, as the prophets had foretold.

Such is already the Johannine interpretation of Jesus' trial and passion. "Though he had done so many signs before them, yet they did not believe in him; it was that the word spoken by the prophet Isaiah might be fulfilled: 'Lord, who has believed our report, and to whom has the arm of the Lord been revealed?' Therefore they could not believe. For Isaiah again said, 'He has blinded their eyes and hardened their heart, lest they should see with their eyes and perceive with their heart, and turn for me to heal them.' "[26]

The murder of Christ is thus explained by the whole of the past history of the Jewish people. It is the natural consequence and culmination of an uninterrupted series of transgressions, of grave offenses and crimes that demonstrate the people's unworthiness. This proof is repeated ad nauseam throughout patristic literature.[27] It is already there in outline in Stephen's tirade before the Sanhedrin: "You stubborn people, with your pagan hearts and pagan ears. You are always resisting the Holy Spirit, just as your ancestors used to do. Can you name a single prophet your ancestors never persecuted? In the past they killed those who foretold the coming of the Just One, and now you have become his betrayers, his murderers."[28]

To a people whom their own history, written by divinely inspired men, portrayed as criminals and sinners one may legitimately attribute, in the present, any crime and any deficiency. The old accusations, which sprang originally from pagan malevolence, gain a new lease of life under the pens of Christians. They also gain a new virulence. They thus continue, in a revived form, the traditional animosity of the Greco-Roman world, lately Christianized. Juster has prepared a catalogue of the principal taunts thrown at the Jews during ancient times.[29] It is interesting to note, as Juster does, that almost every one the pagans manufactured is reused by the Christians. Both pagans and Christians charge the Jews with turbulence and a tendency to revolt. Apion and Celsus tax them with having committed sedition.[30] St. John Chrysostom calls them *ethnos polemopoion*.[31] The Latin Church writers echo this with *rebellantes Judaei*.[32] Pagans and Christians alike declare them to be bitterly envious, headstrong, and mean-spirited. As far as invective is concerned, the continuity between pagans and Christians is as close as it could well be.

There are, however, some charges the Christians are reluctant to take up, perhaps because the same charges had too often been made against themselves. If they are made at all, it is with circumspection, and generally in a sense that differs significantly from the spirit in which they were originally intended. There is, for example, the accusation of misanthropy. Tacitus denounces Jews and Christians on this score in identical terms. It is curious to see Origen defending the Jews against the charge and declaring that, far from detesting pagans, they reserve their hatred for the Christians, who have forsaken idols for the worship of the true God.[33] In later writers the complaint reappears, but always in this new form. The Jews hate Christianity, not the human race. Under the Christian empire these two views tended to become confused. This second reworking of the idea is no less characteristic.

Again, Christian polemists make interesting distinctions between the charges the pagans formulated against the Jews. For instance, the accusation that the Jews worship angels appears from both sides,[34] but the Jewish distaste for images, which had so impressed the pagans,[35] does not appear in the Christian list of charges, even in an age in which the use of icons had already been initiated in the Church. Neither is the Sabbath idleness condemned by Christians, because as an image of the Sunday rest it contained nothing that a Christian would find scandalous. The fundamental institutions of Judaism, such as circumcision and the dietary regulations, which roused the sarcasm of the pagans, are not in themselves denounced by the fathers. They are denounced because the advent of Christianity has rendered them void, and in maintaining their attachment to them, the Jews are once more displaying their spirit of disobedience. It is true that Tertullian says, *Haec et nos risimus aliquando,* but this is in an attempt to emphasize the fact that Christians are not Jews, but are gentiles by birth. He adds shortly afterwards, *De vestris sumus.*[36] He is in any case speaking of biblical truths and not of the rites themselves. And what he says about them applies to the pagan period in the lives of the converts. These truths the Church has made its own. As for the Jewish rites, however odd they may seem to a Christian who has come from a pagan background, their divine origin forbids him to laugh at them.[37]

The accusation that the Jews worship the ass, which is a commonly reiterated theme of pagan polemic,[38] is absent altogether from that of the Christians. The reasons are perfectly clear. The Church recognized the sancitity of the Jerusalem Temple, and any suggestion that a grotesque and idolatrous worship went on there would have been blasphemous. Besides, it would be understandable if the Christians, who had had the same slander thrown up at themselves, had been reluctant to throw it back at the Jews, even though the Jews had sometimes joined in the calumny when the pagans gave the lead. The Jews might have hoped, by turning this stupid accusation off on to the rival cult, to have been rid of it themselves for the future. The Christians, by contrast, had nothing to gain. All the world was aware of the connection between Christianity and Judaism, and mud of this kind, if thrown by Christians at the Jews, was likely to come off on themselves. It was better policy to join the Jews in demonstrating the accusation's inanity. Tertullian tells how a certain Jew of Carthage walked down the street one day carrying a caricature of Christ, decorated with an ass's ears, and bearing this inscription: "Onocoetes, the God of the Christians."[39] But he elsewhere recounts, following Tacitus, the legend of Jewish ass worship, and takes the trouble to refute it, adding, *Atque ita inde praesumptus opinor, nos quoque, ut judaicae religionis propinquos, eidem simulacro initiari.*[40]

The same explanation may be given for the fact that the accusation of ritual murder, which the pagans brought against both Jews and Christians, was not made by Christians against Jews until a relatively late date. It did not really flourish until the Middle Ages.[41] Prudence and, it may be supposed, simple honesty moved the Christians thus to pick and choose a little among the weapons the pagan world bequeathed to them.

But though the Christians sometimes modified the traditional complaints, they did not neglect to augment their list of charges by drawing on the ancient catalogues of accusations and calumnies. These may have originated for the most part in Alexandria, but they had been peddled across the empire and had become common coin. When the much-discussed epithet that Claudius applied to the Jews, "the plague of the world," turns up word for word in the same form in an anti-Jewish homily by St. John Chrysostom, it is not a mere coincidence.[42] Having started life in some pamphlet or other, it very likely became part, both in Antioch and Alexandria, of the popular repertoire of anti-Semitic slogans. The fact that it reappears after more than three centuries in the second document demonstrates how tenacious the old prejudices and hatreds were, in spite of the religious revolution that had intervened, and how fixed were the formulae in which they were expressed. Christians too, in the early years of the Church, had heard themselves described in the same sort of terms. That they did not turn these slanders against the Jews until the very end of the fourth century, when there was no longer any risk of exposing themselves to the same vilifications, is not fortuitous. By that time they could speak in the name of the whole gentile world, which had been called and adopted in place of the Jews.

III

There is, however, more to Christian anti-Semitism than a simple plagiarizing, or even adaptation, of pagan themes. Both in its spirit and its methods it displays considerable originality.

One of the most striking characteristics of Christian anti-Semitism is its subordination of social accusations to moral and religious ones. It is not the supercilious insularity of the Jews that chiefly annoys the Christians, nor even the narrowness and jealousy of their self-sufficient community. Their primary accusation is that the Jews are addicted to all the vices, and that under cover of their scrupulous observance of the law they are really immoral and irreligious.

Here again the Christian polemists are not entirely independent of their pagan predecessors. The charge of impiety is a repetition, in suitably revised form, of the old accusation of atheism. This latter charge could hardly be reused as it stood. It would have come oddly from a people who themselves fell under the same condemnation. Those who professed belief in the God of Abraham, Isaac, and Jacob could scarcely associate themselves with the criticisms that the gentiles made. However, they could and did see in the beliefs and practices of post-Christian Judaism an aberration, a caricature of true religion, and in the last analysis a form of worship not far removed from idolatry.[43] In the eyes of the pagans Jewish atheism was repaid by the hatred of the gods. Posidonius of Apamea calls them μισουμένους ὑπὸ τῶν θεῶν.[44] Similarly, for the Christians Israel's rejection is evidence of her impiety.[45] This is one of the basic themes not only of popular anti-Semitism but of learned polemic.

Not that accusations of immorality and, in particular, of debauchery, are lacking from the old pagan repertoire of anti-Jewish slanders. Tacitus, for example, insists that the Jews are libertines: *projectissima ad libidinem gens*.[46] However, it is not among the commonest accusations. Among the Christians, on the contrary, it appears with special frequency, and for the fourth-century Christian authors immorality is a characteristic Jewish failing.[47]

This assertion too had earlier been thrown up at the Christians. When turned against the Jews, it can be explained otherwise than by pure malice. It is an exaggerated expression of the conflict between Jewish and Christian conceptions of sexual morality. The period was one in which the ascetic ideal, an ideal that set a high value on virginity, was gaining ground in the Church. Now, this ideal was quite foreign to the religious tradition of Israel, and remained incomprehensible, not to say quite disgusting, to the Jews. In opposition to it, they exalted the ideal of family life, as illustrated by the patriarchs. And they quoted the ancient biblical command, "Be fruitful and multiply." For them procreation was a duty, and an abundant offspring the sign of divine favor. Tacitus again expresses it for us: *generandi amor*.[48] Whereas Christians, or at least Christians of a certain kind, sought a remedy against the temptations of the flesh in absolute chastity, the Jews were content with the obligation of conjugal fidelity. What the decalogue and the rabbis condemned was not sexual activity, but simply adultery.

It is understandable that the ascetic party, seeing the Jews exalt the ideal of the conjugal life, should regard them as advocates of debauchery. It is equally conceivable that their views, thus expressed, might have provided material for popular malice to work on, popular malice needing little encouragement in this particular direction. We have evidence from a number of sources that in the Eastern countries, where there was a large Jewish population, and where there was still close contact between the adherents of the rival cults, this very question was the subject of keen debate. Aphraates, for example, devotes one of his homilies, which are such a rich source of instruction on the subject of Jewish-Christian relations, to the subject of virginity. His object is to arm the faithful against Jewish attacks, for the Jews, he says, "because of their sensuality and their carnal desire," rebel against this virtue and by cunning insinuations turn the simple away from it. They laugh at those who practice it and say to them, "You are unclean, because you do not take a wife. We are holy, because we have assured our posterity."[49]

We know also that the monks, who became a weighty influence in the history of the Eastern Church after the fourth century, made themselves foremost in the struggle against the Jews. They were the militant anti-Semites. And it was they who were largely responsible for the reputation for debauchery the Jews acquired. And part of the reason, we may imagine, that so many of the fathers take up the accusation, is that they were in close touch with monastic circles.[50]

It is against the same background that we must evaluate the accusation, rarely made by the pagans, of Jewish greed. Christians, by contrast, were loud in their complaints that the Jews were fond of money, of luxury, of the pleasures of the table, and of every form of wealth.[51] This was a feature of the Jewish mentality the pagans had not noticed, for if they had noticed it, they would not have been slow to include it in their criticisms. It is very difficult to believe that in a relatively short interval of time, at a period when the Christian authorities had not confined the Jews to activities such as moneylending, which Christians were forbidden to take part in, this love of money and its equivalents should suddenly have become so characteristic of the Jews. It is not that this accusation was leveled against the Jews alone. When Jerome reproaches one of the Jews who taught him Hebrew, a famous rabbi, for having charged too much for his lessons,[52] and goes on to denounce the Jews in general for being fond of money and good living, these accusations must be set against the same author's concession, elsewhere, that they were generous to the poor, even the Christian poor.[53] Besides this, he condemns the Romans as well as the Jews for cupidity,[54] and says that the Syrians are worse than either of them.[55] It is wise not to accept these generalizations without reserve. And as Parkes has pointed out,[56] none of the sermons against usury that have come down to us from this period makes any mention of the Jews.

But in any case, St. Jerome and, in differing degrees, the others who pass such strictures on the Jews are all ascetics, who affect to despise the good things of this world. For men such as these, at what point did a taste for money or for gluttony begin? Coming from them, the accusation carries the same weight as the claim that the Jews were libertines. But quite apart from thoroughgoing asceticism, there was a real difference between Christian and Jewish ideals at this point.[57] The former rested upon a pessimistic view of the world and of life in it, regarding them as part of the empire of evil. Contempt for the flesh was only one aspect, though the most important aspect, of this fundamental attitude of renunciation. For the Jews, on the contrary, the creation was good, and it was legitimate for men to enjoy the good things God had placed at their disposal. Success in worldly affairs was, like a large progeny, a sign of God's blessing. The Jews expected a reward for the righteous in this world. The Christians did not anticipate it until the next.

Nevertheless, this was only one aspect of Judaism, just as asceticism was only one aspect of Christianity. Christianity, in coming to terms with "the world," arrived at a mode of life that was noticeably similar to that of contemporary Judaism.[58] Conversely, Judaism by no means ignored the idea of righteous suffering. It had discovered the hard way, throughout its history, that God's chosen ones were never far removed from tears and persecution. Job is just as typical of Judaism as are the patriarchs, full of years, of satisfaction, and of wealth. Jewish morality was no more inclined than that of the Christians to make material felicity the infallible criterion of virtue. When the Christian polemists emphasized with such satisfaction the vices of the Jews, they were far from taking a detached and objective view. They spoke under the influence of hatred and were looking through the distorting glass of asceticism.

But the really characteristic contribution of Christianity to anti-Semitism lay in its methods of argument and its techniques of combat. Whereas the accusations of the pagans were generally reproduced gratuitously and without proof, the Christian writers proceeded to back them up with texts of scripture. The Old Testament was an arsenal of which they made free use. Their accusations are supported by invective drawn from holy writ.

This anti-Semitic exegesis of the Bible had two different objects. It endeavored to show that the criticisms the Church had made of the Jews since the murder of Christ were in conformity with the Jewish character. Their own recorded history and the writings of their own prophets bore witness that the self-styled chosen people had never been anything other than a pack of villains. Conversely, by projecting into the present the most conspicuous features of the prophetic indictment of Israel, and by picking out the most questionable episodes from Israelite history and dwelling on them alone, it lent weight to the accusations that were made against contemporary Judaism and justified the malice with which the Jews of its own day were met.[59]

Thus the Jew, as the animosity of his enemies painted him, was no longer the Jew as he appeared in front of them but the Jew against whom the Lord had declaimed in the past, and whose shortcomings and vices the prophets, the instruments of God's anger, had denounced. The portrait of the Jew was built up by pasting together verses of the Bible. The complaints the inspired writers had made were torn from their contexts of time and place and, combined into a single portrait, provided all the evidence that could be wished for of the utter depravity of the people of God. Thus was created the picture of the eternal Jew, a conventional figure, a literary fiction. And, as a Jewish critic comments bitterly,[60] it was the prophets, the flower of Israel, who involuntarily were responsible for the hatred the early Church stirred up against their brethren.

The Bible provided the Christians with a repertoire of offensive and damaging epithets with which they invariably accompanied every mention of the Jews. Though the "perfidy" of the Jews, which the Good Friday liturgy had immortalized, reflects the memory of the death of Christ,[61] the majority of the other descriptions applied to the Jews are drawn from the Old Testament. A few pagans had explored this source already, but their attempts had been no more than isolated exercises. In the Church, however, daily familiarity with the sacred books made the harvest particularly easy to gather.

One of the commonest epithets is "the stiff-necked people," which occurs a number of times in the sacred text.[62] In ancient Christian literature, from Stephen's speech onwards, the phrase had a noteworthy career. It was meant to express the headstrong determination in pursuit of sin that led the Jews to reject the Messiah. Augustine and Ambrose use it, as does Julian the Apostate, whose use of it bears witness to his thorough knowledge of the Bible.[63] It appears in Commodian.[64] Its popularity among their enemies is attested by the Jews themselves. R. Abun claims in the fourth century that "the gentiles reproach us as the stiff-necked people."[65] The description becomes in its repetitiveness an almost Homeric epithet.

Jewish stubbornness, persisted in, has resulted in blindness. This theme naturally recalled the words of the Psalmist: "They have eyes, but see not; they have ears, but do not hear." The Psalmist, of course, was speaking of the idols, but the Christians readily overlooked this and used the words as if they described the Jews. Thus St. Ambrose, drawing attention at the same time to the traditional "perfidy" of the Jews, says: *Sciebat durae cervicis populum Judaeorum, lapsu mobilem, humilem, perfidia promptiorem, qui aure audiret et non audiret, oculis videret et non videret, lubrico quodam infantiae levem et immemorem praeceptorum.*[66] This stubborn adherence to error and evil and this blindness are signs of a more deep-seated failing. The Jews are carnal creatures, insensitive to the life of the spirit. This is demonstrated by their conception of religion. They have interpreted in an absolutely literal way precepts whose value is entirely symbolic. And they repudiated Christ and Christianity when they arrived because they had failed to recognize their prefigurations in scripture. Their whole religion is based on a gross misconception. The epistle of Barnabas develops this argument at length. Most later writers, without exactly taking over his point of view, reuse different components of his argument. The theme is one of the most hackneyed in ancient apologetic.

Stubborn, carnal, and murderous, the Jews were assuredly both the prey and the instruments of the evil one. Everything they did, whether in the profane or the religious sphere, was a standing offense to God. Their prayers and psalms were like the inarticulate cries of animals, *grunnitus suis et clamor asinorum,* according to Jerome's gracious description.[67] No adjectives are too strong, no comparisons too odious to be applied to the Jews. Gregory of Nyssa provides us with a notable enough specimen of these vitriolic tirades: "Murderers of the Lord, murderers of prophets, rebels and full of hatred against God, they commit outrage against the law, resist God's grace, repudiate the faith of their fathers. They are confederates of the devil, offspring of vipers, scandal-mongers, slanderers, darkened in mind, leaven of the Pharisees, Sanhedrin of demons, accursed, utterly vile, quick to abuse, enemies of all that is good."[68]

IV

But the master of anti-Jewish invective is without question St. John Chrysostom. In him all the complaints and all the insults are gathered together. It is here that we see most plainly the fusion of the several elements that went to make up the Christian polemic: the themes of popular anti-Semitism, the specifically theological grievances, the use of biblical texts. And all these are presented with such violence and at times such a coarseness of language as to be without parallel. This anti-Semitism pervades the whole of Chrysostom's work, but it inspires especially his eight *Homilies against the Jews.*[69]

The first of these homilies is perhaps the most characteristic. It opens with the traditional accusations. The Jews, says Chrysostom, who had been overwhelmed with benefits by God, rejected them all. They had been sons of God, by adoption, and they became like dogs. No people could be more mean than this, for they managed to exasperate God not only by breaking the law but even by observing it. When they ought to have kept it, they broke it. Now that it has been abrogated, they obstinately insist on maintaining it. They have always resisted the Holy Spirit.

They are stiff-necked. They have broken the yoke of Christ, though it was a light one. They have made themselves no better than senseless beasts.[70]

This comparison is one the author keeps on invoking. Like beasts, the Jews are voracious, gluttonous.[71] All their vices are derived from this. And now we have a text supporting the accusation: "Israel ate and was filled and became fat, and the beloved kicked."[72] The Jews, being dominated by gluttony and drunkenness, have fallen into the worst evils. Like well-fed cattle incapable of work, they are no longer fit for anything but slaughter.[73]

The catalogue of criticisms is extended further. The Jews are gluttons, drunkards, and carnal-minded even while they are fasting. Their fasts are in any case an insult to God. Their Day of Atonement is an opportunity for indecent festivities. They dance barefoot in the marketplaces. They gather choirs of effeminate young men and motley collections of women of doubtful reputation. They collect in the synagogue people from the stage and theater, for synagogue and theater are on much the same level.[74]

At this point we may imagine there were signs of protest among the audience. Chrysostom is aware of having momentarily gone too far and begins to defend himself in advance against objections. Let no one accuse him of impertinence. He has done no more than quote prophecy: "You maintained a prostitute's bold front, never thinking to blush."[75] For those carried away by their polemical enthusiasm, the Bible's metaphor became a literal statement of fact. The orator seizes on it, warms to his theme, and insists: "The place where you find a harlot is called a brothel; or rather, the synagogue is not only a brothel and a theater but a brigands' cave and a wild beasts' den."[76] The prophet once more provides support: "Do you take this temple that bears my name for a robbers' den?" And again, "I have abandoned my house, left my heritage. . . . For me my heritage has become a lion in the forest."[77] God has abandoned the Jews. They have disowned the Father, crucified the Son, and refused the help of the Holy Spirit. Cave of brigands? No! Worse than that. Their synagogues henceforth are the seat of demons and the place of idolatry—and not only their synagogues, but their souls. And here Chrysostom, reminded that some Christians think of the rites of the Jews as solemn rituals, and that they visit their assemblies and treat them as holy places, launches into an astonishing diatribe in which the comparison between Jews and animals is further worked out. "They live only for their belly, their mouths always gaping; they behave no better than pigs or goats in their gross lasciviousness and excessive gluttony. They only know one thing, namely, how to gorge themselves and fill themselves up with drink."[78]

Chrysostom turns next to the Judaizers, whom he tries to convince of the horrifying nature of their behavior. But he soon leaves them to make a fresh onslaught on the Jews, the cause of all the trouble. How can anyone have anything to do with these miserable, demon-possessed creatures, brought up on crime and murder? One had much better fly from them. And here we have reiterated, though in a more brutal and naked form, the famous formula from Claudius's letter to the Alexandrians: shun them "like filth and like a universal plague."[79] What transgressions have they not committed? The Psalmist tells us that they burned their sons and daughters to satisfy the demons.[80] The author's indignation builds up and his wrath rises, and again the Jews are compared with beasts. They are wilder than any beast,[81] for beasts sometimes give their lives to save their young, but the Jews have massacred theirs with their own hands in order to honor demons. Which ought to anger us more, their impiety or their cruelty? But even apart from this, their every action expresses their bestial nature: "Sex-crazed stallions, each neighing for his neighbour's wife."[82] Have they not, in their lasciviousness, surpassed even the most lustful of senseless animals?"[83]

What more can be said of them? They are guilty of "expropriation, covetousness, abandoning the poor in their need, and profiteering."[84] A whole day would not be long enough to deliver a catalogue of their vices. They were completely consumed by them even before the murder of Christ, but his murder has set the seal on their abominable behavior. And even after this, Christian people will go and associate with the criminals, will deliver themselves, soul and body, to the demons! The sermon culminates in a moving appeal to the Judaizers. Let them cease this behavior, which can lead only to their own loss! Let everyone apply himself to bring them back into the right way by persuasion, or if necessary by force.

The homilies that follow are devoted to theological discussion of particular points, and their tone is more restrained. It is only in the sixth homily that the polemic again takes an aggressive turn. Chrysostom proposes to expatiate on the present misery of the Jews. Ezekiel is witness that they have always been sinners. They worshiped the calf, tried to kill Moses, blasphemed against God, and sacrificed their children to demons. In spite of all this, God showered upon them signs of His favor. If now they have ceased to practice idolatry and no longer put to death their prophets or their own children, why are they in permanent exile? It is because they killed Christ. This was the supreme act of wickedness, which has left them no hope either of forgiveness or of amendment of life. Their lot henceforward is to be shame and misery. The Christians, by contrast, the followers of him whom they killed, are exalted. Once Christ was dead, prophecy came to an end in Israel, the temple was destroyed, sacrifices ceased, the priesthood vanished. Let not the present Jewish Patriarchs contradict this! They are not priests, but pirates, "traffickers, profiteers, sated with every sort of fraud." [85]

Jewish worship is genuinely divine in origin, and was once worthy of respect, but it is now no more than a caricature of what worship ought to be. "Everything the Jews now do is a grotesque joke, at once laughable and disgusting." [86] The presence of the holy books is not enough to make the Synagogue holy. Christ himself said of the temple that the Jews had made it into a brigands' cave, and that in spite of the fact that it contained the ark and the divine spirit. What shall we say then of the Synagogue of our own day, where nothing goes on except impiety? It is "now a brothel, place of all evil-doing, resort of demons, devil's citadel, ruin of souls, precipice and abyss of perdition. Everything that can be said of it falls short of what it deserves." [87]

The methods by which Chrysostom blackens the Jews are apparent enough. When he is not simply retailing gross and gratuitous slanders, he is taking prophetic condemnations, isolating them completely from the context in which they are recorded and the circumstances in which they were uttered and from which they derive their meaning, and applying them to the present. The texts that speak appreciatively of Israel, in which the Bible abounds, are never called in evidence. This one-sided exegesis, used by the author's undoubted oratorical skill, turns the Jew into an eternal figure, a type; and it is a monstrous, villainous figure, calculated to inspire in all who look at it a proper horror. [88]

Chrysostom's use of metaphor is especially noteworthy. One example will be sufficient. The author emphasizes the intemperance of the Jews at the beginning of the first homily, and he returns to the theme more than once. Everything suggests that we are meant to take the accusation in its simple, ordinary sense. But the accusation of gluttony is in fact based on the text of Deuteronomy I quoted above. As for the charge of drunkenness, its basis is even more infirm. Chrysostom himself, having lightly asserted that the Jews are given to drunkenness, explains in passing, at the end of the cycle of homilies, that it should be understood metaphorically. "So passes the Jews fast, or rather the Jews' drunkenness. For," he goes on, "it is possible to get drunk even without wine."[89] For these things too may be classified as drunkenness: anger, sensuality, avarice, love of honor. And with even better justice may we call "drunkard" the impious man who blasphemes against God and resists the law, which is to say, the Jew. "For drunkenness means nothing other than departure from the path of reason, derangement of mind, loss of the soul's health." And the basis of this entire accusation is, as far as can be discovered, a single text, originally intended in its true sense: "They are drunken, but not with wine."[90]

We should be justified in speaking of bad faith if it were not perfectly obvious that Chrysostom, carried away by the intensity of his anger, has not himself made any clear distinction between real drunkenness and the metaphorical kind of which he is speaking. The two ideas are muddled in his own mind, just as the two vices, in his eyes, are combined in the twisted personality of the Jew.

The same may be said of the accusation of debauchery and the slanderous complaints made against the Synagogue. The prophet had said to his people, "You maintained a prostitute's bold front." There is a tacit syllogism connecting this text with the treatment of the Synagogue as a place of ill-repute. The Jews, who are compared to a prostitute, frequent the Synagogue. Now, the place where prostitutes live is called a brothel. Hence, the Synagogue is a brothel.[91]

Once the fire of his anger has been damped, Chrysostom is perhaps not taken in by his own arguments. But by the time he cools down, he has already done quite enough to confirm the reputation for debauchery and vice with which popular imagination had credited the Jews.

The procedures Chrysostom employed had a not unremarkable career in the history of the anti-Jewish controversies. Some of their results were very serious. It is these methods which explain, for example, the recrudescence of the accusation of ritual murder, which reappeared in the Middle Ages, and which has contributed so much to the misfortunes of the Jews. Pagan anti-Semitism was already familiar with this charge, and extended it, quite naturally, to take in the Christians too.[92] The same accusation has been made in our own time against the Freemasons. It is the sort of slander that popular hatred produces spontaneously. But the insistence with which mediaeval Christianity employed it against the Jews, usually, be it noted, in connection with the Feast of Unleavened Bread, suggests that there was a special reason for it in this case. There seems to be no connection between this particular rite and ritual murder except for one very, very tenuous one provided by a biblical text. Oort has recently shown[93] that the origin of the accusation is to be sought, in all likelihood, in the *Altercatio Simonis Judaei et Theophili Christiani,* which is dated at the beginning of the fifth century.[94] This dialogue ends, in accordance with the usual plan of such works, with the conversion of the Jew. The occasion of the conversion is a discussion about unleavened bread. "Prove to me," says Theophilus to Simon, "that scripture forbids you to drink the wine of the Christians, and I shall show you how it forbids to us the wine of the Jews and their unleavened bread."[95] The Jew is unable to quote any text in his support. The Christian, however, produces several. Concerning the unleavened bread, he quotes: "Your hands are covered with blood"; concerning the wine: "Their stock springs from the vinestock of Sodom and from the groves of Gomorrah: their grapes are poisonous grapes." And again, "Their feet run to do evil, are quick to shed innocent blood."[96] The Jew, finding the argument conclusive, is baptized.

Once having recognized this as its point of departure, it is easy to see how the allegation of ritual murder developed. Hands covered with blood are, of course, the hands of criminals. This is how Theophilus understands the matter. "See with what feet and what hands you prepare the wine and the unleavened bread," he cries, commenting on his quotations. From this it is only a short step to saying that the hands became thus soiled in the preparation of the rite itself. Oort rightly notes that in areas where there was a large Jewish element, popular superstition had always credited the rites of unleavened bread with magical properties. The non-Jews were readily impressed by the rituals, to them very mysterious indeed, that accompanied both the preparation and the consumption of the bread.[97] At the same time they had always ascribed great potency to human blood, especially to the blood of children, in the preparation of sorcerers' spells and potions. It was therefore very natural for the pagan populace to assume that children's blood was a component of the *mazzoth*. The accusation of ritual murder grew up, beginning with a text of scripture as its point of departure, by the application of this method of exegesis, whose most notable exponent is St. John Chrysostom.

Chrysostom represents, in respect of his anti-Semitism, an extreme case in the early Church. His passion in the cause, and the violence of his invective, are without parallel in the literature of the first few centuries. This is explained partly by the individual temperament of the author and partly, as we shall later have occasion to see, by the local situation. It is a specifically Antiochene phenomenon. But if the case is an extreme one, it is not a unique one. Every time the subject of the Jews crops up in the Christian writings of the period, Chrysostom's attitude and methods reappear.

The anti-Jewish state of mind was not confined to the principal officers and scholars of the Church, and did not find expression only through them. We not only have the diatribes of Chrysostom and the more or less veiled insinuations of other ecclesiastical writers. We have the liturgy itself. This is a matter to which Juster has drawn attention,[98] though in such a way that he scarcely presents us with a fair picture of the facts. One gets the impression from reading his work that there are anti-Jewish elements to be found throughout the liturgy. He asserts: "Anti-Jewish polemic in the Church was repeated almost as often as the divine service itself. It was thus driven into the minds of the believers and shaped their entire way of thinking. Being thus reinforced day by day, anti-Jewish sentiments hardened in their minds."[99]

A close study of the liturgical texts themselves does not support this conclusion. In fact, not only are diatribes against the Jews, and even wounding epithets applied to Israel, rare, but allusions of any sort to the Jews are fairly thinly spread. They do, however, collect quite thickly around certain points in the liturgical year, and especially around the celebrations of holy week.

For this reason, Juster's conclusions concerning the difference between pagan anti-Jewish polemic and the Christian variety need some modification. The pagan polemic, he says, consists of "the mere publication of literary works" of an "abstract and aristocratic" kind. He contrasts this with the Christian polemic against the Jews, which he describes as "propagandist, and retailed daily among the populace." For the Christians introduced it "into divine worship, in which solemn and almost dramatic context its impact would be reinforced by all the means which liturgy has at its disposal to move the mind and the emotions."[100] This analysis, it seems to me, divorces the anti-Jewish writings from the popular sentiment in which they were rooted. The roots of pagan anti-Semitism went very deep, and Juster does not recognize this. It is hardly to be supposed that in areas where there existed a large Jewish population anti-Semitism was the exclusive prerogative of intellectuals. The masses shared it, in full measure. At the same time Juster errs, when he speaks of the part played by the liturgy, in exaggerating the importance of anti-Semitism in the Church.[101]

Nevertheless, there was a fundamental difference between the anti-Semitism of pagans and that of Christians. We must give Juster credit for perceiving this, even if he has not noted very accurately what the difference was. Christian anti-Semitism, insofar as it was officially espoused by the Church, did have a sanction as well as a coherence that the pagan sort always lacked. It was used to serve theological ends and it was given theological backing and encouragement. It did not base its arguments on ascertainable facts, not even, for that matter, on the hearsay evidence of popular gossip, but on a particular kind of exegesis of the biblical writings, an exegesis that interpreted them in the light of the death of Christ as a long indictment of the chosen people. Where pagan anti-Semitism was, for the most part, spontaneous and unorganized, that of the Christians was devoted to a well-conceived end. Its aim was to make the Jews abhorrent to all, to sustain the dislike of those in whom the Jews already aroused dislike, and to turn the affections of those who were well disposed.

Let us recall Chrysostom. The Christian, he says, must shun them "as a plague which has afflicted the world." He must follow the example of the martyrs who, because they loved Christ, hated the Jews, for it is not possible to love the victim without hating his murderers. Whereas pagan sentiment accused the Jews of misanthropy, the Church actually practiced it on them. It strengthened the barriers that Jewish religious observances had already erected between Israel and the outside world, its intention being to safeguard believers from contact with these dangerous creatures. The mediaeval ghetto was to be the result, not simply of Jewish particularism, but of the Christians' systematic exclusion of the Jews from Christian society. There was no ghetto in antiquity. But

Christian anti-Semitism, as I have just described it, entailed some of the same consequences, which I must now draw attention to.

V

In the first place, anti-Jewish feelings stimulated by Christian polemic issued quite naturally from time to time in outbursts of violence against the Jews either against their persons or against their property.

In this context we must not forget that there were occasions on which the Jews themselves stirred up trouble. There were times when the measures the Christians took might fairly be represented as reprisals. But this judgment applies mainly, and perhaps only, to those geographical areas in which Jews felt numerically strong enough to take the initiative, and these areas naturally became fewer and fewer as Christianity extended its grip upon the empire. By the fourth century the most that the Jews could generally do was to seize the occasion of the Christians' doctrinal dissensions and intervene in their quarrels, quarrels that were often enough attended with actual violence. At Alexandria, for example, they took the part of the Arians against the orthodox.[102] And when the orthodox party emerged triumphant, the Jews suffered the same ill-treatment as the vanquished Christians. But their intervention in Christian quarrels is not an adequate explanation of the large number of cases in which violence was directed against the Jews alone. There can be no doubt that the imprecations hurled at them from the pulpit by ministers of the Church, if they were not deliberately designed to incite violence, certainly worked to that end, acting as a dangerous leaven in the minds of the masses.

The fairly frequent pogroms that took place in the cities of the East during the pagan period continued after Constantine. It cannot be said, however, that they became any commoner. On the other hand, the general harassing of Jews did tend to become more widespread and more frequent from century to century, though whether this was a result of the decisions of imperial authority or whether it sprang from popular feeling and the initiative of local authorities we do not know.

Within the chronological limits of the present inquiry the clearest instance of the persecution of Jews is their expulsion from Alexandria in A.D. 414 This took place at the instigation of the Patriarch Cyril, against, it appears, the wishes of the prefect. This expulsion was accompanied by the confiscation of both the private and the communal property of the Jews, in particular by the confiscation of synagogues.[103]

This hostility to the synagogues is characteristic of Christian anti-Semitism. During the pagan era the destruction of synagogues was uncommon. Indeed, the only such case that is firmly attested is the destruction of the synagogues of Alexandria under Caligula, and it appears in a series of violent measures enacted against the Jewish community of Alexandria as a whole.[104] During the Christian period, on the contrary, such actions became significantly more frequent. It was Judaism in its capacity as a religion that aroused the hostility, and this is demonstrated by the choice of the places of worship as the principal objects of attack. In exactly the same way, Christians attacked the temples of the dying paganism. Pagan sanctuaries and Jewish synagogues were both alike temples of error. It was therefore not only legitimate but meritorious to destroy them or appropriate them for the true worship.

Numerous instances of confiscation or destruction, generally destruction by fire, are attested throughout the fourth and fifth centuries, both in the West and in the East. The local Church authorities usually gave such proceedings tacit condonation or open approval. Sometimes they even went so far as to instigate the action. At Tipasa in Africa the synagogue became at the beginning of the fourth century the Christian Church of Saint Salsa.[105] At about the same period the bishop of Dertona in Spain led his people in an attack on the synagogue, which he then turned into a church.[106] It was most likely by a similar act of violence that the synagogue at Antioch, which marked the tomb of the seven Maccabaean brothers, passed into Christian hands along with its relics in the second half of the same century.[107] At the beginning of the fifth century, at Edessa, Bishop Rabbula turned the synagogue into the Church of Saint Peter.[108]

Instances of destruction are equally numerous. At Rome in A.D. 388 the usurper Maximinus attempted to force the Christians to rebuild a synagogue they had set fire to. By so doing, he lost both their sympathy and the favor of their God.[109] At Magona in Minorca in A.D. 418 the transfer of the relics of a Saint Stephen, a victim of Jewish persecution, resulted in a violent outburst of anti-Semitism, stimulated by the bishop and clergy. An attempt to take over the synagogue was foiled by the Jews' determined stand, but by a subterfuge they were drawn away from the building and it was sacked and burned.[110] In the East incidents of this kind, particularly numerous during the fifth century, were most often due to the fanaticism and aggressiveness of the monks. In Palestine at the beginning of the century a certain Barsauma, assisted by forty *illuminati,* a species of brigand monks, seems to have made a specialty of exploits of this type. He carried on his activities without disturbance for forty years, finishing off his destructive work, when opportunity presented itself, by massacring Jews.[111] When during the same period, Theodosius II tried to restore to the Jews of Antioch the synagogues taken from them by the Christians, he was severely reprimanded by St. Symeon Stylites and forced to abandon the project.[112]

The most famous and the most characteristic episode is that of the synagogue at Callinicum, which was a small town in Mesopotamia. The incident took place in A.D. 388 and was in itself quite trivial. The Christian population of the town, prompted by the bishop, set fire to the synagogue. The civil authorities informed Theodosius, who sent a rescript laying on the bishop the obligation to indemnify the Jewish community and to rebuild the synagogue at his own expense. He further ordered that those who had set fire to the building should be bastinadoed. St. Ambrose, on becoming acquainted with the imperial decision, immediately intervened.[113] Full of indignation, he condemned the stand the emperor had taken as sacrilegious. A Christian prince has no right thus to show favor to the Jewish error. It is legitimate to set fire to synagogues. If the laws forbid it, it is because they are bad laws. This being so, it is a duty to disobey them, and Ambrose, if he had known earlier of such a prohibition, would have felt compelled to set fire to the synagogue of Milan. God himself has already approved the destruction of these edifices. Let Theodosius therefore revoke his decision! Let him abrogate his rescript! It will redound to his eternal salvation and that of his sons.

As is well known, the matter did not stop there. Theodosius at first persisted in his policy and Ambrose took him to task publicly, in church, during divine worship. He threatened him, if he did not relent, with exclusion from the communion.[114] An argument ensued. The emperor attempted to justify himself, but finally submitted. A second rescript moderated the severity of the former one, and then a third followed, which abrogated both, and annulled the award of reparations that had originally been made to the Jews in Callinicum.

The episode is a significant one. It is only one incident, but it throws light on the whole problem of the latent opposition between Church and State and the encroachment of the ecclesiastical authorities on government and administration. Theodosius behaved at the beginning as a pagan emperor would have done, anxious to maintain order and justice and treating his subjects with equality. His action was based on respect for the accepted rights of the Jews to practice their own religion freely and was aimed at protecting their places of worship. For Ambrose, on the contrary, to show goodwill toward the Jews, or even simple equity, was inconsistent with the profession of Christianity. A Christian emperor had no business to be holding an equal balance between truth and error. It was his job to use the power God had given him in the service of his faith.[115] If he was prevented from doing this by the law, or by the principles of justice on which it was based, then he must change the law or annul it. The law had in any case been handed down from pagan times.

In any event, it was the Church that had the last word. The episode of the synagogue of Callinicum enables us thus to put our finger on another consequence of ecclesiastical anti-Semitism, namely, its effect on imperial legislation concerning the Jews. Both Juster and Parkes in turn have dealt fully with this aspect of the matter. All that I need to do is to emphasize the essential points.

That the ecclesiastical authorities did influence legislation concerning the Jews is not open to doubt. Just as in matters relating to the various heresies the imperial code is more often than not simply an echo of the conciliary canons, so in matters relating to Judaism each amendment to the legislation is made in response to the intervention of one ecclesiastical dignitary or another. St. Ambrose brought about a modification of the law concerning the protection of synagogues.[116] St. John Chrysostom was the moving spirit behind several anti-Jewish laws promulgated by Arcadius, and Arcadius reverted to a more liberal policy as soon as the patriarch had been expelled from Constantinople.[117] To look at the legislation affecting Jews as it develops through the successive texts of the Theodosian Code is to be immediately aware of the increasing hold religion exercised over politics.

The influence of religion appears in the very expressions that the law uses to denote Judaism. It uses offensive terms that are not compatible with the objective neutrality which one expects in legal documents. The tone it uses is that of the anti-Jewish pamphlets.[118] It is manifest that for the man who drew up these laws the Jews are no longer merely one element in the population of the empire, but have become that detestable brood who murdered Christ. That is to say, they have become for him what they are for the ecclesiastical polemists. At every point, as Juster remarks, the legal texts betray a theological motivation for their anti-Jewish dispositions.[119]

And it is not only the tone of the texts that betrays the increasing influence of the Church. Their very spirit and intent is seen to be progressively modified in a direction that is more and more unfavorable to the Jews. Christian apologetic demanded that the Jews and Judaism should continue to exist. They were witnesses. But it demanded that they should exist in misery, that they should enjoy a precarious status, a diminished existence that would mark them out as the people who were once chosen, but now condemned.

The protection the pagan empire had granted to the persons and property of the Jews was thus relaxed. The law became more indulgent toward those who did them injury or violence, but more severe toward their own shortcomings.[120] And already there appears the desire to harass the Jews in their cult activities, and without altogether withdrawing the protection the Synagogue had previously enjoyed, to make things difficult for it. From this point of view, the affair at Callinicum marks a major new departure.

Up to this time the destruction of synagogues had fallen under the censure of the law.[121] It had at least entailed as reparations the rebuilding of the edifice by the guilty parties and, where appropriate, corporal punishment. This is the law Theodosius applied initially at Callinicum.[122] Although in this instance he capitulated to Ambrose, the law nevertheless continued for a time unchanged. Legally, the destruction of synagogues remained a crime. In fact, the law was violated constantly and with impunity, for the ecclesiastical authorities encouraged people to break it and hindered any attempt to enforce it. The fact that the texts prohibiting the destruction of synagogues continued to be republished is evidence that the legislators were unable to enforce obedience to them.

From one edition to the next, moreover, the severity of the laws is moderated. In A.D. 393 some years after Callinicum, Theodosius published a reminder that Judaism was not forbidden by law and that therefore the destruction of synagogues ought to be punished.[123] But he modified the procedure so that what had been a crime that must be remitted to the imperial tribunal now became a matter for the jurisdiction of local authorities. The laws of 397, 412, and 418 again recall in general terms the protection the synagogues enjoy. The second forbids their confiscation, the third forbids incendiarism.[124] Contemporary events, which I have referred to above, show that these texts often remained a dead letter.

The next step is that the imperial authorities make a fresh concession to the Church, in accepting the seizure or destruction of synagogues as a fait accompli, about which nothing could be done. In three laws published during the space of a few months, all of them in the year 423, there is no longer any question of restitution, or of rebuilding at the expense of those responsible.[125] Those responsible, which is to say the Christian communities or their leaders, are required to restore merely the cult objects, or, in cases where these have already been appropriated to Christian use, to pay the value of them. They are obliged, in addition, to provide ground where the Jews may, at their own expense, build a new synagogue.[126] These legal texts, with their astonishing indulgence toward the guilty, and their undisguised discrimination against the Jews, surely acted as a tacit encouragement to repeat the violent actions they were ostensibly designed to punish.

Already by this date another law was in force, and had probably been so for several years, for the laws of 423 cite it. It forbade the Jews to build any new synagogues (except in the instances provided above) and even to repair or improve the old ones.[127] Repair was only allowed on the grounds that the building was in danger of collapse, and special authorization had to be given for it. If a synagogue was illegally built or repaired, the authorities were to see that it was pulled down.[128] A later *novella* of Theodosius II allows the transformation of such an illicit synagogue into a church, and lays a heavy fine on its constructors.[129] It was for an infringement of this law, amongst other misdemeanors, that the Patriarch Gamaliel was deprived of his honorary prefecture.

It was, however, only by slow degrees that the Christian emperors, having inherited from their pagan predecessors the duty of protecting the Jews, turned to bullying and harassing them. Constantine seems scarcely to have departed at all from the traditional policy. The important changes occur in the second half of the fourth century, for the most

part after the reign of Julian. They are partly to be explained as a
reaction against Julian's pro-Jewish policies. Even then resistance is not
lacking. It is possible that Chrysostom's frantic anti-Semitism had of-
fended the court of Arcadius and contributed to his disgrace.[130] Theodosius only capitulated in the Callinicum affair under threat of ecclesiastical discipline and eternal punishment. Furthermore, what he had lost
on the roundabouts he attempted to regain on the swings, by suppressing
the political activities of the monks who were the chief instigators of
anti-Jewish violence: *Monachi multa scelera faciunt,*[131] as he puts it.
Later legislation reflects similar hesitation, and sheds abundant light on
the suppressed conflict between civil and religious authority. Measures
that tend to protect the Jews alternate with those which shelter Christians from their missionary activity. The result of all this was a confusion
about their standing; from which confusion, we may imagine, they
derived no benefit whatever. It is nevertheless true that the imperial
authority, though it was vacillating and from the outset less dependable
than in the pagan era, did manage sometimes to exercise a certain
restraint upon the violence of Christian anti-Semitism.

   Theology, for its part, set its own limits to anti-Semitism. Even after
the coming of the Christ whom they rejected, the Jews had a place to fill
and a part to play. They were, as we have seen, witnesses, *testes iniqui-
tatis suae et veritatis nostrae.*[132] So then, at the same time as it encouraged both official and popular anti-Jewish attitudes, the Church did
have an eye to the survival of Judaism and the Jews. Hatred must not be
pushed to the point at which the Jews were exterminated.

   The law takes account of this theological necessity. In the legal texts
the preamble commonly justifies the privileges accorded to the Jews
either in the name of toleration or on the grounds of their antiquity. But
as Juster points out,[133] these motives could just as readily have been
appealed to to protect pagans, but the Church was not slow to persecute
them. The decisions of the councils freely associate Jews with heretics,
and the imperial legislation speaks of both in the same breath. But this
juxtaposition does not quite amount to an assimilation of the one category to the other. The Jews are accorded the right to exist, a right that
was denied to heretics, and, after Theodosius, denied to pagans also. In
practice, the leading party in the Church, whether it happened to be
Arian or orthodox, always maintained the protected status of the Jews,

albeit in a precarious and doubtful condition. And it did this, even though at the same time it might behave quite pitilessly toward its Christian opponents.

Furthermore, it was not only the cold reason of the theologians that placed some restraint on the wilder excesses of anti-Semitism. It must in fairness be acknowledged that the imprecations and hatred did leave room for more benevolent sentiments, more in keeping with the gospel. When an author fulminates against the Jews, allowance must always be made for the exaggeration of rhetoric and oratory. The word is often more violent than the thought.

St. Jerome, for whom Judas is the image of Judaism,[134] overwhelms the Jews with sarcastic remarks and offensive epithets,[135] but the animosity these reprobates *(Judaici serpentes)* inspire in him is not carried over into his personal relations with Jewish individuals. Just as well-known bishops were able to be on sympathetic, even friendly terms, with pagans, so Jerome was in constant touch with rabbis. He asked them for lessons in Hebrew (though he did swear about the price they charged),[136] which implies a certain confidence not only in their competence but in their intellectual probity. And his daily meeting with them for the lessons presupposes at least a minimum of human politeness and amity. It is possible to represent this as an accommodation that the exigencies of life demanded, as a utilitarian adaptation of behavior. All the same, one cannot help noticing here and there among the patristic writings evidence of a sympathy that, though qualified, is real enough, even when it takes the form of pity. Christian charity is on occasion displayed toward the despised Jews, who, it must be remembered, cherished the same feelings for the "Nazarenes" as the Christians, for the most part, did about them.

The Church held it to be a duty to pray for the Jews, and the fathers frequently recall the fact. Israel had prepared the way for the Church and the Church owed its existence to her. St. Paul had stressed this. Speaking of the Church as a wild olive shoot, grafted on to the Jewish stock, he had asked the Christians not to boast over Israel.[137] His thought, and the image in which it was expressed, was often taken up, as was his assertion of Israel's eventual redemption, in the mercy of God. Thus St. Jerome says: *Nos in radicem ipsam inserti sumus; nos rami sumus, illi radix. Non debere maledicere radicibus, sed debemus orare pro radicibus nostris.*[138] And St. Augustine similarly: *Nec superbe glorie-*

mur adversus ramos fractos. Sed potius cogitemus cujus gratia et quanta miseric ordia et in qua radice inserti sumus.[139]

Amongst the fragmentary knowledge of God that the Jews possessed there existed yet a portion of truth. Christian opinion readily assented to the qualified praise that the apostle accorded them: "I bear them witness that they have a zeal for God, but not according to knowledge."[140] St. Augustine likewise gives them credit for their fidelity to what they believe. When all other peoples adopted paganism, they alone remained unshakably attached to their law, and no power on earth can prevent them from being Jews.[141] They are recognized as possessing other qualities too. St. Ambrose, for example, declares: *Judaei habent castimoniam,*[142] and his testimony provides us with an additional reason for treating with reserve the allegations of sensuality and carnal excesses that are brought against the Jews. We have already noted that St. Jerome mentions in passing the Jews' generosity in giving alms. It is true that these praises are scattered and grudgingly given. Such as they are, however, they provide a welcome counterweight to the virulent diatribes of Chrysostom.

Some of the fathers,[143] even though they are sparing of actual praise, betray a relative sympathy by the moderate tone in which they speak of the Jews, and by the absence of complaints that others make so freely. If this falls short of sympathy, it speaks at least a laudable desire to be just and moderate, and conveys a genuinely human feeling.[144]

The differences of outlook that appear in the writings of the fathers and show that the picture was not uniformly dark are also reflected in popular Christian opinion during the period. It is going too far to say, as Parkes does, that anti-Semitism in the period was not a popular phenomenon, but something artifically worked up by the ecclesiastical hierarchy.[145] If the Christian populace so many times threw itself into the attack on synagogue after synagogue, it was not because it passively accepted orders given from above. The mass of believers, who were of gentile birth, had not on conversion shed their pagan feelings of dislike toward the Jews. If the anti-Jewish polemic was so successful, it was because it awakened latent hatreds and appealed to feelings that were already there.

This, however, is only one aspect of the matter. We learn from Chrysostom that among the people "many stand in awe of the Jews and even today treat their religious institutions with reverence."[146] We can-

not know how these two tendencies, toward hatred and toward sympathy, were balanced. But having weighed the information we have at our
disposal, it seems safe to say that the anti-Jewish bias of official ecclesiastical circles was counterbalanced by equally well-marked pro-Jewish
sentiments among the laity and among some of the clergy too. Or rather,
it is the existence of the pro-Jewish sentiments among the laity that is
the real explanation of Christian anti-Semitism. Anti-Semitism was the
defensive reflex of the orthodox hierarchy to the Jewish danger, the
Jewish disease.

Whatever the emperor Claudius thought, and his opinion was shared
by the pagan world at large, this disease did not consist simply of
unsociability and turbulence, issuing in civil disorder and seditious conspiracy. The symptoms of the disease were analyzed with minute care by
Chrysostom, and he finds it to be essentially a moral and religious
malady. With Israel it is congenital, but it is transmitted also to Judaizing
Christians.[147] When the Jewish sickness is regarded in this light, as a
contagious thing, anti-Semitism takes on the character of therapy.

We are here very close to the real roots of the phenomenon. The vices
of the Jews, whether real or imagined with the help of biblical texts, the
murder of Christ—these are not the real grounds for hatred. They are
merely the arguments that are used to stimulate or to reinforce hatred. If
the Jews are painted so black, it is because to too many of the faithful
they appeared at first sight not sufficiently unattractive. The most compelling reason for anti-Semitism was the religious vitality of Judaism.

This vitality showed itself in a negative way in the doggedness with
which the Jews opposed the Christian gospel. It was shown more positively in the lasting power of Jewish beliefs, and especially of Jewish
rites, to draw an important minority of Christians from the very bosom
of the Church. It was shown in the attraction the Synagogue and its
message still managed to exercise over the believers. This was the first
and great complaint, rooted neither in the biblical past nor in the bygone
days when the gospel was first preached, but in the present situation.
The Synagogue was an ever-present reality. The caricature the gospels
offer us in place of a portrait of the Pharisees expresses the disappointment and distress of the newborn Christianity, and was produced in an
epoch when the doctor of the law had been responsible for the failure of
the mission to Israel. Similarly, the anti-Semitism of the Church, or at
least those elements in it which are original and specifically Christian,

expresses the Church's annoyance at Israel. For Israel, far from either abdicating or being converted, continued to make her influence felt within the Church's own confines, and she did so, sometimes by making a serious effort, and sometimes without even trying.

Religious competition seems to have played the same sort of part in the rise and development of Christian anti-Semitism as has been ascribed to economic competition in the rise of modern anti-Semitism. The extreme form it took can only be explained in terms of a still active proselytizing movement and of the survival of numerous forms of syncretism between the two religions.

NOTES

1. Mommsen, *Röm. Geschichte,* 5:519.
2. For a recent exposition of the subject and bibliographical notes, see Pauly-Wissowa, "Antisemitismus," *RE, Supplement,* 5:3–43. The essential texts are brought together in Reinach's collection. See the work of Fischer and Kittel, *Das antike Weltjudentum,* which is anti-Semitic in tone.
3. Ovid, *Ars Amat.,* I. 415, Reinach, *Textes,* p. 248. Other examples may be found in Juster, *Les Juifs,* 1:172, n. 4. The terra cotta caricatures found frequently in the Rhineland which date from the third and fourth centuries (see Fischer and Kittel, *Weltjudentum,* pp. 167–219) are not necessarily modeled exclusively on Jews. They may be intended to ridicule Semites in general, especially Syrians, who were very widespread in the empire.
4. *Hist. Aug., Alex. Sev.,* 28.
5. Josephus, *Contra Apionem,* 2, 4, 33, Reinach, *Textes,* p. 128.
6. This is what Juvenal's *graeculus esuriens* refers to (*Sat.,* 3. 78). For the Greeks, it was the Egyptians and Phoenicians who were famed for their money and their trading: Plato, *Republic,* 4. 436, *Laws,* 5. 316. For Polybius (6. 46) it was the Cretans and Carthaginians (6. 56) who were distinguished by their unbridled love of gain. On Carthaginian greed, see the Latin authors cited by Gsell, *Histoire Ancienne,* 4:217. Peoples subject to Rome often attributed the Roman conquests to the lure of material profit as well as to the desire for domination and the love of glory. See, for example, the discourses of Jugurtha, *Romanos injustis profunda avaritia* (Sallust, *Jug.,* 81. 1) and of Calgacus: *Raptores orbis . . . si locuples hostis est, avari, si pauper, ambitiosi* (Tacitus, *Agric.,* 30). Texts cited by Fuchs, *Geistige Widerstand* p. 17, and nn. 52, 53. See Jerome, in *Is.,* 2. 8 (*PL,* 24. 48): *Nihil Judaeorum et Romanorum gente esse avarius.* The aiming of this charge at the Jews is not earlier than Christianity.

7. *Jam pridem Syrus in Tiberim defluxit Orontes* (Juvenal, *Sat.,* 3. 60). The reference is to the entire East, Greece included. For Egypt, see Tacitus, *Hist.,* 1. 11: *Superstitione ec lascivia discordem et mobilem, insciam legum, ignaram magistratuum.*

8. Vopiscus, *Vita Saturnini,* 8. On the question of authenticity, Labriolle, *Réaction païenne,* pp. 51 ff.

9. Juster, *Les Juifs,* 2:251–322.

10. See texts relating to the diverse professions taken up by Jews in Fischer and Kittel, *Weltjudentum,* pp. 53–58, and notes p. 222. Agriculture would take first place, especially in Egypt and Asia Minor. See Lietzmann, *Geschichte der alten Kirche,* 1:73.

11. Martial, 12, 57, 13; Juvenal, 3. 12 ff., 6. 542 ff. Reinach, *Textes d'auteurs grecs et romains,* pp. 289 ff.

12. Josephus, *Contra Apionem,* 1:12, brings out the contrast between trading people and the Jews.

13. The Western diaspora was hardly affected by it. The troubles provoked among the Jews of Rome by the first Christian preaching (Suetonius, *Claudius,* 25, Acts 18:2) were not concerned with the traditional kind of Messianism. What Heinemann calls political anti-Semitism arose out of fear that the Jews were becoming too powerful, and was really only found at Alexandria.

14. In this belief the place of the Messianic hope seems to have been quite modest, as far as the Jews of the dispersion were concerned. The wider Judaism had little time for this strictly national side of the religion. On the other hand, the place of "Messianic" aspirations in pagan spirituality in that era is well known. The Sibylline Oracles show that this expanded Messianism provided some common ground.

15. *Quanta concordia.* Cicero, *pro Flacco,* 28:66; see Josephus, *Contra Apionem,* 2.19, Tacitus, *Hist.,* 5. 5, Reinach, pp. 238, 306. On Jewish xenophobia, see Reinach, especially pp. 56 (Posidonius of Apamea), 63 ff. (Apollonius Molon), 133 (Apion), 176 (Philostratus), and 255 (Trogus Pompeius).

16. Tacitus accuses both Jews (*Hist.,* 5:5) and Christians (*Annals,* 15:44) of hatred of the human race, in exactly the same terms. See Minucius Felix, *Octavius,* 8–9, who sums up the principal complaints made by the pagan masses against the Christians after having brought exactly the same ones against the Jews. On Jewish ritual murder, see Apion, Reinach, *Textes,* p. 132. On Christian ritual murders, Eusebius, *HE,* 5, 1, 26.

17. They are analyzed by Heinemann, "Antisemitismus" pp. 22 ff. The author remarks (p. 37) that Greek scholarship was not very interested in Judaism. When the Greeks did exhibit interest, as in the case of Hecataeus of Abdera and Posidonius of Apamea, it was with a certain sympathy for Jewish monotheism. This stream of thought, albeit soon contaminated with anti-Semitic criticisms, is continued, however, by Celsus, who praises the Jews for their sense of tradition (*Contra Celsum,* 5.35) and by Porphyry (Eusebius, *Praep. Ev.,* 9. 10). See Labriolle, *Réaction païenne,* p. 458.

18. The development is clearly perceptible in the second century. Tacitus is equally hard on both religions (see above, n. 16). The anti-Jewish strand of thinking loses its virulence after Juvenal, and meanwhile the "first uneasiness" about Christianity is becoming more clearly apparent (Labriolle, *Réaction païenne.* chapter 2) working up to the great offensive by Celsus, who takes the Jews as his allies. The development of public opinion is a step ahead of the attitude of the authorities (see pp. 41 ff.).

19. Acts shows clearly this halo of sympathy which Judaism had acquired and from which Christianity benefited.

20. See especially Rom. 10:1, 11:1–32.

21. On John's anti-Judaism, see M. Goguel, *Introd. au N.T.,* pp. 537 ff.

22. See p. 70.

23. John, 19:12, 15.

24. E.g., Eusebius, *Vita Const.,* 3.24; Gregory of Nyssa, *Or.,* 5 (*PG,* 46. 685); Asterius of Amasa, *Hom. in Ps.,* 5.16 (*PG,* 40. 424) and especially John Chrysostom; see p. 219.

25. Thus Origen, *Contra Celsum.* 4. 32.

26. John 12:37–40.

27. Most frequently, however, outside the works that are properly anti-Jewish polemical ones, where the proof ran a serious risk of missing the mark.

28. Acts 7:51 ff.

29. Juster, *Les Juifs,* 1:45, n. 1.

30. Josephus, *Contra Apionem,* 2. 5; Origen, *Contra Celsum,* 3.5. Reinach, pp. 130, 166.

31. *Contra Jud. et Gent.,* 16 (*PG,* 48. 835). As a good subject of Rome, Chrysostom regards the Jewish rebellions against Rome as criminal: *In Matt. Hom.,* 43.3 (*PG,* 57. 461). Juster, *Les Juifs,* 2:184.

32. Juster, *Les Juifs,* 1:47, nn. 1, 10.

33. *Hom. 1 in Ps.,* 36 (*PG,* 12.1321). See p. 469, n. 99.

34. Origen, *Contra Celsum,* 1. 26, 5. 6; *Kerygma Petri,* in Clement of Alexandria, *Strom.,* 6, 5, 41; Aristides, *Apol.,* 14. On the reality of this worship, references in Bousset/Gressmann, *Religion des Judentums,* p. 330. See pp. 345 ff.

35. E.g., Tacitus, *Hist.,* 5. 5, Reinach, p. 308; see Reinach's index, under "idolâtrie."

36. *Apol.,* 18. 4.

37. Except for out-and-out allegorizers, such as Barnabas.

38. Josephus, *Contra Apionem,* 2. 7; Tacitus, *Hist.,* 5. 3–4, etc; Reinach, *Textes,* pp. 50, 58, 121, 131, 139, 304, 334.

39. *Ad Nat.,* 1. 14. See Minucius Felix, *Octavius,* 19, and the famous Palatine graffito, *DAC,* 1:2, 2024, whose interpretation is otherwise controversial.

40. *Apol.,*16. 3.

41. Juster, *Les Juifs,* 2:204, and Oort, *Ursprung der Blutbeschuldigung.*

42. *Hom.,* 1 (*PG,* 48. S52). See Simon, "A propos de la lettre de Claude aux Alexandrins," *Bull. Fac. Lettres Strasb.,* 1943, pp. 175–83.

43. *Diognetus*, 3. See C. Th., 16, 8, 7: *sacrilegi coetus;* other texts in Juster, *Les Juifs*, 1:45, n. 1.

44. Reinach, *Textes*, p. 57.

45. See *p. 169*.

46. *Hist.*, 5. 5, Reinach, *Textes*, p. 307.

47. Jerome, *Comm. in Ezek.*, 1, 4, 13; *in Is.*, 44:6; *Ep. ad Gelas.*, 121 (*PL*, 25, 49; 24. 438; 22. 1034). Augustine, *Tract. 3 in Joh.*, PL, 34–35. 1404). Ambrose, *Ep.*, 74. 3 (*PL*, 16. 1255). Asterius of Amasa, in *Ps. 5 Hom.*, 17 (*PL*, 20. 351) and especially the invective of Chrysostom; see pp. 217 ff.

48. *Hist.*, 5. 5.

49. *Hom.*,18.1 and 9. Lucas, *Geschichte*, pp. 38 ff., rightly sees the question of asceticism as one of the essential points of conflict between Jews and Christians.

50. On the part played by monasticism, see Parkes, *Conflict of Church and Synagogue*, pp. 225 ff.

51. E.g., Jerome, *in Is.*, 2. 8:*Praef. ad Os.*; *Ep.*, 121 (*PL*, 24, 45, 25. 855, 22. 1006). It is likely that the Patriarchs' way of life and their privileged financial position, which often made them excessively rich, helped to give rise to this complaint, which was then extended to their flock.

52. *Praef. in Job.*, 1.

53. *Ep.*, 52.

54. See n. 6.

55. *In Ez.*,27. 16 (*PL*, 25. 266).

56. Parkes, *Conflict of Church and Synagogue*, p. 192.

57. On this antagonism and the differences with regard to sexual morality, see *Lehren des Judentums*, 3:135–200, especially 181 ff., and 1:206 ff.

58. The roles were sometimes reversed. Certain Christian authors see ascetic preoccupations in the dietary prohibitions and condemn them for that very reason: *Deus ventre non colitur nec cibis.* See Lukyn Williams, *Adversus Judaeos*, pp. 303 ff. See Novatian, *De Cibis Judaicis*, 5 (*PL.* 3. 96).

59. The leitmotif of the entire argument is already present in Stephen's speech: "As your fathers did, so do you" (Acts 7:51). See Ps. Ambrose, *Serm.*, 7. 4 (*PL*, 17. 639): *Hoc autem non recens in ipsis sed inveteratum et originarium malum est.*

60. Lucas, *Geschichte*, p. 37.

61. For references to liturgical sources see Juster, *Les Juifs*, 1:334, n. 4. To L. Canet's study, mentioned on p. 335, n. 1, add E. Peterson, "Perfidia judaica," in *Ephemerides liturgicae*, 1936, pp. 296-311. The word *perfidia* in theological parlance does not precisely correspond to our word *perfidy*. It refers rather to an offense against the faith. But it still has an injurious meaning, and it is easy to slip from one meaning to the other.

62. Especially Exod. 33:3, 34:9; Baruch, 2:30, 33.

63. Augustine, *Adv. Jud.*, 9 (*PL*; 42. 57); Ambrose, *Ep.*, 74. 3 (*PL*, 16. 1255); Julian, *Contra Gal.*, Neumann's edition, p. 201.

64. *Carmen Apol.*, passim, e.g., 261: *Gens cervicosa nimis. See Instr.*, 1. 38, 1. 40.
65. *Ex. R.*, on 32:7. Wünsche's edition, p. 300.
66. *Ep.*, 74. 3 (*PL*, 16. 1255). See Ps. Augustine, *de Epiphania serm.*, 132 (*PL*, 38–39, 2008): *Caeci ad intelligendum, duri ad credendum;* Maximus of Turin, *de Epiphania, Hom.*, 25 (*PL*, 57. 279): *Quousque, Judaee durissime, obtusa aure, clausis oculis et perfido corde persistis?* See Commodian, *Inst.*, 1. 37.
67. *In Amos*, 5. 23 (*PL*, 25. 1054).
68. *In Christi resurr. orat.*, 5 (*PG*, 46. 685). When the author accuses the Jews of repudiating the faith of their fathers, he is taking up the idea of an original Christianity and identifying it with the true religion of Israel. The accusation is an odd one, if one remembers the commoner complaint that the Jews have an unseasonable attachment to defunct customs.
69. The chronology of these sermons was established first by Usener (*Weihnachtsfest*, pp. 233–47) and corrected by Schwartz, *Ostertafeln*, pp. 169–84. Advancing strong arguments, he places sermons 1 and 2 in the autumn of A.D. 386, sermon 3 in January 387, and nos. 4–8 in the autumn of 387. What we have, then, is a double cycle connected with the Jewish New Year festival in two successive years (the third sermon, against the protopaschites, being in some respects outside the series).
70. *Hom.*, 1. 2 (*PG*, 48. 846). The complaint is founded on Hos. 4:16.
71. *Ibid.*, 846.
72. Deut. 32:15. The quotation is from the LXX, which at this point is not very literal.
73. *Hom.*, 1. 4 (*PG*, 48. 848).
74. *Ibid.*, 847. The orator, though he does not actually quote the texts, evidently has in mind the ideas developed in Ezek. 16 and Hos. 1–2.
75. Jer. 3:3.
76. *Hom.*, 1 (847). Jerome, similarly, commenting on the imprecations in Hos. 2:4–7, calls the Synagogue a harlot, *fornicaria* and *adultera: Comm. in Os.* 1. 2 (*PL*, 25. 830). But Chrysostom goes further. For Jerome there is hardly any question of its being anything but a metaphor. The Synagogue signifies an abstraction, viz., Judaism. Chrysostom is speaking of the Synagogue as an actual place of worship, and sees it as genuinely a place of abomination. It is interesting to note that according to rabbinic tradition, amongst the calamities that will herald the coming of the Messiah is the woe that "the Synagogue will be used for prostitution." References in Bonsirven, *Jud. Pal.*, 1:401.
77. Jer. 7:11, 12:7.
78. *Hom.*, 1. 4, (*PG*, 48. 848).
79. See p. 211.
80. Ps. 106:37.
81. *Hom.*, 1:6 (*PG*, 48:852).
82. Jer. 5:8 (LXX text).

83. *PG* 48. 853.
84. *HOM.,* 1. 7 (*PG,* 48. 853).
85. *Hom.,* 6. 5 (*PG,* 48. 9111).
86. Ibid., 913.
87. Ibid., 915.
88. This is an idea dear to Chrysostom. The Jews are an abomination in the sight of all men. See *Exp. in Ps.,* 8. 3. (*PG,* 55. 110).
89. *Hom.,* 8. 1 (*PG,* 48. 927). For the same equation of fasting and drunkenness, see *Hom.,* 1. 2 (ibid., 846).
90. Isa 29:9.
91. Once Chrysostom's procedure has been analyzed, the accusations he formulates against the Synagogue of his own day can be evaluated with proper scepticism. When he speaks of the Synagogue as a theater, and describes it as a resort of evil-livers, what he actually means is simply that Synagogue worship provided a solemn performance that attracted the pagan society of Antioch. It is no more than a translation into polemical language of the statement made earlier by Josephus, concerning the taste that the people of Antioch, and those of Damascus too (*B.J.,* 2, 20, 2), had for things Jewish. There may well have been among this pagan public some who went because it was the fashionable thing to do. But can this be laid to the charge of the Jews themselves? And could not the same sort of people be found in contemporary Christianity? The use of the word *theater* may also be explained by the liking that Jews of the period displayed for spectacle of all sorts (texts in Juster, *Les Juifs,* 2:240, n. 6). There seems, moreover, to be some play on words, with σκηνή (scene) and σκηναί (Tabernacles). See the beginning of *Hom.* 7.
92. See p. 205.
93. Oort, *Ursprung der Blutbeschuldigung;* see above, n. 41.
94. *PL,* 20. 1165–82. See Lukyn Williams, *Adversus Judaeos,* pp. 298–305.
95. *Altercatio Simonis et Theophili,* 28.
96. Isa. 1:115, 59:7, Deut. 32:32.
97. On the interest in the unleavened bread among the mass of Christians, and its connection with magic, see p. 355.
98. Juster, *Les Juifs,* 1:322–37.
99. Ibid., p. 335.
100. It is going too far to think of the diatribes that some of the homilies contain as elements that are properly a part of the liturgy. The tenor and the tone of the homily are essentially variable, affected by the time, the place, and the speaker. There is no immutable law of homilies that directs that they be always anti-Semitic. They were so only on occasion.
101. Juster, *Les Juifs,* 1:335 ff. Juster tends, perhaps unconsciously, to treat this purely literary anti-Semitism as if it were something artificial. By doing so, he exonerates pagan opinion and throws the entire responsibility on the Church. The same tendency is apparent in Parkes' work.

102. See Athanasius, *Ep. Encycl.*, 3 (*PG*, 25. 228); Theodoret, *HE*, 4. 18 ff. (*PG*, 82:1163 and 1175): H. M. Gwatkin, *Studies of Arianism* (Cambridge, 1882), pp. 57–9; Duchesne, *Histoire ancienne*, 2³:200, 263. Doctrinal sympathies may have made such collusion easier. But it was only relatively speaking that the Arians were more tolerant of Jews than the orthodox; the legislation of Constantius, for example, does not show any signs of it. At Alexandria religion does not seem to have been the deciding factor. See Parkes, *Conflict of Church and Synagogue*, pp. 182 ff.

103. Socrates, *HE*, 7, 13 (*PG*, 67. 760). See Juster, *Les Juifs*, 2:176.

104. Philo, *Leg. ad Gaium*, ch. 20; *in Flacc.*, 8.

105. *Passio St. Salsae* (French translation in Monceaux, *La vraie Légende dorée* (Paris, 1929), pp. 299–326). See *REJ* 44:8 ff.; *DAC*, 1:346.

106. *Acta Sanctorum*, II, 483.

107. See Simon, *Polémique anti-juive de S. Jean Chrysostome*, pp. 413 ff.

108. *Edessa Chronicle*, 51. Other refs. in Juster, *Les Juifs*, 1:464, n. 3.

109. Ambrose, *Ep.*, 40. 23 (*PL*, 16. 1109).

110. St. Severus, *Ep.* (*PL*, 20. 731 ff.).

111. See Nau, in *REJ* 83:184 ff.; Parkes, *Conflict of Church and Synagogue*, p. 232.

112. Evagrius, *HE*, 1, 13 (*PG*, 86. 2456); Metaphrastes, *Life of St. Symeon Stylites* (*PG*, 114. 381).

113. It is from him that we have our information about the affair. *Ep.*, 40 (*PL*, 16. 1101). For detailed analysis of the letter, see Juster, *Les Juifs*, 1:462, n. 3. See Palanque, *Saint Ambroise et l'Empire Romain*, pp. 205–7.

114. *Ep.*, 41 (*PL*, 16. 1120). Palanque, *Saint Ambroise et l'Empire Romaine*, pp. 214–17.

115. Ambrose expresses the same attitude to paganism in connection with the affair of the altar of victory: *Christianus imperator aram solius Christi didicit honorare. . . . Vox imperatoris nostri Christum resultet, et illum solum quem sentit, loquatur. Quia cor regis in manum Dei* (*Ep.*, 18. 31).

116. In his view, legislation concerning synagogues was naturally the province of the ecclesiastical authorities. *Ep.*, 40. 7.

117. See *C. Th.*, 2, 1, 10; 12, 1, 165, which contain laws made following Chrysostom's arrival in the capital. By contrast, after his departure, *C. Th.*, 16, 8, 15 (404). Juster, *Les Juifs*, 1:231, n. 7.

118. *Feralis secta, nefaria secta: C. Th.*, 16, 8, 1 (315); *nefanda superstitio:* 16, 9, 4 (417); *abominandi Judaei:* 16, 8, 26 (423); *sacrilegi coetus;* 16, 8, 7 (357); *foedum taetrumque Judaeorum nomen:* 16, 8, 19 (401).

119. Juster, *Les Juifs*, 1:227, n. 5.

120. Ibid., 1:230–2 and 2:178–82.

121. Ibid., 1:462.

122. Ambrose, *Ep.*, 40, 6, 18.

123. *C. Th.*, 16, 8, 9 (493).

124. *C. Th.*, 16, 8, 2:. . . . *eorumque synagogas in quiete solita permanere.* 16, 8, 20: *quae Judaeorum frequentari conventiculis constat quaeque synago-*

garum vocabulis nuncupantur, nullus audeat violare. 16, 8, 21: *non passim eorum synagogae concrementur.*

125. February, April, and June. C. Th., 16, 8, 25, 26 and 27.
126. C. Th., 16, 8, 25; *Pro his loca eis, in quibus possint extruere, ad mensuram videlicet sublatarum, praeberi.*
127. The law forbidding new buildings is of uncertain date. For discussion see Juster, *Les Juifs,* 1:469, n. 2. The prohibition of the restoration of buildings is recalled in *Nov. Theod.,* 3:3.
128. C. Th., 16, 8, 22 (415).
129. *Nov. Theod.,* 3. 3.
130. Lucas, *Geschichte,: p. 19.*
131. Ambrose, *Ep.,* 41. 27 (*PL,* 16. 1120). See the measures taken by Arcadius to forbid them access to the towns. C. Th., 16, 3, 1–2; 9, 40, 16; 11, 30, 57.
132. Augustine, *in Ps. Enarr.,* 1:21 ff. (*PL,* 36–37, 765). See p. 92.
133. Juster, *Les Juifs,* 1:227.
134. *In Ps.* 108 (*PL,* 26. 1224).
135. See *In Is.,* 11. 6 and 58 (*PL,* 24. 150 and 582); *Ep.,* 121 (22, 1006); *Contra Ruf.,* 3. 25 (22. 493; *In Ezek.,* 38 (25. 370).
136. See p. 185.
137. Rom. 11:17 ff.
138. *In Ps.,* 77 (*Anecd. Maredsol.,* 3, 2, 196).
139. *Tract. Adv. Jud.,* 15 (*PL,* 42. 63).
140. Rom. 10:2.
141. *Contra Faust.,* 12. 13 (*PL,* 42. 261). This retrospective praise, which is transformed in the present into blame for hanging on to an outmoded law, reappears in Gregory of Nazianzus in his panegyric on the Maccabees, *Or.,* 15 (*PG,* 35. 912).
142. *Enarr. in Ps.,* 1 (*PL,* 15. 1032). Chrysostom himself has to recognize certain moral qualities in the Jews. *Hom.,* 6. 2 (*PG,* 48. 906 ff.).
143. E.g., Eusebius in *Praep. Ev.,* and *Dem. Ev.* See A. Puech, *Littérature grecque chrétienne,* 3:195. Similarly St. Augustine, but less clearly. See, however, Blumenkranz, *Judenpredigt,* pp. 186 ff.
144. In general, the writers anterior to the fourth century preserve a far more courteous tone than those who follow. For example, Aristides (*Apol.,* 14:2 ff.) pays homage to Jewish monotheism and Jewish charity. "They practice love for men, and pity towards the poor; they redeem prisoners and bury the dead." Political opportunism may have played its part here, at a time when Judaism was recognized and protected whereas Christianity possessed no legal status. So also may propagandist considerations; not having yet lost all hope of converting the Jews, the Christians could be generous. Taking it all in all, the attitude of the early Church toward the Jews is quite comparable, in all its aspects, to that of Islam toward the revealed religions, Judaism and Christianity, which it claims to supersede as well as to surpass.

145. Parkes, *Conflict of Church and Synagogue*, p. 193.
146. *Hom.*, 1. 3 (*PG*, 48. 847).
147. *Hom.*, 1. 1 (*PG*, 48. 845). See *Hom.*, 2 (859). On the two conceptions, pagan and Christian, of the Jewish evil, see Simon, *A propos de la lettre de Claude*, pp. 177–78.

5

The *Adversus Judaeos* Tradition in the Church Fathers: The Exegesis of Christian Anti-Judaism

Rosemary Radford Ruether

The primary materials for studying the attitudes towards the Jews in the Church Fathers are the *Adversus Judaeos* writings.[1] These writings are remarkable for their preservation of the archaic "testimonies tradition." The earliest Christian scripture before the written New Testament was the Jewish Bible, or "Old Testament," Christologically interpreted. Along with this Christological interpretation of the "Old Testament" there developed from the beginning an anti-Judaic "left hand." This anti-Judaic "left hand" of Christological interpretation was designed to show why the Jewish religious community, from which Christianity got both its Scripture and its messianic hope (which it believed to be fulfilled in Jesus), did not accept this "fulfillment" of its own tradition. In effect the Church sought to discredit the rival rabbinic exegesis of this same Scripture and to build up a case against the Jewish religious community and its teachers in order to confirm its own faith as the authentic culmination of the Jewish religious tradition.[2]

Both the Christological and anti-Judaic exegesis of the Old Testament preexisted and formed the hermeneutical basis of the New Testament itself. But this tradition continues and expands in the Church Fathers as a collection of themes and proof-tests designed to prove that Jesus is the Christ predicted by the prophets and that the Jewish community, which

Reprinted by permission of the State University of New York Press from *Aspects of Jewish Culture in the Middle Ages,* ed. Paul E. Szarmach, Albany, 1979, 27–50.

rejects this faith, is both blind and reprobate. The Old Testament itself continues to be the basic Scripture for this hermeneutical work, although in the patristic collections and treatises one or two New Testament references may be added to the Old Testament testimonies. (Even though in this paper I will follow the Christian convention of referring to the Jewish Scriptures as the "Old Testament," I must note at the outset that this very term itself is a Christological and anti-Judaic *midrash* on the Jewish Scriptures.)

The *Adversus Judaeos* writings include simple catalogues of testimonies arranged by theme with a minimum of exposition, such as Cyprian's *Three Books of Testimonies Against the Jews,* the *Contra Judaeos* by the sixth-century Spanish Father Isidore of Seville, or the *Selected Testimonies from the Old Testament Against the Jews* by Pseudo-Nyssa. They also include treatises on particular themes, such as Novatian's diatribe "On Jewish Meats," or attempts to gather all the themes systematically, such as Tertullian's *Adversus Judaeos* or Justin Martyr's *Dialogue with Trypho.* The anti-Judaic sermon or series of sermons was another favorite form, the most famous of which is the eight sermons against the Jews preached by John Chrysostom in 386–87. The dialogue treatise gave rise to a whole series of imitations, some of which may have actually been written as a result of arranged disputations between Jews and Christians and some of which are literary conventions. In neither case, however, do we get much sense of what the Jewish spokesmen might have said in their own defense. The Jewish protagonist is a straw figure for the Christian apology. The dialogue form can even be elaborated into a liturgical drama.[3] But throughout these writings from the second to the sixth century the arguments themselves remain fairly continuous and fixed. My purpose in this paper will be to provide a systematized summary of the main anti-Judaic themes which appear in these writings and are, therefore, generally accepted as a part of the content of Christian theology. One must remember that this represents the basic hermeneutical tradition of the Church. All theological writing and preaching were based on this Christological interpretation of the Old Testament, and so, although these themes are specifically summarized in this particular genre of writings, they are assumed as the background of and referred to in every teaching that touched on the Jews. Since a cornerstone of Christian faith was that it fulfilled the messianic predictions of the prophets and that the Church was the New Israel replacing the Old, it was difficult to preach or teach anything without referring to this tradition in some way. The *Adversus Judaeos* tradition, then, informed the prevailing way that the Christian community was taught to look at not only the Jews of the New Testament times, but also Jewish history back to Abraham and the Jewish community of its own times. In the fourth century Christianity became the established religion of the Christianized Roman empire. The anti-Judaic doctrines were then translated into a theological-juridical principle for defining the status of Jews vis-à-vis the Church in Christendom. It is at this point that we find the connection between the patristic exegetical anti-Judaism and anti-Semitism as a legal, sociopolitical practice in Christian society.

The anti-Judaic themes typically fall into two major groupings: a) the rejection of the Jews and the election of the gentiles, and b) the inferiority and spiritual fulfillment of the Jewish law and cult. Included in this is the rationale for the Christian messianic, spiritualizing intepretation of the Jewish Scriptures themselves.

The reprobation of the Jews is based ultimately on the assertion that they rejected Jesus as the Christ. But, as in the New Testament, the Church Fathers project this act of apostasy backward so as to make it the culminating and final act of a history that is a trail of crimes and perfidies. This is not a recent forgivable misstep. The Jews have ever been apostate from God. The rejection and murder of Christ is the foreordained conclusion of the evil history of a perfidious people. With the death of Christ the Jews are said to have "filled up the measure of their sins."

The basic form of this idea is to see Jewish history as a heritage of rejecting and killing the prophets, of which the rejection and killing of Christ, the final prophet, are the climax. The theme, begun in the New Testament and carried on in the patristic writings, paints a picture of the Jews as a people who never heard the prophets, always rejected the prophetic message and refused to repent, and finally killed the prophets. The prophets themselves are divorced from the Jewish people and are made the heritage of the Church. An historical view of Scripture as a divinely written book keeps the Church from raising the question of how the prophetic books could have been accepted and preserved by that same people who never "heard the prophets."

The list of the crimes of the Jews had been considerably expanded in the Church Fathers, however. The Jews are also idolators, law-breakers, and evil-doers of every kind. Their proclivity for idolatry and vice is presumed to have been picked up during their stay in Egypt. The Mosaic law, with its cultic and dietary commandments, is seen as a curb upon their Egyptian depravity. God restrained their inordinate appetites with dietary laws and gave them a regulated cult to "innoculate" them against even worse idolatry. Eusebius sums up the matter by saying, "Everything that Moses forbade they had previously done with restraint."[4]

Once out in the desert they were unable to shake off the evil habits picked up in Egypt and fell straightway into idolatry. The Golden Calf is cited as a chief case for this mania for idols. It is the paradigm of their rejection of God, which must finally lead to God's rejection of them. Indeed Barnabas believes that God has already abrogated the covenant with the Jews in favor of the future Church at the time of the Golden Calf, a view found also in the Stephen section of the Book of Acts.[5] Some writers also hint that they resisted Moses and even tried to kill him, but this theme is not prominent, perhaps because of the contradictory desire to deprecate the Mosaic tradition as well.[6]

When in the Promised Land, the Jews continued to run after idols. Every prophetic text that rebukes the people for rebelliousness, unfaithfulness, and "whoring after foreign gods" can be ransacked to provide proof of what the Jews were like in those times. Since the gentile Church itself had recently come from paganism, this would seem to be a dubious charge. But the Fathers surmount this by a remarkable piece of historical compression whereby the proclivity of the Jews for idols is contrasted with the "faithful gentiles," who have turned from idols to the worship of the true God in the Christian Church. As Tertullian puts it:

According to the divine Scriptures the people of the Jews quite forsook God and did degrading service to idols and abandoning Divinity, surrendered to images. . . . And, in later times, in which the kings were governing them . . . they did again worship golden kine and groves and enslave themselves to Baal. Whence it is proven that they have ever been guilty of the crime of Idolatry, whereas our lesser or posterior people quit the idols . . . [and] has been converted to the same God, from whom Israel, as we have shown above, departed.[7]

The prophetic texts can also provide proof of a full array of other crimes: blasphemy, rebelliousness, adultery, and general sensuality. This theme of Jewish sensuality can be fused with the ontological dualism of Christian theology that describes the Jew as a man of the outward letter, a carnal, this-worldly man, as contrasted with the Christian, a man who belongs to the age of the Spirit. Ephrem the Syrian especially draws on the language of Hosea to describe the Synagogue as a harlot, cast off by God because she was "wanton between the legs." Jerusalem is equated with Sodom and Gomorrah.[8] John of Damascene says that God gave the Jews the Sabbath as a time-bound observance because of their "grossness and sensuality" and "absolute propensity for material things," as contrasted with the Christian whose worship belongs to the eschatological or eternal day.[9] Ps. 106:37 especially is used to paint an extraordinary picture of the Jews as infanticides, cannibals, and people who sacrifice their children to idols.[10] The method employed here is to take the prophetic denunciation out of the context and to attribute it, in an absolute manner, to all Jews, then and now.

The purpose of this catalogue of crimes is to demonstrate that their history tends toward and culminates in the final apostasy of the Jews, which is the rejection and death of the Messiah. The nature of the Jews is fixed as one of monstrous evil and rejection of God, logically culminating in the murder of God's Son and justifying God's final rejection of them. God's efforts on their behalf have always been futile. In his forbearance he sends prophets, whom they reject and murder. With the death of Christ the final "evidence is in" that the Jews are not suitable to be God's people. They are then unequivocally rejected for a second people who are the true heirs of the prophets, namely, the gentile Church, which does accept God's Word.

The crime of killing the Messiah is seldom explicitly called "deicide" in the pre-Nicene Fathers, although this is implicit as soon as Jesus is defined as "Son of God" in the metaphysical sense. Most Fathers regard this as the crime of rejection of the final messianic envoy in the line of the martyred prophets. To reject the Christ is to reject the promised salvation and to put oneself beyond the pale of God's designated means of redemption. With the more developed Nicene theology, the character of the crime could be magnified. The Jews are described as enemies of God who commit a cosmic act of treason and *lèse majesté* against the Sovereign of the Universe. Killing Christ is a cosmic regicide. This theme particularly develops after the Constantinian establishment, when Christian theologians begin to identify the emperor with the Vicar of Christ on earth. Chrysostom specifically calls this a sin of "deicide" *(Theoktonian)*.[11]

This proof of the Jews' evil nature, developed by reading prophetic denunciations one-sidedly, was presumed to apply to contemporary Jews also. Since no such evidence of infanticide or gross sensuality does, in fact, seem to characterize their communities, the Church Fathers must explain this, either by hints that such things happen secretly or that, even though they are less evil externally than they used to be, they are actually worse spiritually because of their rejection of Christ. Chrysostom especially plays on his dialectic. Formerly they were prone to every vice and lawlessness, but God kept trying to convert them. Now that they are utterly cast off, they insist on strictly observing all the details of the Law. But since God has now abrogated the Law, this is simply a new perversity on their part. When God wanted them to keep the Law, they would not. Now that God has abolished it, they insist on keeping it. Either way they always do whatever God does not want them to do.[12]

The method of proof-testing this history of Jewish evil consists of splitting the right hand from the left hand of the prophetic message, applying the left hand to the Jews and the right hand to the Church. By this method one gains an unrelieved tale of evil-doing, supposedly characteristic of the Jews, who are divorced from the message of forgiveness and future promise which is applied to the Church. The Jewish Scriptures, which actually contain the record of Jewish self-criticism and repentance, are turned into a remorseless denunciation of the Jews, while the Church itself stands triumphant and perfect, having divorced from itself the heritage of prophetic self-criticism. Anti-Judaism and ecclesiastical triumphalism arise as two sides of the same false polarization of the prophetic dialectic of judgment and promise.

Fundamental to this method is the attempt to prove that, even in the Old Testament, there existed, not one, but two people: an evil apostate people, the Jews, and a faithful people, represented by the heroes and prophets, whose lineage is fulfilled in the future Church. The casting off of the Jews and the election of the gentile Church as the true Israel was known and foretold by the prophets themselves. Only the denunciations of the prophets apply to the Jews. The future promises apply to the Church, not to the Jews. There are several images by which this concept of the two peoples is read back into the Jewish Scriptures. The favorite image comes from the motif of patriarchal sibling rivalry. Ishmael and Isaac, Jacob and Esau, Jacob's elder brothers and Joseph, Manasseh and Ephraim foretell the two peoples; the Church claims the authentic lines of Isaac, Jacob, Joseph, and Ephraim, while relegating the cast-off line to the Jews.[13] The favorite test for this is Gen. 25:23: "Two people" are in Rebecca's womb, and "the younger shall overcome the elder and the elder shall serve the younger." The younger people are the gentile Church, which overcomes the elder brother, the Jews, while the elder brother is to be in perpetual servitude to the younger people, the Church.[14]

This image of the two brothers can be made more startling by tracing it back to Cain and Abel. God rejected the sacrifices of Cain, i.e., the Jewish sacrificial system, while accepting the spiritual sacrifice of the Church. The exiled and reprobate status of the Jews can be compared with that of Cain.[15] This becomes a typological ancestor for the myth of the Wandering Jew. As the fourth-century poet Prudentius puts it:

From place to place the homeless Jew wanders in ever-shifting exile, since the time when he was torn from the abode of his fathers and has been suffering the penalty for murder and having stained his hands with the blood of Christ, whom he denied, paying the price of sin. . . . This noble race [is] scattered and enslaved. . . . It is in captivity under the younger faith . . . a race that was formerly unfaithful confesses Christ and triumphs. But that which denied Christ is conquered and subdued and has fallen into the hands of Masters who keep the Faith.[16]

The image of the two brothers could also draw on the Pauline exegesis of the two wives, Sarah and Hagar or Rachel and Leah.[17] Hagar the bondswoman and her children are cast off. She is the type of the fallen, earthly Jerusalem, which is in bondage together with her children— bondage both in the sense of political bondage in exile under the nations (the gentile Church!) and also in the sense of moral bondage to material things. The Church is the eschatological spiritual Israel, which has been freed by Christ.[18] Like Leah, the Synagogue is "weak-eyed," blinded by the "veil" of the Torah, and unable to read the spiritual message of God. This language could be mingled with that of Hosea, which likens Israel to a harlot, to typify the Synagogue as the cast-off harlot in contrast to the Church, the true bride of Christ. This image of the Church as a triumphant bride in contrast to the Synagogue who stands with broken staff and rejected air, a blind over her eyes, was a favorite motif depicted on medieval cathedrals.[19]

The contrast between the old Israel and the Church is typically assimilated into a contrast between Jews and gentiles. There is little attempt to retain Paul's concept of a Jewish remnant into which the Church is ingrafted. The relation becomes one of straight substitution. This too was foretold by the prophets. God's promise to Abraham that he would be a father "to many nations" is cited to prove that the true descendants of Abraham are not the Jews, but the nations, i.e., the gentiles.[20] All the texts about Israel as a light to the nations, and about the future sway of the Davidic king over the nations, all praise for non-Hebrew people in contrast to unfaithful Israel, are taken up to prove a promised people who are to be called out from among the gentiles. On the other hand, all the enemies of the prophets and the Davidic king must be read to refer to the Jews. This means, at times, a very selective reading of the Psalmic texts, especially since the enemies which the Davidic king is to conquer and disperse must be read as Jews, while the nations that he is to inherit and rule over must be regarded as the future gentile Church! Needless to say, in the original text both the enemies and the nations to be conquered generally refer to outside peoples.[21]

The future promises of the conversion of the gentiles are regarded as proof of the prediction of the gentile Church. This gathering of a faithful people from among the gentiles the Church Fathers (and the New Testament) regard as a fulfillment of the messianic expectation of the ingathering of the "nations" to Zion at the time of redemption. This again requires extraordinary distortion of the original text, for there the Israel which is chastised and the Israel whose messianic fulfillment is predicted are one and the same, while the Church must read the messianic ingathering of the gentiles in an antithetical relation to the chastisement of Israel![22]

After the Constantinian establishment this concept of the universal ingathering of all nations can be identified with the ecumenical empire and the Roman *pax*. Eusebius especially identifies Christendom with the millennial reign of the Messiah over the earth. Like the Davidic king, the Christian emperior reigns "from sea to sea and from the River to the ends of the earth." All nations gather into this Kingdom of Christ, except the Jews, who alone are in exile "under their enemies." But since their enemies are now the gentile Church, the reversal of Jewish messianic hope becomes total. All nations are redeemed at the coming of Christ except the Jews![23] This blending of messianic fulfillment and Roman universal empire gives the Christian mission to all nations a highly imperialistic character. The mission of the Church becomes one of universal conquest. The success of the Church becomes a proof of divine favor and fulfillment, while the sufferings of the Jews proves their disfavor with God. Needless to say, when Christians are persecuted, the opposite standards are applied, and Christian suffering becomes holy martyrdrom.[24] By the same token the suffering of the Jews is denied any commonality with martyrdom. Chrysostom particularly insists that the "martyrs especially hate the Jews for the reasons that they love so deeply the One who, by them, was crucified," while Jewish suffering is the blame-worthy suffering of thieves, grave robbers, and sorcerers.[25]

The climactic theme of the *Adversus Judaeos* tradition is that Jewish reprobation is a permanent and irrevocable condition. The left hand of Christian victory and messianic ingathering of the nations is Jewish exile and servitude "under the nations," now transformed into the New Israel. This exile is to last until the end of time. As evidence of their rejection the Jewish Law has been revoked by God, and they are perverse for continuing to observe it. Their cultic center is destroyed. Temple, priesthood, and sacrificial system have all been terminated. The Jews, therefore, celebrate the festivals illegitimately in the Diaspora. The destruction of the temple *cultus* signifies the end of the only legitimate vehicle of worship which God gave to the Jews, indicating that all access to God for them is now cut off.

This view of the destruction of the Temple demands again a double standard for judging similar developments in the Church and the Synagogue. The noncultic worship of the Church is regarded as the fulfillment of that universal spiritual worship among the nations predicted by the prophet Malachi (1:10–11).[26] As the Church's worship becomes more and more cultic, it is assimilated into the lineage of the Old Testament priesthood. The Synagogue, in turn, survives the demise of cultic worship and creates a form of worship centered in the home and in the assembly for prayer and study. But this noncultic worship, which likewise is scattered among all nations, is strictly denied any legitimacy. The Church uses such texts to prove that its own dispersed and noncultic worship was predicted by the prophets, as the divinely ordained successor to the Temple. With a kind of Sadducean literalism, Christians identified valid Judaism with the temple cult and Aaronite priesthood, declaring their fall to be the abrogation of legitimate Jewish religious existence, while reserving the spiritualizing interpretation of prayer and sacrifice for themselves. The rabbis, on the other hand, interpreted this same passage in Malachi to refer to the Synagogue, where the sacrificial cult was superseded by the better worship of "prayer, thanksgiving, and deeds of loving kindness."[27]

Chrysostom, who is anxious to erect Christianity into a new temple *cultus* and sacrificial priesthood, endlessly vilifies the Synagogue as a place of diabolical worship and castigates the Jewish community for carrying on the ancient festivals after the temple cult has fallen. The permanent destruction of the Temple is the keystone of his argument that religious Judaism has been abrogated, and its continuation is illegitimate in God's eyes and tantamount to the worship of the devil. Julian the Apostate made a promise to the Jewish community to rebuild the Temple. The Christian Fathers erect a myth around this event, claiming that the Jews tried to rebuild the Temple three times, but their impious efforts were miraculously beaten back by God each time.[28]

The divinely ordained state of the Jews from Christ until the end of time is that of preservation—but in a state, not of positive divine election, but of negative bondage under divine wrath. The desolation of Jerusalem, the exile of the Jews, and their now inferior status within Christian society are the proofs of divine wrath. The book of Daniel is searched to show that three captivities were predicted. The first two had precise time limits, and the restoration promised the Jews has already been fulfilled in their restoration after the Egyptian and Babylonian captivities. But the third exile has no time limit and is to last until the end of history.[29] The Temple will never be rebuilt. The Jews will never be restored to Jerusalem or the Promised Land. Their exile, dispersion, and bondage under their enemies is their permanent condition until the Second Coming of Christ, when they will have a final chance to repent and acknowledge their error. In vain do the Jews look for a Messiah to deliver them from captivity.

The Church Fathers frequently cite a mistranslated text from Ps. 69:24, "Their back bend thou down always," to characterize this condition of misery that is to be the lot of the Jews in the Christian era. As the second-century Father Hippolytus puts it:

'Let their eyes be darkened that they see not.' And surely ye have been darkened in the eyes of your soul with a darkness utter and everlasting. For now that the true light has arisen, ye wander as in the night and stumble on places with no roads and fall headlong, as having forsaken the way that says, 'I am the Way.' Furthermore hear this yet more serious word: 'And their back do thou bend down always.' That means, in order that they be slaves to the nations, not 430 years, as in Egypt, nor 70 years, as in Babylonia, but bend them to servitude, He says 'always.' How do you indulge vain hopes, expecting to be delivered from the misery that holds you?[30]

Several Church Fathers connect circumcision with this state of reprobation and divine exclusion from return from exile. Circumcision was not given as a mark of divine favor, but with a view to this future status of exile so that the Jews might be recognized and excluded from Jerusalem. Hadrianic law, following the Bar Kochbar revolt, had indeed excluded Jews from reentering Jerusalem. But since other Semitic peoples, such as Egyptians, were also circumcized, and since this only applied to men, this link of exclusion from Jerusalem with circumcision is peculiar. Its purpose seems primarily polemical, namely, to reverse the significance of circumcision as a sign of election and to make it instead a mark of Cain, thus fixing the Jew in a state of permanent wandering.[31]

The continued hope of the Jews for the coming of the Messiah especially enrages some Church Fathers. Several hint that Jews actually know that the Messiah has come, since their own Scriptures tell them so. Their pretense of looking for another simply reflects their unwillingness to repent of their evil ways.[32] The Messiah for which they look must be the Devil or the Anti-Christ. The idea that the Messiah for whom the Jews look is the Anti-Christ was also incorporated into the baptismal ritual for converted Jews in early medieval times.[33] This notion was to continue to reap deadly fruit up to modern times, when the forged *Protocols of the Elders of Zion,* incorporating the idea that the Jews hope and work for a coming reign of the Anti-Christ, came to stand for the entire myth of the International Jewish Conspiracy.[34]

These theories on the election of the gentile Church and the reprobation of the Jews were supplemented by a second cycle of material, which attempted to prove that Christianity supersedes and spiritually fulfills the Law. Christian exegesis deals with the Law and the cult by claiming that the Jewish understanding of these things is unworthy and "carnal," while the Christian possesses the spiritual realization of that which the Jew clings to in a merely outward way. But beyond this there is also the assertion that the Law and cult themselves were intrinsically unworthy and were given by God for a punitive rather than a redemptive purpose. Both of these assertions rest on the claim that the Jewish teachers cannot interpret Scripture. The Jews see only the letter, while the Christians discern the true spiritual meaning.

The Patriarchs obeyed the universal natural Law from the heart. This was a Golden Age of Virtue. The Patriarchs were not Jews, but like the Christians a universal race. Abraham was the father, not just of the Jews, but of "all nations." The universal, spiritual law of Christ is the restoration of this original spiritual religion of patriarchal mankind. The Mosaic law was given only after the Jews fell into abysmal vice during their stay in Egypt. Its purpose was not to lift the Jews to a higher level, but to restore them to that minimal humanity from the bestiality into which they had fallen. It was given to restrain vice, not to inculcate virtue. It was a special, preparatory training for the Jews, who are worse than the rest of mankind. But it has now been revoked by God, and the Jews are contumacious to continue to observe it.[35]

But even though the Christians do not keep the Law outwardly, they are the true Law keepers because they fulfill it inwardly and spiritually. They possess the new Law of inward obedience promised by Jeremiah. They possess the circumcision, not of flesh, but of the heart—the circumcision of repentance.[36] They understand that the dietary laws refer not to avoidance of particular animals, for how could animals, who are all a part of God's creation, be unclean? The real meaning of these laws is an allegory. They refer to the various brutish habits which we are to avoid.[37] (This allegorical interpretation of dietary laws was a favorite apologia in hellenistic Judaism, which Christianity has taken over in an anti-Judaic manner.)[38] Christians observe not the external Sabbath, which belongs to temporal creation, but the eschatological Sabbath of the New Creation.[39]

So, too, the cult was given to cure the Jews of the abominable idolatry into which they had fallen. God knew that they could only be restrained from their lust for idols by giving them a regulated cult of their own. But this cult was limited to Jerusalem, so it could not be spread to other peoples. And now that it is abrogated, Judaism has been definitively terminated.[40] It is Christianity which spiritually fulfills the cult, not in the sacrifice of bulls and rams, but in the spiritual sacrifice of the contrite heart, a spiritual temple which can be spread to all peoples. Judaism, as we have seen, made a similar claim for the Synagogue as the spiritual successor to the Temple.

This concept of supersession and spiritual fulfillment of the law and the cult is based on the dualism between the temporal and the eschatological, which is fundamental to the theology of Paul, to the Epistle to the Hebrews, and to the theology of the Gospel of John.

But in New Testament theology this concept is based on the belief that Christianity represents the eschatological Israel in the sense that it is the beginning of the age of redemption that will soon bring this present era of temporal history to an end. In the Church Fathers, however, this dualism between the historical and the eschatological eras has been historicized so that it becomes a dualism between the old era of unredeemed man, typified by Judaism, and the new historical era of the Church. One draws a line across history at the time of Jesus, which is treated as though it coincides with a transition from sin to grace, from an earlier era of outwardness, carnality, and unbelief, to a new era of inwardness, spirituality, and faith. The Jews receive the negative side of all these dualisms. The Jews are the men of the letter, vis-à-vis Christian spiritual hermeneutic. The Jews are the carnal men confined in their moral lives to a carnal level of existence, vis-à-vis Christians, who live on a higher plane, morally and ontologically. Jews are blind vis-à-vis Christian belief. But this moral and ontological dualism is also treated as though it were a temporal or historical sequence, so that everything Jewish becomes obsolete and has no further right to exist now that its spiritual fulfillment in Christ has come. The earlier revelation only predicts and symbolizes outwardly that which has now been fulfilled inwardly. It has become obsolete, now that its spiritual realization has taken place. As St. Augustine puts it, the Jews "have remained stationary in useless antiquity."[41]

Like the similar dualism between judgment and promise that assigns judgment to the Jews and promise to the Church, this dualism of letter and spirit, as Jewish and Christian eras and forms of humanity, has been a fatal flaw in Christian theology. Judaism is programmatically denied any dimension of inwardness and spirituality. Jews are made morally inferior and historically obsolete. Cultural obliteration of ongoing Jewish history is programmed into Christianity. This still characterizes Christian education and its secular derivatives. But Christianity, in turn, becomes docetic and is unable to deal realistically with its own bodily and historical existence. The constant splintering of Christianity into perfectionist sects is one side of the Christian inability to deal with its own finitude. On the other side there is the institutional triumphalism of Catholic Christianity, which constantly covers up the actual faults of the Church with a theory of spiritual perfection and infallibility that remains invisible to the outward eye.

This anti-Judaic tradition grew into a fixed standpoint between the second and fourth centuries and was to remain the hermeneutical tradition for identifying the Jews in Christian theology in every sermon, biblical exegesis, and theological treatise down through and including Martin Luther's diatribe on the "Jews and Their Lies." In the fourth century the Church was transformed from a persecuted sect into the established religion of the Christianized empire. With this change the anti-Judaic tradition ceased to be a private battle between Church and Synagogue and became the basis of a new legal and social view of the Jews expressed in law and custom. Within the framework of what now was official social policy, the Church decreed misery and cultural obliteration of the Jew, but not physical extermination. Indeed the ambivalence of Christian theology toward the Jew is that it demanded, simultaneously, the ongoing preservation of the Jews, but only in a status of reprobation, clearly visible by their external social oppression, serving as a continuing witness to the divine favor of the Church and as an ultimate witness to the coming of Christ at the end of time. It was from this contradiction that the tragic history of the Jews in Christian society was to descend to increasingly worsening levels of jealous concern and paranoid projection.

Today it is incumbent upon the Christian Church to take responsibility for this history and to acknowledge clearly its own responsibility for creating and fostering it. This has been done so far only superficially. The Christian Church has been willing to prune back the wilder growths of anti-semitic rhetoric, but it has been unwilling to deal with the roots of this growth in its own theological structures of faith in Jesus as the Christ whom the Jews "rejected." The Christian Church must do this to become honest about its own history and to attempt very belatedly to rectify its relation to the Jewish community. But just as much it must do this in order to correct a fatal flaw in its own theological structures. In other words, anti-Judaism, unlike Jewish self-defense against Christianity, is not just an external problem of relations with another community, but an internal problem of its own understanding of its faith. The theology of messianic fulfillment, once and for all, 2000 years ago created a world view peculiarly fraught with internal suppressions of reality and external projections of the unredeemed side existence upon others, archetypally the Jews. Body and Spirit, works and faith, outward letter and inward meaning, Judgment and Promise, particularism and universalism, sinful and gracious existence: all these dualisms, which must properly be understood dialectically, were split into Christian and Judaic opposites. The unredeemed side of every dualism is projected upon the Jews, the triumphalistic self-righteous side on Christianity. This tendency to paranoia and perfectionism in Christian theology is the internal flaw that has continually marred Christianity's ability to speak the gospel as a message of truthful self-understanding. To correct this flaw we must go back to the root and reexamine Christology itself, that is to say, that theology of fulfilled messianism which continually impedes our ability to speak truthfully about our own ongoing, unredeemed existence in an unredeemed world.

NOTES

1. Rosemary Ruether, *Faith and Fratricide: The Christian Theological Roots of Anti-Semitism* (New York, 1974).
2. I. Rendel Harris, *Testimonies,* I,II (Cambridge, 1961).
3. Arthur Lukyn Williams, *Adversus Judaeos* (Cambridge, 1935).
4. Eusebius, *Demonstrations of the Gospel* I, 16,17.
5. Epistle of Barnabas 4:8; Acts 7.
6. John Chrysostom, *Orations Against the Jews* 6,2; Origen, *Contra Celsus* II, 75.
7. Tertullian, *Adversus Judaeos in Ante-Nicene Fathers* III (New York, 1926) ed. A. Cleveland Coxe, pp. 151–52.
8. Ephrem, *Rhythm Against the Jews* 12.
9. John Damascene, *On the Orthodox Faith* IV, 23 ("On the Sabbath").
10. John Chrysostom, *Orations Against the Jews* 6, 2 and 5, 6.
11. *Ibid.,* 1,7.
12. *Ibid.,* 4,2 and 6,6–7.
13. Maximinius, *Treatise Against the Jews* I.
14. Cyprian, *Three Books of Testimonies Against the Jews* I,19,21; *Epistle of Barnabas,* 13:2–4; Tertullian, *Against the Jews* I; Irenaeus, *Against the Heresies* 4,21,2; Augustine, *Against the Jews* 7(9), etc.
15. Aphrahat, *Demonstrations Against the Jews* 16,8; Ephrem, *Rhythm Against the Jews* 8.
16. Prudentius, *Apotheosis* II. 541–50, ed. and tr. H. J. Thomson (Cambridge, Mass, 1949–53).

17. Gal. 4:21–31; Rom. 9:13.
18. Augustine, *Against the Jews* 5 (6); Cyprian, *Testimonies* I, 20.
19. Wolfgang S. Seiferth, *Synagogue and Church in the Middle Ages: Two Symbols in Arts and Literature* (New York, 1970).
20. Rom. 4:11; Epistle of Barnabas 13:7; Justin, *Dialogue with Trypho* 119.
21. Tertullian, *Against the Jews* 12,13.
22. Ephrem, *Rhythm Against the Jews* 20.
23. Eusebius, *Oration on Constantine* 16, 4–8; Chrysostom, *Demonstration to the Jews and Gentiles that Christ is God.*
24. Aphrahat, *Demonstrations Against the Jews* 21.
25. John Chrysostom, *Orations Against the Jews* 6,2.
26. Justin Martyr, *Dialogue with Trypho* 117; Tertullian, *Against the Jews* 5; Augustine, *Against the Jews* 9(12).
27. Jacob Neusner, *Aphrahat and Judaism* (Leiden, 1971), p. 174.
28. Chrysostom, *Orations Against the Jews* 5,10–11.
29. Lactantius, *Divine Institutes* 4,11,18; Hippolytus, *Expository Treatise Against the Jews* 6; Aphrahat, *Demonstrations Against the Jews* 19; John Chrysostom, *Orations Against the Jews* 5,1,5; 6,12, etc.
30. The same passage appears often in Augustine; cf. *Against the Jews* 5(6), and 7(10); *City of God* 17,19 and 18,46. The Hebrew text is difficult to understand.
31. Justin Martyr, *Dialogue with Trypho* 16; Tertullian, *Against the Jews* 3; Irenaeus, *Against the Heresies* 2,16,1.
32. Hippolytus, *Refutation of all Heresies* 9,25; John Chrysostom, *Orations Against the Jews* 5,9–10; Augustine, *Against the Jews* 18(34); Eusebius, *Demonstrations of the Gospel* 8,2.
33. James Parkes, *The Jew in the Medieval World* (London, 1938), pp. 304, 394–400.
34. Norman Cohn, *Warrant for Genocide: The Myth of the Jewish World Conspiracy and the Protocols of the Elders of Zion* (New York, 1966).
35. Eusebius, *Demonstrations of the Gospel* 1,2,16–17; Tertullian, *Against the Jews* 2; Novatian, *On Jewish Meats* 3.
36. Deut. 10:16; Jer. 4:4; 9,26; Rom. 2:25,29; Gal. 5, etc. Epistle of Barnabas 9:1–5; Justin Martyr, *Dialogue with Trypho* 24; Tertullian, *Against the Jews* 3; Cyprian, *Testimonies* 1,8; John Chrysostom, *Orations Against the Jews* 2,1; Isidore of Seville, *Against the Jews* 2,16.
37. Novatian, *On Jewish Meats* 3; Justin Martyr, *Dialogue with Trypho* 20.
38. Aristeas, 128–170; Philo, *De Specialibus Legibus* 4,106–8; *Agr.* 145.
39. John Damascene, *On the Orthodox Faith* 4,23; Epistle of Barnabas 15:8–9; Justin Martyr, *Dialogue with Trypho* 21; Tertullian, *Against the Jews* 4; Augustine, *Against the Jews* 2; Aphrahat, *Demonstrations Against the Jews* 13,13.
40. Chrysostom, *Orations Against the Jews* 4,7.
41. Augustine, *Against the Jews* 6(8).

II

THE MIDDLE AGES

6

The Roman Church and the Jews

B. Blumenkranz

A. THE POSITION OF THE JEWS

After the establishment of the Germanic successor-states to the Western Roman Empire, the Jews enjoyed at first much better conditions than they had known under the Christian Emperors. Although the new states were not wholly secular (for Christianity was still the religion of the majority of the people, and even to a certain extent the state religion), they were willing to grant a broad measure of toleration to religious minorities, and from this both Jews and heretical Christians alike benefited. Similarly, as far as differences of race were concerned, the widely varying populations of each state were able to enjoy peaceful coexistence. The personal basis of the Germanic juridical system guaranteed all men equality before the law, while allowing them to follow their ancestral traditions.

In each country, the native populations and the Roman *provinciales* lived side by side with the newly arrived Teutonic settlers. As far as legal status was concerned, the Jews still counted as Romans. However, in the successor-states to the Empire, Roman law survived in the form of the "Breviary" of Alaric. This modified considerably the anti-Jewish legislation of the Theodosian Code, and also omitted the harsh provisions of the Code of Justinian (which, in any case, had no currency in the Western Empire). Moreover, in this society, where there were already so many other differences of legal staus, there was a tendency to attenuate

Reprinted by permission of Massada Press, Jewish History Publications from *The Dark Ages: The Jews in Christian Europe, 711–1096,* ed. Cecil Roth, Jerusalem, 1966, 69–99.

the differences amongst those subject to Roman law; thus the anti-Jewish provisions of this legal system fell rapidly into abeyance.

Spain was the only country to follow a different policy, but here again the attitude towards the Jews forms part of a general attitude. Following the conversion of the Visigothic Kings to Catholicism, there had been a relentless drive towards unification in all spheres: national, legal, and religious. A heavy price for this had been paid by some ethnic minority groups—more vulnerable than the Jews because they lived concentrated in one region—for, in their case, national unification was achieved by their physical extermination. The Jews escaped a similar fate, not only because they were scattered throughout the whole kingdom, but also because they were indispensable to its economic and administrative life. In legal and religious affairs, however, they were subjected to harsh measures inflicted by those in power. The responsibility for this policy was actively shared with the King by the nobility and the Catholic hierarchy, who took part in the successive Councils over which the King usually presided. The clergy raised scarcely any objections when faced with the question of the forced conversion of Jews. What they did was to recognize the *fait accompli* and help to draw up regulations designed to ensure that the neophytes became permanent adherents of the faith which they had been forced to accept. Although, legally, the Jews now ceased to exist as a group, the "New Christians" took over their position. Distrust of these unwilling converts resulted, however, in a succession of discriminatory laws, so that, finally, the gulf which divided these so-called Christians from their nominal coreligionists was more marked than that separating Jew and Christian elsewhere during this period.

Indeed, except in Visigothic Spain, Jews and Christians are everywhere recorded at this time as living peaceably together. Apart from religious belief there was no notable factor which divided the one group from the other. Both spoke the same language, both lived in the same districts, and both followed the same professions. There was little difference in their names. By and large, each played the same part in public life.

The Church was inevitably perturbed by this state of affairs. When, as was generally the case, it was not able to participate directly in legislation, as it could in Spain, or exercise territorial power, as it did for a time in parts of Italy under Gregory the Great, then it laid down its own laws for the faithful, which were to be enforced by spiritual sanctions. It is clear from the body of legislative texts which were thus produced that the two constant preoccupations of the Church were to prevent Jews from proselytizing and to encourage their conversion to Christianity.

Any hold which Jews might have over the faithful was to be destroyed; and to this end legislation was passed against mixed marriages (Councils of Orleans 533, Clermont 535, Orleans 538, Toledo 589, Toledo 633), against Christians participating in Jewish meals (Councils of Vannes 465, Agde 506, Epaone 517, Orleans 538, Mâcon 583, Clichy 626/7), and against the admission of Jews to public office, especially that of judge (Councils of Clermont 535, Mâcon 583, Toledo 589, Paris 614/5, Clichy 626/7, Toledo 633). Above all, measures were taken against the possession of Christian slaves by Jews. First, circumstances where legal justification might be found for taking these slaves from their Jewish masters, with or without compensation, were multiplied; then, finally, Jews were prohibited altogether from owning Christian slaves (Councils of Orleans 538, Orleans 541, Mâcon 583, Toledo 589, Clichy 626/7, Toledo 633, Chalon-sur-Saône ca. 650, Toledo 656, and various letters of Pope Gregory the Great).

Restrictions imposed on Jewish worship betray the same preoccupations. The object was to prevent it from being too conspicuous, which was why, for example, the chanting of Psalms in the streets during funeral processions was forbidden (Council of Narbonne 589). Synagogues already in existence were, theoretically, allowed to remain, unless nearby Christian churches found them a nuisance. On the other hand, the Jews were prohibited from building new synagogues, and also from embellishing or enlarging those already standing.

The Church was also afraid that the Old Testament might attract some Christians to Judaism. It saw cause for concern when the faithful, in following Old Testament precepts, found themselves in agreement with the Jews. Christians were attracted especially by the idea of the Sabbath day of rest. They were warned against this tendency by one of the Frankish Councils (Orleans 538), as well as in a letter which Gregory the Great addressed to the people of Rome.

Conversely, the Church made various attempts to force the Jews to observe Christian festivals to some degree at least, forbidding them, first, to appear in public during Easter (Councils of Orleans 538, Mâcon 583), and secondly, to work on Sunday (Council of Narbonne 589).

The Church considered that even merely formal observance of Christian feasts on the part of the Jews would be a first step towards their conversion. To this end Jewish attendance at Church was encouraged (Council of Valence 524). In the early days, the sincerity of converts was still a reason for anxiety, and quite a long probationary period was imposed on Jewish candidates for baptism (Council of Agde 506). Later, however, any method of persuasion or of bringing pressure to bear, especially the promise of material advantages, was accepted in order to increase the number of converts. Gregory the Great was fully aware that converts won in such a fashion were likely to prove poor Christians, but he consoled himself with the thought that their children would be better ones.

Theoretical objections were often expressed to baptism by force (letters of Gregory the Great; Council of Toledo 633); but two things were always lacking. First, a definition of "force" was never given. The threat of being driven from the country, for instance, was not considered to be unjustifiable violence. Secondly, no sanctions were taken against Christians who administered forcible baptism, nor was any compensation offered to the Jew who suffered such treatment. This was not all, for Jews who had been won for the Church in such a way were forced to remain faithful to the religion which had been imposed upon them against their will. A whole series of decisions taken at successive Councils of Toledo (633, 653, 655, 681, 693, 694) affirm this principle, and regulations were enacted to ensure that such Jews did, in fact, become conforming Christians. Nevertheless the sincerity of their faith never ceased to be questioned, and probably rightly so.

The decisions which we have just mentioned applied, in general, to certain limited areas and periods of time. Indeed, they were scarcely ever readopted in the collections of canons which circulated in the early centuries of the High Middle Ages. When the Church had to define its attitude towards the Jews, texts were borrowed from the ancient collection wrongly considered to be acts of a Council of Laodicea. The three canons of this pseudo-Council of Laodicea did bear reference to the Jews, but they were intended to apply simply to Christians. The latter were forbidden to abstain from work on the Sabbath, thus practising the Jewish custom, or to accept gifts at Jewish festivals (probably presents at the feast of Purim), or, finally, to accept the Jews' unleavened bread, or "participate in their profanities" (meaning, perhaps, Christian participation in the feasts on the Sabbath or the Seder on Passover Eve).[1] Not until the 7th century was well advanced did any canonical collection include, at the same time, canons of the pseudo-Council of Laodicea and regulations enacted by the Frankish and Visigothic Councils.[2]

B. THE PAPAL ATTITUDE AND POLICY

From the beginning of the 8th to the end of the 11th century, the Church had no general policy towards the Jews except insofar as missionary activities were concerned. When any given situation necessitated the framing of a policy, it was the local ecclesiastical authorities who laid it down rather than the Pope at Rome.

During the period which concerns us more than sixty Popes succeeded one another, and the sources for a study of their policies are very extensive: the *Liber Pontificalis,* the writings of historians and hagiographers, not to mention the Popes' own voluminous correspondence. Nevertheless, in all this material, there are merely ten or so texts, concerning only seven Popes, which tell us anything of general policies towards the Jews, or even of isolated reactions to specific situations. This slight amount of evidence, in which, moreover, contradictory attitudes are to be seen, prevents us from speaking of any general Papal doctrine with regard to the Jews in this period. Yet in other spheres, as, for example, the problem of the relations between Church and State, a definite policy on the part of the Holy See does emerge at this time. Here already is proof of the fact that the Jewish problem was considered to differ from place to place, to be the product of an ever-changing context calling for a different solution in each case, without it being possible to define any general rule of conduct.

Stephen III (768–772), in a letter to Aribert, archbishop of Narbonne, and the bishops of Septimania and the Spanish Marches, protested vigorously against the fact that the Jews could possess landed property in or near towns, alongside Christian properties, and that the Frankish kings should have confirmed their right to do so.[3]

Hadrian I (772–795), in a letter addressed to the Bishops of Spain, complained of having learnt about that country that many "who call themselves Catholics live together with Jews and unbaptized pagans, not only drinking and eating with them, but practising divers other errors."

Hadrian exhorted the Bishops to see that nothing was done in contradiction to the rules enacted by the Fathers.[4]

This same Pope insinuated that there was scarcely any distinction to be made between iconoclasts and Jews. In his letter to Constant and Irene, where he speaks of images, he did not go so far as to call his royal correspondents "Jews," but implied as much in the turn which he gave to his argument. After explaining that the Christian did not worship things of wood, he went on to refute the objection of those who claimed that God had forbidden the worship of the work of man's hands. He pretended here to be taking up a Jewish objection, and consequently he went on: "Tell me, O Jew, is there nothing on earth, after it was created by God, which is not made by the hand of man?" And the Pope quoted as examples Noah's Ark, the altar with all its attributes, the cherubim and winged creatures, all made by the hand of man and yet at the command of God. In a letter to Charlemagne, again speaking of images, Hadrian I compared heretics to Jews, using passages taken from patristic literature.[5]

Nicholas I (858–867) reproached those who departed from Catholic orthodoxy for thereby drawing nearer to Jewish practice.[6] Arguing that the Catholic sacraments had a value in themselves, independent of the person administering them, he recognized the complete validity of baptism performed by a Jew.[7] He warned the newly converted Bulgars against interpreting the Old Testament literally and following its precepts, especially insofar as Sabbath rest was concerned.[8]

Leo VII (936–939) was consulted, after 937, by Frederick, Archbishop of Mainz, over the question of whether the Jews should be forcibly baptized, or whether they should rather be expelled. The Pope, in his reply, counseled him to neglect no opportunity of preaching the true word to them. If the Jews agreed to believe and to be baptized, the Church would render thanks to the Lord. If, on the other hand, they refused to accept the Christian faith, the Pope authorized the Archbishop to expel them, to save faithful Christians from contact with these enemies of God. But, in any case, they were not to be compelled to be baptized.[9]

According to a Hebrew source, John XVIII (1003–1009) intervened at the instance of the eminent French Jew, Jacob ben Jekuthiel, when the Jews of France and Germany were suffering a particularly fierce persecution. Not only had they been accused of secret dealings with the

Moslems, but also of carrying on missionary activities which must have been extremely indiscreet, since even a Catholic priest in Germany had just been won over to Judaism. The despatch of a high Papal dignitary to the scenes of the troubles is said to have put a speedy end to them.[10]

In calling for vengeance for the destruction of the Holy Sepulcher, Sergius IV (1009–1012) made no mention of the Jews, although, in the violent anti-Jewish movement which we have just referred to, they had been accused of being indirectly responsible for this act. One passage in his appeal might be interpreted as being hostile towards them. This is where he recalls the war against the Jews conducted by Vespasian and Titus. The Christian crusade, he asserted, would be victorious, as the campaign of these two Romans against Jerusalem was victorious. It had been their mission then to avenge Christ; for this reason, although they had never been baptized, they yet obtained as a divine reward the Imperial crown and the remission of their sins.[11]

By contrast, Alexander II (1061–1073) intervened in the Jews' favor. He took up their defense when, in 1063 and 1065, their lives and property were menaced both by the Spanish "crusaders" and by the Normans in Italy—as it seems, at the time of their expedition to Sicily. In an encyclical addressed to the Bishops of Spain (or of Gaul) the Pope declared that he was glad to learn that they had protected the Jews against violence from the forces marching against the Moslems of Spain. It was the ignorance of these people, he said, if not their greed, which made them seek the death of those whom Divine Providence had intended to be saved. The Pope recalled the example of Gregory the Great, who, in like manner, had protected the Jews against those who had wished to persecute them, and even against a bishop who had wanted to destroy one of their synagogues. There was, he added, a profound difference between the Moslems and the Jews. It was lawful to make war on the former, for they harried Christians, and drove them from their cities, but not on the latter, who were everywhere willing to be of service.[12]

In a letter to Bérenger, Viscount of Narbonne, the Pope congratulated him on having protected the Jews under his jurisdiction from the threat of death. For, he added, God abhors the shedding of blood and the murdering of the wicked. A letter, addressed at the same time to Geoffrey, Archbishop of Narbonne, congratulated him in turn for having prevented violence being done to the Jews, and exhorted him to continue, if necessary, his pacifying influence.[13]

The reforming activities of Gregory VII (1073–1085) embraced a multitude of problems, but only once was he concerned with the Jews. Did he voluntarily neglect the Jewish problem, in order to give all his attention to more urgent tasks? Or did he intend to tackle the question when political and other difficulties had been dealt with? The only time he actually intervened in the Jewish problem was in a letter addressed in 1081 to Alfonso VI, King of León and Castile, exhorting him to prevent the Jews from exercising any power over the Christians in his realm. To submit Christians to Jews was, he said, equivalent to oppressing the Church and exalting the Synagogue, and in wanting to please Christ's enemies, the King was showing contempt for Christ himself. Let him beware of offering to his God and Creator an affront which he would not have tolerated himself.[14]

As we have seen, these Popes were not greatly concerned with the Jewish problem. In their polemics against doctrinal errors within the Church, they seem, at times, to put the partisans of these errors on the same footing as the Jews. This was what Hadrian I had done with regard to the iconoclasts, Nicholas I with regard to the Photinians and those who wished the Sabbath to be observed as a day of rest. Warnings were issued (notably to the Christians of Septimania and the Catholic kingdoms of Spain) against over-intimate relationships with Jews. Certain Popes, for example Hadrian I, Stephen III, and Gregory VII, protested against Christians eating with them or living in over-close proximity, as well as against allowing them to hold public office and own landed property.

Unless an implicit invitation to violence against the Jews is to be seen in Sergius IV's preaching of a Crusade, Leo VII was the only Pope to authorize the employment of forceful methods of conversion (in this instance the threat of expulsion). On the other hand, John XVIII and Alexander II openly defended the Jews—in each case, at the time of movements which were distant precursors of the Crusades.

There may have been few instances of the Popes ever adopting a concrete policy towards the Jews, but Christian legend has striven to make up for this lack. The end of the 11th century saw the birth of the legend telling how Boniface IV (608–615) started a discussion between Christians and Jews. A miracle, the restoration of a pious blind man's sight, came in the nick of time to convince the Jews who had refused to be swayed by verbal arguments alone. Five hundred of them are then supposed to have asked for baptism, and the rest to have left the city of Rome in headlong flight.[15] Another story, although related by a contemporary, Adémar of Chabannes, seems no more deserving of credence. The ordeal in the form of an earthquake which was suffered by the city of Rome on Good Friday, 1020, was supposedly brought about by an act of sacrilege committed by the Jews. The cataclysm began, it was said, when they were holding up a crucifix to ridicule. The Pope, Benedict VIII, informed of the matter by a Jewish witness, condemned the perpetrators of the crime to death, and the fury of the elements abated as soon as they had been executed.[16]

There are also Jewish legends concerning the Papacy. Shortly after this period, but still in the Middle Ages, there arises the story of a Pope of Jewish origin. The son of a liturgical poet, Rabbi Simeon the Great of Mainz (ca. 1000), he is said to have been stolen from his parents at an early age and brought up as a Christian. Trained for the Church, he finally became Pope, but when he learnt of his origins he returned to Judaism, at first in secret and then openly, thus causing a great scandal among the Christian people of Rome.[17]

C. CHURCH COUNCILS

Decisions of Church Councils referring to the Jews are relatively much less frequent in this period than during the first three centuries of the High Middle Ages. From 465 to 694, within the space of 230 years, over twenty Councils, mainly Frankish and Visigothic, had enacted legislation with regard to the Jews. There were scarcely twenty which did so in a period nearly twice as long between the beginning of the 8th and the end of the 11th century. But on the other hand, the acts of such Councils henceforward affected the whole of Western Christianity. We find that they took place in Italy, Germany, and even Hungary, as well as in France and Spain (reference here and below is to Christian Spain, the greater part of the Peninsula being, of course, still Moslem).

The Roman Council of 743 forbade marriage between a Christian woman and a Jew, as well as the sale of Christian slaves to Jews.

In 755 the Council of Ver (between Paris and Compiègne) readopted the decision of an earlier Council directed against the transference of

Jewish Sabbath observances to Sunday, and in this connection we note that the Council of Friuli (796/7) mentions that the Sabbath rest was observed by Christian peasants in North Italy. The reformative Council of Paris in 829 stressed its concern over the attraction which this Jewish custom might hold for Christians. The observance of the Lord's Day was reinforced by prohibiting markets, lawsuits, work in the fields, or the transportation of goods on this day. If the Jews, who observed the Sabbath only in a material fashion, abstained from work in the fields on that day, without being forced to do so by any temporal power, how much more should Christians keep Sunday, it was argued.

It was almost certainly on the initiative of Amulo that the Council of Meaux and Paris, 845–846, put forward for the approval of Charles the Bald what amounted to an anti-Jewish statue. Amulo's secretary, Florus of Lyons, had compiled a huge collection of anti-Jewish canons, prohibiting Jews from proselytizing their slaves, preventing them from holding public office, constructing new synagogues, or appearing in public at Easter time, etc. Moreover—a step which was rarely adopted—several Visigothic canons were also included warning Christians not to accord their protection to Jews, and providing for the separation of Jewish children from their parents. Finally—the only fresh piece of legislation concerning the Jews which this Council originated—there was a canon prohibiting the exportation of slaves to Moslem lands by Jewish or by Christian merchants.[18]

This strongly anti-Jewish collection of texts reveals the state of opinion among Catholic clergy at this time, but it had no bearing on the actual legal condition of the Jews, for it remained a draft which never in fact became law. The canons were submitted to Charles the Bald, but he rejected the anti-Jewish texts *en bloc,* and none of them figured in the series of canons promulgated by him at the Diet of Epernay in 846.

The Council of Pavia, in 850, did not directly forbid the Jews to hold the offices of tax-collector or judge, but forbade Christians to allow them to do so. Likewise, at the provincial Council of Metz in 888, the Jews of Metz were mentioned in a rescript which was addressed to the Christians, reminding them of the ancient prohibitions against sharing meals with Jews or accepting food from them.

As had happened at the Council of Meaux and Paris, another vast collection of ancient canons referring to the Jews was assembled by a Council which was held in the south of Italy towards the end of the 9th century. Christians were warned against the observance of the Sabbath rest and against sharing meals with Jews, and the Jews were prohibited from holding public office and from owning Christian slaves. A new canon forbade the Jews from working in public on Sunday, and warned Christians to watch over all their womenfolk lest they should commit adultery with Jews. From the proceedings of the Council of Erfurt in 932 we know of a discussion between Jews and Christians in Jerusalem, followed by a proposal for the forcible baptism of the Jews in Europe and, apparently, their exclusion from certain commercial activities.[19] The Council of Coyanza (in the diocese of Oviedo) in 1050 forbade Christians to eat with Jews or to live together with them in the same houses.

At the Council of Gerona, in 1068, estates in the hands of Jews which had formerly belonged to Christians, were subjected to payment of the Church tithe. The Council held in this same town in 1078 repeated this clause.

At the Council of Rouen, held in 1074 in the presence of William the Conqueror, the prohibition against Jews possessing Christian slaves was extended to include their employment of Christian wet-nurses.

Finally, in 1078 a Roman Council again banned the Jews from holding public office, and in 1092 a Council at Szabolcs (a castle in Hungary on the far side of the Theiss) forbade mixed marriages, the possession of slaves, and working on Sunday.

The following facts emerge from the legislation of these Councils when viewed as a whole. Of the two preoccupations which had inspired earlier makers of canon law, namely, preventing Jewish proselytism, and encouraging the conversion of Jews to Christianity, the former concern now predominated. It is also clear that this ecclesiastical legislation was rarely backed by the authority of the state. It was addressed to Christians, and it was they who would incur the penalties, not the Jews. In another connection, there was a tendency to extend the scope of such prohibitions as those preventing Jews from owning Christian slaves, making this include free-born domestic servants such as wet-nurses. The same desire to prevent over-close relationships between Jews and Christians led also to the provision which forbade them to live in the same building side by side. Not only mixed marriages, but also extra-marital relations between Jews and Christian women were strictly forbidden. In the case of those regulations aimed more directly at the Jews, there was a similar tendency to widen their scope and make them more explicit. The prohibition of Sunday work, for example, was made to include not only the more obvious work in the fields, but also tasks undertaken in the home. Although this legislation did not go so far as to deny Jews the right to own land, it did affirm that their holdings were subject to tithe. Certain restraints placed on the freedom of Jews to trade were a particularly serious innovation.

We have just seen how the Council of Meaux and Paris in 845–846, and that held in South Italy at the end of the 9th century, assembled a vast collection of ancient texts concerning the Jews. Here is revealed a clear tendency towards the elaboration of a code of laws which should be applicable to them. We see this same tendency at work in the general collections of canon law which were to be compiled in the West, and which included a growing number of anti-Jewish texts, grouping them together.[20]

A 10th century compilation called "The Collection of Nine Books," when dealing with baptism, confirmation, etc., also gives rules concerning Jews, heretics, and apostates. Texts borrowed in the main from Gregory the Great, the pseudo-Council of Laodicea, and even from Roman law, establish the rules to be observed when Jews are converted to Christianity, and prohibit Jews from owning Christian slaves, and Christians from taking part in Jewish festivals.

In the first half of the 10th century, a priest from Mainz, Gerard, made a collection of canon laws referring to the Jews at the request of the Archbishop Frederick. Here we find extracts from the letters of Gregory the Great, especially forbidding the owning of slaves, and there is also a large fragment from the projected anti-Jewish statute compiled by the Council of Meaux and Paris.[21]

When, early in the 11th century, the celebrated canonist Burchard, Bishop of Worms, drew up—or had drawn up for him—the Decree which bears his name, he inserted in it (mainly in the fourth book, which deals with baptismal questions and confirmation) an important series of anti-Jewish canons. Finally, towards the end of the 11th century, when Yves of Chartres in turn composed his Decree, he brought together a larger number of anti-Jewish canons than ever before. There were more than forty, twenty-five of which were grouped together in the thirteenth book, and they formed a veritable code for the Jews. In addition to the laws so often encountered prohibiting the owning of Christian slaves, proselytizing, holding public office, etc., we also find Jews debarred from pleading in a court of law, and giving medical treatment to Christian patients, etc.

D. CHRISTIAN PROSELYTIZATION

Throughout the whole of this period there was missionary rivalry between Jews and Christians. Although Jewish proselytism in the High Middle Ages had no organized basis, it was nonetheless actively carried on by individuals. It is particularly significant in this connection that the most fervent missionaries for Judaism were recruited from among the proselytes themselves.

In the course of their missionary rivalry, Jews and Christians did not restrict themselves to preaching to the pagans, but also sought to convert the adherents of the opposing faith. More or less the same methods were employed by both sides, ranging from doctrinal preaching and discussions to bribery and even violence, whether open or masked.

Although religious polemic was not exclusively inspired by missionary aims, as we shall presently see, nevertheless Christians often attempted to make it serve their propaganda purposes. In 1010, for example, Alduin, Bishop of Limoges, commanded certain Catholic scholars to engage in discussions with the Jews of his town in the hope of persuading them to be baptized.[22] Again, at some time between 1068 and 1072, Peter Damian expressed his belief in the usefulness of such discussions. At the request of a correspondent called Honestus, he composed a sort of manual for use by Christians in such encounters. However, they should not engage in this activity, he counseled them, merely to seek vainglory, but only if there was a hope of creating a desire for conversion on the part of their opponent.

Polemical writings did not always pass directly into the hands of the adversary for whom they were ostensibly intended. They also served to provide Christian disputants with telling arguments which they could use in discussions. The *Liber contra Judaeos* written by Amulo in 846[23] was not simply a petition to the Emperor Charles the Bald requesting discriminatory legislation against the Jews; it also contained a lengthy exposition of dogma, giving such religious arguments as were commonly opposed by the Jews, accompanied by the Christian refutation of the Jewish position. Although at first sight this would seem to be merely a piece of occasional writing, it was widely diffused, and reproduced in numerous manuscripts. A similar work was Agobard's *De superstitionibus judaicis* (826/7), not however more widely read than any of his other anti-Jewish pamphlets.

Miracle stories too could often be made to furnish arguments for the Christians in religious discussions, especially when they related incidents concerning Jews and their miraculous conversion.[24]

Besides the literary productions of this period, however, medieval Christianity also had at its disposal the writings of previous centuries. Anti-Jewish literature from the days of the Fathers of the Church was recopied innumerable times. Even a heterodox writer like Tertullian had the fortune to be re-edited at this time. Other texts, of obscure origin, were provided with a false literary identity in order to endow them with greater authority. The literary production of Cyprian and Augustine became in this way immeasurably augmented. In order to make these ancient texts fit the needs of the day, they were often abridged, cut about, and, most important, translated into popular speech, since Latin had become incomprehensible to the mass of the people. Such was the fate of the collection of proof texts which Isidore of Seville had compiled as a veritable manual for Christian controversialists.[25]

We must also mention briefly the fact that Church buildings and the services performed within them had a certain missionary value in themselves. Burchard of Worms at the beginning of the 11th century was very much aware of this, and for this reason inserted in his Decree an ancient canon of the Council of Valence (524) which was intended to encourage churchgoing by the Jews.[26]

It is normal for a sincere Christian to be convinced of the efficacy of his prayers as a means of bringing about the conversion of the Jews. The prayer *pro Judaeis* was certainly originally interpreted in this way. It occurs in the liturgy for Good Friday in a series of prayers for the conversion of the pagans and the return to Catholicism of heretics. Nothing in this prayer, not even the epithet *perfidi* (which here means simply "unbelievers") was in the first place derogatory to the Jews.[27] But from the 8th century onwards the meaning of the prayer acquired an anti-Jewish bias. At first the genuflexion was suppressed, and the malicious explanation given for this was that a Christian in praying for the Jews should not genuflect because on the same day of Good Friday the Jews had mocked Jesus by genuflecting to him. Later, the sense of the prayer was altered through the gradual shift in the meaning attributed to *perfidi,* from "unbeliever" in the religious sense to "perfidious" in the moral one.

Another part of the service, the sermon, was made to serve missionary purposes. If necessary the Jews were to be forced to go and listen to it, while Catholic priests were to preach in the synagogues as well. On the initiative of Agobard, this procedure was adopted between 816 and 822–5 at Lyons, at Chalon-sur-Saône, and at Mâcon. Between 937 and 939, Pope Leo VII recommended similar tactics to Frederick, Archbishop of Mainz, as we have seen. Should these sermons be unsuccessful, the unbelievers were to be expelled. A few years earlier, in 932, Pietro Candiano II, Doge of Venice, had called on the Church Council which met at Erfurt under Henry I to offer the Jews the alternatives of baptism or exile.[28]

Forcible baptisms also occurred during the violent anti-Jewish persecutions in France and Germany at the beginning of the 11th century, when revenge was taken for the collusion which was said to have existed between Jews and Moslems against the Christians. As during the Crusades proper at the end of the same century, these baptisms were imposed by brute force of the most cynical nature. The only alternative offered was death. Yet although the violence in this case equaled that used in Spain in the 7th century, at least there was not the same stubborn determination on the part of the Christians to make those who had been unwillingly baptized continue in their new faith. The chief witness of the drama recounts that as soon as the storm had passed, those Jews who had accepted baptism only as a matter of form, returned openly to the faith of their fathers.

About 1066, Eberhard, Archbishop of Trier, is said to have threatened the Jews of his city with expulsion if they did not accept baptism. We are told that the Jews only eluded this menace by laying a curse on the Archbishop which brought about his death. However, it would seem that the threat of conversion itself no less than the story of the Jewish spell were a later fabrication dating from the time of the Crusades. But it is true that the date attributed to these supposed happenings was approximately that of similar acts of violence performed by the Spanish "crusaders" and by the Normans in Italy. We should remember that Pope Alexander II had to make representations to Landulph, Prince of Benevento, censuring such conduct. "No one should be forced to serve

Christ," he wrote, "but let every man reach his own decision according to his own free will."

As always, it was children in particular who suffered from this odious practice of forcible baptism. Between 816 and 822–5, Agobard had had recourse to this method. As well as forcing the Jewish communities of Lyons and the neighboring towns to attend missionary sermons given in the synagogues by Catholic priests, he concentrated on winning over their children to baptism. He called the latter together in the absence of their parents, and rapidly achieved the result he desired: fifty-three children yielded to his urgent entreaties and declared themselves ready to be baptized. But their Jewish parents immediately complained to the Imperial Court. *Missi dominici* sent by Louis the Pious intervened and possibly also the *Magister Judaeorum,* the Imperial functionary specially charged with Jewish affairs. It would seem that Agobard was then forced to release his prey, and, what is more, he was called before the Emperor to justify these actions which were held to be illegal.[29]

As the power of the central authority in France broke down, the protection accorded to the Jews ceased to be so effective. There is a case which amounts to nothing less than kidnaping which occurred in Mâcon in the mid–11th century, and this may well have been not an isolated incident. One year at Easter time there was no Christian child to baptize during the Easter vigil, as was the custom, and Count Geoffrey found an expedient way out of the difficulty by carrying off a little Jewish boy called Jacob and bringing him to the church, where he and his wife stood as godparents to this little forced convert. In Germany the authorities actively opposed such methods. Henry IV threatened to impose the heavy fine of twelve golden pounds on any Catholic missionary so overzealous as to attempt to convert children in this way.[30]

On the Jewish side the validity of enforced baptisms was denied. Those who returned to Judaism were considered never to have abandoned their faith. Rabbis threatened that any who held the past conduct of former converts against them would be anathematized. And those who had not had the opportunity to return to the faith of their forefathers openly, but would have desired to do so, were still mourned after their death as if they had died as good Jews. They were given all the funeral honors normally accorded to the Jewish dead; indeed, even during their lives, though outwardly they might appear to be Christians, they were still considered to be Jews. It was to such forced converts that

Rashi applied the Talmudic dictum: "Even though he sinned, he remains a Jew" (Sanh. 44a). He affirmed, and most authorities followed him on this point, that Jewish converts to Christianity were still to be regarded as Jews; consequently they were to be taken into account where the obligation of levirate was concerned, and they were also to enjoy full rights of inheritance. Of course, forced converts who continued to observe Jewish practices in secret were *a fortiori* held to be still Jews. A Jewish account of the Crusades affirms that "those who speak evil of them sin, as if they were speaking ill of God Himself."[31]

If we exclude these forcible conversions, which sometimes affected large numbers of Jews, the success of Christian missionary activities was slight, especially in view of the huge effort expended. Agobard is bitter in his laments on this score: "In spite of all the humanity and kindness we display towards them, we do not succeed in bringing over one of them to our faith."[32] When, twenty years later, Hincmar of Rheims was writing of preparation for baptism, he dealt exclusively with the case of converts from paganism without even mentioning the Jews, who were too few to merit attention. The same attitude is to be seen a little while later in the treatise on the catechism for which Angilmodus was responsible.

Here and there cases of sincere conversion to Christianity occurred, though information with regard to them is fragmentary. Yet even if the number of such cases were multiplied many times over, it still would not be possible to speak of a movement on the part of the Jews towards conversion to Christianity.

E. JEWISH PROSELYTIZATION

Although, as we have just stated, Jewish missionary activities were never organized on any formal basis in the High Middle Ages, this did not mean that they were any the less effective. Not only did Jews vie with Christians in attempting to convert the pagan masses, but they also directed their activities towards their adversaries, the Christians.

There was, as we shall see, an element of disinterested intellectual search for truth in medieval religious polemics. But when arguments were intentionally simplified and directed at simple folk, it can safely be assumed that this was done, not with a view to discussion, but with the concrete objective of winning over new adherents. Agobard, Fulbert of

Chartres, Peter Damian, and many others beside, noted that it was often ignorant Christians who were led into religious argument by the Jews.[33] The Jews lead some simple folk so far astray, says Agobard, that they come to believe in their hearts that it is only the Jews who are the people of God, that it is they who strictly observe religious precepts, and that their faith is better than that of the Christians.

There is nothing surprising in the fact that practically nothing has come down to us of Jewish writings intended for use in these missionary activities. An unrelenting censorship was brought to bear on them over the centuries. Nevertheless, a few precious fragments are preserved from a missionary pamphlet written by a renowned 11th century convert from Christianity, Wecelin, in which he attempted to persuade other Christians to follow his example.[34] In addition, thanks to the correspondence of the famous 9th century convert, Bodo-Eleazer, with the Catholic Paulo Alvaro of Cordova, it is possible to form some idea of the nature of the polemical and missionary literature which Bodo-Eleazar wrote for his former coreligionists; we shall deal with this below.

The two cases just quoted are instances of Latin texts which would have been immediately accessible to Christians. But we must also include in the literature of Jewish propaganda a Hebrew text intended to provide Jewish disputants with debating points likely to shake the faith of Catholics. This was the work dealing with the life of Jesus called *Tol^edot Yeshu*.[35] In the present state of studies it is not possible to say exactly when the first redaction of this work was made, but it is evident from the lengthy extracts given by Agobard and Amulo that fairly full versions were in circulation in the West from the 9th century onwards. In this parody of the Gospels, all the transcendental mysteries of Catholic belief concerning Jesus were reduced to human, banal, and even mean dimensions. Christians who found their faith undermined thereby would, it was doubtless hoped, seek satisfaction for their religious needs in Judaism.

A characteristic common to all these Jewish propaganda tracts is their aggressiveness, bitterness, and even violence. Conditions of life for the Jew were harsh, and this harshness showed through in his manner of argumentation, whether offensive or defensive. Even his jokes turned easily into macabre farce, and his ironical smiles became twisted grimaces. The very tone of Jewish propaganda itself warned those to whom it was directed of what would await them if they paid heed to it: a state of ceaseless struggle.

Without making any conscious efforts, the Jews found that their very way of life was often sufficient in itself to attract Christians. The lower classes with their frugal existence must have regarded the ways of their Jewish neighbors with envy: the weekly feast of a semi-liturgical character on the Sabbath, the marking of Purim by an exchange of gifts and of Passover by the eating of unleavened bread. The Church was conscious of the attraction Judaism had for Christians, and set them on guard against it. The same prohibitions were repeated again and again: the faithful were not to eat with Jews, they were not to accept presents at their festivals, and, above all, they were not to eat their unleavened bread. These prohibitions are of ancient date, going back to the canons of the so-called Council of Laodicea, and to those of Elvira. But they are repeated time and again by innumerable Councils and in collections of canons, as we have seen.[36]

From the case of Agobard, Archbishop of Lyons, we know how the sermon, as part of the Catholic church service, was used to warn the faithful against over-close relationships with Jews. Agobard maintained a correspondence with a number of other bishops to urge upon them the necessity of taking such action. His brother-bishop, Nibridius of Narbonne, was told how Agobard went the length and breadth of his diocese to spread counterpropaganda against the Jews in public sermons and exhortations. It is not fitting, he said, that the Church, that chaste virgin, the Bride of Christ, should seek out the feasts of courtezans; in banqueting in company with Jews she ran the risk of contracting divers vices, or, even worse, of endangering her faith. Christians were prohibited from eating with Jews or living with them, to prevent them from being corrupted in their faith and falling into the erroneous ways of the Jews through such constant intercourse. For often, when Christians shared the Jews' earthly fare, they were tempted by their spiritual nourishment as well.

As far as the Sabbath day of rest was concerned, Christians came to desire it for themselves, even without the influence of the Jews.[37] When one remembers the working conditions prevalent in the ancient world, one can easily understand that acquaintance with the Old Testament was enough in itself to create the desire for a weekly day of rest. For, even when the canonical regulations on Sunday observance were strictly adhered to, they spared the worker only from labor in the fields, and not from numerous other tasks in the farmyard or the house. Christians tended frequently either to apply to Sunday the regulations referring to the Jewish Sabbath (evidence of this tendency is to be found as early as the 6th century in the deliberations of a Church Council which was opposed to the practice), or else they simply observed the Sabbath as such. As we have seen, peasants in the district of Friuli at the end of the 8th century observed the Sabbath rest. In the second half of the 9th century, the recently converted Bulgars wished to do likewise until dissuaded by Nicholas I.

In order to further their own missionary aims, it was alleged that the Jews themselves did not hesitate to employ means of coercion. If necessary, they were ready to make use of the authority given them by such public offices as they might hold. Amulo complained of the actions of tax-collectors. Abusing their powers, they were said to be especially harsh towards poor ignorant Christian peasants until finally, by the promise of reduced assessments, they were able to persuade them to forswear their religion.[38]

Even more common was the exercise of similar pressure by a Jewish master on his slaves. Even if he was not concerned with the lofty purpose of propagating the Jewish religion, a Jewish master had purely material reasons for bringing about the conversion of his slaves to Judaism, for it was only after conversion that they were held to be suitable for all kinds of work, particularly the preparation and handling of food and wine. Moreover, when their paganism had been replaced by some form of belief, there was less fear that they would become converts to Christianity (or Islam, as the case might be), with the manumission which that would have entailed.

But it is also true that, quite apart from questions of personal interest, considerations of broader scope made the conversion of slaves desirable. One Talmudic text, for example, calls the acquisition of slaves a pious work, for by it more men can come to know the God of Israel (Yer. 'Av. Zara I,1, p. 39b). Conversely, Jews were strictly forbidden to sell their slaves to Gentiles, for they would thus be deprived of their chance of worshiping God.[39]

Jewish and Christian missionary activities resembled each other even to the extent that the Jews were also ready to make use of brute force when the opportunity arose, as, for example, in Moslem Spain in the mid–9th century. Bodo-Eleazar is in this case alleged to have obtained from the Moslem authorities the promulgation of an edict, in about 847, which forced Christians to choose between death or conversion to either Judaism or Islam.[40] Not only those Christians domiciled in Spain were affected by this measure, but also any who happened to be traveling through the country. Although Moslems, as well as Jews, benefited from this forced conversion, the primary object was to deprive Christianity of any legal status.

The Christian population of Spain urged Charles the Bald of France to demand that the Moslem authorities put an end to these measures, and that he should request the extradition of Bodo-Eleazar. In virtue of the fact that the edicts affected foreign Christians, the intervention of a foreign prince was justified, at least on behalf of his own subjects. Charles the Bald, like other Frankish princes, was eager to put himself forward as defender and protector of isolated Christian communities living in Moslem territory. His intervention can only have had as its aim to put an end to the persecution of Christians—and in this it was probably successful. It is, however, most unlikely that he really demanded the extradition of Bodo-Eleazar, and even less likely that he was in fact extradited.

The convert, Bodo-Eleazar, has already been mentioned more than once. He was a deacon at the Court of Louis the Pious, where he must have met Jews who led him to doubt the truth of Christianity and later convinced him of the truth of Judaism.[41] Slowly he formed his resolve to break with the Church and become a Jew. But he dared not carry out his project on Christian soil. In order to seek asylum in Moslem territory, he invented the pretext of a pilgrimage to Rome. For such a pious purpose his prince furnished him not only with ample provisions for his journey, but with a retinue into the bargain. Once on the way, Bodo took a southwesterly rather than southeasterly route. Even before he was across the Pyrenees, he had openly professed Judaism, and forced his nephew, who was traveling with him, to follow his example. When he arrived at Saragossa, he had himself circumcised, changed his name from Bodo to Eleazar, let his beard grow, and took a wife.

This conversion created a scandal. Partly because of Bodo's former status as member of the Imperial Court, but even more because of his actions after conversion, the affair became the subject of diplomatic exchanges, and therefore engaged the attention of political pamphleteers as well as historians.

The same thing happened with regard to the cleric in the household of a Duke Conrad, Wecelin, who was converted to Judaism at the beginning of the 11th century. He was perhaps a man less in the public eye than Bodo, but because of a polemical and missionary pamphlet which he addressed to his former coreligionists as soon as he was converted to Judaism, his case too caused an uproar.

The scandal must have been great indeed, if Christian authors felt obliged to mention these conversions. Their first thought would have been to throw a cloak of decent silence over them in order to avoid speaking of such sharp denials of the Catholic claim to exclusive possession of the truth.

Such was the reason for the silence of Catholic authors with regard to the religious adventures of Andreas, Archbishop of Bari.[42] From 1078 onwards all mention of his name in Christian sources ceases. One might have thought that he had died then, and indeed some have thought so. But he was dead only insofar as the Church was concerned, for he had turned from Christianity to Judaism, and to do so in safety he fled to Egypt. Even from that distance the force of his example was great, for a number of his flock also went over to the Jewish faith.

It is only by sheer good fortune that we know of these events through the recent discovery of a Hebrew document, written by one of those who followed Andreas' example. Towards the end of the 11th century, a young Catholic priest of Norman stock, called John, who was then living at Oppido, became convinced of the truth of Judaism. As soon as he had become a Jew, taking the name of Obadiah, he was denounced, imprisoned, and threatened with death. Luckily, he managed to persuade his jailer to allow him to escape, but had in turn to flee for his life to Moslem territory. It is in the circumstantial relation of his own religious adventures that we learn, incidentally, of those of Archbishop Andreas.

Other Jewish sources, namely the Hebrew accounts of the Crusades, tell of the heroic death in 1096 of two proselytes, one at Mainz, and the other at Xanten, However, Christian sources are usually too embarrassed by the subject to mention converts to Judaism, and Jewish authors discreetly avoid the topic as well. In any case, historical documents are usually silent concerning the doings of common folk; yet it was precisely from the lower strata of society—slaves, day-laborers, the common people—that Jewish proselytes were recruited. As they passed unnoticed by their contemporaries, we are denied the knowledge of their names or their number.[43]

F. POLEMICAL LITERATURE

Relations between Jews and Christians in the High Middle Ages were not governed entirely by the mutual animosity which their rival missionary activities engendered. Frank and sincere friendship existed at the same time between them. As religious groups, they were not separated by a hostile frontier. Over the dividing line between them, ideas were exchanged and discussed in a spirit of amicable curiosity. The tone of religious polemic varied, and might be grave and serious, wild and passionate, or light and almost playful.[44]

Grave and serious: the best example of this is the discussion which took place in London between Gilbert Crispin, Abbot of Westminster, and a Jew from Mainz, some time before 1096.[45] From the outset the two disputants agreed to have no regard for the plaudits of the audience, but, together, to seek out truth and reason. By common agreement, the Old Testament and pure reasoning were taken as the bases of argument. Urbanity and courtesy were the keynotes of their debates, although Jew and Christian each did his best to present his case as forcibly as possible, making use of all the resources of dialectics. Gilbert Crispin was governed by the same sentiments when he wrote his account of the discussions. There is no other document by a Christian author which sets out the Jewish arguments so frankly, even those most embarrassing to the Christian.

Wild and passionate: this is the tone of the epistolatory exchanges between Bodo-Eleazar and Paulo Alvaro of Cordova.[46] The bitterness is understandable for, on the one hand, Bodo-Eleazar displayed all the zeal typical of a recent convert, and, on the other hand, the Catholic, Paulo Alvaro (though himself of Jewish descent), allowed himself to be carried away by anger and resentment when confronted with someone whom he considered—and called—an apostate. Eleazar explained that when he left the Church "he left a faith which was reprehensible, abject, lying, accursed, horrible and detestable, abominable and vile." Not wishing to be outdone, Paulo Alvaro returned the compliment by calling his adversary "the enemy of God, profaner of Divine law, violator of churches, stealer of sacred objects."

Light and even playful was the tone of a discussion, nonetheless serious, which took place at the Court of Conrad II about 1031, between his personal physician and Wazo, later Bishop of Liège. What was at stake was not the conversion of the loser to the faith of the victor, but simply a jug of wine staked by the Christian against one of the Jew's fingers. When Wazo was declared the winner, and the finger adjudicated to him, he laughingly offered to allow the Jew use of it until such time as it might please him to demand payment of the wager.

Fulbert of Chartres, in three successive sermons at the beginning of the 11th century, gave his flock a number of arguments to be used against the Jews in any discussions they might have with them. His remarks are enlivened by a tone of *bonhomie* and he even advises his listeners to make use of irony to support their reasoning.[47]

Perhaps we should also mention a disputation in Pavia, some time between 750 and 760, when Peter of Pisa confronted a Jew called Lullus or Julius.[48] A written account of this was circulated, but even by 800 it had been lost. Alcuin, who himself had been present at the discussion, could not find a copy. At the end of the 10th century a Hebrew document tells us of a discussion between a bishop and a rabbi at Oria in South Italy.[49] Even if the exact events spoken of in the Hebrew document are not historical, it is nevertheless proof that such encounters were not uncommon.

The discussion at Oria was limited to the consideration of the accuracy of the Jewish calendar. Another discussion of limited scope took place in Regensburg in the first half of the 11th century on the question of miraculous cures. All we know of another discussion which took place at the end of the century is the story, no doubt fictional, that in the event of a Jewish victory, William Rufus, king of England, promised to be converted to Judaism. When the Jews failed to carry the day, they claimed that it was not argument but prejudice which had prevailed.

If we wish to know what was the subject-matter of Jewish-Christian polemics, we have, besides accounts proper of these debates, a number of other literary sources. Christian authors often compiled what amounted to veritable manuals for the use of Christian disputants; we have already named some of them. The *Altercatio Ecclesiae contra Synagogam*, which first appeared perhaps in England about the middle of the 10th century,[50] belongs to this literary *genre*. We have also mentioned on the Jewish side the life of Jesus called *Tol^edot Yeshu*. To these important texts may be added a very large number of polemical passages which were inserted into exegetical works, historical narratives, sermons, or doctrinal treatises. And just as the Christians continued to make use of the writings of the early centuries of the Church, so the Jews continued to draw upon the Talmud and the Midrash.

By common agreement, the Old Testament was accepted as a basis for argument.[51] But there was no agreement over which books were canonical, which version was to be accepted, or in what way the text was to be interpreted. Gilbert Crispin's Jewish adversary protested vehemently at his use of *Baruch* and, above all, against the way in which he wrongly attributed these apocryphal texts to Jeremiah: "You Christians bring forward, as if they belonged to the Law and the Prophets, texts which are not to be found there at all. Thus, the passage which you attribute to Jeremiah: 'And afterwards did God show Himself upon earth, and conversed with men' (Baruch 3:37) and what follows, was never spoken or written by Jeremiah at all."

Each side accused the other of having falsified the Bible by suppressing certain passages, even whole books, or by adding to the text. Paulo Alvaro affirmed that it was in order to avoid the passages which bear witness to the passion of Christ in the *Wisdom of Solomon* that the Jews refused to give the book a place in the canon. "Everyone knows," he said, "that the Hebrew Bible was falsified after the coming of Christ in order to cut out any particularly telling testimonies concerning Christ, whereby the Jews might be converted. It is obvious that those who hunted down the Author of the Law did not hesitate to distort the Law itself, by means of which they might have been confounded."

Another means of falsifying the Bible, without going so far as to reject a text from the canon, was to allow it to fall out of use. Amulo reproached the Jews with having been led so far in their hatred of Jesus that they sent messengers throughout East and West to make sure that Psalm 18 (Ps. 19 of the Vulgate) should not be recited in the synagogues, because it is wholly concerned with the coming of Christ.

On the other hand, in the anonymous 10th century *Altercatio Ecclesiae contra Synagogam,* when the allegorical figure of the Synagogue demonstrates how and in what Biblical passages she found the advent of the Messiah announced, she is careful to insist that she had not forged these texts herself. Gilbert Crispin's Jewish adversary invited the Abbot of Westminster to agree that "the Law and the Prophets were preserved in their original and authentic form" amongst the Jews. He even went further: everything David and the Prophets said or wrote, they said or wrote in Hebrew, and for the Jews. Consequently, any passage from the

Law or Prophets which is quoted in a form different from that accepted
by the Jews, must come from a false interpretation of the text, and be
devoid of authority.

The basic reason for discord in the discussions about the canon and
the translations of the Bible was the Christological exegesis which Christians desired to impose upon Old Testament texts. At all times, the
exaggerated tendency of Christian exegetes to find in each and every
passage of the Bible a prefiguration of Christ and the Church has met
with argument. Gilbert Crispin aroused lively opposition of this sort
when he quoted Ezekiel 44:2 ff.: "And the Lord said unto me: 'This gate
shall be shut, it shall not be opened, neither shall any man enter in by
it. . .' " and claimed that no one could give a literal explanation of the
passage. The spiritual explanation proposed by him was that the "shut
gate" signified the Virgin, and the words "neither shall any man enter in
by it" meant that the Mother of Christ had known no man before Jesus
was conceived and born. The Jew who was arguing with him burst out
with the retort: "If it is legitimate for Christians to read and interpret
the Scriptures in that way with regard to Christ, then there are certainly
a great many other points you can find, which you can explain in a
similar fashion." Already he had protested at an earlier point: "You are
doing violence to the Scriptures, twisting the meaning in order to find
points attesting to your faith."

As during the early Christian centuries, controversy between Church
and Synagogue centered around three principal problems: the supersed-
ing of the Mosaic Law, the Messianic status or the divinity of Jesus, and
the rejection of the Jews and the election of the Gentiles. These age-old
problems were, however, often seen in a new light when, during the
High Middle Ages, they became related to questions of current interest.
Other topics of debate were also added concerning, for example, the
moral attitudes of the adherents of the respective faith, or their different
ways of worship, etc.

"Synagogue," in the *Altercatio Ecclesiae contra Synagogam,* declared
that not only had the Law not been superseded, but that, according to
Isaiah (60:5), all peoples would be converted to it.[52] Gilbert Crispin's
Jewish adversary was ready, for the purposes of his argument, to accept
the spiritual interpretation which the Christians proposed to put upon
the precepts of the Law. If, as they claimed, the prohibition of pork was
really meant to refer to man's evil proclivities which were symbolized by

the pig, why not, then, abstain both from pork itself, since God ordained it, as well as from what pork signified spiritually? This, he concluded, would be the best way of "fulfilling the Law." Elsewhere, the same controversialist did not hesitate to quote passages from the New Testament to point out the contradiction in the Christian attitude towards the Law. If "the Law is good," he says, quoting I Timothy 1:8, and if it has been given by God, why then introduce distinctions between certain laws which are held to be still binding, and others which are held to have been abrogated?

G. RIVAL CLAIMS

Century after century, almost generation after generation, the Jews made fresh calculations for the date of the coming of the Messiah. No previous disappointment could destroy the ultimate hope.[53] But the Christians were always ready to remind them jubilantly of their past disappointments—so many proofs, so they said, of the vanity of Jewish expectations. Every time in the past when the Jews expected the Messiah to come they have been disappointed, and it will be the same in the future, said Amulo.

For the Jews the expectation of the Messiah and hopes of national independence were intimately bound up with each other. The historical example of the Babylonian Captivity lent comfort and consolation to them in their desolation. Bodo-Eleazar invoked these hopes when he said: "It is not surprising that we are captives, and that, far from Jerusalem, we have no king of our own. For thus we were captive in Babylon, but later we returned to our homeland . . . This, then, is our hope: that the same thing will happen to us again, when God wills." Wecelin invoked those passages of the Bible likely to keep Jewish hopes alive, notably Psalm 105 (Vulgate: 104): 8–9: "He hath remembered His covenant for ever, the word which He commanded to a thousand generations; [the covenant] which He made with Abraham . . ." Or the words of the prophet Isaiah (46:13): "I bring near My righteousness, it shall not be far off, and My salvation shall not tarry; and I will place salvation in Zion for Israel My glory," or again (51:5): "My favor is near, My salvation is gone forth, and Mine arms shall judge the peoples." In answer to Paulo Alvaro's mockery of the Messianic hopes of the Jews, Bodo-Eleazar put forward Ezekiel's sublime vision (chapters

36 and 37). The scattering of the Jews and the punishment of their sins are described, but also, in the allegory of the Valley of Dry Bones, the resurrection of the people of Israel. "See therefore," said Bodo-Eleazar to the Christians, after this long quotation from the Prophet, "that you can find nothing to show that all this shall not come to pass here on earth."

The Messiah that the Jews continued to expect would not only bring the ingathering of the exiles, but also the final victory of Israel over the nations which were then oppressing her. What were these nations worth? Bodo-Eleazar applied to them the expression used by Isaiah (40:15)—they were "as a drop of a bucket" before the Lord. Isaiah (60:2) also announced the fate which awaited them, "for, behold, darkness shall cover the earth, and gross darkness the peoples." In the anonymous *Altercatio,* the allegorical figure "Synagogue" vividly describes the respective roles of the Gentiles and of Israel at the coming of the Messiah: "He will raise up my kingdom above all the kingdoms of the earth, and he will humble all other peoples to be my servants."

Not only did the fate of the Jewish people, still scattered and diminished in numbers, prove that the Messiah had not yet come, but also the absence of other signs which were to accompany his advent. Gilbert Crispin's adversary recalled how Isaiah (2:3) had promised that all peoples would then say: "Come ye, and let us go up to the mountain of the Lord, to the house of the God of Jacob." But at that time it was only the Jews who spoke thus, for the Christians spoke of going to St. Peter's or St. Paul's or St. Martin's, but never "let us go up to the house of the God of Jacob." Isaiah also foretells (2:4) universal peace after the coming of the Messiah. However, the soldiers had not yet beaten their swords into plowshares, nor their spears into pruning hooks. On the contrary, the armorers could hardly satisfy the demands of their customers, and there was scarcely enough iron with which to forge the weapons of war. Of no place on earth could it be said that there nation did not lift up sword against nation. Everywhere man was attacking his neighbors, oppressing them or killing them. Nations fought with all their might, and kingdoms did battle one with another. Everyone was trained up from earliest infancy in the exercise of arms.

The Jews did not agree that Jesus could have been the promised Messiah; they were still less ready to believe that he was God, or that it was even thinkable that God should have been made flesh. Gilbert

Crispin's adversary reminded him that the Jews believed in one God "who was not created in time, nor born of a woman." And he pressed his point: what reason or what Scriptural authority is there to lead me to believe that God would wish to be made man, or that He has already been made man? If in God there is neither variableness nor any shadow of turning, he goes on, amplifying a passage of the New Testament (Epistle of James 1:17), how, then, can such a change take place in Him that God becomes man, the Creator a creature? How can one envisage that the incorruptible should have become corruptible? How can one say of God that He endures for ever (cf. Psalm 102 [Vulgate: 101]: 27) if He can be transformed into a man? If God transcends all limitation, how could He be circumscribed by the pitiful narrow bonds of the human body? If God is infinite, in what sense can one say that He has been contained and limited by human dimensions, enclosed in a mother's womb? After quoting the New Testament, the Jew, in order the more to confound his Christian adversary, borrowed from contemporary Catholic philosophy its definition of God. If God is "that than which nothing greater or more complete can be conceived," what necessity brought Him to share our abject human condition and undergo so many sufferings? Finally, if God had become man, how can His saying to Moses remain true: "For man shall not see Me and live" (Exodus 33:20). It would seem to be a contradiction that God should have made Himself man without being able to be seen by anyone, not even by the mother. Therefore, concluded the Jew, we affirm that it is in no wise permissible to think such things of God, nor to say them, even less to spread them abroad, for neither does reason allow that such a thing be possible, nor is there Scriptural evidence which by any stretch of imagination could be taken to confirm this error.

Another Jewish method of combating Christian belief in the divinity of Jesus consisted in giving all the proofs adduced by Christians a trivial and banal explanation. The Tol*dot Yeshu already mentioned made nonsense of the Virgin Birth. This "ungodly man, the son of an ungodly man," was the son of a pagan father, a certain Pandera, who was supposed to have seduced Mary, from which union Jesus was said to have been born. The Resurrection was similarly scoffed at. If the tomb was found empty, it was because the Jews had dragged the corpse out to insult it, unless it was that flood-waters had swept it away.

The last subject of importance in this controversy was the Christian belief in the rejection of the Jews and the election of the Gentiles as the Chosen People of God.[54] It was argued by Christians that the rejection of the Jews was borne out by their present condition, scattered and powerless as they were, with no rights, no land of their own, and no king, whereas the status of the Gentiles as Chosen People was shown by the expansion of the Church throughout all the world, where she had won over all peoples. In speaking of their Messianic hopes, we mentioned how the Jews believed that, even though they were then scattered powerless over the face of the earth, the Messiah would gather in the exiles and would exalt the power of Israel. But what of the contemporary absence of any Jewish royal power?

The Christians insisted on the point for two reasons. They considered it proof that Jesus really was the Messiah and also that the Jews had been finally rejected by God. And here they brought in evidence a text of Genesis (49:10) which was almost always rendered in the ancient pre-Vulgate Latin version as follows: *Non deficiet princeps de Juda neque dux de femoribus eius, donec veniat qui mittendus est, et ipse erit exspectatio gentium.* He who is to be sent, the hope of all peoples, in short, the Messiah, would not come until the extinction of the Jewish royal house. But that house had been extinct since the time of Herod—another proof that Jesus was indeed the expected Messiah, and that the fall of the Jews from grace was final. Christian authors who made use of this proof-text from ancient times right through the Middle Ages are too numerous to name. But from the time of St. Jerome onwards, and above all during the High Middle Ages, the Jews made a double rejoinder.

First of all, they disputed the translation of the verse quoted by the Christians. The Hebrew text speaks of *shevet* and *u-meḥoqeq* which should be translated "tribe" and "law-giver" instead of "scepter" and "ruler" (or "prince"), as the Christians would have it. This was not the only philological objection raised. Indeed, for the whole passage, and for every word of the passage, countless translations were proposed.

Secondly, even granting the Christian interpretation, the Jews contested the conclusions drawn from it, for, they said, the line of the Jewish royal house had not been broken. This statement is to be found quoted by Isidore of Seville and later on also by Julian of Toledo and by Paschasius Radbertus. The early writers had recourse to the King of the Ḥimyarites to destroy the Christian argument and later it was the King of the Khazars (and sometimes perhaps even Muhammad) who was invoked for this purpose. In the early 11th century the Jews were still claiming the existence of a Jewish sovereign in the Far East. The kingdom of the Khazars had already been destroyed, and possibly it was the legendary reports of Eldad ha-Dani, who had brought to North Africa amazing accounts of independent Jewish tribes, which now provided them with their argument.

As always, the Jews did not restrict themselves to the defensive on this question. From points won, they took the offensive, and arguing from the existence of the Khazar kingdom, not to mention the great masses of mankind already conquered by Islam, they contested the Christian claim that the Church had spread over the whole earth.

That Israel was the Chosen People of God had been proved by the innumerable benefits showered by Him on His people. These were listed by "Synagogue" in the *Altercatio* already mentioned: the Covenant with Israel, the plagues with which God smote the Egyptians, the crossing of the Red Sea, the preservation of the Jews during their wanderings in the wilderness, their entry into the Promised Land . . . To recall these mercies proved to the Jew that he was chosen of old, and reassured him as well for the future. Wecelin, at the beginning of the 11th century, brought the Psalmist to witness (105 [Vulgate: 104]: 8–9): God would never go back on His promise to Israel, for "He hath remembered His covenant for ever, the word which He commanded to a thousand generations; [the covenant] which He made with Abraham."

It is characteristic of Jewish-Christian polemics in the High Middle Ages that the Jew often appears in the role of the attacker.[55] Besides the three principal problems which have just been mentioned, and which were topics created by Christian polemists, the Jew introduced a number of other arguments. Although both the exterior and interior of synagogues were frequently unadorned, sober, even clumsy in style, whereas the churches made a display of their wealth both in their architecture and ornamentation, this was not indicative of the intrinsic value of the two religions. Bodo-Eleazar, as a convert to Judaism, ridiculed the magnificence of the Christian churches. This external and wholly material splendor of the churches was no guarantee of the enduring nature of the Church. One had only to look at the magnificent temples of the pagans, which now stood for nothing. Do you Christians, he asked, build bigger houses for your Jesus than did the pagans for their gods? And developing his sarcastic attack, Bodo-Eleazar delved into memories of his ecclesiastical studies and brought out some verses by the Christian poet, Arator, suggesting that Christians, in the same way as the pagans whom he specifies, would have cause one day to bewail their fate: "Woe is me, suddenly, before my eyes, shrines built long ago and the noble edifice of the temple are falling in ruins."

The Jews also attacked Christian worship of saints. We have just seen how Gilbert Crispin's Jewish adversary referred ironically to the way Christian churches were set under the protection of such and such a saint, so that they were the houses of Peter or of Paul, but not of God. Wecelin, at the beginning of the 11th century, with the added verve of the neophyte, spoke of "Peter, John, or Martin, or those other devils you call saints." This objection was summarized most succinctly and forcefully by the Jew who started a discussion with a simple peasant who had come to pray to the relics of St. Mansui to cure his paralyzed son: "What help can you expect from someone who is himself dead and lifeless?" He could be of more help himself, he said, for he was very much alive.

Christian respect for sacred images was also condemned. According to Gilbert Crispin's adversary, the verse in Psalm 97 (Vulgate: 96):7: "Ashamed be all they that serve graven images," was to be applied to Christians, for they served images and gloried in their idols. "Sometimes you represent God himself as pitifully nailed to the cross, a thing which is terrible merely to look upon, and you adore this."

Debates within the Church, whether about the use of unleavened wafers in the Eucharist, or the value of the Eucharist itself, or about so many other problems of doctrine or practice, gave the Jews an opportunity to reproach the Christians with lack of unity in their faith. The importance of such discussions was exaggerated by Bodo-Eleazar, who claimed to have seen at the Court of the King of the Franks fourteen Christians arguing, each one with a different conception of Christian worship.

The moral conduct of the faithful was also the object of Bodo-Eleazar's none-too-discreet curiosity. In order to confound the Christians yet further he had no hesitation in retailing his own misconduct and debauchery when he was a Christian—and, even worse, a Catholic priest. He accused himself of having then "taken delight in the sweet embraces of numerous women" whom he had known within the precincts of the Church itself.

H. REPERCUSSIONS

In the history of relations between the Church and the Jews, the High Middle Ages in the West is an exceptional period. Generally speaking, at no other time were relations between the two communities so relatively smooth—and this without the Jews having to renounce any of their beliefs and practices, even the right to conduct missionary activities. It is true that the canons of Church Councils tended to accentuate the division between Jews and Christians, in order to save the latter from contacts which might have imperiled their faith. The Church also wished to see a further decline in the social status of the Jews, in the hope of facilitating missionary activities among them. It wanted its cause to be adopted in civil legislation, and canon law to become the law of the state. However, the Carolingian Princes particularly, and also the rulers of the Germanic Empire, gave effective protection to their Jewish subjects against such pretensions. Furthermore, the actions of the Councils had merely local reference, and were only rarely supported by the Papacy. What is more, the Papacy sometimes gave support to the Jews during local persecutions as was to be the case also in later periods.

The difference between conditions in this period and the next is well illustrated by the iconographical representations of the conflict between Church and Synagogue, so frequently found at all times in the Middle Ages. In the High Middle Ages, these two figures do not occur among church statuary or in bas-reliefs and frescos. But from Carolingian times onwards, they are often found on ivories, where Synagogue has not yet been given the humiliated role which she was to have later—blindfold, with her lance broken, and the tablets of the Law slipping from her grasp. The Carolingian artists do not show her as vanquished, but as combatant, and whether represented in an attitude of haughty disdain, or openly expressing anger and contempt, she is always accorded a certain proud nobility. This artistic representation is a faithful reflection of the social condition of the Jews which was, as we have seen, a not unsatisfactory one.

The reason for the generally favorable attitude of the civil authorities towards the Jews was because in the High Middle Ages—apart from Visigothic Spain in the 7th century—the state was partly a secular institution. The Jews were part of medieval society, and not merely a group on the fringes. But from the beginning of the 11th century the position began to change. As a foreboding of the Crusades, civil and religious affairs became much more closely associated. Henceforward, in their warlike activities, Christians in the West had a common religious purpose, and the Jews were necessarily excluded from it. This exclusion was followed by an attitude of mistrust which turned to hatred. At the outset the Jews were merely prevented from taking up arms against an external enemy, but they were finally accused of sympathy for that enemy, and of having secret contact with him. Once this identification of Jew with enemy had taken place, it is not surprising that the military effort directed against the Moslems was first unleashed against the Jews.

NOTES

1. These canons were repeated in the canonical collection *Quesnelliana*, which circulated in Gaul from the end of the 6th century; also in the *Breviatio canonum* of Fulgentius Ferrandus, which dates from before 546; and in the collection of Cresconius, of the end of the 6th or 7th century. On these collections, cf. P. Fournier and G. Le Bras, *Histoire des collections canoniques en Occident*, 2 vols., Paris, 1931–32, *passsim*.

2. The collection known as the *Hispana*, arranged first chronologically, later systematically by subjects; cf. Fournier and Le Bras, *op. cit.*

3. The letter of Stephen III in *PL*, vol. 129, col. 857. It was common for Jews to hold land during the High Middle Ages, cf. B. Blumenkranz, *Juifs et chrétiens dans le monde occidental, 430–1096*, Paris, 1960, pp. 22–31; on land-owning at Narbonne in particular, see above, pp. 157–8.

4. Cf. *idem, Les auteurs chrétiens latins du moyen âge sur les Juifs et le Judaïsme*, Paris, 1963, no. 128c. The reference to the rules enacted by the Fathers indubitably refers to the collection of Denis le Petit, which appeared in a new and enlarged edition under the auspices of Hadrian. Known as the *Dionysio-Hadriana*, it contained, like its model of the 5th century, the anti-Jewish canons of the pseudo-Council of Laodicea.

5. Cf. Blumenkranz, *Les auteurs chrétiens*, nos. 128 a, b. Through a mistaken reading, S. W. Baron, *A Social and Religious History of the Jews* (2nd ed.), New York and Philadelphia, 1952–60, IV, p. 6, attributes to Gregory IV a definite attitude concerning the Jews. The canon of the Fourth Council of Toledo, which affirms the validity of forcible baptisms, although it advises against using such methods of conversion, was not taken up by this Pope.

6. Cf. Blumenkranz, *Les auteurs chrétiens*, nos. 169 c, d. Nicholas I's reproach was directed at the followers of Photius or at those who, confusing the

Jewish and Christian liturgies, wished to sacrifice a lamb during the Easter mass.

7. *Ibid.*, no. 169 b.

8. *Ibid.*, no. 169 a. Nicholas I refers to Gregory the Great's letter where this question had already been decided; cf. *ibid.*, no. 89.

9. Cf. *ibid.*, no. 186. For the episode, see Cecil Roth, ed., *The Dark Ages: The Jews in Christian Europe, 711–1096*, World History of the Jewish People 2.2, New Brunswick, N.J., 1966, p. 167.

10. The Hebrew account in the De' Rossi MS. 563, no. 23, at Parma, has been published in *Magazin für die Wissenschaft des Judenthums*, 3 (1876), in the Hebrew section *Ozar Tob*, pp. 46–8; A. M. Habermann, *Gᵉzerot Ashkᵉnaz uᵉẒarᵉfat*, Jerusalem, 1945, pp. 19–21; in a French translation: H. Gross, *Gallia Judaica*, Paris, 1897, pp. 71–3 (summary); S. Schwarzfuchs, *Evidences*, 6 (1954), No. 41, 36–7. Gross, *op. cit.*, p. 72, identifies the Pope whom Jacob b. Jekuthiel is supposed to have approached in 1007 as Gregory V. In fact the eventful pontificate of Gregory V is to be ascribed to the end of the 10th century (996–999). The fact that John XVIII sent a legate, the Bishop of Piperno, to France is attested in the Pope's correspondence; cf. P. Jaffé and W. Wattenbach, *Regesta pontificum romanorum* (2nd ed.), Leipzig, I, 1885, nos. 3958–61. It is true that, according to these sources, the object of the legate's mission had nothing to do with the anti-Jewish persecution. The persecution is also attested in Latin sources: Raoul Glaber, *Hist.*, 3, 7 (*PL*, vol. 142, cols. 657–9); cf. Blumenkranz, *Les auteurs chrétiens*, no. 220; Adémar of Chabannes, *Hist.*, 3, 47 (*PL*, vol. 141, col. 60), etc.; *Les auteurs chrétiens*, nos. 213, 215 b; cf. also Roth, ed., *op cit.*, pp. 147–8. On the conversion to Judaism of the Catholic priest Wecelin, see below, note 42 and the sources cited there.

11. The text of the encyclical was published for the first time by J. Lair, *Bibliothèque de l'Ecole des Chartes*, 18 (1857), 251; most recently by A. Gieysztor, *Towarzystwo Naukowe Warszawskie* (Wydział II, Nauk historycznych, społecznych i filozoficznych), Warsaw, 1948, p. 82; and *Medievalia et Humanistica*, 6 (1950), 33–4. The latter questions the authenticity of the text which he places at the end of the 11th century.

12. Cf. Blumenkranz, *Les auteurs chrétiens*, no. 227.

13. *Ibid.*, nos. 228, 229. See Roth, ed., *op. cit.*, pp. 159–60, 371–2.

14. *Ibid.*, no. 238.

15. *Ibid.*, nos. 234, 235.

16. *Ibid.*, no. 214. It is surprising that, according to this story, the Pope did not inflict punishment for this alleged crime upon the whole community of Jews in Rome, but only upon those who are supposed to have been convinced of their "culpability."

17. Cf. *Germania Judaica: von den ältesten Zeiten bis 1238*, ed. by I. Elbogen. A. Freimann and H. Tykocinski, Breslau, 1934, pp. 204, 221, with H. Vogelstein and P. Rieger, *Juden in Rom*, Berlin, I, 1896, pp. 296 ff., and the sources to which they refer, notably A. Jellinek, *Bet ha-Midrasch*, Vienna,

V, 1873, pp. xxxviii, 148 ff.; VI, 1877, pp. xxxiii, 137 ff., together with different versions of this legend. Even before the 12th century when Anacletus II, of authentic Jewish descent, attained the honorable position of being at least Antipope, Gregory VII had already been suspected of being of Jewish extraction. His true origins did not make matters easier for him. Even today this question is still not resolved: cf. the most recent contribution of G. B. Picotti, "Della supposta parentela ebraica di Gregorio VI e Gregorio VII," *Archivio storico italiano*, 100 (1942), 3–41.

18. For the Councils here mentioned see—in addition to J. D. Mansi, *Sacrorum conciliorum nova et amplissima collectio*, Paris, 1900 ff. (repr. Graz, 1960 ff.), *passim;* and C. J. Hefele and H. Leclercq, *Histoire des conciles*, Paris, 1907 ff., *passim*—also B. Blumenkranz, "Deux compilations canoniques de Florus de Lyon et l'action antijuive d'Agobard," *Revue historique de droit français et étranger*, 33 (1955), 227 ff., 560 ff. See also Roth, ed., *op. cit.*, pp. 130, 140–1.

19. See Roth, ed., *op. cit.*, p. 37 and pp. 116–7.

20. See references to editions and MSS. in Fournier and Le Bras, *op. cit.*, *passim*.

21. Cf. Blumenkranz, *Les auteurs chrétiens*, no. 187.

22. Cf. *idem, Juifs et chrétiens*, pp. 68 ff., 162 ff.; and *Les auteurs chrétiens*, nos. 213, 232.

23. *Ibid.*, nos. 139–144, 165.

24. Cf. B. Blumenkranz, "Juden und Jüdisches in christlichen Wundererzählungen," *Theologische Zeitschrift*, 10 (1954), 417 ff.

25. Cf. *idem*, "Vie et survie de la polémique antijuive," in *Studia patristica*, Berlin, 1957, I (= *Texte und Untersuchungen zur Geschichte der altchristlichen Literatur*, vol. 63), pp. 460 ff.

26. Cf. *idem., Juifs et chrétiens*, pp. 84 ff.

27. Cf. *idem.*, "Perfidia," *Archivum Latinitatis Medii Aevi (Bulletin Du Cange)*, 22 (1952), 157 ff.

28. Cf. *idem., Juifs et chrétiens*, pp. 99 ff. See above, p. 37, and below, p. 116.

29. See Roth, ed., *op. cit.*, pp. 137–40. Cf. Blumenkranz, "Deux compilations canoniques," *loc. cit.*

30. The Mâcon episode is related in the *Necrologium eccl. s. Petri Matiscon*, Lyons, 1874, App. 6, pp. 75–6; for the prohibition of forcible baptism of children, and its sanctioning by Henry IV, see *MGH, Dipl. reg. et imp. Germ.*, 6, 2, pp. 546, 548–9.

31. For the interpretation given by Rashi and the Tosafists to Sanh. 44a, cf. J. Katz, *Tarbiz*, 27 (1958), 203 ff.; the other references are to be found in *Juifs et chrétiens*, pp. 137 f.

32. *Ibid.*, pp. 138 ff.

33. *Ibid.*, pp. 162 ff.

34. *Ibid.*, pp. 164 ff.; and B. Blumenkranz, "Un pamphlet juif médio-latin de polémique antichrétienne," *Revue d'histoire et de philosophie religieuses*, 34 (1954), 401 ff. See Roth, ed., *op. cit.*, pp. 93, 96.

35. Cf. particularly the numerous studies of S. Krauss, from *Das Leben Jesu*

nach jüdischen Quellen, Berlin, 1902, to "Une nouvelle recension hébraïque du Toldot Yešu," *REJ,* 3 (103) (1938), 65 ff. (See the notes to p. 65 of that article for the author's other writings on this text).

36. Blumenkranz, *Juifs et chrétiens,* pp. 171 ff.
37. *Ibid.,* pp. 175 ff.
38. *Ibid.,* pp. 177 ff.
39. For a recent study on Jewish proselytizing of slaves, see Ben Zion Wacholder, "The Halakah and the Proselyting of Slaves during the Gaonic Era," *HJ,* 18 (1956), 89 ff.; cf. also, by the same author, "Attitudes towards Proselytizing in the Classical Halakah," *ibid.,* 20 (1958), 77 ff.
40. Blumenkranz, *Juifs et chrétiens,* p. 208; and *idem,* "Du nouveau sur Bodo-Eleazar?" *REJ,* 12 (112) (1953), 35 ff.
41. *Ibid., loc. cit.;* and *Les auteurs chrétiens,* nos. 210–12.
42. For Wecelin, see Alpert de St. Symphorien-de-Metz, *De diversitate temporum,* 1, 7; 2, 22–4 *(PL,* vol. 140, cols. 457, 484 ff.); *Les auteurs chrétiens,* nos. 210, 211. For the most recent studies on the conversion of Andreas, archbishop of Bari, and of John-Obadiah, cf. S. D. Goitein. " 'Obadyah, a Norman Proselyte," *JJS,* 4 (1953), 74 ff.; A. Scheiber, "The Origins of 'Obadyah, the Norman Proselyte," *ibid.,* 5 (1954), 32 ff.; L. Musset, "Un prêtre normand converti au Judaïsme," *Bulletin Soc. Antiqu. Normandie,* 53 (1955–6), 363 ff.; B. Blumenkranz, "La conversion au Judaïsme d'André, Archevêque de Bari," *JJS,* 14 (1963), 33 ff.; N. Golb, "A Study of a Proselyte to Judaism who Fled to Egypt at the Beginning of the 11th Century," *Sefunot,* 8 (1964) (Itzhak Ben-Zvi Memorial Vol.), 87 ff.; *idem,* " 'Obadiah the Proselyte," *The Journal of Religion* (Chicago), 45 (1965), 153–6; *idem,* "Notes on the Conversion of European Christians to Judaism in the Eleventh Century," *JJS,* 16 (1965), 69–74; N. Allony, *Sinai* (Hebrew), 57 (1965), 43–55. There has been further discussion of the episode and of the two protagonists in the Hebrew daily *Haaretz* (Tel Aviv), June 11 and July 2, 1965.
43. Blumenkranz, *Juifs et chrétiens,* pp. 209 ff.
44. *Ibid.,* pp. 213 ff.; cf. also the Introductions to the critical editions, *Altercatio Ecclesiae contra Synagogam, texte inédit du Xe siècle,* Strasbourg, 1954, pp. 5–24, 46–8; *Gisleberti Crispini Disputatio Iudei et Christiani,* Utrecht, 1956 (Stromata patristica et mediaevalia, vol. 3), pp. 10–11.
45. Cf. also B. Blumenkranz, "La 'Disputatio Judei cum christiano' de Gilbert Crispin, abbé de Westminster," *Revue du moyen âge latin,* 4 (1948), 237–52.
46. Cf. *idem, Les auteurs chrétiens,* nos. 157–60; and "Un pamphlet juif médio-latin de polémique antichrétienne," *loc. cit.*
47. Cf. *Les auteurs chrétiens,* nos. 222, 204–6; cf. also *idem,* "A propos du (ou des) 'Tractatus contra Iudaeos' de Fulbert de Chartres," *Revue du moyen âge latin,* 8 (1952), 51–54.
48. Cf. *Juifs et·chrétiens,* pp. 68 ff., 162 ff.
49. See Roth, ed., *op. cit.,* p. 104.

50. *Op. cit.*, pp. 216 f.
51. *Ibid.*, pp. 222 ff.
52. *Ibid.*, pp. 279 ff.
53. *Ibid.*, pp. 243 ff.
54. *Ibid.*, pp. 272 ff., 227 ff.
55. *Ibid.*, pp. 279 ff; and B. Blumenkranz, "Die jüdischen Beweisgründe im Religionsgespräche mit den Christen in den christlichlateinischen Sonderschriften des 5. bis 11. Jahrhunderts," *Theologische Zeitschrift*, 4 (1948), 119 ff.

7

The Papal Bull *Sicut Judeis*

Solomon Grayzel

1. ITS DEVELOPMENT

Most of the popes during the Middle Ages had occasion to issue formal
statements about the position of the Jews and the practice of Judaism in
the midst of Christian society. Such statements generally revolved about
some issue of the moment, whether to protect Jews against a specific
danger threatening them from Christians, or to repress their presumably
expanding influence and activity which were considered a threat to
Christianity, or to grant them privileges, or to rescind those already
granted. Such letters, or Bulls, dispatched by various popes were addressed to secular rulers or to the clergy generally or particularly.

There was one such Bull which differed from these others in several
important respects. For one thing, it was in the category of a statement
of general policy, dealing with matters of faith and religious discipline
and expressed in the form of a warning and exhortation addressed "To
all faithful Christians." This is why it was sometimes called a *constitutio,*
to distinguish it from letters conferring privileges or grants and from
administrative orders.[1] As such, this Bull, which began with the words
Sicut Judeis, was entered into the collection of Church formulations
from which Canon Law was drawn.[2] Moreover, it appears to have been
repeated more frequently than any other papal utterance concerning the
Jews: being used by six popes during the twelfth century (including

Reprinted by permission of E. J. Brill from *Studies and Essays in Honor of Abraham A.
Neuman,* ed. Meir Ben-Horin, Bernard D. Weinryb, and Solomon Zeitlin, Leiden, 1962,
243–80.

Innocent III), by ten popes during the thirteenth, by four popes during the fourteenth (including an anti-pope), and by three during the fifteenth century. It is to be noted that it was used most frequently during the century of the papacy's greatest influence and that, as we shall see, it was subjected to increasing modification as time went on.

The basic text of the Bull ran as follows:[3]

Even as the Jews ought not have the freedom to dare do in their synagogues more than the law permits them, so ought they not suffer curtailment of those [privileges] which have been conceded them.

This is why, although they prefer to persist in their obstinacy rather than acknowledge the words of the prophets and the eternal secrets of their own scriptures, thus arriving at an understanding of Christianity and salvation, nevertheless, in view of the fact that they have begged for our protection and our aid and in accordance with the clemency which Christian piety imposes, we, following in the footsteps of our predecessors of happy memory[4] ... , grant their petition and offer them the shield of our protection.

We decree that no Christian shall use violence to force them into baptism while they are unwilling and refuse, but that [only] if anyone of them seeks refuge among the Christians of his own free will and by reason of faith, his willingness having become quite clear, shall he be made a Christian without subjecting himself to any opprobrium. For surely none can be believed to possess the true Christian faith if he is known to have come to Christian baptism unwillingly and even against his wishes.

Moreover, without the judgment of the authority of the land, no Christian shall presume to wound their persons, or kill them, or rob them of their money, or change the good customs which they have thus far enjoyed in the place of their habitation. Furthermore, while they celebrate their festivals, no one shall disturb them in any way by means of sticks and stones, nor exact forced service from any of them other than such as they have been accustomed to perform from ancient times. Opposing the wickedness and avarice of evil men in such matters, we decree that no one shall dare to desecrate or reduce a Jewish cemetery, or, with the object of extorting money, exhume bodies there interred.

Should anyone, being acquainted with the contents of this decree, nevertheless dare to act in defiance of it—which God forbid—he shall suffer loss of honor and office or be restrained by the penalty of excommunication, unless he make proper amends for his presumption. We desire, however, to place under the protection of this decree only those [Jews] who do not presume to plot against the Christian faith.

The central ideas of this Bull were not new even at its first appearance, during the pontificate of Calixtus II (1119–1124). More than six hundred years earlier, Theodoric the Ostrogoth, basing himself on characteristic

Roman respect for custom and precedent, expressed some of these ideas in a letter to the Jews of Genoa (ca. 500).[5] He said:

Even as, when petitioned, we like to give due consent, in the same measure we dislike it when, because of our favor, laws are evaded, especially in such matters as we believe involve religious reverence . . . We therefore decree, by the authority of these presents, that you may erect a roof over the old walls of your synagogue, thus [in response] to your petition granting permission in so far as imperial regulations permit;[6] but no decorations of any kind may be added and there must be no overstepping the limits by extending the structure . . . We cannot command religious faith, for no one can be forced to believe who is unwilling to do so.

The great Pope Gregory I, toward the end of the sixth century, expressed himself to the same effect:[7] Jews were entitled to have a place "where they can observe their ceremonies unhindered"; and the pope added: "We forbid that the said Jews be unreasonably burdened and afflicted; they must, rather, be permitted to live in accordance with Roman Law . . ." Moreover, a few years later Pope Gregory began one of his letters with the very sentence which became the characteristic opening for the famous Bull here under discussion.[8] The Jews of Rome having submitted to the pope a complaint by their fellow Jews of Palermo, the pope urged the bishop of that diocese to make sure that justice was done to the Jews of his district. The prestige which Pope Gregory I enjoyed throughout the subsequent history of the Church thus fortified the principle of continuity which he asserted with regard to the Jewish position.

To the continuity of the regulations under which they lived and their right to unhindered worship, the Bull *Sicut Judeis* added a warning against attempts to convert the Jews by force. As we shall see below, the first issuance of the Bull in its developed form was probably connected with the outbreak of forced conversions incidental to the First Crusade. It was therefore necessary if the Jews were to be protected, for the Church to refute the argument that the persistence of Judaism or, as churchmen were likely to express it, "the stubbornness of the Jews," was contrary to God's will. Basing themselves on the strong condemnation of Jesus' opponents in the Gospel stories, the Church Fathers had minced no words when referring to the unwillingness of their Jewish contemporaries to give up Judaism.[9] "Blind" and "hard" were mild words used by Augustine.[10] On the other hand, it was Augustine himself who interpreted Psalm 59: 12 as a warning by Jesus not to kill the Jews, who are God's witnesses and whose lowly status and dispersion are punishment enough for their sins.[11] How then was their conversion to be attained? Tertullian, in the second century, when the Christian Church was still subject to persecution, had argued that religion must be accepted freely or not at all.[12] Similarly Lactantius, a century later, asserted that nothing was essentially more voluntary than religion.[13] Theodoric's letter cited above reflected the same sentiment. Pope Gregory I insisted on several occasions that the proper way to seek the conversion of Jews was not by force or threats but by mildness and persuasion.[14] He berated a bishop of Naples for interfering with the Jews in the observance of their holidays, since such interference not only fails to bring them nearer to conversion but also violates ancient usage.[15]

Pope Gregory's repeated warnings indicate how difficult it was to restrain an aroused mob and overzealous churchmen. He himself on one important occasion was not altogether consistent in upholding the objections to conversion by force and under threat.[16] His triumphant letter to King Reccared, hailing the entry of the Visigothic kingdom into the Catholic fold, speaks of the attempt of the Jews to bribe the king to leave them alone, but has not a word of criticism about the element of compulsion in the situation. Evidently even the saintly Pope Gregory was not ready to include destitution and exile in his definition of force. On the whole, the idea that conversion should be the result of peaceful efforts remained alive during the early Middle Ages. Popes Gregory IV (828–44) and Leo VII (936–9) expressed themselves to the same effect.[17] Pope Alexander II (1061–73), in a letter to the bishops of Spain in connection with the Reconquest,[18] quoted Gregory I's view that conversion should be achieved by peaceful methods, that the Jews must not be killed, and that synagogues should not be destroyed.

It is thus clear that a substantial part of the Bull *Sicut Judeis* had a long history by the time of its first issuance about the year 1120. The prohibition of physical violence directed against the adherents of Judaism and of physical force in the effort to convert them antedated the Bull by many centuries. The other gross forms of attack and persecution—such as pelting Jews and their synagogues with stones and the desecration of cemeteries—had certainly not been unknown before the twelfth century,[19] but had now become characteristic enough of local Christian-Jewish relations for the popes to take note of them.[20] It was not sufficient to make general statements about not changing the "good customs" that had obtained; specific examples had to be listed.

2. ITS PROMULGATION

The relationship of this Bull to the Jews of Europe is a matter of great interest. It is reasonable to assume that the situation which called the Bull forth was the disastrous result of the First Crusade, which so radically changed the status of the Jews.[21] Murder, pillage and forced conversions accompanied the march of the crusaders across central Europe. Although the reversion to Judaism on the part of forced converts was permitted by the civil authorities, on the assumption that with the passing of the storm everything would return to normal, the zeal aroused by the preaching of the crusade belied any such prospect. The General Peace, proclaimed for the Empire in 1103, for the first time classed the Jews with those who were in need of special protection.[22] Civil protection, moreover, was hardly enough in a situation created by an excess of religious emotionalism, and an appeal to the pope must have suggested itself soon after the events of 1095–6. Pope Urban II had remained strangely silent in the face of the ugly events which he had been instrumental in arousing. The anti-pope Clement III was decidedly unsympathetic and had even protested against the reversion of the forced converts.[23] At the same time, the unsettled conditions both in the Empire and in Rome which the popes of the legitimate succession faced made an appeal to them impossible.[24] Peaceful conditions for the papacy did not return until several years later after the election of Pope Calixtus II in 1119. The Jews of the Empire then had an opportunity to elicit a general statement of papal protection.

The above order of events constitutes a plausible theory,[25] but unfortunately there is no way of proving its truth. No actual copy of Calixtus' Bull is in existence; knowledge of its issuance is based on the mention of Calixtus as the first among the predecessors of the many popes[26] who are credited with it. One cannot tell, therefore, whether Pope Calixtus gave any indication of the people to whom the Bull was addressed or of the situation that caused its promulgation. If its wording was the same as that given above, it gave no hint of the ravages caused by the crusaders. Another view seems to be more cogent, namely, that the Bull was asked for and given to the Jews of Rome. The turbulence of the city during the first quarter of the twelfth century made the need for such special protection obvious;[27] and subsequent popes repeated the Bull as an act of grace to their own Jewish subjects. One may assume that the Bull's extension to other Jewish communities came during the reigns of Calixtus' successors, perhaps during the time of later councils and crusades.[28]

The second pope to issue the Bull was Eugenius III (1145–53). During his reign the Second Crusade was in progress, and the Jews of various parts of Europe were suffering in consequence. This pope would certainly have heeded their plea had the Jews turned to him for protection, since Bernard of Clairvaux, the most venerated Churchman of that day, had come out strongly in defense of the harassed Jews.[29] Yet Eugenius' Bull—assuming that it also did not differ from the *Sicut Judeis* issued by his successors—in no way reflects a situation like that of the attacks by crusaders. He, too, one must assume, granted the Bull to his Jewish subjects in the city of Rome who hailed him upon his entry into the city.[30]

There is no record of the next two popes issuing the Bull, perhaps because their relations with the city of Rome were not sufficiently peaceful. Alexander III, however, did issue it some time during his comparatively long reign of twenty-one years (1159–81).[31] For the first time one may assume that other Jews, besides those of Rome, were concerned with the document. A Jew by the name of Yehiel, scion of an important scholarly family, served Pope Alexander as financial advisor, and he may well have sensed the threat of hostile legislation emerging from the forthcoming Third Lateran Council. He may have acted as intermediary for Jewish communities who felt insecure and prevailed upon the pope to dispatch the Bull *Sicut Judeis,* originally given to the Jews of Rome, to such other places as France and England.[32]

It may be assumed therefore that, while the Jewish community of Rome continued to play the dominant role in obtaining the re-issuance of the Bull *Sicut Judeis* as soon as possible after the accession of a new pope, knowledge of the Bull had penetrated beyond Italy and that, by the latter part of the twelfth century, the Jews of the rest of Europe saw in it a statement that could be turned into a ready defense. The Church, too, now recognized it as more than an act of grace on the part of a pope after his ceremonious entry into the city. Of the three popes who followed Alexander III—Lucius III (1181–5), Urban III (1185–7) and

Gregory VIII (1187)—only the first spent a few months in Rome, and these were troubled ones; they had no chance to issue the Bull. But Clement III (1187–91) did issue it, and his Bull was preserved as a guide to Canon Law.[33] It was also issued by his successor, Coelestine III (1191–98),[34] and thereafter by almost every pope practically to the end of the thirteenth century: Innocent III,[35] on September 15, 1199, in the second year of his reign; Honorius III,[36] on November 7, 1217, in his second year; Gregory IX,[37] on May 3, 1235, in his ninth year, perhaps because his hold on the city of Rome was not really secure till that year;[38] Innocent IV,[39] on October 22, 1246, and again on July 9, 1247, in his fourth and fifth years; Alexander IV,[40] on September 22, 1255, in his first year; Urban IV,[41] April 26, 1262, in his first year; none by Clement IV (1265–68);[42] Gregory X,[43] October 7, 1272, and possibly again on September 10, 1274, in his first and third years; none by the three following popes who died within months after their election; Nicholas III,[44] on August 2, 1278, in his first year; Martin IV,[45] on August 2, 1281, in his first year; Honorius IV (1285–7) and Nicholas IV (1288–92), dates unknown.[46]

There were no further renewals of the Bull until 1348. One reason for this, during the rest of the final decade of the thirteenth century, may have been the personalities of the two men who occupied the Papal Throne: the non–politically minded Coelestine V, who soon resigned, and the highly politically minded Boniface VIII. The latter may have refused to issue the Bull because of the growing influence of the Inquisition, which found it an annoying limitation on the inquisitors' desire to extend their jurisdiction over the Jews. Pope Boniface may not even have been asked to renew it because the Jews of Rome were in no position to approach the pope.[47]

It is clear from the above—from the dates of issuance and from the fact that copies of the Bull are found in various parts of Europe—that the Jewish community of Rome had in some way made itself responsible for obtaining the Bull and for paying the fees involved. Other Jewish communities could thereupon obtain copies from the Papal Chancery on payment of a separate fee, but without going to the trouble and expense of making the initial approach,[48] certainly more difficult for non-residents of the city. The procedure was facilitated by the wording of the Bull's address, which generally was the simple formula *Universis Christifidelibus* (To All Faithful Christians), or some modification of it, rather than to the Christians of any specific city or region. Nor did the thirteenth-century Bull indicate the Jewish community that had asked for protection. This may also explain in part why two of the popes enumerated above are credited with two issues of the *Sicut Judeis,* though in each case one of the issues contains additional protection.

3. ITS EXPANSION

The popes, for their part, looked upon the Bull *Sicut Judeis* as a statement of general Church policy. Pope Innocent III emphasized this attitude by adding a prefatory statement to the *Sicut Judeis* which he granted early in his reign. Always desirous of acting in accordance with neatly regulated theological principles, he saw in this Bull, not only the limits within which Jewish life was to be lived, but also the bounds of his own authority respecting the "Jewish perversion of faith" *(perfidia Judeorum).* He consequently felt that he must explain his issuance of the Bull, and he set the tone for it by harking back to Augustine.[49] His introductory statement read as follows:[50]

> Although the Jewish distortion of the faith is deserving of thorough condemnation, nevertheless, because the truth of our own faith is proved through them, they must not be severely oppressed by the faithful. So the prophet says, "Thou shalt not kill them, lest in time they forget Thy Law"; or, more clearly put: Thou shalt not destroy the Jews completely so that the Christians may not possibly forget Thy Law which, though they themselves fail to understand it, they display in their books for those who do understand.

Pursuing the same thought of the Church Father, Innocent III, in a letter to Philip-Augustus of France, eloquently urged the repression of the Jews, but he began by restating the old principle that their dispersion and subjection are pleasing to God.[51] In fact, apart from the Bull *Sicut Judeis,* Pope Innocent III issued no communication favorable to the Jews; nevertheless, he who had ordered the extermination of the Albigenses warned crusaders and other Christians against doing the Jews physical harm.[52]

With few exceptions, other popes who issued the Bull did, when requested, extend additional protection by means of letters directed to princes and Churchmen in various parts of Europe where persecution of the Jews was rampant. But what is especially interesting in this connection is the fact that such protection was also extended by means of additions to the *Sicut Judeis*. This happened on three occasions in the thirteenth century and more frequently thereafter. If, therefore, one assumes that by the thirteenth century this Bull was meant to define Church policy, the additions to it must have been looked upon by those who made them as elaborations of that policy.

Before discussing the three additions, it may be helpful to cite instances when separate Bulls were issued on a subject which later became the substance of an addition to the *Sicut Judeis*. We have seen that in 1235 Pope Gregory IX granted the Jews a *Sicut Judeis* Bull. It appears to have afforded insufficient protection to the Jews of France and England, who then found themselves in dire straits. A year later, Pope Gregory IX therefore responded to their plea and issued a more direct warning to their persecutors, thereby gaining the reputation of having been bribed by the Jews.[53] Graetz connects these two Bulls with a ritual murder accusation at Lauda.[54] Such a connection with the ritual murder libel was made by the next pope, Innocent IV, who had also granted a *Sicut Judeis*. He, too, like his predecessor, speaks with horror about the cruelties perpetrated against the Jews by men who were obviously more interested in gain than in truth.[55]

No wonder that Pope Innocent IV thereupon decided to add the prohibition of the ritual murder charge to the list of those actions against the Jews prohibited by Church policy. On July 9, 1247, he granted a second *Sicut Judeis* in which the following was added immediately before the final penalty clause:[56]

. . . exhume bodies there interred. Nor shall anyone accuse them of using human blood in their religious rites; for they are instructed in the Old Testament against the use of blood of any kind, not to speak of human blood. Since, however, at Fulda and elsewhere many Jews have been killed on account of this suspicion, we, by the authority of these presents, strictly forbid the recurrence of this charge in the future. If anyone . . .

The next addition was made by Pope Gregory X. Innocent's warning had done no good; cases of ritual murder accusation multiplied during the long interregnum in the Empire and spread to countries on its periphery.[57] Gregory X's statement on the subject was therefore longer and more detailed, so that the Bull itself appears almost like an introduction to the refutation of the charge which resulted in such barbarities. Moreover, even where the accused Jews were brought to trial, the judicial hearings were a farce, since a number of Christians were always on hand to testify against them. It was necessary, therefore, to re-assert the existing judicial procedure in which a mixed group of witnesses was required to condemn a Jew for murder.[58] This, too, was introduced into an expanded *Sicut Judeis*. The new material was introduced immediately after the prohibition against changing the old customs:[59]

... from ancient times. Furthermore, we decree that the testimony of Christians shall not avail against Jews unless a Jew is among the Christian witnesses, since Jews [alone] cannot act as witnesses against Christians. For it happens from time to time that Christian children are lost and the enemies of the Jews thereupon accuse them of having stealthily kidnapped and murdered these Christian children and of having performed a sacrifice of their hearts and blood. Or the parents of the children, or other Christians who are enemies of the Jews, secretly hide these children so as to be able to accuse the Jews; and, in order to be able to extort sums of money from them as a means of purchasing freedom from torture, they make the totally false assertion that the Jews were the ones who had secretly and stealthily kidnapped the children and killed them and had sacrificed their hearts and blood. Since their Law clearly and explicitly prohibits them from sacrificing, eating and drinking blood, or tasting it even from animals of cloven hoof—as has been repeatedly proved before our court through Jewish converts to our faith—the frequent arrest and imprisonment of such Jews has been contrary to justice. We ordain that Christians must not be heard against Jews in such cases, and we order that the Jews arrested on this empty charge be freed from prison and that the Jews be not hereafter arrested on the basis of this empty charge, unless, perchance—which we do not believe likely—they are caught red-handed. We ordain that no Christian shall introduce any innovation with respect to them, but that they shall remain in the position and status which has been theirs from the days of our predecessors in times gone by till our own day ...

A situation of still another kind, though also connected with witnesses and the judicial process, was the subject of an addition to *Sicut Judeis* by Pope Martin IV in 1281. The zeal of the inquisitors in ferreting out heresy made them try to extend their operations to Jews. They justified their going outside the confines of Christianity in a number of ways: a hostile Christian might accuse his Jewish neighbor or creditor of sacrilege or blasphemy or ritual murder; or a Jewish convert to Christianity might be found to have continued his contacts with members of his Jewish family, thus laying them open to the charge of trying to lure him back into the Jewish fold. The latter charge became especially frequent during the second half of the thirteenth century as a result of the many ritual murder libels and the ensuing riots with their inevitable forced conversions. A number of papal pronouncements bear on the subject of safeguarding the Christianity of the converts.[60] But Pope Martin IV was also convinced that this situation, like the charge of ritual murder, encouraged false accusations and false testimony, especially since the usual procedure was to force confession out of the accused rather than make the accuser prove his charge. His addition to the *Sicut Judeis,* therefore, attempted to make such accusations more risky; it also made it possible for a convert to move about with greater freedom, provided he had nothing to do with his former family.

Pope Martin's addition was inserted just ahead of the penal clause, and read as follows:[61]

... exhume bodies there interred. We also desire and decree that no inquisitor of the evil of heresy, or anyone else whatever his office, shall exert compulsion on the said Jews or on anyone of them on any man's petition; but that he who accuses them must give and submit to the court a guarantee [of trustworthiness] similarly secure. If the crime of which the Jew is accused is not proved, the accuser shall be subject to the same penalty to which the accused was bound and it shall be inflicted on him. And if a baptized Jew has converse with some other Jew whom he does not recognize, he shall not be held for punishment. If any-one ...

None of these three additions to the Bull *Sicut Judeis* during the thirteenth century acquired the force of Church policy either to the extent of being repeated by subsequent popes or of being included in the *Corpus Juris Canonici*. In fact, the one concerned with the inclusion of a Jew among the witnesses testifying against another Jew in a criminal case was tacitly contradicted in a pronouncement of the Council of Vienne which was included in the *Corpus*.[62] What these additions point up is that the situation of the Jews by the end of the thirteenth century was—as we shall indicate below—beyond any aid from the vague generalizations contained in the Bull *Sicut Judeis*. Its granting had become a formality; and the long and specific additions to it, like that of Gregory X on the ritual murder libel, even went contrary to its nature as a *constitutio*. When the Jews of any part of Europe cast about for help from the imminent danger stemming in part from religious fanaticism, they would turn to the pope for a statement bearing on the specific problem which faced them. They frequently elicited such a statement,[63] quite apart from the Bull *Sicut Judeis*. When the Jews asked the protection of their secular ruler, they would submit a copy of the *Sicut Judeis,* sometimes one issued long before, but generally accompanied with a more specific papal protest against their persecution.[64] There were popes who, as far as is known, did not issue a *Sicut Judeis,* yet offered protection on a definite issue. Pope Boniface VIII, for example, one of the very few popes in the thirteenth century without a *Sicut Judeis* to his credit, responded to the request of the Jews of Rome for protection against the inquisitors who, claiming that every Jew was "powerful" and therefore in a position to intimidate witnesses, refused to let accused Jews see the names of the people who had testified against them, thus interfering with their defense.[65]

4. ITS DECLINE

It is quite possible that, had the popes' residence in Rome remained uninterrupted, they would have continued issuing the official Bull of protection as part of the formality of their accession. But the prolonged absence of the popes from Rome during the so-called Babylonish Captivity broke the custom. At the same time, the Jews outside of Rome had learned that there was no advantage in obtaining the Bull's confirmation. There is hardly a trace of the wording of *Sicut Judeis* in the protective pronouncements of the first two popes (John XXII and Benedict XII) permanently resident in Avignon.[66] Its first reaffirmation in full was made by Pope Clement VI in 1348.[67] This was the year of the Black Death, when the Jews, accused of poisoning the wells of drinking water, were subjected to great cruelty and slaughter. Messengers came to Avignon from various parts of Europe and pleaded for protection. But again it was felt, presumably both by the Jews and by the pope, that the statement in *Sicut Judeis* was hardly specific enough to meet the situation. A second Bull was therefore issued a few months later, referring back to the above Bull, repeating the substance of its usual preamble, summarizing the rest and then continuing to refute the charge of poisoning the drinking water and demanding that the persecutions cease. Addressed to the higher clergy, it began as follows:[68]

Even though we properly scorn the Jewish perversion of the faith, because they, persisting in their stubbornness, refuse to understand the words of their own prophets and the mysteries of their own scriptures and so accept the Christian faith and the promise of salvation, nevertheless, we recognize that the said Jews are to be tolerated, since the Prophet Isaiah bore witness that in time to come their remnant would be saved. To them, therefore, invoking our protective guardianship and the kindliness of Christian piety, we, following in the footsteps of our predecessors of blessed memory, the Roman pontiffs Calixtus, Eugenius, Alexander, Clement, Celestinus, Innocent, Gregory, Nicholas, Honorius, and Nicholas IV, have caused the shield of our protection to be granted, decreeing, among other things, that: No Christian shall dare, for whatever reason, to wound or kill these Jews without the judgment of the lord or officers of the country or region which they inhabit, or carry off their property, or exact forced service from them excepting such as they have been accustomed to perform for them in time gone by. Whoever, knowing the contents of this decree, attempts to act to the contrary shall lay himself open to the loss of honors and office or be punished by excommunication, unless he takes care to correct his presumption by means of the proper amends—as is clearly stated in those same letters.

Recently widespread rumor has made us aware . . .

One may note that this summary of the Bull *Sicut Judeis* does not contain any direct reference to forced conversion or to interference with the synagogue. It may be that Pope Clement VI simply emphasized life, property and forced services because these were the earmarks of the persecutions of the day; nevertheless, the missing items are significant.

Another restatement of *Sicut Judeis* in its practically unmodified form was issued by Pope Urban V, in 1365.[69] It may have been asked for by the Jews of France, who had but recently been readmitted to that country in restricted numbers. Thus, the Bull was issued, during the Babylonish Captivity, twice in its usual form and once in considerably modified form.

The return of the popes to Rome might have been expected to bring about a revival of the Bull's use at the beginning of a papal reign; but this did not happen. The Bull was not issued by Urban VI. There is evidence of its issuance by Pope Boniface IX (1389–1404), who showed his favor to the Jews on a number of occasions.[70] The Avignon pope Clement VII, on the other hand, issued the Bull twice. The first time, in 1379,[71] therefore soon after his accession, it was intended perhaps as a symbolic assertion of legitimacy, since it revived an ancient custom. It concerned the Jews of Avignon and, after the usual beginning, deviated to guarantee their safety and their peaceful possession of communal property. The anti-pope issued it a second time, in its usual wording, in 1393,[72] perhaps in connection with events in Spain, where under existing circumstances it was bound to be meaningless. But the next two popes of the Roman succession, Innocent VII and Gregory XII, did not issue any *Sicut Judeis,* although the former ratified all the privileges that had been granted the Jews by his predecessors.[73]

By the time of Pope Martin V (elected in 1417), some two centuries of experience had shown that the basic regulations of the Bull *Sicut Judeis* were no longer relevant. The traditional idea that protecting the Jews was a matter of Christian piety could not be abandoned, but the areas of protection were now quite different. The Bull had long ceased to be a practical *constitutio* and had become just another papal pronouncement, subject to the vagaries of politics in an ecclesiastically turbulent age.

Once the Great Schism had been healed, it was but natural for the popes, Martin V and his successor Eugenius IV, to seek to re-establish the power and influence of the papacy.[74] Their vacillating attitude toward the Jews was a manifestation of the conflict between their innate sense of fairness and their desire to show unchallengeable zeal for the Church, between their attempt to retain the support of the princes and their desire not to re-arouse the conciliar movement. Pope Martin appeared at first unfavorably disposed toward the Jews; but he soon changed his mind, under the urging of some civil authorities[75] who called his attention to the deteriorating condition of the Jews as a result of the activities of the preaching monks and the inquisitors. In the course of his reign, he issued a considerable number of pronouncements about the Jews.[76] Those between the years 1418 and 1422 were on the whole in their favor; and two of them bore unmistakable resemblance to the *Sicut Judeis,* commencing with the usual formula but then turning to matters of more immediate concern.

The first of these, issued in Mantua in 1419,[77] was in behalf of the Jews of northern Italy. After stating that they must not be molested in their synagogues nor forced into baptism, it goes on to add that they must not be compelled to violate their Sabbaths and holidays, although they should not be allowed to work openly on Christian festivals; the wearing of the Jewish Badge should not be made harsher than it had been in their respective places of habitation; and they must be permitted to do business with Christians. The Bull ends on the usual note that it was intended for the protection of only those Jews who do not plot against Christianity.

Almost exactly four years later,[78] Pope Martin issued a second *Sicut Judeis,* this time addressed to all Christians and applying to Jews everywhere. After the usual beginning and mentioning a number of the predecessors who had issued the Bull, he further motivates its issuance by pointing out that preachers to the Christians threaten with excommunication those who have any dealings with the Jews, even to the extent of making a fire for them or nursing their children, and that Christians stir up riots against the Jews by accusing them of poisoning wells, mixing blood with their matzot, and bringing calamities on mankind. Thus ill-treated, Jews are discouraged from joining the Christian faith. The pope reminds the Christians that the Jews are preserved by God in order to provide testimony for the truth of Christianity and that the prophets had said that a remnant of them would be saved. He therefore goes on to forbid preachers to preach against them, to urge that they be treated with kindness, to permit them to have converse with Christians, to prohibit injuring their persons or property, to let them enjoy the privileges granted or to be granted them, to place them under civil or ordinary ecclesiastical (rather than inquisitorial) authority, so as not to subject them to exactions or molestations. Furthermore, lest the contents of this decree be kept from public knowledge, he orders that it be copied by the notary and be made known to all. The Bull, of course, contains the usual limitation to those Jews who do not plot against Christianity.

The issuance of so broad a privilege, on top of various other favorable pronouncements for the Jews—even of those of Spain—and other restrictions of the zealous preachers,[79] appears to have aroused a storm of protest. Within the year, Pope Martin rescinded the Bull and imposed restrictive regulations.[80] This hostile attitude prevailed, on the whole, till 1429, when it underwent another sudden change. At the beginning of that year, the pope issued a Bull of protection which outdid the *Sicut Judeis* of 1421 in the extent of protection and the number of privileges granted.[81]

There are two striking differences from the usual about this document. One is in the wording of the preamble. The Bull does not begin with the words *Sicut Judeis*, but with *Quamquam Judei*. It expresses the thought that, although the Jews choose to remain obdurate in their refusal to recognize the truth of Christianity, nonetheless the Church tolerates them as witnesses of Jesus and in the hope that Christian kindness will lead them to baptism. The predecessors who granted protection by the usual Bull are mentioned, but not enumerated. The introductory words of *Sicut Judeis* occur somewhat later in the document, as a preface to the actual grant of protection and privilege. The second striking difference between this Bull and *Sicut Judeis* is its use in behalf, not of all Jews, but of the Jews of Italy. Perhaps this accounts for its departure from the customary beginning, namely, that *Sicut Judeis* as a formula had acquired the tradition of universal application. One may speculate on the possibility that the pope, having bound himself in 1421 not to extend this privilege to the Jews of all lands, did not consider it a breach of his promise nor an irritant to zealous Churchmen in other lands to issue a Bull of protection to the Jews of Italy so much more directly under his control.

The rest of the document follows pretty closely the *Sicut Judeis* of 1421, the language being somewhat stronger. But the few new items deserve mention. Inquisitors are warned not to proceed against Jews unless they are found acting contrary to the interests of Christianity. Jews are not to be compelled to listen to a Christian religious service. They may buy and sell houses, land and goods, and carry on other business with Christians. They may send their sons to general schools to study and open schools of their own. They may settle their disputes in their own way, and any civil authorities who judge their lawsuits must be above suspicion of taking the law into their own hands. All this concludes with a rather strong penal clause, although it is stated, of course, that the whole applies to such Jews as do not plot against Christianity.

Not since the days of Gregory I had a pope issued a Bull in favor of the Jews so broad in its outlook or so opposed to the prevalent course of the relationships between the Synagogue and the Church. It was a courageous act for the pope thus to have set himself against the opinion-making preachers and the conciliar party among the Churchmen who, at the Council of Basel, acted to rescind all privileges granted the Jews.[82] Eugenius IV, Pope Martin's successor and apparently just as well disposed to the Jews, followed a more circumspect course. Early in February 1432 he issued a *Sicut Judeis* which harked back to the thirteenth-century model.[83] Following the usual sequence of clauses, if not the exact wording, the Bull offers two novel additions toward the end. One refers to territory under papal government and orders that the collection from the Jews of taxes, subsidies and the like, be made through Jews designated by the Jews themselves. The second new statement, of general application, sets forth the principle that those who do not enjoy the freedom and privileges of a place should not be subjected to reprisals imposed on it, unless, of course, the Jews were the cause of the new burdens. This was not the only protective Bull issued by Pope Eugenius. He repeated several of the favorable clauses included in his predecessor's Bull of 1429, such as the prohibition against stirring up the populace by means of hostile sermons.[84] He even challenged the hostility of the Spanish clergy by coming to the defense of the hard pressed Jews of the Iberian Peninsula.[85] Yet such were the political conditions of the time, of which the pope had to be constantly aware, that he was compelled to change his attitude completely and in 1442 issued a Bull which was as hostile to the Jews as Pope Martin V's of 1429 had been favorable.[86] To be sure, this Bull was directed to Castile and Leon, but the pope's attitude to Jews elsewhere became also considerably cooler than it had been. The pressures for a change of policy had apparently mounted.

There were, to be sure, letters of protection issued by various successors of Eugenius IV during the fifteenth century and more rarely in the centuries which followed. They were directed most often in favor of the Jews of Italy. Thus Nicholas V (1447–1455) showed evidences of vacillating just as his two predecessors had done.[87] So, too, Pope Pius II (1458–1464) harked back to some of the efforts of Martin V to make life easier for Italian Jews.[88] Pope Sixtus IV (1471–1484) made a valiant effort to halt the incitements against the Jews connected with the Simon of Trent ritual murder libel.[89] A century later, Pope Paul III (1534–1549) still went back to the privileges granted by Martin V to the Jews of Poland, Bohemia and Hungary.[90] These and other popes, sometimes in words and more often in spirit, recalled privileges and protective utterances ultimately derived from the Bull *Sicut Judeis*. The Bull itself, however, was not repeated.[91]

5. ITS EFFECTIVENESS

We have seen the Bull *Sicut Judeis* grow from expressions of personal opinion on the part of theologians and popes into an organized statement of Church policy. As such it was used in the course of the twelfth and especially of the thirteenth centuries to define the relations between Jews and Christians. It began as the grant of a privilege to the Jews of Rome by the popes who were their direct sovereigns. Soon Jews elsewhere learned to use it to re-inforce their request for protection from the local authorities. It evidently helped the Jews greatly in times of distress, especially during the period when the popes were the undisputed masters of Church policy, the recognized guides of public morals, and the respected advisors, if not the suzerains, of emperors and kings. Even then the Bull did not stop all persecution, expulsion or forced conversion; but its effectiveness decreased as time went on, because of conditions inherent in the evolving situation of European society and economics, and because of the weaknesses inherent in the Bull itself.

The changes in the position of the Jews during the Middle Ages constitute too vast a subject for discussion here.[92] They became increasingly dependent on emperors, kings and the civil authorities of the towns. They became the pawns of political and economic policy. Their economic usefulness had to be balanced against the political dangers of retaining them as a small but conspicuous minority of a different religious faith. To this was added the situation within the Church during the fourteenth and fifteenth centuries: the crying need for reforming the papacy and the growing power of the monastic orders, exercised through their preaching and exerted through the Inquisition. The religious as well as the secular clergy sought to maintain and extend their emotional hold on the population and could not, therefore, acquiesce in a policy of active toleration, such as the Bull originally implied, and pressed for its reduction to mere theoretical toleration. A theological doctrine calling for a *status quo* in human relations could hardly prevail against the turbulent forces of that day.

The Bull began by asserting that the Jews must continue living under established custom. Nevertheless, popes themselves modified the rules under which Jewish life was to be permitted. The introduction of the Badge was one such change. Innocent III prescribed it at the Fourth Lateran Council; but, aware that it was an innovation, he justified it on the basis of the biblical command of *tzitzit*.[93] This principle of visible separation grew into the prohibition of social contacts and eventually evolved into fixed ghettos.[94] Changes in the regulation of court procedure were another departure from established custom of which the Bull *Sicut Judeis* spoke.[95] The condemnation of the Talmud, first ordered by the Church in the thirteenth century, was certainly a clear interference with the time-honored right of the Jews to practice their religion as guaranteed by the Bull.[96] So, too, was the increasing resort to conversionist sermons by permitting monks to invade synagogues on the Sabbath.[97] Restrictions multiplied, while ancient customs were weakened.

An important example of the Bull's failure to make its point is the nice distinction which the Church drew between forced and voluntary conversion. The statement in the Bull is perfectly clear: baptism must be accepted willingly. Yet the meaning of the thought became doubtful early in the Middle Ages. Pope Leo VII, about the middle of the tenth century, for example, advised the Archbishop of Mainz to hold the threat of expulsion over the heads of the Jews.[98] The clergy at the time of the crusades may or may not have deplored the numerous forced conversions which resulted from those semi-religious movements, but they said nothing about their being invalid, and an anti-pope considered it unheard of for permission to be granted to these forced converts to return to their original faith.[99] The Church claimed that, baptism being a sacrament, it would be blasphemous to think that it could be disregarded. But this was not the difficulty; the real difficulty, as far as the Jews were concerned, was the narrowness of the interpretation of the term "forced." By the end of the thirteenth century, nothing short of death was considered sufficient objection to baptism.[100] The popes, to be sure, continued to plead against the use of force, but they never disqualified the results. They did not, in fact, go beyond a plea in their objections to this and to other violations of the Jewish status outlined in the Bull. The penal clause,[101] contained in this Bull as in practically all others, was rarely, if ever, enforced. No one, as far as one can tell, was actually removed from office or made to suffer excommunication for converting Jews by force or even for the tortures and murders to which they were subjected throughout the bleak years of the Middle Ages.[102]

The final source of weakness which made the *Sicut Judeis* all but inoperative was the statement toward its conclusion which limited its application to such Jews as plotted no injury to the Christian faith. It seems like a natural enough limitation for those days. In effect, however, it opened the doors wide to anyone who plotted against the Jews. With this as an excuse, on the basis of false accusations or exaggerations, any restriction or condemnation could be justified. The bitter invective levelled against the Jews in the Bulls imposing restrictions offers a sharp contrast to the mild and reasonable exhortations of the *Sicut Judeis*.[103]

What was left of the Bull *Sicut Judeis* on the eve of the Renaissance and the Reformation was the one basic principle: Thou shalt not kill them, lest my people forget. . . . It is a fact that the papacy never abandoned this fundamental teaching, largely motivated by theology. The attitude soon to prevail was best exemplified by the anti-pope Benedict XIII, in his Bull of May 11, 1415.[104] After a long series of restrictions calculated to make life for Jews all but impossible, he concludes with an appeal, almost in the words of Gregory I, that the Jews must be attracted to Christianity with kindness and Christians must refrain from molesting them. In this context, the words, which had been so eagerly sought after in the twelfth and thirteenth centuries, sound hollow, dead, a mockery of every hope of humane co-existence. Hardness and restriction eventually won the day everywhere during the Counter-Reformation.

One may conclude that it is an exaggeration to speak of the Bull *Sicut Judeis* as the papal pronouncement that protected the Jews during the Middle Ages. It may have done so in its early days when it still reflected the actual relationship between Christians and Jews. Later protection was the result rather of the general political and economic conditions which, even while undermining the Jewish position, guarded the Jews against total destruction. To the extent to which papal protection was effective, other pronouncements, more direct in their nature, played a greater role, especially those decrees which strengthened the hands of secular and religious princes. Probably the greatest protection offered by the Church was its constant reminder of human decencies and its reference to the Jewish people as an integral part of the Divine Plan. Christianity's unwillingness to surrender completely to its Greek heritage and its retention of its heritage from Judaism thus contributed to the survival of the Jewish people.

NOTES

1. *See* Reginald L. Poole, *Lectures on the History of the Papal Chancery* (Cambridge 1915), pp. 40 f., 117 f. The term *constitutio* must not be confused with "constitution" as used currently.
2. *Corpus Juris Canonici*, Decretalia Gregorii IX, Lib. V, tit. vi, c. ix., where it is headed "Constitutio pro Judeis."
3. For the text, in addition to the *Corpus Juris*, as above, *see* S. Grayzel, *The Church and the Jews in the 13th Century* [hereinafter to be referred to as

C & J] (Philadelphia 1933), pp. 92–5, no. 5. Apart from additions and substantial modifications, which will be discussed below, this text varied slightly in wording in every issue.

4. At this point those predecessors were listed who were credited with the issuance of the Bull. Sometimes one or more names were overlooked.

5. Migne, *PL,* 69, col. 561; *cf.* James Parkes, *Conflict of the Church and the Synagogue* (London 1934), pp. 208 ff.

6. For imperial Roman legislation on the subject of synagogue building see *Codex Theodosianus* 16. 8. 25 and 27. *Cf.* Parkes, *ibid.,* p. 182. *See also* Peter Browe, "Die Judengesetzgebung Justinians" in *Analecta Gregoriana,* vol. viii (Rome 1935).

7. September/October, 591: Jaffe 1157; *Monumenta Germaniae Historica (MGH),* Regesta Gregorii I, Bk. II, no. 6.

8. To Bishop Victor of Palermo, in June, 598: Jaffe 1514; *MGH,* Reg. Greg. I, Bk. VIII, no. 25 — Sicut Judaeis. . . . The same thought, using more or less the same words, is expressed in another letter of Gregory dealing with the same subject: *see* Jaffe 1562; *MGH, ibid.,* Bk. IX, no. 38.

9. *See,* for example, Marcel Simon, *Verus Israel* (Paris 1948), especially chapter viii, "L'antisemitisme chrétien."

10. *See* Bernhard Blumenkranz, *Die Judenpredigt Augustins* (Basel 1946), pp. 186 ff.

11. *De civitate Dei* 18, 46. In KJ the verse reads: "Slay them not, lest My people forget; scatter them by Thy power and bring them down, O Lord our shield." *Cf.* Blumenkranz, *op. cit.,* p. 208.

12. Migne, *PL* 69, quoted in the note to col. 56.

13. *Ibid.*

14. *MGH, ibid.,* Bk. I, no. 34; Jaffe 1104; March 16, 591, to the Bishop of Terrason in southern France. Again, in June of the same year, he wrote to another bishop warning him that converts by force were likely to revert to their old religion and become more devoted to it than ever: *MGH, ibid.,* Bk. I, no. 45; Jaffe 1115. Cf. *ibid.,* Bk. IX, no. 195; Jaffe 1722, where Pope Gregory says that overzealous clerics must be made to understand that *magis utenda est ut trahatur ab eis velle, non ut ducantur inviti,* which is an almost verbal precursor of the statement in the bull *Sicut Judeis.*

15. *MGH, ibid.,* Bk. XIII, no. 15; Jaffe 1879; November, 602, to the Bishop of Naples.

16. *MGH, ibid.,* Bk. IX, no. 228; Jaffe 1757; August, 599.

17. Migne, *PL,* 132, col. 1083; Aronius, *Regesten zur Geschichte der Juden im fränkischen und deutschen Reiche bis zum Jahre 1273* (Berlin 1902), no. 125; *cf.* Salo W. Baron, *A Social and Religious History of the Jews* (2nd ed., New York and Philadelphia 1957), vol. iv, p. 6.

18. Migne, *PL* 146, p. 1386; Mansi, *Sacrorum Conciliorum Amplissima Collectio,* XIX, col. 964; Jaffe 4528, addressed to all the bishops of Spain.

19. *Cf.* Bernhard Blumenkranz, *Juifs et Chrétiens dans le monde occidental: 430–1096* (Paris 1960), esp. pp. 97 ff.

20. For such occurrences in Rome, *see* the description of the turbulence in that city in Vogelstein u. Rieger, *Geschichte der Juden in Rom* (Berlin 1896), vol. i, pp. 218–21.

21. Guido Kisch, *Forschungen zur Rechts- und Sozialgeschichte der Juden in Deutschland während des Mittelalters* (Zurich 1955), pp. 17 f.

22. Guido Kisch, *The Jews in Medieval Germany* (Chicago 1949), p. 109; James Parkes, *The Jews in the Medieval Community* (London 1938), p. 106; Aronius, no. 314a, p. 141.

23. Migne, *PL* 148, col. 841. Aronius, no. 204: . . . *quod inauditum est et prorsus nefarium.* But the anti-pope had no word of regret for the method by which the conversion had been obtained.

24. *Cf.* F. X. Seppelt, *Papstgeschichte* (Munich 1949), pp. 112 ff.

25. Simon Dubnow, *Weltgeschichte des jüdischen Volkes* (Berlin 1926), vol. iv, p. 407, takes the view that the Bull was issued for the benefit of the Jews in general. Most others who dealt with the subject of the Bull *Sicut Judeis* made the same assumption: *cf.* Peter Browe, *Die Judenmission im Mittelalter und die Päpste* (Miscellanea Historiae Pontificiae, vol. vi, Rome 1942), pp. 235 f. Aronius, no. 313a inclines to connect its first issuance with events in France.

26. The first Bull extant is that credited to Pope Alexander III (1159–81).

27. Vogelstein und Rieger, pp. 219 ff. Baron, *op. cit.* pp. 7 f. and n. 3 on pp. 235 f., while agreeing that it was given at the request of the Roman Jews, connects it with fears concerning possible enactments at the approaching First Lateran Council in 1123. If so, it would seem to indicate that the Jews of Rome were acting in behalf of all the Jews of Europe.

28. Walter Holtzmann, "Zur päpstlichen Gesetzgebung über die Juden im 12ten Jahrhundert" in *Festschrift Guido Kisch* (Stuttgart 1955), p. 221 n. 3, points out that non-Roman recepients of the Bull are first mentioned in connection with the Bull issued by Pope Alexander III.

29. Aronius, nos. 242–249.

30. Vogelstein u. Rieger, *op. cit.*, p. 223.

31. Jaffe 13973; Aronius, no. 313a.

32. Vogelstein u. Rieger, *op. cit.*, p. 225. Holtzmann, *loc. cit.*, mentions the archbishops of Reims and of Canterbury among those to whom the Bull was addressed. Baron, *op. cit.*, p. 238 n. 9, doubts the connection with the approaching meeting of the Third Lateran Council. This does not invalidate the possibility of Yehiel's intervention with the pope in behalf of the more distant Jewish communities.

33. Jaffe 16577; Aronius, no. 334; *see* n. 2 above.

34. Aronius, no. 344. He, like his predecessor, is mentioned in the *Sicut Judeis* of Innocent III.

35. Potthast 834; *C & J*, pp. 92 ff., no. 5.

36. Potthast 5616; *C & J*, pp. 144 f., no. 35.

37. Potthast 9893; *C & J*, pp. 218 f., no. 81.

38. *Cf.* Seppelt, *op. cit.*, p. 142.

39. Potthast 12315; M. Stern, *Päpstliche Bullen über die Blutbeschuldigung,* pp. 14 ff.; *C & J*, pp. 260 ff. and 274 f., nos. 111 and 118. *Cf.* G. Bondy and F. Dworsky, *Zur Geschichte der Juden in Böhmen, Mähren und Schlesien von 906 bis 1620* (Prague 1906), vol. i, pp. 25 ff.

40. Fidel Fita, *España Ebrea* (Madrid 1890), part II, p. 87, drawn from *Boletin de la Real Academia de la Historia,* 36–7 (1900), pp. 16–18.

41. N. Ferorelli, *Gli Ebrei nell' Italia meridionale* (Turin 1915), p. 53; Vatican Archives, Armarium II, 38, fol. 22r–24v.

42. The existence of such a document has as yet not been indicated. For Pope Clement III's attitude toward the Jews, *see* S. Grayzel, "Jewish References in a Thirteenth-Century Formulary," *JQR,* vol. xlvi (1955), 58.

43. Bondy and Dworsky, *op. cit.,* no. 27; Stern, *Päpstliche Bullen,* pp. 18–22; *idem, Urkundliche Beiträge,* pp. 5–7; L. Ennen, *Geschichte der Stadt Köln* (Cologne 1863), p. 64.

44. B. and G. Lagumina, *Codice diplomatico dei Giudei di Sicilia* (Palermo 1884–1909), vol. i, pp. 119 ff., no. 82.

45. *Ibid.,* pp. 117 f., no. 81.

46. Vatican Archives, Armarium XXXI, 72, fol. 307v., gives a *Sicut Judeis* in which the last two predecessors mentioned are Nicholas and Honorius, thus indicating that Honorius IV issued the Bull and that this was a copy of the document prepared for Nicholas IV who was Honorius IV's immediate predecessor. Nicholas IV is also mentioned as the last in the series of predecessors in the Bull issued by Clement VI: Regesta Vaticana 187, fol. 21r.; *cf.* Reynaldus, ad a. 1348, 33. *See* n. 68 below.

47. On the condition of the Roman Jews during the last decade of the 13th century, *see* Vogelstein u. Rieger, *op. cit.,* pp. 252–8.

48. For a brief reference to fees *see* R. L. Poole, *The Papal Chancery* (Cambridge 1915), p. 134. On expenses incurred in the process of asking for papal protection *see* Grayzel, *JQR,* vol. xlvi (1955), 64.

49. *See above,* n. 12.

50. *C & J*, pp. 92 f.

51. Potthast 2373, January 16, 1205; *C & J*, p. 104.

52. Potthast 5257; *C & J*, p. 142, no. 32.

53. *C & J*, pp. 218 f., no. 81 and n. 2; and *ibid.,* pp. 226 ff., Potthast 10243.

54. Graetz, *Geschichte,* vol. vii, p. 92 and n. 4 at end of the volume.

55. Pope Innocent IV had issued his *Sicut Judeis* in October 1246. The following May he sent a series of letters concerning the ritual murder charge: to the Archbishop of Vienne, on May 28, 1247: *C & J*, pp. 262, no. 113 and 114; to the King of Navarre and Count of Champagne, June 12 and July 6, 1247: *ibid.,* nos. 115 and 117; to the Archbishops and Bishops of Germany, July 5, 1247: *ibid.,* no. 116.

56. *C & J*, pp. 274, no. 118.

57. Graetz, *Geschichte,* vol. vii, p. 148, calls them an almost annual occurrence. Boleslav of Poland prohibited the libel in 1264: *cf.* Aron Eisenstein, *Die Stellung der Juden in Polen im 13ten und 14ten Jahrhundert* (1934),

pp. 34 ff. On the possibility, if not the likelihood, of Pope Clement IV crediting the libel, *see* Grayzel, "Formulary etc.", *JQR,* vol. xlvi (1955), 58 ff.

58. *Cf.* Kisch, *The Jews in Medieval Germany,* pp. 260 ff.

59. Stern, *Blutbeschuldigung,* pp. 18–23; *idem, Urkundliche Beiträge,* pp. 5–7; Bondy and Dworsky, *op. cit.,* vol. i, pp. 32–4, no. 27.

60. The Bull *Turbato corde* was repeatedly issued at the request of inquisitors in various parts of Europe: Clement IV, 1267, Potthast 20095, I. H. Sbaralea, *Bullarium Franciscanum* (Rome, 1759–68), III, 127; Gregory X, 1274, Potthast 20798, Th. Ripoll, *Bullarium FF. Praedicatorum* (Rome, 1729–40), I, 517; Martin IV, 1281, Bibliothèque Nationale, Fond Doat 37, fol. 193 ff., *cf. REJ,* III, p. 218, no. 53; Nicholas IV, 1288, Potthast 22795, E. Langlois, *Les Registres de Nicholas IV,* p. 62, no. 322, *REJ,* III, p. 220, no. 66; again in 1290, Potthast 23391, *Registres,* p. 511, no. 3186. An extract from a Bull bearing on the same subject, which may have been a repetition of *Turbato corde* issued by Pope Boniface VIII, found its way into the *Corpus Juris Canonici,* Decretalium lib. V, tit. II, c. xiii. *Cf.* Browe, *Judenmission,* pp. 258 f. Note that this Bull by Martin IV was issued only a few months before the *Sicut Judeis* under discussion.

61. Lagumina, *op. cit.,* pp. 117 f., no. 81.

62. The ecumenical Council of Vienne was held from October 1311 to May 1312. The decision was included in the Clementinarum lib. II, tit. VIII, c. 1.

63. Every pope who reigned for any length of time during the second half of the 13th century, with the exception of Clement IV, and most of those of the 14th century as well, had occasion to issue protective pronouncements for the Jews.

64. The Jews would submit the documents for inspection by the local authorities, who would then incorporate these documents in an edict of their own. For example, Rudolph of Hapsburg, in 1275, acknowledged and ratified the Bull *Sicut Judeis* as issued by Pope Gregory X, with its long addition on the subject of ritual murder, as well as the Bull *Lachrymabilem Judeorum* which had been issued by Pope Innocent IV in 1247 and which bore on the same subject; *cf.* Stern, *Blutbeschuldigung,* p. 13 and the references there cited. A similar *Vidimus* is mentioned in Bondy and Dworsky, *op. cit.,* pp. 35–6. The same volume cites an earlier instance, in no. 25, pp. 23–8, where King Premysl-Ottakar II of Bohemia acknowledges seeing and ratifies the *Sicut Judeis* of Innocent IV and the same pope's Bull *Obviare non credimus,* directing the Bishop of Würzburg to oppose the mistreatment of the Jews in his diocese (September 25, 1253: C & J, pp. 292 ff., no. 132). On the other hand, King Martin and Queen Maria of Sicily, on June 28, 1392, acknowledged and ratified the *Sicut Judeis* of Pope Nicholas III of 1278, with no other Bull appended: Lagumina, *op. cit.,* no. LXXXII.

65. *Exhibita nobis,* June 13, 1299, for the Jews of Rome and the same on July

7, 1299, for the Jews of the Comtat Venaissin: Digard, Faucon, Thomas et Fawtier, *Les Registres de Boniface VIII*, vol. ii, cols., 412 and 488, nos. 3063 and 3215: ... *vos asserentes potentes, publicationem huiusmodi vobis aliquando facere denegant, sicque vobis ex hoc debite defensionis facultas subtrahitur* ...

66. Pope John XXII had occasion to speak out for the protection of the Jews when he urged both the civil and ecclesiastical authorities to take strong measures against the participants in the Shepherds' Crusade in 1320: *cf.* S. Grayzel, "References to the Jews in the Correspondence of John XXII," *HUC Annual*, vol. xxiii (1950–1), part 2, pp. 47–52, nos. x–xiii. No. xiii contains the phrase *specia ius sunt in testimonium catholice fidei reservati*. Pope Benedict's efforts to protect Jewish life seem limited to the one instance in 1338 when the Jews of a number of towns in Bavaria were accused of ritual murder and desecration of the Host. The pope suspected that it was a plot and that some of the clergy were involved. He asked Albert of Austria to investigate. *Cf.* Raynaldus ad a. 1138 §18–20; J. M. Vidal, *Les Registres de Benoit XII, Lettres closes et patentes*, p. 571 f., no. 1966.

67. *Sicut Judeis*, July 4, 1348: Raynaldus as a. 1348 § 33 ; Reg. Vat. 187, fol. 21r.

68. October 1, 1348: A. Lang, *Acta Salzburgo-Aquilajensia* (Graz 1903), vol. i, pp. 301–2; Reg. Vat. 187, fol. 20v–21r. Raynaldus, *u.s.*, combines the two Bulls.

Clement VI issued one other Bull on the subject of events connected with the Black Death and mentioning the Jews. It was addressed to the Archbishop of Magdeburg and dealt specifically with the Flagellants, asking for their repression along with the laymen and the clerics who had joined them: *Inter solicitudines*, October 20, 1349; G. Schmidt, *Päpstliche Urkunden und Regesten* (Halle 1886), no. 172; Reg. Vat. 143, fol. 94v–96r.

69. June 7, 1365: Bull. Rom, vol. iii, part II, p. 327; Reg. Vat. 254, fol. 36r. On the position of the Jews of France *see* Parkes, *Community*, pp. 372 f.

70. Browe, *Judenmission*, p. 235, concludes that such a Bull was issued by basing himself on a calculation made by M. Kayserling, *Geschichte der Juden in Portugal* (Leipzig 1867), p. 38. The calculation does not appear convincing. It is in any case unnecessary, since Boniface IX appears among the predecessors enumerated by Eugenius IV in his Bull issued in 1432 as given in Neubauer's note in *JQR*, o.s., vol. ii (1890), 530, though omitted in Stern, *Beiträge*, p. 43, no. 34. Among Boniface IX's many favorable pronouncements were: for the Jews of Velletri, *Licet Judei*, July 12, 1401: Reg. Lat. 89, fol. 185v–186r; for the Jewish settlers in Calabria, *Etsi Judeorum*, June 26, 1403: Reg. Lat. 108, fol. 99r.–v.; for the Jews of Rome, guaranteeing their peaceful possession of property, *Religioni convenit*, in 1403: Vernet, "Le Pape Martin V et les Juifs," *Revue des Questions historiques*, vol. 51 (1892), no. 68.

71. Konrad Eubel, "Zu dem Verhalten der Päpste gegen die Juden," *Römische Quartalschrift*, 13 (1899), p. 30, no. 2.
72. *Ibid.*, 17 (1903), p. 184, no. 3.
73. Addressed: *Universis Judeis utriusque sexus ubilibet commorantibus: Quamvis potius*, August 1, 1406: Reg. Vat. 334, fol. 186v.
74. *Cf.* L. Elliott Binns, *The Decline and Fall of the Medieval Papacy* (London 1934), pp. 202–4; Seppelt, *Papstgeschichte*, pp. 183 ff.
75. Salomon Kahn, *Une Bulle inédite de Martin V* (Nimes, n.d.), p. 4. On the influence of King Sigismund *see* Max Simonsohn, *Die kirchliche Judengesetzgebung im Zeitalter der Reformkonzilien von Konstanz und Basel* (Breslau 1912), p. 20.
76. Vernet, in the article cited above, lists 84 items.
77. Stern, *Beiträge*, no. 11; Raynaldus, ad a. 1419, § 2; Simonsohn, *op. cit.*, p. 23, gives the date as January 31; Vernet, *op. cit.*, p. 411, no. 9. The preamble also contains the phrase *quia imaginem Dei habent*. This *Sicut Judeis* was not as inclusive as the one given by Pope Martin at Constance, on February 12, 1418, *Quamvis potius*, addressed to the Jews of Germany and Savoy in response to their petition seconded by King Sigismund. The papal Bull approved a highly favorable list of privileges granted them by the papal vice-chamberlain Ludovicus Alamandi. *See* Stern, *op. cit.*, nos. 9, 10; Vernet, *op. cit.*, nos. 5, 6.
78. Stern, *op. cit.*, no. 21; Vernet, *op. cit.*, no. 24; Raynaldus, ad a. 1422, § 36; dated February 20, 1422.
79. *Cf.* Stern, *op. cit.*, nos. 12, 16, 17; Vernet, *op. cit.*, nos. 19, 21, 22, 22b, 22c. On Martin's relieving the Jews of Spain from the restrictions imposed on them by the anti-pope Benedict XIII, see Stern, *op. cit.*, no. 18; Vernet, nos. 17, 18.
80. For the pressure brought on the pope and for the rumors that became current that he had been bribed by the Jews, see Simonsohn, *op. cit.*, pp. 28–32. For the recall of the favorable Bull, see Stern, *op. cit.*, nos. 24, 25, 26; Vernet, *op. cit.*, nos. 28, 29, 32, 48, 48b.
81. *Quamquam Judei*, February 13, 1429: Stern, *op. cit.*, no. 31; Vernet, *op. cit.*, no. 52.
82. For the Council of Basel, which met in July 1431 and therefore soon after Martin's death, *see* Simonsohn, *op. cit.*, pp. 37–45.
83. Stern, *Urkundliche Beiträge*, no. 34. Only the predecessors of the 13th century are mentioned.
84. *Ibid.*, nos. 35, 38.
85. *Ibid.*, no. 40.
86. Simonsohn, *op. cit.*, pp. 50–4; Vogelstein u. Rieger, *op. cit.*, vol. ii, pp. 11 f.; Raynaldus ad a. 1442 § 15.
87. Stern, *Beiträge*, nos. 30, 40, 41, especially the last which repeats some of the items mentioned in the protective Bulls of his two predecessors on the subjects of preaching and conversion of minors. *See*, on the other hand, the harsh Bull surrendering to John of Capistrano: *Super gregem*, June 23,

1447, in U. Hüntermann, *Bullar. Franciscanum* (n.s.), vol. i, pp. 540–2, no. 1072; also the specific abrogation of Martin V's and Eugenius IV's privileges: March 1, 1451, in Raynaldus, ad a. 1451 § 5. *Cf.* Strack, *The Jews and Human Sacrifice*, p. 257.

88. *Humilibus supplicum*, July 27, 1459, A. Pezzana, *Storia della città di Parma* (Parma 1847), vol. iii, app. VII.

89. *Licet inter causas*, October 10, 1475, in Martene et Durand, *Amplissima Collectio*, vol. ii, cols. 1516 f.

90. Vernet in *RQH*, no. 84.

91. Cardinal Ganganelli, subsequently Pope Clement XIV, in his report on the ritual murder libels in Poland which he made to Pope Clement XIII (1758–1769), cited the *Sicut Judeis* of Innocent IV and the longer version of it issued by Gregory X. *See* Cecil Roth, *The Ritual Murder Libel and the Jew* (London 1935).

92. The literature is too vast for citation at this point. Two basic books are: Otto Stobbe, *Die Juden in Deutschland während des Mittelalters* (Leipizig 1902), and J. E. Scherer, *Die Rechtsverhältnisse der Juden in den deutsch-österreichischen Ländern* (Leipzig 1901); *cf.* Herbert Fischer, *Die verfassungsgeschichtliche Stellung der Juden in den deutschen Städten während des 13ten Jahrhunderts* (Breslau 1951). Guido Kisch, in his *The Jews in Medieval Germany* (Chicago 1949), sums up the subject from a new angle and gives the relevant literature. Much of it to the 13th century is presented in Baron, *A Social and Religious History of the Jews* (2nd ed., New York 1957), vol. iv. For the Iberian states, *see* F. Baer, *Studien zur Geschichte der Juden im Königreich Aragonien während des 13ten u. 14ten Jahrhunderts* (Berlin 1913), and his work on *The Jews in Christian Spain*, in Hebrew and in English.

93. *C & J*, p. 308, no. 10: *cum et per Moysen hoc ipsum eis legatur injunctum.*

94. The prohibition for Jews to have Christian servants and nurses (*cf.* Gregory IX, *Sufficere debuerat*, March 5, 1233: *C & J*, p. 198, no. 69) was gradually broadened and intensified until a ghetto was adumbrated for Carpentras by Gregory XI (*Cum Judei*, September 7, 1376: *Reg. Vat.* 288, fol. 257), compelling the Jews to live separately as they had chosen to live prior to the Black Death. The development reached its culmination in the Bull *Etsi doctoribus gentium* by Anti-Pope Benedict XIII (May 11, 1415) which extended the prohibition to all contacts, economic as well as social, and practically called for a boycott to the death (*cf.* Simonsohn, *op. cit.*, pp. 3–16; Amador de los Rios, *Historia de los Judios de Espana y Portugal* [Madrid 1876], vol. ii, pp. 651 ff.). Gradually the restrictions of this frightful pronouncement became established, despite the objections to it on the part of many of the popes during the 15th century, as indicated above, until it triumphed in terms of expulsion—total expulsion in the case of Spain and partial expulsion to a ghetto in various places in Germany and Italy.

95. The Third Lateran Council ordered that a Christian must be admitted to

testify against a Jew (Decretalia Greg. IX, Lib. II, tit. xx, c. 21; *C & J*, p. 297). By the time of Gregory X, the situation had so far changed that the pope had to insist on the admissibility of Jewish evidence (*see* n. 59 above). Nicholas V, in one of his repressive Bulls in which he returned to the attitude of the Anti-Pope Benedict XIII (February 25, 1450: Stern, *Beiträge,* no. 46) forbids the testimony of Jews against Christians. Calixtus III, on May 28, 1456, prohibited Jews from testifying against Christians, but permitted Christians to testify against Jews (*Si ad reprimendos: Bullar. Romanum,* vol. iii, pt. 3, p. 76).

96. Gregory IX, *Si vera,* June, 1939: *C & J,* nos 95–8; Innocent IV, *Ad instar,* August 12, 1247: *ibid.,* no. 119 and note. *See* further for the 13th century: Clement IV, *Dampnabili perfidia Judeorum,* July 15, 1267: Potthast 20081; Ripoll, *op. cit.,* vol. i, p. 487. Honorius IV, *Nimis in partibus,* November 18, 1286: Potthast 22541; Raynaldus, ad a. 1286 § 25. In the 14th century, the inquisitor Bernard Gui, in 1319, had all copies of the Talmud confiscated and burned in southern France (Ph. Limborch, *Historia Inquisitionis* [Amsterdam 1692], pp. 273 ff.). John XXII ordered its confiscation, on September 4, 1320, following the example of Clement IV: *Dudum felicis recordationis:* G. Mollat, *Lettres communes de Jean XXII,* no. 12238; Grayzel, *HUC Annual,* vol. xxiii, pt. 2, p. 54, no. xvi. For the condemnation by the Anti-Pope Benedict XIII, *see* Simonsohn, *op. cit.,* pp. 4 f. Benedict put the prohibition of the Talmud at the very head of his list. The Reuchlin-Pfefferkorn controversy and the burning of the Talmud in 1553 are beyond our scope.

97. Interference with Jews in their synagogue worship had developed far beyond the attack with sticks and stones mentioned in the *Sicut Judeis.* James of Aragon for a time permitted Paulus Christianus to preach in synagogues (*cf.* Cecil Roth, "The Disputation of Barcelona," *Harvard Theological Review,* vol. xliii [1950], p. 140; Bzovius, *Hist. Eccl.,* ad. a. 1263, no. 16). For similar permission by Louis IX of France, *see* U. Robert, *REJ,* III (1881), p. 216, no. 40. The repeated references by the popes of the 15th century to disturbances by preachers may refer to this attempt to impose conversionary sermons on the Jews. Nevertheless, Pope Nicholas V, on December 20, 1447, permitted the King of Sicily to compel the Jews to listen to such sermons four times a year: Raynaldus, ad a. 1447 § 22.

98. For this and other examples, *see* Browe, *op. cit.,* pp. 142 f.

99. *See* n. 23 above.

100. *See* the answer of Pope Nicholas III to a question addressed to him by some inquisitors of the Provence about Jews who claimed that they had been baptized in fear of death. They later wanted to return to Judaism and the inquisitors threw them into prison; but they still held their ground. The pope ruled that they were not *absolute et precise coacti.* Cf. Bibliothèque Nationale, Fond Doat 37, fol. 191 ff.; *REJ,* III, p. 217, no. 50. For a case in the early 14th century, *see* Grayzel, "The Confession of a Medieval Jewish Convert," in *Historia Judaica,* vol. xvii (1955), pp. 89–120. On the

interpretation of forced baptism as illicit but not invalid, as set forth by Innocent III in 1201, *see* George LaPiana, "The Church and the Jews," *Historia Judaica,* vol. ix (1949), pp. 129 f.; Browe, *op. cit.,* pp. 237 f.; *C & J,* pp. 100–103, no. 12.

101. The clause which begins *Si quis autem:* . . . "If anyone, being acquainted with the contents of this decree . . ."

102. Some of the minor nobility guilty of such murderous deeds were commanded to disgorge their ill-gotten gains (see *C & J,* pp. 264–7), and in the case of the Shepherds' Crusade, the miserable peasants were ordered destroyed partly because of their attacks on the Jews (*see* Grayzel, *HUC Annual,* vol. xxii, no. x and notes). On the other hand, such preachers of death and destruction as Vincent Ferrer and John Capistrano wielded great influence and were eventually canonized.

103. Even so friendly a pope as Martin V spoke, in his restrictive Bull of 1425 (*Bull. Romanum,* vol. III, part 2, p. 453), of *enormitates et scelera detestabilia* which some Jews dare to commit.

104. *See* n. 94 above.

8

The Crusading Movement in Its Bearing on the Christian Attitude towards Jewry

H. Liebeschütz

The history of western Jewry during the Middle Ages from the time of the Carolingians to the Reformation as established by nineteenth-century scholarship is characterised by a downward trend to isolation and degradation. Whilst under Charlemagne Jewish long-distance merchants had provided the royal court and the nobility with luxury goods from the Mediterranean basin, the function of Jewish trade became gradually more and more marginal; at the end of the epoch moneylending on a small scale and pawnbroking formed the main basis of their existence.

Recent research has somewhat qualified this picture. Dr. C. Roth has put an end to any illusion that the early centuries of our civilisation, the Dark Ages, brought security to the Jewish communities; and Prof. Kisch has made use of his comprehensive and profound knowledge of German legal literature to prove that the position of Jews, both in civil and criminal law, was still comparatively normal in the middle of the four-teenth century. But these contributions to a closer understanding of a complex period do not necessitate any fundamental change in interpre-tation.[1] It remains true that the desperate state of European Jewry at the beginning of the modern period had its roots in those three centuries after 1000, when increased population, new techniques of economic exchange, and forms of social organisation adapted to less primitive conditions had brought about an age of expansion.[2] The radical deteri-oration of the Jewish position from the end of the thirteenth century

Reprinted by permission of the *Journal of Jewish Studies* 10 (1959): 97–111.

may have some connection with the stagnation of economic activities and the retrogression of population figures which are at present being much discussed as an important characteristic of the late Middle Ages. But the fact remains that the origin of this catastrophic tendency can be traced back to the preceding centuries of European expansion and prosperity. It was at this time that Jewry was isolated from the rising class of *entrepreneurs* who created and exploited the new opportunities, and concentrated on moneylending.[3] The contrast to development in the eighteenth and nineteenth centuries, when economic expansion prepared the way for emancipation and assimilation, is striking. We shall perhaps understand this fundamental difference better, when we consider the transformation in the religious life of the people in the West which brought medieval civilisation to its maturity. It is from that point of view that this paper reviews some motives behind the Crusades which had a lasting effect on habits and attitudes in the environment of Jewry.

I

We investigate first the fact that from the year 1000 onwards the idea of Christian society became more concrete in men's minds and became associated with emotions which had not been there before. The front facing the outsider showed a greater coherence than had existed in the early Middle Ages. The introduction of Christianity to the Germanic world during the period of migrations had, as its main basis, an alliance between rulers and Church, by which the Christian cult was established and maintained throughout the lands. Even in the time of Charlemagne, when diverse forces were integrated for the first time, it was still the monarchy through which the Church influenced society.[4] The change brought about during the eleventh century meant a more direct and intimate contact between ecclesiastical ideas and institutions on the one hand, and the land-owning class (which established at the same time its character as military nobility) on the other. The impulse for this movement came from political and social conditions in France, where in most regions royal power was almost completely absorbed by the local dynasts; these in great numbers, and of varied importance and rank, lived in their fortified houses throughout the countryside, always in command of armed retainers. Antagonism between neighbours, to be settled by the outcome of private war, was a permanent feature of this society.[5]

In this situation, active prelates felt it to be their duty to "support the commonwealth" or, in less classical and more biblical language, "to protect the peace of the poor, who are gravely suppressed by their rulers."[6] Such intentions led to ecclesiastical legislation in dioceses and provinces. The "poor" and their property were placed under the Church's protection. In this context the word "poor" means all those who, because they were excluded from the privileges of the warrior class, were powerless to safeguard their rights by force of arms. The ecclesiastical leaders were eager to give power to their regulations by securing for them the support of the very class whose activities they wished to curb. After 900 there were not a few noblemen who, in quiet moments, felt the effects of feudal anarchy to be the outcome of human sin, for which those mainly responsible would have to account before the supreme Judge in heaven. It was this attitude which gave the Church the possibility of a new approach to the warrior class. Epidemics and famine after a bad harvest were understood as actions of divine retribution. The teaching of the Bible regarding peace on earth as the fulfilment of God's command made a fresh impact on the mind of the age. It was in this atmosphere that the first religious mass movement in the western Church was brought about. The French prelates convened synods in which the clergy was surrounded by a great number of lay folk, and the barons and knights, carried away by a wave of religious enthusiasm, declared their ready acceptance of the covenants of peace. Men of all strata of feudal society answered with uniform emotion to this call, being greatly stimulated by reports on the miraculous working of relics, which had been collected for these meetings. The biblical idea of God's people had again found concrete representation.[7]

But the dialectic which so often in history has brought about a contrast between intention and effect, had its full play in the ecclesiastical movement of the eleventh century. When the ancient Church had preached *Militia Christi,* it was intended as a paradoxical metaphor. The men of prayer who were described in this way faced death like soldiers in battle, but their way of life had been, in every other respect, in perfect contrast to that of a warrior. But the movement to mobilise religious forces for social betterment and peace made the Church a fighting force in the most literal sense of the word. The peace assemblies had shown the possibility of a direct approach to great numbers of lay people by emotional appeal. After this experience, the idea of rallying the believers against the outsiders became a practical policy. Some assemblies agreed to organise armed resistance against breakers of peace, and we hear of cases in which this programme was followed up.[8] Moreover, the French warrior class developed the ideal of chivalry, which had as the centre of its code the fight in the service of God, and this finally influenced the formation of ruling classes throughout Europe. When in the second half of the eleventh century the Papacy took control of the ecclesiastical reform movement, the conception of *militia Petri* was coined to express the religious vocation of the knights' class. Gregory VII used this idea to mobilise the military forces of western Europe to exercise pressure and even to mobilise them for open war against the monarchy. In this he over-played his hand and finally failed. But the overwhelming success of his second successor Urban II in 1095, when he called for armed pilgrim-age to Jerusalem, proved that the direct contact between Church and warrior class had remained intact.[9] The biblical stories about Israel's fighting in Palestine during the period of the Judges, and especially the conflict of the Maccabees with Antiochus of Syria, became topical as models for the new people of God, fighting on behalf of the right order. The Marchioness Matilda of Tuscany, whose forces fought against the Emperor Henry IV in northern Italy, was praised as the new Jael who was destroying Sisera, and the knight Erlembald, who directed the eccle-siastical rebellion of the artisans in Milan, was styled the new Judas Maccabaeus, because he had taken up the case of God's people against his enemies.[10]

The most lasting result of this development was a stronger feeling of Christian solidarity, which could be mobilised against any whose atti-tude characterised them, in particular circumstances, as outsiders. This possibility would necessarily increase sensitivity towards any group who, of their own will, stood out as permanent antagonists of Christianity. For this attitude Jewry was the classical example in the midst of a world now deeply penetrated in its everyday life by ecclesiastical doctrine.

II

We illustrate this process by a few observations on the interplay of ideas and actions. One of the most important presuppositions of the crusading movement was the fact that, during the eleventh century, the project of unarmed pilgrimage to Jerusalem had become popular—especially among the members of the aristocracy. Already in the thirties this phenomenon had become so striking that people in reflective mood pondered over it, as a change in the world which called for explanation.[11] It was no coincidence that the new trend developed at the very time when ecclesiastical synods legislating for peace were transformed into mass meetings dominated by religious excitement. The "great journey" was the highest achievement of active piety available both to the clergy and to the layman. The pilgrim would expect to receive from Jerusalem and Palestine a palpable contact with the stage on which the history of salvation had been enacted. For the men of this age it was of tremendous significance to experience the decisive spiritual events of the remote past, incorporated into the things of the concrete world and so made accessible to the world of the senses. The pilgrim who saw the reality of the biblical landscape with his own eyes and touched its soil with his own feet, was reassured of the reality of the link between himself and salvation which had been secured through events in that very locality. When, by Urban II's design, the pilgrim became also a warrior with the task of conquering the land of the Bible, a further motive was added: the Christian knight became the soldier and the vassal of his Saviour, and had to fight for the honour of his Lord. The biblical story was being continued, and the knight was enabled to take part in its action. The new active piety of the layman, certainly the product of an ecclesiastical movement, remained nevertheless in contact with feudal thought.[12] The relevance of this trend to the fate of Jewry is obvious. The expedition to Jerusalem, the city which, for Christian piety, stood mainly as a monument of the Saviour's death, would necessarily strengthen feeling against the Jews. The words which a Hebrew chronicler of the time quotes to describe the original intention of Godfrey of Bouillon, one of the leaders of the First Crusade, express this attitude only too well: "He would go on the holy journey while revenging the blood of his Saviour on the blood of Israel, and he would not allow anyone who carries the name of a Jew to escape".[13]

But there was a second group of ideas, which helped to carry the appeal of pilgrimage to Jerusalem and crusade to all classes of the population. Belief in the approaching end of the world had already been part of the religious lore of the ancient Church, but the Fathers had finally come to the conclusion that man must abstain from any speculation as to the date of the final events. The thousand years of the eschatological oracle in St John's *Revelation* were interpreted as the epoch of the Church in the world, and knowledge about the time when the end would come was reserved to God.[14] But the ancient dramatic story of the final conflict between Christian witnesses and the demonic forces incorporated in the Antichrist, continued nonetheless to attract the religious phantasy of men. The intense interest in the life beyond which Christianity brought to every individual, had again and again made people infringe the principle of discretion established by the classical theology of the Church. No devaluation of this form of thought by the failure of calculations and prophecies could endure; readiness to accept the belief in the approaching end of the world was soon restored. The element of messianism which formed a part of this popular belief was an important factor of its vitality. Already in the beginnings of Christian eschatological thought, in St John's *Book of Revelation,* the prophecies about the last days were linked with the conception of the Millennium. In the Latin Church a group of writings was handed down, in which a fictitious author, purporting to have lived in Antiquity, presented well-known facts from the past in the guise of prophecies as a basis for eschatological forecasts. This meant that, as this literature was carried on from one age to the next, the great events of the moment were incorporated into the traditional material.[15] The dramatic conflicts brought about by the course of ecclesiastical reform, especially after the pontificate of Gregory VII, stimulated such adaptation during the last quarter of the eleventh century.

At this epoch an ancient text was enlarged by a typical addition: The messianic emperor of the last days will enforce the baptism of all pagans, and transform their temples into churches. At that moment the Jews will accept conversion and so partake in salvation. Thus all conditions will be fulfilled for the last emperor's journey to Jerusalem, where he will lay down his crown and hand over his empire to God and Christ. In this text the traditional story of the fight with the Antichrist is replaced by the topical theme of the liberation of Jerusalem, summarised by the verse from Isaiah "His tomb will be glorious".[16] The inclusion of Jewry's conversion in the eschatological story goes back, of course, to the famous chapters (ix–xi) in St Paul's *Epistle to the Romans.* There is probably no non-Jewish text that has had a greater impact on Jewish history than these very personal reflections by the Apostle to Gentiles on the parting of the ways between himself and his people.[17]

Another eschatological interpretation of the Crusade shows a certain relationship of type to the text just discussed: here the expedition to Jerusalem is characterised as a preparatory task, necessary for the completion of man's course. It forms part of the version which Abbot Guibert of Nogent, a skilful man of letters, gives of Urban's decisive address at the great assembly of Clermont. The essential idea runs as follows: According to a prophecy in the *Second Epistle to the Thessalonians* (ii:4), the Antichrist will come to Jerusalem and, as his name implies, fight against the Christians—not against pagans or Jews. Consequently the Orient, as the stage whereon the Antichrist has to play his part, must be entirely returned to Christianity before he can appear and so complete the course of the world. Establishment of conformity with Christian belief as sign of the maturity of the human affairs for the coming aeon is again seen as the task in hand.[18]

The identification of Islam with the forces of the Antichrist, most apposite as the myth of the crusading age, had been represented in this literary tradition since the seventh century.[19] We therefore find, about 1100, the Mohammedans described as a type of men who cultivate idols for the purpose of magic. At the same time the French legend of Roland's death and Charlemagne's revenge found its final form as the conflict between Christians and Saracens in the days of the Antichrist.[20]

It is the peculiarity of this form of eschatological thought that the details of its content can be changed, without altering the fundamental tension which it creates in the mind of men. For the Jewish communities this possibility of exchanging the figures in the story made more acute the danger which was latent in every armed expedition against Jerusalem. It needed a small change of emphasis only to transform a voluntary conversion of the Jews at the end of the days, into an impulse to bring about the end of Judaism by every means, including violence and murder.

III

We shall now try to find out how all these trends led to catastrophic action by analysing the circumstances in which the grave persecution of the Rhenish communities originated. Why did it happen just in these regions? Was there a special antagonism between the minority and its environment? It is well known that the events were a terrible surprise for the communities concerned. The report of the anonymous Jewish chronicler has preserved the famous letter written by the "pillars of the world" in Mayence in answer to the French communities, who were terrified by the preparations for the great expedition of armed Christendom. The leaders of German Jewry emphasised their sympathy and reported that they had ordered a day of fasting, to pray for divine intervention in aid of their brethren in danger. But they strongly assert that they themselves in their own lands have not heard anything like the news from France; no sword is hanging over their head.[21] It is easy to take this feeling of security on the eve of a catastrophe as a very strong expression of self-deception. But when we examine the German situation at the time, we must admit that there were factors which make the attitude of the men of Mayence understandable. It is very probable that no religious emotion had changed the surface of life in their surroundings. They lived just outside the borders of the Romance-speaking region, where the crusading movement had swayed the population. The tidal flow running from West to East became weaker as it reached Central Europe. The great armies which carried Urban's plans to success had as their core thousands of knights, organised by the great dynasts in west and south Europe who had handed on to their vassals the Pope's call to action, and had found willing compliance. This kind of mobilisation included Lorraine, the borderland, which belonged politically to the Empire, but by its social structure, recent ecclesiastical development and language also had strong links with the West. It is relevant to our problem that further to the East the German aristocracy remained in a high degree sceptical towards the new ideal of armed pilgrimage and considered the different groups of crusaders passing through the country with suspicion, as people who undertook as certain things which were in fact uncertain.[22] The most obvious reason for this refusal to accept the idea of war motivated by religion was recent experience. During the last two decades before the proclamation of the First Crusade Germany had seen many years of internal warfare, with Henry IV stubbornly resisting the reduction of his royal rights over the Church against the claims of the reformed Papacy and its Canon Law. The Pope's decrees against the King had given a strong impulse to the antimonarchial forces within the nobility. But the consequence of this introduction of religious emotion into the field of feudal politics had been a great increase of knight-fiefs at the expense of the higher nobility, considerable devastations, great disorder in the ecclesiastical administration, and yet no decision. There were at this time still bishops who would not recognise Urban II as the legitimate Pope, and in 1095 Ruthard, the head of the diocese and ecclesiastical province of Mayence, belonged to them.[23]

But the feeling against warlike activity dictated by piety was not restricted to the dwindling ranks of the opposition to the Gregorian Papacy. It was a conservative attitude with deep roots among the prelates of the imperial Church, who, in contrast to France, had formed a political body in association with the crown as their protector for 150 years. The underlying philosophy was formulated about 1030 by a bishop in the western borderlands of the empire, Gerard of Cambrai, whose diocese was under the ecclesiastical jurisdication of the French archbishop of Rheims. He had been urged to join the peace movement which swept France, and to force the nobility of the diocese to subscribe to the oath on the articles of peace. Gerard opposed this demand, because he considered it contrary to the established order of classes, by which Christendom was divided into men responsible for prayers, for agriculture, and for the handling of the sword. And, as he added on another occasion, the ending of war and the vigorous maintenance of peace was the task of kings.[24]

This conservative attitude on the part of the prelates in the imperial Church had prevented them from influencing the secular nobility, their own blood relations, in the same way and with the same vigour as their colleagues in Burgundy and south-west France had influenced their secular neighbours. The Swabian and Saxon nobility had certainly rallied in great numbers to the call of Gregory VII to resist Henry IV by the force of arms, but they had done so for their own reasons, for local interests and traditional rights. They accepted the papal condemnation of the King to justify their own political struggle, but they did not conform to the mental pattern of the western aristocracy which made the Pope's appeal in Clermont successful beyond all expectation. The optimistic attitude taken by the Jewish leaders in Mayence seems, therefore, to have had some reason behind it during the early months of 1096, while the great expedition was in its preparatory stage. The country in which they lived lay outside the movement which was shaking France with its passion. But it was just this situation which accounts for the suddenness of the catastrophe in Germany. The crusading movement in France, under direct control of the Papacy, kept to the rules as they were formulated by Pope Alexander II in 1063, when an enterprise which he organised against the Mohammedans in Spain had led to riots. He had differentiated between the Jews, as subjected infidels who ought to be left in peace, and the Saracens, whose hostility made them objects of a justified attack.

In so doing the Papacy was upholding the ancient principle, already formulated by Gregory I, that no conversion of the Jews ought to be attempted by force and violence.[25] For the great enterprise in the Orient the continuation of this policy was of considerable importance. The expedition had as one of its main conditions of success the preservation of strict discipline on the long journey through Christian, but not too benevolent countries. The task would have been made very much more difficult if, right at the beginning, the leadership had given way to the instincts and emotions of armed men against the almost defenceless and prosperous Jewish communities in their path. The blow which the French communities had foreseen did not, finally, fall on them, because the leader of the feudal army obeyed the rules of the Papacy. Even Geoffrey of Lorraine followed an order of Henry IV not to touch the Jews, because he knew that the excommunicated Emperor was, on this point, in agreement with the *curia:* the duke was content to receive from the Jews material help for his expedition.[26]

But considerations of this type did not operate with the so-called Peasants' Crusade which developed quite unexpectedly in the West, parallel with the mobilisation of the feudal host. It spread mainly from man to man: which means that it was, by its very nature, remote from effective control in accordance with any national plan. The eremitical movement, which during the last decades of the eleventh century had reached France from Italy, had introduced the preaching of radical decisions to the countryside and created some readiness to leave home-steads and fields. Economic factors worked in the same direction. The autumn of 1095 brought a bad harvest. Prices for supplementary food were beyond the reach of the common man in the countryside. The idea of the great expedition appealed to many as the way out. The peasant sold his cattle to obtain the cash he needed for the journey. People, who on one day stood aloof from the movement and criticised others for their unreasonable selling, changed their mind on the next and gave away their possessions at any price available, in order to join the great journey. Other common people put all their belongings on a cart with two oxen and started on the journey with their family. At every town or castle the children asked whether that was Jerusalem.[27]

It was in this atmosphere that the bands of crusaders crossed the Rhine in April and May 1096, i.e. three months before the organised feudal host had gathered.[28] They came from northern France, the lands between the lower Meuse, the Scheldt, and England, and carried the movement into a land where prosperous communities of infidels, forming a long barrier in the path, seemed to offer an ideal object for an enterprise which would establish the preliminary conditions for the coming of the last days. The restraining influence exercised in France by the papal authority had no direct effect here, because there was no officially inspired movement. Peter of Amiens himself still respected the papal ruling about the Jewish communities, when he appeared with the first groups in Cologne in April and started, not without success, recruiting for the popular crusade. Single noblemen offered themselves as leaders. A month later, when another crowd arriving from western Europe was joined by Rhenish people under the command of Count Emicho, the catastrophe came. When the crusaders spared neither women nor children in their attempt to extinguish Judaism in Christian lands by the dilemma of "baptism or murder", the knights of the archbishop of Mayence refused to assist the victims of the attack; they did not wish to fight on the side of the Jews against Christians.[29] They had not joined the Crusade, but they felt sympathy with the enthusiasm for the sake of religion which caused the massacre. After the event the chronicles of the Crusade explained this catastrophe as the outcome of Emicho's greed, and his band was characterised as an unbearable rabble of men and women. Such judgments are quite independent of the chronicler's sympathies or antipathies towards the Jews.[30] They reflect mainly the fact that the Peasants' Crusade of 1096 had been a dismal failure. The majority of its followers did not penetrate beyond Hungary, where the undisciplined bands dissolved, in conflict with king and population. In contrast to the "wheat" of the army, which conquered Jerusalem, they were but the "husks", and their leaders could not escape responsibility.

IV

In the context of Jewish history the character of men like Emicho is less important than the situation in which the catastrophe developed. The attitude of Urban II, though limited in its power, was sincere and was backed by a tradition which can be traced back to Gregory I and St Paul; and it was continued as the official policy of his successors. But the failure to enforce it in Germany was not really the by-product of historical circumstances. The emotional atmosphere, emphasised by the chroniclers as characteristic of the Peasants' Crusade and the cause of its disorders and failure, was really the sign of a changed situation, no longer controlled by the traditional conceptions. The attitude of the knights in Mayence is significant in this respect. This combination of enthusiasm and primitive instincts was rather a presupposition of the Crusades than their consequence. It was one of the elemental factors at the basis of medieval civilisation as it developed fully during the twelfth and thirteenth centuries. Life in the towns, which in this period became more complex and rose to greater importance in society, gave additional emphasis to the feeling of Christian solidarity as it had developed during the eleventh century, and at the same time made the guidance of the masses a permanent problem for the Papacy. The great city churches, designed especially to hold large audiences listening to popular sermons, became a lasting monument of this situation. In this world the religious outsider was felt much more intensely to be an abnormality than had been the case in the more loosely knit society of the early Middle Ages. The enthusiasm for the Crusades, always intermittent, died down at the end of the thirteenth century.[31] But the image of Jews and Judaism, in which the ancient antagonism of Synagogue and Church had come to life once more, had a much longer life than had the movement which had brought it to the surface.

It remains true that the change of the Jewish position in western society since the eleventh century had social and economic causes, which had no direct link with the *religious* history of the age. The new merchant class arose by shaping the institutions of its environment according to its needs; with its guild organisation it established an efficient instrument both for long distance trade and for the production of marketable goods by a very much increased artisan class. European trade was now carried actively into the basin of the Eastern Mediterranean, whereas in the previous period the chain of Jewish communities had served as the main link. The new organisation of commerce outclassed the older one by its greater efficiency. The change over to moneylending as the main function of the Jews was an escape route, dictated by the pressure of a new economic situation which allowed them precarious opportunities.

But this whole development was determined by the fact that the Jews remained outside the more intensely developed corporate life which carried on this economic expansion of Europe. And there is no doubt that the absence of religious conformity was the barrier on both sides. Both the increase of the emotional element and the deeper penetration of religious motives into everyday life increased the emphasis on group differentiation, while the concentration of the Jews on the money trade, which was outlawed for Christians by the rules of the Church, made the Jew more than ever the symbol of forces to be fought by Christian doctrine and preaching. The consequences were to dominate the fate of Jewry in the western world for many centuries. This aspect of the fully developed medieval civilisation accounts for the contrast between its impact on Jewish history and that of the parallel movement of European expansion during the late eighteenth and nineteenth centuries. Enlightenment and free enterprise gave Jewry the possibility to become an active partner in the transformation of the world by industry and world trade, while the Gothic age, with its papal monarchy, preaching friar and the commercial policy of its guilds and cities, had finally meant exclusion for the Jew. It was the lasting result of the forces which had prepared the minds of men for the Crusade.

NOTES

1. C. Roth, *"European Jewry in the Dark Age: A Revised Picture"* in *HUCA*, XXXII, 2 pp. 151–170. S. W. Baron, *A Social and Religious History of the Jews*, IV (1957) p. 282 has accepted Roth's results with some qualifications. His own most important contribution to this question is offered by his chapter: "The psychological after-effects", pp. 139–149. But Roth in his final conclusions (p. 167) *confirms* the traditional view about the social position of the Jews before and after the crusades. The contrast between their status and function during the Carolingian period and the conditions which developed after the twelfth century are indeed striking. The problem remains to date the turning-point. In this respect the catastrophe of 1096,

despite the gravity of its impact, may be a symptom rather than a cause of the change which had developed during the eleventh century.

2. *Cambridge Econ. Hist.*, II pp., 338–349; 456–458 (1952). F. Roerig, *Die europäische Stadt im Mittelalter* (1955).

3. Y. Renouard, *Les Hommes d'Affaires Italiens du Moyen Age* (1949), p. 38. An early testimony to moneylending as the characteristic function of the Jews is Bernard of Clairvaux' letter (no. 365, Migne *P.L.* 182, col. 564), written in connection with his action to stop the anti-Jewish riots during the preparations for the second crusade in 1146.

4. An attempt to sketch the relationship between popular belief and the ideas behind the ecclesiastical policy of the government in the age of Carolingian Renaissance will be found in *Arch. f. Kultur-gesch.*, XXXIII (1950), pp. 28–32.

5. Marc Bloch, *Société féodale*, II (1940), pp. 194–213. H. Mitteis, *Der Staat des hohen Mittelalters* (1943), pp. 144–155. H. Dannenbauer, *Politik und Wirtschaft in der Kaiserzeit*, in *Grundlagen der mittelalterlichen Welt* (1958), p. 444 f.

6. *Chronicon Cameracense et Atrebatense, Mon. Germ. Hist. S.S.* VII, p. 477, Fulbert of Chartres, *Ep.* 44 Migne *P.L.* 141, col. 224B. L. C. Mackinney, *The People and Public Opinion in the Eleventh Century Peace Movement, Speculum*, 5 (1930). The fundamental discussion of these ecclesiastical experiments to reform society against the background of religious change is by C. Erdmann, *Die Entstehung des Kreuzzugsgedankens* (1935). I may add here that this eminent historian, who died at the end of the war, was an uncompromising and courageous champion of truth under the Nazi rule.

7. Rodulfus Glaber, *Historiarum libri quinque*, IV, cap. 5, Migne *P.L.* 142, col. 678f. The biblical influence is brought out well in the *Hymn on Peace* by Bishop Fulbert, Migne *P.L.* 141, col. 349, *Gaudeat lancea falx, gaudeat spatha/Devenire vomer/Pax ditat imos, pauperat superbos* (cf. *Is.* ii: 4, *Mic.* iv: 3).

8. *Les miracles de Saint Benoit*, ed. E. de Certain (1856), pp. 192–193; discussed by Erdmann, pp. 56 ff.

9. Erdmann, pp. 134–165.

10. Bonizo, *Liber ad amicum* VIII and VI, *Mon. Germ. Libelli de Lite* I, pp. 620, 5; 599,3; a survey in P. Alphandéry, *Les citations bibliques chez les historiens de la première croisade, Revue de l'Histoire des Religions*, 99 (1929), pp. 139–157.

11. Rodulfus Glaber IV, 6, Migne, *P.L.* 142 col. 681f. The whole phenomenon is discussed by E. Joranson, *The great German Pilgrimage of 1064–1065*, in *The Crusades and other historical Essays presented to D. C. Munro* (1928), pp. 3–43.

12. A. Waas, *Politik und Kultur in der Geschichte der Kreuzzüge*, in *Die Welt als Geschichte*, XI (1951) pp. 225–248. The same author's *Geschichte der Kreuzzüge* I/II (1956) contains the most up-to-date bibliography.

13. Solomon bar Simon, in A. Neubauer and M. Stern, *Hebräische Berichte*

über die Judenverfolgungen während der Kreuzzüge, with German translation by S. Baer (1892), p. 87. Criticism of text and translation by I. Elbogen in *Festschrift für M. Philippson,* pp. 6–24; I. Sonne, *R.E.J.,* 96 (1937), pp. 113–156.

14. Augustine, *De civitate Dei,* XX, cap. 7–9. For the interpretation of the famous chapter 20 of *Revelation* and its history, see W. Bousset, *Kommentar zur Offenbarung Johannis* (1906) pp. 56–70.

15. Edited by E. Sackur, *Sibyllinische Texte u. Forschungen* (1898).

16. *Is.* xi: 10. C. Erdmann, *Endkaiserglaube und Kreuzzugsgedanken im 11. Jahrh,* in *Zeitschrift. f. Kirchengesch.,* 51 (1932), pp. 411ff. A. Scharf's recent article in *JJS,* VII (1956), pp. 59–70 on a Hebrew text from the Byzantine world shows well the impact of Christian eschatological expectation on contemporary Jewry. But in the first paragraph of his English text I should like to restore D. Kaufmann's translation "German Jews" for *'ashkenazim* instead of "Franks", which Scharf, following J. Star, prefers. But people who have come in masses with their wives and all their money (p. 60), are Jews, not crusaders; and the objections raised can be solved by a change in the position of the inverted commas.

17. See a recent discussion of these chapters by A. Oepke, *Das neue Gottesvolk* (1950), pp. 213–218.

18. *Gesta Dei per Francos,* II, cap. 4, Migne *P.L.* 156, col. 700A.

19. Ps.-Methodius, introduction and text by Sackur, *op. cit.,* pp. 40; 46; 82; 86.

20. C. D. Munro, *The Western Attitude towards Islam during the Period of the Crusades,* in *Speculum,* VI (1931), pp. 329 ff. K. Heisig, *Geschichtsmetaphysik des Rolandliedes,* in *Zeitschrift. f. Rom. Philologie,* LV (1935), pp. 38–40; 68–71.

21. Neubauer, Stern, Baer *op. cit.,* p. 170.

22. Ekkehard of Aura, *Hierosolymita,* cap. 9. ed. Hagenmeyer (1877), pp. 109 ff.; a parallel text in *Chronicon Universale, Mon. Germ. S.S.* VI, p. 214.

23. Ruthard joined Urban's side when Henry IV made him responsible for his failure to protect the Jews. See A. Hauck, *Kirchengesch.* III (1920), pp. 880, n. 7; and the monograph by Sara Schiffmann, *Heinrich IV und die deutschen Juden zur Zeit des ersten Kreuzzugs,* Berliner Dissert. 1931.

24. *Gesta episc. Canmerac.* II, cap. 27; 32; *Mon. Germ. S.S.* VII, pp. 474; 485. The chronicler confirms the bishop's attitude with the observation that almost none of those who had signed the peace pact remained free from perjury.

25. Alexander II to the Spanish bishops, Migne *P.L.* 146, col. 1386D. *Registr. Gregori I., Mon. Germ. Epist.* I, p. 72; II, p. 183.

26. Neubauer, Stern, Baer, *op. cit.,* p. 88.

27. Guibert, *Gesta Dei per Francos,* III, 3. Migne *P.L.* 156, col. 704B.

28. Albert of Aix, *Liber Christianae expeditionis* II, 26, Migne *P.L.* 166, col. 407. H. v. Sybel, *Gesch d. ersten Kreuzzuges* (1881), pp. 193–212; F. Duncan, *The Peasants' Crusade,* in *Amer. Hist. Rev.* 26 (1921), pp. 450–

453; P. Alphandéry, *La Chrétienté et l'Idée de Croisade* (1954), pp. 43–72.

29. This attitude of the *milites* is described by Analista Saxo, *Mon. Germ. S.S.* VI, pp. 729, 22. The Jewish report (Neubauer, Baer *op. cit.*, p. 95) is shorter, but by comparing the Bishop's servants with the broken reed of *Isaiah* xxxvi: 6, implies the same meaning as does the Christian chronicler. The most recent surveys are by E. Dietrich, *Das Judentum im Zeitalter der Kreuzzüge, Saeculum* III (1952), pp. 94ff; P. Alphandéry, *op. cit.*, pp. 73–79.

30. Bernold, *Chronicon, Mon. Germ. S.S.* V. p. 464, 20; Albert of Aix *op. cit.*, col. 407; Ekkehard, *Hierosolymita op. cit.*, p. 126. Ekkehard's *Chronicon Universale* adduces the well known story that Emicho's soul, after his death during a baronial feud in Germany, had to join a group of souls which appeared in the region of Worms under the fiery burden of the arms by which they had once sinned. *Mon. Germ. S.S.* VI, p. 261.

31. See P. A. Throop, *Criticism of the Crusade. A Study of Public Opinion and Crusade Propaganda* (1940).

9

The Jews in Christian Europe

Lester K. Little

In the eleventh century, when Latin Christendom for the first time achieved a self-conscious unity, there remained within its borders one group of people, the Jews, who were immune to the moral condemnations by the clergy of those who engaged in monetary transactions. It was in the same century that European Jews began to settle in towns, to engage extensively in commerce, and to specialize in the money trade. They gained such a reputation for expertise in the handling of money that they eventually became identified with money and moneylending in the Christian consciousness. And since these were the objects of profound ambivalence on the part of Christians, such an identification carried dangerous risks.

1. MONEYLENDERS

The first millennium of Christian-Jewish relations was marked by an uneasy coexistence, at times tense and hate-filled but rarely violent. In territories controlled by Germanic tribes, where Roman law no longer afforded its protection, the Jews' legal status depended entirely upon the will of the king. During the post-Carolingian period, the Jews came under the control of various feudal lords, ecclesiastical and lay. When the meagre urban and commercial activity of the Carolingian era waned,

Reprinted by permission of Cornell University Press and Grafton Books, a division of William Collins & Sons, U. K., from *Religious Poverty and the Profit Economy in Medieval Europe,* by Lester K. Little, Ithaca and London, 42–57. Copyright © Lester K. Little 1978.

withdrawal to the land became nearly complete. This was necessarily as true of Jews as of anyone else.

While the Jews did not, of course, lose their identity in this period, they probably came nearer to merging into the rest of the European population than at any other time before the nineteenth century. Everywhere Jews settled, they used the local language. If their well-educated leaders knew Hebrew, the fact is no more remarkable than the fact that a few Christians learned Latin; it had little to do with separating a Jewish from a Christian community. Whereas Jews tended to adopt local names, many Christians favoured the use of Old Testament names. Jews did not distinguish themselves by wearing any special clothing, nor did they look different from their Christian neighbours. The historical record, at least, shows that Christian writers did not describe Jews as having any peculiar physical characteristics, and Christian artists did not render Jewish subjects, such as members of the Holy Family, with what they thought to be peculiarly Jewish attributes. There is no trade or profession of the period that one can identify as either a normal or the exclusive Jewish occupation.[1] There were some Jews engaged in commerce—like those mentioned in a tenth-century charter on behalf of 'Jews and other traders' at Magdeburg—just as there were some non-Jewish merchants, as the same phrase from the same charter attests.[2] Like other early merchants, Jewish merchants gave credit and performed rudimentary banking operations. Other Jews owned rural properties and were integrated into the rural economy.

With the fundamental changes in the economy that we have been discussing came a changed status for the Jews, who were selling their rural lands (which had most likely undergone a notable increase in value) and moving to towns. The concern of ecclesiastical authorities as to whether property actually or formerly owned by a Jew is subject to the payment of a tithe testifies to the importance of Jewish property ownership.[3]

In towns the Jews lived together in one street or neighbourhood, as at Worms, where there was a Jewish quarter by the close of the tenth century. The first walled Jewish neighbourhood on record was provided in 1084 by Rudiger, the Bishop of Speyer. In the following century the walled ghetto became a standard feature of the European town.[4] While the Jews continued to know and use the prevailing local language, just as their ancestors had done, many Jewish communities in the twelfth century decided to give instruction in Hebrew to all of their children, girls as well as boys.[5] In such ways the Jewish identity became increasingly distinct.

The same age gave rise to distinctive forms of dress for Jews, such as the tall, conical hat. Christian ecclesiastical legislators sought to remove all doubts and ambiguities by imposing certain external badges as a way of indicating a Jew. Circular yellow patches or else six-pointed stars, about the size of a man's hand, were to be worn conspicuously. The fact that Jews were generally not recognizable by either physical appearance or clothing is confirmed by the insistent demands of church councils, beginning with the Fourth Lateran in 1215, that Jews identify themselves with these badges.[6]

This newly sharpened identity aids in the sketchy process of assembling a notion—it can be little more than that—of the size and locus of the European Jewish population. From before the start of *reconquista,* there had been Jews in Christian Spain. In the tenth century, there were Jewish communities in Catalonia, in Castile, and in the far western part of the peninsula, near Coimbra. Jews owned rural properties in every major principality. In the eleventh and twelfth centuries, they also appeared everywhere engaged in various professions and trades alongside Christians. The most important urban settlements were at Barcelona, Zaragoza, Burgos, and Toledo. Only during the thirteenth and fourteenth centuries did Jews become more and more involved in professional moneylending, and even then not exclusively.[7] Most Italian Jews were concentrated in a few relatively large communities in the South, while the rest were spread thinly over the central and northern sections. When Peter Damian agreed to write a treatise against Jews, he did so reluctantly, preferring to write against the vices of the age, 'for these enemies are always with us, while Jews have now almost ceased to exist.'[8] A traveller to Italy in the 1160s found only two Jews at Genoa, while he claimed that there were twenty Jewish families in Pisa and about 200 in Rome. The number of Jewish people in Venice is set by historians at about 1,000. Prior to the middle of the thirteenth century, there were relatively few Jews in the important communities of northern Italy. From that time on they appeared from countries north of the Alps, often as bankers.[9]

Without interruption since Carolingian times there had been concentrations of Jewish people in the towns along the Rhine and the other rivers of western Germany. They owned and managed arable land; they worked as artisans, merchants, and—already in the eleventh century— moneylenders. The spread of Jews eastward in the twelfth and thirteenth centuries was part of the German drive to colonize the lands to the east; afterwards it resulted from the expulsions from the western kingdoms. The Rhenish communities were also responsible for colonizing the Netherlandish towns. There were Jews in Louvain by 1220 at the latest, and in several neighbouring cities within a few decades; they all seem to have emigrated from Rhineland and, barring a few medical doctors, all were professional moneylenders.[10]

Two hundred and forty twelfth-century Jewish communities have thus far been identified in the territories that comprise modern France. Most of the important northern and north-eastern towns had Jewish residents.[11] The Jews established in England by the Norman conquerors apparently came from Rouen; those still at Rouen in 1096 experienced one of the early pogroms.[12] Reims had a Jewish quarter at least as early as 1103. A Jewry Street with a synagogue and 24 houses owned by Jews ran for a block in the centre of the Ile-de-la-Cité in Paris. Yet there were far more important Jewish populations in the southern towns, especially in Provence and Languedoc. The heaviest concentration of communities was in the Vaucluse; 26 communities lay within a 30-mile radius of Carpentras. Arles, with several hundred Jews, was known for its many distinguished rabbis. Jews figured prominently in the commerce of Marseilles, though for raising capital they had to seek out Christian moneylenders. One of the oldest, largest, and wealthiest communities in the region flourished at Narbonne. At Peripignan, where there is no reference to Jews prior to 1185, a Jewish community appeared and increased to about 300 or 400 people by the late thirteenth century, giving Perpignan one of the largest communities north of the Pyrenees. A very few of these Peripignan Jews were artisans or merchants; nearly all were moneylenders. Peripignan, and Rousillon generally, underwent a considerable expansion at this time, and a large part of the capital and financial talent required was apparently coming from southern French Jewish communities. In a case brought before the court of a small Provençal town in the thirteenth century, the accusation against a Christian usurer stated that there were many Christian usurers in that place who were worse than the Jews. Thus moneylending—hardly an exclusive preserve of the Jews—was becoming the virtually exclusive occupation of Jews.[13]

In England, the Jews held a more conspicuous position in financial matters but could never surpass the Christian moneylenders or escape the immediate and strict control of the king. The strongest European monarchy had been established in England before the effects of the Commercial Revolution were felt there. When the Jews arrived in England, they did so late in the eleventh century under the aegis of the Normans and were made to live together in London near the Tower. Only during the disorderly reign of Stephen (1135–54) did they start to settle elsewhere. When most widely dispersed, towards the middle of the thirteenth century, the Jews were settled in 21 towns and altogether made a community of perhaps 3,000 people. As elsewhere, a few of these people were artisans and merchants, but most heads of families were moneylenders. The principal development for the English Jews came around the year 1180. Until then, Henry II borrowed from them on a modest scale in order to compensate for a lapse in his regular income or to cover an extraordinary expense; apparently Henry repaid these loans. After 1180, Henry tallaged the Jews; that is, he taxed them arbitrarily. An exchequer of the Jews was organized; each Jewish community was to have a leader, a 'priest (or bishop) of the Jews', as he was called, whose duties probably included negotiation of tallages with the royal government. The genius behind this method of collecting revenue lay in the confluence of the following facts: (1) virtually every class and group in English society held loans from the Jews; (2) the Jews had no choice except to a pay a tallage; (3) the only way they could get their money was to insist on payment of debts due; (4) while this insistence would perhaps provoke hostility, the Jews remained under royal protection; and (5) the Jews could thus drain off a layer of money from the population at large and pass it on to the royal treasury without the king's having to get approval to levy a tax or his having to pay the costs of collecting a tax. Therefore the Jews, prior to the development of a general and regular system of taxation, had in effect, if unofficially, become royal tax collectors. Under Henry II and Richard, the arrangement gave satisfaction to all parties involved; its abuse by John eventually frustrated all parties. Considerably smaller tallages were taken from the Jews by Henry III and Edward I; meanwhile these kings sought ways to get taxes by consent and Edward began the policy of borrowing regularly from Italian bankers.[14]

With allowances made for local variations, remarkable changes, begun in the eleventh century, had thus taken place in the condition of European Jewry. Jews entered virtually every phase of the new commercial activity, including moneylending. 'All Jews,' observed Hermann of Cologne in the following century, 'are becoming involved in commerce.'[15] But that streak of exclusiveness that began to appear in various merchant guilds had the effect of restricting Jews more and more to the field of finance, where they were allowed to operate, though not without competition and a strong measure of control.[16]

By the thirteenth century, the Jews had become a people—still very small in number—living in the midst of Latin Christian society and almost exclusively in towns; practising a religion different from the prevailing one; being distinguished by certain forms of clothing and badges; increasingly self-conscious about its own spiritual and cultural heritage; and in disproportionate numbers deeply involved in the money trade. This involvement placed the Jews in a peculiar situation vis-à-vis Christians.

2. INFERIORS

The relative stability and charity that characterized Christian-Jewish relations in the post-Carolingian era began to deteriorate in the eleventh century. This deterioration is seen in numerous instances of unrestrained physical violence directed against individual Jews or against entire Jewish communities. Deterioration is seen, also, in the practice of forced baptism and its concomitant executions and suicides. It is seen in the many varieties of insult that Christian society added to the injuries it had inflicted upon the Jews. Some insults were sanctioned by popular myth, others by formal public ceremony. Finally, an age relentless in its pursuit of precise legal definitions gave expression to these deteriorated relationships in the form of new laws, new constitutions, and new legal principles.

In the years 1009 and 1010 the Jews of Orléans and Limoges were ordered to choose either to go away, to be converted to Christianity, or to be killed. Practically none was converted but many apparently fled, and a few took their own lives.[17] The unusual phenomenon of a Christian being converted to the Jewish religion was itself the cause of an expulsion. When a duke's chaplain was converted in 1012, the Emperor Henry II expelled the Jewish community from Mainz. Henry's gesture can be interpreted as a warning to potential Jewish proselytizers, but perhaps it was also an angry admission of humiliation at the fact that a relatively important cleric had given in to the 'errors of the Jews.'[18]

At Toulouse in the eleventh century, there was a legend about some Jewish traitors who, more than a century earlier, had given over their town to the advancing armies of Islam. One can understand that civic pride might keep alive such a story of defeat, if there were a clearly established case of treachery involved. But it was a curious civic pride that at Toulouse invented a defeat—for the Moors never took Toulouse —in order to punish the descendants of the supposed traitors. In any event, to perpetuate the memory of this tale, tradition ordained that a Jew stand before the Basilica of St Stephen on Easter Day and be ceremoniously struck in the face; one year the appointed Jew died from the blow. This cruel practice came to an end early in the twelfth century, but only through commutation by an annual money payment to the clergy. Similar traditions and their commutations are recorded at Béziers, Arles, and Chalon-sur-Saône.[19]

In Castile, in a moment of governmental weakness shortly after the death of Sancho the Great in 1035, the burghers of Castrojeriz launched an attack against the neighbouring town of Mercatillo. They killed 60 Jews and forced the remaining Jews to return with them to Castrojeriz.[20] The Spanish Reconquest provided the occasion for knights to pass through southern France and Catalonia; a group of knights on their way through in 1063 attacked several Jewish communities, killing and despoiling as they went. At Narbonne, the archbishop's Jewry was open to these armed pilgrims; indeed the archbishop apparently did nothing to deter them in their cruel mission. The viscount, on the other side of the city, protected his Jews against the outsiders, as did members of the Spanish clergy generally. Pope Alexander II condemned the behaviour of the Archbishop of Narbonne and the knights, and he lauded the viscount and the Spanish clergy. He reminded all parties of God's displeasure at any person's spilling of human blood. Yet he went on to distinguish the case of the Jews, who live peacefully among Christians and whom the mercy of God had predestined to be saved, from that of the Saracens, who had persecuted the Christians and driven them out of their own cities and lands. There could be no condoning of the knights' behaviour, whether caused, as Alexander said, by rash ignorance or by blind cupidity. Still, such behaviour became part of every major expedition against the Saracens, and so in this respect as in virtually all others, the Spanish experience of the eleventh century served as a model for the crusades.[21]

The best known of the attacks on the Jews that coincided with the first crusade took place in the Rhine Valley. Like the Viscount of Narbonne 30 years before, Bishop John of Speyer stood by the Jews of his city in May 1096. He assembled an armed force to protect the Jews, whom he gathered in a castle, and in this way effectively frustrated the designs of the crusading bands. A few weeks later the Jews of Worms faced a similar test but with a less helpful bishop. Whether in their own homes or in the episcopal palace, the Jews of Worms were slaughtered. Cologne, Metz, Mainz, Trier, Bamberg, and Prague were among those cities where this pattern was repeated.[22]

From the description given by Guibert of Nogent of the massacre at Rouen in September of 1096 comes the classic formulation of the crusaders' rationale: it would be putting things in the wrong order for them to set out first to travel great distances eastward to fight the enemies of God when the greatest enemy of all was there before their very eyes. They herded the Jews together in a place of worship (ecclesiam)—a church perhaps, but more likely a synagogue—and then slaughtered them all, sparing only those willing to accept Christianity.[23]

Greater emphasis has been placed traditionally on the German rather than the French massacres, perhaps because of the imbalance in extant source materials on the subject. Yet recent study has yielded specific details about a massacre inflicted by crusaders from Languedoc and Provence upon the Jews of some Provençal community, perhaps Monieux, a small town in the Vaucluse. Such a case gives some credence to the assertion of Richard of Poitiers that the crusaders, before going off to the Holy Land, exterminated in many massacres the Jews of virtually all Gaul, apart from those who were willing to be baptized.[24]

The Second Crusade followed the pattern established by the First, with the addition of an influential crusade preacher, who urged attacks against Jews. A Cistercian monk named Ralph travelled throughout 'those parts of Gaul that touch the Rhine and inflamed many thousands of the inhabitants of Cologne, Mainz, Worms, Speyer, Strasbourg, and many other neighbouring cities, towns, and villages to accept the cross. However, he heedlessly included in his preaching that the Jews whose houses were scattered throughout the cities and towns should be slain as foes of the Christian religion.'[25] St Bernard had to be called in to silence

this Ralph, a task he succeeded in accomplishing only with great difficulty, due to the fervour of Ralph's popular following. Bernard flatly
opposed the pogroms but in his own way he helped foster the mentality
that was so receptive to the preaching of Ralph. He argued that Christians should not kill Jews 'for they are living tokens to us, constantly
recalling our Lord's passion.'[26] This was a traditional argument, but a
provocative one also, and as such it represented a significant choice on
Bernard's part. Moreover, his intervention in the disputed papal election
of 1130 reveals a deeply hostile attitude towards Jews. The candidate he
opposed, Anacletus, was the great-grandson of a Jew who had been
converted to Christianity. Jewish ancestry had not prevented the future
Anacletus from being a student at Paris, a monk at Cluny, a priest, a
loyal supporter of the papal reform party, a cardinal, a papal legate, or
the leader of the majority in the college of cardinals. None the less,
Bernard wrote to the Emperor Lothair, saying: 'it is well known that
Jewish offspring now occupies the see of St Peter to the injury of Christ.'[27]

The Second and Third Crusades added several English towns to the
list of localities that experienced pogroms. In the autumn of 1189 a wave
of persecution broke out in London and spread throughout most of the
country. In March 1190, virtually the entire Jewish community at York
was wiped out. Their houses were pillaged, their records destroyed, and
the streets were strewn with their corpses.[28]

The signs of things to come can be seen in the policies of Philip
Augustus. Shortly after the coronation in 1180, as Rigord tells it, he had
'the Jews throughout all France seized in their synagogues and despoiled
of their gold and silver and garments, as the Jews themselves had spoiled
the Egyptians at their exodus from Egypt.'[29] The Jews of the royal
domain were imprisoned and then released only upon payment of a
ransom of 15,000 marks. Next Philip cancelled four-fifths of all debts
owed by Christians to Jews, and had the remaining one-fifth paid to the
royal treasury. The final step, taken in 1182, was the confiscation of all
Jewish property and the expulsion of the Jews from his lands. Philip
readmitted the Jews under very carefully regulated conditions in 1198,
but the pattern of future treatment of the Jews had been set.

The trampling underfoot of European Jews took place on an intellectual as well as a physical plane. Works by Peter Damian, Gilbert Crispin,
and Peter of Blois, to name just a few, follow a well established pattern
of citing Old Testament texts, especially Messianic passages, and then

trying to prove that the Messiah had come.[30] The *Tractatus contra Judaeorum inveteratam duritiem* ('Treatise Against the Unyielding Obstinacy of the Jews') by Peter the Venerable, Abbot of Cluny from 1122 to 1156, contained a chapter on 'the Absurd and Utterly Stupid Tales of the Jews.'[31] Consistent with his remarkable achievement of having the *Koran* translated into Latin, so that Christian scholars would no longer need to rely on nonsensical notions about the religion of Islam, but rather could give serious attention to the authentic text of Islam, Peter here dealt at length with Talmudic scholarship. He showed how Christian and Jewish understanding on particular biblical passages was at variance and then attacked the Jewish interpretations.

One of the allegorical themes of romance literature was the contrasting relationship of the Old Law with the New, and of Synagogue with the Church.[32] In the thirteenth century the legend of the wandering Jew came to the West, first in an Italian chronicle entry for 1223 and then in Roger of Wendover's *Flores historiarum* five years later.[33] Liturgy also registered a shift in attitude around 1200 when in the Good Friday service the congregation was instructed not to kneel during the prayer for the Jews (urging their ultimate conversion); the faithful continued to kneel, however, for the other solemn prayers.[34]

The inferior status of Jews was intellectualized by Christians in pictures as well as words, with the use of such signs as the tall pointed hat and the circular badge, but more significantly with the use of such attributes as the hook-nose and the crafty eye. In representations of Christ's passion, Jews are implicated at every stage. Not only are the soldiers who take Jesus in the garden prominently hook-nosed Jews; Pilate is shown as a Jew, and the same is true of those who nail Jesus to the cross, of the one who puts the sponge with vinegar to his mouth, and of the one who pierces his side. The allegorical figure of Synagogue found in several hundred works in France and Germany suffers an astonishing array of indignities; and in the thirteenth century, the theme of Jews sucking at the teats of a sow first appeared in Germany.[35]

The legal position of the Jews declined in the course of the second feudal age from an insecure but negotiable status of virtual equality to one of abject servility. This same decline coincided with the period of the coalescing of feudal principalities into entities that in everything but name were sovereign states. Papal lawyers in about 1120 drew up a *Constitutio pro Judaeis,* which established basic guarantees for Jewish life and religion, but with the ambiguous provision that papal protection was reserved for those Jews who did not plot against the Christian faith.[36] Beginning in the late twelfth century, most of the urban charters in Aragon and Castile asserted that 'Jews are the slaves of the crown and belong exclusively to the royal treasury.'[37] Similar statements were formulated by French, English, and imperial lawyers.[38]

In such a climate of thought it is not surprising to find Abbot Peter the Venerable wondering 'whether a Jew is a human being, for he will neither accede to human reasoning nor yield to authoritative statements that are divine and from his own tradition. I do not know, I say, whether that person is human from whose flesh the heart of stone is not yet removed.'[39]

The treatment accorded Jews, the money-specialists of Christian society, was thus in thought as well as deed increasingly cruel in the course of the eleventh, twelfth, and thirteenth centuries. As justification for this cruel treatment, Christians added the insult of regarding the Jews as inferiors, as some class of sub-human beings. They wrote tracts to prove the point, extended the argument with pictorial and plastic representations, and fixed the point by law. All of these themes, depictions, and laws are understandable in the light of Christian violence against the Jews. But why did all of this violence occur in the first place?

3. SCAPEGOATS

Any attempt to explore the motives behind Christian violence against Jews must take into account the evolution of attitudes and feelings, as distinguished from overt actions and carefully reasoned theological and legal statements. These are revealed indirectly through such sources as the charges made against Jews, the associations made between Jews and filth, or the changing image of Judas.

The charge of ritual murder is made in the story told by Chaucer's prioress. In her story, a pure, fair-haired, golden-throated, seven-year-old choir-boy, son of a poor young Christian widow, is set upon in the ghetto by a filthy Jew who lives in a dark alley, who slits the boy's throat, and then dumps the body in a latrine, which the Jews continue to use.[40] Whereas Chaucer was writing in the latter part of the fourteenth century, the first actual charge of ritual murder was made in Norwich in 1144, when the body of a young boy was found on Good

Friday and the story quickly spread that the boy had been crucified by Jews. This crucifixion was not the random act of a few local Jews but, according to the story, the carefully contrived action of the collectivity of European Jewry, carrying out a plan conceived at an assembly of rabbis held at Narbonne in the previous year.[41]

Similar charges were made at Gloucester in 1168, Bury St Edmunds in 1181, Winchester in 1192, Norwich again in 1235, and, most notably, Lincoln in 1255. The English did not monopolize the ritual murder charge: it is encountered at Blois in 1171 and at Pontoise and Zaragoza in 1182. At Würzburg, in 1147, the body of a Christian was discovered in the Main and the Jews bore the blame and cost of this unexplained Christian death with several Jewish lives. These are but a few of the charges that were made, and they continued as persistently in the thirteenth century as in the twelfth.[42] Many of them coincided with preparations for crusading expeditions, and these expeditions were in turn, as previously pointed out, almost invariably accompanied by massacres of Jews. Every few years and in various places there would be an eruption of Christian hostility towards the Jews. Then Christians would create the fantasy that Jews had murdered a Christian child, a point usually embellished with hideous detail. The convenience of such a charge was that Christians could then project their own guilt on to the Jews and accordingly punish the Jews, as befits murderers. At Blois, in 1171, 38 Jews were burned at the stake. At Bray-sur-Seine, in 1191, there were 100 Jewish victims. Nineteen Jews were hanged without trial in connection with the Lincoln affair of 1255.[43]

The charge of profaning the sacred host was made against some Jews at Belitz, near Berlin, in 1243; the local Jews were taken into custody and burned to death. There were many such cases in Germany, but relatively fewer in other parts of Europe. The charges vary in detail, although the main point is that the Jews got hold of a consecrated wafer and then subjected it to some iniquitous treatment.[44] The charge of host profanation fulfilled two functions for Christians. First, it permitted them to project on to Jews their doubts about transubstantiation, a doctrine long in the making and finally declared dogma only as recently as the year 1215. There was never a period in which this doctrine enjoyed universal acceptance. The feast of Corpus Christi was established in 1264 to foster its propagation, and little more than a century later Wyclif launched his frontal attacks against it; these attacks were

kept up by others right through to the Reformation. The Corpus Christi
plays also served to bolster popular belief in the miracle of transubstatia-
tion. They showed Jews driving nails into consecrated wafers, thus
making them bleed. The dramatic tension was built around this very
point, but of course Jews did not have to wonder whether a consecrated
wafer were really the body and blood of Christ; that was a problem,
instead, for Christians.[45] The second function fulfilled by the charge of
host profanation was that it marked an improvement over the ritual
murder charge, for it dispensed with the problem of finding a corpse and
of identifying the victim.[46]

The charge that Jews contaminate wells and streams was heard in
Germany occasionally before 1300, but more generally coincided with
the natural disasters that struck Europe during the fourteenth century.[47]
By then there was an old tradition of associating Jews with filth and of
considering them to be filthy. Peter the Venerable complained to King
Louis VII that when a church was robbed of a chalice, the thief would
sell the stolen object to a Jew and the Jew would in turn do things to the
chalice 'horrendous to contemplate, detestable to mention.'[48] The government of Louis' son and successor included in its rationale for expelling the Jews in 1181 a charge that Jewish pawnbrokers committed
disgusting acts with Christian liturgical vessels that had been pawned
with them.[49] Matthew Paris recorded the tale of a wealthy English Jew
who kept an image of the Virgin inside his latrine where he defecated on
it repeatedly.[50] A French counterpart of this story told of a Parisian Jew
who fell into the public latrine; he reminded the friends who rushed to
help him that it was the Sabbath and thus that they should wait. When
the king heard of this he ordered his guards to keep the friends away
from the latrine on the following day so that the Lord's day would not
be violated. And when the Jews came to the unguarded latrine on
Monday, their friend was dead.[51] A thirteenth-century Austrian poet
claimed that thirty Jews could saturate even the largest principality with
their stench; and a contemporary Flemish poet related the murder of a
Christian boy by 'the dirty Jews, the stinking dogs' *(die vule Jueden, die
stinkende Honde)*.[52]

The association of filth and faecal matter with one's enemies, a common enough phenomenon, takes on special significance in the present
case in two ways. First, it places the Jews in the company of that foul-
smelling creature, the devil. At a critical moment when a converted Jew

was baptized, that is, when he abandoned his allegiance to the devil and became a servant of Christ, he was thought to lose his foul smell in the purifying waters of baptism.[53] The personified figure of Synagogue is often shown with the devil; the Church of Christ is set in opposition to the Synagogue of Satan. Secondly, this association calls to mind the connection between filth and money, and indeed one often finds a representation of avarice, seated before his coffer and counting coins, a devil with his tongue sticking out lounging nearby, and he, avarice, bearing the standard attributes of a Jew.[54] One of the twelfth-century dialogues between Synagogue and Church had Synagogue make the charge that Christian rulers and clerics did not demonstrate in their own lives what was generally regarded as Christian holiness. The reply given by Church was notable by the way it ignored this point and also by its counter-charge to Synagogue: 'one could never calculate the extent of your avarice; there is no limit to your evil-doing.'[55]

The personage who more than any other became the epitome of an avaricious man was Judas. 'Judas sold Christ,' explained Thomas of Froidmont, 'out of cupidity.'[56] Matthew Paris distinguished between the burdens of guilt borne by Paul and Peter on the one hand, and, on the other, by Judas. With Paul the problem was ignorance; with Peter it was a matter of weakness, which in turn generated fear; with Judas the problem was iniquity, and in particular, cupidity.[57] All of the standard forms of dress for identifying a Jew were applied to Judas, while at the same time he absorbed the attributes of avarice as well.[58] He was also referred to in the Holy Thursday *tenebrae* service as 'that most vile of merchants.'[59] Little was known about the early life of this person until a Latin 'Legend of Judas' was composed in the twelfth century (followed shortly by vernacular versions throughout Europe). The legend includes accounts of fratricide, patricide, and incest (with his mother), all as a prelude to his betrayal of Christ.[60] The importance of these amplifications of the story of Judas lay in the fact that he served, for Christians, as a symbol of all Jews; in the words of one monastic author: 'these things that have been said concerning Judas the traitor extend to the entire Jewish people.'[61]

The principal mechanism at work in the complicated web of Christian-Jewish relations was projection. This is easy to see in a statement such as Guibert of Nogent's claim that the Jews were responsible for clerical immorality in his time, giving the reason that Jews were known to introduce clerics to the company of the 'villainous prince' and to teach them to serve him.[62] The charge of ritual murder, although more complicated, can be examined in the same light. There are no extant records of widespread killings of Christians by Jews in this period; all that we have in this connection are the elaborately fanciful tales of ritual murder, filled with their airs of conspiracy and perversion. Meanwhile, there is the long irrefutable record of the pogroms, and since, as previously pointed out, the ritual murder charge usually accompanied a pogrom, we are permitted to see that charge as a projection of guilt (and at the same time a justification) for the pogrom. Christians, not able to justify and accept the reality of their violent behaviour towards the Jews, and thereby feeling guilty, projected their guilt on to them rather as one casts an image on to a mirror, and then they attacked in them that which they had found intolerable about themselves.

But reports of pogroms usually included mention of destruction done to property as well as harm done to persons. Some accounts specifically state that the financial records of the Jews were destroyed.[63] When official pogroms or expulsions took place governments were careful to preserve Jewish financial records, for the pattern in such cases was for the governments to demand payment into the royal or seigneurial treasury of a portion of the amount previously owed the Jews.[64] No such interest restrained the perpetrators of the relatively unorganized pogroms. Blind hatred based on religious fanaticism might have stimulated the flow of energy in many of those who attacked Jews and Jewries, but the fact remains that these attacks—whether consciously or not—served the common end of destroying the written evidence of Christians indebtedness to the Jews. The attacks on Jewish communities—against both property and persons—consisted of more than a cycle of violence, guilt, projection, and more violence. Christians hated Jews because they saw in Jews the same calculating for profit in which they themselves were deeply and, in their own view, unjustifiably involved. It was above all the guilt for this involvement that they projected onto the Jews. The Jews functioned as a scapegoat for Christian failure to adapt successfully to the profit economy.

Peter the Venerable's complaining to the king about what Jews did to stolen liturgical vessels reveals a concrete case of such projection. First of all, he did not emphasize the stealing as a problem; otherwise the discussion would presumably have turned to the protection of churches and the punishment of thieves. Further indication that this was not a critical problem is the rationale for expulsion later promulgated by the royal government, in which theft was not mentioned; the problem was purely one of what Jewish pawnbrokers did to liturgical vessels. In the second place, what Peter did emphasize was the imaginary problem of what Jews did to pawned objects, 'imaginary' not because it could not happen but because he made no specific charge and because there are no such formal charges extant against Jews. And third, Peter's statement diverts attention from the reality that liturgical vessels were being pawned. The reality was that treasure was being transformed into specie. The reality was that someone was undergoing the experience of taking sacred vessels to a perhaps sordid shop and haggling over their precise monetary value in order to realize that treasure in the form of cash.

This reality, moreover, was not hypothetical. The abbey of Cluny, as we shall see, ran heavily into debt in Peter's time, to Jewish moneylenders among others, and when one of the abbey's most generous benefactors passed by there in 1149 to help reduce their debt again, he found that a cross he had presented to the abbey some years before had been stripped of its outer layer of gold.[65]

Peter the Venerable did not participate in pogroms or advocate them. People less well educated and less morally responsible than he gave vent to their feelings of anxiety in all-out attacks against Jewish communities. But Peter in his own way, through the terrible bitterness that his writings display, gave expression to an inner confusion that he could hardly have understood or explained. Little wonder, then, that he doubted whether Jews were human. When Louis VII was preparing to go on crusade (and the Jew-baiter Ralph was preaching), Peter wished the king well but also expressed doubt about whether the expedition, even if successful, would be useful, because enemies far worse than the Saracens lived in their very midst. Immediately he added that he was not suggesting that these worse enemies, the Jews, be killed, for God had condemned them to be preserved in a life worse than death. His idea, though, was that the Jews be made to pay the costs of the forthcoming expedition. And this was just, he argued, because the Jews were wealthy and yet they did not work. Their storage bins were filled with produce and their cellars with wine. Their purses were filled with money and their chests with gold and silver. Yet they did not earn this great wealth by working on the land, nor did they get it from serving as soldiers or in any other honourable and useful position. They got it by stealing from Christians and by receiving goods stolen from Christians by thieves.[66] Apart from the gratuitous accusation about stealing, this was an essentially accurate, if rough, description of those who were successful in the new economy. The other great monastic leader of the twelfth century, St Bernard, explicitly identified the entire money trade with the Jews. He knew but could not fully accept the reality of Christian involvement in the money trade. 'We are pained to observe', he wrote, 'that where there are no Jews, Christian moneylenders "Jew", or "Judaize" (judaizare), worse than the Jews, if indeed these men may be called Christians, and not rather baptized Jews.'[67] Bernard thereby gave new significance to a hitherto innocuous Latin verb, judaizare, which meant merely to proselytize and to convert people to Judaism, a counterpart to the verb 'to Christianize.'[68] The money trade, the crucial activity of the Commercial Revolution, was thus now considered to be exclusively the work of the Jews. Christian moneylenders were really Jews.

It was both inaccurate and unfair to regard commercial activity, especially moneylending, as the exclusive preserve of Jews, for the Jews always formed a tiny minority of the people so engaged. And yet the main function of the Jews in the Commercial Revolution was to bear the burden of Christian guilt for participation in activities not yet deemed morally worthy of Christians. Christians attacked in the Jews those things about themselves that they found inadmissible and that they therefore projected on to the Jews. Guilt led to hostility, and hostility to violence, which led to a need for rationalizing the violence, and this rationalization led to a deeper hostility and still more violence, and so the fateful cycle turned.[69] Joined to this guilt that was felt by some was a more simple anxiety about the disorders and uncertainties of urban life and about the behaviour of those increasingly separate, marginal people, the Jews; anxiety itself, quite apart from guilt, can breed hostility. And simpler still was the anger of those who felt oppressed by moneylenders.

Religious enthusiasm alone would not have constructed the elaborate device of limiting the Jews to occupations thought by Christian moralists to be sinful and then harassing the Jews for doing their jobs. The particular occupations chosen are themselves most revealing. Presumably the Jews could have been forced to haul water or clean the streets or till the soil. But more complicated Christian feelings were responsible for setting the Jews up in finance and then attacking them bitterly for their involvements in finance.

Early in the twelfth century, Rupert of Deutz inquired: 'Tell me, who are they who gather wicked avarice in their homes more than the Jewish people'?[70] Rupert's prudently rhetorical question remained undisturbed by the obvious answer. Midway through the century, St Bernard made his revealing assertion that all moneylenders, even Christian moneylenders, are Jews. By the late twelfth century, the new needs of both business and government for a system of credit collided head on with the old moral and legal prohibitions against usury. As there was still no yielding on the side of morality or legality, certain Christian princes, in particular the kings of France and England, who remained in firm and exclusive control of 'their Jews', created the fiction that some of the Christian moneylenders, clerical as well as lay, living under their jurisdiction, were Jews—'their Jews', of course—thus enabling them to operate at the prince's pleasure, free from harassment by any other authority.[71] Political power in this way brought to the surface and lent support to a myth that had originated in projection.

NOTES

1. B. Blumenkranz, *Juifs et chrétiens dans le monde occidental, 430–1096* (Paris, 1960), part 1.
2. Cited by Duby, *Warriors and Peasants* (London, 1974), p. 134.
3. S. W. Baron, *A Social and Religious History of the Jews*, 2nd ed., 13 vols. (New York, 1952–67), IV, 164; Blumenkranz, *Juifs et chrétiens*, p. 20.
4. *Regesten zur Geschichte der Juden im fränkischen und deutschen Reiche bis zum Jahre 1273*, ed. J. Aronius (Berlin, 1902), no. 168.
5. M. Güdemann, *Geschichte des Erziehungswesens und der Cultur der abendländischen Juden während des Mittelalters und der neureren Zeit*, 3 vols. (Vienna, 1880–88), I, 92–106.
6. *COD*, p. 266.
7. Y. Baer, *A History of the Jews in Christian Spain*, tr. L. Schoffman, 2 vols. (Philadelphia, 1961–6), I, 39–110; I. Loeb, 'Le nombre des Juifs de Castille et d'Espagne au moyen âge,' *Revue des études juives*, XIV (1887), 183; L. Poliakov, *De Mahomet aux Marranes* (Paris, 1961), p. 127; Baron, *History*, IV, 34. Cf. G. Jackson, *The Making of Medieval Spain* (New York, 1972), pp. 99–110; and J. L. Schneidman, *The Rise of the Aragonese-Catalan Empire, 1200–1350*, 2 vols. (New York, 1970), II, 419–20.

8. *PL*, CXLV, 41.
9. C. Roth, *The History of the Jews in Italy* (Philadelphia, 1946), pp. 74, 83; and 'Genoese Jews in the 13th Century', *Speculum*, XXV (1950), 190–1. Cf. Baron, *History*, IV, 24–6.
10. G. Caro, *Sozial- und Wirtschaftsgeschichte der Juden im Mittelalter und der Neuzeit*, 2 vols. (Leipzig, 1908, 1920), I, 171–4; J. Stengers, *Les juifs dans les Pays-bas au Moyen Age* (Brussels, 1950), pp. 9–16.
11. B. Blumenkranz, 'Géographie historique d'un thème de l'iconographie religieuse: les représentations de *Synagoga* en France', in *Mélanges offerts à René Crozet*, ed. P. Gallais and Y.-J. Riou, 2 vols. (Poitiers, 1966), pp. 1141, 1143. R. Chazan, *Medieval Jewry in Northern France: A Political and Social History*, The Johns Hopkins University Studies in History and Political Science, 91st series (Baltimore, 1973), pp. 207–220.
12. Guibert of Nogent *De vita sua* ii.5 (*PL*, CLVI, 903).
13. N. Golb, 'New Light on the Persecution of French Jews at the Time of the First Crusade', *Proceedings of the American Academy for Jewish Research*, XXXIV (1966), 12; I. Loeb, 'Les négociants juifs à Marseilles au milieu du XIIIe siècle', *Revue des études juives*, XVI (1888), 73–83; J. Regné, 'Etude sur la condition des juifs de Narbonne du Ve au XIVe siècle', ibid., LVIII (1909), 75–105, 200–25; R. W. Emery, *The Jews of Perpignan in the Thirteenth Century: An Economic Study Based on Notarial Records* (New York, 1959), pp. 11–13, 16–25. For Manosque, in Provence, see J. Shatzmiller, *Recherches sur la communauté juive de Manosque au moyen age, 1241–1329*, Etudes juives, XV (Paris, 1973), p. 139. A study of the royal inquests in the middle of the thirteenth century shows that three-fourths of all complaints against Jews had to do with loans; see G. Nahon, 'Le crédit et les Juifs dans la France du XIIIe siècle,' *Annales E. S. C.*, XXIV (1969), 1121–48.
14. H. G. Richardson, *The English Jewry Under Angevin Kings* (London, 1960), pp. 63, 93–4, 121, 161–75; P. Elman, 'Jewish Trade in Thirteenth Century England', *Historia Judaica*, I (1938), 91–104; 'The Economic Causes of the Expulsion of the Jews in 1290', *Economic History Review*, VII (1937), 145–54; W. E. Rhodes, 'The Italian Bankers in England and their Loans to Edward I and Edward II', chap. 5 of *Historical Essays*, ed. T. F. Tout and J. Tait (Manchester, 1907), pp. 137–68; R. W. Kaeuper, *Bankers to the Crown: The Riccardi of Lucca and Edward I* (Princeton, 1973).
15. Hermannus quondam Judaeus *Opusculum de conversione sua* ii (*MGH, Quellen zur Geistesgeschichte*, IV, 72); 'Siquidem omnes Iudei negotiationi inserviunt.'
16. Baron, *History*, IV, 184–5; Caro, *Sozial- und Wirtschaftsgeschichte*, I, 434.
17. J. W. Parkes, *The Jew in the Medieval Community: A Study of his Political and Economic Situation* (London, 1938), pp. 37–9; Adhémar of Chabannes *Historiarum libri III* iii.47 (*MGH, SS*, IV, 136–7).
18. Alpertus *De diversitate temporum* i.7 (ibid., 704).
19. Adhémar of Chabannes *Historiarum libri III* iii.52 (ibid., 139); Parkes, *Jew*

in the Medieval Community, pp. 43–4; Blumenkranz, *Juifs et chrétiens*, pp. 55–6.

20. Baron, *History*, IX, 35.
21. *PL*, CLXVI, 1386–7.
22. L. Poliakov, *The History of Anti-Semitism*, I, tr., R. Howard (New York, 1965), pp. 43–6; Baron, *History*, IV, 94–106.
23. Guibert of Nogent *De vita sua* ii.5 (*PL*, CLVI, 903).
24. Poliakov, *Anti-Semitism*, p. 42; Golb, 'New Light'; cf. Richard of Poitiers in *HF*, XII, 411. Chazan, *Medieval Jewry*, p. 28, stresses that 1171 was a more decisive moment for the northern French Jewry than 1095–6.
25. Otto of Freising *Gesta Frederici imperatoris* i.37–9, ed. G. Waitz, 3rd ed. (Hanover and Leipzig, 1912), pp. 58–9.
26. Otto of Freising *Gesta* i.40 (ibid., pp. 59, 61–3).
27. H. Bloch, 'The Schism of Anacletus II and the Glanfeuil Forgeries of Peter the Deacon of Monte Cassino', *Traditio*, VIII (1952), 159–264.
28. Baron, *History*, IV, 124–6.
29. Rigord, *Gesta Philippi Augusti* xii–xiv, ed. H.-F. Delaborde (Paris, 1882), pp. 24–7.
30. B. Blumenkranz, *Les auteurs chrétiens latins du moyen age sur les juifs et le judaisme* (Paris, 1963); A. Williams, *Adversus Judaeos: A Bird's-Eye View of Christian Apologiae Until the Renaissance* (Cambridge, 1935), pp. 366–74, 400–7.
31. *PL*, CLXXXIX, 507–650.
32. M. Schlauch, 'The Allegory of Church and Synagogue', *Speculum*, XIV (1939), 448–50.
33. G. K. Anderson, *The Legend of the Wandering Jew* (Providence, 1965), pp. 18–22; MP, V, 341–2.
34. L. Canet, 'La prière "Pro judaeis" de la liturgie catholique romaine', *Revue des études juives*, LXI (1911), 213–21; and R. Fawtier, 'The Jews in the "Use of York" ', *Bulletin of the John Rylands Library*, V (1918–20), 381–5.
35. B. Blumenkranz, *Le juif médiéval au miroir de l'art chrétien* (Paris, 1966), pp. 85, 105–109; W. S. Seiferth, *Synagogue and Church in the Middle Ages: Two Symbols in Art and Literature*, tr. L. Chadeayne and P. Gottwald (New York, 1970), pls. 1–65; I. Shachar. *The 'Judensau': A Medieval Anti-Jewish Motif and Its History*, Warburg Institute Surveys, V (London, 1974).
36. S. Grayzel, *The Church and the Jews in the XIIIth Century*, rev. ed. (New York, 1966), pp. 76–8, 92–5.
37. Baer, *Jews in Christian Spain*, I, 44–5, 85, 88–90.
38. G. I. Langmuir, ' "Judei nostri" and the Beginning of Capetian Legislation', *Traditio*, XVI (1960), 203–30; F. Pollock and F. W. Maitland, *The History of English Law*, 2nd ed., 2 vols. (Cambridge, 1905), I, 468; Poliakov, *Anti-Semitism*, p. 76; G. Kirsch, *The Jews in Medieval Germany: A Study of Their Legal and Social Status* (Chicago, 1949), p. 133.
39. *Tractatus contra Judaeorum inveteratam duritiem* iii (*PL*, CLXXXIX, 551).

40. G. I. Langmuir, 'The Knight's Tale of Young Hugh of Lincoln', *Speculum*, XLVII (1972), 459–82.
41. Thomas of Cantimpré *Bonum universale de Apibus* ii.29.17, ed. G. Colverenius (Douai, 1627), p. 145.
42. J. Tractenberg, *The Devil and the Jews: The Medieval Conception of the Jew and Its Relation to Modern Antisemitism* (New Haven, 1943), pp. 124–39; Poliakov, *Anti-Semitism*, pp. 56–64.
43. Langmuir, 'The Knight's Tale', pp. 464–9.
44. Tractenberg, *Devil and the Jews*, p. 114; Baron, *History*, XI, 164–70.
45. K. Young, *The Drama of the Medieval Church*, 2 vols. (Oxford, 1933), I, 492–539; E. K. Chambers, *The Medieval Stage*, 2 vols. (Oxford, 1903), II, 133; V. A. Kolve, *The Play Called Corpus Christi* (Stanford, 1966), pp. 33–56; F. E. Barnes, 'The Background and Sources of the Croxton Play of the Sacrament', The University of Chicago, Ph.D. dissertation, 1926; and D. Devlin, '*Corpus Christi:* A Study in Medieval Eucharistic Theory, Devotion, and Practice', The University of Chicago, Ph.D. dissertation, 1975.
46. G. I. Langmuir, 'From Xenophobia to Prejudice: The Emergence of Anti-Semitism in the Thirteenth Century', paper delivered at the annual meeting of the American Historical Association, Toronto, 29 December 1967.
47. Baron, *History*, XI, 158–64; Tractenberg, *Devil and the Jews*, pp. 97–108.
48. Letter 130 (*LPV*, I, 327–30).
49. *HF*, XII, 215; cf. Rigord, cited above, n. 29.
50. MP, V, 114–15.
51. Poliakov, *Anti-Semitism*, p. 124.
52. Güdemann, *Geschichte des Erziehungswesens*, I, 145; Stengers, *Juifs dans les Pays-bas*, pp. 55–6.
53. Tractenberg, *Devil and the Jews*, p. 48.
54. Blumenkranz, *Le juif médiéval*, p. 45.
55. Pseudo-Gilbert Crispin *Disputatio ecclesiae et synagogae*, ed. E. Marténe and U. Durand, *Thesaurus novus Anecdotorum*, 5 vols. (Paris, 1717), V, 1497–1506.
56. Thomas of Froidmont [Bernard] *Liber de modo bene vivendi* xlv (*PL*, CLXXXIV, 1266).
57. MP, III, 163.
58. On the tympanum at Conques, Judas hanged has a moneybag suspended from his neck in the manner of avarice personified.
59. Young, *Drama of the Medieval Church*, I, 101–2.
60. P. F. Baum, 'The Medieval Legend of Judas Iscariot', *Publications of the Modern Language Association of America*, XXXI (1916), 481–632; on p. 497 Baum discussed the manuscript known as Lc, from the late twelfth or early thirteenth century, which was almost certainly in the possession of Bury St Edmunds. Cf. W. Creizenach, *Judas Ischarioth in Legende und Sage des Mittelalters* (Halle, 1875).
61. Othlon de Saint-Emmeran *Liber de cursu spirituali* vii (*PL*, CXLVI, 160):

'. . . quae de Iuda traditore sunt dicta, congruunt iudacio populo. . . .' Cf. Geoffrey of Vendôme *Opuscula* vii (*PL*, CLVII, 222).

62. Cited by B. Monod, 'Juifs sorciers et hérétiques au moyen age', *Revue des études juives*, XLVI (1903), 237–45.

63. Golb, 'New Light', p. 18; Parkes, *Jew in the Medieval Community*, pp. 64, 371.

64. Ibid., pp. 367–82.

65. Georges Duby, 'Le budget de l'abbaye de Cluny entre 1080 et 1155', *Annales E. S. C.*, VII (1952), 169–70; L. Voss, *Heinrich von Blois, Bishof von Winchester (1129–71)*, Historische Studien, CCX (Berlin, 1932), pp. 114–15.

66. Letter 130 (*LPV*, I, 327–30).

67. *Ep.* ccclxiii (*PL*, CLXXXII, 567): 'Taceo quod sicubi desunt, pejus judaizare dolemus Christianos, feneratores, si tamen Christianos, et non magis baptizatos Judaeos convenit appelari.'

68. Du Cange, *Glossarium mediae et infimae latinitatis* (Niort, 1887), IV, 437.

69. I found the following instances of scholars working towards a similar interpretation: O. Fenichel, 'Elements of a Psychoanalytic Theory of Anti-Semitism', in *Anti-Semitism, A Social Disease*, ed. E. Simmel (New York, 1946), p. 29; R. M. Loewenstein, *Christians and Jews: A Psychoanalytic Study*, tr. V. Damman (New York, 1951), p. 84; F. G. Friedman and K. Rahner, 'Unbefangenheit und Anspruch: ein Briefwechsel zum jüdisch-christlichen Gespräch', *Stimmen der Zeit*, CLXXVIII (1966), 81–97, especially p. 85 where Friedman is writing; and G. Langmuir, 'Anti-Judaism as the Necessary Preparation for Anti-Semitism', *Viator*, II (1971), 388.

70. Rupert of Deutz *Commentaria in duodecim prophetas minores: in Habacuc prophetam* ii (*PL*, CLXVIII, 616): 'Quisnam ille est, qui congregat, vel congregavit avaritiam malam domui suae, magis quam populus Judaicus . . .?'

71. See the complaint by Peter the Chanter *Verbum abbreviatum* (*PL*, CCV, 158); discussed by J. W. Baldwin, *Masters, Princes, and Merchants: the Social Views of Peter the Chanter and his Circle*, 2 vols. (Princeton, 1970), I, 298–300.

10

The Medieval Conception of the Jew: A New Interpretation

Cecil Roth

The problem which I am endeavouring to solve in this paper is one which must have impressed many other students of the Middle Ages, but which I have never seen formulated—that of the amazing mentality which contemporary literature, records, and chronicles appear to ascribe to the Jew. Close examination shows that according to these sources he does not seem either to think or to act like other human beings. His behaviour in matters of the utmost significance is completely irrational. He is proof, apparently, not only against logic and argument, but even against ocular demonstration. Nevertheless, he is prepared to maintain his absurd opinions, and to persist in his preposterous conduct, to the death. He is, of course, depicted as an enemy of Christendom—that goes without saying. But he gives expression to his enmity under circumstances, and in a fashion, conceivable in no ordinary man: and he persists in his attitude even when publicly proved in the wrong.

Let us take, as a point of departure, the curious spectacle presented by the mediaeval "Disputations" between Jews and Christians. In most cases, these are misnamed. I am not for the moment alluding to the fact that they were so one-sided, that the verity of Christianity was assumed by the sponsors to be beyond all question, and that any fair debating reply on the part of the Jews to the obloquy heaped upon their heads would be characterised, and punished, as blasphemy. Quite apart from this, these discussions did not necessarily centre upon the merits and

Reprinted by permission of the Jewish Theological Seminary of America from *Essays and Studies in Memory of Linda R. Miller*, ed. Israel Davidson, New York, 1938, 171–90.

verities of the two faiths. They were in many instances attempts to prove *from the Talmud and kindred writings* (the italicised clause is all-important) that the Messiah promised in the Bible had already appeared in the person of Jesus. This was the case, in particular, in the Disputation of Tortosa in 1413/4—the most spectacular of all those of the Middle Ages —when the apostate Mestre Geronimo de Santa Fé pitted himself against the flower of Spanish Jewish scholarship, in the presence of the anti-Pope Benedict XIII and his *curia*. On this occasion, the efforts of the champion of Christianity were concentrated in an endeavour to convince his opponents, not out of the Bible, but out of Rabbinical literature, that the Christian religion was the true one, and Jesus the Messiah. This argument postulated, in effect, that the Rabbis of the first centuries of the Christian era had admitted the Messiahship of Jesus, realised the verity of Christianity, and even given their ideas literary expression, while at the same time organising Judaism as a separate faith, based upon the denial (not to say the blasphemy) of the Redeemer whom they knew to have appeared![1]

All this appears to the modern mind utterly absurd. There are, as it seems to me, three possible explanations. One is to deny the authenticity of the records—which in the case just mentioned, at least, are unimpeachable. The second is to question the sanity of the theologians who put forward this point of view, of the Pontiff and Prelates who applauded it, and of the Christendom which admitted it. Yet the mediaeval mind was as keen, as logical, and as eminently reasonable as is ours. The last alternative is to discover the premise which permitted this line of argument, and (as we shall see) much else traceable to it.

I have found it, I think, in the conception which I now wish to submit for consideration. We are accustomed, at the present time, to the phenomenon of the person who does not conform to the state religion. Even in rigidly Catholic countries, such as Portugal or Italy, non-Catholics are known and tolerated. The Jew is regarded in consequence simply as a Dissenter—different perhaps in degree, but not essentially in kind, from the Wesleyan or the Baptist or the Adventist. In the Middle Ages, of course, the picture was entirely different. In Western Europe, where the most important Jewish communities were to be found, the Catholic Church was everywhere supreme. The residue of the old Pagan faiths had been rooted out, or else forced to conform. Heresy was fiercely suppressed. The only exception which qualified the universal homogeneity of faith was, therefore, the Jew. The very conception of Dissent being strange, he could not be fitted into that category. He was not a heretic— one who professed himself a Christian, but refused to conform to Catholic doctrine. Moreover, he knew the Scripture; he lived among Christian people; he was not ignorant of Christianity. He was in this respect completely dissimilar from the benighted, ignorant Paynim. He was neither a heretic on the one hand, nor a heathen on the other. He was something more—an unbeliever: nay, *a deliberate unbeliever*. Unlike the unfortunate Hindu or Moslem who had never known the truth, he was one who, knowing the truth, refused to recognise it.

Here we have, as I believe, the solution to the problem which I have endeavoured to propound. This explains why the verities of Christianity might be proved from the Talmud; for the Rabbis of that age realised them and did not scruple to put them on record in their recondite Aramaic compilations, for the information (not, of course, for the guidance!) of posterity.

The Jews (so many Christians argued) had witnessed the life and activities of Jesus. They had seen all the prophesies of their ancient seers fulfilled in and by him. They had personal experience of the miracles by which his claims were so amply substantiated. But, in spite of all this, they refused to give him the recognition which was his due. They had gone further. They had crucified him, because he did not live up to the standard of earthly splendour which they had anticipated. Their mediaeval descendants, had they been present at the time, would *ex hypothesi* have acted in a precisely similar manner, for the attitude was one inherent in the Jewish nature in all ages.

The perpetuation of the enmity against them, generation after generation, was not therefore entirely unreasoning nor (granted the premises) illogical. The Jews were not blamed (as is generally believed) simply for the crime committed by their ancestors. They were blamed for a crime which was the inevitable outcome of their stubborn national temperament—one which, had circumstances permitted, they themselves would certainly have condoned, and which they were prepared to repeat at any time, if they had the opportunity. The "unbelieving Jew" (not the unbelieving Mussulman, or the unbelieving heathen) thus became a byword. After the Forced Conversions in Spain and Portugal, in the fourteenth and fifteenth centuries, the same physical and moral characteristics which had marked the Jews, and the same qualities of deliberate misbelief, were considered typical of the New Christians, their descendants:[2] and in the long succession of anti-Semitic literature written to assail the Marranos of the Peninsula, exactly the same charges figure. It is not suggested that this was the universal conception of the Jew—Gregory the Great, or St. Bernard of Clairvaux, or Thomas Aquinas, obviously thought differently. But it must have been a very widespread conception, particularly among the less educated; and it explains a good deal in the mediaeval religious mentality which otherwise remains incomprehensible.[3]

There were numerous natural signs which clearly indicated to the popular mind that the Jews were a race apart, cursed for all eternity. The Jews had tails—a superstition credited in remote parts even now. They were distinguished from the rest of mankind by a bloody flux and a peculiar odour, which disappeared automatically on the administration of the waters of baptism! This was enough, surely, to make rational beings realise the error of Judaism. But the Jews were not rational beings, and it was preposterous to regard them as such.

A striking illustration of this attitude is provided by the story of Ahasuerus, the Wandering Jew. When Jesus was on his way to crucifixion, according to an almost universal mediaeval legend, a Jewish shoemaker pushed him and told him tauntingly to go on. In punishment, the Saviour in turn condemned him to go on forever, 'till I come back.' In consequence, the Wandering Jew was believed immortal. He re-appeared at intervals throughout the Old World and the New, but could not die. No person, assuredly, could have had more convincing proof than this eye-witness of the Messiahship and Divinity of Jesus. But, notwithstanding this fact, the Wandering Jew remains eternally a Jew. He does not profess repentance. He is dressed in characteristic Jewish garb; and he never accepts Baptism.

In this, as in so much else, the Wandering Jew is typical of his people: for the Jews of more recent times were as intentional in their disbelief as their ancestors had been at the time of the Crucifixion. The pretensions of Jesus were incontrovertibly proved (it was considered) from the Holy Writ; but the Jews did not scruple to tamper with many such passages in the hope of obscuring the evidence. In the heyday of the Renaissance, an Italian Jewish scholar named Lazaro de Viterbo felt impelled to write a treatise for the Cardinal Sirleto vindicating the integrity of the Hebrew Scriptures. St. Jerome himself accused them of suppressing the doctrine of the Trinity in a number of verses of the Prophets. St. Justin asserted that they eliminated certain incriminating statements from Ezra and Nehemiah. Even in the year 1932, a Catholic scholar could express implicit belief in this charge.[4] Under the circumstances, it is little wonder that, in the Middle Ages, the Jews were suspected of wholesale suppression and misinterpretation of any Biblical prophecies which might prove them in the wrong. They *were* in the wrong. They knew it. But they staunchly refused to admit it, even at the cost of eternal suffering in this world and the next.

It was not only the Scriptures that they were willing to distort for their own ends. As we have seen, they were as unscrupulous in their treatment, and their interpretation, of their own recondite Jewish authorities. The controversies which center upon them were thus no ordinary disputes. They were attempts to tear away the veil of hypocrisy behind which the Jews had taken refuge, and to show the world that their own teachers realised (even if they did not recognise) the essential truth of Christian doctrine. Similarly, the earliest Christian students of Hebrew, Pico della Mirandola and Johannes Reuchlin, were able to justify their interest in such suspicious lore only by demonstrating that, though the Jews refused to admit it, Jesus was plainly indicated in the Kabbalah.

Nor was it from the Talmud and the allied literature alone that the Jews could be confuted. Their great historian, Josephus, bore eloquent testimony to the life and miracles of Jesus. Naturally, they not only refused to pay attention to these passages, but in case of need would even suppress them. An anecdote of Giraldus Cambrensis (*Opera* VIII. 65), describing an alleged episode of the twelfth century, is eloquent in this respect:

"But it is thus clear how great is the malice of the Jews, and how obstinate and obdurate is their teaching against their own weal, that even the testimony of their historian, whose books they have in Hebrew, and consider authentic, they will not accept about Christ. But Master Robert, the Prior of St. Frideswide at Oxford, whom we have seen, and who was a man old and trustworthy, whose latter years coincided with our earlier ones, was a man of letters and skilled in the Scriptures, nor was he ignorant of the Hebrew tongue. Now he sent to diverse towns and cities of England in which Jews have dwelling, from whom he collected many Josephuses written in Hebrew, gaining them with difficulty, since they were acquainted with him because of his knowing the Hebrew tongue. And in two of them he found this testimony about Christ written fully and at length, but as if recently scratched out; but in all the rest removed earlier, and as if never there. And when this was shewn to the Jews of Oxford summoned for that purpose, they were convicted and confused at this fraudulent malice and bad faith towards Christ."[5]

One of the most common, most tragic, and most widely believed of all charges brought against the Jews in the Middle Ages was that of desecrating the Host. From the thirteenth century down to the eighteenth, this accusation continually made its appearance in various parts of Europe, and was the occasion for massacres, expulsions, and judicial murders galore. It was alleged that the consecrated elements were stolen and ritually outraged by torture, stabbing, or flagellation. This is, perhaps, the most preposterous of all accusations of the sort. It is perfectly obvious that such action in a Jew would be completely paradoxical. It pre-supposes a degree of belief in the supernatural qualities of the sacrament which he could not conceivably hold, if he retained his religious convictions. If (as the result of some curious mental aberration) he desired to show his contempt of Christianity in some tangible manner, an unconsecrated wafer (obtainable with far less difficulty and danger) would have served his purpose equally well. So, at least, would appear to the modern mind.

But the mediaeval point of view was quite different. Of course, the Jew believed in the supernatural qualities of the Host—no rational being could do otherwise. Of course, he was perfectly aware that after consecration the Wafer became transformed into the very Body of Christ. It was for that very reason that he desired to get it into his possession and to torture it, making it know once again the sufferings of the Passion. The offense was generally said to come to light because of the astounding reactions of the Host to its maltreatment. It would spontaneously rise into the air, or bring about an earthquake, or above all—in a majority of cases—shed blood in discernible quantity (a phenomenon for which a scientific explanation is in fact available, in the *micrococcus prodigiosus* which may appear on stale food kept in a damp place). On one occasion, we are informed, while some Jews were burying pieces of a pierced host in a meadow, the fragments changed into butterflies, which began to heal cripples and restore the sight of the blind. On another, they fluttered out of a swamp, and a herd of grazing oxen did homage before them. On another, when the wafer was being burned in a stove, angels and doves flew out. In an early legend, we are told that the wafer whimpered like an infant on being pierced. Similarly, in another account, the blood is said to have splashed over the foreheads of the Jews who were engaged in the torment, leaving an indelible mark which betrayed their crime.

In consequence of tales such as these, myriads of innocent persons perished in the long centuries which followed the first tragedy at Belitz (near Berlin) in 1243, when a large number of Jews were burned at the stake on the spot subsequently known as the *judenberg*. Yet in barely a single one of these instances is it reported that any individual was sufficiently impressed by the miracle to request baptism, even though this would almost certainly have saved his life.[6] Sometimes they are reported to have been surprised, but no more than a Christian would be at a similar happening. Why was this? The answer is not difficult to find on the hypothesis which I am attempting to propound. They knew that the Host actually *was* the body of Christ (it was for this reason only that they went to such risks to obtain it). It was therefore natural, even in their eyes, that it should react in a human fashion when cut with knives or tortured. There was no reason why, on that account, they should change their attitude towards Christianity, which was one of deliberate defiance; and they mounted the pyre or the gallows still continuing in their sacrilegious negation of what they knew to be true.

Closely akin to this accusation in its essential paradoxicality and incredibility was another of a like nature. A charge frequently brought up (not so much, it seems, against the Jews themselves, as against the New Christians or Marranos, who were left behind in the Peninsula when the Jews were expelled) was that of scourging and otherwise maltreating crucifixes or images of the Madonna, as part of a religious ceremonial. Thus, for example, the principal sufferers in the great Auto-dé-Fé held at Madrid on July 4th 1632, were the supporters of a secret synagogue which had been discovered in the Calle de las Infantas.[7] Part of the procedure at these illicit assemblies is said to have been the flogging of an effigy of Christ. It manifested its sufferings by shedding blood, and thrice chiding the delinquents. It might have been imagined that, under such circumstances, the latter would have repented wholeheartedly of their misdoing. Instead, they consumed the object with fire. Inquisitors and Grandees of Spain vied with one another in their zeal to destroy the building in which so heinous an action had taken place; and the Capuchin convent subsequently erected on the site was known as La

Paciencia, in remembrance of the patience with which Christ had borne the indignities inflicted upon his image.

The case was not dissimilar with regard to the alleged Ritual Murders, committed on the person of an innocent child. With regard to this ghastly libel, which unhappily still haunts the Jews in many parts of the world even at the present day, a great deal of confusion has arisen, through which the real issue has become obscured. The terms 'ritual murder' and 'blood accusation' are today used interchangeably. They actually denote, however, two completely different conceptions. The Blood Accusation is the charge levied against the Jews of obtaining Christian blood (generally, but not invariably, as the result of homicide) for use in manufacturing their unleavened bread or other ritual requirements at the Passover period. The motive, according to Thomas of Cantimpré in his *Bonum Universale de Apibus,* was rational enough. Ever since the Jews had called out to Pilate, 'His Blood be upon us and on our children', they had been afflicted with haemorrhoids. A sage had informed them that they could be cured *solo sanguine Christiano*—that is, through the blood the Messiah whom they had rejected. Through wilful blindness, however (here we find further support for the hypothesis I am endeavouring to establish in this paper), they preferred to interpret this advice literally. Hence some congregation in each province (the choice being made, according to another account, by a conference of Rabbis which assembled at Narbonne) undertook to slaughter a Christian each year in order to obtain blood for distribution amongst their co-religionists far and near.

Why, however, was this imagined crime associated with the Passover? And why was the putative victim always, or almost always, a boy, hardly ever being ascribed to the opposite sex? In order to answer these questions, we must direct our attention to the other conception which (as I have shown elsewhere[8]) is the earlier—that of Ritual Murder. In spite of all the efforts of the Council of Nicaea, the Jewish Passover still approximates to, and sometimes even coincides with, the Christian Easter. It is with this that the atrocious charge levelled against the Jews was originally associated, the Passover connexion and the consumption of blood (now considered axiomatic) being later developments. Christian Europe was first made acquainted with the idea in 1144, on the occasion of the discovery of the body of little William, a tanner's apprentice, in a wood outside Norwich. The day, on which the murder was said to have been committed, was the Wednesday in Holy Week (March 22nd). This happened in that year to coincide with the *second* day of the Jewish feast, when the major solemnities were already concluded. According to the envenomed oration made before the Synod by the priest Godwin, as reported by Thomas of Monmouth, the outrage was so fixed because of the incidence of the occasion, not in the Jewish but in the Christian calendar *(dominice passionis ebdomada)* on which account the Jews were bound to carry out such practises *(ex dierum quibus tale quid a iudaeis fieri debuerit habitudine)*. The murder of the child was thus in imitation of the Passion, and without any connexion with the Passover on the one hand or with the ritual use of the Blood on the other. These two elements began to figure only at a later period, after the close approximation of the Jewish and Christian solemnities began to be noted; and for a long time, though the two ideas were confused, the earlier remained paramount.

It must be admitted that, granted the premises (that is, the Jew's deliberate disbelief and his hatred of the Messiah whom he had wittingly rejected and slain), the earliest idea is the more logical; and it enables us to realise at last the origin of what has hitherto seemed a particularly stupid and pointless libel. It enables us to see why the alleged victim is always a boy, and never a girl. It explains the origin of so many of the grotesque accompanying details which are so frequently found—e. g. the perpetration on the victim of tortures reminiscent of the Passion, and the conclusion of the outrage by a reenactment of the Crucifixion. It provides the clue, moreover, to one mysterious sequel which had previously been peculiarly perplexing. The victims were generally revered by the populace as martyrs; and in some instances the Church itself unwillingly acquiesced. The cases of 'St.' William of Norwich, 'St.' Andreas of Rinn, 'St.' Hugh of Lincoln, 'St.' Simon of Trent, and El Santo Niño de la Guardia (dramatised by Lope de Vega) will readily come to mind: yet they are only a few out of many. In these cases, there is one detail which appears supremely illogical. A child of three or four years, perhaps, as yet unexposed to the trials and temptations of existence, can hardly have had the opportunity to shew supernal perfection in his daily life. The mere fact that he was put to death, unwillingly, at the hands of the Jews would not appear to give him *per se* a title to the adoration of the faithful, any more than falling in battle against the Saracen did to the average Crusader. If, however, the children were purported to be slain, not merely in a spirit of hatred or in order to obtain their blood, but as a quasi-religious ceremony in imitation of the Crucifixion (exactly similar, therefore, to the alleged crime of Desecrating the Host), it is obvious that the case was different. Something of the divinity of Jesus himself descended upon the innocent boy, who had ostensibly suffered in a ceremonial reenactment of his Passion. Beatification (in the popular heart, at least) was thus a foregone conclusion.

In these instances, too, it may be noted, the conduct of the Jews after the discovery of the alleged outrage is significant. The crime was generally said to be made manifest by miracles performed by the tortured body. Thus, when 'Little St. Hugh' was martyred at Lincoln in 1255, it was found impossible to bury the corpse, which rose spontaneously, time after time, to the surface of the ground. On the other occasions, the body gives out a sweet odour, or the child continues to chant the *Ave Maria* (as in Chaucer's "Prioress's Tale"), or the church bells ring without human agency. But such phenomena seldom persuaded the Jews of the exceptional heinousness of their action—a fact of which they were already abundantly aware; and they were considered willing to stage a similar parody without qualms in the following year. How different all this was from the attitude of ordinary non-Christians, who would go in droves to the baptismal font for conversion to Christianity in consequence of the slightest manifestation of supernatural phenomena! Nothing, indeed, was generally required to open the eyes of the latter to the light but the preaching of any earnest missionary—whose main difficulty, according to the Chronicles, was to secure a hearing. It was not, therefore, that the Jews did not believe in Christianity, in the same sense as Moslems or heathens did not believe in it. It was that they were constitutional antagonists of Jesus Christ—of a Jesus whom they knew to have existed and to have been justified in his Divine claims, but whom they had crucified rather than admit to be their king.

The Jews, then, deliberately rejected Christianity, while realising to the full the implications of their attitude. Small wonder then, that their professions of religion were not always taken seriously. They were hardly considered to be, in fact, worshippers of the Most High. They were followers rather, in a literal sense, of Beelzebub, on whose support and favour they counted to save them from the Divine anger which was the natural consequence of their sins.

Conscious misbelievers such as these were plainly less than human.

Individuals whose whole life was a perpetual conflict against Jesus and his followers were capable of any crime, imaginable or unimaginable. They were prepared to assassinate without compunction any of their co-religionists, or even their own children, who desired to pass over to Christianity. They did not scruple to butcher non-Jews for the purposes of their infernal rites. At time of pestilence, it was they who had poisoned the wells. At time of war, they were prepared to betray Christendom to the Moslems or to the Tartars. They exported large quantities of weapons from Germany to arm the latter, concealed in barrels. Their physicians were suspected of the intention of murdering all patients who came under their charge. (There was a New Christian physician in Lisbon who was said to have boasted that he had brought about the death of no less than 2,000 true sons of the Church in the course of his professional career). They were the declared enemies of God, of the Christian faith, and of the human kind.

The popular mediaeval conception of the Jew, as a deliberate miscreant rather than as a mere unbeliever, thus explains to some extent the bitterness, as well as the psychology, of the persecutions of that age. When persons of this nature were concerned, it was impossible to feel consideration or fellow-feeling. They could hardly be considered human beings, and human sentiments were out of place where they were concerned. Atrocity could be repaid with atrocity. They might be expelled and despoiled, without compunction, by any Christian monarch, who, in persecuting them, performed a duty rather than committed a crime. They could be attacked and exterminated by the mob, with no more hesitation than a pack of wolves. On the assumption advanced in the foregoing pages, it is possible to acquit the ordinary man of the Middle Ages of unreasoning cruelty in his relations with a people whom he was encouraged to consider in so distorted a light, but not our own contemporaries, who have revived an equally preposterous conception in this enlightened age.

NOTES

1. The contemporary records are too prolix to permit the quotation in full of passages to prove this point. Cf. however Moses Nahmanides' account of the Disputation of Barcelona of 1263, in J. C. Wagenseil's *Tela Ignea*

Satanae (Altdorf, 1681), p. 30: 'Then again said Brother Paul [i.e. Pablo Christiani, the Christian protagonist] that in the Talmud it is written that the Messiah is already come; and he brought evidence from the Midrash on the Lamentations of Jeremiah . . . Then again Brother Paul (may his name be blotted out!) said that it is stated explicitly in the Talmud that Rabbi Joshua ben Levi [learned from the Prophet Elijah that the Messiah was to be found among the sick in Rome] . . . And he is Jesus.' See also F. Baer's study on the Disputation of Tortosa in *Spanische Forschungen,* and his documents, p. 331: 'Talmudice auctoritates per magistrum Jeronymum contra judeum allegate . . .'

2. In the case of the 'Old Christian' Martyr of the seventeenth century, Don Lope de Vega, who was of unsullied *limpieza,* it was suggested that the milk imbibed from the breast of his Marrano foster-mother sufficed to infect him permanently with Jewish disbelief!

3. More than one Pontiff and scholar of the Middle Ages, indeed, went out of his way to teach that the Jews were men like any others, and should be treated as such. Clearly, this was intended to controvert the popular view of the Jew here outlined.

4. *The Dublin Review,* XCVI (1932), p. 233.

5. Dr. Robert Eisler ingeniously, though unconvincingly, suggests that the MSS in question actually contained an elaborated version of the *Testimonium Flavianum,* such as may be found in the Slavonic Josephus.

6. Considering the inherent dangers, it was difficult even for mediaeval naivety to ascribe an adequate reason for such behaviour on the part of the Jews. One was found, sufficiently preposterous to fit the crime, in the assumption that the blood which flowed from the Host could cure the Jews of their unpleasant smell, the *foetor judaicus,* or endow them with the roseate complexion denied them by nature!

7. H. C. Lea, in his *History of the Inquisition in Spain,* 4 vols. (London, 1922), III. 130/1 and 310, duplicates this episode, ascribing some lurid details to 1732.

8. *The Feast of Purim and the Origins of the Blood Accusation* in *Speculum,* October 1933.

11

Scholarship and Intolerance in the Medieval Academy: The Study and Evaluation of Judaism in European Christendom

Jeremy Cohen

Recent developments in the field of literary criticism have emphasized the influence of texts and textual traditions in shaping the world views of individuals and the cultures of societies. Perceptions of meaning, structure, and authority in literature, as well as the extent of its accessibility, reflect and contribute to manifold components of a community's ethos, ranging from the political and socioeconomic to the religious and intellectual. It follows that new methods for studying particular texts, or any alteration in the prevailing level of familiarity with them, may ultimately affect existing patterns of interpersonal relations and hitherto regnant ideologies in a given culture. Viewed within the context of the rise of urban schools and universities in high medieval Europe, the orientation of Christian scholars to the biblical and rabbinic literature of the Jews offers a fascinating case in point. Christianity had always acknowledged its debt to the Old Testament,[1] but the medieval church could not forget that a community of unbelievers—a people unique in its ability to withstand Christianity's conquest of the Roman world and to secure legal standing in Western Christendom nonetheless—served as the guardian of the original Hebrew text of the Old Testament and maintained the most literal observance of its precepts. Modern scholars

Reprinted by permission from the *American Historical Review* 91 (1986): 592–613.

have long recognized that, as the focus of medieval intellectual creativity shifted from monastery to urban school. Christian concern for the *Hebraica veritas* and rabbinic exegesis of the Bible increased markedly. This process had several implications for scholarly method and religious ideology. As their interest in Hebraic texts rose, Christian scholars of the period came to espouse the view that these texts, to serve as a valid source of religious and historical knowledge, had to be measured against the beliefs and instruction of contemporary Jews. Yet when influential churchmen, true to the Scholastic spirit of their age, turned to these beliefs as a subject for academic scrutiny in their own right, they perceived that such a comparison threatened to undermine established notions of the relationship between the church and the synagogue. Ultimately, medieval theologians realized the need for a new approach to the Jews and their textual traditions, attuned to historical reality but compliant with the demands of fundamental Christian doctrine.

I believe that there is a linkage between the intellectual awakening of the twelfth and thirteenth centuries, on the one hand, and simultaneous changes in Christian anti-Judaism, on the other. Granted, this period witnessed important political and socioeconomic developments that directly influenced the way Europeans treated the Jews—along with changes in the Jewish posture toward Christians and their faith—but the present discussion will not concern them. Rather, it will investigate three contemporaneous trends in high medieval culture that contributed to an increase in Christian anti-Judaism: (1) methodological advances in Christian scholarship (ever present in this period) and the gradual emergence of theology as an independent academic discipline; (2) the Christian pursuit of Hebraic scholarship and literalist exegesis of the Old Testament; and (3) the increasingly hostile ideological stance of the church toward the European Jewish community. Each of these developments has received ample consideration in recent scholarly literature, but the nature of their interdependence still awaits explication.[2] Focusing on the nexus between method and ideology in the study of religious texts, I propose to assess the significance of that interdependence prior to the career of Anselm of Canterbury and the First Crusade, in the midst of the cultural ferment and experimentation that characterized the twelfth century, and through the high Scholastic attempts at intellectual synthesis in the thirteenth century.

Despite the exceptional and admittedly significant portents of change in Christian exegesis that appears in some eleventh-century Christian polemics, the study of Christian doctrine before the twelfth century consisted principally of the reading and figurative interpretation of the Bible. Removed from the hubbub of urban life, monastic scholars evidently did not feel the need—nor had they developed the means—to approach theology as a science in itself. They perpetuated the Augustinian notion that religious truth could be derived entirely from the text of Scripture, if only that text were properly understood.

This idea affected the Christian attitude toward the books of the Jews. Above all, it insured the centrality of the Old Testament—and, by extension, the opposition between the Old Testament and the New—in the study of theology. It also militated against the maturation of biblical exegesis as an academic discipline just as it impeded that of theology. If the Bible had to meet all of the theologian's needs, those needs a priori colored his appreciation of the scriptural text. According to Augustine, the perfection and goal *(plenitudo et finis)* of the Bible and biblical study were the love of God. Such a consideration not only relegated non-canonical texts to a markedly inferior status but also determined the appropriateness of literal or figurative exegesis for any specific passage of Scripture. Augustine explained simply to his readers, "Whatever in the word of God cannot be related in its literal sense to moral virtue or doctrinal truth you may recognize as figurative." As a result, Heiko Oberman correctly observed, there was "no objective standard by which to separate the literal sense—or the clear places in Scripture—from the allegorical sense—or the obscure places." This distinction was not grounded in the text but was "largely dependent on the relation of the reader to God."[3] No wonder that the historical study of Scripture was largely neglected during the early Middle Ages or that churchmen generally failed to procure the tools that would have promoted it—in the case of the Old Testament, familiarity with the Jewish traditions that embodied it and knowledge of Hebrew. Instead, because of their preoccupation with the contrast between church and synagogue, Catholic theologians identified the literal meaning of Mosaic law with all that the Christian covenant of grace had supplanted. In that case, the interest of pedant or antiquarian aside, how could the literal sense of the Old Testament enhance appreciation of Catholic doctrine? Therefore, if many publicly advocated the study of Hebrew for the sake of understanding the Bible, few bothered to act on their own advice.[4]

Alongside this valuation of the Old Testament developed a particular Christian attitude toward the medieval Jew who followed its precepts. Augustine had also instructed that the Jew had survived—and should survive—in Christendom, precisely because he maintained the biblical tradition that bespoke the truth of Christianity.[5] And, if doctrinal considerations shaped Christian understanding of Jewish Scripture, so too did they mold the Christian conception of the Jews, an idea similarly out of touch with historical reality. Beryl Smalley aptly noted "how deeply the spiritual interpretation will penetrate language, thought, politics, and finally everyday life. The types are so real and so familiar that they may be used as arguments from authority, as well as for illustration. Their influence may be beneficent or sinister. The Synagogue is always opposed to the Church as darkness to light, and gradually this type becomes identified with the living Jew. . . . Philo's 'wise architect' [of allegorical exegesis] had built a prison for the Jewish people."[6]

The *Adversus Judaeos* tradition in patristic and medieval theology, through which the church asserted its legitimacy and validity, was serviced by the existence of Jews who typified life under the Old Testament. Doctrinally, the Jew had to remain, in Augustine's words, "stationary in useless antiquity," thereby bearing unconscious witness to the authenticity of the new Israel. This belief at the root of classical Christian theology helped insure the toleration of the Jews in early medieval Europe, but it prolonged Christian ignorance of the postbiblical, rabbinic religion that characterized medieval Jewish life, despite the legacy of classical rabbinic midrash that pervaded the methods and structures of patristic exegesis.[7]

Anti-Jewish polemicists of the early Middle Ages accordingly took little notice of the contemporary Jew, not because he was inaccessible to them but because, his proximity notwithstanding, he served little purpose in their arguments. These generally constituted an annotated list of biblical passages, usually from the Old Testament, which attested to the basic doctrines of Christian theology and which might depict the triumph of the church and the present subjugation of the Jews as foretold in Israelite prophecy.[8] Fulbert of Chartres, for example, whose three polemical sermons against the Jews undertook to prove their messianic hopes wrong and the doctrines of Christianity correct, relied entirely on biblical evidence. Like most medieval authors before him, Fulbert did

not intend his polemic for use against a live Jewish audience but presented Jewish arguments—readily available in earlier Christian literature—as a foil, in order to strengthen the faith of his Christian listeners.[9]
And, as late as the mid-eleventh century, Peter Damian, himself an avid
exponent of reform in the Western Church, authored two anti-Jewish
treatises that similarly rehashed the usual scriptural testimonies and their
established patristic interpretations. Of note are Damian's naive confidence that his biblical citations would triumph—in an actual face-to-
face debate—over "every insanity of Jewish depravity" and his telling
remark that disputing with contemporary Jews should not rank high
among the priorities of the church.[10]

This relatively stagnant approach to the study of Jewish texts underwent dramatic change in the twelfth century. Lawyers, exegetes, and
philosophers recognized more clearly the problem of conflicting authorities in the heritage of the church and offered a variety of solutions for
reconciling them. Systems of rational analysis became the principal
methodology in the exposition of sacred doctrine, challenging the procedure and substance of much patristic teaching based solely on the
figurative interpretation of Scripture. The Crusades, which also reawak-
ened Europe to the problematic status of the Jew, generally broadened
the social, economic, and cultural frontiers of European Christendom.
Cities, industry, and commerce were all on the rise and with them a new
urban locus for the study of theology, a setting that inevitably increased
the interaction between Christian scholar and Jew. Those who cultivated
Christian spirituality no longer confined themselves to the monastery
but turned directly to the natural world, seeking to understand it, to
rationalize it, and to incorporate all of its facets into the totality of
Christian life. The rebellion against patristic methodology, the insistence
on a more scientific explication of texts, the demand that religious ideas
bespeak the *realia* of history—all of these contributed to a renewed
interest in and the greater influence of Jewish books in twelfth-century
Christendom. With instructively different evaluations of the phenomena,
Beryl Smalley, Henri de Lubac, M. D. Chenu, and others have all demonstrated the burgeoning of literalist exegesis of the Old Testament, the
widening tendency to view the observance of Mosaic law as meritorious
and justificatory in its own time, and the greater use of Mosaic precepts
to explain and authenticate contemporary Christian institutions and
practices. Concern for the *Hebraica veritas* gained prominence in Chris-

tian Old Testament commentary, and exegetes began to involve themselves in the study of the Hebrew language, either with the help of
converted Jews or with that of medieval rabbis, who were themselves
placing greater emphasis on the literal meaning of Scripture *(peshat)*
rather than on its homiletic sense *(derash)*. Yet Christian commentators
sought far more than linguistic instruction from the Jews. For who could
better understand the primary meaning and significance of the Old
Testament than those who continued to observe and promulgate the
literal sense of its teachings? Beryl Smalley put it well: "When the
medieval scholar talked to a Rabbi he felt that he was telephoning to
the Old Testament." [11] Literal-minded commentators borrowed extensively from rabbinic scholars and from rabbinic literature, with the
paradoxical result that in the realm of Christian exegesis evidence gleaned
from contemporary Jewish sources frequently was deemed authoritative
prima facie. The forthrightness and ease with which Hugh of St. Victor,
his student Andrew, Peter Comestor, and Stephen Harding (to list only
a few) justified their instruction from rabbis, juxtaposed rabbinic traditions with traditional Christian exegesis, and even preferred the former
over the latter has been much discussed in recent scholarship, but it still
cannot fail to astound the student of Christian-Jewish relations. [12]

One would expect that the perception of the medieval Jew as spokesman for the Old Testament would have reinforced the anti-Jewish tone
of earlier polemics, grounded as they were in the premises that the
biblical character of Judaism had not changed since antiquity and that
the Jews therefore served to convey the meaning of their Scriptures to
the Christians who tolerated them. Most of the extant Christian polemics from the twelfth century do validate this assumption. Some, to be
sure, incorporate the conciliatory, rationalistic approach of Anselm of
Canterbury, who asserted that the Jews could have rejected Jesus and
Christianity only out of blind ignorance, which actually lessened their
guilt for the crime of deicide; as rational human beings, the Jews needed
only effective enlightenment to the truth. [13] Others, such as the popular
and influential *Disputatio Judei et Christiani* of Gilbert Crispin, also
manifest the rising frequency of intellectual exchanges between Christians and Jews, as well as a growing familiarity with Jewish responses to
the Christological teachings of the church; the author of a theological
treatise of the school of Abelard actually quoted Scripture in Hebrew as
he appealed to the Jews to convert. [14] Nevertheless, as a general rule, the

Jews continued to be typed as theological relics, the proponents of a carnal understanding of scriptural prophecy, which Christianity had supplanted and replaced. The language and arguments of the polemics remain overwhelmingly biblical. Polemicists failed to comprehend the historical significance and interpretative character of the evolving rabbinic tradition that regulated contemporary Jewish life and that had emerged only after the birth of Christianity. As a result, they showed little interest in undermining the status of the Jew within Christian society, either through active proselytism or through forms of physical persecution.[15]

Even Peter Alfonsi's *Dialogue* with Moses the Jew (Peter's name before he converted from Judaism to Christianity), noted for its reference to a number of postbiblical talmudic homilies, conforms to this general pattern.[16] Peter stated at the outset that he composed his polemic in order to defend his recent conversion against Jewish charges of sacrilege, intellectual error, and opportunism. He never challenged the propriety of Jewish survival in Christendom, and he pursued his dialogue not with other prospective converts but solely with his alterego Moses. The debate ultimately concerns the correct interpretation of Scripture. Peter openly acknowledged that the Jews were the followers *(cultores)* of Mosaic law—their misinterpretation of it notwithstanding—and he acceded to Moses' request that in citing the Bible he make use of the *Hebraica veritas.* He devoted eight of the twelve chapters of his polemic to a justification of Christianity on primarily scriptural grounds. Only in the first three chapters did Peter turn to rabbinic texts to demonstrate his disenchantment with Judaism. "Show me," demanded Moses, "how it seems to you that the Jews have erred in the interpretation of the [Old Testament] Law, and that you indeed understand better." Pointing to the frequently anthropomorphic midrashim, a series of which he proceeded to criticize, Peter responded: "Inasmuch as you see them attending solely to the superficial meaning of the Law, expounding the text not according to the spirit *[spiritualiter]* but according to the flesh *[carnaliter],* whence they are deceived by the greatest error." Yet, while alleging that continued rabbinic adherence to the literal meaning of the Old Testament drove him away from the Jewish community, Peter actually cited an array of figurative, imaginative homilies that ranged far and wide beyond the letter of the biblical text.[17] Here lies the crux of the issue. From Peter's Christian perspective, any Jewish interpretation of the Old Testament was necessarily literal and thus to be distinguished from the true, spiritual, Christological reading of Scripture, for such was the role of the Jews in the divine economy of salvation. Although his Jewish upbringing and education should have enabled Peter to reveal the postbiblical character of contemporary Judaism to his Christian coreligionists, the demands of Augustinian theology weighed so heavily in his reading of Jewish texts that he could not. In his assessment of Jewish Scripture, Peter Alfonsi anticipated the judgment with which Peter of Blois prefaced his own anti-Jewish polemic. If, as Richard W. Southern has argued, this other Peter embodied much of the distinctive intellectual spirit of the twelfth century, we can appreciate his words as encapsulating the still-prevalent approach to the Jews and their books. "Even today the Jews are to be allowed to live, because they are our enslaved book-bearers *[capsarii]*, as they carry around the prophets of the law of Moses for the assertion of our faith. Not only in their books but also in their faces do we read of the passion of Christ." [18]

A new interest in Hebrew and rabbinic exegesis among Christian scholars, coupled with the need to retain the conviction that Judaism was essentially a fossil of biblical antiquity, raised serious questions and caused concern among various churchmen of the High Middle Ages. Did the use of Jewish sources as *auctoritates* conform to the underlying premises of Christian anti-Jewish polemic? Could granting a particular measure of truth to Jewish texts alter the Christian perception of contemporary Judaism? If rabbinic interpretation of the Old Testament was assumed to convey its literal meaning, positive Christian valuation of the *Hebraica veritas* and its historical sense could cast a presumption of significance and legitimacy on Jewish traditions, and this might in turn undermine the basic contrast between carnal Judaism and spiritual Christianity at the heart of the *Adversus Judaeos* tradition. The opposition between the letter and the spirit of the law had always been the foundation of Christianity's claims to validity, and this opposition had facilitated the conception of Judaism as stationary and antique, which had prompted seeking Jewish help on the literal sense of the Old Testament in the first place. When a Christian exegete of the twelfth century expounded the historical meaning of a biblical passage, perhaps even at the neglect of its Christological meaning, or when he approached a rabbi for advice in interpreting such a text, he assuredly did not deem his action an admission of the rectitude of Judaism. Yet in attributing relevance and importance to the contemporary Jewish understanding of the letter of the law, his exegesis could be construed as subverting the very set of theological assumptions that had spawned it.

One can thus appreciate the fear of literalism of Richard of St. Victor, himself a Hebraist, when he read the commentaries of Andrew of St. Victor and his successors.

I have come upon a certain treatise of Master Andrew, which he wrote in explanation of Isaiah . . . , in which I have found several things imprudently taken for granted and argued in an unorthodox manner [minus catholice]. For in many instances in his treatise, the opinion of the Jews is cited as if it were not merely the Jews' but his own—and true. On the passage, "Behold a virgin will conceive and bear a son," he raises the questions or objections of the Jews and does not resolve them; and it appears as though he has given them victory, because he has left them [that is, their objections] as if they were insoluble. In matters of this sort those more informed are scandalized and those less informed are defamed, inasmuch as even today there are those among his students who explain the aforementioned prophecy not in terms of the blessed Mary, but rather concerning a certain prophetess.[19]

One ought not to conclude that Andrew of St. Victor either denied the belief in the Virgin Birth or even challenged its allegorical prefiguration in Isa. 7:14. Enthusiastically applying his Hebraic knowledge to his commentary on an Old Testament text, he simply allowed his penchant for literalism to run free of theological concern and constraint. Nevertheless, Richard of St. Victor did compose his *De Emmanuele* to redress Andrew's error, which from Richard's perspective revealed not only a preference for the historical over the figurative interpretation of a single prophetic verse but also the ostensive preference of the literalist exegetes, indignantly dubbed *judaizantes nostri,* for Judaic over Christian hermeneutic. In Richard's view, Andrew and his disciples had interpreted the Old Testament independently of the New, paying little heed to the dictates of Catholic doctrine and ecclesiology, thereby enhancing the stature of Judaism at Christianity's expense. Richard's sentiments accompanied the transmission of Andrew's commentaries into the thirteenth and fourteenth centuries and are echoed even today in the monumental *Exégèse médiévale* of Henri de Lubac.[20]

If the new literalism of twelfth-century commentators like Andrew might undermine hallowed Christian teachings, the frequently concomitant reliance on rabbinic interpretations in explaining a scriptural text posed a related theoretical problem. His innocence notwithstanding, a churchman who sought instruction from a contemporary rabbi might unintentionally accredit the traditions of postbiblical Judaism, tacitly acknowledging that they embodied a meaningful understanding of the Old Testament. Yet, properly understood, rabbinic traditions also demonstrated that Judaism had not remained "stationary in useless antiquity" ever since the day of the crucifixion, as Augustine had presumed, and it was Augustine's assumption that had provided primary theological justification for tolerating Europe's growing Jewish community, as well as for the church's claim to have inherited God's biblical covenant from a stagnant, moribund Judaism. Medieval Christians hitherto owed most of their minimal knowledge of rabbinic traditions to Jerome, who considered them (as Peter Alfonsi did) an extension of the Jews' Old Testament perspective on divine and prophetic revelation.[21] The enthusiasm with which some prominent Christian exegetes now sought rabbinic instruction awakened doubts among others. In his gloss on a canon of Gratian's *Decretum,* which asserted the authority of the Hebrew text of the Old Testament, Rufinus reworked a statement of Jerome to establish that contemporary Jewish books were no longer trustworthy. Jerome himself had emphasized that the Hebrew text of the Old Testament contained important evidence of the truth of Christian doctrine not found in Greek or Latin translations, unless the Jews had later distorted various passages that Christian polemicists had used against them. Rufinus maintained that such corruption had taken place on a grand scale, that now, because of the deceit of Jews who lived after the birth of Christianity, the Latin biblical text was more trustworthy than the Greek, the Greek more than the Hebrew. His concern was soon echoed by a series of influential canon lawyers: Johannes Faventinus, Huguccio, the author of the *Glossa palatina,* and Joannes Teutonicus.[22]

As I have argued elsewhere, the view of rabbinic Judaism as having deviated from its biblical predecessor came to maturity in the mendicant anti-Jewish polemic of the thirteenth century.[23] Twelfth-century churchmen did not perceive the extent and substance of talmudic literature and thus generally did not realize the troublesome ramifications that a new literal exegesis posed. Some writers, like Peter the Venerable of Cluny and the exegete Herbert of Bosham, did attempt to confront rabbinic teaching directly, but they failed to recognize the inconsistencies and contradictions in their treatments of the Jews and their traditions. In

their studies of Herbert's commentary on Jerome's Hebrew Psalter, Beryl
Smalley and Raphael Loewe have illustrated the impressive scope of this
English scholar's Hebraic and Judaic knowledge. Impelled to understand
the literal sense of Scripture despite its admitted inferiority to the spiritual, Herbert acquired facility in Hebrew and even Aramaic. He consulted contemporary rabbis, perused Jewish biblical commentaries and
medieval textbooks on Hebrew grammar, and appears actually to have
read from the Talmud and works of classical rabbinic midrash, and his
work displays a remarkable familiarity with the subtleties of rabbinic
hermeneutics, as well as with the history of the Masoretic Text. He did
not shy away from criticizing Jewish opinion or from expressing sympathy with Richard of St. Victor's rebuke of *judaizantes nostri.* Yet knowledge gleaned from Jewish books remains the primary *auctoritas,* the
foundation for Herbert's understanding of the Old Testament. He accused Christian commentators of corrupting the Hebrew text to support
their messianic arguments. When he did understand a Psalm Christologically, he rarely took the time to expound it doctrinally, and he still
evinced greater interest in the rejected Jewish teaching. He seems to have
been completely at ease with Christological interpretation only when he
could support it with rabbinic evidence: Christian exposition of the
literal sense, his method suggests, should ideally comport with Jewish
exegesis.[24] It is of particular significance, then, that Herbert's commentary itself provided fuel for the argument to invalidate rabbinic interpretations of Scripture, for he also suggested that rabbinic traditions embodied a heretical departure from the true, antique religion of biblical
Israel. On a number of occasions, Herbert noted the differences in the
beliefs and practices of ancient and medieval Jews; at times he accused
contemporary rabbis of deliberately obscuring their ancestral traditions.
Commenting on Ps. 2, he wrote:

Modern Jewish scholars state that things in the Psalm . . . were explained by
their ancient masters as pertaining to the messiah. They themselves do furnish
the truth in their senseless little explanations; but, piecing together statements of
the Psalm on the spur of the moment, as if they in fact wrote them, they prefer
that *Quare fremuerunt etc.* [that is, Ps. 2] be interpreted these days with regard
to King David—so as not to assent to ecclesiastical opinion, and to condemn
the men of the Church. It is indeed the error of a perverse, depraved generation
and its obstinate hatred of the truth, which prefers to deviate from its own
masters and the authority of its sages, knowingly and intentionally to distort the

Scriptures, so as not to espouse their ecclesiastical interpretation which its own ancient masters actually held![25]

Herbert neither recognized nor followed the implications of his logic. To the end of his life, he remained ambivalent toward the Judaic understanding of Scripture—maintaining his valuation of the literal sense and, accordingly, obliged to justify the persistence of his Christian faith.

Even though he lacked Herbert's Hebraic knowledge, Peter the Venerable, in his lengthy polemic against the Jews, also accused the postbiblical rabbis of abandoning the divine precepts of Scripture for the sake of the illegitimate teachings of men.[26] In particular, Peter criticized a number of talmudic homilies, whose logical absurdities and anthropomorphisms, he maintained, revealed the bestial, satanic character of contemporary Judaism. He voiced the rationalist spirit of his age, but in a line of argument diametrically opposed to that of Anselm of Canterbury. For Peter, since the Jews spurned the blatantly rational truth of Christianity, they must have been less than human, and their blasphemous Talmud was to blame.[27] Peter attributed little value to a knowledge of Hebrew; Greek and Latin translations of the Bible afforded Christians precisely the same entrée to the truth, while the teachings of Jewish tradition were grossly unacceptable.[28] He proclaimed to the Jews:

I extend to you before the whole world, O beastly Jew, that book of yours— yes, your book, that Talmud of yours, that illustrious doctrine of yours, which is to be preferred to prophetic books and all authentic teachings. . . . The Jewish Talmud cannot be that book of which it is said, "in thy book they are all recorded" [Ps. 139:16]. . . . Who besides Satan can teach such absurd things, and who besides the Jew can listen to, if not believe, them—that the reading of the Talmud can prejudice the power of God, that the incredible recitation of an infernal book can impede the will and mandate of God? For is that book of yours, O Jew, holier than the five books of Moses, holier than the books of the prophets, better or more worthy? . . . You have fought for so long against divine books with diabolical ones, and you have striven to tinge and obscure heavenly doctrine with the smoke of the infernal pit.[29]

Some historians have concluded that Peter hereby repudiated the conception of the Jew and Judaism that gave rise to the literalist exegesis of the twelfth century, that for him the medieval Jew was no longer the Jew of the Bible and rabbinic religion was nothing less than a perversion of real Judaism.[30] Yet a careful reading of Peter's anti-Jewish pronouncements reveals inconsistency and ambivalence. Like those of Herbert of Bosham, his comments suggest that contemporary Judaism and the religion of the Old Testament were not the same, but, without direct access to the Talmud, he failed to perceive the implications of his polemic. The Jews accordingly remained the guardians of the biblical books and tradition, distinguished for the unity and steadfastness of their loyalty to Mosaic law.[31] Their Talmud may have manifested a "bovine intellect," but Peter persisted in the traditional estimation of the Jews as blind to the truth of Scripture rather than as cognizant and deliberately unfaithful.[32] The Talmud, in other words, perpetuated the pre-Christian religion of ancient Israel, carnal understanding of the Bible and all. Rabbinic Judaism, albeit abominable, did not depart from the letter of the obsolete Mosaic covenant; it was not a heresy. In Peter's view, the "blasphemous, sacrilegious, ridiculous, and false" doctrine of talmudic Judaism emerged when Israelite prophecy ended; it antedated Jesus and thus comprised at least part of the religious outlook that Christianity came to replace.[33] Peter, therefore, could identify the Talmud's homilies with "the endless fables, and the traditions utterly foreign to the law of God, of which the Lord said to the Pharisees in the Gospel [Matt. 15:7], 'You have abandoned the precepts of God for the sake of your own traditions.' " Just as Peter Alfonsi had ignored the figurative, imaginative character of rabbinic Aggadah, so, too, Peter the Venerable attributed the error in talmudic interpretation to a mentality that insisted on interpreting a sacred text only literally, admitting "neither metaphor, nor allegory, nor any of the customary modes of figurative speech, through which all these things may rightfully be interpreted as applying to God."[34] European Jews still played their instructive part in the divine economy of salvation. "There is fulfilled in you, O wretched people, what your apostle by birth, ours in terms of doctrine, said of such things: 'The time will come when they will not stand wholesome teaching, but follow their own fancy and gather a crowd of teachers to tickle their ears. They will stop their ears to the truth and turn to mythology' [2 Tim. 4:3–4]."[35] Peter's anti-Jewish writings display no desire to promote proselytism; he consistently reaffirmed that the Jews ought not to be killed. Bearing the mark of Cain, the Jews should surely be subjugated and oppressed, but their traditions had not yet been judged incompatible with their toleration by Christian society.[36]

Thirteenth-century Scholasticism brought the academic discipline of theology to maturity. The innovative methodologies of previous generations, who were propelled by an unquenchable thirst for discovery and investigation, successfully transformed theology into a science, emancipated from the curricular and methodological prejudices of the church fathers. Schoolmen of the thirteenth century capitalized on the flurry of translations from Arabic and Greek into Latin, attempting to assemble all available knowledge in their exposition of sacred doctrine, just as they banded together in universities to formulate the intellectual syntheses that marked the age. No critical faculty was left uncultivated in what Jaroslav Pelikan had dubbed "the reintegration of the Catholic tradition." And the *summa,* the hallmark of thirteenth-century scholarship, was not complete without a reconciliation of all conflicting arguments, from authority or from reason, or without an intellectually compelling fusion of seemingly discordant ideas and texts. Significantly, the Scholastic synthesis did not rest in the ivory tower; it attempted to create a harmony between theory and practice, to apply the logic and conclusions of theological scholarship to social structures and individual lives. Scholasticism accordingly contributed to the flowering of an applied or missionary theology, intent on converting the infidel, rehabilitating the heretic, and insuring that all components of an organismically conceived Christian society worked toward the interests of the whole in every avenue of life. Schoolmen not only recovered, restored, and scrutinized ancient biblical and patristic texts but also developed new reference tools and methods of indexing these materials, which facilitated their availability to and utility for preachers as well as academicians. If the theological masters collected and studied works of Greek and Muslim philosophers, they also strove to eliminate all challenges to the Christian world view posed by these works. They implemented ecclesiastical directives to restrict the dissemination of dangerous ideas—above all those of Aristotle—and they condemned their colleagues who pursued the logic of Averroism beyond the limits of Christian responsibility. The *summa,* the universities, and the friars of the new mendicant orders who sought to realize the totalistic vision of their age—whether as academicians, preachers, inquisitors, or missionaries—all gave expression to the same ideological premise: intellectual activities were appropriately governed by Christian principles and directed toward Christian ends.[37]

These developments precipitated noteworthy changes in Christian attitudes toward the Jews and their books. Freed in some measure from its traditional enslavement to the exposition of Christian doctrine, thirteenth-century biblical exegesis refined its theories of signification in literary texts, formalizing the distinction between literal and spiritual senses and placing greater emphasis still on the former. Recognition of the value of the *Hebraica veritas* became more widespread; the number of Christians adept in Hebrew increased markedly; and schools of clerics labored to correct the text of the Vulgate, a process in which their acquaintance with the Hebrew Masoretic Text often proved significant.[38] The new Aristotelian rationalism also infused vitality into the endeavor to understand Old Testament teaching as purposeful in its original context. At the same time, however, new polemics appeared that rejected the contemporary Jew as no longer valuable in illuminating or enhancing the encounter between Latin Christendom and the Old Testament. The church's scholars gained considerable familiarity with postbiblical rabbinic tradition, and they now could perceive the historical evolution that separated antique biblical Judaism from the religion of medieval Jewry. Some deemed the European Jewish community unfit for toleration on theoretical grounds, given its abandonment of the stagnant, Old Testament way of life with which Augustine had justified its preservation. No longer was Judaism a mere foil that facilitated the Christological assertions of the polemicist. Anti-Jewish polemic assumed a much more direct and aggressive character; it aimed to undermine the presence and security of the Jew in a properly ordered Christian society. In all of this, one can discern an awakening to ideological inconsistencies that appeared to underlie the twelfth-century valuation of rabbinic instruction in Christian exegesis, and an effort to resolve them. Christian scholars finally grew sensitive to the interplay of their use of Jewish tradition with the logical demands of their *Adversus Judaeos* polemic.

The most telling evidence of these developments remains the well-known assault of the thirteenth-century church on the Talmud. Indicted before Pope Gregory IX by an embittered Jewish apostate, Nicholas Donin, in 1236, the Talmud was denounced in a series of papal bulls in 1239 and 1244, burned in Paris under papal direction in 1242, subsequently condemned by a commission of prelates and university masters in 1248, and attacked repeatedly by the church during the later Middle Ages.[39] The ecclesiastical treatment of the Talmud exemplifies the predilection of church scholars in the high Scholastic period to discover, to scrutinize, to understand, to classify, and actively to employ the contents of all available texts in their syntheses. Donin may have served as an important catalyst in the emergence of the church's new stance toward rabbinic Judaism, but the extent and impact of the new attitude quickly transcended the limited sphere of his personal influence. Two hundred years earlier, even someone like Donin could not have elicited the forceful response enunciated by the papacy in the 1230s and 1240s, and, even without Donin, the ideological climate of thirteenth-century Christendom was such that a careful investigation of contemporary Jewish belief and practice was only a matter of time. It is telling that, in the realm of metaphysics, thirteenth-century Christian philosophers expended great energy to grapple with the systems of Arabic and Jewish thinkers, so like and yet unlike their own, feeling compelled to assimilate them and to overcome them simultaneously. The Jew Moses Maimonides thus commanded respect as a philosophical authority in the Christian academy; his philosophical formulations served as a model for blending Aristotelian science with faith in the God of the Bible and for demonstrating the limits of rational inquiry. William of Auvergne and Thomas Aquinas frequently appropriated the rationalist Maimonidean exegesis of the Mosaic commandments, asserting their rightfulness and purpose in their original setting and thereby promoting the Christian study of the Old Testament in its literal sense.[40] Nevertheless, this positive estimation of Maimonidean thought did not prevent Dominican inquisitors from burning the works of Maimonides as heretical, Thomas Aquinas from reproaching him for abandoning the literal meaning of Scripture, and Giles of Rome from condemning him for forsaking the rational truth of biblical revelation.[41] Given such an intellectual climate, the amplitude and theological-historical implications of talmudic literature provoked a swift, deliberate reaction.

The Christian encounter with the Talmud demonstrates that growing numbers of influential churchmen were acquiring an interest in rabbinic texts and recognizing the importance of greater familiarity with them. On the one hand, a rabbinic interpretation of Scripture continued to inform Christian understanding of the literal, historical sense of the Old Testament. On the other hand, in its discovery of the Talmud, the thirteenth-century church also discerned the postbiblical character of rabbinic tradition and perceived the threat that it posed to the Augustinian notion of what the Jews and their books were supposed to be. Talmudic and midrashic texts thus had to be mastered and persecuted at the same time; whatever utility they proffered had to be liberated from the biblically inauthentic—and therefore ultimately intolerable—contemporary Jewish community that preserved and defended them. William of Auvergne, Albert the Great, and Hugh of St. Cher openly applied their knowledge of rabbinic sources in their writings, and yet they all participated actively in the Parisian condemnations of the Talmud. Raymond de Peñaforte—who served as papal confessor when Gregory IX received Donin at the curia, who stood at the helm of the Order of Friars Preachers when the Dominicans played a leading role in the *auto-da-fé* of 1242 against the Talmud, and who clearly shared the view of contemporary postbiblical Judaism as a heretical departure from the biblical norm—vehemently advocated that clerics study Hebrew and use rabbinic sources in preaching to the Jews. Raymond opened a number of schools for training mendicant friars in Hebrew, and Pablo Christiani and Raymond Martini, his two best-known disciples, both based their polemics against the Jews on the premise that rabbinic texts bespoke the truth of Christianity.[42] Most significantly, as the church grew more conscious of the complex linkage between its attitude toward Judaic learning and its treatment of the Jews, it began to voice concern over this troublesome relationship. The *Summa theologiae* attributed to Alexander of Hales weighed the evils of the Talmud against the positive testimonial function served by the Jews' presence in Christendom. "Since they must observe the doctrine of that book as law," the treatise concludes, "their books, in which blasphemies are contained, are to be burned"—although the Jews and their legitimate Old Testament rites did warrant toleration.[43] Later in the 1240s, when the Jews protested to the papacy over the ecclesiastical attack on the Talmud, the key issue set the alleged postbiblical—and therefore heretical—nature of rabbinic literature against the Christian duty to endure the survival of biblical Judaism. Popes Gregory IX and Innocent IV had deemed the Talmud a distortion of Judaism and had consigned it to the flames. As a result, Innocent later recounted to Louis IX of France,

the Jewish masters of your kingdom recently asserted before us and our brothers, that without that book which in Hebrew is called "Talmut," they cannot understand the Bible and their other statutes and laws in accordance with their faith; we then, bound as we are by the divine command to tolerate them in their Law, thought fit to have the answer given them that we do not wish to deprive them of their books if as a result we should be depriving them of their Law.

Innocent added that he had designated the chancellor of the University of Paris, Eudes of Chateauroux, to inspect rabbinic books, and "of these he should tolerate such as he will find may be tolerated, in accordance with the [aforementioned] divine command."[44] The legatine commission convened at the University of Paris and condemned the Talmud for its "innumerable errors, abuses, blasphemies, and wickedness." The language of this formal pronouncement was terse, but Eudes argued more discursively in an earlier letter responding to the papal demand for his investigation.

The said books were full of errors, and . . . the veil covers the heart of these people to such a degree, that these books turn the Jews away *not only from an understanding of the spirit, but even of the letter,* and incline them to fables and lies. From this it is clear that the Jewish teachers of the Kingdom of France uttered a falsehood to Your Holiness and to the sacred fathers, the Lords Cardinals, when they said that without these books, which in Hebrew are called "Talmud," they cannot understand the Bible and the other precepts of their laws, in accordance with their faith.[45]

Despite recent scholarly protestations to the contrary, the charge of talmudic heresy—that the books under indictment obviated Jewish fidelity even to the letter of the Old Testament—remained at the heart of ecclesiastical concern, both during the thirteenth century and beyond.[46] One must also note that Eudes did not rest with his summary condemnation of the Talmud and his insistence that it not be restored to the Jewish community. As chancellor of the University of Paris, he also supervised a massive effort by clerics to study the Talmud and present those of its contents with a potential interest to a Christian reader in a manner befitting his needs. The result was a written compilation over two hundred folio pages long, usually entitled *Extractiones de Talmut,* which first amassed in the order of their appearance some two thousand talmudic texts deemed noteworthy, then grouped them under thirteen subject classifications (for example, "Concerning the authority of the law which is called 'Talmud,' " "Concerning blasphemies against Christ and the Blessed Virgin," and so forth), and finally appended some shorter lists, including a collection of texts about the mechanisms of the rabbinic legal system.[47] Eudes' undertaking manifests the Scholastic inclination for using texts to serve the higher purposes of Christendom. Discoveries in the classroom demanded packaging that would facilitate their application in the world at large—in the case of the Talmud, to the pastoral interpretation of Scripture, the mendicant mission to the Jews, and the justification for persecuting Jewish books. As Richard Rouse and Mary Rouse have concluded, "Tools [which afforded easier access to important texts], mendicants, and (to a large degree) university are all responses to the same demand, the Church's need for a clergy properly trained and provided with the necessary books to preach and to minister to a Christian society."[48]

A sharp distinction between the utilitarian employment of Jewish exegesis and the tacit countenance of an inherently illegitimate rabbinic tradition also pervades the biblical commentaries of the Parisian master Nicholas of Lyra, whose academic career spanned the late thirteenth and early fourteenth centuries. Nicholas accepted the Thomistic definition of the literal sense of the Old Testament as that which its writer consciously intended, but he argued that such an intention could indeed have been Christological. The primary meaning of the same biblical text could therefore include both historical and Christological dimensions.[49] Throughout his postils, Nicholas drew extensively on the glosses of Rashi (Solomon ben Isaac of Troyes, 1040–1105) and on other rabbinic works. Yet, avoiding the logically problematic conclusions of earlier Hebraists, Nicholas did not entangle his knowledge of Hebrew in the a priori legitimization (whether expressed, implicit, or even unintentional) of the instruction of European rabbis. His Hebraica did not depend on the Jews.[50] He advocated and pursued Hebraic study in the service of exegesis even in the absence of the Jews, who were expelled from France in 1306, and he maintained that talmudic Judaism and its contemporary spokesmen had deviated deliberately from the faith of their antique biblical forebears and were essentially heretical as a result. One could no longer casually presume Jewish exegesis to be authoritative. In the prologue to his monumental *Postilla litteralis*, Nicholas decried the obfuscation of the literal understanding of Scripture in his day, which he attributed primarily to the errors of scribes and translators. "In order to attain the literal truth in the Scripture of the Old Testament, one must resort to the books of the Hebrews." In the same passage, however, Nicholas echoed the warning of Rufinus. "In this one must still be cautious indeed with regard to those passages in Old Testament Scripture which speak of the divinity of Christ and its consequences. The

Jews have corrupted some of them in defense of their error." To his explanation for adducing the literalist commentaries of Rashi, "who among the Hebrew doctors has spoken most reasonably," Nicholas juxtaposed a reminder to his readers that absurd Judaic teachings ought not to be condoned.[51] Rashi himself elicited rebuke from Nicholas for concealing the Christological truth of the Bible, and Nicholas typically substantiated his charges with references to other texts of presumably ancient Jewish interpretation that the medieval rabbi had deliberately abandoned. For example, to "the error of the Hebrews, who say that in these three chapters [of Isaiah], namely 7, 8, and 9, mention is not made of Christ," Nicholas responded, "In order to disallow this falsehood and to declare the truth, one must depend above all on the Aramaic translation [of the Old Testament] which among the Hebrews is called 'Targum' and is of such great authority among them that no one has dared to contradict it." Nicholas similarly cited the Septuagint to disclose Rashi's corruption of Isa. 9:5 and the glosses of Rabbi Moses ha-Darshan of Narbonne to refute Rashi's exegesis of Ps. 79. All of these sources, Nicholas believed, antedated the talmudic heresy.[52] Rashi's "perversity" allegedly led him to self-contradiction in the understanding of Isa. 55:5. And, in his discussion of Ps. 2, Nicholas echoed the polemic of Herbert of Bosham; he indicted Rashi for openly conceding the messianic message of the text and for demanding at the same time that "for the sake of responding to the heretics [that is, Christians] it be expounded as concerning David."[53] Rashi epitomized for Nicholas the most learned of contemporary Jews *(Judei moderni),* whose Hebraic knowledge could serve the Christian exegete of the Old Testament but whose adherence to deviant talmudic Judaism merited outright condemnation and rejection. Nicholas accordingly clarified and reiterated the warning of Richard of St. Victor against overestimating the reliability of Jewish biblical interpretation. The *Postilla* denounces Andrew of St. Victor for joining Rashi in his *perversitas,*[54] chastises those Catholic doctors who, like Andrew, "Judaize" more than Rashi himself ("magis Iudaizant quantum ad hoc, quam ipse Rabbi Salomo"),[55] and even faults an interpretation of Thomas Aquinas for favoring the error of the Jews over the doctrine of the church.[56] As Hebraist, commentator, and theologian, Nicholas succeeded not only in appropriating literalist exegesis from medieval Jews but also in recognizing the ideological dangers in according their texts intrinsic value.

It is instructive that in the period of the most intense Christian study of Judaica new polemics undermined the security of European Jewry. Whereas in the early medieval period ignorance of rabbinic teaching had perpetu- ated the nonaggressive *Adversus Judaeos* polemic of the church fathers, which was grounded in the notion of a Jewish religion that had remained stagnant and moribund since the first century, the growing interest in traditional Jewish learning ultimately led to disavowal of the old presup- position and its logical implications. A more direct and hostile type of polemic emerged, and alongside it a new Christian view of Jewish his- tory, one that perceived a major qualitative transformation in the nature of Judaism and Jewish literature since the end of biblical times and the birth of Christianity. Such a schema underlay the novel idea of Thomas Aquinas and Nicholas of Lyra that first-century Jews actually recognized Jesus as Messiah and Son of God but spitefully killed him nonetheless. It facilitated the aggressive proselytizing of Raymond de Peñaforte and his confreres, as evidenced in the monumental *Pugio fidei* of Raymond Martini.[57] And, in terms of the new bifurcation between the literal truth of Scripture and the beliefs of contemporary Jews, this notion was expressed quite succinctly by William of Auvergne. In his *De legibus,* William first affirmed the primacy and authenticity of the literal—as opposed to the prefigurative—meaning of the Old Testament:

Why was it necessary for the law to express a spiritual meaning, at a time when we were not yet in existence? And after the Christian Church was established, it was truly not necessary that the law speak to us figuratively, since the truth of the Gospel itself had come to us clear and unconcealed. So by all means it is necessary that such things [Old Testament precepts] had a literal sense. And it is most improbable that the entire Jewish nation, the people of the law—in which everyone, from the most distinguished to the most obscure, was trained in the law and studied it—for so many thousands of years, would not have detected such an error [that is, that they understood the law incorrectly].

Yet contemporary Jews, continued William, no longer understood this literal truth.

If anyone should ask why the Jews themselves today do not accept what we have stated and written concerning the ostensive absurdities [of the truly rational Mosaic laws], we would respond that at the time of their enactment, [their reasons] were most apparent to the [Jewish] sages. Yet this knowledge vanished from among the Jews, because of the passage of time, their suffering, their dispersion, and above all their neglect of the study of the law. Such neglect was caused in part by the greed to which they are certainly prone, and in part by the love of Gentile philosophy.[58]

In the high medieval academy, increased study of a minority viewpoint led not to greater toleration but to greater bifurcation between the circumscribed value of such an outlook and its despised protagonists. Twelfth- and thirteenth-century scholars may well have refined numerous hermeneutic techniques in pondering the significative character of theological language. Yet, as G. R. Evans has noted in a recent monograph, modern standards of textual criticism eluded them, inasmuch as their reading of a text still had to fit the predetermined mold of their theology. Modes of interpretation may have changed, but not the fundamental doctrinal assumptions that antedated them.[59] For the medieval Jew, the results were dire. As Scholasticism facilitated an understanding of his books, it nearly eliminated his theologically grounded utility in European Christendom.

NOTES

1. The term "Old Testament," befitting the theological perspective of the Christian subjects of this essay, has been used for convenience.

2. The following works were of particular importance in laying the basis for this study. On Scholasticism and the academic study of theology, see Martin Grabmann, *Die Geschichte der scholastischen Methode,* 2 vols. (1909–11; reprint edn., Berlin, 1956); M.-D. Chenu, *La théologie au douzième siècle,* Etudes de philosophie médiévale, vol. 45 (Paris, 1957), and *La théologie comme science au XIIIᵉ siècle,* Bibliothèque thomiste, vol. 33 (3d edn., Paris, 1957); Gordon Leff, *Medieval Thought: St. Augustine to Ockham* (Chicago, 1957); R. W. Southern, *Medieval Humanism and Other Studies* (Oxford, 1970); Jaroslav Pelikan, *The Growth of Medieval Theology (600–1300),* The Christian Tradition, vol. 3 (Chicago, 1978); G. R. Evans, *Old Arts and New Theology: The Beginnings of Theology as an Academic Discipline* (Oxford, 1980); Robert L. Benson and Giles Constable, eds., *Renaissance and Renewal in the Twelfth Century* (Cambridge, Mass., 1982); and Stephen C. Ferruolo, *The Origins of the University: The Schools of Paris and Their Critics, 1100–1215* (Stanford, Calif., 1985). On Christian Hebraic scholarship and biblical exegesis, see Beryl Smalley, *The Study of the Bible in the Middle Ages* (3d edn., Oxford, 1983); Henri de Lubac, *Exégèse médiévale: Les quatre sens de l'écriture,* Théologie, vols. 41–42, 59 (Paris, 1959–64); Herman Hailperin, *Rashi and the Christian Scholars* (Pittsburgh,

Pa., 1963); Aryeh Grabois, "The *Hebraica veritas* and Jewish-Christian Intellectual Relations in the Twelfth Century," *Speculum*, 50 (1975): 613–34; and G. R. Evans, *The Language and Logic of the Bible: The Earlier Middle Ages* (Cambridge, 1984). On anti-Jewish polemic, see Lena Dasberg, *Untersuchungen über die Entwertung des Judenstatus im 11. Jahrhundert* (Paris, 1965); Amos Funkenstein, "Ha-Temurot be-Vikkuah ha-Dat she-bein Yehudim le-Notsrim ba-Me'ah ha-12" (Changes in the Patterns of Christian Anti-Jewish Polemic in the Twelfth Century), *Zion*, new ser., 33 (1968): 125–44; Ch. Merchavia, *Ha-Talmud bi-R'i ha-Natsrut: Ha-Yahas le-Sifrut Yisra'el shele-Ahar ha-Miqra ba-ʿOlam ha-Notsri b-Imei ha-Beinayim [500–1248]* (The Church versus Talmudic and Midrashic Literature, 500–1248) (Jerusalem, 1970); and Jeremy Cohen, *The Friars and the Jews: The Evolution of Medieval Anti-Judaism* (Ithaca, N.Y., 1982).

3. Augustine, *De doctrina christiana*, 1.84–85, 3.33–34, CSEL 80:30, 62–63, 88; and Heiko Augustinus Oberman, *Forerunners of the Reformation: The Shape of Late Medieval Thought* (New York, 1966), 283–84.

4. On Christians' knowledge of Hebrew, see Berthold Altaner, "Zur Kenntnis des Hebräischen im Mittelalter," *Biblische Zeitschrift*, 21 (1938): 288–308; and Matthias Thiel, *Grundlagen und Gestalt der Hebräischkenntnisse des früheren Mittelalters*, Biblioteca degli studi medievali, vol. 4 (Spoleto, 1973).

5. Augustine, *Tractatus adversus Judaeos*, PL 42: 51–67; *De civitate Die*, 18.46, 20.29; *Sermo*, 200.2, PL 38: 1030; *Enarrationes in Psalmos*, 58.1.21–22, CCSL 39: 744; and *De fide rerum invisibilium*, 6.9, CCSL 46: 15–16. Also see Bernhard Blumenkranz, *Die Judenpredigt Augustins: Ein Beitrag zur Geschichte der jüdisch-christlichen Beziehungen in den ersten Jahrhunderten* (1946; reprint edn., Paris, 1973), and "Augustin et les Juifs; Augustin et le judaïsme," *Recherches augustiniennes*, 1 (1958): 225–41.

6. Smalley, *Study of the Bible*, 25–26.

7. On the influence of rabbinic midrash on patristic exegesis, see, among others, Harry Austryn Wolfson, *The Philosophy of the Church Fathers* (2d edn., Cambridge, Mass., 1964), 24–96 *passim;* and Raphael Loewe, "The Jewish Midrashim and Patristic and Scholastic Exegesis of the Bible," *Studia patristica*, 1 (1957): 492–524.

8. Amos Funkenstein, "Basic Types of Christian Anti-Jewish Polemics in the Later Middle Ages," *Viator*, 2 (1971): 373–75. On early medieval anti-Jewish polemic, see A. Lukyn Williams, *Adversus Judaeos: A Bird's-Eye View of Christian Apologiae until the Renaissance* (Cambridge, 1935), bks. 4–5; Bernhard Blumenkranz, *Les auteurs chrétiens latins du moyen âge sur les juifs et le judaïsme* (Paris, 1963); and Heinz Schreckenberg, *Die christlichen Adversus-Judaeos-Texte und ihr literarisches und historisches Umfeld (1.–11. Jh.)*, Europäische Hochschulschriften ser. 23, vol. 172 (Frankfurt am Main, 1982). R. W. Southern maintained that early medieval Spanish Christian scholars adopted a similarly affected ignorance toward Islam. Southern, *Western Views of Islam in the Middle Ages* (Cambridge, Mass., 1962), 25.

9. Fulbert of Chartres, *Tractatus contra Judaeos*, PL 141:305–18. Also see

Blumenkranz, *Les auteurs chrétiens latins*, 237–43. On the availability of Jewish interpretations of Gen. 49:10 (the main text of Fulbert's sermons) in earlier Christian writings, see Adolf Posnanski, *Schiloh: Ein Beitrag zur Geschichte der Messiaslehre* (Leipzig, 1904), chaps. 4, 14.

10. Peter Damian, *Antilogus contra Judaeos, PL* 145:41; "Si Christi miles esse, et pro eo viriliter pugnare desideras, contra carnis vitia, contra diaboli machinas insignis bellator arma potius corripe; hostes videlicet, qui nunquam moriuntur: quam contra Judaeos, qui jam de terra pene deleti sunt." For Damian's *Antilogus*, see *PL* 145: 41–58. For a companion work, see *Dialogus inter Judeum requirentem, et Christianum, e contrario respondentem, PL* 145: 57–68. On both *opuscula*, see David Berger, "St. Peter Damian: His Attitude toward the Jews and the Old Testament, *Yavneh Review*, 4 (1965): 80–112; and Blumenkranz, *Les auteurs chrétiens latins*, 265–71.

11. Beryl Smalley, *Hebrew Scholarship among Christians in XIIIth Century England as Illustrated by Some Hebrew-Latin Psalters*, Lectiones in Veteri Testamento et in rebus judaicis, vol. 6 (London, 1939), 1.

12. Smalley herself wrote that what "drove scholars to study the literal sense of the Old Testament" is "one of the darkest problems connected with the twelfth-century revival"; Smalley, "An Early Twelfth-Century Commentator on the Literal Sense of Leviticus," *Recherches de théologie ancienne et médiévale*, 35 (1969): 98.

13. For example, see Anselm, *Cur Deus homo*, 2.15. Also see R. W. Southern, *Saint Anselm and His Biographer: A Study of Monastic Life and Thought, 1059–c. 1130* (Cambridge, 1963), chap. 3, and "St. Anselm and Gilbert Crispin, Abbot of Westminster," *Medieval and Renaissance Studies*, 3 (1957): 78–115. For a work at least worthy of mention in connection with this genre of rationalist polemic, see Peter Abelard, *Dialogus inter philosophum, Judaeum et Christianum*, ed. Rudolf Thomas (Stuttgart, 1970).

14. See Crispin, *Disputatio Judei et Christiani*, ed. Bernhard Blumenkranz, Stromata, vol. 3 (Utrecht, 1956); and *Ysagoge in theologiam*, in *Ecrits théologiques de l'école d'Abélard: Textes inédits*, ed. Arthur Landgraf, Spicilegium sacrum lovaniense: Etudes et documents, vol. 14 (Louvain, 1934), esp. 126–62. On Crispin, see R. J. Z. Werblowsky, "Crispin's Disputation," *Journal of Jewish Studies*, 11 (1960): 69–79; and Anna Sapir Abulafia, "An Attempt by Gilbert Crispin, Abbot of Westminster, at Rational Argument in the Jewish-Christian Debate," *Studia monastica*, 26 (1984): 55–75. On the widespread popularity of the polemic, see Blumenkranz, "La *Disputatio Judei cum Christiano* de Gilbert Crispin, abbé Westminster," *Revue du moyen âge latin*, 4 (1948): 237–52; and David Berger, "Gilbert Crispin, Alan of Lille, and Jacob ben Reuben: A Study in the Transmission of Medieval Polemic," *Speculum*, 49 (1974): 34–47.

15. Berger, "Gilbert Crispin"; Margaret Schlauch, "The Allegory of the Church and the Synagogue," *Speculum*, 14 (1939): 448–64; and M.-H. Vicaire, " 'Contra Judaeos' meridionaux au début du XIIIᵉ siècle: Alain de Lille,

Evrard de Béthune, Guillaume de Bourges," in *Juifs et judaïsme de Langue-doc*, Cahiers de Fanjeaux, vol. 13 (Toulouse, 1977), 269–93.

16. Peter Alfonsi, *Dialogus Petri et Moysi Judei*, PL 157: 535–672.

17. *Ibid.*, 540. Subsequently, Peter wrote that, because the statements of the biblical prophets were often obscure, they should be interpreted allegorically if their literal sense would cause readers to veer from the path of reason ("talia . . . quae secundum litteram accipientes a rationis tramite exorbite-mus, ea allegorice interpretamur"). The rabbis, however, did not perceive God properly ("non cognoverunt, ut oportuit, Deum"), and they therefore erred by interpreting prophetic teaching literally. Precisely in this regard Peter believed that he understood Scripture better than the Jews—that is, as reason would demand ("prout sanus exigit sensus"). *Ibid.*, 553.

18. Peter of Blois, *Contra perfidiam Judaeorum*, PL 207: 825. Also see South-ern, "Peter of Blois: A Twelfth Century Humanist?" in his *Medieval Humanism*, 105–32.

19. Richard of St. Victor, *De Emmanuele*, PL 196: 601–02. On the understanding of Scripture in a "Catholic sense," see Pelikan, *Growth of Medieval Theology*, 36–39.

20. See Beryl Smalley, "A Commentary of Isaias by Guerric of Saint-Quentin, O.P.," *Miscellanea Giovanni Mercati*, 2 vols., Studi e testi, vols. 121–22 (Vatican City, 1946), 2:391–95, and "Ralph of Flaix on Leviticus," *Recherches de théologie ancienne et médiévale*, 35 (1968): 52–68; Nicholas of Lyra, *Postilla litteralis*, in *Biblia sacra, cum glossis, interlineari et ordinaria, Nicholai Lyrani Postilla, ac moralitatibus, Burgensis additionibus, et Thoringi replicis*, 6 vols. (Venice, 1588), 3: 148FGH, 4: 21FGH–22BC, 89FG, 336B, 381G; and de Lubac, *Exégèse médiévale*, pt. 2, vol. 1: 362–67.

21. De Lubac, *Exégèse médiévale*, pt. 2, vol. 1: 140–41, 238–47; Funkenstein, "Ha-Temurot be-Vikkuaḥ ha-Dat," 138 n. 49; and Merchavia, *Ha-Talmud bi-R'i ha-Natsrut*.

22. Jerome wrote in his preface to the Pentateuch: "Sicubi tibi in translatione videor errare, interroga Hebraeos, diversarum urbium magistros consule: quod illi habent de Christo, tui codices non habent. Aliud est si, contra se, postea, ab Apostolis usurpata testimonia probaverunt, et emendatiora sunt exemplaria latina quam graeca, graeca quam hebraea." A. Gasquet *et al.*, eds., *Biblica sacra iuxta latinam vulgatam versionem ad codicum fidem*, 16 vols. (Rome, 1926–81), 1: 68–69. Gratian had accordingly recorded: "Libris veterum ebrea volumina, novis greca auctoritatem impendunt"; *Decretum*, D. 9, c. 6. Yet Rufinus wrote: "In tempore primitivo, antequam ecclesia per omnes partes orbis propagaretur, incorrupta erant et integra volumina Hebreorum atque Grecorum, procedente vero tempore, cum admodum christianus populus cresceret et multorum hereses in ecclesia germinarent, tam ab ipsis Iudeis ecclesie invidentibus quam ab hereticis hebraica et greca exemplaria corrupta sunt, sed magis hebraica quam greca, magis greca quam latina"; *Summa decretorum*, ed. Heinrich Singer (Paderborn, 1902), 23. Compare the citation and questionable interpretation of Rufi-

nus's gloss in Grabois, *"Hebraica veritas,"* 625–26. Also see the comments on *Decretum*, D. 9, c. 6, in Johannes Faventinus, *Summa Decreti*, Biblioteca Vaticana, Reg. lat. MS. 1061, f. 53ra; Huguccio, *Summa Decreti*, Admont Stiftsbibliothek, MS. 7, f. 11v; *Glossa palatina*, Biblioteca Vaticana, Reg. lat. MS. 977, f. 3vb; and Joannes Teutonicus, *Glossa ordinaria*. I am grateful to Steven Horwitz of the Institute of Medieval Canon Law at the University of California, Berkeley, for supplying me with photoprints of the relevant portions of the manuscripts cited.

23. Cohen, *The Friars and the Jews*, and "The Jews as the Killers of Christ in the Latin Tradition, from Augustine to the Friars," *Traditio*, 39 (1983): 1–27.

24. Beryl Smalley, "A Commentary on the *Hebraica* by Herbert of Bosham," *Recherches de théologie ancienne et médiévale*, 18 (1951): 29–65; and Raphael Loewe, "Herbert of Bosham's Commentary on Jerome's Hebrew Psalter," *Biblica*, 34 (1953): 44–77, 159–92, 275–98.

25. Smalley, "A Commentary on the *Hebraica*," 57. It should be noted, in all fairness, that Andrew of St. Victor had denied the validity of rabbinic exegesis on a number of occasions but never so thoughtfully or convincingly as Herbert does here—hence the criticism of Andrew for Judaizing. See Smalley, *Study of the Bible*, 157–59.

26. Peter the Venerable, *Adversus Judeorum inveteratam duritiem*, CCCM 58. In addition to the studies of polemic cited above, see Saul Lieberman, *Sheqiʿin* (A Few Words on Some Jewish Legends, Customs, and Literary Sources Found in Karaite and Christian Works) (2d edn., Jerusalem, 1970), 27–42; Manfred Kniewasser, "Die antijüdische Polemik des Petrus Alphonsi (getauft 1106) und des Abtes Petrus Venerabilis von Cluny (+1156)," *Kairos*, new ser., 22 (1980): 49–76; and the introduction of Yvonne Friedman, CCCM 58: vii–lxx.

27. Peter the Venerable, *Adversus Judeorum inveteratam duritiem*, CCCM 58: 57–58: "Patet ergo quia non ab huiusmodi canibus, sed a Iudaeis longe hiis deterioribus Christus ad occisionem ducendus a propheta praedictus est. Et quoniam fere idem est vel adversus nugacissimas fabulas et primo auditu contempibiles se quemquam disputando effundere, vel inanem aerem crebis ac validis ictibus feriendo vires lassare, sufficiat quod dictum est. Ad illud redeat sermo, propter quod de Iudaicis fabulis, quibus plus cunctis erroneis hominibus abundant, istud assumptum est. Est autem illud quod probare sermo intenderat, immo quod iam tam auctoritate, quam ratione probauerat. Christum temporalem regem intelligi non debere. Christi regnum terrenum, et finiendum accipi non oportere. Sufficere quidem possunt omni homini ad huius rei certitudinem quae praemissa sunt. Sed quia cum Iudaeo, qui nescio utrum homo sit, michi sermo est, adhuc aliqua addenda sunt. Nescio plane utrum Iudeus homo sit, qui nec rationi humanae caedit, nec auctoritatibus divinis et propriis adquiescit."

28. *Ibid.*, 99, 144–45.

29. *Ibid.*, 125–26, 128, 139, 186. In a polemic against Islam, Peter even blamed

the infidelity of Muhammad on the Jews and their rabbinic fables; Peter the Venerable, *Summa totius haeresis Saracenorum,* in James Kritzeck, *Peter the Venerable and Islam,* Princeton Oriental Studies, vol. 23 (Princeton, N.J., 1964), 206, and, in the English translation, 131–32: "And in order that the whole fullness of iniquity should come together in Mohammed, and that nothing should be lacking for his damnation and that of others, Jews were joined to the heretic. And lest [Mohammed] become a true Christian, the Jews, craftily providing for this man eager for novelties, whispered to Mohammed not the truth of the scriptures, but their own fables in which they abound even now. Thus Mohammed, instructed by the best Jewish and heretical doctors, produced his Koran and wove together, in that barbarous fashion of his, a diabolical scripture, put together both from the Jewish fables and the trifling songs of heretics."

30. Amos Funkenstein forcefully maintained that Peter, breaking with the precedent set by Jerome, ceased to consider rabbinic Judaism a mere corollary of a literal understanding of Scripture. Peter, argued Funkenstein, instead considered "the Talmud the Jewish equivalent of the New Testament—that is, a different *nova lex*—and that, all would agree, was heresy"; "Ha-Temurot be-Vikkuaḥ ha-Dat," 140.

31. Peter the Venerable, *Liber contra sectam sive haeresim Saracenorum,* in Kritzeck, *Peter the Venerable,* 252–53. Granted, the immediate purpose of this passage, in which Peter stated that Jews everywhere maintained copies of the same biblical books, is to counter Muslim assertions of the ancient loss and subsequent corruption of Scripture, but the implication that the Jews remained faithful to a canon of authentic, antique texts is unavoidable.

32. Peter the Venerable, *Adversus Judeorum inveteratam duritiem,* CCCM 58: 1, 32, 42–43, 70, 89.

33. *Ibid.,* 186.

34. *Ibid.,* 152. Ludolf of Saxony echoed Peter's understanding of Matt. 15:7. See Ludolf of Saxony, *Vita Jesu Christi,* 1.88, 4 vols. (Paris, 1878), 2: 314–19.

35. Peter the Venerable, *Adversus Judeorum inveteratam duritiem,* CCCM 58: 159.

36. See *ibid.,* 141–42; and Peter the Venerable, *Letters,* ed. Giles Constable, 2 vols. (Cambridge, Mass., 1967), 1: 327–30. The lack of an urgent call for proselytism may in fact help explain the abusive tone of Peter's anti-Jewish pronouncements, in comparison to the softer tenor of his anti-Muslim polemic, whose purpose was perhaps conversion. See Kritzeck, *Peter the Venerable,* 21–23, and chaps. 3–5 *passim;* and Kritzeck, "Peter the Venerable and the Toledan Connection," in Giles Constable and James Kritzeck, eds., *Petrus Venerabilis, 1156–1956: Studies and Texts Commemorating the Eighteenth Centenary of His Death,* Studia anselmiana, vol. 40 (Rome, 1956), 176–201.

37. See Jean Leclercq, "The Renewal of Theology," in Benson and Constable, *Renaissance and Renewal,* 68–87; Nikolaus Haring, "Commentary and

Hermeneutics," in *ibid.*, 173–200; Richard H. Rouse and Mary A. Rouse, "*Statim invenire:* Schools, Preachers, and New Attitudes to the Page," in *ibid.*, 201–25; Marie-Thérèse d'Alverny, "Translations and Translators," in *ibid.*, 421–62; Pelikan, *Growth of Medieval Theology,* 270–84; R. W. Hunt, "Manuscripts Containing the Indexing Symbols of Robert Grosseteste," *Bodleian Library Record,* 4 (1953): 241–55; Charles M. Radding, "Evolution of Medieval Mentalities: A Cognitive-Structural Approach," *AHR,* 83 (1978): 577–97; and Caroline Walker Bynum, *Jesus as Mother: Studies in the Spirituality of the High Middle Ages* (Berkeley and Los Angeles, 1982), 13, 82–109. On the Scholastic attempt to displace marginal and deviant elements in Christian society, see John Boswell, *Christianity, Social Tolerance, and Homosexuality: Gay People in Western Europe from the Beginning of the Christian Era to the Fourteenth Century* (Chicago, 1980), pt. 4.

38. Among others, see Smalley, *Study of the Bible,* chap. 6; Raphael Loewe, "The Medieval History of the Latin Vulgate," in P. R. Ackroyd *et al.,* eds., *The Cambridge History of the Bible,* 3 vols., (Cambridge, 1963–70), 2: 148–52; Samuel Abraham Hirsch, *Early English Hebraists: Roger Bacon and His Predecessors* (London, 1905); and Altaner, "Zur Kenntnis."

39. Yitzhak Baer, "Le-Viqqoret ha-Vikkuḥim shel R. Yeḥi'el mi-Paris ve-shel R. Moshe ben Naḥman" (The Disputations of R. Yechiel of Paris and of Nachmanides), *Tarbiz,* 2 (1931): 172–87; Judah M. Rosenthal, "The Talmud on Trial," *Jewish Quarterly Review,* new ser., 47 (1956): 58–76, 145–69; Solomon Grayzel, "The Talmud and the Medieval Papacy," in Walter Jacob *et al.,* eds., *Essays in Honor of Solomon B. Freehof* (Pittsburgh, Pa., 1964), 220–45; Merchavia, *Ha-Talmud bi-R'i ha-Natsrut,* 227–420; and Cohen, *The Friars and the Jews,* chaps. 6–7.

40. Beryl Smalley, "William of Auvergne, John of LaRochelle and St. Thomas Aquinas on the Old Law," in *St. Thomas Aquinas, 1274–1974, Commemorative Studies,* 2 vols. (Toronto, 1974), 1: 10–71; Jacob Guttmann, "Der Einfluss der maimonidischen Philosophie auf des christliche Abendland," in W. Bacher *et al.,* eds., *Moses ben Maimon: Sein Leben, seine Werke und sein Einfluss,* 2 vols (1908; reprint edn., Hildesheim, 1971), 1: 135–230; and Wolfgang Kluxen, "Maimonides im lateinischen Abendland als Beispiel einer christlich-jüdisch Begegnung," in Paul Wilpert, ed., *Judentum im Mittelalter: Beiträge zum christlich-jüdischen Gespräch,* Miscellanea mediaevalia, vol. 4 (Berlin, 1966), 146–66. On Aquinas's resulting theological evaluation of Mosaic law, see, among others, Yves M.-J. Congar, "Le sens de l'économie salutaire dans la 'théologie' de S. Thomas d'Aquin *(Somme théolgique),*" in Erwin Iserloh and Peter Manns, eds., *Festgabe Joseph Lortz,* 2 vols. (Baden-Baden, 1958), 2:73–122; M.-D. Chenu, "La théologie de la loi ancienne selon Saint Thomas," *Revue thomiste,* 61 (1961): 485–97; Amos Funkenstein, "Gesetz und Geschichte: Zur historisierenden Hermaneutik bei Moses Maimonides und Thomas von Aquin," *Viator,* 1 (1970): 147–78; and Shlomo Pines, "Saint Thomas et la pensée juive médiévale:

Quelques notations," in G. Verbeke and D. Verhelst, eds., *Aquinas and the Problems of His Time,* Mediaevalia lovanensia, ser. 1, vol. 5 (Louvain, 1976), 118–29.

41. On the inquisitorial burning of Maimonides' works, see Cohen, *The Friars and the Jews,* 52–60 and nn. 1–15. Among the works that Cohen cited, see, especially, the intriguing arguments of J. L. Teicher; Teicher, "Christian Theology and the Jewish Opposition to Maimonides," *Journal of Theological Studies,* old ser., 43 (1942): 68–76. For Aquinas's rebuke of Maimonides, see Aquinas, *In IV Sententiarum,* 48.2.3, ad 6; and Hans Liebeschütz, "Eine Polemik des Thomas von Aquino gegen Maimonides," *Monatsschrift für die Geschichte und Wissenschaft des Judentums,* 80 (1936): 93–96. Also see Giles of Rome, *Errores philosophorum,* 12.1–11, ed. Josef Koch and trans. John O. Riedl (Milwaukee, Wis., 1944), 58–67.

42. Cohen, *The Friars and the Jews,* 62, n. 20, 103–69, and "The Jews as the Killers of Christ," 26.

43. Alexander of Hales, *Summa theologiae,* 2–2.161.1, 5 vols. (Quaracchi, 1924–48), 3: 729. For a translation, see Robert Chazan, ed., *Church, State, and Jew in the Middle Ages* (New York, 1980), 44–46. Also see Jacob Guttmann, "Alexandre de Hales et le judaïsme," *Revue des études juives,* 19 (1889): 224–34; W. Lampen, "Alexander von Hales und der Antisemitismus," *Franziskanische Studien,* 16 (1929): 1–14; Venicio Marcolino, *Das Alte Testament in der Heilsgeschichte: Untersuchung zum dogmatischen Verständnis des Alten Testaments als heilsgeschichtliche Periode nach Alexander von Hales* (Münster, 1970); and Smalley, "William of Auvergne," 25.

44. Solomon Grayzel, ed., *The Church and the Jews in the XIIIth Century* (rev. edn., New York, 1966), 275.

45. *Ibid.,* 278–79 n. (emphasis added). For a list of the masters who signed the report of the legatine commission, see Heinrich Denifle, *Chartularium universitalis parisiensis,* 4 vols. (Paris, 1889–97), 1: 210–11.

46. See Joel E. Rembaum, "The Talmud and the Popes: Reflections on the Talmud Trials of the 1240s," *Viator,* 13 (1982): 203–23. Arguing that Innocent IV in 1247 dropped the charge of heresy from the papal opposition to the Talmud, Rembaum dismissed the significance of Innocent's own decretalist commentary—which rationalized the papal condemnations of the Talmud on the basis of its deviation from the Mosaic law—with the unconvincing suggestion that "it is possible that he formulated this statement on the basis of Gregory's bulls of 1239 and his own letter of 1244 prior to his being approached by the Jews in 1247." *Ibid.,* 216 n. 81. Innocent wrote his commentary on the *Decretales* between 1246 and 1254. In the case of such an accomplished scholar, one may not assume that the final version of his work would have undercut the theoretical basis for his own actions only several years earlier. See Innocent IV, *Commentaria . . . super libros quinque decretalium,* ad X.3.34.8, 2 vols. [Frankfurt, 1570], 1: 430; and Ch. Lefebvre, "Sinibale dei Fieschi (Innocent IV)," in *Dictionnaire de droit canonique,* 7 vols. (Paris, 1935–65), 7: 1031. Rembaum failed to

come to grips with the arguments of Benjamin Z. Kedar. See Kedar, "Canon Law and the Burning of the Talmud," *Bulletin of Medieval Canon Law,* 9 (1979): 78–83. And Rembaum overlooked the fact that the rationale of Innocent's commentary for the burning of the Talmud was echoed in the subsequent commentaries on the same decretal by Hostiensis, Joannes Andreae, and Franciscus Zabarella, by the fourteenth-century inquisitor Nicholas Eymeric, and by commentators at the court of the fifteenth-century antipope Benedict XIII. See Eymeric, *Directorium inquisitorum,* 2.46.3–4 (Rome, 1578), 244–45; and A. Domingues de Sousa Costa, "Canonistarum doctrina de Judaeis et Saracenis tempore Concilii constantiensis, *Antonianum,* 40 (1965): 55–70.

47. The earliest extant copy of the *Extractiones* is in the Bibliothèque Nationale, Paris, lat. MS. 16558. For a detailed description of the manuscript, see Merchavia, *Ha-Talmud bi-R'i ha-Natsrut,* chap. 13.

48. Richard H. Rouse and Mary A. Rouse, *Preachers, Florilegia, and Sermons: Studies on the Manipulus Florum of Thomas of Ireland* (Toronto, 1979), 6–7.

49. See, for example, Nicholas's discussion of the biblical instructions for preparing the original paschal sacrifice; *Postilla litteralis,* on Exodus 12.1, 13.10, in *Biblia sacra, cum glossis,* 1: 145F–146B, 150GH: "One must understand the burning of the paschal lamb, as well as other sacrifices, in two respects. One concerns the [historical] moment, namely, the situation of the people departing from Egypt. The second is the signification *(figuratio)* of the lamb, designating the passion of Christ, which was prefigured in them [that is, the sacrifices]. The Apostle [Paul] accordingly states, 'Everything happened to them as a sign *(in figura)'* [1 Cor. 10:11]; and Rabbi Solomon states—and likewise the ancient Hebrew doctors—that all the prophets prophesied exclusively concerning the days of the Messiah. Therefore, since Moses was the greatest prophet, everything which he wrote is ordained for Christ; and as a consequence, there is a twofold meaning *(duplex est sensus)* in [the instructions for] offering the paschal lamb: One is the situation of the people departing from Egypt; this is literal and first [in time], and this I intend to explicate first. The other is the prefiguration of Christ who would someday suffer, and on this meaning I shall touch briefly at the end. For although this is last in chronological order, it is nevertheless primary in intention—like an objective, in relation to those things which have been ordained toward an objective *(sicut finis respectu eorum, quae sunt ad finem ordinata)."* The most extensive studies of Nicholas and his reliance on Hebraic sources remain those of Herman Hailperin. See Hailperin, *Rashi and the Christian Scholars,* esp. 184–91, "Nicholas de Lyra and Rashi: The Minor Prophets," in *Rashi Anniversary Volume,* American Academy for Jewish Research Texts and Studies, vol. 1 (New York, 1941), 115–47, and "The Hebrew Heritage of Medieval Christian Biblical Scholarship," *Historia Judaica,* 5 (1943): 133–54. On the text adduced in this note, see Oberman, *Forerunners of the Reformation,* 286.

50. Compare the conclusion of Herman Hailperin; Hailperin, "Yaḥaseihem shel Ḥakhmei-ha-Notsrim 'el Ḥakhmei Yisra'el, ve-Hashpaᶜato shel RaSh"I ᶜal Mefarshei ha-TaNa"Kh ha-Notsriyim" (Intellectual Relations between Christian and Jew with Special Reference to Rashi and Nicolas de Lyra), *Proceedings of the Rabbinical Assembly of America*, 7 (1940): 223. Hailperin wrote that, even if "all the Jews in the world of that day were to have converted to Christianity, Christian scholars [that is, Nicholas] would not have ceased to deal with Hebraic studies and Hebraic culture in the least."

51. *Biblia sacra, cum glossis*, 1: 3GH.

52. *Ibid.*, 3: 203FGH–204B, 4: 21FGH, 24GH–25BCD. The notion that a full acceptance of Targumic interpretations of Old Testament prophecies would lead directly to Christianity still appears in modern Christian scholarship. See, for instance, Roger le Déaut, *The Message of the New Testament and the Aramaic Bible (Targum)*, trans. Stephen F. Miletic, Subsidia biblica, vol. 5 (Rome, 1982), 43–55. "Frequently the Aramaic translations represent real theological progress (especially in so far as explicitation is concerned) when compared to the Hebrew text. As such, they form one stage towards the revelation of the New Testament." Déaut's disclaimer of sympathy with the medieval polemicists notwithstanding, he, too, suggested that rabbinic tradition deliberately suppressed Aramaic translations in early Jewish biblical interpretation and that these could have served to bring Jews closer to the church. "But the primary interest of the Aramaic versions is that they could be understood as a *praeparatio evangelica* ('preparing the way for the Gospel'). The best proof of their usefulness for understanding the content itself of the New Testament and Christian apologetics resides in the defiance and in the growing opposition of the Rabbis against this type of writing, leading to only one 'authorized' recension, which conformed to official teaching, namely the Onkelos translation of the Torah and the recension of Jonathan ben Uzziel for the Prophets." Déaut, *Message of the New Testament*, 43, 54, 51.

53. *Biblia sacra, cum glossis* 3: 88DEFGH, 4: 89H–90B.

54. On Isa. 53, see *ibid.*, 4: 89FG.

55. On Ps. 44 (Ps. 45 in the Masoretic Text), see *ibid.*, 3: 148FGH. On Hos. 2:15 (Hos. 2:17 in the Masoretic Text), see *ibid.*, 4: 336B. On Mic. 5:2 (Mic. 5:1 in the Masoretic Text), see *ibid.*, 4: 381G.

56. *Ibid.*, 4: 21FGH–22BC. Concerning the nonmessianic, Jewish interpretation of Isa. 8:3, Nicholas reported: "Hoc dictum videtur sequi Thomas de Aquino in quadam postilla, quae sibi attribuitur tanquam ex eius dictis reportata, ubi solvuntur argumenta que solent fieri ad contrarium. . . . Hoc dictum videtur nimis favere errori Hebraeorum. . . . Solutiones Thomae . . . non valent: quia falsum assumunt." For Aquinas's statement, see his *In Isaiam prophetam expositio*, 8.1, in Stanislaus Eduard Fretté and Paul Myaré, eds., *Opera omnia*, 34 vols. (Paris, 1874–80), 18: 722–25.

57. Cohen, "The Jews as the Killers of Christ," 19–27.

58. William of Auvergne, *De legibus,* chap. 15, in *Opera omnia,* 2 vols. (Paris, 1674), 1: 46–47. Also see Jacob Guttmann, "Guillaume d'Auvergne et la litterature juive," *Revue des études juives,* 18 (1889): 243–55; and Smalley, "William of Auvergne," 27–46.
59. Evans, *Language and Logic of the Bible,* 164–67.

III

THE REFORMATION

12

Against the Jews

Mark U. Edwards, Jr.

The older Luther's polemics against Jews provide the greatest challenge
to those who wish to view, or at least to treat, the later polemics as
essentially theological tracts encumbered with some incidental, nontheo-
logical matter. For even the most stalwart advocates of this "theological
approach" find it necessary in the case of the anti-Jewish treatises to
acknowledge that external events shaped their argument and that they
can only be properly understood within their historic context. Yet why
should this be true of the anti-Jewish treatises and not of all Luther's
other writings? We shall return to this question after examining the
context and content of these most problematic treatises of the older
Luther.[1]

THE ANTI-JEWISH HERITAGE

The rivalry between Christians and Jews, and its attendant hatred and
violence, is as old as Christianity itself.[2] The earliest Christians were all
Jews, as was Jesus himself. Christianity began as a sect within Judaism,
a sect that claimed to be the true heir of God's promises to the people of
Israel. These early Jewish Christians believed that Jesus was the messiah
promised to the Jews, and that with his coming, his death, and his
resurrection the old covenant between God and Israel had ended and a

Reprinted by permission of Cornell University Press and E. J. Brill from *Luther's Last
Battles: Politics and Polemics, 1531–46,* by Mark V. Edwards, Jr., Ithaca and Leiden,
1983, 115–42. Copyright © 1983 by Cornell University Press.

new covenant had begun. Most Jews remained unconvinced, and understandably, they resented Christian claims that, if taken seriously, relegated non-Christian Judaism to the wastebasket for superseded religions. These conflicting claims led to violence and to attempts at repression. In Jerusalem a Christian Jew named Stephen was stoned for blasphemy. Later, a Jew named Saul, who had reportedly held the coats at Stephen's stoning, was on his way to Damascus to organize the imprisonment of Christians there when a vision of the resurrected Jesus converted him to Christianity. In such an atmosphere hostility grew, and Christians began drawing invidious parallels between the Israelites who had refused to accept the prophets of old and the Jews of their own day who refused to accept Jesus as the messiah. "Like fathers, like sons," Luke records Stephen to have said. "Was there ever a prophet whom your fathers did not persecute? They killed those who foretold the coming of the Righteous One; and now you have betrayed him and murdered him, you who received the Law as God's angels gave it to you, and yet have not kept it" (Acts 7:51–53). When Matthew recorded his gospel, Christians in his circle held all Jews responsible for Jesus's execution, the Jews are reported by Matthew to have cried out to a man: "His blood be on us, and on our children" (Matthew 27:26).

The Saul who had persecuted Christians became the Paul who brought his own version of Christianity to non-Jews, to Gentiles. Soon the Christians at Jerusalem and elsewhere were hotly divided over the question whether Gentile Christians had to observe Jewish customs as their Jewish Christian brothers and sisters did. Paul argued that they did not; Peter at first disagreed, and then, reportedly, came over to Paul's position. In letters on this issue Paul stigmatized Jewish observances as "dead law," and contrasted such "works righteousness" with the "divine righteousness through faith in Christ."

With all their conviction that Jesus was the messiah promised in the Scripture, the early Christians were hard pressed to explain a very embarrassing fact. If Jesus was the messiah promised to the Nation Israel, why had so few of the Jews, the Nation Israel, accepted him as this promised messiah? Paul ruminates on this question in his last extant letter, his letter to the Romans. He first suggests that the Nation Israel must be understood spiritually, rather than literally. Not entirely satisfied with this solution, he invokes God's inscrutable will: "The pot has no right to say to the potter, Why did you make me this shape?" Not entirely satisfied with this solution either, Paul finally settles on a mystery:

For there is a deep truth here, my brothers, of which I want you to take account, so that you may not be complacent about your own discernment: this partial blindness has come upon Israel only until the Gentiles have been admitted in full strength; when that has happened, the whole of Israel will be saved. . . . (Romans 11:25–26)

So by the end of the apostolic period, Jews in the eyes of Christians were adherents to a covenant that was no more, that had been replaced by a new covenant revealed by Jesus Christ. They were a rejected people, guilty of the murder of the prophets and of God's own Son. They were under God's wrath, a Christian view that was reinforced by the destruction of the Temple and Jewish Jerusalem in 70 and 135 A.D. At the end of time they would convert to Christianity. In the meanwhile they would serve as examples of God's wrath over those who forsake him.

With the end of an autonomous Jewish state, Jewish authorities lost the opportunity to harass their Christian rivals. With the beginning of the Christian empire under Constantine and his successors in the fourth century, Christian authorities gained the opportunity to persecute their Jewish rivals and every other non-Christian group. From the time of Constantine to our own twentieth century, Christians have made frequent use of this opportunity.

The medieval West was a society of corporations, of voluntary and involuntary communities bound together by mutual responsibility. The greatest corporation of them all, embracing all the West, was the church. In its midst existed only one foreign body, only one smaller corporation that failed to acknowledge the truth of its beliefs: the Jews. For the medieval theoretician the Jews were to be tolerated within the Christian community for the witness they gave by their suffering to the truth of Christian claims. They were responsible for Christ's death; they showed forth God's wrath towards his rejected people. To the common people, who heard their preachers describe the Jews in these, if not in much worse terms, the Jews were also the one body within their midst that did not fit in. Dietary observances kept Jews and Christians from sharing meals. Religious convictions and laws on both sides prevented intermarriage. The areas of life in which Jews and Christians could interact on a daily basis were few even in the early Middle Ages. With time the opportunities for interaction became ever more limited as Christian corporations, guilds and communes, forced Jews out of agriculture, out of commerce, out of industry and into some of the most disreputable occupations, such as petty moneylending and pawnbroking. Limited to such occupations, most Jews came to be seen by Christian townspeople and peasants as greedy, grasping, and immoral.

In the crusades, popular suspicion and dislike came together with religiously-based contempt and hatred. Some who marched to free the Holy Lands from the Infidel thought it only proper to deal first with the enemy in their midst. If one could kill for religion in the Holy Land, one could kill for religion in Western Europe. And so, over the protests of bishops on the scene and the pope in Rome, the crusaders began their crusade with the murder of thousands of Jews living in the Rhineland and along the route of march. About this time stories first began circulating about ritual murder of Christian children by Jews, about the poisoning of wells by Jews, about Jewish contempt for the Virgin Mary. Life, which had hardly been easy for Jews up to the eleventh century, became more difficult. Years could pass with nothing more for them to cope with than the traditional Christian contempt and insults, and then suddenly violence and death would visit a Jewish community.

And there were always the attempts by Christians to convert the Jews to the "true faith." Not infrequently the Jewish community would be hauled into the local church or cathedral to hear an impassioned sermon by a visiting bishop or mendicant friar on the truth of Christianity and the futility of Jewish beliefs. "Why has your God forsaken you?" was one of the most popular questions posed the Jews. "Why have you been in exile and suffered for so many years?" Of course, the answer the preacher gave was that the old covenant was ended, that Jesus was the promised messiah, and that the Jews suffered so because of their sin of rejecting their Christ. And then the preacher would parade a list of passages in the Old Testament that Christians believed pointed to Jesus as the Christ.

Some Jews were convinced and converted to Christianity. Some Jews were unconvinced, but were baptized anyway by force. Once baptized, they could not return to Judaism without suffering the penalties for apostasy. Most of the Jews probably left the sermon as unconvinced as they came, glad that the humiliating ordeal was over and not likely to be repeated for a while.

During the Middle Ages Jews enjoyed periods of relative peace and periods of active persecution and exploitation. In the Holy Roman Empire Jews became "imperial serfs," property of the emperor, under his protection (such as it was) in exchange for heavy payments.[3] The fifteenth century, the century before the Reformation, was a bad century for Jews both within and without the empire. In 1421 they were expelled from Austria, in 1424 from Cologne, in 1432 from Saxony, in 1435 from Speyer, in 1440 from Augsburg, and by 1499 from Würzburg, Mecklenburg, Magdeburg, Nuremburg, Esslingen, and Ulm. Beginning in 1470 they were driven out of the Archbishopric of Mainz. Bavaria began expelling its Jews in 1450, Württemberg in 1498. This list of expulsions could be easily multiplied several times over.[4]

Not only were there relatively few Jewish communities left within the empire, those that did remain were subject to severe legal restrictions, to economic exploitation by rulers, and to harassment and persecution by populace and authorities for alleged magical and demonic activities. The most extreme of these accusations, one leveled with some frequency in the late fifteenth and sixteenth centuries, was that Jews murdered Christian children for their blood to be used in the Passover celebration and in various magical activities.[5] An example of such an accusation illustrates one of the popular beliefs about Jews in Luther's day.

In 1503 near Freiburg in Breisgau browsing oxen uncovered the body of a young boy who had obviously bled to death. Suspicion immediately fell on the child's father, who was an accused thief. We have two accounts of what then occurred: an anonymous rhymed verse account entitled *A horrible, shocking story of an ungodfearing, insane, and desperate Christian man, who sold . . . his own flesh and blood to the soulless, godless, god-betraying Jews,*[6] and an allegedly eyewitness report by Johann Eck, Doctor of Theology at the University of Ingolstadt and Luther's most prominent Catholic opponent.[7] At first the father pleaded ignorance. When the corpse of his son was brought into his presence, however, it began to sweat blood.[8] The father then confessed that he had sold his son to two Jews for ten gulden, believing that they would only take some of the child's blood but not kill him. But the child died from the bloodletting.

At this point the anonymous author adds that the authorities decided to verify this confession. When questioned under torture, however, the father changed his account. Now he said that he himself had bled his child, hoping to sell the blood to the Jews, who, he had heard, would pay well for Christian blood. He had never made the sale, however, because after he collected the blood he realized belatedly that the Jews would believe that he was hoaxing them, that the blood came from an animal rather than a Christian child, and that he could not prove otherwise. So he threw the blood away.

Not sure which confession to believe, the authorities decided, as they usually did with charges of ritual murder, to arrest all the Jews of the territory and submit them to questioning, also under torture. The Jews, however, maintained their innocence. Unable to extract a confession, the authorities were forced to release them. The father, however, was sentenced to be drawn and quartered, as well as to be torn with red hot tongs. At the time of his execution he recanted his earlier confession, and returned to his claim that it was the Jews who had murdered his child, not himself.

Eck now picks up the narrative once more. He claims to have seen the murdered child himself and to have touched the child's stab wounds with his own fingers. He also saw the father executed and heard his dying confession that the Jews had stabbed his son to death.

Eck harbors no doubts about the authenticity of this ritual murder. The anonymous author, although he relates information that should have given him pause, is also convinced of the Jews' guilt. He attributes the father's second confession, that he himself had murdered his child, to the influence of the devil.[9] He is further convinced that the father, since he returned to his original claim that the Jews had committed the murder, died a Christian bound for ultimate salvation.[10]

This incredible story is only one of several alleged ritual murders related in the anonymous account and in Eck's treatise. It illustrates well, however, the improbability of the charge of ritual murder, while at the same time it shows that even highly educated men such as Johann Eck firmly believed such libels. Eck's whole treatise, *Refutation of a Jewbook in Which a Christian, to the Dishonor of All Christendom, Claims That Injustice is Done the Jews in the Accusation That They Murder Christian Children*, published a year before Luther's most infamous treatises, is dedicated to proving, in reply to a Lutheran skeptic, that Jews did murder Christian children for their rituals; that they did desecrate the eucharistic host; and that they did do such things as poison wells and bewitch animals and ruin crops.[11] These were the convictions of a scholar, writing in this case for a popular audience.[12]

Such, then, were the conditions when, in 1513, Martin Luther began lecturing on the Psalms at the University of Wittenberg. There were Jews left in the empire, clinging to survival in small territories often controlled by a bishop or abbot. The large territories and most of the imperial cities had expelled their Jews some years earlier. Only on rare occasions did Luther encounter Jews; he never lived in close proximity to them, but he inherited a tradition, both theological and popular, of hostility toward them. He lived within a larger community, Western Christendom, which saw the Jews as a rejected people, guilty of the murder of Christ, and capable of murdering Christian children for their own evil purposes. And he lived within a local community that had expelled its Jews some ninety years earlier. Despite this heritage of suspicion and hostility, Luther's first treatise on the Jews advocated that they be treated in a friendly manner and denounced the treatment they were currently subjected to.

THAT JESUS CHRIST WAS BORN A JEW

Before the 1538 publication of *Against the Sabbatarians* Luther had published only one treatise concerning the Jews, his 1523 treatise, *That Jesus Christ Was Born a Jew*. The treatise was occasioned by the report that Duke Ferdinand had charged that Luther denied Mary's virginity before and after Christ's birth. However, the treatise went beyond a simple refutation of these charges to explain the reasons from Scripture that induced Luther "to believe that Christ was a Jew born of a virgin." With this Luther had hoped that he might "entice some Jews to the Christian faith."

For our fools, the popes, bishops, sophists, and monks—the gross asses' heads —have treated the Jews to date in such fashion that he who would become a good Christian might almost have to become a Jew. And if I had been a Jew and had seen such oafs and numbskulls governing and teaching the Christian faith, I would have rather become a sow than a Christian.

For they have dealt with the Jews as if they were dogs and not men. They were able to do nothing but curse them and take their goods. When they were baptized, no Christian teaching or life was demonstrated to them, rather they were only subjected to papistry and monkery. When they then saw that Judaism had such strong scriptural support and that Christianity was nothing but twaddle without any scriptural support, how could they quiet their hearts and become true good Christians? I myself have heard from pious baptized Jews that if they had not in our time heard the gospel, they would have remained life-long Jews under their Christian exterior. For they confess that they never yet have heard anything about Christ from their baptizers and masters.

It was his hope, Luther had continued, that if the Jews were dealt with in a friendly fashion and were instructed carefully from the Holy Scripture, "many of them would become true Christians and would return to the faith of their fathers, the prophets and patriarchs." To reject their beliefs so absolutely, allowing nothing to remain, and to treat them solely with arrogance and scorn, frightened them away from true Christianity.[13]

In the first part of the treatise Luther had laid out at some length the scriptural basis for his belief that Mary was perpetually virgin and that Christ, as the seed of Abraham, was a true Jew.[14] Next, out of an expressed desire to "serve the Jews so that some of them might be brought to their own true faith which their fathers had had," Luther had offered to the Jews and to those who dealt with the Jews some scripturally based arguments to show that Jesus was the Jews' awaited messiah.[15] Somewhat surprisingly, Luther had argued that at first it was enough to convince the Jews that Jesus was the true messiah. Later they could learn how he was also true God.[16]

Luther had closed with an appeal to his fellow Christians:

Therefore, I would request and advise that one manage them decently and instruct them from the Scripture so that some of them might be brought along. But since we now drive them with force and slander them, accuse them of having Christian blood if they don't stink, and who knows what other foolishness, so that they are regarded just as dogs—what good can we expect to accomplish with them? Similarly, that we forbid them to work, do business, and have other human association with us, so that we drive them to usury—how does that help them?

If we wish to help them, we must practice on them not the papal law but rather the Christian law of love, and accept them in a friendly fashion, allowing them to work and make a living, so that they gain the reason and opportunity to be with and among us [and] to see and to hear our Christian teaching and life.

If some are obstinate, what does it matter? After all, we too are not all good Christians. Here I will let matters rest until I see what I have accomplished.

The missionary tendency of this treatise is apparent from the citations quoted. Luther had obviously hoped that at least some and perhaps an appreciable number of Jews might convert to Christianity once they were exposed to the Protestant faith. While the renewed gospel was given time to do its work, patience and tolerance was to be shown the Jews. This very patience and tolerance was meant to further this missionary goal.[17]

JOSEL OF ROSHEIM

Although Luther had relatively little to say about the Jews during the late 1520s and the early 1530s, there is evidence that sometime before 1536 three learned Jews had visited him and, on the basis of their rabbinic tradition, had taken issue with the interpretation Luther placed on various messianic passages in the Old Testament. Already disappointed about the meager success of his missionary efforts, Luther was so frustrated by this conversation that he vowed not to enter into such a dialogue again.[18] But this issue, the proper interpretation of messianic passages in the Old Testament, remained much on his mind during his final years. From the beginning of the Genesis lectures in 1535 Luther took great pains not only to insist on the Christological interpretation of the Old Testament,[19] but specifically to insist that the Old Testament testified to the trinity and to the incarnation. In this he adopted as his own the arguments of the Old Testament exegetes of the late Middle Ages and especially those of Nicholas of Lyra, Paul of Burgos, and Matthew Döring. He continued his debate with rabbinic exegesis in his 1538 *Three Symbols* and in his "Schmalkaldic Articles." In these publications he once again claimed Old Testament passages as witnesses to the trinity and to the incarnation. In these same treatises his anger began to show through. His tone is shrill, and abusive remarks about the Jews are more pervasive.[20]

On 6 August 1536 Elector Johann Friedrich, for reasons that cannot now be ascertained, issued a mandate forbidding Jews to settle or do business in Electoral Saxony or even to travel through electoral lands.[21] Although there is no evidence that Luther had instigated this mandate, his subsequent refusal to intervene in behalf of the Jews indicates that he approved of it.[22]

In early summer 1537 Luther remarked at table that he had received a letter from a certain Jew who had requested that Luther secure a safe-conduct allowing him to enter Electoral Saxony.[23] This Jew was none other than Josel of Rosheim (ca. 1478–1554), the officially designated spokesman for the Jews within the empire.[24] It was in his capacity as a representative of his people that Josel wished to enter Electoral Saxony to confer with Luther and Elector Johann Friedrich about the recent mandate against the Jews. He brought with him very favorable letters of recommendation, one from Wolfgang Capito to Luther himself, the other from the magistrates of Strasbourg to Elector Johann Friedrich.[25] These recommendations notwithstanding, Luther remained true to his earlier resolve not to enter into further dialogue with the Jews. He refused to intercede for Josel. To his table companions he exclaimed, "Why should these rascals, who injure people in goods and body and who estrange many Christians [from Christianity] with their superstitions, be given permission? For in Moravia they have circumcised many Christians and called them by the new name of Sabbatarians. So it goes in those regions where Protestant preachers are expelled . . . I'll write this Jew not to return."[26] In his letter to Josel, Luther spelled out briefly his position toward the Jews.[27] He claimed that just as his 1523 treatise *That Jesus Christ Was Born a Jew* had greatly served all Jewry, he would have very gladly interceded with the elector on Josel's behalf. But since the Jews so shamefully misused such service of his and undertook things which were intolerable to Christians, they had themselves deprived Luther of all influence that he might have had with the princes and lords. In his heart he had always felt, and still did, that the Jews should be treated in a friendly fashion so that God might look graciously upon them and bring them to their messiah, but not so that they should become worse and strengthened in their effort through Luther's favor and influence.[28]

Some of this letter seems to harken back to the position expressed in *That Jesus Christ Was Born a Jew*. He is still advocating friendly treatment of the Jews, and he appears not to have abandoned entirely his hope for Jewish converts, although he expects their numbers to be small. At the same time there is a harshness in this letter not found in the 1523 treatise. And he refused to help Josel. Apparently, Josel was no more successful with others and had to return home without having an audience with the elector and without having the mandate against the Jews modified or lifted.[29]

AGAINST THE SABBATARIANS

Luther's first major attack on the Jews, made in his last years, was an open letter entitled *Against the Sabbatarians*[30] and addressed to a good friend. It was first published in March 1538. The "good friend" was Count Wolfgang Schlick zu Falkenau. The count had sent Luther word that Jews had been proselytizing in Bohemia and Moravia and had convinced some Christians that they should be circumcized, that the messiah had not yet come, that the Jewish law was eternally valid, and that it should be observed by Gentiles. Until he had time for a lengthier reply, Luther intended with this open letter to explain how these arguments of the Jews should be refuted with Holy Scripture.

The letter began by saying that the Jews had been made very stubborn by their rabbis so that they were very hard to win over. For when one developed a convincing argument on the basis of Scripture, they retreated from Scripture to their rabbis and said that they had to believe their rabbis just as Christians believed their pope and decretals. This, Luther said, was his own personal experience with them. Accordingly, in order to strengthen Christians in their faith the "good friend" should produce the old and irrefutable argument that Nicholas of Lyra and others had utilized.

Jews should be asked what was the sin for which God was so horribly punishing them. For there was God's promise (as the Jews themselves boasted) that their law should endure forever, that Jerusalem should be God's own residence, and that both the princes of the house of David and the priests of the tribe of Levi should always remain before God. Yet this and other promises had remained unfulfilled for fifteen hundred years. Now since it made no sense to accuse God of not keeping his promise and of having lied for fifteen hundred years, the Jews had to be asked what was wrong. They would have to answer that their sins were responsible.

Whatever sin the Jews might point to, it would not help their case. For in Jeremiah 31 God announced that he wished to make a new covenant or law, unlike the covenant or law of Moses, and that he would not be hindered in this by their sins.[31] In fact, it was precisely because they had not kept the old covenant that He wished to make a new covenant which they could keep.

This showed that the Jews were lying when they claimed that the advent of the messiah was delayed by their sins. God's promises were now contingent upon the Jews' behavior. The conclusion seemed inescapable to Luther:

Now since it is clear and obvious that the Jews cannot name any sin for which God should so long delay his promise and thus make Himself a liar, and even if they were able to name one or more [sins], nevertheless God's word made them liars, for He assured them that He did not wish on account of their sins to abandon His promise to send the messiah and to maintain the throne of David for ever and ever, it follows inescapably that one of two things must be true: either the messiah must have come fifteen hundred years ago or God must have lied (God forgive me for speaking so shamefully) and not kept His promise.[32]

God's promise had been kept and the messiah had come in the person of Jesus of Nazareth. The promised new covenant was fulfilled in Christ. The sin of the Jews for which they were suffering such a long and horrible punishment was their rejection of Christ as the promised messiah.

In the second part of the letter Luther examined the reported boast of the Jews that their law was eternal and should be observed by the Gentiles. He said that the coming of the messiah some fifteen hundred years earlier had marked the end of the old law. Moreover, for fifteen hundred years the Jews themselves had been unable to keep the law in its entirety because of the destruction of the temple and their exile from Jerusalem.

When Jesus stated that he had not come to abolish the law, Luther continued, he had not the ceremonial law in mind but rather the Ten Commandments. But the essence of the Ten Commandments had spread throughout the world well before Moses, Abraham, and all the patriarchs. This was especially true of the first commandment. All the pagans bore witness in their writings to the universal validity of the Ten Commandments. Only the commandment concerning the seventh day or Sabbath was a temporally limited addition, suited to the Jews at that time and, like other specifically Jewish, temporally bound laws, had since fallen into disuse.

Each of these arguments was drawn out and buttressed with careful examination of the appropriate texts from Scripture. Luther was uncompromising in his insistence on the error of the Jews, but his language is still, for the most part, temperate and restrained. His hope, he told his "good friend," was that he had provided sufficient material to allow the friend to defend himself against the Sabbatarians. If the friend were unable to convert the Jews, then he should consider that he was no better than the prophets, who were always killed and persecuted by the Jews. It appeared to Luther that God had truly forsaken the Jews and that they were no longer God's chosen people.

THE ATTACKS OF 1543

In 1543 Luther published three treatises against the Jews and Jewish exegesis: *On the Jews and Their Lies, On the Ineffable Name and on Christ's Lineage,* and *On the Last Words of David.*[33] These three treatises are best understood as three parts of one major statement. The first treatise, *On the Jews and Their Lies,* was written in response to a letter from Count Schlick of Moravia. In May 1542, the count had sent Luther a treatise (now apparently lost) in which a Jew, in dialogue with a Christian, attacked Jesus, the Virgin Mary, and Christian exegesis of the Old Testament,[34] and the count had requested that Luther refute this Jewish treatise. Luther's second treatise, *On the Ineffable Name and on Christ's Lineage,* was announced in the first treatise, while the third treatise, *On the Last Words of David,* was announced in the second. In fact, these last two treatises are more addenda to the first than independent treatises in their own right. All three draw upon the same sources, especially the writings of Nicholas of Lyra, Paul of Burgos, Raymund Martin, and Salvagus Porchetus. Together these treatises make up Luther's last testament against the Jews and the Jewish interpretation of the Old Testament.[35]

Luther introduced *On the Jews and Their Lies* with the confession that he had intended to write nothing more about or against the Jews. But because he had learned that Jews were still enticing Christians to become Jews, he had issued this book so that he might be numbered among those who had resisted the Jews and had warned Christians against them. It was not his intention, he wrote, to quarrel with the Jews or to learn from them their exegesis of Scripture, which he already knew well. Much less was it his intention to convert the Jews, for that, he claimed, was impossible. Nicholas of Lyra and Paul of Burgos had already faithfully described and powerfully refuted the Jews' filthy interpretation of the passages in question. In any case, their efforts had not at all helped the Jews, who had become progressively worse.[36]

After briefly rehearsing the argument he had developed at length in *Against the Sabbatarians*,[37] Luther took up several claims and boasts allegedly made by the Jews. First, he said, the Jews gloried in their claim of physical descent from the noblest people on earth, Abraham, Sarah, Isaac, Rebecca, Jacob, the twelve patriarchs, and the holy people of Israel. Further, they boasted and thanked God that they were created human beings rather than animals, Israelites rather than Goyim (Gentiles), and men rather than women. But, Luther replied, women were also human beings and made in the image of God. Furthermore, in Genesis 17, when God instituted circumcision, he damned all flesh regardless of lineage. As far as physical birth was concerned, Esau or Edom was as noble as Jacob, Ishmael as noble as Isaac, but what good did physical descent do them? All Gentiles were descendants of Noah through Japheth as the Jews were through Shem, and thus had equal claim to honor, nobility, and glory. In any case, all people, Jew and Gentile, were conceived and born in sin, and were accordingly born under God's wrath and condemnation and could not be God's children simply on account of nature or birth.[38]

Second, he continued, the Jews claimed superiority over others and despised them because of the covenant of circumcision. But circumcision in itself contained no holiness or power. Moreover, in Genesis 17 Moses stated that Abraham was ordered to circumcise all males in his house including sons and servants and even slaves. This meant that as far as physical circumcision was concerned, Ishmael and his descendants, among other descendants of Abraham and his household, had as much right to boast as the Jews. Circumcision did not make the Jews God's chosen people. According to Moses (Deut. 4 and 12; Leviticus 26) and Jeremiah (chapters 4 and 9), true circumcision was of the heart, not of the flesh. Furthermore, the Old Testament was full of individuals such as Job and people such as the Ninevites who were converted yet remained uncircumcised. As St. Paul taught, circumcision as a work in itself could not save. It was given as a sign, covenant, or sacrament so that those circumcised should hear and obey God's promise and word. Apart from the word of God, it was nothing. Their perversion of circumcision was like the papists' perversion of the sacraments. The papists like the Jews had fallen into works righteousness.[39]

Third, the Jews were greatly conceited because God had spoken with them and given them the Law of Moses on Mount Sinai. Indeed, they had entered into a marriage with God through the Law and had become His bride. But it was apparent from the Old Testament histories that they had become a besmirched bride, an incorrigible whore and wicked slut with whom God continually had to scuffle, tussle, and fight. This applied not only to the wicked Jews of the past but also to the Jews of Luther's own day, since their fifteen-hundred-year exile and suffering proved that they were one with the whoring Jews described in the Old Testament and not God's people. To have God's word meant nothing. The devils in hell had God's word. At issue was the fact that the Jews failed to keep God's word. Outward obedience to the Law of Moses, apart from obedience to the Ten Commandments, meant nothing. Moses himself was aware that no one could keep God's commandments except those whose sins God forgave. This required a man who bore our sins for us. It was of this man that Christians spoke and taught. It was of such a man that the prophets and apostles spoke and taught.[40]

Fourth, the Jews boasted that God had given them the land of Canaan, the city of Jerusalem, and the Temple. But God had dashed this conceit through the king of Babylon, the king of Assyria, and the Romans. The Jews failed to recognize that all this had been given them that they might obey His commandments. They wished to be God's people by reason of their deeds, works, and external condition and not out of sheer grace and mercy as all prophets and the true children of Israel had to be. They were like the papists, Turks, and fanatics, who all claimed to be the church on the basis of their own notions and without respect for the one true faith and obedience to the divine command. By their own deeds they wished to become God's people.[41]

Relying heavily on Nicholas of Lyra and Paul of Burgos, Luther in the second, and lengthiest, part of the treatise examined the conflicting interpretations of various prophetic texts in the Old Testament. These texts were interpreted by Christians as referring to the messiah and as showing this messiah to be Jesus of Nazareth. Luther gave greatest attention to the prophecy concerning "Shiloh" in Genesis 40; the "last words of David" concerning an "everlasting covenant" in 2 Samuel 23; the "consolidation of the Gentiles" prophesied in Haggai 2; and the "seventy weeks of years" discussed in Daniel 9. The Jews, Luther wrote, were so convinced that the messiah had not yet come that even if all the angels and God Himself said otherwise, the Jews would not believe them. Much less were they willing to listen to Christian exegetes and even former Jews, although these exegetes had so mightily overcome the arguments of the Jews. "But their accursed rabbis, who know better indeed, so wantonly poison their poor youth and common people and turn them from the truth. For I believe that if such writings were read by the common man and the youth, they would stone all their rabbis and hate them worse than we Christians do."[42] Judgments similar to this were sprinkled throughout this section. Luther had little use for Jewish exegesis and considered the rabbis to be knowingly and wantonly mis-interpreting the Scripture.[43] Despite these asides, most of this second section was devoted to serious, although often unoriginal, exegesis. Lu-ther added his own distinctive theological perspective when he repeat-edly insisted that these messianic promises, these promises of grace, were unconditional—that they were dependent not on the actions of men as some Jewish exegetes argued but solely on divine truth and grace.

In the third section Luther dealt with alleged Jewish slanders against the Virgin Mary and her son, Jesus. He accused the Jews of claiming that Jesus was a magician and instrument of the devil and that he worked his miracles by the power of the "ineffable name" (Shem Ham-phoras). Using cabalistic numerology, the Jews changed Jesus' name into an insult and perverted the conventional Jewish greeting into a curse on Christians. They called Jesus a whore's son and Mary a whore, although they knew better. They claimed that Mary had conceived while men-struating, which meant that her offspring, Jesus, was insane or a de-mon's child, and they perverted Mary's name into the word for manure pile. Luther recounted, without unequivocally accepting as true, some of the crudest charges traditionally lodged against the Jews: that they poi-soned wells and that they kidnapped children, pierced them with nails, and hacked them into pieces. He believed them guilty in thought and deed of shedding the blood of the messiah and his Christians.

The Jews' claim that they were held captive by the Christians was a "thick, fat lie." They were free to leave Germany; their departure would be a blessing, for their presence was a plague on Germany. They had been expelled, Luther pointed out, from numerous countries and cities: France, Spain, Bohemia, Regensburg, Magdeburg, and other places. It was in fact the Christians who were held captive to the Jews' usury. The Christians held the Jews captive as he, Luther, held captive his kidney stone and other afflictions.

From this list of indictments Luther swung immediately into a series of harsh recommendations to secular authorities on how to deal with the Jews. Their synagogues and schools should be burned and whatever would not burn should be buried. Their homes should be destroyed. All their prayer books and Talmudic writing should be taken from them. Their rabbis should be forbidden to teach. Their safe-conducts on highways should be revoked. Their usury should be forbidden and their money taken from them.[44] They should be put to work in the fields so that they earned their living by the sweat of their brows. Better yet, they should be expelled after a portion of their wealth had been confiscated. Luther rejected angrily the argument that the Jews were an indispensable financial resource to governments. The benefit failed to outweigh the blasphemy and harm done by the Jews. It was the duty of the secular authorities, Luther insisted, to implement these recommendations. It was the duty of the ecclesiastical authorities to warn and instruct their congregations about the Jews and their lies.

In the closing section of the treatise, Luther ridiculed the Jews' hope for a messiah who would give them a worldly kingdom but not redeem them from death. He would prefer to be a sow, who had no terror of death, he said, than to have such a messiah. He juxtaposed unfavorably the spiritual kingdom of the Christian messiah to the worldly kingdom sought, he claimed, by the Jews. In the final paragraphs he rehearsed the miracles that bore witness to the truth of the Christian faith, and he repeated his arguments concerning Old Testament passages he believed referred to Jesus Christ.

In March 1543, Luther published what amounted to an appendix to *On the Jews and Their Lies*. Entitled *On the Ineffable Name and On Christ's Lineage*, this treatise was composed of two unrelated sections. In the first section Luther translated into German and discussed what Salvagus Porchetus had written in his *Victory Against the Impious Hebrews* about the power of the "Ineffable Name" *(Shem Hamphoras)*. In the second part Luther reconciled the lineages of Christ given in Matthew and Luke and discussed the various Old Testament texts that he believed referred to the virgin birth of the messiah.[45]

The combined treatise was written, Luther said, to expose to German

Christians the devilish lies of the Jews and especially the lies of the
rabbinic exegetes and, further, to show those Christians who were considering becoming Jews what fine articles of Jewish faith they would
have to believe. The treatise was not directed at the Jews themselves
since Luther had given up all hope of their conversion. A few of their
number might yet be saved, he wrote, but the great majority of the Jews
were so stubborn that to convert them would be like converting the devil
into an angel, hell into heaven, death into life, and sin into holiness.[46]

Luther began section one with a translation of the eleventh chapter
from part one of Porchetus' treatise. In this chapter Porchetus claimed
that the Jews were so hostile toward the miracles of Christ that, out of
their wickedness, they had fabricated a mendacious book about Christ.
In this book they claimed that Jesus had performed all his miracles
through the power of the "ineffable name" which he had obtained
through trickery. In short, Jesus was no more than an evil magician.

After reproducing this legend from Porchetus, Luther spent the rest of
section one ridiculing the legend and the Jews who, he claimed, believed
such superstitions. It was "shit" like this, he said, that the Jews were
taught by their rabbis and had to "kiss, gobble down, guzzle, and
worship." With frequent vulgar asides, Luther explained the cabalistic
reasoning that he alleged was behind this legend, asserted that contemporary Jews still believed such shameful lies and blasphemies, and charged
that, in fact, the Jews were the worst of blasphemers and idolaters, in
attributing divine power to mere letters. The devil had possessed the
Jews and made them his captive. That was why they believed such
foolishness, lies, and blasphemy. It would not have been surprising, he
wrote, if God's wrath had long ago consigned the Christians to the abyss
of hell along with the Jews for tolerating in their midst such accursed,
manifest blasphemers of God. The only possible excuse was that they
had not known of the Jews' horrible deeds. "But from now on," Luther
warned, "you dear princes and lords who protect and tolerate Jews
among you, be aware of what you're doing. I do not wish to be responsible for the consequences!"[47]

In contrast to Luther's other writings against the Jews, section one of
this treatise is singularly devoid of any edifying theological, exegetical,
or historical comments. Even by Luther's standards the vulgarity is
excessive and unusually humorless. Offering his standard apology to
critics of his polemics, Luther replied to the "merciful saints among us

Christians who think that I am being too coarse and tasteless towards the poor wretched Jews in dealing with them so disdainfully and sarcastically" that the devil was the Jews' master.

In contrast to the first section, the second section of the treatise, although containing various characterizations of rabbinic exegesis as "Judas' piss," "Jewish sweat," and other excrementa, is relatively restrained in its vulgarity. More important, it contains extensive discussion of Christian and rabbinic exegesis of crucial passages in the Old Testament. Luther's aim was to show that various Old Testament passages had predicted that a New Testament would succeed and fulfill the Old. He also offered a thoughtful explanation of how the genealogies in Matthew and Luke could be reconciled with each other. He discussed in some detail what he believed to be the proper exegesis of various Old Testament passages traditionally interpreted by Christians to refer to the virgin birth. Although sarcastic and abusive asides are scattered throughout the text, the discussion is for the most part substantial and designed to refute rabbinic exegesis of the same passages. In contrast to the first section, this section can be rightly characterized as an exegetical and theological work rather than an anti-Semitic tract.

On the Last Words of David,[48] published in the late summer of 1543, was even less an anti-Jewish treatise than was the second section of On the Ineffable Name and On Christ's Lineage. In fact, the few critical asides in the treatise are aimed at rabbinic exegesis and not at contemporary Jews in general. This does not mean that Luther had changed his mind as to the threat he thought the Jews posed or as to the harsh treatment he thought they should receive. On the contrary, the intense antagonism Luther bore the Jews continued to the end of his life and even found violent expression in his last public sermon.[49] On the Last Words of David just happens not to be a polemical treatise. Instead, it is a detailed discussion of those passages in the Old Testament that he believed attested unequivocally to the Christian Trinity and to the incarnation of the Word in Jesus Christ. As such, it is a fascinating example of Luther's theologically based hermeneutics and Christocentric interpretation of the Old Testament. It is also a rich source for his understanding of the Trinity and of the incarnation including the communication of idioms between the divine and human natures of Christ. But it is not, properly speaking, a polemic and thus need not detain us further.

The reaction of contemporaries to Luther's anti-Jewish writings indicates fairly clearly that his readers saw a significant difference between the early and the later treatises. *That Jesus Christ Was Born a Jew* appears to have been received with favor among Protestants, Jews, and Jewish converts (Marranos). Some Marranos in the Netherlands may even have translated the work into Spanish and sent copies to their brethren in Spain. The treatise may have even reached Palestine.[50] It may also have encouraged several South Germans to work for the amelioration of the treatment of the Jews.[51] On the other hand, it may have lent some support to the Catholic charge, aired, for instance, at the Diet of Augsburg in 1530, that the Protestants had learned their doctrine from the Jews.[52]

The later tracts met with more criticism. Catholics, not surprisingly, were sharply critical. For instance, at the 1545 Diet of Worms several Catholic deputies reportedly characterized *On the Ineffable Name* as a "hateful book, as cruel as if it had been written in blood," and argued that it incited the rabble to violence.[53] Understandably, Jewish reaction was also unfavorable. Josel of Rosheim twice petitioned the Strasbourg magistrates concerning these tracts. The magistrates agreed to forbid a second printing within their jurisdiction of *On the Jews and Their Lies*, apparently out of concern for the violence it might engender. They also agreed to urge the ministers "not to preach turmoil from the pulpit"— this in response to the report that the pastor of Hochfelden had attempted to incite his congregation against the Jews.[54]

Protestant reaction was mixed. Melanchthon sent a copy of *On the Jews and Their Lies* to Landgrave Philipp of Hesse with the mild recommendation that the book contained "much useful teaching."[55] When he sent a copy of *On the Ineffable Name,* however, he failed to add a similar recommendation.[56] It is hard to say whether this indicates disapproval; generally speaking, Melanchthon was uncomfortable with the violent tone of many of the writings of the older Luther.[57] Andreas Osiander of Nuremberg appears to have been critical of the work, although unwilling to confront Luther with his objections.[58] Luther's Zurich opponents, the authors of the 1545 *True Confession,* branded Luther's *On the Ineffable Name* as "swinish" and "filthy," and remarked that had it been written by a swineherd and not by a famous shepherd of souls, there might have been some although little excuse for it.[59]

This last criticism is interesting since it appears to focus on Luther's language rather than on his arguments or recommendations. It would be informative to know what their judgment would have been on such works as the anonymous *A Horrible, Shocking Story* and Eck's *Refutation of a Jew-Book,* which employed more moderate language to express their attacks on Jews but which in their substance were more hostile and, from our perspective at least, more libelous than Luther's works.[60] Martin Bucer, together with a group of Hessian theologians, published a memorandum in 1539, addressed to Landgrave Philipp, that offered recommendations for the treatment of Jews in Hesse that were more moderate in language but still very harsh in their effect.[61] There is no guarantee that the Zurich theologians would have shared Bucer's views, but the presumption seems reasonable that on this point Bucer and the Zurichers would not have been far apart.[62] In fact, few treatises were produced in this period that had much favorable to say about the contemporary Jews. Even Andreas Osiander's memorandum arguing against the charge that Jews committed the ritual murder of Christian children was published anonymously, perhaps for fear of criticism such "moderation" and "reasonableness" might provoke.[63]

Fortunately, no Protestant prince attempted to put all Luther's recommendations into practice. Several did, however, take some measures against the Jews as a result of Luther's writings. In May 1543 Elector Johann Friedrich revoked some concessions he had made to the Jews in 1539. He cited as his reason for doing so Luther's recent treatises, which had opened his eyes to Jewish proselytizing and to their attacks on Christianity.[64] Johann of Küstrin, Margrave of Neumark, similarly revoked the safe-conduct of Jews under his jurisdiction.[65] And Landgrave Philipp added several new restrictions to his *Order Concerning the Jews* of 1539.[66]

If publishing statistics are any guide, then the 1523 treatise had a broader appeal, both quantitatively and geographically, than did any of the four later treatises.[67] *That Jesus Christ Was Born a Jew* saw thirteen editions, ten in German and three in Latin translation.[68] Four of these editions were issued in Wittenberg, two in Augsburg, two in Basel, two in Strasbourg, and one in Speyer. In contrast, the four later treatises saw a combined total of only fifteen editions, eleven of which were published in Wittenberg, three in Frankfurt, and one in Augsburg. *On the Ineffable Name* was reprinted most, with seven German editions, five published in Wittenberg and two in Frankfurt. It is unclear why this treatise should have been the one most reprinted of the four later treatises; perhaps its sensational first half, recounting Porchetus's tale of Christ the magician, appealed to the curious.[69] *On the Last Words of David* saw only two printings, while *Against the Sabbatarians* and *On the Jews and Their Lies* saw three printings each.

In general Luther's polemics were reprinted less frequently during these later years than in the earlier stages of the Reformation. Nonetheless, these statistics suggest that even among the polemics of his last years, the anti-Jewish treatises may have been less "popular" and "sought after" than the other major polemics of his late years.[70] To give a standard for comparison: *Against Hanswurst* saw four printings,[71] *Against the Papacy at Rome* saw six,[72] *Admonition to Prayer Against the Turks* saw ten,[73] and *Short Confession on the Supper* saw six.[74] In terms of reprintings, then, only *On the Ineffable Name and on Christ's Lineage* exceeded these other polemics of Luther's old age.

THEOLOGY AND HISTORY

In recent years some scholars have insisted that Luther's attitude toward the Jews can be understood *exclusively* from the presuppositions of his theology. Wilhelm Maurer is foremost among advocates of this view, both for the strength of his argument and for the care with which he examines all of Luther's pronouncements on the Jews.[75] According to Maurer, *That Jesus Christ Was Born a Jew* was not a missionary tract, and *Against the Sabbatarians* and the three treatises of 1543 were not simply anti-Jewish libels. He believes that the 1523 treatise may be best described as a "Christological study of the human nature of Christ" with an "apologetic missionary tendency." And he describes *Against the Sabbatarians* as the beginning of a theological discussion concerning the Christian understanding of the Old Testament that is continued in the interrelated anti-Jewish treatises of 1543. These late treatises were "theological treatises" and "belong first and foremost to the history of theology."[76]

Undergirding these "theological" treatises, Maurer argues, were four basic theological principles or presuppositions that remained constant through Luther's career, from the Psalms lectures of 1513–15 to the last sermon of 1546.[77] These principles or presuppositions derived from Luther's theology of justification by faith alone with its distinction between law and gospel, judgment and faith. The principles were (1) that the Jews were a people suffering under the wrath of God; (2) that without divine intervention they were incorrigible and impossible to convert by human effort; (3) that their religion remained perpetually hostile to Christianity and could not cease blaspheming God and Christ; and (4) that there existed a "solidarity of guilt" between Christians and Jews: a common suffering under God's wrath, a common resistance to Christ, a common attempt to gain one's own righteousness and salvation apart from Christ, a common need for grace.

What changed over Luther's career, Maurer contends, was not these theological principles or presuppositions but rather the practical and legal conclusions Luther drew from them. Maurer, following historians before him, suggests a number of political and religious matters, perceived by Luther in a new light or to which he attached new importance, that may collectively account for this change of mind. Although always concerned over the problem of usury, for example, Luther became even more concerned over *Jewish* usury in his later years. He also appears to have shared his society's suspicions that the Jews favored the Turks and were assisting them against the Christians. Direct personal experiences may have played a role: for example, problems with Jewish converts and a frustrating debate in the early 1530s with three learned Jews over certain messianic passages in the Old Testament. Reports of Jewish proselytizing, of Judaizing sects within Christianity, of messianic movements among the Jews may have fed his ire and increased his concern over the effect Jews had on society. Most important of all, of course, was his determined effort to preserve the Christological interpretation of the Old Testament from the historicizing exegesis of the rabbis and the Christian Hebraicists who followed the rabbinic lead.[78]

Maurer places the harsh recommendations themselves in their theological context. At issue was the matter of blasphemy. For Luther a Protestant territory was Christian not to the extent that its inhabitants were Christian but to the extent that it refused to tolerate anti-Christian teaching in public. By the mid-1530s Luther had abandoned his belief that Jewish blasphemy against Christ and God was confined to the privacy of the synagogue. Having encountered Jewish propaganda and received report of active Jewish proselytizing, Luther became convinced that the Jews and their blasphemy were a threat to the public good. His demands—that the synagogues be burned and buried, that Jewish prayer books and the Talmud be destroyed, that rabbis be forbidden to teach, and that Jewish worship be forbidden—stem from his belief that Jewish teaching and preaching contained blasphemy.[79]

These harsh recommendations were for Luther an expression of "rough mercy" *(scharfe Barmherzigkeit)* that might save a few Jews from the flames of hell,[80] while "soft mercy" (such as that expressed in his 1523 treatise) only made the Jews worse and worse.[81] "Rough mercy" was the paradoxical action of God in judgment and grace. The Christian preacher was to proclaim this from the pulpit; the Christian authorities were to carry it into practice.[82]

The central concern of the late treatises was not, however, these political and economic expressions of "rough mercy." Luther's late anti-Jewish writings were attempts to defend and maintain theologically and exegetically the Christian sense of the Old Testament and to refute competing Jewish exegesis. Maurer argues at length that Luther was attempting to found a new school of exegesis that would direct the research efforts of the Christian humanist Hebraists. In these treatises Luther was concerned fundamentally with the perpetual problem of the relation between the Old and the New Testaments.[83]

The attractiveness of this "theological" explanation of Luther's attitude toward the Jews obviously goes beyond its ability to account for Luther's beliefs and behavior. For one thing, it makes clearer the inappropriateness of *racial* anti-Semites claiming Luther as a patron of their cause. Luther identified a Jew by his religious beliefs, not by his race. (Identification of a Jew by his race is, in any case, a concept foreign to the sixteenth century.) If a Jew converted to Christianity, he became a fellow brother or sister in Christ. For racial anti-Semitism religious belief is largely irrelevant. For example, under National Socialism a person was considered Jewish if either of his grandparents were Jewish, whatever his religious convictions. Scholars who point this out are not condoning religious anti-Semitism. They are pointing out only that the logic of religious anti-Semitism leads to attempts at conversion, not to genocide.

A "theological" explanation as presented by Maurer also allows the modern scholar to conclude that the theology itself does not necessarily lead to the political and economic recommendations Luther actually recommended to the rulers of his day. For example, Maurer characterizes Luther's harsh recommendations as an "anachronism," "utopian but also hopelessly reactionary," an "unrealizable remnant of medieval tradition."[84] Luther's attempt to separate Christians from Jews is judged "a mistaken decision that was deeply grounded in the social reality of his time and that, furthermore, reveals a deficiency in his understanding of history."[85] For Maurer, Luther's *theological* considerations remain valid to this day,[86] while in the social and political realm, he was fighting a "losing battle."[87] In short, this distinction allows contemporary theologians to embrace Luther's theology without also having to embrace his anti-Semitic practices.[88]

Maurer is certainly right to insist that the primary subject of the later treatises, whether viewed quantitatively or qualitatively, was the proper exegesis of the Old Testament. He is also right to insist that, when doing critical theology, one must distinguish between the essential assertions of Luther's theology and their specific application, which may have been conditioned by the circumstances of the sixteenth century. As Maurer realizes, Luther's theology of justification and the conclusions one draws from it remain of central importance for the Jewish-Christian dialogue of today.[89] In this dialogue it would not do to confuse "accidents" with "essence."

From an historical perspective, however, this "theological" evaluation of Luther's attitude toward the Jews is unsatisfactory. Sixteenth-century readers of Luther's treatises, and even Luther himself, could not have distinguished between what Maurer termed the "essential theology" of the tracts and the "remnants of medieval tradition" that they also contained. For Luther and for his contemporaries the "remnants" of prejudice and discriminatory treatment were in logic and in practice tied to the theological description of the Jews as a God-forsaken people suffering under divine wrath. Theology and practice reinforced each other. So twentieth-century scholars may conclude that for the purposes of twentieth-century theology those aspects of Luther's theology that twentieth-century theologians deem essential need not entail the practical recommendations that Luther made. But the historian must insist that *Luther* saw a clear relationship between the two. To be sure, the historian may also conclude that Luther was illogical or that he was using his theology to rationalize beliefs and prejudices that he and his society shared. Nevertheless, for the historian the distinction between "essential theology" and "medieval remnants" tells more about the twentieth than about the sixteenth century.

Neither the vulgarity nor the violence nor the charges of satanic motivation nor the sarcastic mocking is unique to these treatises. If anything, Luther's 1541 *Against Hanswurst* and his 1545 *Against the Papacy at Rome, Founded by the Devil* contain more scatology, more sallies against the devil, more heavy sarcasm, and more violence of language and recommendations. The polemics of the older Luther against Turks and Protestant opponents are only slightly more restrained. Against each of these opponents—Catholics, Turks, other Protestants, and Jews —he occasionally passed on libelous tales and gave credence to improbable charges. In all these respects Luther treated the Jews no differently than he treated his other opponents.[90]

With many of these other polemics the vulgarity and harshness may have been a deliberate rhetorical tactic. The language was consistent with the general tenor of the polemical contest. But can the same be said of the anti-Jewish treatises? Ostensibly, Luther was replying to a Jewish treatise that defamed Christ, the Virgin Mary, and Christianity in general. Unfortunately, this treatise is now lost, so that it is not possible to evaluate its rhetoric and style of argumentation. There were some anti-Christian Jewish writings produced in this period, but not enough to allow us to locate Luther's work within a polemical contest between Christians and Jews, even assuming there was such a contest.[91] In any case, this is not really necessary since the treatises were explicitly aimed not at the Jews but at fellow Protestants. In this respect his anti-Jewish writings have more in common with his attacks on Protestant opponents than with his attacks on Catholics and Turks.

For Luther the Catholics and Turks were *external* threats, coming from outside the Reformation movement itself. Also they were threats closely bound up in politics. This can be seen from the fact that the treatises against Turks and Catholics were almost all written at the request of Elector Johann Friedrich and reflect the political interests of the elector and his fellow members of the League of Schmalkalden. In contrast, in his attacks on Sacramentarians and Jews he was worried primarily about *internal* subversion, about the threat these opponents posed from within the movement. The Sacramentarians claimed to be fellow Christians and to be in essential agreement with Luther, and yet they denied the real presence in the Lord's Supper. The internal threat they posed is obvious.[92]

Significantly, Luther also viewed the Jews, or rather Jewish exegesis, as more an internal than an external threat.[93] It was, after all, to counter Jewish efforts to proselytize Christians (or to counter Judaizing sects within Protestantism) that Luther wrote his *Against the Sabbatarians*. Of greater threat, however, was the challenge posed by Jewish exegesis of the Old Testament. Luther believed his Christological interpretation of the Old Testament and his Christian interpretation of various messianic Old Testament passages to be of vital importance to his theology. Jewish exegetes challenged both. And, increasingly, Protestant theologians and translators were adopting the exegetical opinions of the Jewish exegetes.[94]

In the later anti-Jewish treatises Luther attempted to dissuade fellow Protestants from employing rabbinic exegesis. He attacked the exegesis itself, using historical, scriptural, and theological arguments. But he also employed his rhetorical skills to attack its source: the Jews themselves. To discredit the message it helps also to discredit the messenger.

There is another significant dimension to Luther's anti-Jewish treatises that links them with the other polemics of his later years. Heiko Oberman has recently pointed out that Luther's anti-Jewish polemics cannot be understood properly apart from his apocalyptic beliefs. Luther believed that he was living on the eve of the Last Judgment, that with the establishment of the Reformation and exposure of the papal antichrist within the church the devil had unleashed his last, most violent attack on the true church. The devil's servants in this final assault were the papists, the fanatics, the Turks, and the Jews. Luther saw it as his duty in this apocalyptic struggle to attack the devil with all the vehemence at his command and to defend the church against all the devil's thrusts. His attacks on the Jews, Oberman insists rightly, cannot be understood properly apart from this apocalyptic context.[95]

To insist on the importance of context for a proper understanding of Luther's anti-Jewish treatises is not merely good history. It also makes it more difficult for modern anti-Semites to exploit the authority of Luther's name to support their racist beliefs. This is all to the good. But we cannot have it both ways. If the anti-Jewish treatises cannot be divorced from their context without serious distortion, then the same should be true for his other writings. It is not intellectually honest to pick and choose.

NOTES

1. The literature on Luther's relation to the Jews is so vast that a monograph recently appeared on the literature itself (Johannes Brosseder, *Luther's Stellung zu den Juden im Spiegel seiner Interpreten. Interpretation und Rezeption von Luthers Schriften und Äusserungen zum Judentum im 19. und 20. Jahrhundert vor allem im deutschsprachigen Raum* [Munich, 1972]. See also Kurt Meier, "Zur Interpretation von Luthers Judenschriften," in *Vierhundertfünfzig Jahre lutherische Reformation, 1517–1967* [Berlin/Göttingen, 1967], pp. 233–52; C. Bernd Sucher, *Luthers Stellung zu den Juden. Eine Interpretation aus germanistischer Sicht* [Nieuwkoop, 1977], pp. 125–99). For reasons that will become apparent, I have found most useful the following works: Wilhelm Maurer, "Die Zeit der Reformation," in *Kirche und Synagoge,* edited by Karl-Heinrich Rengstorf and Siegfried von Kortzfleisch, (Stuttgart, 1968), 1:363–452; and C. Bernd Sucher, *Luthers Stellung zu den Juden.* During the final stages of revision before publication I received a copy of Heiko A. Oberman's *Wurzeln des Antisemitismus: Christenangst und Judenplage im Zeitalter von Humanismus und Reformation* (Severin und Siedler, 1981). Developing an analysis similar in some respects to my own but in considerably more detail, this fascinating monograph places Luther's writings back within their historic context and thus corrects many of the more exclusively theological studies.

2. Of the vast literature on the history of the Jews and of Jewish-Christian relations, I have found most useful Rosemary Radford Reuther, *Faith and Fratricide: The Theological Roots of Anti-Semitism* (New York, 1974); Alan Davies, ed., *Antisemitism and the Foundations of Christianity* (New York, 1979); Salo Baron, *A Social and Religious History of the Jews* (New York, 1957–73), vols. 2–15; Guido Kisch, *The Jews in Medieval Germany: A Study of Their Legal and Social Status* (Chicago, 1949).

3. See Kisch, *The Jews in Medieval Germany,* pp. 107–68.

4. Maurer, "Die Zeit der Reformation," pp. 367–69; Oberman, *Wurzeln,* pp. 52–55, 99–104.

5. In 1144 the Jews of Norwich in England were accused of murdering a young Christian boy named William. This is the first of a series of such accusations made through the Middle Ages and into our own times. See Baron, *A Social and Religious History,* 11:146–57.

6. *Ein grausame, erschrockenliche geschicht von einem vngotzförchtigem verrucktem vnnd verzweyfelten Christen man, der sein eigen fleiss vnd blüt, sein natürliches kind ein junges kneblin den Seellosen. Gottlosen, Gotts verretterschen Juden verkaufft vnc zü kauffen geben hatt . . .* (n.p.,n.d.), pp. Aii(v)–Ci(v). The copy of this tract found in the British Library [STC 4033.c.50(6)] has the date 1544 penned on the title page. I suspect that the treatise was originally published at an earlier date. The libel I am recounting

occurred in 1503. Another murder treated in this account, to which the anonymous author claims to have been an eye-witness, apparently occurred in 1504 [see p. Dii(v))]. In any case, the verses appear to have been written before Emperor Maximilian's death in 1519 [see p. E(v)].

7. Johann Eck, *Ains Judenbüechlins verlegung: darin ain Christ, gantzer Christenhait zü schmach, will es geschehe den Juden vnrecht in bezichtigung der Kristen kinder mordt* (Ingolstadt: Alexander Weissenhorn, 1542), pp. Biii(v)–Biv(v).

8. Eck only says it sweated (p. Biv).

9. *Ein grausame, ershrockenliche geschicht,* p. Bii.

10. Ibid., p. C(v).

11. In 1540 the Jews of Tittingen and the surrounding area were accused of murdering a young peasant boy (Selma Stern, *Josel of Rosheim, Commander of Jewry in the Holy Roman Empire of the German Nation* [Philadelphia, 1965], pp. 180–83). While hearings were taking place at the court of the Bishop of Eichstätt, two Jews from Sulzbach presented the Episcopal Counselors with an anonymous treatise defending Jews against the accusation of ritual murder. Its author was probably Andreas Osiander of Nuremberg (Moritz Stern, ed., *Andreas Osianders Schrift über die Blutbeschuldigung* [Kiel, 1893]). Eck was then commissioned by Albrecht of Leonrod, one of the councilors of the Bishop of Eichstätt (*Verlegung,* pp. Aii(v)–Aiii), to issue a written Refutation to this treatise. The resulting publication was some 189 pages, and dealt at length with Osiander's arguments, citing in the process numerous alleged ritual murders, even explaining the use to which the blood was put, and detailing other sinister practices of the Jews. Eck was aware that the author of the treatise was a Lutheran, and expressed the hope that princes, lords, and cities would come to recognize the bad tree that could produce such bad fruit (*Verlegung,* p. Aiii). He even suggested at one point that Osiander was the author (*Verlegung,* p. Div).

12. Since the treatise was written in German, I infer that Eck had a popular audience in mind. Most of his writings were in Latin (see "Verzeichnis der Schriften Ecks," in *Corpus Catholicorum* [Münster, 1930], 16:LXXII–CXXXII).

13. As the apostles, who were Jews, had treated the pagans in a brotherly fashion, so the Christians should treat the Jews in a similarly brotherly fashion "so that we might convert some." After all, Luther had reminded his readers, we are the pagans and they are the blood relatives of Christ (WA 11:314–15).

14. WA 11:316–25.

15. WA 11:325–36.

16. WA 11:336.

17. It is unlikely that Luther had abandoned his *theological* conviction that any conversions stood not in man's power but in God's. But he had already experienced the incredible successes of the heady early years of the Reformation. He thought of himself as an instrument of God's to reveal the

purified gospel. While faith was always in God's power, not in man's, God used men to bring other men to faith. Perhaps He would use Luther to bring some of the Jews, perhaps even many of them, to their true messiah. The relative optimism of this position was, however, short lived. When the rush of Jewish converts did not occur, he returned to his theologically based pessimism. The Jews were under God's wrath. Their punishment made them even more stiff-necked. Some might yet find their true messiah, but they would be few. The rest were the devil's children, enemies of the true church of God.

18. WATR 3, 3512b. WATR 4, 5026 and 4795. WA 53:461. Cf. WA 50:515. Cited in Maurer, "Die Zeit der Reformation," pp. 398–99.

19. To summarize briefly: Luther believed that the true church of God had been established even before the Fall when God commanded Adam to eat from every tree except the tree of the knowledge of good and evil. When Satan had tempted Adam and Eve, and they had fallen, God had immediately announced the promise of the blessed seed that would crush the head of the serpent. The saints of the Old Testament lived and taught this faith in the promise of the seed of the woman. "They gave the exact same sermons that we in our time present to the church and community of God, except that they taught about the future Christ who was yet to come, but we say of him: 'Christ has come,' while they said: 'He will come' " (WA 44:635). For this reason Luther interpreted the Old Testament Christologically and saw all promises by God in the Old Testament as referring to Christ. Hence the saintly Jews of the Old Testament were part of the true church, living by faith in God's promise. But the New Testament revealed how most Jews had rejected their promised messiah, crucified him, and persecuted his followers. With these actions they had drawn down upon themselves God's wrath. The history of postbiblical Jewry was for Luther the history of God's implacable wrath over a rejected and forsaken people. Their life of suffering was a continuous witness to the judgment and power of God. Their conversion lay in God's power, not in man's. Some might yet accept the true messiah, Jesus Christ. But God's wrath and their suffering actually made the majority worse and more obstinate.

For a description of how this view develops, see, among others, Scott Hendrix, *Ecclesia in Via. Ecclesiological Developments in the Medieval Psalms Exegesis and the Dictata Super Psalterium of Martin Luther* (Leiden, 1974); James Samuel Preus, *From Shadow to Promise: Old Testament Interpretations from Augustine to the Young Luther* (Cambridge, MA, 1969); Jaroslav Pelikan, *Luther the Expositor* (St. Louis, 1959); Heinrich Bornkamm, *Luther und das Alte Testament* (Tübingen, 1948).

20. E.g., WA 50:273–83.

21. C. A. H. Burckhardt, "Die Judenverfolgung in Kurfürstentum Sachsen von 1536 an," *Theologische Studien und Kritiken* 70(1897):593–98.

22. See the following discussion of his correspondence with Josel of Rosheim.

23. WATR 3:441–42.

24. See Stern, *Josel of Rosheim.*
25. WABr 8:76–78. For a discussion of these letters, see Stern, *Josel of Rosheim,* pp. 155–57, 303n7, 304n8.
26. WATR 3:441–42.
27. For the following, see WABr 8:89–91.
28. Luther had not fully abandoned his missionary hopes, for he announced in · this letter that if God granted him the opportunity, he intended to write a booklet about this to see if he couldn't win a few from Josel's paternal tribe of holy patriarchs and prophets and bring them to their promised messiah. This promised treatise may be his *Against the Sabbatarians* (see WABr 8:91n4).
29. See Stern, *Josel of Rosheim,* p. 162.
30. WA 50:312–37.
31. "Behold, the time is coming, says God, when I shall make a new covenant with the house of Israel and with the house of Judah, not like the covenant which I made with their fathers when I took them by the hand and led them out of Egypt, [the covenant] which they did not observe and I had to force them [to observe]. But this shall be the covenant that I shall make with the children of Israel after this time, says the Lord: I will put my law into their hearts and write it in their minds, and they shall be my people, and I will be their God. And no one shall teach and say to his brother or to another, 'See, know the Lord,' for they shall all know me, both the great and the small, says the Lord. For I will forgive them their misdeeds and will no longer think of their sins" (translated from Luther's German).
32. WA 50:318.
33. WA 53:417–552, 53:579–648, 54:28–100.
34. WA 53:417.
35. For more on the background of these treatises and their sources, see WA 50:309–11, 53:412–14, 53:573–75, 54:16–24, as well as the literature cited in note 1 above.
36. WA 53:417.
37. WA 53:418–19.
38. WA 53:419–27.
39. WA 53:427–39.
40. WA 53:439–46.
41. WA 53:446–48.
42. WA 53:449.
43. At one point he related how he had personally debated such passages with three learned Jews. These Jews, Luther claimed, when they were unable to refute Luther's exegesis of the texts, had fallen back on the authority of their rabbis. For this reason, and on account of their blasphemies, Luther wished to have nothing further to do with them (WA 53:461–62).
44. Some amount could be returned to converts to Christianity so that they might support themselves.
45. The Jewish treatise that had prompted Luther's *On the Jews and Their Lies*

had apparently also maintained that it could not be proved that Jesus was of the tribe of Judah since Matthew traced the genealogy of the tribe of Judah to Joseph rather than to Mary. It was to refute this claim that Luther composed the second section.

46. WA 53:579–80.
47. WA 53:587–609, quote on pp. 605–6.
48. WA 54:28–100.
49. See WA 51:152–53, 166–67, 195ff.; WA 54:17–18.
50. Carl Cohen, "Martin Luther and His Jewish Contemporaries," *Jewish Social Studies* 25(1963):201. Benzing (Josef Benzing, *Lutherbibliographie: Verzeichnis der gedruckten Schriften Martin Luthers bis zu dessen Tod* [Baden-Baden, 1966]) does not list this Spanish translation, and I have been unable to verify its existence.
51. WA 54:24.
52. Stern, *Josel of Rosheim*, p. 95. See also Eck's *Verlegung*.
53. Stern, *Josel of Rosheim*, p. 307n6.
54. Stern, *Josel of Rosheim*, pp. 192–93, 196–99.
55. CR 5:21.
56. CR 5:76–77.
57. See, for example, his evaluation in his funeral oration for Luther (CR 11:727–28). See also Gustav Mix, "Luther und Melanchthon in ihrer gegenseitigen Beurteilung," *Theologische Studien und Kritiken* 74(1901):458–521; and Wilhelm Pauck, "Luther und Melanchthon," in *Luther und Melanchthon*, ed. Vilmos Vajta (Göttingen, 1961), pp. 11–31.
58. CR 5:729; WA 53:574.
59. "So ist vorhanden Luthers Schwynins katigs Schemhamphoras, welches so es geschriben wäre von einem Schwynhirten, nit von einem berrümpten Seel hirten, etwas doch ouch wenig entschuldigung hette." *Wahrhaffte Bekanntnuss* (Zurich, 1545), p. 10r. For a brief discussion of this treatise, see my *Luther and the False Brethren* (Stanford, 1975), pp. 194–96.
60. Stern characterizes Eck's treatise as "the most abusive to have been written against the Jews even in that 'Age of Grobianism'." (Stern, *Josel of Rosheim*, p. 183). It certainly makes for grisly reading.
61. Martin Bucer et al., *Ratschlag Ob Christlicher Obrigkeit gebüren müge, das sie die Jüden, vnter den Christen zu wonen gedulden, vnd wo sie zu gedulden, welcher gestalt vnd mais* (Erfurt, 1539). The pastors recommended that Jews be barred from all forms of employment except the most lowly and degrading, so that they would be constantly aware of their status.
62. See Oberman, *Wurzeln*, esp. parts I and II, for the linkage between anti-Jewish and reform sentiments held by Catholics and Protestants.
63. See n. 5, above.
64. Burkhardt, "Die Judenverfolgung," p. 597.
65. Stern, *Josel of Rosheim*, p. 195.
66. Stern, *Josel of Rosheim*, pp. 199–200.
67. The following statistics are drawn from Benzing, *Lutherbibliographie*, num-

bers 1530–1542, 3293–3295, 3424–3426, 3436–3442, 3448–3449. One of the German editions of *Against the Sabbatarians* was printed in Augsburg by Alexander Weissenhorn, who, a year later in 1539, moved to Ingolstadt where he published much of the Catholic controversial literature issuing from that center including the only two editions of Eck's *Verlegung* ("Verzeichnis der Schriften Ecks," in *Corpus Catholicorum* [Münster, 1930], 16:CXXIX; Josef Benzing, *Buchdruckerlexikon des 16. Jahrhunderts (Deutsches Sprachgebiet)* [Frankfurt a.M., 1952], pp. 14, 81). Did he perhaps have a special animus toward Jews? Or is this just a coincidence?

68. As noted above, I have been unable to identify the Spanish edition mentioned by C. Cohen (see n. 50).

69. There is some circumstantial evidence to support this suggestion. One of the two Frankfurt publishers of this treatise was Hermann Gülfferich, who generally specialized in popular literature for home and school (Benzing, *Buchdruckerlexikon,* p. 52).

70. Gordon Rupp has found some solace in *On the Jews and Their Lies* being a "worse seller" (Gordon Rupp, "Martin Luther and the Jews," *Nederlands Theologisch Tijdschrift* 31[1977]:130).

71. Benzing, *Lutherbibliographie,* numbers 3369–3372.

72. Benzing, *Lutherbibliographie,* numbers 3497–3502.

73. Benzing, *Lutherbibliographie,* numbers 3378–3387.

74. Benzing, *Lutherbibliographie,* numbers 3458–3463.

75. Maurer has published two major essays on Luther's attitude toward the Jews: Wilhelm Maurer, *Kirche und Synagoge. Motive und Formen der Auseinandersetzung der Kirche mit dem Judentum im Laufe der Geschichte. Franz Belitzsch-Vorlesungen 1951* (Stuttgart, 1953); and Maurer, "Die Zeit der Reformation" (see n. 1). There are some significant differences between the two essays (see Brosseder, *Luther Stellung zu den Juden,* pp. 270–75). In the later essay Maurer places less stress on the missionary aspects of the 1523 treatise and more on its Christological thrust. Brosseder, *Luthers Stellung zu den Juden,* follows Maurer on most points.

76. Maurer, "Die Zeit der Reformation," pp. 388–89, 407, 416, 427.

77. In recent reviews of the literature this general line of argument is given the title "change and continuity": meaning that Luther's practical recommendations concerning the Jews change while his theological view of their status remains constant throughout his career (Meier, "Zur Interpretation von Luthers Judenschriften"; Brosseder, *Luthers Stellung zu den Juden,* pp. 35–36 and *passim;* Sucher, *Luthers Stellung zu den Juden,* pp. 125–69). The weight of scholarly opinion now seems to favor this view.

The main competing interpretations, identified first with Reinhold Lewin's *Luthers Stellung zu den Juden* (Berlin, 1911), argues that there are one or two changes in Luther's attitude towards the Jews, changes manifested in his interest in converting them, in the treatment he advocated towards them, and, perhaps, even in some theological issues concerning their status within divine history and in relation to Christianity. Lewin identified two changes:

in the period to about 1521 Luther was indifferent toward the Jews or hostile only on a theological level; then for a time, reaching its high point in the 1523 *That Jesus Christ Was Born a Jew,* he was sympathetic toward the Jews and harbored optimistic hopes for their conversion; finally, in the latter part of his life, he became actively hostile on both a theological and practical level. The grounds offered for these changes are normally psychological, particularly Luther's disappointment that his 1523 treatise largely failed in its missionary attempt.

One attraction of this interpretation, quite apart from its merits in dealing with the evidence, is that it allows its proponents to choose which is Luther's "true" position: the relatively tolerant and sympathetic attitude of 1523 or the hostile position of the older Luther.

Although neither interpretation was immune from misuse in the service of Nazi anti-Semitism (Meier, "Zur Interpretation von Luthers Judenschriften," pp. 235–40; Brosseder, *Luthers Stellung zu Den Juden,* p. 259), the great majority of such propagandistic uses favored the view of change put forward by Lewin (Brosseder, *Luthers Stellung zu den Juden,* p. 259). But whereas Lewin applauded the statements of the early 1520s, the Nazi propagandists argued that the statements of the old Luther represented his authentic position. For these propagandists it was convenient to depict Luther as a man who was originally friendly toward Jews but, learning from bitter experience, became one of the greatest anti-Semites of all time (see Brosseder, *Luthers Stellung zu den Juden.* esp. pp. 156ff.).

78. Maurer, "Die Zeit der Reformation," pp. 388–89, 407, 416, 427.
79. Maurer, "Die Zeit der Reformation," pp. 397–400.
80. WA 53:522.
81. WA 53:525.
82. Maurer, "Die Zeit der Reformation," p. 426.
83. Maurer, "Die Zeit der Reformation," pp. 416, 407–15.
84. Maurer, "Die Zeit der Reformation," pp. 428, 421.
85. Maurer, "Die Zeit der Reformation," p. 427.
86. Maurer terms them *"unverlierbare."*
87. Maurer, "Die Zeit der Reformation," p. 421.
88. Not all theologians are comfortable with this approach. Aarne Siirala writes: "Is not the structure of the Lutheran consensus presented above the structure of a rationalization? It may be understandable as a reaction against those interpretations in which Luther has been blamed for modern anti-Semitism or made a scapegoat for the holocausts of our generation. But the attempt both to find a scapegoat and an interpretation of history in terms of a rationalization, in which a certain present position is defended by repressing and avoiding certain facts of history, is a sign of an escape from facing one's own loyalties and disloyalties in the present. To characterize Luther's attitude toward the Jews as 'religious,' 'biblical' or 'theological' does not clarify this complex issue. Even the Inquisition, for example, claims to be all that, but in that case we are ready to see in it a pathological element in the

perversions of the generations in question" (Aarne Siirala, "Luther and the Jews," *Lutheran World* [1964]:356).

89. Maurer, "Die Zeit der Reformation," pp. 375–76.

90. Maurer, "Die Zeit der Reformation," p. 380, also makes this point.

91. See Hayim Hillel Ben-Sasson, "The Reformation in Contemporary Jewish Eyes," *Proceedings of the Israel Academy of Sciences and Humanities* 4(1971):239–326; and Cohen, "Martin Luther and His Jewish Contemporaries." I have not been able to consult E. Zivier, "Jüdische Bekehrungsversuche im 16. Jahrhundert," in *Beiträge zur Geschichte der deutschen Juden. Festschrift . . . Martin Philippson* (Leipzig, 1916), pp. 96–113.

92. See my *Luther and the False Brethren* for details.

93. Maurer argues that from the late 1520s on the Jews are seen by Luther as no longer having any connection with adherents to the gospel. They are now seen as part of a common front comprising papists (including heretics), unbelieving Jews, and Turks (Maurer, "Die Zeit der Reformation," p. 395). Although this is true for the Jews themselves, Jewish exegesis is seen as a threat from within the Reformation movement.

94. See Maurer, "Die Zeit der Reformation," pp. 414–15, 436–38.

95. E.g., Oberman, *Wurzeln*, pp. 155–56.

13

John Calvin and the Jews

Salo W. Baron

Unlike Martin Luther and most other German reformers, John Calvin had few, if any, contacts with contemporary Jews. The first twenty-five years of his life he spent in his native Picardy, Paris, or Orléans long after the expulsion of the Jews from France. Nor did he have many occasions to encounter Jews during the last quarter century of his life and his increasingly dictatorial regime in Geneva. Jewish sojourn in that Swiss city had been cut short by its city council's decree of expulsion of December 1490, which was carried out ruthlessly during the harsh winter season of January 1491. So few Jews had visited Geneva in the following decades that when, in 1547, two travelers passed through the city on their way from Flanders to Venice, the Council ordered a study of the regulations affecting such temporary sojourn, regulations which had evidently gone into oblivion during the intervening years. While we do not hear of Calvin's personal participation in this debate, it stands to reason that nothing of such significance for religious conformity could have escaped the attention of Geneva's theocratic ruler.[1]

Nor did the issue of Jewish "usury," which so greatly embittered the relations between the two faiths throughout western Europe, play a particular role in the Geneva reformer's attitude to the Jews. Apart from the physical absence of Jewish moneylending in Calvin's immediate environment, his view differed sharply from the traditional ecclesiastical

Reprinted by permission of the American Academy for Jewish Research from *Harry Austryn Wolfson Jubilee Volume on the Occasion of His Seventy-fifth Birthday,* English section, Vol. 1, Jerusalem, 1965, 141–63.

rejection of any kind of interest. In his comment on the crucial passage in Luke 6:35 he stated clearly: "No Scriptural testimony exists which would totally condemn usury. For that sentence of Christ which the populace regards as most unequivocal, namely *mutuum date nihil inde sperantes* [in Luke 6:35], has been gravely distorted."[2] Not that Calvin altogether favored moneylending. True, many Genevans had long made a living from that occupation and in several ordinances, confirmed in 1547, the city council of Geneva officially set the allowable maximum of interest rate at 5 percent. Certainly no legislation adopted by the city during Calvin's regime could have been promulgated without at least his tacit approval. Yet he refrained from clearly stating his position on this issue which loomed increasingly large in that period of rising capitalism. Occasionally he indulged digs at contemporary Jewish greed and repudiated the Jews' privileged position with respect to charging interest to non-Jewish borrowers. In his comment on Isa. 60:6–7, where the Jews had been promised great "abundance" and that the "wealth of the nations shall come unto thee," Calvin observed: "Under the pretext of this prophecy, the Jews stupidly devour all the riches of the earth with their unrestrained cupidity." In a sermon of 1556 he also declared that the fact the Jews had once been allowed to charge usury to the heathen nations, does not mean that "today they may aggrieve and molest God's children."[3] In any case, his attitude to moneylending was so ill-defined that it readily lent itself to divergent interpretations and opened the road for the subsequent Calvinist blanket approval of profits derived from banking.[4]

However, Calvin was undoubtedly impressed by the anti-Jewish teachings of most German reformers. True, Martin Luther's crudely anti-Jewish attacks of 1542–46 were not fully accessible to him because of his limited knowledge of German. He apparently studied only those works by Luther, whom he never met in person, which were available in Latin or French translation.[5] But during his sojourn in such German-speaking cities as Basel and Strasbourg and particularly during his semi-political appearances at the assemblies of Frankfort, Hagenau, Worms and Regensburg, Calvin must have discussed with German theologians various contemporary problems including those related to Jews. In Strasbourg, in particular, the vaunted religious tolerance of the city administration, (greatly influenced by the humanist Jacob Sturm), if not of its famous theologians, attracted a great many religious persecutees and was conducive to sociopolitical as well as theological debates of all kinds.[6]

Among the German theologians it was particularly Martin Bucer (Butzer) who exerted a deep and permanent influence on Calvin's thinking. This generally rather gentle Strasbourg theologian had many harsh things to say about Jews, particularly in connection with a debate between Landgrave Philip of Hesse and the Hessian theologians in 1538. Theretofore Bucer seems to have had but few direct relations with Jews. Several years later (in 1546) he was sharply to remonstrate against the imputation that he was of Jewish parentage. But when approached by his Hessian theological disciples, he took a definite anti-Jewish stand. He helped them prepare an extensive memorandum to answer the Landgrave's seven-point program, which was rather friendly to the Jews. After claiming that it was the general duty of civil rulers to protect the true religion and that the Jewish people had been both dishonest and long condemned by God, Bucer and his associates stressed particularly the country's losses occasioned by the economic rivalry between Jewish and Christian merchants. Their proposals, known as the "Cassel Advice," demanded, therefore, both religious and economic safeguards. The Jews were to pledge themselves not to harm Christians, to have no religious disputations with them, to attend Christian sermons, and, most significantly, to discontinue their reliance on the Talmud. They were also to be forbidden to engage in moneylending, commerce or industry and forced to make a living only from menial labor. In this connection the Hessian clergy coined the well-known simile of the sponge-like function of Jewish moneylending which first sucked up the country's wealth and was subsequently squeezed dry by the authorities. When the Landgrave rejected these proposals as too extreme and argued against them also on theological grounds, he received an urgent letter from Bucer, pointing out his alleged theological errors.[7] It was unavoidable that Bucer's anti-Jewish views should also affect Calvin who happened to spend most of his involuntary exile from Geneva in those very years 1539–41 in Bucer's close proximity at Strasbourg.[8]

CALVINUS JUDAIZANS

Like other reformers, Calvin naturally had to take a stand on the differences between Judaism and Christianity. Not surprisingly, the late medieval and early modern sectarian struggles frequently resulted in each faction accusing the other of "judaizing." This practice, which in ancient times had led Roman emperors to speak in official decrees of the "new Jew," Nestorius, and which in the sixth century had made opponents of Patriarch Paul of Antioch call him "Paul the Jew," repeated itself during the Albigensian revolt and subsequently during the sectarian conflicts of the Protestant Reformation.[9]

Calvin and his associates were particularly prone to hurl that accusation at their opponents, especially Miguel (Michael) Servetus, whose anti-trinitarianism smacked, in fact, of Jewish as well as of Muslim teachings. "It is, indeed," reads one of Calvin's articles of accusation addressed to the syndics of Geneva in 1553, "an abomination to see how this wretched man [Servetus] excuses the Jews' blasphemies against the Christian religion, and he approves and extols the miserable words of the Muslims that the three persons in the Trinity or, as he styles them, three gods, were unknown to the Fathers and are sons of Beelzebub."[10]

As was usual in such cases, the accusers did not have to be consistent. Almost in the same breath Calvin appears as the defender of the Old Testament against calumnies by Servetus, such as that ancient Judea had really been a very poor country, and as denouncer of Servetus' too great indebtedness to Jewish Bible commentators. Indubitably, Servetus was a much better student of Hebrew than Calvin and most other reformers and made good use of such Jewish commentaries as those of Rashi and David Kimhi which enjoyed a great vogue among other Christian Hebraists as well. Curiously, Calvin often accused his enemy of having borrowed a "Jewish" interpretation from the commentary of a good medieval Catholic, Nicholas de Lyra. This denunciation was not so completely far-fetched, however, for Nicholas had indeed extensively borrowed from Rashi's *Commentary*.[11] This series of denunciations constituted, of course, but a part of the Calvinist campaign against Servetus which resulted in the latter's burning at the stake in 1553—that permanent blemish on the dark dictatorial regime of the Geneva reformer.[12]

Servetus reciprocated in kind. Just as his anti-trinitarianism had served as the main target for the Calvinists, so did he turn the tables on his archopponent by pressing charges based on Calvin's emphasis upon "Jewish legalism." There is no question, indeed, that Calvin, who had been trained for the practice of law, rather than of theology, and who was building in Geneva what his fellow reformer, John Knox, admiringly called the "maist perfigt schoole of Chryst that ever was in the earth since the days of the Apostiliis," was greatly attracted to the Old Testament law which he tried to imitate as much as possible in his new Christian republic. With his usual fervor Servetus declaimed, "You [Calvin] place the Christians on a par with the vulgar Jews." Calling the Mosaic law an "irrational, impossible, tyrannical law," Servetus thundered, "And to that law you wish to make us adhere equally today." He further appealed to Calvin to desist from "twisting that law to apply to us and from violently agitating for its observance, as if you were dealing with the Jews." In another context he bluntly accused Calvin that he overlooked that in the New Covenant a new and living way was inaugurated and had thus "shocked me with your true Jewish zeal." These accusations were not silenced by Servetus' death, and, in 1595, Aegidius Hunnius published a polemical pamphlet under the characteristic title of *Calvinus Judaizans*. Curiously, some of the main shafts were aimed at Calvin's doctrine of the Trinity. Hunnius claimed that his work would show "the Judaic glosses and corruptions wherewith John Calvin did not hesitate to corrupt in a detestable fashion the passages and the most celebrated testimonies in Holy Scripture concerning the glorious Trinity." [13]

Perhaps egged on by such accusations, Calvin often went out of his way in attacking not only the ancient Jews but also his Jewish contemporaries, particularly in their persistent adherence to their traditional interpretation of the Bible. He did not hesitate from time to time to accuse Jews of fraudulently corrupting the biblical texts. True, he never budged from his insistence on the basic trustworthiness of the extant texts of the Law of Moses. Referring to contemporary queries as to how, after the burning of all books by Antiochus Epiphanes, they were again speedily available after the cessation of hostilities, Calvin exclaimed, "But even though all wicked men as if conspiring together, have so shamelessly insulted the Jews, no one has ever dared charge them with substituting false books." Nevertheless some minor textual falsifications, especially in the books of Prophets and the Hagiographa, were still possible. Calvin believed that Jewish scribes, even if supported by all extant Hebrew texts, could not be trusted, particularly wherever an original reading might have had Christological implications. While suggesting, for example, an emendation in Ps. 22:17, he exclaimed: "I do not labor here in order to convince the Jews whose stubbornness is indomitable to the last ditch [ad rixandum]. I merely wish to show how unjustly they have disturbed Christian minds because of their different reading of this passage." [14] In another context he accused the Jews of knowingly denying the Old Testament's testimonies concerning Christ. "But they are not only foolish and stupid but also frenetic." All of this was, in his opinion, merely a sign that God had struck them with blindness, "and if I wished to persist in refuting their errors there would be no end." [15]

Understandably, it was the Book of Daniel with its messianic predictions which lent itself particularly well to Calvin's exposition of his general outlook on history and the delineation of the alleged differences between ancient Israel and post-Christian Jewry. Needless to say, the Geneva reformer unquestioningly accepted the traditional date of that book. In a long overlooked brief statement of 1555, Calvin expressly stated that Daniel had accurately predicted the events unfolding during the following two centuries "for he had so clearly specified the persons, the mores and nature, as well as the circumstances of their actions, that one is bound to conclude that he was a true spokesman of God before whom all matters are ever present." [16]

Here Calvin ran up against the commentary on Daniel by Don Isaac Abravanel which had attracted wide attention also among Christians. It is possible that Calvin knew Abravanel's comment only from second hand. At his first mention he refers to his friend Antonius Cevallerius as having suggested to him the name of "Barbinel who appears to be ingenious above all other" Jewish commentators. Here Calvin attacked particularly Abravanel's six arguments against the identification of Daniel's Fifth Monarchy with the reign of Jesus Christ. In various other comments Calvin likewise attacked Abravanel with his accustomed vehemence calling him an "impostor," "a dog," and the like. He denounced Abravanel's "hallucinations," particularly also in the reconstruction of ancient history. Apart from the usual theological and dogmatic controversies, Calvin went into great lengths in proving that Abravanel's repudiation of Josephus, whom he himself avowedly not always followed, was completely unjustified. Of course, he rejected Abravanel's chronology, doubtless taken over from Ibn Daud's twelfth-century Chronicle, that two centuries had passed between the death of Christ and the destruction of the Temple. "How great is his ignorance!"[17] Elsewhere, too, Calvin attacked the Jewish messianic expectation as too materialistic. In one of his sermons he declared that the Jews imagine that the Messiah would "come into the world in order to bring an abundance of goods so that they may have a bellyful to eat, that there shall be no wars, that each should rest and indulge in various delights; this is how the Jews have depicted their savior." But he had to admit that the very Apostles were not completely free of that "fantasy."[18]

Not surprisingly, some homiletical interpretations of Scripture current among contemporary Jews lent themselves as special targets for Calvin's verbal arrows. Not drawing any distinction between what the Jews themselves considered the ordinary meaning of Scripture and the various folkloristic and homiletical elaborations by ancient and medieval rabbis, Calvin's logical mind could readily indulge in sharp attacks upon such Jewish "fantasies." In his comment on Isa. 48:21 he declared that "according to their custom, Jews mix in here stupid fables and invent miracles which never occurred. This is not merely the result of their ignorance but audacity, for they easily allow themselves to invent whatever appears favorable to them even if it lacks all reason." In another context he derided the Jews' identification of Canaanites with contemporary Illyrians, Germans, and even Frenchmen, because the ancient Canaanites had allegedly migrated into western Europe. "They already understand Zerphat to connote Spain" (Calvin evidently received wrong information about the contemporary Hebrew use of Ṣarefat vs. Sefarad). These identifications, with a long folkloristic history behind them, furnished Calvin the opportunity of assailing the Jews who "are not abashed by anything and incongruously bring together frivolous matters.... They are also garrulous about subjects unknown to them. They do it all for no reason but deception [delectus]."[19] In all these matters Calvin drew no distinction between the ancient homilists who, through imaginative hermeneutics, tried to deduce moral lessons from Scripture, and his Jewish contemporaries who were perfectly aware of the difference between aggadic and allegorical interpretations on the one hand, and the ordinary meaning of the biblical texts. As a matter of record, in the perennial Judeo-Christian polemics Jews were often accused by their opponents of "materialism" precisely because of their rigid adherence to the literal meaning of Scripture.

The last quoted passage from Calvin's *Commentary* on Matthew is exceptional in so far as, through drawing in the Jewish interpretation of Isa. 7:14, Calvin had the opportunity of controverting a Jewish exegesis relating to the New Testament, an opportunity which rarely offered itself in connection with his commentaries on that Testament. Here he could only elaborate the differentiation between Israel before Christ and the Jewish people's repudiation of the Christian messiah as stated in the New Testament and in its interpretation by the Church Fathers. Like his predecessors, Calvin saw in pre-Christian Judaism essentially a preparation for the Christian message. "It ought to be known," he declared, "that to whatever places Jews had been expelled there also was diffused with them some seed of piety and the odor of a purer doctrine." But, as a rule, Calvin emphasized the anti-Jewish and toned down the pro-Jewish statements in the New Testament. Even the well-known pro-Jewish utterances of Paul in his Epistle to the Romans are twisted in Calvin's interpretation to convey an essentially anti-Jewish message. In this respect we find a considerable difference in emphasis between Calvin's *Institutes* and his commentaries. The former work, written before Calvin achieved domination in Geneva, though it was frequently revised, hews rather closely to the traditional interpretation. Discussing Romans 9 and 11, the reformer observes:

Nevertheless, when Paul cast them down from vain confidence in their kindred, he still saw, on the other hand, that the covenant which God had made once for all with the descendants of Abraham could in no way be made void. ... Therefore, that they might not be defrauded of their privilege, the gospel had to be announced to them first. For they are, so to speak, like the first-born in God's household. Accordingly, this honor was to be given them until they refused what was offered, and by their ungratefulness caused it to be transferred to the Gentiles. Yet, despite the great obstinacy with which they continue to wage war against the gospel, we must not despise them, while we consider that, for the sake of the promise, God's blessing still rests among them.

Against this deliberately cautious, but sympathetic interpretation, we find that in his *Commentary* on Rom. 11:28–32, he argues inconclusively back and forth the pro- and anti-Jewish elements in this passage, but finds its main meaning in the fact that "their [the Jews'] greatest

crime consisted in their lack of faith *[incredulitas]*." Elsewhere, too, he
contends that the Jews still "wish to have tangible *[ad oculos]* evidence
of divine power in connection with every miracle."[20]

In his sermons Calvin could even more freely allude to contemporary
Jews, while using historical developments or biblical interpretations as a
foil. In the crucial matter of the Deuteronomic prohibition of interest,
Calvin delivered in 1555 an important sermon arguing that the distinction between the "brother," to whom no interest could be charged, and
the "stranger," from whom one could collect it, no longer held true. But
rather than contend that, after the advent of Christ, all men had become
brothers and hence usury was prohibited to all, Calvin, who had also
rejected the underlying Aristotelian view of the unproductivity of money,
taught that moderate interest could be charged to all borrowers except
persons in utter penury. This classical tirade of the Geneva reformer
included the following statements:

> For God wished to withdraw the children of Abraham from the rest of the
> world; He had united them into one body and wished to be their chief. There
> was good reason, therefore, for their maintaining [that unity] and that they
> should be more inclined to support one another. From that condition the Jews
> took occasion to trap all those who have little, for they interpret all the Scriptural
> promises to their advantage. . . .
> For example, when it is said 'Ye shall rule over many nations' they conclude
> therefrom: It is permitted to us to exercise any kind of tyranny and to devour
> the heathens for they are uncircumcised, polluted, and in no way belong to God,
> and that we should extract from them everything possible without sparing them.
> Even the word of the priest [Deuteronomist] they understood as meaning that
> they create no difficulty for them [the Jews] to charge to a stranger as much
> usury as he can stand without any regard for equity. . . . [In contrast thereto] we
> [the Christians] should preserve equity and righteousness toward all men and
> have pity and compassion for all.

All of which did not prevent Calvin in the same breath from teaching
that there may be a "special brotherhood" in a community of like-
minded Christians.[21]

DEBATE WITH JOSEL OF ROSHEIM?

Among Calvin's writings there is a small but remarkable tract entitled
Ad quaestiones et obiecta Judaei cuiusdam responsio. Nothing is known
about the circumstances which induced Calvin to write this noteworthy

dialogue, nor about the date of its composition.[22] The content, too, raises many questions. In the first place the Jewish debater reveals an astounding familiarity with the New Testament. True, in the sixteenth century quite a few Jews, particularly before entering a religious disputation with a Christian, familiarized themselves with some of the classical Christian arguments and their scriptural backing. This is true of Don Isaac Abravanel, Abraham Farissol, and a number of other Jewish controversialists. Nevertheless it is quite remarkable that the Jewish debater tried to persuade Calvin through arguments largely borrowed from Christian theology. As if to pay back in kind, Calvin's replies were largely based upon Old Testament passages. While neither debater drew a sharp line of demarcation between the two Testaments, this inverted emphasis by the two contestants is quite remarkable.[23]

Secondly, the Jew's arguments are not only given with much objectivity, a procedure rarely pursued by the Geneva reformer in his controversial pamphlets, but, despite their brevity, they often appear more forthright and logical than Calvin's much longer and quite involved replies. If this Jewish debater had been a figment of Calvin's imagination, as is assumed by most scholars, this discrepancy between query and answer would appear doubly remarkable. Even if logically capable to do so and by his legal training perhaps best prepared to see two sides of any question, Calvin was temperamentally far from inclined to give any opponent an equal chance. It stands to reason, therefore, that Calvin may indeed have heard such a presentation by a Jewish spokesman and tried to invalidate it by his replies. In that case the most likely period for the composition of this tract would appear to be the time of his sojourn in Strasbourg in 1539–41 and particularly his visit to Frankfort in 1539. Here he may indeed have encountered Josel of Rosheim, the chief defender of German Jewry at that time, who often sought direct contacts with the religious and political leaders of both warring camps. Though primarily a businessman, Josel was a well-informed controversialist who could stand his ground in any religious disputation. In fact, in his *Diary* Josel records the "disputations he had held with many Gentile scholars [in Frankfort in 1539] to prove to them from our holy Torah against the words of Luther, Bucer and his faction" the groundlessness of the latter's anti-Jewish accusations. Among the Protestant controversialists, Josel informs us in another context, there arose one who attacked him in a "violent, angry and menacing" harangue. Josel replied calmly: "You, a learned man, wish to threaten us poor people? God, our Lord, has preserved us from the days of Abraham. He, in His grace, will doubtless preserve us also from you." It would quite fit Calvin's temperament to have made such a menacing speech against the Jewish apologist of a new type he had encountered, probably for the first time in his life.[24]

Be this as it may, even Calvin's replies are written without his customary rancor. We need not expatiate on the whole gamut of the theological questions raised by the Jewish debater in the twenty-three queries here reproduced. For the most part they deal with the long-standardized arguments concerning the messiahship and divine character of Jesus, the earlier prophetic "testimonies" for it, and the Jewish participation in Jesus' crucifixion. Of more direct contemporary interest was the question relating to the perpetuity of Jewish law. Citing the Old Testament passages concerning the eternal validity of the law which must not be added to, nor subtracted from, and illustrating it by the law of circumcision, the Jew pointed out that Jesus' assertion "I am not come to destroy, but to fulfill" the law (Matthew 5:17) was clearly controverted by the Christians' repudiation of circumcision. To which Calvin answered by referring to several Old Testament passages indicating that in the messianic age many laws would be abrogated. As is well known, the problem of the abrogation of the law in the messianic period had already been the subject of debate during the sectarian strife of the Second Commonwealth and remained the bone of contention in the medieval Judeo-Christian religious controversy.[25]

Another intriguing contradiction was pointed out by the Jewish debater. He referred to the contention that the messiah was to be the king of peace, whereas "from that time on the world had not ceased from being at war." He also cited the contradiction between Isaiah's prediction "that the government may be increased, and of peace there be no end" (9:6) and Jesus' assertion, "Think not that I am come to send peace on earth: I came not to send peace but a sword" (Matt. 10:34). To which Calvin could only reply by pointing out that many prophetic predictions concerning Israel's glorious future had not come true and that there could never be peace so long as there were stubborn evildoers. "Foremost among men are the Jews who through their perversity show that they wish to have no peace with God."[26]

Perhaps most relevant to the contemporary conflicts was the Jew's final query:

I ask those who contend that we are in this Exile because of Jesus' execution, but this is not true because we had been in Exile before his death. If it be true what is written that, in the hour of his death Jesus begged his Father and said, 'Father, forgive them; for they know not what they do' [Luke 23:34] and if Father and Son are identical and both have the same will, then certainly that iniquity was condoned which he himself had forgiven.

In his reply Calvin could only harp on the theme of the Jews' obstinacy in persisting in their error and the numerous sins their forefathers had previously committed, as is attested by the numerous prophetic denunciations. These cumulative sins over generations have sufficiently accounted for the sufferings of the people of Israel since it went into exile.[27]

With all this fury Calvin showed himself, on the whole, somewhat more merciful toward the Jews, as well as the Muslims, than toward Christian heretics. True, the passage in the first edition of his *Institutes* which had criticized the use of force to attract Jews or Turks to Christianity was omitted in later editions. Yet nowhere did Calvin advocate the use of fire and brimstone against Jews as he did against Servetus and other Christian heretics, in whom he rightly saw the real threat to his own position and the future of his Church. He seems to have been satisfied, on the whole, with keeping the Jews out of Geneva and with echoing the long-accepted anti-Jewish polemics. He certainly made no direct effort to undermine the position of those Jewries which still persisted in Germany. Nor did his correspondence with friends in Poland in any way interfere with the remarkable expansion, numerical, economic and cultural, of Polish Jewry, then entering into its golden age. He evidently was willing to let the Polish Protestants take care of their own Jewish question.[28]

IMPACT OF CALVINISM

John Calvin may thus be quoted as a classical example of heroes making history in a way unknown to, and unintended by them. If Calvin's own tyrannical temperament often played havoc with his best intentions—he himself once admitted to having an irritable bent of mind and conceded that "here I have gravely sinned for I have been unable to keep moderation"[29]—and led to the establishment of his despotic theocratic regime in Geneva, the ultimate outcome of his reformatory work was the very opposite. Even as an immediate reaction to the execution of Servetus many voices were heard in Switzerland and elsewhere condemning this first inquisitorial "act of faith" on the part of Protestant believers in individual conscience. As a sequel to Servetus' martyrdom appeared, in particular, that distinguished collection of utterances, both old and new, concerning the freedom of conscience which was assembled by Sebastian Castellio, another victim of Calvin's dictatorship. The latter's *Concerning Heretics* sounded a clarion call for the general liberty of conscience which, though muted for a while by the clash of arms during the Wars of Religion, nevertheless ultimately helped to tip the scale for religious toleration in the western world.[30] Needless to say, the Jews, whose position in sixteenth-century Europe might seriously have been endangered by the spread of Calvin's wrathful denunciations, unwittingly became major beneficiaries of the ensuing trend toward religious liberty.

Calvin's influence was even more directly felt in the new appreciation of religious "legalism." A statement like that in his *magnum opus,* "Here is the function of the law by warning men of their duty, to arouse them to a zeal for holiness and innocence," could have been penned by any contemporary rabbi. Also his long elaboration of the Decalogue, to which he devoted fully fifty-nine chapters, and his emphasis that the intention behind the act is as important as the act itself, were wholly in line with long accepted rabbinic teachings. Perhaps the rabbis would not have followed him fully in the practical application of the lesson he derived from the last three commandments, "Murder that is of the soul consists in anger and hatred; theft, in evil covetousness and avarice; fornication, in lust." They certainly were not quite so ready to prosecute men for evil thoughts as was the Geneva dictator and his most zealous followers. But many of their teachings had great affinity to those of a reformer who had, to all intents and purposes, abandoned Pauline antinomianism in favor of Old Testament legalism. In fact, so closely did Calvin adhere to the Jewish interpretation of the Ten Commandments that he reemphasized the Jewish prohibition of imagery in a way shared by few of his confreres. Unlike Luther, he left the second commandment intact, requiring no readjustment in subsequent numbers made necessary by Luther's compromise with Catholic imagery in worship.[31] It is small wonder, then, that the disciples of Calvin in many lands so eagerly turned for enlightenment to the Old Testament. With the newly awakened humanist recognition of the relevance of the original language for the understanding of any ancient text, Calvinist divines and scholars in many lands became some of the foremost Christian Hebraists of the following two centuries. Calvin's own commentaries on the Old Testament, with occasional asides concerning certain Hebrew words, and his admission that the rabbinical interpreters of Scripture were strong in grammar if not in theology, could not but help stimulate among his disciples the interest in the Hebrew Bible and its rabbinic exegesis.[32]

If these spiritual bridges facilitated the rapprochement between Protestantism and Judaism, the effects of the Calvinist doctrines on the socioeconomic and political life of the western world even more enduringly narrowed the chasm separating the two faiths. The original sweeping theses by Max Weber and Werner Sombart concerning the far-reaching relationships between the Protestant ethic or the Jewish spirit and the rise and evolution of modern capitalism have rightly been toned down by the assiduous, more detailed work of later scholars. However, the historic fact that both Protestants and Jews contributed much more than their share to the rise of capitalist institutions and the so-called capitalist "spirit" has remained unimpaired. These activities by bankers and merchants of both faiths may have stimulated competition and economic rivalries between them which at times created new tensions. But these were more than counter-balanced by the ensuing opening of new lands and new economic avenues for the Jewish wanderers.[33]

No less paradoxical were Calvinist influences on the rise of western democracy and the separation of state and Church. He who succeeded in establishing in Geneva a powerful dictatorship which suppressed many existing democratic liberties and in erecting a dominance of the Church over the state in a way unparalleled elsewhere in contemporary Europe, nevertheless became the fountainhead of much of the democratic and republican thought in western Europe and America. Perhaps because of this very overstraining of the power of theocracy, Calvin also helped bring into the world the doctrine of total separation of state and Church. It has been shown that his theory demanded the intervention of the state in religious affairs only for the purpose of a one-time suppression of heresy and the establishment of a righteous regime. Having accomplished this task, the state was to withdraw into its own sphere and leave the Church in exclusive control of all spiritual affairs. From here was only one step to the doctrine of separation between the two institutions, which became doubly necessary because of the growing sectarian discord within the Protestant camp.[34]

Last but not least was the fact that, equally unwittingly, Calvinism escaped the temptation of becoming linked up with the rising European nationalism. If Erastianism became one of the greatest drawbacks of the modern Protestant evolution, and the involvement of the Lutheran churches in the increasingly authoritarian princely regimes and soon also in the German nationalist agitation, opened up threatening vistas for the universal teachings of Christianity in its Protestant reinterpretation, Calvinism avoided these pitfalls. In part this non-involvement stemmed from Geneva's small size which prevented it from forming a base for an independent national movement. More importantly, in its French Huguenot wing and in its large following among the English "dissenters," it commanded allegiance among persecuted religious minorities which refused to surrender their religious identity to the national solidarity with the respective majorities. From the outset, therefore, Calvinism represented an international movement, in part an interterritorial diaspora, very much resembling in its socioreligious structure that of the persecuted Jewish minority. These deep affinities between the two groups far transcended the differences so harshly emphasized by the founder.[35]

In short, the total effect of Calvin's anti-Jewish preaching resembled that of the ancient prophecy of Balaam. The Geneva reformer, too, set out to curse the Jews, but in the end turned out to have blessed them.

NOTES

1. J. A. Galiffe, *Matériaux pour l'histoire de Genève*, 2 vols. (Geneva, 1829 [1830]), I, 167; Achille Nordmann, "Histoire des Juifs à Genève de 1281 à 1780," *REJ*, LXXX (1925), 1–41, esp. pp. 38 f. See also Emile Doumergue, *Jean Calvin, les hommes et les choses de son temps*, 7 vols. (Lausanne, 1899–1927), III, 252 f. (also offering interesting data on the Jewish quarter in Geneva). It is possible, however, that in his numerous sermons Calvin may have referred to Jews and Judaism more frequently than is now known. Perhaps further progress of H. Rückert's ed. of *Johannes Calvins Predigten* (which, begun in 1936, has been resumed in 1958 in the so-called *Supplementa Calviniana,* sponsored by the World Presbyterian Alliance), will yield some new data on the Jewish question, too, from the hundreds of still unpublished homilies of the reformer. See the example from his sermon on II Sam. 22, cited *infra,* n. 20. However, many sermons doubtless are irre-

JOHN CALVIN AND THE JEWS   395

trievably lost. The Geneva Library, which in the early eighteenth century still owned 44 vols. of Calvin's homilies in MS, now possesses only 12. See the latest review of the extant MSS in Georges A. Barrois' introd. to his ed. of Calvin's *Sermons sur le livre d'Isaïe Chapitres 13–29* (Neukirchen, 1961), Vol. II of the series, pp. xx ff.

2. Calvin's "De usuris," reproduced among his "Consilia" in his *Opera quae supersunt omnia*, ed. by Wilhelm Baum, *et al.*, 59 vols. (Brunswick, 1863– Berlin, 1900), (Corpus reformatorum, XXIX–LXXXVII), X, Part 1, cols. 245 ff.; his comments on Deut. 15:7–10, 23:19–20, *ibid.*, XXIV, 679 ff.; XXVII, 325 ff.; XXVIII, 111 ff.; and the controversial interpretations thereof, cited *infra*, nn. 4 and 21. See also Théodore Reinach, "Mutuum date nihil inde sperantes," *Revue des études grecques*, VII (1894), 52–58, suggesting a relatively slight emendation of the text in Luke.

3. *Opera*, XXVIII, 117; XXXVII, 358. The editors were quite justified in includ- ing the Genevan ordinance of 1547 among Calvin's works, *ibid.*, X, Part. 1, cols. 56 f.

4. This issue has preoccupied many leading students of both economics and Protestant theology. See esp. Karl Holl, "Zur Frage des Zinsnehmens und des Wuchers in der reformierten Kirche" (1922), reprinted in his *Gesam- melte Aufsätze zur Kirchengeschichte*, 4 vols. (Tübingen, 1928), III, 385– 403; Henri Hauser, "A propos des idées économiques de Calvin," *Mélanges d'histoire offerts à Henri Pirenne*, 2 vols. (Brussels, 1926), I, 211–24; and particularly André Bieler's recent comprehensive analysis of *La Pensée écon- omique et sociale de Calvin*, with a Foreword by Anthony Babel (Geneva, 1959). See also Ernst Ramp's comparative study of *Die Stellung von Luther, Zwingli und Calvin zur Zinsfrage* (Diss. Zurich, 1949), esp. pp. 81 ff., 106 ff.; and Charles H. George, "English Calvinist Opinions on Usury, 1600– 1640," *Journal of the History of Ideas*, XVIII (1957), 455–74.

5. See Wilhelm Niesel, "Verstand Calvin deutsch?" *Zeitschrift für Kirchen- geschichte*, XLIX (1930), 343–46.

6. See the data assembled by Klaus Rudolphi in *Calvins Urteil über das poli- tische Vorgehen der deutschen Protestanten nach seinem Briefwechsel* (Mar- burg, 1930); Philippe Dollinger, "La Tolérance à Strasbourg au XVIe siè- cle," *Hommage à Lucien Febvre*, 2 vols. (Paris, 1953), II, 241–49.

7. Martin Bucer, *Der CXXX Psalm* (Strasbourg, 1546), p. 2; *idem, Von den Juden, ob und wie die unter den Christen zu halten sind* (Strasbourg, 1539), (reproducing the respective memoranda); Max Lenz, ed., *Briefwechsel Phi- lipp's des Grossmüthigen von Hessen mit Bucer*, 3 vols. (Leipzig, 1880–91), I, 55 ff. These data are analyzed by Siegmund Salfeld in *Die Judenpolitik Philipps des Grossmütigen* (Frankfort, 1904); and by Hastings Eells in his "Bucer's Plan for the Jews," *Church History*, VI (1937), 127–35. On Bucer's utterances on the Jewish question and his likely encounter in Frankfort, in 1539, with Josel of Rosheim, see Harry Bresslau, "Aus Strassburger Juden- akten," *Zeitschrift für die Geschichte der Juden in Deutschland*, V (1892), 307–44; and Selma Stern, *Josel von Rosheim: Befehlshaber der Judenschaft*

im Heiligen Römischen Reich Deutscher Nation (Stuttgart, 1959), esp. pp. 125 ff. See also, *infra*, n. 24; and the study by J. V. Pollet, *Martin Bucer: étude sur la correspondance avec des nombreux textes inédits*, Vol. 1 (Paris, 1958), which includes an interesting correspondence of 1542 between Conrad Pellican, Boniface Auerbach and Bucer about the need of a translation of the Koran for missionary purposes, similar to the use made of Hebrew studies to combat the Jewish interpretations (pp. 181 ff.). See also the rich *Bibliographia Bucerana* assembled by Robert Stupperich and appended to Heinrich Bornkamm's succinct analysis of *Martin Bucers Bedeutung für die europäische Reformationsgeschichte* (Gütersloh, 1952).

8. Much has been written about Bucer's influence on Calvin's theological and economic thinking and also the impact of the Strasbourg environment upon the Genova reformer. See esp. Georg Klingenburg's Bonn theological dissertation, *Das Verhältnis Calvins zu Butzer, untersucht auf Grund der wirtschafts-ethischen Bedeutung der beiden Reformatoren* (Bonn, 1912); Wilhelm Pauck, "Calvin and Butzer," *Journal of Religion*, IX (1929), 237–56; and Jean Daniel Benoit, et al., *Calvin à Strasbourg, 1539–1541* (Strasbourg, 1938).

9. See the early examples cited in my *A Social and Religious History of the Jews*, 2d. ed. (New York, 1952 ff.), III, 5 ff., 229 f. nn. 1 and 4.

10. "Clarissimis syndicis, et amplissimo Senatui Genevensis Reipublicae dominis nostris colendissimis . . ." in Calvin's *Opera*, VIII, 555 f.

11. See the data assembled by Jakob Guttmann in his "Michael Servet in seinen Beziehungen zum Judentum," *MGWJ*, LI (1907), 77–94; and Louis Israel Newman in his *Jewish Influence on Christian Reform Movements* (New York, 1925), pp. 511 ff. Nor did Calvin hesitate, in his meeting with Melanchthon in Frankfort in 1539, to criticize the Lutheran liturgy as too "Jewish." See his letter to his closest friend, Guillaume Farel, of April 1539 in his *Opera*, X, Part 2, col. 340.

12. The relations between the two reformers, illumined in particular by their extant correspondence and the final trial and death of Servetus, have intrigued many scholars. Of the large literature on the subject we need but mention R. Willis's older but still useful *Servetus and Calvin: a Study of an Important Epoch in the Early History of the Reformation* (London, 1877); and Roland H. Bainton, *Hunted Heretic: The Life and Death of Servetus, 1511–1553* (Boston, 1953). See also the noteworthy eloquent, though somewhat exaggerating, description of the conditions in Geneva under Calvin's dictatorship by Stefan Zweig in *The Right to Heresy: Castellio against Calvin*, English trans. by Eden and Cedar Paul (New York, 1936). It may be noted that even some of those who were horrified by Servetus' execution were far from embracing the doctrine of religious toleration. The clergy of the Vaud district across Lake Geneva may have condemned the proceedings as illegal and irreligious and yet when, in 1554, the Academy of Lausanne contemplated inviting the distinguished scholar, Immanuel Tremellius, a baptized Jew of Ferrara, to serve as its professor of Hebrew, the Berne

authorities rejected him solely because of his Jewish descent. See H. Vuilleu-
mier, "Les hébraisants vaudois au seizième siècle," *Recueil inaugural* of the
University of Lausanne (1892), p. 64; Achille Nordmann, "Les Juifs dans
les pays de Vaud, 1278–1875," *REJ,* LXXXI (1925), 163.

13. Servetus' Thirty Letters to Calvin in the latter's *Opera,* VIII, esp. Letter XXV,
cols. 703 ff. (at the end citing Maimonides); also Letter XIV, col. 675;
Newman, *Jewish Influence,* pp. 588 ff.

14. Calvin's *Institutes of the Christian Religion,* i.8, 9–10, English trans. by
Ford Lewis Battles, ed. by John T. McNeill, 2 vols. (Philadelphia, 1960),
(The Library of Christian Classics, XX–XXI), I, 88 f., with reference to I
Macc. 1:56–57; his *Commentary* on Ps. 22:17 in his *Opera* XXXI, 228 f.

15. *Commentary* on Dan. 7:27 in his *Opera,* XLI, 82.

16. See the fragment reprinted by Hans Volz in his "Beiträge zu Melanchthons
und Calvins Auslegung des Propheten Daniel," *Zeitschrift für Kirchengeschichte,* LXVII (1955–56), 116 ff.

17. Calvin's *Commentary* on Dan. 2:39, 44–45; 4:10–16; 7:27; 9:24–26, in
his *Opera,* XL, 597 f., 603 ff., 658; XLI, 81 ff., 167 ff., 172 ff., 184 ff. See
Abraham ibn Daud, *Sefer ha-Kabbalah* (Book of Tradition) in *Mediaeval
Jewish Chronicles,* ed. by Adolph Neubauer, I, 60 ff.; *idem, Zikhron dibre
malkhe Yisrael ba-bayit ha-sheni* (Memoir on the History of the Jewish
Kings during the Second Temple), (Mantua, 1513 ed.), and my remarks
thereon in *A Social and Religious History of the Jews,* 2d. ed., VI, 207 f.,
210, 428 ff. nn. 70 and 73.

18. Calvin's Sermon XLIII on Dan. 12:1 in his *Opera,* XLII, 113 f. In general,
Calvin was not too articulate in depicting the messianic expectations allegedly held by the ancient prophets, nor did he describe in any detail his own
view of the final end of days after the second coming of Christ. See Heinrich
Berger, *Calvins Geschichtsauffassung* (Zurich, 1955), esp. pp. 239 f.

19. *Commentary* on Isa. 38:8, 48:21; Obad. vv. 19–20; Mic. 5:1–2; Hab.
2:45; Hag. 1:1; Matt. 1:22–23, etc., in his *Opera,* XXXVI, 653; XXXVII, 187
f.; XL, 66; XLVIII, 198 ff., 368 f., 551; XLIV, 80 f.

20. See his *Institutes,* IV, 16, 14, in the English trans. by F. L. Battles, II, 1336
f.; his *Sermon XIV* on Evangelical Harmony, and his *Commentaries* on Acts
17:4; Rom. 7:4–5, 9:30, 11:28–32; I Cor. 1:23–24 in *Opera,* XLVI, 167 f.;
XLVIII, 395; XLIX, 172 ff., 192 f., 228 f., 327 f. Time and again Calvin
reverts to this theme of the election and repudiation of Israel. In his sermon
of Jan. 9, 1563 he launched an attack on both Jews and papists and declared
with something of a sigh that "the Church will thus always have enemies
which she will be unable to chase out." See his *Predigten,* ed. by H. Rückert,
I, 679. It also was more than a merely archaic reference when, discussing
the sale of Joseph by his brothers, Calvin declared that the Jews could not
place the responsibility for that act on a few individuals, but that in fact this
crime brought infamy to the whole people. In the context of a commentary
on Acts (7:9, *Opera,* XLVIII, 135) such an observation doubtless recalled to
the minds of most Christian readers the idea of the responsibility of the

whole Jewish people for the crucifixion of Jesus. This combination appeared,
indeed, in such contemporary Passion plays as that of Augsburg, a predecessor of the later famous Passion play of Oberammergau. Here the Jews,
trying to persuade Judas to betray Jesus, are made to assert that they had
saved up the thirty pence from the time when Joseph had been sold by his
brethren. See the text ed. by A. Hartmann in *Das Oberammergauer Pas-
sionsspiel in seiner ältesten Gestalt* (Leipzig, 1880), vv. 213–20; and Hans
Carl Holdschmidt, *Der Jude auf dem Theater des deutschen Mittelalters*
(Emsdetten, 1935), (Die Schaubühne Quellen und Forschungen zur Theater-
geschichte, XII), p. 106. Incidentally, Bucer, too, had found the disparage-
ment of Paul's Jewish contemporaries useful for his own purposes, such as
the defense of his high appreciation of the Graeco-Roman pagan writers.
See H. Strohl, *Bucer, humaniste chrétien* (Paris, 1939), (Cahiers of the
Revue d'histoire et de philosophie religieuses, XXIX), pp. 17 ff.

21. Calvin's second sermon on Deut. 15:7–10 in his *Opera*, XXVII, 325 ff.
Other passages relating to usury have led Benjamin N. Nelson to find in
them the opening to "the road to universal otherhood," namely the permis-
sibility of interest among members of the same faith. See his *The Idea of
Usury: From Tribal Brotherhood to Universal Otherhood* (Princeton, 1949),
pp. 73 ff., 141 ff.; and the critique of this interpretation by Charles H.
George in his aforementioned essay in the *Journal of the History of Ideas*,
XVIII, 456 ff. See also *supra*, n. 4.

22. *Opera*, IX, 653–74. This tract seems to be identical with a letter by Calvin
to which J. F. A. de le Roi refers in *Die evangelische Christenheit und die
Juden*, 3 vols. (Karlsruhe, 1884), I, 44. See also Jacques Courvoisier's observations thereon in his "Calvin et les Juifs," *Judaica*, II (1946–47), 203–8.

23. See H. H. Wolf's dissertation, *Die Einheit des Bundes. Das Verhältnis von
Altem und Neuem Testament bei Calvin* (Halle, 1941), (typescript, *non
vidi*).

24. Josel of Rosheim's *Diary*, published by Isidor Kracauer in his "Rabbi Josel-
mann de Rosheim," *REJ*, XVI (1888), 92; *idem, Trostschrift an seine Brüder
wider Buceri Büchlein*, published by Ludwig Feilchenfeld in his *Rabbi Josel
von Rosheim. Ein Beitrag zur Geschichte der Juden in Deutschland im
Reformationszeitalter* (Strasbourg, 1898), pp. 180 ff., App. XVI. The fact
that the Jewish controversialist fails to mention Calvin by name is the less
astonishing as the Genevan reformer lived at that time as a fairly obscure
French refugee and Genevan exile in Bucer's entourage in Strasbourg. When
Josel published his *Letter of Consolation* (the Hebrew original of which is
regrettably lost) in reply to Bucer's aforementioned pamphlet in the Hessian
controversy, no one could have foretold that shortly thereafter the Genevan
population would change its mind and reinvite the reformer to its leading
pulpit, thus giving him the opportunity to play his stellar role in the history
of the Reformation. In fact, Calvin's name occurs but rarely in the contemporary German sources relating to the conferences of 1539–41. If the
frequent use of New Testament sources by Calvin's Jewish spokesman

militates against his identification with Josel who, in his other recorded disputations, seems to have relied exclusively upon the words of the Hebrew Bible, we must remember that both Josel's *Diary* and his *Letter of Consolation* were written in Hebrew for Jewish audiences. Josel may have omitted here the arguments from the New Testament which were unfamiliar to them and possibly might have been resented by the unsophisticated masses. On Calvin's role in the German assemblies and his participation in the religious disputations, see F. W. Kampschulte, *Johann Calvin, seine Kirche und sein Staat in Genf,* 2 vols. (Leipzig, 1869–99), esp. I, 328 ff., 333 n. 1, 338 f.; and E. Doumergue's uncritical observations in his *Jean Calvin,* II. See also Selma Stern, *Josel von Rosheim,* esp. pp. 138 ff.; and *supra,* nn. 7–8.

25. A. Diez Macho, "Cesará la 'Tora' en la edad messianica?" *Estudios biblicos,* XII (1953), 115–58; and other data cited in my *A Social and Religious History of the Jews,* 2d. ed., II, 73 f., 161 f., 298 f., 360 f. n. 25; V, 124, 193 f., 347 n. 54, 380 ff. n. 58.

26. Query viii in *Opera,* IX, 663. This problem, too, had often engaged Jewish and Christian controversialists in their mutual recriminations. See my *History,* V, 118.

27. Query xxii in *Opera,* IX, 674. The problem of Exile had likewise engaged the attention of controversialists of both faiths since ancient times.

28. One must bear in mind, of course, that in Poland Calvinism represented but one of many rivaling Protestant factions which, under the existing conditions of relative religious freedom, fought one another as vigorously as they combated Catholicism. Even Servetus, particularly after his martyr's death, gained a wide following there. In 1557, Simon Zacus, the superintendent of the Calvinist community of Vilna, bitterly complained of the spread of all kinds of heresies, such as those of the Anabaptists, the Libertines, the Schwenkfeldians, and the New Arians of the school of Servetus and his Polish follower, De Goniadz. Cited by Stanislaw Kot in "L'influence de Michel Servet sur le mouvement antitrinitarien en Pologne et en Transylvanie" in the collection of essays, *Autour de Michel Servet et de Sebastien Castillon,* ed. by B. Becker (Haarlem, 1953), pp. 72–129, esp. p. 78. See also Gottfried Schramm's review article of the literature relating to the "Antitrinitarier in Polen, 1556–1658" in *Bibliothèque d'humanisme et renaissance,* XXI (1959), 473–511. This certainly was not the time for the Polish Calvinists to antagonize the ever growing, but strictly neutralist, Jewish population in the country.

29. Calvin's letter to Farel of October, 1539 in his *Opera,* X, Part 2, col. 398. See also Fritz Büsser, *Calvins Urteil über sich selbst* (Zurich, 1950), p. 54.

30. Roland H. Bainton, ed., *Concerning Heretics. Whether They are to be Persecuted and How They are to Be Treated. A Collection of the Opinions of Learned Men both Ancient and Modern. An Anonymous Work attributed to Sebastian Castellio. Now First Done into English, Together with Excerpts from Other Works of Sebastian Castellio and David Joris on Religious Liberty* (New York, 1935), (Records of Civilization, XXII). See

also the aforementioned confrontation of Castellio with Calvin by Stefan Zweig in *The Right to Heresy.*

31. Calvin's *Institutes,* ii.8, 6; iii.19, 2 in Battles's English trans. I, 372, 835; the comments thereon by Marc-Edouard Chenevière in his Geneva dissertation, *La Pensée politique de Calvin* (Paris, 1937), pp. 61 ff., 99 ff.; and by Fritz Büsser in *Calvins Urteil,* pp. 36 f. See also J. V. Bredt, "Calvinismus und Judentum," *Der Morgen,* III (1927), 243–50.

32. Calvin's *Commentaries* on Ps. 22:17; Dan. 4:10–16, in his *Opera,* XXXI, 228 f.; XL, 858.

33. It may be of interest to recall here the initial debates on the Weber thesis by Felix Rachfahl, Eugen Troeltsch and Weber himself. See Felix Rachfahl's "Calvinismus und Kapitalismus," *Internationale Wochenschrift,* III (1909); Troeltsch, "Die Kulturbedeutung des Calvinismus" (1910), reproduced in his *Gesammelte Schriften,* IV, 783–801; Weber, "Antikritisches zum 'Geist' des Kapitalismus," *Archiv für Sozialwissenschaft und Sozialpolitik,* XXX (1910), 176–202. The subsequent literature on both the Weberian and the Sombartian theses is enormous and need not be repeated here.

34. See esp. Hans Baron's twin essays, *Calvins Staatsanschauung und das konfessionelle Zeitalter* (Munich, 1924), (*Historische Zeitschrift,* Beihefte 1), esp. pp. 48 ff., 115 ff.; and "Calvinist Republicanism and Its Historical Roots," *Church History,* VIII (1939), 30–42; as well as Josef Bohatec's more detailed analysis of *Calvins Lehre von Staat und Kirche, mit besonderer Berücksichtung des Organismusgedankens* (Breslau, 1937).

35. See my *Modern Nationalism and Religion* (New York, 1947), (or paperback ed., New York, 1960), esp. the chapter on "Protestant Individualism," pp. 117 ff.

14

The Burning of the Talmud in 1553, in Light of Sixteenth-Century Catholic Attitudes toward the Talmud

Kenneth R. Stow

By decree of the Roman Inquisition,[1] the Talmud was publicly burned at Rome in the early Fall of 1553.[2] In the succeeding months other Italian cities confiscated and burned the Talmud in compliance with this decree.[3] Historians have regularly explained this decree as the result of a dispute between the two Venetian publishers, M. Guistiniani and E. Bragadoni. Both had published the *Mishneh Torah* in 1550, but Bragadoni's edition also contained the recently completed commentary of R. Meir Katzenellenbogen of Padua. Commercial rivalry led Giustiniani to propose to ecclesiastical authorities that they scrutinize the commentary of R. Meir in Bragadoni's edition for improprieties. He also hired apostates to argue his point. Bragadoni retaliated in kind. These apostates then exceeded their original commission, and, when the case was heard before the Inquisition, they attacked the Talmud on the grounds that it contained blasphemies against Christianity. The Inquisition responded by condemning the Talmud and decreeing its destruction.[4] Eight months later Julius III issued the bull *Cum sicut nuper*[5] to ensure the enforcement of the Inquisition's decree. Hence, the 1553 burning has been identified as an attack on the Talmud's alleged blasphemies and, thus, like its thirteenth-century predecessor in which the papacy had likewise significantly participated,[6] as a typical manifestation of the

Reprinted by permission of Librairie Droz S. A., Genève, from *Bibliothèque d'Humanisme et Renaissance* 34 (1972): 435–49.

Church's zeal to dispose of literature which both threatened[7] and insulted[8] Catholicism.

An order to burn the Talmud was also issued in 1415. Although the instigator of this assault was probably the Franciscan, Vincent Ferrer,[9] the actual order to burn the Talmud was given by the Avignonese pope, Benedict XIII, in his bull *Etsi doctoris*.[10] Benedict's primary concern in condemning the Talmud was not, however, identical with that of the thirteenth-century Gregory IX and Innocent IV. The overall purpose of *Etsi doctoris* was to establish machinery to effect the mass conversion of the Jews.[11] Accordingly, Benedict declared:

... since it is manifest ... that the prime cause of the Jewish blindness ... is a certain perverse doctrine, which was formulated after Christ and which the Jews call Talmud ... we have had this Talmud most carefully examined. As a result, because we desire to remove the whole veil from their eyes..., we have edicted that no one ... should presume to hear, read, or teach that doctrine.[12]

But this supposition, that the prohibition of the Talmud would promote a radical increase in conversions, was never tested in practice. Instead, as in the 1260's and 1270's in Spain, copies of the Talmud were subjected to expurgation.[13] Most likely, Benedict's theory had encountered opposition from those who adhered to the principle developed by Raymund Martini in his *Pugio Fidei*,[14] namely, that the Jews could be persuaded to convert if the truth of Christianity were proved to them from rabbinic literature. The compromise of expurgation was then effected.[15] Even so, the fact does remain that in 1415, actions taken *vis-à-vis* the Talmud, especially on the part of the papacy, were primarily directed toward the promotion of conversion and not toward the eradication of blasphemy and insult.

The papal involvement in the burning of the Talmud in 1553 could thus have been motivated by two disparate, yet not mutually exclusive precedents. The decree of condemnation[16] issued by the Roman Inquisition, which had been revived in 1542 as a direct arm of the papacy,[17] reveals clearly which of these two precedents was considered the more cogent. To be sure, the alleged presence of blasphemies in the Talmud and the necessity of eradicating them receive considerable attention in the interior paragraphs of the decree. Seen in terms of the propositions contained in the introductory paragraph of the decree, however, these interior paragraphs are merely explicative of that first paragraph, in which the Inquisitors state:

We have considered that nothing would be more conducive to their illumination than if we were able to lead them away from their impious and inane doctrines to the scrutiny of sacred letters (which they falsely assert they study), where they would be able to discover and know the hidden treasure of their salvation, God granting to us that the veil be removed from their hearts.[18]

The Inquisitors prefaced this statement, moreover, by declaring that since the task of the Inquisition is to bring men to recognize the light of truth, it must concern itself with the blind perfidy of the Jews. Hence, the remarks on blasphemy explain why the Inquisition has decided to destroy the Talmud in order to fulfill what it considers its principal function in its dealings with Jews, namely, the pursuit of their conversion. Like Benedict XIII, the sixteenth-century Inquisitors viewed the contents of the Talmud as an essential fomentor of Jewish obstinacy. While the publishers' feud and the ensuing charges of blasphemy assuredly precipitated the condemnation of the Talmud, the simple elimination of blasphemy was not the purpose underlying the Inquisition's act.[19] Indeed, the convert accusers themselves may have argued the conversionary function of the destruction of the Talmud.[20]

The Inquisition's decree was not, however, universally obeyed. Hence on May 29, 1554 Julius III issued the bull *Cum sicut nuper*. Its unmistakable purpose was to reaffirm both the theory and the procedure enunciated by the Inquisition in the fall of 1553. In the bull's proemium Julius complains that while some copies of the Talmud have indeed been burned, he is disturbed because other copies still exist, in defiance of the Inquisitional order. These Talmuds too must be consumed.[21] Moreover, he adds:

We do not, in the future, permit the Jews (who are tolerated by the Holy Mother, Church, so that at some time, led by our kindness and by the breath of the Holy Spirit, they may convert to the true light of Christ) to be vexed by anyone [in the matter of their books], provided they . . . do not contain blasphemy.[22]

Understood in the light of the entire bull, this statement establishes that the fundamental Church goal of converting the Jews demands that Hebrew books containing nothing detrimental to Christianity may alone be permitted,[23] while those containing blasphemies against Christianity must be prohibited. The importance of conversion as a factor for determining which books Jews may read is revealed in the clause "Jews are tolerated . . . so that . . . led by our kindness . . . they may convert." Traditionally, papal bulls had declared: "although they refuse to convert, Jews are tolerated"; the clause: "tolerated, so that. . . ," appears for the first time in *Cum sicut nuper*.[24] With this clause Julius III indicates that in distinction to the policies of his predecessors, every constituent procedure of his Jewry policy, beginning with toleration itself, ought to be predicated on the usefulness of that procedure in promoting conversion. Juxtaposed to a determination about books and also to a reference to the Inquisitional order of 1553, this clause indicates Julius III's complete identification with the purpose of the Inquisition in its attack on the Talmud. Accordingly, in his list of papal actions taken between 1542 and 1593 to encourage conversions, the Jesuit, Antonius Possevin, includes the issuance of the bull *Cum sicut nuper*.[25]

Joseph ha-Kohen, too, seems aware of Julius III's motivations. Even more, in his *'Emeq ha-Bakha'* he suggests that the burners of the Talmud had calculated the possible effect of that burning correctly. Ha-Kohen may indeed view affliction of Jews as the basic reason behind the punitive measures effected by the papacy during the 1550's,[26] and he assuredly does portray Paul IV (1555–59), the Chief Inquisitor in 1553, as Pharaoh reborn to embitter the lives of the Jews.[27] Nevertheless, ha-Kohen expresses a graver fear when he writes of the Jewish mission to Julius III which begged that pope to allow the publication and study of books other than the Talmud.[28] He prays for God's help, because under the present circumstances, that is, with the Talmud burned, Jews do not have the strength to defend themselves.[29] More telling, when he records the death of Julius III, ha-Kohen refers to the pope as the one "who wished to lead us to apostasy, who ordered our glorious books to be burned. . . ."[30]

Not as pronounced as the remarks in the *'Emeq ha-Bakha'*, but still indicative of the threat to Judaism posed by the burning is the plaint of R. Menahem Porto: "This too [the Talmud], the delight of our eyes, in whose shadow we thought we could survive among the nations, has been made into firewood."[31] Similarly, R. Immanuel of Benevento mourns the loss of the Talmud and expresses anxiety that the Kabbalah[32] too may be prohibited: "If we should lose this too, what would the man whose Torah is his way of life do in his desolation? From what book could he come to know the Glory of God?"[33]

Immanuel, in fact, touched on exactly what the papacy and the Inquisition had in mind when they attacked the Talmud. What Immanuel saw as the Glory of God, however, they saw as the Talmud's lies. Nowhere is this theory more explicitly set forth than in the *De Sola Lectione,* written in 1555 by the Jesuit Francisco de Torres,[34] one of the more influential Catholic scholars of the sixteenth century, particularly on questions of censorship.[35] The work is addressed to the Inquisitors, and its main theme is that the Inquisition must pursue to its conclusion the policy initiated by the burning of the Talmud.[36] Hence, the Inquisitors must not neglect:

What is particularly necessary for the salvation of the Jews. Indeed, for the glory of Christ I will state boldly what I feel: if you do not interdict to the Jews all the remaining commentaries of the Jewish tradition, all of which . . . tend not only to make vanity of our cross and glory, but also both to hold the Jews back from embracing the faith and to lead them away from the observances of the Christians, I fear lest you will be charged with their blindness at the horrible judgment of the last day.[37]

Once these books are removed, however, it will soon result that the more they are without that wisdom of their princes, that is, the rabbis, so much the more will they be prepared and disposed to receiving the faith and the wisdom of the word of God.[38]

For when that wisdom—or rather the insanity of their traditions, of the Jewish fables, and of the commentaries—has been blotted from memory, they will easily understand the mysteries of Christ, and the prophecies of his advent, as that of Jacob, the most famous of all: "Non auferretur sceptrum de Iuda, etc."[39]

[Indeed, when they had the Talmud, the Jews used to claim:] That those wise men (the rabbis) should be considered the "Duces de femore Iudae."[40]

[Therefore,] how are you able to attend to saving their remnant if you do not remove that which brings them to grief? Are the Jews not insane enough by themselves, and are the Jews not blind enough, that you have to allow them that which teaches them insanity?[41]

De Torres' arguments were accepted. In 1557 the Inquisition, which was then strictly controlled by Paul IV,[42] prohibited the Jews from possessing any religious work in Hebrew except the Bible.[43] And in 1559 Paul IV published an Index of Prohibited Books which included the Talmud and all its commentaries.[44] It was also Paul IV, who, as Chief Inquisitor, had been most responsible in 1553 for arguing the conversionary value of burning the Talmud. Of a certainty, then, the beliefs and opinions expressed by de Torres are those which the papacy and the Inquisition both held and acted upon when first they decreed the destruction of the Talmud and when later they condemned all rabbinic works.

The burning of the Talmud was in reality only one aspect of a multifaceted conversionary program organized by the later sixteenth-century papacy.[45] The first component of the program was the *Domus cathecumenorum* which was established at Rome in 1542.[46] Then, in 1555, in the proemium of his bull *Cum nimis absurdum,* Paul IV declared that since the Church tolerates the Jews so that it may lead them to convert, it must establish a Jewry policy conducive to attaining that goal.[47] Apparently, Paul IV believed that the establishment of a ghetto and a prohibition on Jewish ownership of real property, both of which *Cum nimis* prescribed, would inaugurate such a policy. The establishment of this conversionary program was completed by Gregory XIII in 1584. His bull, *Sancta Mater Ecclesia,* required all Jews to attend weekly missionary sermons.[48] In addition, from 1568 on, Cardinal Sirleto, the protector of the *Domus cathecumenorum,* was empowered to supervise, besides the *domus,* the enforcement of both *Cum nimis* and the decrees against Jewish books, hence centralizing the control of the conversionary policy in the hands of one man.[49] Nor was this policy unsuccessful. The later sixteenth century witnessed a marked increase in the number of converts from Judaism to Christianity.[50] Thus the evidence which vigorously argues that the papacy and the Inquisition attacked the Talmud for conversionary reasons becomes conclusive.

Papal Talmud policy did not, however, remain static during the second half of the sixteenth century. In 1554, while maintaining the Talmud ban, Julius III specifically permitted non-blasphemous Hebrew books to circulate.[51] But the Inquisition, together with Paul IV, effectively reversed this decision in 1557 by forbidding Jews to possess any Hebrew book except the Bible.[52] Then, in 1564 Pius IV apparently abandoned prohibition and announced that the Talmud would be tolerated if it were censored and if the name, Talmud, were removed from its title page.[53] He also issued a letter making the ownership of other Hebrew books lawful, provided they contained no blasphemies.[54] Pius V, however, renewed in 1566 the decrees of 1553 and 1557.[55] Similarly, in 1581 Gregory XIII ordered the confiscation of all Hebrew books,[56] although earlier in his reign he had considered the alternative of censorship.[57] Sixtus V renounced his predecessor's confiscatory policy, and during his reign (1585–90) preparations were actually made for a new edition of the Talmud, which was to be published in accordance with the stipulations of Pius IV.[58] This edition never appeared. Indeed, in

1592 in a letter to the Inquisition and in the 1593 bull, *Cum hebraeorum malitia,* Clement VIII renewed the 1557 ban on all Hebrew books except the Bible.[59] And in 1596 he wrote to the Inquisition that he had completely rejected the notion that the Talmud could be expurgated and allowed to circulate.[60] The 1596 Index reflects this decision and prohibits the Talmud entirely.[61] Indeed, after 1553 Hebrew printing in Rome effectively ceased until 1810.[62]

These policy fluctuations did not reflect personal whim. What they reflected is the influence exerted by the diffusion during the later sixteenth century of diverse opinions on the value, both positive and negative, of rabbinic literature. It is, of course, impossible, without access to minutes of consistory meetings and without knowledge of private unrecorded conversations, to determine which of these opinions most influenced papal circles at any given moment. Yet, once these opinions have been examined, it will become evident that each fluctuation could have been based on one of these opinions and that the frequency of the fluctuations can only be explained by the number and diversity of these opinions. It will also become evident that no fluctuation of itself gives reason for concluding that any particular pope had deviated from a Talmud policy whose primary goal was the promotion of conversion.

At one extreme, there were those who, like Possevin and de Torres, demanded that the Talmud and its commentaries be burned to promote conversion. Writing in 1557, the Udinese jurisconsult, Marquardus de Susannis, discusses and praises the burning of the Talmud in the context of an essay on the proper method of inducing the Jews to convert. While he never explicitly asserts it, the context makes his belief in the conversionary efficacy of book burning perfectly clear.[63] This belief, moreover, was not confined to the 1550's, or even to the sixteenth century. In a gloss of the 1564 bull, *Cum pro munere,* the early seventeenth-century canonist, Flavius Cherubinus, concluded that: "[The Jews] must not be permitted to read prohibited books through which their impiety is encouraged or increased and their conversion is delayed."[64] And in 1629 the Inquisitor, Cardinal Scaglia, wrote to Cardinal Paelotto in Vienna, requesting that he urge the Emperor to prevent his officials from allowing Jews to possess copies of the Talmud. For in Asia and Africa where copies abound, "they prove the greatest impediment to conversion."[65]

The belief in the conversionary efficacy of Talmud burning could not have developed, however, were it not that the almost universal Christian evaluation of the Talmud was a hostile one. Even those who voiced no opinion on the question of burning lambasted the Talmud. In his tract on crimes, the late sixteenth-century jurist Tiberius Decianus calls the Talmud reprehensible, "since it contains execrations and horrendous blasphemies against Christ, our Lord . . . One cannot hear [these books read] without [feeling] the greatest horror and [uttering] curses."[66] Most indicative of commonly held sentiments is the attitude toward the Talmud taken by the sixteenth-century theologian, Io. Ludovicus Vives of Valencia, in his *De Veritate Fidei Christianae,* which attempts to prove the truth of Christianity by refuting gentile arguments. When he refers to the derogatory fables about Jesus supposedly found in the Talmud, he merely announces his unwillingness to refute them. He apparently assumes that the fabulous and blasphemous nature of the Talmud is general knowledge.[67] Indeed, the Talmud was attacked even by those who, as will be seen, argued that parts of the rabbinic corpus itself were valuable instruments for persuading Jews to convert. That staunchest proponent of the conversionary value of rabbinic literature, the Franciscan, Petrus Galatinus, conceded, albeit by inference, that the Talmud contained many false statements.[68] The Ferrara notary, Hadrianus Finus, admonishes the Jews to recognize that "their codices, which they call the Talmud . . . are replete with falsities, iniquities, and impieties."[69] The convert Dominican, Sixtus of Siena, defends the Kabbalah on the one hand, but vigorously denounces the travesties of the Talmud on the other.[70] And the controversial theologian of the early seventeenth century, Tommaso Campanella, accuses the Babylonian Rabbis of having filled the Talmud with demonic illusions.[71]

This universally hostile evaluation, especially of Talmudic attitudes toward Christianity, served as the underpinning for the belief held by such men as de Torres, de Susannis and Scaglia that the destruction of the Talmud would promote conversion. Thus, de Torres argues that destroying the body of rabbinic writings would remove from the Jews that "which tends to make vanity of our cross,"[72] and "that which teaches them insanity."[73] Indeed, the 1553 Inquisition order itself is based on precisely this assumption.[74] Similarly, de Susannis accuses the Talmud of containing wickedness and *deliramenta.*[75] And Cardinal Scaglia condemns the Talmud as a horror of horrors which the Emperor should totally extirpate, not allowing such poisonous sprouts to flourish in his Empire.[76] However, although these charges were made to support a conversionary argument, the men who made them were certainly aware that the Talmud had been burned in the thirteenth century for the express purpose of eliminating its blasphemies. Hence, while the Talmud was condemned in the sixteenth century specifically to foster conversions, the widespread acceptance of accusations which had originated in the thirteenth century must have stimulated the sixteenth-century condemnation all the more.

The Talmud question was further complicated by a problem which involved Catholics alone. In his gloss on *Cum pro munere* Cherubinus indicates that Christians, as well as Jews, may not read works which contain confutations of the Christian faith and provoke impiety.[77] He is, of course, referring to the Talmud. Moreover, Cardinal Scaglia warns that the existence of Talmuds in many places in Germany foments schism.[78] In other words, both Cherubinus and Scaglia are concerned lest a freely circulating and freely read Talmud corrupt not only Jews, but Catholics too.

In addition, while Cherubinus and Scaglia were undoubtedly perturbed by Talmudic statements directly offensive to Christianity, sixteenth-century Talmud critics had also resurrected the thirteenth-century accusation that the Talmud contains ideas offensive to monotheistic theology in general.[79] Indeed, they renewed the same specific charges and supported them with the same Talmudic texts. Assuredly drawing on the mid–thirteenth-century *Extractiones de Talmud,* Hadrianus Finus asserts that the God of the Talmud is not the True God, because, according to a statement of "R. Ioanna nomine R. Joseph" found in "Benedictionum, cap. i," God prayed. Prayer predicates a superior to whom one prays, but the True God has no superior.[80] Tommaso Campanella too reiterates this charge, as well as others.[81] The Talmud, he says, impugns the wisdom of God and makes Him *ignorantiorem Rabbynis* when it records God's admission of defeat by the Rabbis in an halakhic dispute in which He sided with R. Eliezer against the Rabbis.[82] Campanella, moreover, formalizes these charges, something which had not been done previously, by framing them in strict theological terminology.

> In these books, [he says], a God is predicated who is not the God of Gods and prime, but second, subject to whom I know not. Indeed, the Talmudists have made their God neither omnipotent, nor omniscient, nor the prime will, but often impotent, often ignorant, and often criminal.[83]

By thus passing judgment on these charges as a whole, Campanella illustrates definitively another possible reason for an attack on the Talmud. A Church which had become overly sensitive to even the nuances of theology could not permit free access to the gross theological errors which the Talmud allegedly contains.[84] To be sure, an attack for general theological reasons would take most into consideration the possible effect of the Talmud on Christians. It is, however, equally certain that such an attack could only exacerbate the difficulties besetting the Jews who were laboring to effect the recision, or at least the modification of the decrees ordering the Talmud's proscription.

Nevertheless, despite the accusation of theological perversity and even despite the charges of blasphemy, there were Christians who vigorously argued that they must be allowed to read the Talmud. No less a man of the establishment than the Spaniard Bartolomeo de Valverde, the chaplain of Philip II, wrote to Sirleto in 1584 asking the Cardinal, who was also a member of the Congregation of the Index, to renew the permit allowing him to possess forbidden books. His research, Valverde complained, would otherwise be curtailed, especially since a new edition of the Index was about to appear on which were listed the works of many saints and, "lamentable loss, all the commentaries of the Jews."[85] This situation, however, Valverde continues, should never have occurred, and would not have, except for the fact that "those who have been entrusted with this matter [the new Index] . . . are completely unskilled in Greek and Hebrew letters and ignorant in judgment."[86]

According to Andreas Masius, the Flemish scholar of Hebrew and Greek, the attack on the Talmud and on Hebrew literature will result only in the greatest damage to Christianity.[87] The Bible in particular is continually misinterpreted by those who know it through translations alone.[88] Hence, early in 1554 he beseeches the Venetian Senate to refrain, despite its edict condemning the Talmud,[89] from burning the works he has purchased, but has not yet received from the Venetian publishers of Hebrew books.[90] Masius, in fact, represents an extreme, arguing wholeheartedly all his life against the prohibition and destruction of Hebrew books. As is to be expected, his efforts provoked a harsh reaction among those unequivocally opposed to the circulation of the Talmud, and accordingly, Pius V, one of rabbinic literature's severest opponents,[91] included Masius' name on the list of dangerous authors and placed his commentary of Joshua on the Index.[92] On the other hand,

Masius' writings, especially those claiming that Christian studies required a knowledge of Hebrew and of rabbinic literature, reflect the growth of a counter-pressure to the argument that Christians must not be allowed to read the Talmud. Indeed, although by no means so all-inclusive as those voiced by Masius, Valverde's complaints too substantiate the existence of this counter-pressure. They also reveal that this pressure grew in response to more than the theoretical issue of the danger, as opposed to the value of rabbinic literature to Christian scholars. As Dejob points out,[93] and as is illustrated clearly by Valverde's 1584 letter, men like Valverde objected not to the institution of censorship itself, but rather to its management by ill-trained and inconsistent censors. This objection held, moreover, irrespective of the origin of the censored material. Thus, the question of the permissibility of rabbinic literature was further complicated by entanglement in the imperfect practical mechanics of the Catholic Restoration. And, undoubtedly, the arbitrary censorship affected Jews as adversely as it affected Christians.[94]

At the same time, the Christian desire to study rabbinic works certainly advanced the possibility that this literature would not remain totally outlawed. The real impetus for rehabilitating the Talmud and rabbinic works came, however, from those who, in diametrical opposition to the Inquisition, argued that "above all, it is necessary to know that the perfidy of the Jews ought to be eliminated by using their Talmudic writings."[95] Indeed, Masius, whose defense of the Talmud's value for Christian scholars was surely linked to his estimation of its conversionary value, reproaches the Inquisition in a letter to Cardinal Pighinus because, at the advice of two base converts:

> You so precipitously passed a sentence eternally ignominious to the apostolic throne and eternally damnable to Christian affairs because of the gain which would otherwise have accrued from the conversion of the Jews. . . . No book is more appropriate to convince the Jews than the Talmud; to assert the opposite is ridiculous. I had, moreover, begun to collect materials [from the Talmud] for a book which would have won the Jews for Christianity. But in my great indignation at your bungling, I threw it all into the fire.[96]

It is, however, in the *De Arcanis* of Petrus Galatinus, which antedates the burning of the Talmud by forty years, that the most thorough advocacy of the conversionary value of rabbinic literature is found. Hence, the full title of the work: *Opus toti Christianae Reipublicae maxime utile, de arcanis catholice veritatis, contra obstinatissimam Iu-*

daeorum nostrae tempestatis perfidiam: ex Talmud, aliisque hebraicis
libris nuper excerptum: et quadruplici linguarum genere eleganter con-
gestum.[97] The *De Arcanis* is divided into twelve books, the last eleven of
which attempt to defend and prove the truths of Christianity by drawing
on the Bible and rabbinic literature.[98] The first book, accordingly, demonstrates why rabbinic literature offers such proof. In essence, Galatinus
argues that the Rabbis with the greatest authority lived soon after the
Babylonian exile and received their doctrine from the prophets themselves, whose pupils and successors they were. Therefore, it is not strange
that these Rabbis wrote about the truths of the Christian faith, and that
all of these writings have been variously placed in the Talmudic books.[99]
After the Resurrection, moreover, many Rabbis saw the words of the
prophets fulfilled in Christ and adhered to him in both faith and deeds,
as, for instance, Gamaliel the Elder,[100] whose sayings have great authority among the Talmudists.[101] Even the Rabbis of that period who held
fast to their perfidy unwittingly wrote of the truth of Christ. And it is
chiefly from their writings that the Talmudic codex is compiled.[102] Thus,
there is nothing more appropriate and efficacious than the Talmud for
both confuting the Jews' arguments and convincing them to convert.
Indeed, what could be more pleasant to the Christian than to rip the
sword from the hands of his enemy and to sever the head of the Infidel,
as did David himself, with his own weapon![103] Hence, the Talmud
should be acceptable to Christians.[104]

In addition, trying to base his argument on solid canonical tradition,
Galatinus declares that at the 1311 Council of Vienne, Clement V decreed that the Talmud should be translated into Latin so that once
Catholic scholars were familiar with its contents, they could use the
Talmud to propagate Christianity among Jews.[105] Clement V had indeed
ordered the establishment of chairs in Hebrew, Arabic and Chaldean at
various universities in the hope that the studies carried on and the
translations made by the holders of those chairs would result in increased conversions.[106] He had not, however, said a word about the
Talmud. Aware of this fact, Galatinus argues that Clement V could have
meant only the Talmud, for the Bible had long before been translated
into Latin.[107] Apparently this argument gained a number of adherents.
In 1566 Sixtus of Siena found it necessary, in the course of his thorough
denunciation of the Talmud, to upbraid Galatinus' claims about the
Vienne decree as mere nonsense.[108] Again, in 1629, Cardinal Scaglia

attempted to refute Galatinus by asserting that the 1311 decree certainly did refer only to the Bible.[109] What thus becomes clear is that the defenders of opposing Talmud policies were debating with each other publicly and that these debates extended over a hundred-year period. Hence, there is reason to assume that the contrary opinions advanced by the Talmud's partisans and foes were in large measure responsible for the fluctuations which occurred in later sixteenth-century papal Talmud policy.

The argument explicitly favoring the use of the Talmud as a conversionary tool was undoubtedly enhanced by the appearance during the sixteenth century of writings which did not address themselves specifically to the question of retaining or destroying the Talmud, but which did propose, as the major theologian Cardinal Robert Bellarmine succinctly put it, that "there is a greater possibility of urging the Jews [to convert] by the use of Hebrew writings than by the use of writings in Latin or Greek."[110] Perhaps most interesting, because its contents are suggestive of the activity which went on in the Roman *Domus cathecumenorum* and also of the type of argument which was used there to persuade cathecumens that their choice was correct, is the work of the convert Fabiano Fioghi. His *Dialogo fra il cathecumino e il Padre Cathechizante,* which was written in 1582 while he was a lector at the Roman *domus,* is a catechism for recent converts. Accordingly, it is based not on the writings of Christian theologians, but on Biblical and rabbinic texts.[111] Thus, for example, Fioghi attempts to prove the validity of the Trinity from the *Zohar, Sefer Yetsirah,* and *Midrash Tehillim.* He uses no specific text from the *Zohar,* but asserts that the three persons of the Trinity are represented by the first three Spheres.[112] *S. Yetsirah,* he claims, refers to the Trinity in the verse: "There are three lights, a pre-existing light, a shining light, and an illuminating light; even so, all three are but one."[113] This verse, however, is found in none of the versions of *S. Yetsirah.*[114] Fioghi's excerpt from *Midrash Tehillim,* though, is legitimate; it was also used by Raymund Martini in the thirteenth century.[115] The expression, "God, God, the Lord" (Ps. 50,1), he notes, is explained in *Midrash Tehillim* as the three names with which God created the world.[116] And while the Rabbis did not explicitly affirm their conversion in this Midrash, he explains, they by no means denied the Trinity, but in effect confirmed it.[117] The entire *Dialogo* follows this pattern.

In like fashion, the first eight books of Hadrianus Finus' *In Iudaeos*

Flagellum [118] employ texts from the Bible and rabbinical works to demonstrate Christian truths and quell Jewish objections. The truth of the second person of the Trinity, Finus writes, is seen in the commentary of Nachmanides on the word *Breshith*. For Nachmanides interprets that word as " 'In wisdom,' which is the principle of principles [i.e., the Word, the Son] . . . He thus verifies that wisdom was conceived by God, and, as a consequence, he signifies that God has a son." [119] Similarly, Finus proceeds, *Midrash Ruth* states that it was revealed to Adam that the messiah would be the son of God. [120] And *'Ekh'a Rabb'a* and *Breshith Rabb'a* of R. Moshe ha-Darshan both tell of a conversation between a Jew laboring in his field and an Arab. The Arab announces the arrival of the Messiah. The Jew asks the Messiah's name. Menachem, the Arab replies. Then the Jew asks his father's name. Answer: Hezekiah, which name Finus translates as "Deus fortis." With this second question Finus considers his case proved. [121]

The ninth book of the *Flagellum*, however, in apparent contradiction to the first eight, denounces the Talmud. By adhering to that work, Finus declares, the Jews not only abandon, but also subvert the Law of Moses. [122] For the Talmud is a diabolic law, which is their own creation, a false doctrine, which they ought to eschew. [123] Indeed, if the Jews learned that the Talmud abounds with impieties and recognized the error of following its precepts, they would surely convert. [124] In the *Flagellum*, then, the argument to conserve and the opposing argument to destroy the Talmud in order to foster conversion have coalesced. More than that, Finus has obviously combined significantly older opposing arguments. His claim that rabbinic texts can perform a conversionary function derives from Raymund Martini's thirteenth-century *Pugio Fidei*, [125] and his claim that the Talmud is a creation of the Jews, a *nova lex,* first appeared in France during the thirteenth century. [126] In addition, Finus enlarged on this latter claim by suggesting that if the Jews rid themselves of the Talmud, they would convert, thus integrating the *nova lex* charge with the stance taken by Benedict XIII in 1415. [127] Nor was Finus alone among his contemporaries in integrating stances. Combining the thirteenth-century French and thirteenth-century Spanish positions, although, unlike Finus, remaining solidly in favor of destruction, de Torres asserts:

It is one thing for the Jews to profess the Law, another to corrupt the Law which they are permitted to profess. The Church permits the profession of the

Law so that perhaps we may win them; the corruption of the Law it does not permit.[128]

Fioghi appears to have combined the *nova lex* charge with the theory of the *Pugio Fidei*. While he holds that rabbinic texts are the optimum conversionary tools, and never attacks the Talmud *per se,* he finds it difficult to convince the Jews that they have wandered from the True Law, for they believe that they do observe the Law of Moses.[129]

The most interesting and perhaps the most explicit combination of arguments is found in the *Quod Reminiscentur* of Tommaso Campanella. On the one hand he states:

[The Talmud] is a new Scripture, superceding the Scripture of Moses and the Prophets . . . From reading it the Jews have become blind so that they cannot sense goodness or wisdom.[130] . . . Indeed, because they live by the doctrine of the impious Talmud, having deserted the Law and the Prophets, the Jews are unable to believe.[131]

But on the other hand, he seems to have carried these combinations to absurdity when, in summation of his tract, he declares:

[With the arrival of the Golden Age] you will be convinced, even from the Talmud itself, that the messiah has come; . . . and that you can in no way recognize the messiah unless you desert the Talmud and adhere anew to the Scriptures of Moses and the Prophets.[132]

No matter what the combination, however, it is clear that it was structured by first modifying and then integrating the conversionary or potentially conversionary elements found in opposing arguments in order to fashion a more effective conversionary program.

The tendency to combine arguments was, moreover, quite strong. The existence of two Talmud arguments which both had the same end, the promotion of conversion, but which differed on whether the conservation or the destruction of the Talmud would achieve that end virtually made it impossible to espouse one argument while ignoring the other. Even the genuinely single-minded Galatinus admits that the Christian reception of the Talmud to exploit its conversionary value should be limited to accepting only its truths. In particular, Talmudic distortions of Scripture must be pilloried and also corrected.[133] Herein lies, moreover, the essence of the concept which, although unspoken, permitted Finus to assume an apparently self-contradictory stance and which, incidentally, also explains precisely the incorporation of the *nova lex* charge into the argument for destruction. The Talmud which is to be condemned is only the rabbinic concoction which obfuscates the true Talmud and hinders conversion. As put most forcefully by Joseph de Voisin[134] in his prefatory observations to the 1687 edition of the *Pugio Fidei:*

> How many ancient traditions in which the mysteries of our faith are set forth have the Jews removed from the Talmud? How many of these which they were unable to delete have they buried over with circumlocutions? How many commentaries have they forced onto us, how many contrary expositions of Scripture? And these offenses of the Midrashim and Aggadoth are well known, so that not even the Jews can deny them.[135]

The true and acceptable Talmud, that which will convince the Jews, is the remainder, which contains the statements of those Rabbis who allegedly recognized and duly recorded the truth of Christ and thus, as Galatinus, for instance, asserts,[136] adhered to the True Law.

Hence, intrinsically reflecting both sides of this concept, Galatinus declares:

> The more recent Jews,[137] whose impious perfidy has blinded them, turn the true sense of divine Scripture against us, and wage war on us. But we will easily convince them [of Christianity's truth] by using the traditions of the ancient Talmudists, which speak quite clearly on these matters in their explanation of the Law and Prophets.[138]

Similarly, the concept of a true and false Talmud explains the seeming absurdity of Campanella's statement that the Jews would be convinced through the Talmud, yet could not be convinced until they had abandoned it.[139] Campanella intends that statement to be read in the light of a preceding one in which he expresses the novel idea:

> Because of [the Talmud's] errors, we advise you [Jews] that since the Rabbis wrote whatever they pleased [in the Talmud], you ought to call a Council of all the most learned for the purpose of examining the doctrine of the Talmud; and we shall provide you with aid and advice.[140]

It is thus the purified Talmud which will convince the Jews, but the spurious product of the later Rabbis which must first be abandoned.

The most unusual expression of this dichotomous evaluation of rabbinic literature is found in the *Bibliotheca Sancta* of Sixtus of Siena. Sixtus explicitly differentiates the pernicious lies of the Talmud[141] from the saving truths of the Kabbalah.[142] By means of the Kabbalah, he claims, "Christians can stab Jews with their own weapon."[143] Indeed, when the Talmud was burned at Cremona in 1559, he insisted, successfully, that Kabbalistic tracts be spared.[144] Not satisfied, however, with the simple differentiation between the Talmud and the Kabbalah, Sixtus subdivided the latter into a true and false Kabbalah. He even argued this issue with the Inquisition.[145] Certainly in response to the Inquisition's condemnation of the Kabbalah in 1562,[146] Sixtus wrote in 1566 that the true Kabbalah:

Is a more secret exposition of divine law, received by Moses from the mouth of God, and by the Fathers from the mouth of Moses in continuous succession, received not written, but orally. This Kabbalah returns us from the earthly to the heavenly.[147]

The origins of this dualistic view of rabbinic literature must probably be sought in the attempt made in fifteenth-century Spain to harmonize the views of Benedict XIII and the *Pugio Fidei*.[148] For the fifteenth-century attack on the Talmud ended in the expurgation of Hebrew books. And in the sixteenth century the use of this dualistic view as the rationale for harmonizing opposing Talmud arguments based on thirteenth- and fifteenth-century traditions was undoubtedly most responsible for the imposition of censorship on Hebrew books. Indeed, Galatinus' formulation of the dualistic view explicitly requires the correction of errors.[149] The dualistic view, moreover, explains why in the bull *Cum sicut nuper,* Julius III imposed that form of censorship which bans certain books while permitting others.[150] The usual explanation of the clause in *Cum Sicut nuper* which permits the ownership of non-blasphemous Hebrew books is that Julius III was influenced, in one way or another, by a Jewish delegation.[151] Yet Julius III's decision was more likely prompted by reading Masius' arguments in his letter to Cardinal Pighinus.[152] It is not unreasonable to assume that Pighinus, one of the two Inquisitors who had opposed the 1553 decree of condemnation,[153] had shown Masius' letter to the Pope. Impressed on the one hand by the letter, but unprepared on the other hand to disregard the contentions of the Inquisition, Julius III compromised. He reaffirmed the ban on the Talmud, but approved the use of other rabbinical works, while at the same time—and this is the crucial point—explicitly asserting that he had acted to promote conversion.[154]

The brunt of the censorship which was imposed on rabbinic works, however, took the form of expurgation. To be sure, a large censorship apparatus was established during the Catholic Restoration to expurgate and condemn heretical and blasphemous works no matter what their origin.[155] The actual censorship procedures, moreover, were often carried out by untrained and hence inconsistent censors.[156] Certain facts, however, confirm that the motivation for expurgating Hebrew books was not merely the usual motivation for censorship, that is, the desire to protect Catholicism.[157] Most important, the major attempts at censorship were made in the late 1570's under the direction of Cardinal Sirleto with Robert Bellarmine serving as chief censor.[158] Sirleto, of course, was superintendent of all conversionary activities, and Bellarmine was an avowed member of the faction which proposed the use of rabbinic works as a conversionary tool. In addition, the censor's manual compiled in 1596 by the apostate monk, Laurentius Franguellus, contains a list of rabbinic passages which, according to Franguellus, prove the Transfiguration and the Divinity of Christ.[159] Franguellus most probably expected censors using his manual to place a hand with an outstretched index finger next to these passages in accordance with the usual custom for calling the attention of the reader to significant points.

In 1578, moreover, the Polish Jew, Simon of Gambs, contracted with the Basle printer Froben to have a new edition of the Talmud printed.[160] The contract stipulated that the edition would be prepared in conformity with the provision of the 1564 Index that the Talmud would be tolerated only if it were expurgated and then only if it appeared without the name, Talmud.[161] Accordingly, the censor Marcus Marinus de Brescia was dispatched from Rome, with the approval of none other than Sirleto.[162] The resulting edition was not only so disfigured that Simon had to be taken to court before he would accept the volumes, but, in addition, the margins were filled with Catholic interpretations of the Talmudic texts.[163] It seems difficult not to suspect that at Sirleto's instigation, de Brescia had attempted to prepare an instrument with which to implement the idea that a purified Talmud was the optimum means for promoting conversion.

The theoretical concept underlying censorship, the dualistic view which propounded the existence of both a true and a false Talmud, surely represents the ultimate refinement in sixteenth-century thought about the Talmud. The existence of this concept, moreover, demonstrates why the sixteenth-century papacy was able to reverse its Talmud policy so often without deviating from its overall policy of conversion. For underlying this concept is the supposition that any position taken *vis-à-vis* the Talmud can be turned into a conversionary one. Thus, irrespective of whether his Talmud policy was influenced by the argument for destruction, the argument for conversion, or by a combination of arguments, any pope of the later sixteenth century was able to justify that policy, both to himself and to others, as one whose primary objective was the promotion of conversion.

NOTES

1. A copy of this decree is found in M. Stern, ed. *Urkundliche Beiträge über die Stellung der Päpste zu den Juden* (Kiel, 1893), number 100, p. 98.
2. A. Yaari, *Srēfath ha-Talmud b'Italiah* (Tel-Aviv, 1954), 16 gives the date as Rosh ha-Shannah, Sept. 9, 1553; Franc. Albizzi, *De Inconstantia in Fide* (Amsterdam, 1683), Part I, 295 gives the date as Succoth, Sept. 2, 1553.
3. See S. W. Baron, *A Social and Religious History of the Jews* (henceforth, *SRH*), (Phila., 1969), XIV, 29–31; R. N. Rabbinowicz, *Ma'amar 'al Hadpasath ha-Talmud*, ed. M. Haberman (Jerusalem, 1952), 59 ff.; A. YAARI, *Srēfath ha-Talmud b'Italiah*, 16–21; and Joseph ha-Kohen, *'Emek ha-bakh'a*, ed. M. Letteris (Cracow, 1895), 128–30.
4. For a detailed discussion of this dispute, see D. W. Amram, *The Makers of Hebrew Books in Italy* (Phila., 1909), 254–64; see also *SRH* XIV, 29, H. Graetz, *Dibrē Ymē Israel*, trans. S. Rabbinowicz, VII, 245, W. Popper, *The Censorship of Hebrew Books* (New York, 1899), 31–37, F. H. Reusch, *Der Index der Verbotenen Bucher* (Bonn, 1883), I, 45 ff., Rabbinowicz, *Ma'amar*, 59, and Yaari, *Srēfath ha-Talmud*, 7–8.
5. May 29, 1554; in *Bullarium Diplomatum . . . Taurensis Editio* (Henceforth, *B.R.*), (Turin, 1857–72), VI, 482. The Talmud policy of Julius III's successors in the sixteenth century will be discussed below.
6. On the burning of the Talmud in Paris in the 1240's, see esp. Ch. Merchavia, *The Church Versus Talmudic and Midrashic Literature, 500–1248* [in Hebrew] (Jerusalem, 1970), 446–52, for papal letters; I. Loeb, "La Controverse de 1240 sur le Talmud," *Revue des Etudes Juives,* I (1880), 217–61, II (1881), 218–70, III (1881), 39–57, and J. Rosenthal, "The Talmud on Trial," *Jewish Quarterly Review,* N. S. XLVII (1956–57), 145–69, for texts revealing clearly that the motive for burning was the Talmud's alleged blasphemies and insults; S. Grayzel, *"The Church and the Jews in the XIIIth. Century* (Phila., 1933), 339–43, on the role of Nicholas Donin, and for copies of letters sent to local officials in France

ordering the destruction of the Talmud because of its blasphemies; and A. Funkenstein, "Changes in the Patterns of Christian Anti-Jewish Polemics in the 12th. Century," [in Hebrew,] *Zion,* XXXIII (1968), 137–39, on the additional thirteenth century charge that the Talmud was a *nova lex,* not the true Law of Moses, and hence fit for condemnation.

7. In addition to the works cited in nn. 3 & 4, *supra,* see esp. P. Browe, *Die Judenmission im Mittelalter und die Päpste* (Rome, 1942), 39, and K. W. Hoffmann, *Ursprung und Anfangstätigkeit des ersten päpstlichen Missioninstituts* (Münster, 1923), 50–51. While pointing to the heavy conversionary bias of later sixteenth century papal Jewry policy, both Browe and Hoffmann view the papal attack on the Talmud as part of the general Catholic Reformation assault on threatening literature.

8. The proposition claiming that the Talmud was burned in the thirteenth century because of its insults to Christianity is reinforced by noting that prevention of insult is central to the canons dealing with the Jews issued in that period. See E. Friedburg, ed., *Corpus Iuris Canonici* (Leipzig, 1879–81), X. 5, 6 *De Iudaeis;* and the explication of X. 5, 6 in M. de Susannis, *De Iudaeis et Aliis Infidelibus* (Venice, 1558), Part. I, chap. 4.

9. See Y. F. Baer, *A History of the Jews in Christian Spain* (Phila., 1966), II, 166–69 & 229.

10. The text of this bull is published in I. Döllinger, ed., *Beiträge zur politischen, kirchlichen, und Kulturgeschichte der sechs letzten Jahrhunderte* (Regensburg, 1863), II, 393–403.

11. The bull proposes disputations, missionary sermons, and the deprivation of jurisdictional autonomy to prove to the Jews that the prophecy of Gen. 49:10, "The sceptre will not be removed from Judah, etc. . . ," has been fulfilled. See *ibid.,* 393, 396 & 401. The bulls of Gregory IX and Innocent IV had in fact declared that the Talmud is said to be *(dicatur esse)* the prime cause which keeps the Jews in their perfidy and that the Jews teach their children the Talmud and not the Bible because they fear that from the Bible their children will perceive the truth of Christianity (see Merchavia, *The Church,* 446–52). But as Merchavia notes (*ibid.* 228), these phrases are indeed only hearsay, as the words *"dicatur esse"* indicate. In distinction to *Etsi doctoris,* which announces its conversionary intent in its proemium, the thirteenth century bulls speak of conversion only as an afterthought.

12. Döllinger, *Beiträge,* 394.

13. Baer, *History,* II, 229.

14. Raymundus Martini, *Pugio Fidei Adversus Mauros et Iudaeos* (Leipzig, 1687). On Martini's theory, see Funkenstein, "Anti-Jewish Polemics," 137–39. On the authenticity of many of the rabbinic passages cited by Martini, see Y. F. Baer, *History,* 1, 167, 185 & 411, n. 54, who claims they are forgeries, and S. Lieberman, "Raymund Martini and his Alleged Forgeries," *Historica Judaica,* V (1943), 87–102, who claims they are authentic.

15. This suggestion is prompted by the fact that a similar compromise was effected in the sixteenth century. Cf. S. Lieberman, *Shkiin* (Jerusalem, 1939), 43, where he suggests that Martini's arguments were instrumental in preventing the burning of the Talmud in Spain in the 1260's.

16. See Stern, *Urkundliche Beiträge,* number 100, p. 98.

17. G. Buschbell, *Reformation und Inquisition in Italien um die Mitte des xvi Jahrhunderts* (Paderborn, 1910), *passim,* and esp. 221.

18. Stern, *Beiträge,* 98.

19. The only modern historian who seems aware of this fact is G. Sacerdote, "Deux Index Expurgatoires de Livres Hebreux," *REJ* XXX (1895), 268–69.

20. Hoffmann, *Ursprung,* 48, makes this suggestion, but at the same time dissociates the purpose of the converts from that of the papacy and the Inquisition.

21. *B.R.,* VI, 482.

22. *Ibid.*

23. An explanation of this clause will be given below.

24. For the old formula see e.g. Potthast number 834 (Grayzel, *The Church,* 92), the bull *Licet perfidia* (Sept. 15, 1199) of Innocent III: "Licet in sua magis velint duritia perdurare, quam prophetarum verba . . . cognoscere, atque ad Christiane fidei . . . pervenire, . . . ipsorum petitionem admittimus." This formula was repeated through the fifteenth century, in particular in those bulls known as the *Constitutiones pro Iudaeis,* which defined the Jewry policy of a given pope. See S. Grayzel, "The Papal Bull Sicut Iudeis," *Studies and Essays in Honor of Abraham A. Neuman,* eds. M. Ben-Horin, et al. (Leiden, 1962), 243–80.

25. Antonius Possevin, *Bibliotheca Selecta . . . ad salutem omnium gentium procurandum* (Cologne, 1607), Bk. IX, p. 391. This entire work, as its title indicates, deals with conversionary methods. Book IX deals, in particular, with the proper method for converting Jews.

26. *'Emeq,* ed. Letteris, 128–34.

27. *Ibid.,* 133.

28. On this mission see *SRH,* XIV, 31, and Popper, *Censorship,* 37–38.

29. *'Emeq,* 130.

30. *Ibid.,* 131.

31. In his introduction to the second edition of the *Tur 'Orah Hayim* (Venice, 1564), reprinted in Yaari, *Srēfath,* 34.

32. The attitudes of sixteenth century Christians towards the Kabbalah will be discussed below.

33. In the introduction to the *Ma'arekheth 'Elohuth* (Mantua, 1558), reprinted in Yaari, *Srēfath,* 37. Also see Yaari, 22–39, for statements of general despair made by late sixteenth-century Jewish authors, all of which betray a fear for survival without the Talmud, or at least a fear for the continuation of Jewish life as they knew it.

34. Francisco de Torres, *De Sola Lectione Legis, et Prophetarum Iudaeis cum*

Mosaico Ritu, et Cultu Permittenda, et de Jesu in Synagogis Eorum ex Lege, ac Prophetis Ostendendo, et Annunciando. Ad Reverendiss. Inquisitores. Libri Duo. (Rome, 1555).

35. On de Torres and censorship see Ch. Dejob, *De L'influence du Concile de Trente sur la litterature et les beaux-arts chez les peuples catholiques* (Paris, 1884), 32, 50, & 53. De Torres' major literary effort was translating numerous Greek polemics into Latin: for a bibliography of these see C. Sommervogel, *Bibliothèque de la Compagnie de Jésus* (Strasbourg, 1898), VIII, 113–26. De Torres was also a major canonist and served on the commission which edited Gregory XIII's "Editio Romana" of Gratian's *Decretum;* see Friedberg, *Corpus Juris,* I, lxxvii.

36. The *De Sola Lectione* is divided into two books. The first deals with rabbinic literature and the second with the organization of a preaching mission whose purpose would be to convert the Jews by proving Christian truth to them from the Torah and the Prophets.

37. *De Sola Lectione,* 6–7.

38. *Ibid.,* 9.

39. *Ibid.,* 10.

40. *Ibid.,* 11.

41. *Ibid.,* 12.

42. See L. Christiani, *L'Eglise à l'époque du Concile de Trente* (Paris, 1948), 150 f., and H. Daniel-Rops, *The Catholic Reformation,* trans. J. Warrington (New York, 1964), I, 127 ff.

43. Hoffmann, *Ursprung,* 59.

44. Reusch, *Der Index,* I, 48.

45. See Browe, *Judenmission,* passim, and esp. 39–50, and Hoffmann, *Ursprung,* passim. Indeed, Hoffmann's thesis is that the first truly organized mission to the Jews arose in the sixteenth century. Hoffmann, however, as well as all others who have studied later sixteenth-century papal Jewry policy (cf., e.g., I. Sonne, *Mi-Pavolo Ha-Revi'i 'ad Pius Ha-Hamishi* [Jerusalem, 1954], introduction; H. Vogelstein and P. Rieger, *Geschichte der Juden in Rom* [Berlin, 1895], II, 142–189; C. Roth, *The History of the Jews of Italy* [Phila., 1946], 291–309: A. Milano, *Storia degli ebrei in Italia* [Turin, 1963], 244–262; and Baron, *SRH,* XIV, 32–59) has failed to recognise that conversion was the organizing and driving force behind all aspects of that policy. This fact my study of the *De Iudaeis et Aliis Infidelibus* of Marquardus de Susannis has demonstrated; see K. R. Stow, *Catholic Thought and Papal Jewry Policy, 1555–1593* (New York, 1976). Indeed, as my study has also shown—contrary to the common assumption —prior to the sixteenth century the papacy had not actively sought to promote large scale conversion, but had always spoken of the mass conversion of the Jews in passive terms, as an event which would occur in the distant future. The terminology of later sixteenth-century bulls changes, however, and calls for the active pursuit of mass conversion. Cf. n. 21, *supra.* This change, along with the establishment of a conversionary pro-

gram, indicates that in distinction from the policies of their predecessors, the popes of the later sixteenth century were the first ones to pursue a Jewry policy whose goal was mass conversion.

46. Hoffmann, *Ursprung*, 9–67, discusses the *Domus* at length.

47. July 15, 1555. *B.R.*, VI, 498.

48. Sept. 1, 1581. *B.R.*, VIII, 487–89.

49. See Ch. Dejob, "Documents tirés des papiers du Cardinal Sirleto," *REJ*, IX (1884), 77–91.

50. See A. Milano, *Il Ghetto di Roma* (Rome, 1964), 303–04. Milano cites no specific figures for the period 1542–1600; he does, however, state that the number of converts for 1634–1700 was 1,195, and for 1700–1790, 1,237, and he then adds that the number was higher in the later sixteenth century.

51. *Cum sicut nuper, B.R.*, VI, 482.

52. Popper, *Censorship*, 13, and Reusch, *Der Index*, I, 48.

53. F. Reusch, *Die Indices Librorum Prohibitorum des 16 Jahrhunderts* (Tübingen, 1886), (This work, a collection of texts of Indices, is not to be confused with the synthetic *Der Index*), 279: "Thalmud Hebraeorum eiusque glossae, annotationes, interpretationes et expositiones omnes; si tamen prodierint sine nomine Thalmud et sine injuriis et calumniis in religionem christianam, tolerabuntur." (Entry from the 1564 Index, which carries Pius IV's bull of approbation).

54. See M. Radin, "A Papal Brief of Pius IV," *Jewish Quarterly Review*, N.S. I (1910–11), 113–21.

55. POPPER, *Censorship*, 53–54.

56. *Ibid.*, 66.

57. *Ibid.*, 56, and Sacerdote, "Deux Index," 262 f.

58. Yaari, *Srēfath*, 12 ff., and Reusch, *Die Indices*, 518.

59. See Albizzi, *De Inconstantia*, 292, for the 1592 letter, and F. Cherubinus, *Compendium Bullarii . . . ab Leone Primo usque ad Paulum V* (Rome, 1623), Tom. 3, p. 6, for the 1593 bull.

60. See Albizzi, 296.

61. Reusch, *Die Indices*, 536–37. Reusch, *Der Index*, I, 51, notes that the determination of the 1596 Index remained in force for over two hundred years.

62. Popper, *Censorship*, 29–30.

63. Marquardus de Susannis, *De Iudaeis et Aliis Infidelibus*, Part III, chap. 1, pars. 48–50. Two thirds of the *De Iudaeis* contain a synthetic examination of the canons and Roman laws which together form the basis for medieval Italian common law Jewry law. The remaining third is a conversionary polemic.

64. Cherubinus, *Compendium*, II, 22: "Non . . . permittenda est lectio librorum prohibitorum, quibus eorum impietas, vel foveretur, vel augeretur, vel conversio retardaretur. . . ." *Cum pro munere* is the bull of Pius IV authorizing the 1564 Index; see Reusch, *Die Indices*, 243–45.

65. Albizzi, *De Inconstantia*, 297: ". . . n'abbonda grandemente l'Asia, e l'Africa,

ove sono di grandissimo impedimento alla converzione de' popoli ..."
(296–98 contain the whole letter of Card. Scaglia.)

66. Tiberius Decianus, *Tract. Criminalis* (Venice, 1614), 333.

67. Io. Ludo. Vives Valentini, *De Veritate Fidei Christianae* (Basle, 1543), 243–45. The work is divided into five parts, three of which are directed toward "gentile" (i.e., non-European) arguments, one toward Muslim arguments, and one toward Jewish arguments.

68. Petrus Columna Galatinus, *De Arcanis Catholice Veritatis* (Frankfurt a. M., 1602), 23^r.

69. Fini Hadriani Fini Ferrariensis, *In Iudaeos Flagellum* (Venice, 1538), 553^r.

70. Sixtus of Siena, *Bibliotheca Sancta* (Venice, 1566), 110 ff., in defense of the Kabbalah, and 125 ff., against the Talmud.

71. Romano Amerio, ed., *Per la conversione degli Ebrei*, (Part III of Campanella's four part conversionary tract, *Quod Reminiscentur*, completed in 1618), (Florence, 1955), 95.

72. De Torres, *De Sola Lectione.*

73. *Ibid.,* 12.

74. Cf. discussion above.

75. De Susannis, *De Iudaeis*, Part III, chap. I, par. 48.

76. Albizzi, *De Inconstantia*, 297.

77. Cherubinus, *Compendium*, II, 22, schola 1.

78. Albizzi, *De Inconstantia*, 297.

79. See J. Rosenthal, "The Talmud on Trial," 155–59, for a list of these charges and for the Talmudic texts on which they were based. For a history of Christian attacks on Talmudic theology, see S. Lieberman, *Shkiin*, 27 f. & 42 f.; Y. Baer, *A History of the Jews in Christian Spain*, (in Hebrew) (Tel-Aviv, 1959), 200 ff.; and especially Ch. Merchavia, *The Church Versus Talmudic and Midrashic Literature, passim.*

80. Finus, *Flagellum*, 576^r. For the charge as found in the *Extractiones* and as supported by a text from *Brakhoth*, 7a, see Rosenthal, "The Talmud on Trial," 158.

81. See Campanella, *Per la Conversione*, 97 ff.

82. *Ibid.,* 98. See Rosenthal, "The Talmud", 159, for the thirteenth-century charge and the supporting text, *Bab'a Mtsi'a'ª*, 59b, which text Campanella also refers to.

83. Campanella, *Per la Conversione*, 97.

84. See Stern, *Urkundliche Beiträge*, number 100, p. 98, for the 1553 Inquisition decree, which condemns the Talmud for blasphemies against humanity, against Mosaic law, and against Christ, and which also forbids Christians, besides Jews, from reading the Talmud.

85. In Dejob, *De L'influence*, 77.

86. *Ibid.,* 77.

87. Excerpts from Masius' letters appear in J. Perles, *Beiträge zur Geschichte Aramäischen und Hebräischen Studien* (Munich, 1885), 226: Letter of Feb. 19, 1554 to Marc. Ant. de Mula, Venetian ambassador to the Imperial

court: ". . . die Entscheidungen . . . nicht ohne grossten Schaden für die Christenheit beseitigt werden können." (Perles' translation; M. Lossen's *Briefe von A. Masius,* which has the Latin texts, was unobtainable. Where, however, Perles provides the Latin, I will cite that rather than the German.)

88. *Ibid.,* 229: Letter of Feb. 25, 1554 to the Roman prelate, Octav. Panagathus.

89. See Stern, *Urkundliche Beiträge,* number 104, p. 104, for a copy of this Oct. 21, 1553 edict.

90. Perles, *Beiträge,* 226: Letter of Feb. 19, 1554.

91. Cf. discussion above.

92. Perles, *Beiträge,* 229.

93. On the entire subject of erratic censors and censorship, see Dejob, *De L'influence,* 78 ff.

94. On erratic censorship of Jewish books, see Sacerdote, "Deux Index," 289 ff.

95. Galatinus, *De Arcanis,* 10ᵛ.

96. Perles, *Beiträge,* 224: Letter of Dec. 24, 1553 to Cardinal Pighinus.

97. Of special interest is the letter of approbation given the work by Emperor Maximillian and printed in the preface. It thanks Galatinus for defending his counsellor, Reuchlin. Moreover, the format of the work is a dialogue between Galatinus, Reuchlin, and Hoogstraten. Taking the nature of the work into consideration, these two facts suggest that in at least one of its phases, the Reuchlin controversy was really a controversy over the value of burning or conserving the Talmud to promote conversion and, hence, a prelude to the controversy of the later sixteenth century in Italy. On the Reuchlin controversy, see Baron, *SRH* XIII, 182–90, and the literature cited in Baron's notes. On Reuchlin's desire to promote conversion, see G. Kisch, *Zasius und Reuchlin* (Stuttgart, 1961), *passim.*

98. By rabbinic literature Galatinus, as many of his contemporaries, meant all Hebrew religious works, including the Kabbalah. Cf. discussion below. As is apparent from reading Joseph de Voisin's marginalia in the 1687 edition of the *Pugio Fidei,* Galatinus drew heavily from that work; indeed, de Voisin claims that Galatinus copied some sections almost verbatim.

99. *De Arcanis,* 11ᵛ.

100. There are indeed legends, based on Paul's claim in Acts 22:3 that Gamaliel was his teacher, that Gamaliel was in some way involved with Christianity. See M. Avi-Yonah, *Bimē Rom'a u'Biz'antiyon* (Jerus., 1946), 159, where he reports that Christians sacked Gamaliel's grave to obtain the relics of "Paul's teacher." The idea that Gamaliel was an outright convert may be Galatinus' own. De Voisin, in *Pugio Fidei,* 961, claims that the chapter of the *De Arcanis* in which this idea is found is composed from original materials. Galatinus, moreover, makes no attempt to support this idea with textual evidence.

101. *De Arcanis,* 16ᵛ.

102. *Ibid.,* 16ᵛ.

103. *Ibid.*, 23ʳ.

104. *Ibid.*, 23ʳ.

105. *Ibid.*, 23ʳ.

106. See Friedberg, *Corpus Iuris*, Clem. 5, 1, 1, for the decree incorporated into the canons. On the relatively small effects of this decree, see Browe, *Judenmission*, 271–74.

107. *De Arcanis*, 23ʳ.

108. Sixtus of Siena, *Bibliotheca Sancta*, 125.

109. Albizzi, *De Inconstantia*, 297.

110. St. Robert Bellarmine, *Opera Omnia* (Frankfurt n. M., 1965 photo.), *Controversiae*, Vol. 1. ch. 2: "E codibus Hebraeis magis urgeri posse iudaeo, quam ex Latinis et Graecis". See Sacerdote, "Deux Index", 262–63, and cf. discussion below on Bellarmine's role in the censorship of Hebrew books, a fact which probably accounts for the above remark.

111. F. Fioghi, *Dialogo fra il Cathecumino et il Padre Cathechizante* (Rome, 1582).

112. *Dialogo*, 17ᵛ–18ʳ.

113. *Ibid.*, 19ʳ.

114. The two basic versions of *S. Yetsirah* are found in the Lewin-Epstein (Jerus., 1965) photograph of the 1806 edition; many editors. This edition also contains the variations used by Jos. Karo and Shabbetai Donnolo. A critical edition was attempted by L. Goldschmidt, *Das Buch der Schöpfung* (Frankfurt a. M., 1984), but G. Scholem, *Les Origines de la Kabbale*, trans. J. Loewenson (Paris, 1966), 34, n. 9, calls it arbitrary. However, since Fioghi does indeed offer a Hebrew text it must be assumed that he copied it from another book with the name, *Sefer Yetsirah*, or that he simply copied the name of his source incorrectly.

115. *Pugio Fidei*, 494.

116. *Dialogo*, 16ᵛ, where Fioghi cites *Midrash Tehillim*, 140ᵃ (ed. Buber, Vilna, 1891).

117. *Dialogo*, 16ᵛ–17ʳ.

118. Published at Venice in 1538, but written more than twenty years earlier. See G. Tiraboschi, *Storia della Letteratura Italiana* (Rome, 1783), VI¹, 268.

119. *Flagellum*, 437.

120. *Ibid.*

121. *Ibid.* Cf. *Pugio Fidei*, 349, for Finus' source. His support text is: *'Ekh'a Rabb'a*, chap. 1 v. 16, p. 44b (ed. Buber, Vilna, 1899), and *Breshith Rabb'a* of R. Moshe ha-Darshan, ch. 30, v. 41 (Cf. S. Liebermann, *Shkiin* [Jerus., 1939], 86, for this version of *Breshith Rabb'a*).

122. *Flagellum*, 553.

123. *Ibid.*, 559.

124. *Ibid.*, 553.

125. Cf. discussion above on the nature of the *Pugio Fidei*.

126. See Funkenstein, "Anti-Jewish Polemics," 137–39.

127. Cf. discussion above.
128. De Torres, *De Sola Lectione*, 35.
129. Fioghi, *Dialogo*, 1b.
130. Campanella, *Per la Conversione* (*Quod Reminiscitur*, Part III), 96.
131. *Ibid.*, 116.
132. *Ibid.*, 147.
133. Galatinus, *De Arcanis*, 23.
134. The late date of this preface does not diminish the value of the following citation, which has, moreover, been cited primarily for its forcefulness, but which, in fact, also reflects previous thought; cf. n. 71, *supra*. On J. de Voisin, a French theologian who flourished in the mid-seventeenth century, see H. Hurter, *Nomenciator Literarius Theologiae Catholicae* (Innsbruck, 1907), IV, 427. He was also the author of *Theologia Judaeorum, sive opus, in quo Christiana religio fuisse priusquam Christus veniret ex hebraeorum libris ostenditur, errores vere Judaeorum coarguuntur, in 4.* (1647).
135. De Voisin, in *Pugio Fidei*, 77b.
136. Cf. discussion above.
137. The overall context of book I of the *De Arcanis* makes it clear that by "more recent Jews" Galatinus means most Rabbis who lived after the Tannaitic period.
138. Galatinus, *De Arcanis*, 28.
139. Cf. discussion above.
140. Campanella, *Per la Conversione*, 113.
141. Sixtus of Siena, *Bibliotheca Sancta*, 125ff. For a full description of this work, and for a biography of Sixtus, see Hurter, *Nomenclator*, III. 80 f.
142. On other Christian students of the Kabbalah in the sixteenth century, and on the desire to use the Kabbalah to promote conversion, see J. Blau, *The Christian interpretation of the Kabbalah in the Renaissance* (New York, 1944), 17–30, 41–77: F. Secret, "Les Jésuites et le Kabbalisme chretien à la Renaissance," *Bibliothèque d'Humanisme et Renaissance* XX (1958), 542–55; Secret, "Les Dominicains et la Kabbale Chrètienne à la Renaissance," *Archivum Fratrum Praedicatorum* XXVII (1857), 321–36; and J. W. O'Malley, *Giles of Viterbo on Church and Reform* (Leiden, 1968), 67–83.
143. *Bibliotheca Sancta*, 110ᵛ: ". . . Christiani Iudaeos suis telis confodiant."
144. See Graetz, *Dibrē Ymē Israel*, VII, 262.
145. See Secret, "Les Dominicains," 328.
146. On this condemnation see Amram, *Censorship*, 328. The Inquisition had, in fact, approved the 1558 Mantua edition of the *Zohar* (*ibid.*, 328). The 1562 condemnation surely reflects a change of mind on the part of the Inquisition about the "truth" of the *Zohar's* contents. Indeed, the rabbinical synod which met at Padua in 1554 had debated whether the Church would condemn the Kabbalah as blasphemy or urge, even decree, its publication and teaching as beneficial to conversionary activity. See

I. Sonne, ed., *Mi-Pavolo ha-Revi'i 'ad Pius ha-Hamishi* (Jerus., 1954), 123–25, and S. Assaf, *Texts and Studies in Jewish History* (Jerus., 1946), 236–46.

147. *Bibliotheca Sancta,* 110ᵛ: "Est [autem Kabala] secretior divinae legis expositio, ex ore Dei a Moyse recepta, et ex ore Moysis a patribus per continuas successiones non quidem scripto, sed viva voce suscepta ... quae rursum nos ducat a terrenis ad coelestia."

148. Cf. discussion above.

149. Cf. discussion above.

150. Cf. discussion above.

151. See Reusch, *Der Index,* I, 49.

152. Cf. discussion above. Masius' letter was written on Dec. 24, 1553, and the bull was issued May 29, 1554.

153. See Amram, *Makers of Hebrew Books,* 263.

154. It is not improper to assume that Pius IV's 1564 decision to allow the circulation of an expurgated Talmud was based on similar reasoning.

155. On sixteenth-century censorship in general, see Dejob, *De L'influence,* 144–50, 153 ff.

156. Cf. discussion above.

157. For detailed discussions of the censorship of Hebrew books, see Popper, *Censorship,* 56–65, Reusch, *Der Index,* I, 50–51, and Sacerdote, "Deux Index," *passim.*

158. Popper, *Censorship,* 58 f., and Sacerdote, "Deux Index," 259, 262.

159. On this manual see Sacerdote, 271–72.

160. See Reusch, *Der Index,* I, 50. For a detailed analysis of both the events leading up to the publication of this edition and also of the appearance and quality of the printing itself, see J. and B. Priis, *Die Basler Hebräischen Drucke,* 1492–1866 (Olten und Freiburg im Br., 1964), p. 175–212, esp. p. 177–186, and also p. 175 for a bibliography of the various writings which discuss this event. Cf. also A. Nordmann, "Geschichte der Juden in Basel," *Basler Zeitschrift für Geschichte und Altertumskunde,* 13 (1914), p. 27–32.

161. See Reusch, *Die Indices,* 279.

162. Popper, *Censorship,* 56. Popper, in fact, seems to go so far as to suggest that the idea to print the Talmud in 1578 had a Christian origin.

163. See *Ibid.,* 56–60, for a discussion, with examples, of censored passages and of passages given Christian interpretations.

IV

THE JEWISH RESPONSE

15

At the Crossroads: Tannaitic Perspectives on the Jewish-Christian Schism

Lawrence H. Schiffman

INTRODUCTION

The purpose of this study is to determine why it is that Judaism, after tolerating sectarianism and schism for the entire length of the Second Temple period,[1] elected to regard Christianity as another religion entirely. This study will concentrate on the attitude of Judaism in the pre-Christian and early Christian periods to Jewish identity and the nascent Christian Church. It will seek to understand why Christianity was not simply regarded as one of the sects, and why, when, and how Judaism sought to dissociate itself fully from Christianity.

The research presented here will be largely based on tannaitic evidence for two reasons. First, by the time Judaism and Christianity made their final break, it was the tannaitic tradition which was almost completely representative of the Jewish community in Palestine and that segment of the Diaspora which remained loyal to its ancestral faith. Second, the evidence available does not indicate any differences of opinion regarding Jewish status between the various sects of the Second Commonwealth and later tannaitic traditions.[2] This is not to be dismissed as an argument from silence. In almost all aspects of halakah

Reprinted in part by permission of Augsburg Fortress Publishers from *Jewish and Christian Self-Definition,* vol. 2, ed. E. P. Sanders, Philadelphia, 191, 115–17, 138–56. Copyright © 1981 Fortress Press, Philadelphia. This chapter has been expanded into a book-length study by Lawrence H. Schiffman entitled *Who Was a Jew? Rabbinic and Halakhic Perspectives on the Jewish Christian Schism,* Ktav Publishing House, Hoboken, 1985.

known from both Second Commonwealth and tannaitic sources, variations and differences of opinion do exist.

It can be argued that it is purely by coincidence that disagreèments regarding the subject of Jewish identity did not come down to us. It is most likely, however, that there were none. Indeed, contention regarding the very notions of who was a Jew and who a Gentile would have been of such great importance as to figure prominently in the sources. Further, nothing could have served as a more forceful polemic than to accuse opposing sects of not being Jewish. Yet despite all the sectarian animus found in various texts from or about the Second Commonwealth period,[3] even the most virulent never accuse the members of other groups of having left the Jewish community. Sinners they were, but Jews all the same.[4]

What then caused the Jews of the tannaitic period to reject the Christians? Let us examine how the Jews viewed their own identity and how they evaluated Christianity and the Christians within this framework. (Beyond our concern will be the attitude of the Christians to Judaism and the self-definition of the early Christian communities.)

The causes of the Jewish-Christian schism may be classified in two categories—doctrinal and socio-historical. In Judaism the doctrinal factors are expressed through the halakah, the Jewish legal system. Therefore, it will be necessary to understand the halakic definitions of the born Jew and the convert. Some knowledge of the tannaitic legal view of heresy will also be important. The traditions to be examined must also be dated as precisely as possible to be certain that they do, in fact, form part of the background for the parting of Judaism and Christianity.

The socio-historical factors are the result of the evolution of Judaism and Christianity in this period. Specifically, the Jewish attitude towards Christianity was influenced greatly by the changes that took place in the emerging church during the first two centuries of this era. Only by considering these changes will it be possible to understand why Jewish self-definition led the Jews to regard Christians first as heretics and later as members of a separate and distinct religious community.

It is in the nature of all societies and groups that certain formal or informal regulations exist regarding membership in the group and the behaviour of the members. Religious groups, in addition to adherence to their codes of behaviour and belief, also make additional requirements for membership or rites of initiation. These procedures may differ depending on whether the member stands in hereditary relationship to other members or whether he is an entirely new member, usually termed a convert. The requirements for membership or entry into religious groups would have no significance if they were only arbitrary or accidental. But we know them to reflect the perceptions of the group about its own identity and nature. We can, therefore, learn a great deal about a religious group from the study of its regulations for membership or conversion. We can understand how the group characterizes itself and its relationship to the society within which it functions. Conversely, we can compare the perceptions of the society at large to the group's requirements and regulations. Is the group's image of itself consistent or inconsistent with that of outsiders, and what do outsiders consider the basic character of the religious group?

Within this framework the following study will seek to determine what the requirements were for hereditary membership in the tannaitic Jewish community, and how one could enter the Jewish people as a convert. From these regulations we shall see what the rabbis regarded as the essence of Judaism and Jewish identity. The history of the legal practices we encounter will be examined to see how far back the tannaitic approach can be traced.

Most important is the establishment of the halakic definitions of a Jew which existed in the period in which Christianity developed. After we consider how one may enter the Jewish people, we shall ask whether it is possible to leave or to be expelled from the polity of Israel. We shall see that a Jew continued to be regarded as a Jew by the Tannaim even if he espoused Christianity. The Tannaim, however, did impose legal sanctions upon the early Jewish Christians whom they regarded as transgressors, but Jews nevertheless. Eventually, as the Christians turned further and further away from the halakic definition of a Jew, the tannaitic sources portray a progressive exclusion of the Christians. It is, therefore, the halakah which ultimately determined the expulsion of the Christians from the Jewish community.[5][. . .]

CONVERSION TO JUDAISM

[. . .] Judaism is centred on the Jewish people, a group whose membership is fundamentally determined by heredity. If one is not born a Jew, how can one become a Jew? Here the halakah demands the maximum of commitment, for the convert is literally changing his heredity. He will pass on to his children descent which he did not inherit but rather acquired. For this reason, he must go through an extensive process to acquire fully the main characteristics of what Jewishness is.

He must be committed to the acceptance of the Torah. He himself must stand at Sinai, for Sinai was the formative event in the Jewish historical experience. There he, like the people of ancient Israel, must accept not only the laws of the Torah, but also the rabbinic interpretation or oral Law which, according to the Tannaim, was given at Sinai as well.

He must also identify with the entire historic experience of the Jews. He must understand that his fate is now linked with his new co-religionists, for he has literally switched his heredity to become a part of the Jewish people. He must at the same time acquire the characteristic of charity and kindness which Jews have been proud to maintain.

The male convert must be circumcised, for this is considered the ultimate sign of Jewish identity and of the covenant in which he is now enrolling. Even more important, he is to become a descendant of Abraham, and the Torah has commanded that Abraham's descendants be circumcised.

He must purify himself in a ritual bath, for the Jewish people saw itself, from its earliest origins, as striving to live a life of purity and holiness.

Finally, he must bring a sacrifice, an act which receives the assent of God, for without God's favour and acceptance, no Jew could sustain himself. In bringing the sacrifice, he shows that he is ready to draw near to the divine presence and to come under its wings as a full member of the people of Israel.

HERETICS AND APOSTATES

Thus far the definitions of the born Jew and the convert have been established for the period immediately preceding and contemporaneous with the rise of Christianity. What must be asked now is whether anyone can be excluded from the Jewish people and lose his Jewish status as a result of any beliefs or actions. Indeed, it will be shown conclusively that this cannot occur and that only the criteria described above could serve to indicate who was or was not a Jew in the early centuries of this era.

A word of definition is in order. A heretic in one whose *beliefs* do not accord with those of the established religion to which he claims adherence. An apostate is one whose *actions* are not consonant with the standards of behaviour set by his religious group. We shall have to treat these separately as they involve different halakic categories.

In this context, it would be wise to remember that tannaitic Judaism and, indeed, biblical Judaism are primarily a religion of action rather than belief. Only a small number of beliefs have ever been seen as mandatory in Jewish life, and when compared with the requirements of action and behaviour, it is easy to see that the primary emphasis of Judaism is on the fulfillment of commandments and not on faith.

The starting point for any discussion of heresy in tannaitic Judaism must be the *locus classicus* of mSanh 10.1:[6]

The following[7] are those who do not have a portion[8] in the world to come:[9] the one who says there is no resurrection of the dead,[10] [the one who says] the Torah is not from Heaven, and the *'apiqoros*.[11]

It is this passage which has served as the basis of most claims that Judaism has a creed.[12] This mishnah effectively suggests that those who hold certain beliefs are excluded from the world to come, and that opposite beliefs are normative and required.[13] We shall investigate the specific offences mentioned and show that exclusion from a portion in the world to come does not imply expulsion from the Jewish people.

The case of one who does not believe in the world to come is explained in a baraita in bSanh 90a:[14]

[A Tanna] taught: He denied resurrection of the dead. Therefore, he will not have a portion in the resurrection of the dead.[15] For all the retributions of the Holy One, blessed be He, are measure for measure. . . .[16]

This baraita is noteworthy in that it indicates that the Tannaim understood the phrase 'world to come' as it appears in our mishnah to refer to the period after the resurrection of the dead. For this reason, the baraita substituted the term 'resurrection of the dead' for 'world to come' in recapitulating the content of the mishnah. From mSanh 10.3 we learn that after resurrection there will be divine judgment followed by the world to come. The baraita explains that since the person in question denied the existence of the resurrection of the dead, he will be denied the right to be resurrected. Accordingly, he will not attain a portion in the world to come.

The mishnah is most probably directed against the Sadducees, who, Josephus tells us, did not accept either the immortality of the soul or the idea of reward and punishment after death.[17] Indeed, both of these doctrines are inextricably connected with the doctrine of resurrection as mentioned in our mishnah, and the Pharisees saw resurrection as a prelude to the world to come. Our mishnah states that those Sadducees, who deny resurrection of the dead, would therefore have no share in the world to come.[18]

The second class of non-believers are those who deny the heavenly or divine origin of the Torah. It might be tempting to view the Torah here as a reference to *torah she-be-ʿal peh,* the oral Law, which the Tannaim believed was given to Moses on Sinai along with the written Torah. (Indeed, this meaning might perhaps be attributed as well to the statement of mAbot 1.1 that 'Moses received the Torah from Sinai'.) Unfortunately, we cannot date the use of the term 'oral Law' any earlier than the Yavnean period.[19] Since, as will be shown below, it is likely that this mishnah predates the destruction of the temple, the term 'torah' here is probably limited in meaning to the written law.[20] The person described by our mishnah, therefore, denies the prophetic character of Moses and, in effect, asserts that Moses himself was the author of the Pentateuch.

It is known from Graeco-Roman sources that some classical authors attacked the Torah, claiming that Moses had made it up and formulated divine authorship only in order to assure observance of its laws. Indeed, from Philo of Alexandria and from some much later midrashic sources it seems that some Jews came to believe the same thing.[21] In fact, it is probable that those who wished to substitute the constitution of the Greek *polis* for that of the Torah in Hellenistic Jerusalem did so out of belief that both were man-made, whereas the *polis* offered greater possibilities for advancement, both economic and political.[22] It is most likely that our mishnah is directed against those who, perhaps under Hellenistic influence, have come to deny the divine origin of the Torah. They, therefore, are a class who will not share in the world to come.

How did the rabbis arrive at such a conclusion? The case of the denial of resurrection was understood by the Tannaim as based on the doctrine of equivalent recompense ('measure for measure'). The same doctrine must have motivated the rabbis here. The promise of ultimate bliss in the world to come after resurrection and divine judgment is meant as a reward for observance of the commandments. For Jews this means observance of all the commandments of the Torah. For non-Jews it is sufficient to observe the Noachian laws. Only one who accepts the premise on which the entire system of the commandments is based, the divine origin of the Law, can be worthy of receiving the reward which the life of Torah is meant to assure. Hence, he who denies the divine character of the Law cannot reap its rewards.

The third class excluded for reasons of belief from the world to come is the *'apiqoros*. There can be no question but that this word is derived from Greek *Epikouros*,[23] the name of the famous Greek philosopher (342/1–270 BCE). The only question is whether this term signifies a follower of this philosopher or if it has somehow become a more general term for a heretic. The talmudic definitions of this word,[24] which are based on a Semitic derivation,[25] are amoraic and clearly do not reflect the actual tannaitic usage.

Josephus mentions Epicureans in his discussion of the book of Daniel.[26] There he says that Daniel's correct prophecies show that the Epicureans who deny providence and assert that the world is without a 'ruler and provider'[27] are in error. In other words, to Josephus the Epicurean is one who denies God and his role in the world. It can be assumed that Josephus is using the term 'Epicurean' in the way it was understood by the people of his day. The chronological proximity of the mishnah under discussion to the works of Josephus would lead us to the conclusion that the meaning of *'apiqoros* in our mishnah is this: one who denies God's involvement in the affairs of men and the world.

Why did the *'apiqoros* lose his portion? Indeed, he denied the very basis of the resurrection, divine judgment, and the world to come. For he denied the role of God, even the concern of God, for the affairs of mankind. Hence, he was unworthy to share in the blessings which God had stored up for mankind in the end of days. Again we find the principle of 'measure for measure'.

Against whom were the rabbis polemicizing when they excluded the *'apiqoros* from the world to come? According to Josephus[28] the very same beliefs ascribed to the *'apiqoros* were held by the Sadducees. Now it must again be remembered that Josephus wrote at a time not so far from the composition of this mishnaic statement, and so his descriptions of the Sadducees may be taken as accurate for the last days of the temple. Of course, one must never forget the tendency of Josephus to picture the sects as if they were Greek philosophic schools.[29] Nevertheless, Josephus does testify to an affinity between the views of the Sadducees and the Epicureanism of the very same period. If so, it is safe to conclude that the *'apiqoros* of our mishnah was often a member of the Sadducean group.

If so, we have found that this mishnah describes three forms of heresy, two of which are attributed by Josephus to the Sadducees. Indeed, we must conclude that this mishnah is Pharisaic in origin and polemicized against the Sadducees and certain Hellenized Jews. At the same time, anyone holding these views, regardless of his affiliation with one of the prevalent groups of the Second Temple period, was considered to have lost his portion in the world to come.

Can the statement under discussion be dated?[30] We have omitted from discussion so far the second part of this mishnah in which R. Akiba and Abba Saul add to the list several heterodox *practices* (as opposed to beliefs dealt with in the anonymous first half of the mishnah) which also exclude the transgressor from the world to come.

The qualitative difference between the offences of creed listed in the first anonymous part of the mishnah and the offences of practice listed in the sections attributed to R. Akiba and Abba Saul would tend to support the idea that the original teaching was composed at a time when issues of belief were central, whereas the Yavnean period (the time of R. Akiba and Abba Saul) was one in which there was an attempt to strengthen and standardize practice in order to close ranks and to ensure the survival of Judaism in the aftermath of the destruction of the nation and its temple.[31]

Further, we have seen that the heresies catalogued by this mishnah can all be attributed to or connected with the Sadducees or the Hellenized Jews. It is therefore most probable that the anonymous first clause of the mishnah was composed before the destruction of the temple while Sadduceeism and Hellenism were still issues for the Pharisaic leaders. After all, the Sadducees were to disappear soon after the destruction with the removal of their power base, the central sanctuary in Jerusalem.

Can it be determined from the material presented thus far whether loss of one's portion in the world to come implies also loss of one's status in the Jewish people, or whether the status of a Jew is inviolable regardless of his beliefs? One thing is certain. No intrinsic link can be claimed between Jewish status and the possession of a portion in the world to come. MSanh 10.3, for example, indicates that the men of

Sodom have no portion in the world to come. If a portion in the world to come went hand in hand with Jewish status, why even mention the men of Sodom? Indeed, tSanh 13.2 contains a tannaitic debate about whether the righteous of the nations of the world can have a portion in the world to come. Again, the question of Jewish status and that of a portion in the world to come are separate issues. The fact that certain heretics or non-believers are excluded from the world to come in no way implies expulsion from the Jewish people.

Thus far the offences which disqualified a person from a portion in the world to come were doctrinal. The Tosefta, however, adds several offences of commission. The context is a statement attributed to the House of Shammai in which three classes are delineated: those righteous receiving immediate reward, the average people who will be punished and then receive their reward, and the worst offenders who will be consigned permanently to purgatory. TSanh 12.5 concerns this last group: [32]

But as to the heretics [minim],[33] the apostates [meshummadim], the informers, the 'apiqorsin, those who denied the Torah, those who separated from the ways of the community,[34] those who denied the resurrection of the dead, and everyone who transgressed and caused the public to transgress . . . ,[35] Gehenna[36] is shut in their faces [or 'before them'], and they are punished in its [Gehenna] for ever and ever.

It is easy to see that this passage represents an expansion of the list found in the Mishnah, adding certain offenders whose transgressions had such major consequences as to cause the loss of their portion in the world to come and to bring upon them eternal punishment.

Minim in this context means early Christians. This term as well as the halakic status of this group will be treated in detail below.

While the role of informers in talmudic literature is in need of a thorough study, at least it can be observed that these were people who denounced Jews who practised rituals forbidden during the Hadrianic persecutions and perhaps at other times as well.[37] Such denunciations were extremely dangerous to the Jewish community. For this reason, potential informers were threatened with loss of their share in the world to come in order to deter them from committing this offence.

The term meshummad[38] is usually translated as 'apostate'. While this English word denotes one who forsakes his religion, the Hebrew term meshummad is more complex. Literally, it means one who has been destroyed. We shall see that it refers to one who ignores the commands of the Torah and the demands of Jewish law. According to Lieberman,[39] the term originally referred to those forced to worship idols and only later came to refer to those who committed offences of their own free will. In any case, this wider meaning is already represented in the tannaitic sources before us.

The distinction between the *meshummad le-te'avon,* one who apostasizes for desire of forbidden pleasures, and the *meshummad le-hak'is,* one who does so out of spite, in an amoraic distinction which will not be relevant to this study. This distinction was developed as a response to the ambivalent attitude of tannaitic halakah towards the apostate. This ambivalence was resolved in amoraic times by the assumption that there were two different types of *meshummad.*

Only two tannaitic passages can be presented in an attempt to reach a more exact definition of the *meshummad.* An anonymous baraita in bHor 11a attempts to define which commandments are such that their violation labels the offender a *meshummad:* [40]

Our rabbis taught: If one ate forbidden fat, he is a *meshummad.* And who is a *meshummad?* one who ate[41] animals not ritually slaughtered or afflicted with fatal diseases,[42] forbidden animals and reptiles,[43] or who drank the wine of (idolatrous) libation. R. Jose son of R. Judah[44] says: even one who wears a garment of wool and linen.[45]

This baraita represents the conflation of two sections. The first was an anonymous baraita indicating that one who ate forbidden fat was a *meshummad.* The second asked the question of who was a *meshummad* and answered that one who ate certain forbidden foods fell into this category.[46] To this anonymous definition was added a dictum in the name of R. Jose b. R. Judah to the effect that the wearing of *sha'atnez,* a garment of mixed wool and linen, also qualified the offender as a *meshummad.*

R. Jose b. Judah was a late Tanna, a contemporary of R. Judah the Prince. We have no way of asserting that even the anonymous parts of the baraita are earlier than the last days of the tannaitic period, although no evidence against an early date can be marshalled either.

This definition of a *meshummad* is clearly halakic in character and presents the *meshummad* as one who violated certain dietary restrictions. Indeed, even one who wears mixed linen and wool, in the view of one late Tanna, is a member of this class.

A more general definition is found in a *midrash halakah* based on Lev. 1.2. The version in the Sifra is as follows: [47]

[Speak to the children of Israel and say to them: When any of you presents an offering of cattle for the Lord. . . .] Any: To include the proselytes. Of you: to exclude the *meshummadim*. The text [of the Torah] says children of Israel: Just as Israel are those who have accepted the covenant, so also the proselytes are those who have accepted the covenant. But the *meshummadim* are excluded since they do not accept the covenant.[48] For indeed, they have declared the covenant void. . . .

This statement sees the *meshummad* as the opposite of the proselyte. While the proselyte has undergone acceptance of the Torah as part of the conversion process, the *meshummad* has denied that very covenant, as is evidenced by his actions.

BHull 5a contains a version of this halakic exegesis which is more expansive: [49]

Of you:[50] Not all of you, excluding the *meshummad*. Of you: Among you [Israel] have I made a distinction, but not among the nations. Of cattle: to include people who are likened[51] to cattle. From this they said,[52] it is permitted to receive sacrifices from the transgressors of Israel in order that through them they may come to repent, except from the *meshummad* or one who pours [idolatrous] libations, or violates the Sabbath in public.

Now this midrash halakah is germane to the central issue: Is the *meshummad* considered part of the people of Israel? The midrash answers in the affirmative. Whereas all non-Jews (including idolaters) may send voluntary offerings to be sacrificed in the Jerusalem temple, this right is denied to certain Jews, namely to those who have apostasized to the extent of performing idolatrous worship or violating the Sabbath in public. These *meshummadim* are, therefore, still Jews, for if they were excluded from the Jewish people, their offerings *would* be acceptable. Indeed, this principle is seen by the Tannaim as derived from the Torah itself. There can be no question, therefore, that the *meshummad,* like the heretic and the *'apiqoros,* is never deprived of his Jewish status.[53] Nevertheless, there is a legal disability under which he lives as a consequence of his actions.

TANNAITIC JUDAISM AND THE EARLY CHRISTIANS

It is time to pause to consider the implication for the Jewish-Christian schism of the tannaitic sources studied thus far. The halakic definitions of a Jew in the pre-Christian era have been established: ancestry through the mother or conversion including circumcision for males, immersion, acceptance of the Torah, and sacrifice. These continued to be the only possible ways to enter the Jewish people in the period in which Christianity came to the fore. Further, it was determined that the Tannaim did not view heresy or apostasy in and of itself as negating the offenders' status as a Jew. Indeed, Jewish status could never be cancelled, even for the most heinous offences against Jewish law and doctrine. It is against this background that the tannaitic reaction to the rise of Christianity must be viewed.

As far as the Tannaim were concerned, when Christianity began, it must have appeared simply as a group of Jews, otherwise generally conforming to the norms of the Jewish populace of Judaea, who had come to believe that the Messiah had come in the person of Jesus. As long as the new group preached its gospel primarily among Jews, this view continued to be held by the Tannaim.

While our sources point to general adherence to Jewish law by the earliest Christians in Judaea, we must also remember that some deviation from the norms of the Tannaim must have occurred already at the earliest period. Indeed, the sayings attributed by the gospels to Jesus would lead us to believe that he may have taken a view of the halakah different from that of the Pharisees. Nevertheless, taking into account the halakic material discussed thus far, the Tannaim did not see the earliest Christians as constituting a separate religious community. After all, there was no sin in making the error (as it was to the Tannaim) of believing someone to be the Messiah.[54] In regard to the other deviations that must have occurred, Judaism had long been accustomed to tolerating both differences of opinion and deviation from the norms of observance by its members.

The Pharisees presumably regarded Jesus as yet another false Messiah of a type which was not so unusual in the last days of the Second Temple. Indeed the existence of all kinds of sects and religious leaders was the norm of the day in the Second Temple period as we know from so many sources. Judaism was in what we might call an experimental stage. The biblical tradition was being adapted in many different ways in an unconscious effort to see which approach would best ensure the future of Judaism and of the Jewish people. For this reason, little opposition to the very concept of sectarian divergence existed. Each group argued for its own primacy and superiority, yet no voice called for the unity of the people as a virtue in and of itself. It was in such a context that Christianity arose. It was seen by the Tannaim in its earliest stages as no greater a threat than any other sect, and the halakic regulations discussed above determined the identity of the early Christians as Jews.

This situation changed with the destruction of the temple. Divisions within the people, after all, had made the orderly prosecution of the war against the Romans and the defence of the Holy City impossible.[55] The temple had fallen as a result. Only in unity could the people and the land be rebuilt. It was only a question of which of these sects would unify the populace.

For all intents and purposes the Pharisees were the only sect to survive the destruction. The smaller sects were either scattered or destroyed. The Sadducees had been deprived of the temple, their base of power and authority. Disturbance of the social and economic order wrought by the war deprived the Sadducees of their previous status. This was clearly the time for the entire nation to unite behind the Tannaim, the inheritors of the Pharisaic approach to Judaism. For Pharisaism, with its flexibility in adapting the halakah to new circumstances, would be best fit to deal with the new realities after the unsuccessful revolt and the destruction of the temple.

But where would the Christians fit into this newly constituted Jewish community? The evidence indicates that the Christians, although still Jewish, had only moderate success in winning converts among the Jews of Palestine.[56] At the same time, the nascent church turned more and more to Gentiles as prospective converts.[57] Undoubtedly, some of the new converts were Hellenistic Jews for whom the new religion seemed but a variety of Judaism. On the other hand, the vast majority of the new Christians consisted of Gentiles and the former semi-proselytes.

Of the vast numbers of Graeco-Roman non-Jews who were attracted to Christianity, only a small number ever became Jewish Christians. The new Christianity was primarily Gentile, for it did not require its adherents to become circumcised and convert to Judaism or to observe the Law. Yet at the same time, Christianity in the Holy Land was still strongly Jewish.[58]

While the destruction of the temple was drawing near, the differences between Judaism and Christianity were widening. By the time the temple was destroyed, the Jewish Christians were a minority among the total number of Christians, and it was becoming clear that the future of the new religion would be dominated by Gentile Christians. Nevertheless, the Tannaim came into contact primarily with Jewish Christians, and so continued to regard the Christians as Jews who had gone astray by believing in Jesus.

A new set of circumstances confronted the tannaitic leadership when it reassembled at Yavneh after the war was lost. By this time, the need to close ranks and to face the future as a united community was greater than ever. We shall see, though, that the rabbis still did not elect to see the Jewish Christians as a separate religion. After all, they still met the halakic criteria of Judaism. Instead action would be taken to bar them from officiating as precentors in the synagogue in order to make them feel unwanted there and to exclude their books from sanctified status. Tannaitic law would eventually have to face the Gentile Christians, but the rabbis as yet had little opportunity for contact with them.

JEWISH CHRISTIANS IN TANNAITIC HALAKAH

While our sources show no attempt on the part of the Tannaim to read anyone out of the Jewish people on account of heretical beliefs, the rabbis did impose certain restrictions on those whom they regarded as standing outside the accepted system of Jewish belief. Such heretics who were subjected to legal restrictions are termed *minim*.

While this term itself has been a major scholarly problem, it is now agreed that it was a general term for heretics, applied at various times in the rabbinic period to different groups which presented doctrinal challenges to rabbinic Judaism while remaining from an halakic point of view within the fold.[59] A number of tannaitic restrictions directed against *minim* clearly refer to the early Jewish Christians, as can be shown from their content and date.[60] These regulations show how the rabbis attempted to combat those beliefs they regarded as outside the Jewish pale while never rejecting the Jewishness of those who held them.

The primary area in which the Tannaim imposed restrictions on the Jewish Christians was in regard to the synagogue. The *birkat ha-minim,* the benediction against the heretics, was directed at excluding such people from serving as precentor in the synagogue.[61] Indeed, this restriction probably went a long way toward making the Jewish Christians feel unwelcome in the synagogues and causing them to worship separately.

A baraita in bBer 28bf. states:[62]

Our rabbis taught: Simeon Ha-Faqoli ordered[63] the Eighteen Benedictions[64] before Rabban Gamaliel in Yavneh.[65] Rabban Gamaliel said to the sages: Is there no one who knows how to compose a benediction against the *minim*?[66] Samuel Ha-Qatan stood up[67] and composed it. Another year [while serving as precentor], he [Samuel Ha-Qatan] forgot it[68] and tried to recall it[69] for two[70] or three hours, yet they did not remove him.[71]

Despite some ingenious claims to the contrary,[72] the Gamaliel of our baraita is Rabban Gamaliel II of Yavneh in the post-destruction period. Simeon Ha-Faqoli set the Eighteen Benedictions in order before Rabban Gamaliel as part of the general effort at Yavneh to fix halakah. Rabban Gamaliel asked for a volunteer to compose the benediction against the *minim*. Samuel Ha-Qatan stood up and adapted a previously existing benediction to include the *minim*.[73] In another year, he was called upon to serve as precentor. In the course of the service, he was unable to recite the benediction against *minim*. Nevertheless, even after he spent several hours trying to recall it, the rabbis did not remove him as precentor.

BBer 29a asks why he was not removed. After all, it was the purposes of this blessing to ensure that the precentor was not one of those heretics cursed in the benediction.[74] The Talmud answers that since Samuel Ha-Qatan had himself composed it, it could be assumed that he was not a *min*.

For many years there has been debate about the identity of the *minim*. Most recent opinion sees the term *min* as referring at different times to various forms of heresy that threatened rabbinic Judaism in talmudic times. It is therefore essential to clarify who the *minim* of this benediction are. Palestinian texts of the Eighteen Benedictions from the Cairo Genizah present us with a text of the benediction which elucidates the identification of the *minim*:[75]

For the apostates may there be no hope unless they return to your Torah. As for the Christians and the *minim*, may they perish immediately. Speedily may they be erased from the Book of Life and may they not be registered among the righteous. Blessed are You, O Lord, Who subdue the wicked.

While other specimens of the Palestinian liturgy show slight variation, the Christians and *minim* are always included in this benediction. Some may wish to debate whether the Christians and *minim* here mentioned are to be taken as one group or two. Yet the fact remains that the Christians were included with other apostates and heretics in the Genizah documents.

May we assume that this version of the benediction represents the text as it was recited before the sages of Yavneh? On the one hand, the Palestinian liturgical material found in the Cairo Genizah generally preserves the traditions of Palestinian Jewry in the amoraic period. On the other hand, there is external evidence that this benediction was recited during the tannaitic period and that it included explicit reference to Christians.

Three passages in the gospel of John (9.22; 12.42; 16.2) mention the expulsion of Christians from the synagogue. This expulsion may have been the result of the institution of the benediction against *minim*. Justin Martyr, writing in the middle of the second century CE, says in his *Dialogue with Trypho*, 'You, the Jews, curse the Christians in your synagogues. . . .' Similar testimony comes from Origen (c. 185–c. 254). Epiphanius (c. 315–403) says of the Jews that they curse the Christians three times daily in their prayers. Further evidence is preserved by Jerome (c. 340–420).[76]

This curse could only be found in the Eighteen Benedictions since it would be the only thrice-daily recitation in the synagogue services. If Justin Martyr was referring to this benediction, then we would have confirmation from the mid-second century that the Christians were specifically mentioned in this prayer. Further, while the version before us differentiates *minim* and Christians, it should be remembered that many rabbinic texts speak of the *minim* and clearly designate believers in Jesus. It is most likely, however, that our benediction meant to distinguish Jewish Christians from Gentile Christians, and that the *minim* were Jewish Christians while the *noẓᵉrim* ('Christians') were Gentile Christians.

If this last interpretation is correct, it is possible to trace the development of this benediction. The original threat to Judaism was from Jewish Christianity, and so a benediction against the *minim* (a general term here referring to Jewish Christians) was instituted. At some later date, perhaps by 150 CE but definitely by 350 CE, as the fate of Christianity as a Gentile religion was sealed, the mention of Gentile Christians was added as well to the prayer.

The specific function of the benediction was to ensure that those who were *minim* would not serve as precentors in the synagogue. After all, no one would be willing to pray for his own destruction. It was assumed that the institution of such a benediction would lead ultimately to the exclusion of the *minim* from the synagogue. Such a benediction in its original form can only have been directed against Jews who despite their heretical beliefs were likely to be found in the synagogue. Gentile Christians would not have been in the synagogue or called upon to serve as precentor.

When the separation of the Jewish Christians from the synagogue was accomplished, the prayer was retained as a general malediction and prayer for the destruction of the enemies of Israel. Therefore, the *noṣerim* were also added.

That such a development actually took place in the benediction is clear from the church Fathers.[77] Only in Epiphanius (c. 315–403) and Jerome (c. 340–420) do we find explicit mention of the *noẓᵉrim* in the Graecized form *Nazōraioi* and the Latinized *Nazaraei*. This is because the *noṣerim* were added to the benediction after the time of Justin and Origen, whose accounts of the benediction make no mention of this specific term. By this time, the Roman empire (now Christian) had imposed various anti-Jewish measures. It was only natural to add explicit mention of the Gentile Christians to this prayer.

It cannot be overemphasized that while the benediction against the *minim* sought to exclude Jewish Christians from active participation in the synagogue service, it in no way implied expulsion from the Jewish people. In fact, heresy, no matter how great, was never seen as cutting the heretic's tie to Judaism. Not even outright apostasy could overpower the halakic criteria for Jewish identification which were outlined above.[78] When the method of excommunication was used to separate heretics from the Jewish community in the Middle Ages,[79] even this measure, which was to a great extent a medieval halakic development, did not in any way cancel the Jewish status of the excommunicant. Indeed, regardless of the transgression of a Jew, he was a Jew under any and all circumstances, even though his rights within the halakah might be limited as a result of his actions.

While the benediction against the *minim* was certainly the most important step taken by the Tannaim to combat Jewish Christianity, they also took steps to emphasize that the Christian scriptures were not holy.[80] First, the Jewish Christians themselves wrote scrolls of the Bible (*sifre minim*). The question here was the sanctity of the entire text.

Second, beginning in the second half of the first century, early recensions of the gospels and epistles began to circulate. The sanctity of those sections of these Christian texts which quoted the Hebrew scriptures directly had also to be determined. In view of the role of the gospels and epistles as a vehicle for spreading Christianity, it is easy to understand why the rabbis went out of their way to divest them of sanctity and halakic status.

TShab 13 (14).5 deals with these texts:[81]

We do not save from a fire[82] [on the Sabbath] the gospels[83] and the books of the *minim* [heretics]. Rather, they are burned in their place, they and their Tetragrammata. R. Jose ha-Gelili says: During the week, one should cut out their Tetragrammata and hide them away and burn the remainder. Said R. Tarfon: May I bury my sons![84] If [these books] would come into my hand, I would burn them along with their Tetragrammata. For even if a pursuer[85] were running after me, I would enter a house[86] of idolatry rather than enter their [the Jewish Christians'] houses. For the idolaters do not know Him and deny Him,[87] but these [Jewish Christians] know Him and deny Him. . . . Said R. Ishmael: If in order to bring peace between a husband and his wife, the Ever-present has commanded[88] that a book which has been written in holiness be erased by means of water, how much more so should the books of the *minim* which bring enmity between Israel and their Father Who is in Heaven be erased, they and their Tetragrammata. . . . Just as we do not save them from a fire, so we do not save them from a cave-in nor from water nor from anything which would destroy them.

The passage contains no disagreement regarding what to do if the gospels or other books of the *minim* (texts of the Hebrew scriptures) are caught in a fire on the Sabbath. These books are not to be saved, since they have no sanctity. There is, however, debate regarding what to do with such texts during the week. R. Jose ha-Gelili suggests removing the Tetragrammata and burning the rest. Apparently, he feels that regardless of who wrote it, the Tetragrammaton retains its sanctity. R. Tarfon permits the burning of the texts with their divine names. R. Ishmael agrees with R. Tarfon and supports his view with an analogy to the bitter waters of the suspected adulteress. Further, R. Tarfon regards these Jewish Christians as worse than idolaters; for while a pagan might embrace the new faith, it was a great source of frustration that Jews, raised in the traditions of Judaism, would have done so as well.[89]

In regard to dating, the named authorities in the debate are all Yav-neans who flourished in the period leading up to the Bar Kokhba revolt. We see that the Jewish Christians were using Hebrew texts of the Bible and that already there were early recensions of the gospels in circulation. A decision, therefore, had to be rendered regarding their halakic status.

This Tosefta passage is indicative of the emerging view of the Tannaim. By this time, more and more Gentiles had joined the church, and the scriptures of the Christians had begun to be read in Palestine. The rabbis had to take a stand indicating the heretical nature of these texts in the early years of the first century.

Further reference to the very same texts appears in tYad 2.13:[90]

The gospels and the books of the *minim* ['heretics'] do not defile the hands. . . .

The 'defilement of the hands' was a sign of canonicity in tannaitic texts.[91] Books of the Bible which defiled the hands were holy scriptures. In spite of the appearance of verses from the Hebrew Bible in the gospels, this text indicates that they and even texts of the Hebrew Bible written by *minim* have absolutely no sanctity.

While there is no indication of date in this passage, it seems that it would emerge from the same period as the passage before. Indeed, in the years before the Bar Kokhba revolt, there was a need to accent the illegitimacy of Jewish Christianity. The two passages we have studied here indicate clearly that the transgressions of the *minim* were sufficient to render their texts of the Hebrew Bible unholy. The Tannaim sought in this way clearly to differentiate Christianity from Judaism, but they did not attempt to disavow the Jewishness of the *minim* at any time.

Apparently, then, the Tannaim still regarded the Jewish Christians they knew as Jews even as late as the end of the first century CE. Although by this time Gentile Christians constituted a majority of the believers in the new religion, the impact of this situation had not yet been felt in Palestine, where Jewish Christianity still predominated until the Bar Kokhba revolt.

THE FINAL BREAK

The years between 80 and 130 CE were for the Jewish community of Palestine years of reconstruction of the country and preparation for the Bar Kokhba revolt. Throughout this period Christianity kept growing, and simultaneously its Jewish element was being reduced. While in actual fact the juridical basis for the Gentile domination of Christianity was laid in the time of Paul,[92] the effect of these actions was not actually felt by the Tannaim until the early years of the second century.

By the time of the Bar Kokhba war (132–135 CE), Gentile Christianity had most probably still not taken over the Jerusalem church. As such, the Tannaim would still have seen Christianity as a form of Judaism. When Bar Kokhba began his revolution, in which he was definitely seen by some in a messianic role, the Jewish Christians refused to participate in the rebellion. After all, Jesus was their saviour, and so they could not unite to fight on behalf of another Messiah. Furthermore, they probably shared the view of the church Fathers that the destruction of Jerusalem and Judaea in the Great Revolt of 66–74 CE was a just punishment for the Jewish rejection of the messiahship of Jesus. As a result of this refusal to join in the revolt, Bar Kokhba attacked Jewish Christians and executed many.[93] Subsequently, the attacks of Bar Kokhba, the dislocation of the war, and other factors—some of which are still not clear—led to a large decrease in the number of Jewish Christians in Palestine,[94] and this at a time when the number of Gentile Christians in the Roman world was increasing rapidly.

But the Romans indirectly brought about the final break. When the city of Jerusalem was turned into Aelia Capitolina in the aftermath of the war, Jews, including Jewish Christians, were prohibited from entering the city.[95] Therefore, the newly re-established Jerusalem church was to be an essentially Gentile one. The Roman prohibition of circumcision, probably promulgated before the war but enforced immediately after it, must have discouraged conversion to Jewish Christianity even further. The Jewish Christians, then, dissipated into small sectarian groups, so that after the Bar Kokhba war Christianity was no longer Jewish but Gentile.[96] The rabbis ceased to be dealing with Jews who had gone astray but who fulfilled the halakic requirements of Jewish identity. They now confronted Gentiles who had converted to a religion which had rejected circumcision, Jewish proselytism and the requirements of life under the halakah. Only in this way had Christianity become a separate religion. It was now that the rabbis dealt with Christians as members of a different and hostile religious community.[97]

The ultimate parting of the ways for Judaism and Christianity took place when the adherents of Christianity no longer comformed to the halakic definitions of a Jew. From then on, Christians and Jews began a long history of inter-religious strife which played so tragic a part in medieval and modern history.

NOTES

The author is exceedingly grateful to Professor David Weiss Halivni for his careful reading of the paper and the suggestions he made regarding the rabbinic sources.

1. See my 'Jewish Sectarianism in Second Temple Times', in *Great Schisms in Jewish History* (ed. Jospe and Wagner), 1981, pp. 1–46.
2. For the views of Philo of Alexandria see S. Belkin, *Philo and the Oral Law*, 1940, pp. 44–8. While the evidence is not entirely conclusive, there is no reason to believe that Philo's full-fledged proselyte was any different from that of the Palestinian sages of his time.
3. Much of the material pertaining to the Qumran sect has been collected in C. Rabin, *Qumran Studies*, 1957, pp. 53–70.
4. On the Samaritan schism, see R. J. Coggins, *Samaritans and Jews*, 1975, and F. Dexinger "Das Garizimgebot im Dekalug der Samaritaner," *Studien zum Pentateuch*, 1977, pp. 111–33.
5. A similar conclusion is reached from the Christian sources by M. Smith, 'Early Christianity and Judaism', *Great Confrontations in Jewish History* (ed. Wagner and Breck), 1977, pp. 47–9. Smith writes, p. 48, '. . . the dispute between the Pharisees and the followers of Jesus . . . did not primarily or principally concern the question whether or not Jesus was the Messiah. On the contrary, the matter in dispute was the Christians' non-observance of the law.'
6. Translating MS Kaufmann. While some Mishnah texts begin with the clause stating that all Israel have a share in the world to come, it is clear from the omission of this clause in most manuscripts that it is secondary. We have therefore omitted it from discussion. See E. E. Urbach, *Hazal*, 1971, p. 588 n. 11 (ET, *The Sages* II, pp. 991–2). Finkelstein *(Mabo le-Massektot 'Abot ve- 'Abot de-Rabbi Natan*, 1950, pp. 104–7) takes the view that the original context of this clause and the entire mSanh 10.1 was the introduction to mAbot in its early form as a Pharisaic document. There is, however, simply no way of proving this ingenious theory.
7. Other texts read *'elu*. It might be objected that the *waw* of *ve-'elu* might indicate that it was preceded by the clause concerning the portion of all Israel (above, n. 6), the *vav* serving as the *vav* of contrast meaning 'but'. On the other hand, all the previous chapters begin with *ve-'elu*. Rather, we should see the *vav* here as functioning much like Arabic *fa*. Cf. D. Weiss Halivni, *Mekorot u-Mesorot, Mo'ed*, 1975 p. 526 n. 2**.

8. On *ḥeleq,* see Finkelstein, p. 221, who sees the usage here in a temporal rather than a spatial sense. He understands the word to mean 'future', or 'lot'.

9. On the world to come and its various definitions in rabbinic and medieval Judaism, see Finkelstein, pp. 213–21.

10. Words *min ha-Torah* are added in many texts. Nonetheless, they must be seen as a late addition (Finkelstein, p. 229). The addition was probably made under the influence of the many midrashim attempting to establish the basis of this concept in the Bible. The quotation of this mishnah in pPeah 1.1; 16b shows that this clause was not part of the original text.

11. Transliterated in accord with the vocalization of MS Kaufmann. Cf. E. Ben-Yehudah, *Millon Ha-Lashon Ha-ʿIvrit* I, 1959, p. 349 n. 1.

12. See A. Hyman, 'Maimonides' "Thirteen Principles" ', *Jewish Medieval and Renaissance Studies* (ed. Altmann), 1967, pp. 119–44. For a general bibliography on dogma and creed in Judaism, see Hyman, p. 120 n. 7.

13. The view expressed here is effectively a compromise between the two possibilities discussed in Hyman, 'Maimonides' "Thirteen Principles" ', pp. 112f. On the one hand, it is difficult to accept the view of Maimonides and Joseph Albo that one must affirm these beliefs to have a share in the world to come. On the other hand, Hyman's assumption that on the surface there is no relation between this mishnah and required belief is overstated, especially when one takes into consideration the tenuous relationship of the statement 'All Israel has a share in the world to come' to the rest of the mishnah.

14. Translating the Venice ed.

15. MS Munich here reads 'the world to come', but MS Florence accords with ed. Venice. R. N. Rabbinovicz, *Diqduqe Soferim,* ad loc., prefers the reading of the printed editions. Indeed, it seems that the version of MS Munich has substituted the interpretation for the text itself. Cf. *Ḥiddushe Rabbenu David Bonfil* (ed. Y. Lipshitz), 1966–67, p. 79, and (pseudo-)Ran, ad loc.

16. On the principle of 'measure for measure', see E. E. Urbach, *Ḥazal,* pp. 325f., 386f. (ET, *The Sages,* I, pp. 371f. and pp. 436ff.).

17. Josephus, *Bell.* II. 165. Cf. *Ant.* XVIII.16 and E. Schürer, *History,* § 26.1, ET II.ii, 1898, pp. 13f.; rev. ed., II, 1979, p. 391.

18. Finkelstein, *Mabo',* p. 228.

19. See J. Neusner, 'Rabbinic Traditions about the Pharisees before AD 70: The Problem of Oral Transmission', *JJS* 22, 1971, 1–18.

20. But cf. E. E. Urbach, *Ḥazal,* pp. 254–8 (ET, *The Sages* I, pp. 286–90). If the wider use of Torah could be proven for Palestine before 70 CE, we could say that the 'Torah' in our mishnah and mAbot 1.1 is meant to include the 'traditions of the elders' ascribed by Josephus to the Pharisees. These traditions were a forerunner of the tannaitic oral Law.

21. A. J. Heschel, *Torah min ha-Shamayim ba- 'Aspaqlaryah shel ha-Dorot* II, 1965, pp. 100–45.

22. Cf. V. Tcherikover, *Hellenistic Civilization and the Jews,* 1959, pp. 152–74.

23. S. Krauss, *Griechische und Lateinische Lehnwörter im Talmud, Midrasch und Targum* II, 1964, repr. p. 107.
24. BSanh 99b–100a, pSanh 10.1; 27d. Cf. 'Apiqoros', *'Entsiqlopediah Talmudit* II, pp. 136f. which also contains an excellent survey of the medieval halakic discussion.
25. Cf. Maimonides, *Perush ha-Mishnayot,* ad loc. (ed. Vilna, p. 124a) who derives the word from Aramaic *pqr.*
26. Josephus, *Ant.* X.277–80, Cf. G. Deutsch, 'Apikoros', *JE* I, pp. 665f., and S. Lieberman, How Much Greek in Jewish Palestine?', *Biblical and Other Studies* (ed. Altmann), 1963, p. 130.
27. On these beliefs of Epicurus, see J. M. Rist, *Epicurus,* 1972, pp. 146–8, and G. Strodach, *The Philosophy of Epicurus,* 1963, pp. 52–5.
28. Josephus, *Bell.* II. 164f.; *Ant.* XIII.173.
29. Schürer, *A History of the Jewish People in the Age of Jesus Christ,* §26.1, ET II, ii, 1898, p. 15; rev. ed., II, p. 393.
30. L. Finkelstein sees our mishnah as part of an ancient Pharisaic document going back as far as the 'men of the great assembly', a view which we find difficult to accept. He sees the specific passage under discussion here, however, as being a later addition. At the same time he suggests that it must have been added at a time when Epicureanism was making inroads into the Jewish people. Unfortunately, however, it is not possible to determine precisely the status of Epicurean beliefs among Jews at this time so as to pinpoint the time in which our mishnah was formulated.
31. Accordingly, the word 'even' (Hebrew *'af*) in our passage should be understood as part of the words of the Tannaim, R. Akiba and Abba Saul, rather than as an addition of some redactor. Further, it is extremely unlikely in light of the nature of the doctrinal offences described here that the anonymous clause was formulated in the Yavnean period and was then, at the same time, glossed by R. Akiba and Abba Saul.
32. Translating Zuckermandel's ed. Cf. bRSh 17a, ed. Venice and *Diqduqe Soferim,* ad loc., as well as the discussion in R. T. Herford, *Christianity in Talmud and Midrash,* 1903, pp. 118–25.
33. According to Rashi ad bRSh 17a, in the version of *Diqduqe Soferim* the *minim* here are the *talmide yeshu,* the disciples of Jesus, in other words, the early Jewish Christians.
34. Too general a classification to belong to this list. Delete it with Rashi and *Diqduqe Soferim,* ad loc.
35. The text here mentions Jeroboam and Ahab and then adds two classes of transgressors extremely difficult to explain precisely and not relevant to our study.
36. See B. Kedar, 'Netherworld, In the Aggadah', *EJ* XII cols. 997f. for a treatment of Gehenna in rabbinic texts.
37. Contrast, however, the view of Rashi to bRSh 17a, who sees the offence of the informer as causing financial loss to fellow Jews.
38. The printed editions of rabbinic texts usually read *mumar,* lit. one who was

changed or converted, for the Hebrew *meshummad,* lit. 'one who was destroyed'. Christian censors replaced *meshummad* with *mumar,* which they deemed less offensive. Indeed, the word *mumar* itself is most probably an invention of the Christian censors.

39. *TK* III, p. 402 n. 45.
40. Translating the Venice ed. The version in tHor 1.5, ed. Zuckermandel, seems corrupt and hence we rely on the baraita as preserved by the gemara.
41. MS Munich reads *'okhel . . . veha-shoteh (Diqduqe Soferim,* ad loc.).
42. I.e., an animal that would have died of itself if not slaughtered ritually. Such animals are termed *terefot,* literally 'torn animals', and are forbidden according to halakah.
43. Translating with Jastrow, *šqp.*
44. The reading 'R. Judah' found in some late printed texts is clearly an error. See *Diqduqe Soferim,* ad. loc.
45. Generally termed *sha'atnez* and prohibited according to Lev. 19.19 and Deut. 22.11.
46. The redactor of the baraita in its present form added the *vav* before *'ezehu* which stood in the material before him in order to ease the transition. Nevertheless, the awkwardness as well as the apparent redundancy of the formulation give evidence of its building blocks. Indeed, this redundancy was felt by the Amoraim, who interpreted the first clause to refer to the *meshummad* and the second to the *min.*
47. Sifra Vayyiqra' parashah 2.3 (ed. Weiss, p. 40). On this passage cf. E. P. Sanders, *Paul and Palestinian Judaism,* 1977, pp. 83f. Cf. pShek 1.4 (ed. Krot. 1.5, 46b).
48. Reading *meqabbele berit* with Weiss and MS Rome, Assemani 66 (ed. Finkelstein), New York, 1956.
49. Translating the Venice ed.
50. MSS Hamburg and Rome *(a)* add 'of you' a second time *(Diqduqe Soferim* ad loc.).
51. All MSS read *ha-domin (Diqduqe Soferim,* ad loc.).
52. See D. Weiss Halivni, 'Yesh Mevi 'im Bikkurim', *Bar-Ilan* 7–8, 1969–70, p. 79.
53. Two more passages show that the Tannaim did not consider the *meshummadim,* or for that matter any other transgressors, as non-Jews. Instead, they are listed separately from the *goyim,* the non-Jews. See bAZ 26a–b; bGitt 45b. On apostates in the writings of Philo, see H. Wolfson, *Philo* I, 1968, pp. 73–85.
54. Maimonides, H. Melakhim 11.3 states that R. Akiba and his contemporaries erred in thinking Bar Kokhba (Bar Kosiba) to be the Messiah. Needless to say, no accusation of heresy was lodged against these scholars.
55. Baron, *A Social and Religious History of the Jews,* 1952, II, p. 129. The divisions during the revolt are well documented in D. Rhoads, *Israel in Revolution, 6–74 C.E.,* 1976, pp. 94–149.
56. According to Acts 6.7 the 'number of disciples multiplied greatly in Jerusa-

lem' (RSV). Nevertheless, the picture one gets from Acts is of a small, close-knit group.

57. See F. F. Bruce, *New Testament History*, 1972, pp. 279–90.

58. Cf. Bruce, *New Testament History*, pp. 265–78.

59. D. Sperber, 'Min', *EJ* XII, cols. 1–3.

60. R. T. Herford, *Christianity in Talmud and Midrash*, pp. 361–97; G. Alon, *Toledot ha-Yehudim be-Erets Yisra'el bi-tequfat ha-Mishnah veha-Talmud* I, repr. 1967, pp. 179–92.

61. Cf. Y. M. Elbogen, *Ha-Tefillah be-Yisra'el*, 1972, pp. 27–9, 31, 40; G. Forkman, *The Limits of the Religious Community*, 1972, pp. 90–2.

62. Translated from ed. Venice 30a. Cf. bMeg 17b and Herford, *Christianity in Talmud and Midrash*, pp. 125–35.

63. MS Munich *sidder*.

64. 'Benedictions' is omitted in MS Munich.

65. This is in accord with the view that the men of the Great Assembly composed, but did not place in order the Eighteen Benedictions (L. Ginzberg, *Perushim ve-Ḥiddushim bi-Yerushalmi* I, 1941, p. 322; Halivni, *Mekorot u-Mesorot, Mo'ed*, p. 489).

66. Contrast M. Ydit ('Birkhat Ha-Minim', *EJ* IV, col. 1035), who says that Samuel Ha-Qatan 'revised its text after it had fallen into oblivion'. This is impossible in light of the uses of the verb *tqn* which refers to composition or formulation of a text.

67. MS Florence and some *rishonim* read *yarad* (*Diqduqe Soferim*, ad loc.). This reading seems to be influenced by the continuation of the baraita, which is set in a liturgical context, for *yrd* is a technical term for serving as precentor (*yrd* followed by *lifne ha-tevah*, 'to go down before the ark'). Indeed, the precentors in early synagogues stood at a level below that of the worshippers. We, however, prefer the reading *'md*. The first part of the baraita takes place in the setting of the academy of Yavneh where Rabban Gamaliel sought a Tanna to compose a benediction against the *minim*. The following year, Samuel Ha-Qatan's 'amnesia' occurred in a liturgical context as he was serving as precentor. This view is supported by pBer 5.3 (ed. Krot. 5.4, 9c).

68. While it seems from the context that he forgot the text of this blessing, an amoraic passage in pBer 5.3 (ed. Krot. 5.4, 9c) suggests that he skipped the entire blessing.

69. PBer 5.3 (ed. Krot. 5.4, 9c) in its Aramaic version of our baraita reads: *mashqif 'alehon*, 'he looked at them'. Ginzberg, *Perushim* IV, 1961, p. 276 takes this as indicating that the correct reading is Hebrew *'alehem*. More probably, the Amoraim were confused by this strange use of the hif'il of *šqf* and so modified the object pronoun. The word *bah* clearly refers to the benediction.

70. MS Munich: 'more than two'.

71. Literally, 'bring him up'. Cf. n. 196.

72. Aaron Hyman, *Toledot Tanna'im ve'Amoraim* III, 1964 p. 1148. Hyman

failed to realize that the stories about Samuel Ha-Qatan and Hillel are apocryphal.

73. Joseph Heinemann, *Ha-Tefillah bi-Tequfat ha-Tanna'im ve-ha-'Amoraim*, 1966, p. 142 (ET, *Prayer in the Talmud: Forms and Patterns,* pp. 225f.), and Lieberman, *TK* I, pp. 53f.

74. Cf. Midrash Tanhuma' (ed. Buber), Lev., p. 2a.

75. J. Mann, 'Genizah Fragments of the Palestinian Order of Service', *HUCA* 2, 1925, p. 306, restored in accord with S. Schechter, 'Genizah Specimens', pp. 657, 659.

76. See also Luke 6.22, Forkman, *The Limits of the Religious Community,* pp. 105f., and S. Krauss, 'The Jews in the Works of the Church Fathers', *JQR,* os 5, 1892–93, pp. 130–4.

77. Krauss, ibid.

78. The famous statement, 'An Israelite, though he sins, is (still) an Israelite', although based on bSanh 44a, was not seen as a halakah until much later. See J. Katz, ' 'Af 'al pi she-Ḥata' Yisra'el Hu' ', *Tarbiz* 27, 1957–58, pp. 203–17. Katz takes the view that the use of this statement as a halakic dictum originated with Rashi. On the other hand, halakic use of the statement appears in Midrash ʾAggadah (ed. S. Buber) to Num., p. 162, to indicate that impurity could be contracted by killing a Jewish apostate, since he still retained his Jewish identity despite his transgressions. (The reference is noted in Halivni, *Mekorot u-Mesorot, Nashim,* p. 67 n. 3.) This tradition is without parallel. Since much of the material in this text comes from the school of Moses Ha-Darshan, it seems that Rashi was only reflecting a usage already prominent in the French exegetical tradition. Rashi did not originate the halakic use of this sentence. Cf. also J. Katz, *Exclusiveness and Tolerance,* 1962, pp. 67–81 and the many medieval responsa he cites; L. Ginzberg, *An Unknown Jewish Sect,* ET 1970, p. 105; and G. Blidstein, 'Who is Not a Jew?—The Medieval Discussion', *ILR* 11, 1976, pp. 369–90.

79. The use of bans in talmudic times was intended as a means of discipline. Under no circumstance did they imply any effect on the personal status of the person banned, only on the way he and his neighbours related to one another. Cf. Forkman, *The Limits of the Religious Community,* pp. 92–105.

80. See G. F. Moore, 'The Definition of the Jewish Canon and the Repudiation of Christian Scriptures', reprinted in *The Canon and Masorah of the Hebrew Bible* (ed. S. Leiman), 1974, pp. 115–41.

81. Translating MS Vienna (ed. Lieberman).

82. MSS Erfurt and London omit.

83. So Lieberman, *TK,* ad loc. and S. Leiman, *The Canonization of Hebrew Scripture,* 1976, pp. 190f, n. 511.

84. This is an oath formula.

85. The talmudic *rodef,* 'pursuer', is chasing his victim in order to kill him.

86. *Bayit*, 'house', is probably used here to refer to a temple or house of worship.
87. Ed. princ. and MS Erfurt: *bo*. London omits.
88. Num. 5.23.
89. It should be mentioned in passing that R. Tarfon is not to be identified with the Tryphon with whom Justin Martyr conducted his dialogue.
90. Translating MS Erfurt (ed. Zuckermandel). Cf. Leiman, *Canonization*, p. 109 and notes, and Herford, *Christianity in Talmud and Midrash*, pp. 160f.
91. Leiman, *Canonization*, pp. 102–20.
92. We refer here to the formal legitimization of Gentile Christianity by the church in Jerusalem (Bruce, *New Testament History*, pp. 269f). From the point of view of Rome, the Emperor Nerva (ruled 97–98) exempted the Christians from the *fiscus judaicus*, thereby declaring Christianity a separate religion (Bruce, *New Testament History*, p. 390).
93. Moore, 'Jewish Canon', pp. 123f.
94. Many of the later Jewish Christians in Palestine were in reality Judaizing Christians—not Christians of Jewish halakic status. We speak here, however, of the halakically Jewish Christians.
95. Schürer, *History* § 21.iii. rev. ed., I, 1973, pp. 553–5.
96. Bruce, *New Testament History*, pp. 390–2.
97. For the rabbinic attitude to Christians after Bar Kokhba, see Urbach, *Ḥazal*, p. 485 (ET, *The Sages* I, pp. 543f.).

16

Social and Religious Segregation

Jacob Katz

The reluctance of the halakhists to exclude Christian worship absolutely from the category of idolatry is quite understandable. The gulf which separated the two religions (both in dogma and spiritual outlook) was only one reason for this. Doctrinal differences became the more acute because of the social situation of Jewry in Christian countries. We have had occasion above to define this situation as the position of a minority dependent upon the broader society of which it formed part. This prompted the halakhists, as we have seen, to forgo any attempt to reintroduce the original talmudic laws of segregation in so far as economic activity was concerned. But the same situation induced them to retain the precepts which were designed to prevent the Jewish community from coming into intimate contact with non-Jews in the social and religious spheres. For the Jewish community was now in far greater danger of being absorbed by its social environment than it had been at the time when these precepts originated. The Christian Church was more zealous in its efforts to entice Jews to join its community than any pre-Christian sect or denomination with which Jews had come into contact in previous epochs had been. It possessed better means of persuasion and inducement, since it based its beliefs on the same tradition as Judaism itself, namely the teachings contained in the Old Testament. Lastly, the dependence of the Jewish community on the economic resources and services of its Gentile environment was likely to bring Jews into constant

Reprinted by permission of Jacob Katz from *Exclusiveness and Tolerance: Studies in Jewish-Gentile Relations in Medieval and Modern Times,* by Jacob Katz, New York, 1962, 37–47. Copyright © 1962 by Jacob Katz.

contact with Christians, in a way which exposed them to the influence of the Christian religion.

We shall better be able to appreciate the problem with which Jewish society was confronted if we first survey the more distinct features of their situation. As mentioned above, Jewish communities consisted at this time of tiny groups of ten people, or in most places even fewer; in a few places only did they amount to hundreds. Even more decisive than the restricted numbers of the communities was the lack of variety in occupation and economic position. Reliance on a livelihood derived from the investment of capital in trade or in some other financial undertaking became, in this period, more and more the distinctive characteristic of Jewish economic existence.

The social implication of this was a double one. Firstly, the business dealings of the Jews brought them into close contact with Gentiles of varying status. The picture of the Jew waiting at home for the Gentile to come to borrow money or to pay a debt is a realistic one, at least for the period commencing with the Crusades.[1] But it reflects only one aspect of the situation. In this period many Jews had also to call at the house of the Gentile, to offer their services as traders or money-lenders.[2] On some occasions the Jew followed the Gentile into the law courts as a result of their dealings.[3] For a Jew to be obliged to stay overnight in the house of a Gentile or to eat a meal there was not, perhaps, an everyday occurrence; on the other hand, it was not entirely out of the ordinary.[4] In this way business connexions facilitated social contact.

Social intercourse with Gentiles was indirectly forced upon the Jew to an even greater extent by his inability to supply his needs from Jewish sources alone. The Jewish household was dependent upon the Gentile for its meat, milk, grain, wine, beer, and other foods.[5] Nor could the Jew dispense with the Gentile's services either inside or outside his household. Gentiles were employed as domestic servants as well as for special projects or on particular errands.[6] No Jew was able to harvest his grapes, whether the vineyard was his own or its crop purchased from a Gentile.[7] Jews employed Gentiles as their agents in transferring money, as well as wares and commodities.[8] How pervasive this dependence of the Jewish household on Gentile help was can be gathered from a story derived from a certain French community in the twelfth century: The eve of Passover coincided with the Christian Easter, so that no Gentile help was available and the Jews were therefore unable to bake their *maṣṣoth* in the afternoon ready for the evening, as was their habit in other years.[9]

One would assume that such conditions would be likely to render ineffective any ritual precepts, the intention of which was to keep Jewish and Gentile society apart. The impact of the situation is clearly seen in the way in which the halakhists dealt with the problems so created. The outcome, however, was more in the nature of a change in the function of the ritual than its neglect or abandonment.

Originally, Jewish ritual had fulfilled the function of securing the social segregation of the Jewish community from its Gentile environment. Under 'normal' conditions (where the constitution of a separate Jewish society was feasible), the effect of such ritual was to strengthen the tendency among Jews to rely as much as possible on each other. If the meat, wine, milk, and cheese of the Gentiles were forbidden, the Jew was thrown back, willy-nilly, on his own brethren for the production of these commodities.[10] As under changed conditions this was impossible, the outcome had necessarily to be different. Had the Jews not possessed a deep-rooted conviction of the truth of their religion, and had they not actively sought to maintain their separate identity, the tendencies inherent in medieval conditions would inevitably had ended by breaking down the social barrier erected by Jewish ritual. As it was, Jewish ritual merely underwent certain alterations. We may describe the nature of the change by saying that, from a system of prescriptions which ensured the social cohesion of those who felt bound by them, it became a method of personal conduct enabling the individual to preserve his inward sense of aloofness from those with whom he came into everyday social contact.

This change is clearly reflected in the modifications of the laws concerning segregation. The Mishnah (ʿA.Z., 2. 6) simply states, for instance, that the bread of Gentiles was forbidden to the Jew. In talmudic times the prohibition was not universally observed. It was, however, only under medieval conditions, when Jews could not rely upon production by Jewish bakers, that the eating of Gentile bread was permitted by the authorities.[11] The observance of the former prohibition became a sign of special strictness of ritual conduct, such as was confined to the exceptional few.[12] There was a much more stringent ban on Gentile wine. Being the article of sacred use in libation as well as the medium of close social intercourse and fraternization, it stood under a complete interdict.[13] The talmudic prohibiton included the deriving of any benefit from a Gentile's wine. This ban excluded wine as a possible article of merchandise for Jews and, as we have mentioned in the previous chapter, this would have entailed intolerable economic hardship. The prohibition on drinking, however, was felt to be an indispensable means of social segregation. So it remained forbidden for the Jew to drink a Gentile's wine. As Jews were neither capable of growing their own vines nor of preparing wine without Gentile help, the solution was sought in a division of labour. Gentiles did the preparatory stages of the work. It had to be determined casuistically from which stage in the production the grape juice was considered to be proper wine. From that moment on no one but a Jew was allowed to prepare wine for Jewish use. It is true that such distinctions had already appeared in talmudic discussions. But only in the Middle Ages did the division of the actual work become a usual feature of wine-production.[14]

The weight of the tradition which connected wine, particularly, with sacred worship as one of its media intensified the ritualistic attitude towards it. Logically, one might suppose that other alcoholic drinks such as beer and mead ought to have been placed in the same category as wine. The Talmud did, indeed, mention that they were prohibited, but indicated certain modifications which would make their use permissible under certain conditions.[15] Not being for sacred use, these liquids escaped the emphatic prohibiton which applied to everything connected with idol worship. As beer was the common beverage in the Middle Ages, this was an additional reason for accepting a less ritualistic attitude concerning it. Nevertheless it was on casuistic grounds only that these liquids were excluded from the prohibition. The effect of the exclusion was far-reaching. In fact it was only drinking with Gentiles by way of entertainment that remained forbidden.[16] As, however, some limitations continued to be valid, the observance of these necessarily remained a part of the code of personal conduct in an environment which was deemed to offer attractions liable to seduce the Jew from his religious affiliation.

Similar consequences were entailed by the fact that Jews found themselves compelled, more and more, to rely upon the personal services of free Christian servants who lived with them in the same household. This situation developed only later: until the eleventh century, and occasionally even later, Jews bought slaves whom they then circumcised and so converted into 'half' Jews.[17] In the event of manumission the slave became, with certain very slight reservations, a full Jew, and even while he was a slave he was for ritual purposes regarded as a Jew.[18] He could handle the wine of his owner and do his cooking. Not so the Christian servant, to whom the restrictions of the segregative laws applied.

The halakhists dealt extensively with the situation and the problems arising out of it. Some of them understood quite clearly the incongruity between circumstances as they were and the law which had to be applied to them. For the Gentile, far from being kept at arm's length, was in fact incorporated into the Jewish household.[19] On the other hand, it was also observed that, since the servant was of a lower social status, contact with him would not have the same dangerously attractive influence as would social intercourse between Jews and Gentiles of equal standing.[20] On these grounds it was suggested that servants in Jewish households be exempted from certain ritualistic restrictions. This lenient tendency, however, did not prevail. In the first generations after the problem had become acute there was hesitation on the matter. Some halakhists allowed a Gentile servant to do the entire housework including cooking— thereby disregarding the prohibition of *bishshul nokhri* (cooking done by a Gentile). However, we also have a report of one great authority, Rabbi Eliezer of Metz, who, because of doubt with regard to the *ḥallah* (which must be made from dough prepared by a Jew), would not allow his Gentile servant to do the kneading; this was therefore done by the Rabbi's wife.[21] Such restrictions would, of course, have made it futile to employ domestic help. So in the course of time a middle way was found. The servants were allowed to do all the domestic work, but the Jew or his wife maintained the fiction of participating in every household task done by the servant.[22] Once again we here a method of maintaining personal detachment from Gentile society even while actually living together in the same household with a representative of it.

We would be wrong to assume that this was the result of nothing but a petrified ritualistic attitude. The ritual situation is an accurate expression of the prevalent socio-religious one. A Christian servant was treated humanely in a Jewish household, according to the accepted standards of that time, but such humane conduct was necessarily limited by the nature of the Jewish family. The life of the Jewish family was based on its religious rites and ceremonies, and into these a Christian servant could not have been integrated. The situation is well characterized by the custom of distributing presents on the day of *Purim* to non-Jewish servants also. This practice was objected to by Rashi because it included Gentiles in an act which should have been reserved as a Jewish religious ceremony.[23] The ritual of segregation, even if only a relic, expressed the real nature of this situation.

Since no neutral social sphere was developed in the Middle Ages, social segregation between Jews and Gentiles was merely the logical consequence of their religious separation. To shun the other's religious rites was not merely prudent; avoidance of contact with the visible expressions of the Christian faith became almost an instinct with the Jew, who felt himself endangered spiritually, and perhaps even physically, whenever he encountered a Christian gathering performing its religious rites. We shall find many examples of this in the attitude of the *Ḥasid*. At the reflective level, this trend was both controlled and encouraged by the halakhic tradition. As we have seen above, economic necessity was the reason for dispensing with many prescriptions whose intention was to prevent the Jew from coming into contact with 'alien worship'; and this dispensation was endorsed by the halakhists, although by such endorsement the Halakhah was but bowing to the force of reality, and no principle was established on the grounds of which a general dispensation could have been given. The abrogation of certain details of the law was either an explicit concession to economic necessity or was made as a result of casuistic considerations. These very often entailed a distinction between the 'idols', i.e. the images venerated in Christian worship and their associated ritual objects on the one hand, and the economic value which they represented on the other. If the Christian priest himself quenched the lights which were burning in front of the holy image, or damaged the chalice used in worship, and then sold them to a Jew, did he not himself remove from them their sacral and, in Jewish eyes, obnoxious character?[24] Is not the garment of a priest given in pawn to a Jew to be regarded as the former's private property, even if it is used for the performance of religious ceremonies?[25] From such considerations emerged the obvious tendency to detract from the sacral quality of such objects and reduce them to their economic value. The method of dialectics in vogue in contemporary Jewish as well as Gentile society helped to achieve this objective.

Whether concessions were made by means of such dialectics, or merely in compliance with economic needs, they always retained the nature of a compromise. That 'alien worship' included Christian worship was inherent in the argument, and was sometimes explicitly stated—as, for instance, in the first source, where the problem of lending money on a priest's garments was discussed, by R. Gershom *Me'or Ha-Golah*.[26] The inquirer proposed a solution based on a consideration of the priestly garments as not belonging to the category of 'objects used in alien worship', but simply as the private property of the priest. R. Gershom rejects this view, using, characteristically, the analogy of the garments of the priests of the Temple at Jerusalem, which were regarded as sacred. In the same way, *mutatis mutandis*, the garments of the Christian priest must be regarded as pertaining to the ritual. It is because of the economic need that R. Gershom justifies the granting of permission to lend money on a priest's garments. Those who used dialectical distinctions in order to find a justification betrayed the inconsistent character of their decisions by the qualifications which they attached to them. Some dealings were allowed, but others remained within the scope of the original law. In principle, then, Christian worship was still regarded as 'alien worship' even though the number of exceptions prevented the law of segregation from exercising any practical effect.

At any rate, permission was granted only where economic necessity demanded it, or where the process of neutralization could be facilitated by regarding the sacred objects as mere commodities. The images of Christian worship themselves were never exempted from the prohibition.[27] Reservations were also made where Christian worship was encountered *per se*, especially where no economic interests were involved. R. Eliezer of Metz besought his fellow Jews not to follow a Christian procession in the street for, even if unintentionally, they would thereby be joining in the accepted way of Christian worship. He adds that one could, by dialectical distinction, preclude this from being regarded as real worship, but that 'one should not rely on distinctions'.[28]

After analysis of the above facts, we may make some remarks on the interrelations between the social and religious forces which moulded the destiny of the Jewish community in this period. Economic necessity weighed heavily, and compelled the adjustment of tradition to prevailing circumstances. At the same time no less strong an influence was exercised by tradition, which operated as a corrective to this tendency. Such force was derived from the conservatism inherent in every tradition. This conservatism manifested itself in the retention by the Jewish communities of their historical identity, in spite of changes of environment and conditions and in the face of fierce religious opposition by Christianity. The fact that Rashi identified his community with the Israel of which biblical and talmudic tradition had spoken allowed him to interpret the events of his own time by using terms and concepts drawn from that tradition. The same motive prompted the halakhists to justify the legality of the adjustments in terms of the ancient tradition. In spite of the apparent deviation from older practices, Jewish life was made to appear as a continuation of that of earlier times.

We may now formulate a view as to the real function of the Halakhah in the period in question. Its function was that of holding the balance between the two driving forces, namely the necessary adjustment to new conditions and the preservation of Jewish identity. That the Halakhah followed in the wake of social change has been observed very often by historians.[29] Again and again we have had occasion to refer to instances of this. But the other function, that of safeguarding Jewish identity by means of rationalization, is no less conspicuous a task. It was the achievement of the Halakhah that it prevented the community and the individual from being engulfed by the social and religious life of the Christian environment, by setting a limit to what might be conceded to the force of circumstances. The Halakhah was not responsible for creating the wish for social and religious disengagement. This arose spontaneously, from the community's adherence to its own image of its past as pictured by tradition. The barrier which served as the means of separation was but the logical consequence of the religious or mystical thinking of the Jewish community which accepted this position. The Halakhah was called upon to elaborate the details of the socio-religious separation. It did so by relying upon its own historical sources, and by taking into consideration the prevailing conditions. Its task was, in any case, to regulate and control; not to create, in the sense of producing new religious values or suggesting original social settings.

That the Halakhah was not the originator either of the adjustment or of the state of separateness is corroborated by its method of justification and control which we have repeatedly encountered during our analysis. Before concluding, we may refer to one instance where this characteristic stands out with special clarity.

We possess a fragment of correspondence between two great halakhists of the twelfth century, Rabbenu Tam and his nephew, Rabbi Isaac. The correspondence concerns the problem of wine prepared or touched by a Gentile. As we have seen above, economic conditions made the granting of permission for trading in such wine highly desirable. Rabbenu Tam gave permission and in his ingenious way found a justification for it in the sources. He put forward the suggestion which we have already noticed, namely that the Gentiles of his day did not fall within the category of idolaters in whose wine, during talmudic times, it was forbidden to trade. His correspondent was quite willing to acquiesce in this, but raised the objection that on this supposition one should be consistent and allow the wine of contemporary Gentiles for drinking, which appeared to him as inconceivable. Rabbenu Tam was so impressed with this argument that he withdrew his original ruling and resolved to find another justification for permitting wine as merchandise which would not entail the consequence of its being permitted for drinking also.[30]

One may well query the logic of this controversy. If Rabbenu Tam's original supposition is correct, why do these two halakhists recoil from the consequences of their own thought? The talmudic sources do not make any distinction between the Gentile's wine as an object of trade and as a commodity for personal consumption. If, therefore, the halakhists decided that contemporary Gentiles were not included in the prohibition, they would have been entitled to waive the prohibition for both purposes. That they did not do so was because, even though the two kinds of use were found to be logically on the same level of prohibition, in reality there were opposing interests connected with them. The use of wine for business was an economic necessity, and to grant permission for this purpose did not imply any social contact with non-Jews. The drinking of the wine, however, was regarded as leading to social and even sexual intercourse, as expressed in the concise definition of the Talmud: 'Their wine was forbidden on account of their daughters.'[31] The former concession, therefore, could be accepted, but the latter had to be rejected uncompromisingly. The weightiest factors bearing on the decision were thus the two tendencies, economic and religious, and the arguments of the Halakhah were merely a rationalization.

NOTES

1. Such a situation is reflected in some of our sources, e.g. Eliezer b. Nathan (Raben), Prague edn., p. 148. The much quoted generalization of *Leqeṭ Yosher*, Berlin, 1903, i, pp. 118–19, applies to the author's time, i.e. the fifteenth century.

2. G. Caro, *Sozial- und Wirtschaftsgeschichte der Juden*, 1908–1920, i, pp. 426, 434–5; M. Hoffmann, *Der Geldhandel der deutschen Juden während des Mittelalters*, 1910, pp. 7 ff.; H. J. Zimmels, *Beiträge zur Geschichte der Juden in Deutschland insbesondere auf Grund der Gutachten des R. Meir Rothenburg*, 1926, pp. 46 ff.

3. G. Kisch, *The Jews in Medieval Germany: A Study of Their Legal and Social Status*, 1949, pp. 173–4, 245–7.

4. The lodging of Jews in the house of a *maᶜarufya* (i.e. someone with whom he stands in permanent business relationships) is mentioned in *Ravyah*, 404 (ed. V. Aptowitzer, i, p. 462). Taking a meal is mentioned in *Tosafoth, ᶜA.Z.*, 31b; *᾿Or Zaruaᶜ, ᶜA.Z.*, 163.

5. This is evident from the preoccupation with the ritual problems deriving from this fact, as we shall see later.

6. The charters granted to the Jews furnished this permission: cf. J. Parkes, *The Jew in the Medieval Community*, 1938, pp. 159, 161–3. The repeated ban by the Church on the employment of non-Jewish servants by Jews is rightly interpreted as a sign that the prohibition was not heeded; cf. S. W. Baron, *A Social and Religious History of the Jews*, 1937, ii, p. 41. Internal sources confirm this impression. The problems arising out of Gentiles' presence in the Jewish household are manifold: cf. I. A. Agus, *Teshuvoth Baᶜaley Ha-Tosafoth*, 1954, 26; *Ravyah*, 841; *Tosafoth, Kerithoth*, 9a; *Semag*, p. 167a bottom; *Tosafoth, ᶜA.Z.*, 12a, 61a, &c.

7. See the discussion below of the problem relating to wine touched by a Gentile.

8. *Semag*, p. 167a; *Tosafoth, ᶜA.Z.*, 61a.

9. *Ravyah*, 452; Aptowitzer's surmise (*Mavo᾿ le-sefer Ravyah*, p. 439) that the Jews were themselves forbidden to do work on Sundays is unfounded.

10. Such must have been the result of these precepts in talmudic times.

11. Rabbenu Gershom is the only one who adheres to the original prohibition. S. Eidelberg, *Teshuvoth Rabbenu Gershom Meᵒor Ha-Golah*, 1955, p. 20. Cf. Eliezer of Mainz, 303; *Tosafoth, ᶜA.Z.*, 35b; *᾿Or Zaruaᶜ, ᶜA.Z.*, 187–8; *Rosh, ᶜA.Z.*, 2. 27; *Tosafoth, Beṣah*, 16b.

12. J. Katz, *Exclusiveness and Tolerance: Studies in Jewish-Gentile Relations in Medieval and Modern Times*, 1961, Chap. VIII.

13. Both reasons are stated in B. T., *ᶜA.Z.*, 29b, 36b.

14. Cf. B. T., *ᶜA.Z.*, 55a ff.; Eliezer of Mainz (see n. 1), 309; *Tosafoth, ᶜA.Z.*, 55b, 60a.

15. B. T., *ᶜA.Z.*, 31b.

16. *Tosafoth*, ʿA.Z., 31b; *ʾOr Zaruaʿ*, ʿA.Z., 163; *Rosh*, ʿA.Z., 2. 15.

17. As late as the end of the eleventh century Jews were explicitly allowed to purchase pagan (but not Christian) slaves; see Parkes, *Community*, Appendix, p. 392, para. 8, 10 in Henry IV's charter. The Hebrew sources relating to the problem are listed in S. Assaf, ' ʿAvadim u-seḥar ʿavadim ʾeṣel ha-Yehudim bimey ha-Beynayim', *Beʾoholey Yaʿaqov*, 1943, pp. 236–7. The article appeared previously in *Zion*, iv, 1939, pp. 91–125.

18. Maim., *Hilkhoth Shehiṭah*, 4. 4; cf. *Kesef Mishneh*, ibid.

19. *Tosafoth*, ʿA.Z., 38a; *ʾOr Zaruaʿ*, ʿA.Z., 163; *Mordekhai*, ʿA.Z., 830.

20. It is quoted as a suggestion of an anonymous halakhist by Eliezer of Mainz (see n. 1), according to R. Joel Sirkis, *Bayith Ḥadash, Yoreh Deʿah*, 113; cf. *Sheʾeloth u-Theshuvoth Rashba* (attributed to Ramban), 149.

21. *ʾOr Zaruaʿ*, 1. 760.

22. Eidelberg, *R. Gershom*, 20; Eliezer of Mainz, 303. The actual part of the Gentile's work in the Jewish household is reflected in *Tosafoth*, ʿA.Z., 12a; *ʾOr Zaruaʿ*, ʿA.Z., 124. For the final regulation regarding the employment of Gentile servants see *Shulḥan ʿArukh, Yoreh Deʿah*, 113.

23. I. Elfenbein, *Teshuvoth Rashi*, 1943, 131.

24. *Tosafoth*, ʿA.Z., 14b, 50a.

25. *Tosafoth*, ʿA.Z., 50b. This lenient view was not, however, universally accepted. R. Eliezer of Metz protested against permission being given on such grounds, *Sefer Yereʾim*, p. 37a; cf. 36a.

26. Eidelberg, *R. Gershom*, p. 21.

27. This is implicit in the instances of the exemptions we have noted. Sometimes it is stated explicitly, e.g. Eliezer of Mainz, 289.

28. *Sefer Yereʾim*, p. 128a–b.

29. Lately much stressed by E. E. Urbach in his *Baʿaley Ha-Tosafoth*, 1955, pp. 50, 79, 203, 290, 430; cf. my remarks in *Qiryath Sefer*, 1955, pp. 9 ff.

30. *Tosafoth*, ʿA.Z., 57b.

31. B. T., ʿA.Z., 36b.

17

From Politics to Martyrdom: Shifting Paradigms in the Hebrew Narratives of the 1096 Crusade Riots

Ivan G. Marcus

Sans doute, notre Salomon n'est pas un habile chroniqueur, il n'est qu'un modeste conteur, qui rapporte simplement ce qu'il a entendu.[1]

In the spring of 1096, in response to Pope Urban II's appeal for an armed pilgrimage to Jerusalem, mobs of French and local German Christians attacked Rhineland Jewish communities in Speyer, Worms, Mainz, Cologne, Trier and elsewhere. Both in the Hebrew and Latin narrative accounts, the most striking aspect of these events was less the gruesome slaughter and pillage by the Crusaders than the extraordinary way Jews killed their own families and then themselves in order to avoid baptism. Shocked almost beyond words, the twelfth-century German Churchman, Albert of Aix (Aachen) reported:

> The Jews, seeing that their Christian enemies were attacking them and their children, and that they were sparing no age, likewise fell upon one another, brother, children, wives, and sisters, and thus they perished at each other's hands. Horrible to say, mothers cut the throats of nursing children with knives and stabbed others, preferring them to perish thus by their own hands rather than to be killed by the weapons of the uncircumcised.[2]

In his account, Albert selected the available information about what had happened in the Rhineland and interpreted it from his perspective

Reprinted by permission of Johns Hopkins University Press from *Prooftexts* 2 (1982): 40–52.

as a Churchman. Thus, he goes on to relate that when the Crusader rabble was itself decimated in Hungary, that disaster was a sign of God's judgment. The Christians who had violated Church law by forcibly converting, not to speak of murdering, Jews were themselves justly punished. Although Albert correctly sensed that Jewish mothers preferred to kill their own children "rather than be killed by the weapons of the uncircumcised," he did not fully understand the meaning of the Jewish reactions to the attacks.

Three Hebrew narratives[3] of the events of 1096 do provide such a Jewish perspective. They were written in the early twelfth century shortly after the events they portray, and are based in part on eye-witness and other oral and written reports. The three texts make use of some of the same facts which Albert knew but view them through a specifically Jewish cultural prism. Although Albert expresses shock at the ways Jews killed their own families to avoid Christian contact, the Jewish narrators are principally concerned with interpreting the meaning of those acts of unprecedented martyrdom in traditionally acceptable modalities. The martyrs' actions were such a daring innovation at the time that they prompted an act of literary imagination no less bold. The three Hebrew narratives are literary responses to those events. Whereas the martyrs themselves sought by their actions to justify the ways of God, the narrators who chronicled their actions had, by use of archetypal imagery, to justify the martyrs. In so doing they fashioned rich and complex narratives which invite literary analysis.

Of the three texts, the longest and most complex is ascribed with some probability to an otherwise unknown author, Solomon ben Samson (SS); the second, which contains liturgical poems (piyyutim) with name-acrostics of the distinguished German-Jewish scholar Rabbi Eliezer ben Natan, is most likely his work (EN); and the third, shorter than Solomon's account, is anonymous (A). Although each text is unique in some respects, the three have much material in common and also follow a similar pattern of organization: Each narrator describes first how different Jewish communities were attacked by Crusader mobs and then how the Jews in each responded to the attacks. The three also share a literary heterogeneity: the accounts consist not only of chronological narrative segments, containing specific references to individuals, the dates and places of each attack, but also of a liturgical prose framework.

In view of the number and complexity of these texts, it is not surprising that scholars have been more interested in some aspects of them than in others. Some have tried to isolate the "sources" of each account in order to resolve the textual problem of how the three are related to each other.[4] Others have analyzed the accuracy of the historical facts—names, dates, places—found in the chronological narrative portions.[5] Still others have interpreted the literary motifs in the liturgical framework[6] or considered the narrators' ideological biases.[7]

Although these studies offer important insights into one or more aspects of the narratives, none has attempted a literary reading in which the complete narratives are considered as products of coherent religious imaginations. The classification of the texts as medieval chronicles is one reason for this failure. That term usually denotes texts which contain documentary historical data which are embedded in a theological narrative framework. But the notion that medieval chronicles consist of an almost mechanical combination of "facts" and a "religious narrative framework" is a distortion: Such texts cannot be treated as though the "facts" are preserved in narrative like fossils in amber. Most medieval narrators were not interested in what happened for its own sake. Instead, a monk or a royal biographer or a hagiographer usually made use of what he considered to be facts—especially miracles—in order to demonstrate the wonders of God or of His royal or ecclesiastical servant. What appears to be facts in a medieval chronological narrative, then, should be considered a highly edited version of the "deeds" (*gesta*) which the narrator learned from traditional accounts, hearsay or eyewitness reports. The events actually reported qualify for inclusion only when they fit the narrator's preconceived religious-literary schema.[8] Medieval chronicles are, in this sense, fictions: imaginative reorderings of experience within a cultural framework and system of symbols.

Approaching Hebrew Crusade chronicles as literary works, as fictions of a particular Jewish religious imagination, requires appreciation of their stylistic modalities: In particular, the shape or structure of the entire narrative—the combining of chronological accounts with liturgical prose segments which accounts for the shape of the narrative; the particular symbolic imagery used; and the generic choice of prose rather than liturgical poetry. All are clues for understanding how the narrators express in specific cultural symbols a Jewish interpretation of the events of 1096.

The Solomon ben Samson narrative, to which I shall give the most attention, consists of a highly articulated five-part structure: Two different kinds of narrative are framed by three liturgical interpretations of the narratives. Each community's experience is structured, in effect, as a drama in which a liturgical prologue introduces the first act which then narrates the political events which took place when a particular community confronted the Crusader threat; a liturgical entr'acte separates the political narrative in Act One from the lists of martyrologies in Act Two. Finally, a liturgical epilogue concludes the action by addressing the ultimate meaning of the acts of martyrdom. By constructing each community account in this highly stylized way, the narrator affirms that a fundamental shift took place in the world-view of the Jews he is describing: a shift from politics to martyrdom. The narrator's plan is to justify the martyrs' behavior by describing how they resorted to killing only after exhausting all conventional religious and political alternatives. The narrator makes special use of the liturgical framework to signal to the reader that all aspects of the Jews' behavior were justified.

Moreover, by describing the shocking acts of killing and suicide as a reenactment of the Temple cult,[9] as a symbolic rebuilding of the Temple of Jerusalem in Mainz, the innovative behavior of the martyrs is legitimated by being masked in archetypal symbolism. By invoking the symbols of the Temple cult, the narrator justifies the physical boundary which the martyrs' acts of killing and suicide erected between Jewish bodies, defined as Holy Things (*Kodoshim*), and Christians, characterized in the most graphic imagery of impurity and pollution. Only the members of the Holy Community (*Kehillah Kedoshah*) can be permitted to touch, i.e. to sacrifice, the Holy Things. Hence, it is justifiable for the Jews to try and kill themselves and thereby avoid any physical contact with the Crusader pollutants.

The narrator's effort to legitimate the innovative acts of martyrdom is also reflected in his use of genre, but here two different considerations undercut one another. On the one hand, the narrator adopted a quasi-liturgical mode, perhaps with the hope of perpetuating the account in the permanent liturgy of the community, the German-Jewish rite. On the other hand, the narrator's need to justify the martyrs by bearing witness to their actual deeds led him to record the facts as he knew them in the form of a sequential narrative. But the descriptive detail essential to the prose medium made the liturgical parts unassimilable into the liturgy, which is almost always cast in the most general language of "Israel" and

"God," not of particulars, such as the "Jews of Mainz" and the "Christians of France and Germany." Had the story been written as liturgical poetry, as are parts of Eliezer ben Natan's text and other post-Crusade poems, such versions might have been incorporated into the prayerbook. Perhaps the narrator thought that the formal constraints of the poetic form would distort the "telling" or perhaps he viewed the piyyut, itself an innovative form in comparison with the fixed parts of the liturgy, to be an inappropriate genre for providing traditional legitimation for acts of daring and innovation.

The essential clue to the chronicler's message is the internal shaping of the narrative, especially the division into two "acts," the first political and the second martyrological. These narrative segments differ in several fundamental ways. Whereas the political narrative portrays leaders who are figures of authority in the Jewish community and in the Christian power structure, the martyrologies are all portraits of individual members, regardless of their power and authority, of a particular Jewish community. While the action in the political narrative takes place very much in this world, the martyrologies describe a drama which unfolds between individual Jews and God and which concerns the eternal reward anticipated in the world to come. Lastly, though the political narratives describe Jewish strategies for dealing with Christian power which are conventional, the martyrs' acts of cultic homicide and suicide are radically unanticipated.

Let us consider the presentation of the political events. Modeled in part on the Book of Esther, the initial response of Mainz Jewry is both to abstain "from food and drink for three consecutive days and nights" (Esther 4:16; SS: NS, 1; H, 25; E, 22) and also to intervene politically by an appeal to Gentile power. Thus, upon learning about the earlier attacks on Speyer and Worms, Mainz Jewry organizes a special council to meet the emergency in political terms: " 'Let us elect elders so that we may know how to act' " (SS: NS, 2–3; H, 26; E, 24). The confrontations depicted in the political narratives are between Jewish and Christian political leaders, not between individuals who lack authority. Adopting standard political practices, the elders bribe the bishop, the political authority, in return for promises of protection.

With the mobs still far off, a new danger arises when Duke Godfrey of Bouillon threatens to massacre Jews on his way to Jerusalem. To meet this larger challenge, an appeal to the highest political protector is called for, and Rabbi Kalonimos ben Meshullam, the leader (*parnas*) of Mainz Jewry,

> dispatched a messenger to King Henry [IV] in the Kingdom of Apulia. The king was enraged and sent letters to all of the ministers, bishops and governors of all the provinces of his realm as well as to Duke Gofrey . . . commanding them to do no bodily harm to the Jews and to provide them with help and refuge. (SS: NS, 3; H, 26–27; E, 25)

Throughout the political sections, the narrator depicts a conflict between leaders in authority: the communal elders bribe Bishop Ruthard "who took the entire community into his inner chamber" (SS: NS, 5; H, 29; E, 28); or bribe Count Emicho, the leader of the Crusader mob. When political action fails, the Jewish leaders, weakened from pious fasts, try taking up arms in military defense, but outnumbered and overpowered, again their efforts fail.

In contrast, the martyrology sections describe highly detailed portraits of individual Jewish men and women who defiantly hurl abuse at Chrisitan symbols before enacting precisely orchestrated rites of sacrificial killings. In the political sections, the characters are predictable; they seem to be reading from prepared scripts and playing assigned roles. The martyrs, on the other hand, are fully realized and individuated characters whose responses to events are presented as spontaneous and *ad hoc:*[10]

> Who has seen or heard of an act like the deed of the righteous and pious young Rachel . . . [who] said to her friends, "I have four children. Have no mercy on them." . . . With bitterness she said, "Do not slaughter Isaac before his brother Aaron, or [Aaron] will see his [older] brother's death and run away. . . ." [But] a friend took [Isaac] and slew him. . . . When Aaron saw that his brother had been slaughtered, he cried, "Mother, do not slaughter me," and fled, hiding himself under a box. . . . When this pious woman had finished sacrificing her three [other] children to their Creator, she raised her voice, calling, "Aaron, Aaron, where are you?" She drew him out by his feet from under the box where he was hiding and slaughtered him before the Exalted and High God. Then she put them all on her arms, two children on each side. . . . (SS: NS, 9; H, 34; E, 35–36)

Or,

> The pious Isaac returned to the synagogue to set it aflame and he lit the fire at all the exits. He proceeded from one end to the other, his hands stretched to Heaven to his Father in Heaven praying to God out of the flames in a loud voice. The enemy shouted at him through the windows, "Wicked one, escape from the

fire; you can still save yourself." They extended a pole toward him to help him escape from the fire, but the saint did not want to take hold of it and died in the flame, an innocent, just and God-fearing man. And his soul has found rest in the quarters of the righteous in Eden. (SS: NS, 12–13; H, 37–38; E, 41)

Along with the profound eschatological preoccupation here, one should notice the pronounced absence of evoked recent historical precedents. Here, none is found, and the typological antecedents which are offered (the Akedah;[11] Hananiah, Mishael and Azariah;[12] Rabbi Akiva) are evoked in order to show how far they have been outstripped by present events. The gap between tradition and experience is unconcealable. The message is clear: the martyrologies as they occurred were unprecedented: "Inquire and seek: was there ever such a mass sacrifical offering from the time of Adam?" that is, from the beginnings of created time (SS: NS, 8; H, 32; E, 33).

The prominent role played by women is one of the more striking aspects of the innovative behavior described in the martyrologies. As Albert of Aix noted, women killed their own children and then themselves. Moreover, the narrator gives credit to women for being in the vanguard of the martyrs. Thus in Speyer, "a distinguished pious woman there . . . was the first among all the communities of those who were slaughtered" (SS: NS, 2; H, 25; E, 22). In the imagery in which the martyrdom is cast, women along with men play the role of the male Temple priests in performing the sacrifical cult. Thus, in the martyrdom narratives, women and men are equalized as priests, and this is but one additional innovation in these accounts. In marked contrast, convention obtains in the political narratives: Men rule.

Taken together, then, the differences between the political story and the martyrologies amount to an overwhelming contrast. The question that must be asked is what is the meaning of two such divergent conceptions of reality and how can they credibly apply to the same actors? We can be helped in answering this question by terms offered by discussions in the history of science and anthropology. The notion of paradigms is key. Culturally conditioned models or paradigms, according to Thomas Kuhn, provide different ways of processing experience.[13] Paradigms enable the same people to reorder the world they experience in different ways. Because paradigms are products of specific cultures, they have interested such anthropologists as Victor Turner. One of Turner's studies[14] offers suggestive implications for understanding the two-act dramas which we have described in Solomon's account of the 1096 Crusade riots. Turner analyzed Thomas Becket's murder in the cathedral by the agents of King Henry II of England in light of a basic question: How was it that Thomas, formerly Henry's loyal Chancellor, became alienated from the king after Thomas became Archbishop of Canterbury? Using Kuhn's idea of shifting paradigms, Turner suggests that Thomas "saw" the world in two different ways when he was Henry's Chancellor and when he became Archbishop. Mentally, culturally, and symbolically, Thomas recreated his world when he shifted from one role to the other. Henry did not understand Thomas' new role, and the values and relationships it dictated and took Thomas' behavior to be a betrayal of his former friend's loyalty to him.

Applied to the two stages of the Hebrew Crusade narratives, Turner's analysis suggests that the narrators, if not the protagonists themselves, shifted paradigms during the Crusaders' attacks. Aggressively striving to avoid being defeated by the Christian mobs, the Jews first used political means to check the assaults. When these efforts failed, they adopted a new posture which involved symbolically recreating the Temple in order to deny the Christian mob a victory through forced baptism. Thus, before the Jews "saw" that political action was futile, they behaved like medieval Jews and sought protection from their political rulers; after they interpreted political and military failure as the judgment of God, they reordered their world-view according to a new paradigm, the Temple cult. The same people lived in two cultural worlds because they processed experience through two different cultural grids. The political narratives follow the Esther paradigm of political intercession in the Gentile court. When it becomes clear that there would be no Purim in Germany, the Temple paradigm takes over. Political leaders are replaced by lists of individual martyrs; the court is now the Temple altar; conventional collective Jewish-Christian relations become extraordinary acts of individual defiance which testify to the truth of Judaism and the falsehood of Christianity.

It is by means of the theological-liturgical framework which introduces, interrupts and concludes the two-act drama, that the narrator signals the meaning of each act and justifies the shift from one to the other. The first liturgical section introduces the political narrative by anticipating the defeat "in this world" and offering valid theological reasons why the political and military measures will fail. A minor motif is the cliché that the suffering is a divine punishment for past Jewish sin, but this is immediately dismissed as inadequate:

No prophet, seer or man of wisdom was able to understand how the sin of the people infinite in number was deemed so great as to cause the destruction of so many lives in the various Jewish communities. The martyrs endured the extreme penalty normally inflicted only upon one guilty of murder. Yet, it must be stated with certainty that God is a righteous judge, and we are to blame. (SS: NS, 3; H, 27; E, 25)

The more credible theodicy is the proposal that the suffering was a divine trial of the righteous, not a punishment of the guilty. Like Job, the righteous of Mainz are divinely tested in order to see if they will remain loyal to Him. Thus, when Solomon explains that the mob attacks resulted from a call to pilgrimage issued by the Pope, he refers to him as "Satan," the "Accuser" in the Book of Job who challenges God to subject the righteous man to a supreme trial.[15] Similarly, in Mainz, the righteous suffered because

This was the generation that had been chosen by Him to be His portion, for they had the strength and the fortitude to stand in His sanctuary, and fulfill His word, and sanctify His Great Name in His world. (SS: NS, 2; H, 25; E, 22)

The suffering was so great, so excessive if viewed as a punishment, that it can be explained only as a trial:

How has the staff of might been broken, the rod of glory—the sainted community comparable to fine gold, the community of Mainz. It was caused by the Lord to test those that fear Him, to have them endure the yoke of His pure fear. (SS: NS, 4; H, 28; E, 26)

The second liturgical section continues the motif of providing a theodicy but adds that the martyrs themselves were justified in their unprecedented acts because they acted only after "seeing" that political failure was God's judgment: "The people of the sacred convenant saw that the Heavenly decree had been issued and that the enemy had defeated them . . ." (SS: NS, 6; H, 31; E, 31). The martyrs, Eliezer ben Natan reports, "hastened to fulfill the will of the Creator . . . for lovingly they accepted Heaven's judgment" (EN: NS, 39; H, 75; E, 83). And the anonymously written account also notes:

A venerable student, Baruch ben Isaac was there [Mainz] and he said to us, "Know that his decree has been issued against us in truth and honesty, and we cannot be saved. (A: NS, 52; H, 98, E, 107)

While the theological transitions between the political and martyrological narratives explain why the martyrs were justified, the concluding
theological sections explain the meaning of the acts of martyrdom as
aspects of God's justice. Contrary to facts as they seem, the narrators
declare that the Crusaders will be punished, the innocent victims will be
avenged and God's justice demonstrated:

"God of vengeance, O Lord, God of vengeance, shine forth" [Psalms 94:1]. . . .
Do to them as they have done to us. Then will they understand and take to heart
that . . . for falsehood have they slain our saints. (SS: NS, 16–17; H, 42–43;
E, 48)

The cry for vengeance is a cry for ultimate justice: "The murderers are
marked for eternal obloquy; those murdered . . . are destined for enter-
nal life . . . Amen" (SS: NS, 14; H, 40; E, 44).

In addition to prayers for vengeance which affirm the ultimate triumph
and truth of Judaism over Christianity, there is a second closing motif
which assigns a positive role to the martyrs' deaths in the future. The
narrator prays that

the blood of His devoted ones stand us in good stead and be an atonement for
us and for our posterity after us, and our children's children eternally like the
Akedah of our father Isaac when our father Abraham bound him upon the altar.
(SS: NS, 17; H, 43; E, 49)

Common to the theological-liturgical framework is the theme of justice
and the affirmation not only that God is just but that the martyrs' acts
were justified. The Jews of the Rhineland did not sin but were tested
because they were especially righteous; they committed acts of killing
and suicide only after "seeing" that it was God's will that their political
and military actions fail; and their acts are described as acts of supreme
loyalty, like Abraham's willingness to sacrifice Isaac and are praisewor-
thy because they will ultimately result in just punishment for the Christian perpetrators and less suffering for Jews in need of vicarious atonement.

The narrator also tries to justify and legitimate the martyrs' innovative acts of homicide and suicide by interpreting them as a symbolic
reinactment of the Temple sacrificial cult. In this way, the categories of
purity and impurity, holy and profane are introduced and with them a
justification for the martyrs to draw a boundary around themselves as
Holy Things. Whereas the political narratives depict Jewish-Christian

relations as a fluid boundary—the Jews have their assigned place within the Christian town, protected by the Christian ruler—the martyrologies describe an attempt to avoid any contact whatsoever with Christians.[16]

Jacob Katz has correctly observed that in the martyrdom narratives the Jews, like the Christian Crusaders, act out their sense of religious superiority against members of the other religious community.[17] Far from being described as passive, the martyrs, no less than the political leaders of the Jewish communities, initiate their deaths as symbolic acts of defiance and self-affirmation. They go out of their way to hurl invective upon invective at their Christian attackers, and the imagery denotes the view that Christians are impure and must not be permitted to contaminate the Holy Ones, that is, the martyr-sacrifices. Thus, martyrs decide to kill themselves and refuse "to gainsay their faith and replace the fear of our King with an abominable stock, bastard son of a menstruating and wanton mother . . ." (SS: NS, 7; H, 32; E, 32). The language is hostile and aggressive. Jewish women "taunted and reviled the Crusaders with the name of the crucified, despicable, and abominable son of harlotry, saying, 'In whom do you put your trust? In a putrid corpse?' " (SS: NS, 9; H, 33–34; E, 35).

In light of the impurity and falsehood of Christianity, the martyrs are justified in erecting ritualized boundaries between would-be victims and aggressors. The martyrdom becomes enacted as a form of religious polemic, performed as highly stylized "ritual dramas," in Victor Turner's phrase. Natalie Zemon Davis has pointed out that in Protestant and Catholic urban religious riots in sixteenth-century France, the streets became extensions of religious debates.[18] Religious "polemic" reverted to a symbolically specific form of its literal meaning, "warfare." The narrators describe the encounters between Rhineland Jews and Crusaders as a case of the "rites of violence."

But the ritualization of those "polemics" in the streets of Mainz is culturally specific to Judaism. Although the Akedah image is pervasive, it is less generalized than the symbolism of the Temple cult, of which the Akedah might be considered a failed anticipation. Abraham was ready to sacrifice Isaac on Mt. Moriah, on which Solomon later succeeded in erecting the Temple.

Mainz is compared to Jerusalem throughout the narrative. In one respect, the fall of Mainz is comparable to the destruction of the Second Temple: "For since the day on which the Second Temple was destroyed, their like had not arisen, nor shall there be their like again . . ." (SS: NS, 8; H, 32; E, 33). Mainz was forsaken, just as God "forsook the sanctuary of Shiloh—the Temple in Miniature—which He had placed among His people who dwelt in the midst of alien nations" (SS: NS, 4; H, 27; E, 26). The verse "And the daughter of Zion was shorn of all her splendor" (Lamentations 1:6), we are told, "refers to Mainz" (SS: NS, 6; H, 30; E, 29), and on and on.

More spectacularly, the narrator describes the martyrdom at Mainz and the other lesser communities as a rebuilding of the Temple of Jerusalem. The accounts of the martyrs are told in language which applies to the Temple cult. Thus Mistress Rachel "spread her sleeves to receive the blood, according to the practice in the ancient Temple sacrificial rite" (SS: NS, 9; H, 34; E, 35). Mistress Skolester's son, Isaac, tells his mother, after being forcibly baptised, " 'Mother, I have decided to bring a sin-offering to the God of Heaven. Perhaps I will thereby achieve atonement.' " To do so, he takes his children into the synagogue at night and "there he slaughtered them, in sanctification of the Great Name. . . . He sprinkled some of their blood on the pillars of the Holy Ark . . ." (SS: NS, 12; H, 37; E, 40). Near Cologne, a father tells his son,

"Yehiel, my son, my son, stretch out your neck before your father and I will offer you as a sacrifice to God. I will recite the benediction of ritual slaughter and you will respond, 'Amen.' " (SS: NS, 19; H, 45; E, 52)

Similarly, Samuel ben Gedalia, Yehiel's friend, calls to Menahem, the sexton of the synagogue of Cologne, and asks him to sacrifice him: " 'By your life, take your sharp sword and inspect it carefully so that there be no flaw in it and slaughter me, too, for I cannot bear to see the death of my friend' " (SS: NS, 19; H, 45; E, 52).

In this way, the narrator replaces the Esther paradigm by the Temple imagery and, to a lesser extent, by the Akedah. Both archetypes serve to anchor the martyrs' innovative behavior by masking it in the most ancient archetypes of Jewish piety: Abraham's demonstration of loyalty to God and the Temple cult. By clothing the martyrs in the symbols of the Priests, the narrators justify the boundaries which the martyrs erected between their lives and Christian contamination:

The last survivor shall slaughter himself with his knife at his throat, or shall thrust his sword into his stomach so that the impure ones and the hands of wickedness will not be able to defile us with their abominations. (SS: NS, 21–22; H, 48; E, 56)

Another effort the narrators made to legitimate the martyrs' radically innovative behavior did not succeed. Although the transitions in the narratives are written in liturgical language, the texts did not become part of the liturgy in a lasting way. Only actual liturgical poems could be incorporated into the prayerbook, not narratives about specific events framed in liturgical sections, however moving. The factual parts were needed for a specific theological purpose: By telling exactly what happened, the narrators bore witness to the martyrs' justification for what they did. But by including "the facts," the narrators inadvertently caused their texts to be excluded from the permanent liturgy.

The account which Solomon wrote, finally, conveys a message of consolation about the future. His narrative is designed to leave a feeling of renewal as well as a memorialization of destruction. As noted earlier, the concluding liturgical passages express a hope that the sacrifices of the martyrs may serve as vicarious atonement for Jews in the future. But there is a more immediate message of hope as well. As arranged, the narrative focuses not only on the destruction of the rabbinic elite of Mainz, but also on continuity in Speyer which mainly survived in 1096. Although some fifty per cent of Solomon's account dwells on the martyrdom of Mainz, it begins with the survival of most of Speyer Jewry and contains an appendix about the founding, Crusade experience, and rededication of the Speyer synagogue in 1104.[19] Moreover, that brief local account relates that Speyer had been founded in 1084 after a fire broke out in Mainz and Jews fled there. The point is clear: Thanks to an act of God, there will be continuity in Speyer, despite the losses suffered elsewhere. "It was the Lord's doing to grant us a vestige and a remnant by the bishop's hand" (A: NS, 48; H, 95; E, 101).

Once again, historical accuracy is conveyed for reasons of religious ideology, not because the narrators were interested in the past for its own sake. It is a coincidence that the narrator reports accurate historical information about the political as well as the martyrological events. This is evident in the details about where the attacks occurred and how Jewish leaders responded, and it is also reflected in the final impression the Solomon ben Samson account leaves the reader: Speyer offers German Jewry some hope for a future. Without explicitly saying so, Solomon

or a later editor expressed hope in that the destruction of Mainz/Jerusa-
lem was accompanied by the survival of Speyer/Yavneh.

To be sure, the supreme irony of the narrative lies not in its inadvertently containing accurate historical information, but rather in the way
it demonstrates the truth of Judaism and the falsehood of Christianity.
The narrative shows that the Crusaders, who had set out to restore
Christian hegemony over Jerusalem, never got there;[20] the Jews, whom
the Crusaders tried to destroy en route, were even capable of rebuilding
the Temple in Mainz—their own Jerusalem!

NOTES

1. N. Porges, "Les relations hébraïques des persécutions des Juifs pendant la
   première croisade," *Revue des Etudes Juives* 25 (1892): 189.
2. Quoted in Edward Peters, ed., *The First Crusade* (Philadelphia, 1971),
   p. 103.
3. The standard editions of the Hebrew texts are A. Neubauer and M. Stern,
   eds., *Hebräische Berichte über die Judenverfolgungen während der Kreuzzüge* (Berlin, 1892), with German translation by S. Baer; and A. M. Haberman, ed., *Sefer gezerot Ashkenaz veZarfat* (Jerusalem, 1945), which includes liturgical poems from the period. Shlomo Eidelberg, ed. and trans.,
   *The Jews and the Crusaders: The Hebrew Chronicles of the First and Second
   Crusades* (Madison, 1977), is a complete English translation. These are
   abbreviated in the body of the text as NS, H, and E, respectively.
4. The most recent are Robert Chazan, "The First-Crusade Chronicles," *Revue
   des Etudes Juives* 133 (1974): 237–54 and idem, "The Hebrew First Crusade Chronicles: Further Reflections," *AJS Review* 3 (1978): 79–98. The
   earlier textual studies by Bresslau, Porges, Aronius, Elbogen, Haberman,
   Sonne and Baer are cited in Chazan's first article and in Joseph Hacker, "On
   the 1096 Persecutions" (Hebrew), *Zion* 31 (1966): 225, n. 1.
5. For example, see Shlomo Eidelberg, "The Solomon Bar Simson Chronicle as
   a Source of the History of the First Crusade," *Jewish Quarterly Review* N.S.
   49 (1959): 282–7; Chazan, "Hebrew First-Crusade Chronicles."
6. Shalom Spiegel, *The Last Trial*, translated by Judah Goldin (Philadelphia,
   1967).
7. Especially suggestive are Yizhak Baer, "The 1096 Persecution" (Hebrew),
   Sefer Assaf (Jerusalem, 1953), pp. 126–40; Jacob Katz, "On the Persecutions of 1096 and 1648/9" (Hebrew), *Yizhak Baer Jubilee Volume* (Jerusalem, 1960), 318–37, and Chazan's two studies cited in note 4.
8. See Roger D. Ray, "Medieval Historiography through the Twelfth Century,"
   Viator 5 (1974): 33–59. On the Hebrew chronicles, see Haim Hillel Ben-

Sasson, "Towards an Understanding of the Goals of Medieval Jewish Historiography" (Hebrew), *Historionim ve'askolot historiyot* (Jerusalem, 1963), 29–49.

9. See Baer, "1096 Persecution," p. 136. That the Temple is the central symbolic image in these narratives is an insight of Professor Alan Mintz who kindly shared his reading of these texts with me, a chapter from his forthcoming book.

10. See Chazan, "Further Reflections," pp. 94–96, who stresses the clash of wills and the character portraits in the narratives. I have modified this by restricting the detailed portraiture to the martyrs, not the politicos, and I think it somewhat misleading to characterize the texts as a whole as "this-worldly" without some qualification (p. 95). The narrators never doubt that God permits the events to unfold as they do.

11. Genesis 22.

12. Daniel 1:8–21.

13. Thomas S. Kuhn, *The Structure of Scientific Revolutions* (2nd ed.; Chicago, 1970). See also Ian G. Barbour, *Myths, Models and Paradigms* (New York, 1974), pp. 119–70.

14. Victor Turner, "Religious Paradigms and Political Action," in his *Dramas, Fields and Metaphors* (Ithaca, 1974), pp. 60–97.

15. Job 1–2.

16. See Mary Douglas, *Purity and Danger* (London, 1966).

17. See above, no. 7.

18. "The Rites of Violence," in her *Society and Culture in Early Modern France* (Stanford, 1975), pp. 152–87.

19. On this short text, see Robert Chazan, "A Twelfth-Century Communal History of Spires Jewry," *Revue des Etudes Juives* 128 (1969); 253–57.

20. Chazan, "Further Reflections," p. 88, correctly stresses that the Crusaders' failure to reach Jerusalem in the narratives may be more the result of the narrators' bias than of their knowledge about what happened in 1099.

18

The Jewish-Christian Debate in the High Middle Ages

David Berger

I. ON JEWISH-CHRISTIAN POLEMIC

Polemical literature is one of the liveliest manifestations of Jewish-Christian relations in the Middle Ages. At times calm and almost dispassionate, at other times angry and bitter, religious polemic is a reflection of the mood and character not only of the disputants themselves but of the age in which they wrote and spoke. While the tone of the Jewish-Christian debate ranges from somber to sarcastic to playfully humorous, the underlying issues were as serious to the participants as life itself. Failure on the part of the Christian polemicist could encourage Jews in their mockery of all that was sacred and might engender doubts in Christian minds; failure by the Jew could lead to apostasy and, on some occasions, severe persecution and even martyrdom. Religious arguments could be stimulating and enjoyable, but the stakes involved were monumental.

The *Nizzaḥon Vetus,* or *Old Book of Polemic,* is a striking example of Jewish disputation in its most aggressive mode. The anonymous author collected an encyclopedic array of anti-Christian arguments current among late thirteenth-century Franco-German Jews. Refutations of christological exegesis, attacks on the rationality of Christian doctrine, a critique of the Gospels and Church ritual, denunciations of Christian

Reprinted by permission of the Jewish Publication Society of America from *The Jewish-Christian Debate in the High Middle Ages A Critical Edition of the Nizzaḥon Vetus,* by David Berger, Philadelphia, 1979, 3–32.

morality—all these and more are presented in an exceptionally vigorous style that is not especially scrupulous about overstepping the bounds of civility. Although both the style and comprehensiveness of the book are not altogether typical of Jewish polemic, they make the *Nizzahon Vetus* an excellent and unusually interesting vehicle for the study of this crucial and intriguing dimension of medieval Jewish-Christian relations.

Jewish-Christian polemic begins at the very dawn of Christianity. The reasons for this are built into the essence of the Christian faith, for a religion that was born out of Judaism had to justify the rejection of its parent. Indeed, theological and exegetical approaches which can be labeled polemic can also be seen as the elementary building blocks of the developing faith, since certain early doctrines grew naturally out of a reading of the Hebrew Bible. Isaiah 53, which could easily be read as a reference to the vicarious atonement of a "servant of the Lord," served as an almost inevitable explanation of the paradox of the Messiah's crucifixion. Whether or not Jesus applied such an understanding of this passage to his own career (and he probably did not),[1] this is a case in which a crux of later polemic was read christologically for fundamental, internal reasons.

Some doctrines, of course, did not develop out of the Hebrew Scriptures. Nevertheless, Christian acceptance of the divine origin of those Scriptures, together with an espousal of central beliefs that did not seem to be there, generated a need to explain this omission. Thus, even if Jews had not pressed their opposition to statements concerning the divinity of the Messiah, the virgin birth, or the abrogation of the Law, almost any serious Christian would have tried to find biblical justification for these doctrines. It is, in fact, often difficult to tell when a given Christian argument is directed against Jews and when it is an attempt to deal with a problem raised by the writer's own study of the Bible. This uncertainty applies even to some works ostensibly aimed against the Jews, because the number of such works through the ages seems disproportionate to the threat that Judaism could have posed.[2]

Were Jewish questions, then, the primary factor behind the search for biblical testimonies to Christian truth? Was it, as one scholar has suggested, because of Jewish arguments that Christians became concerned with the conflict between the genealogies of Jesus in Matthew and Luke?[3] Did the incredulous inquiries of Jews inspire the various rationales concerning the need for the incarnation, up to and including

Anselm's *Cur Deus Homo?*[4] The extent of Jewish influence is difficult to determine, but it is clear that such issues would not have been ignored in the absence of Jewish disputants. It is surely evident that when Isidore of Seville, in a work on Leviticus, has a Jew ask why Christians fail to bring sacrifices or observe the sabbatical year, he is raising problems suggested by his own reading of the Bible, and yet Peter Damian transferred these passages without change into a polemical work against the Jews.[5] Christians undoubtedly wrote books against Judaism in response to a challenge actually raised by Jews, but they were also motivated by the internal need to deal with issues that were both crucial and profoundly disturbing.

One approach to the puzzling conflict between the Hebrew Bible and Christian beliefs was a frontal attack. Marcion and other Christian heretics rejected the Jewish Scriptures and subjected them to a wide-ranging critique. In one respect this was a simple and straightforward solution since the problem vanishes entirely; there was no longer any need to engage in point by point exegesis of individual passages. On the other hand, this radical solution of one problem created another even more intractable difficulty. The Gospels, after all, clearly recognized the divine origin of the Hebrew Bible; indeed, many of the biblical testimonies central to later polemic are found in the New Testament. The suggestion that offending New Testament passages be emended was hardly palatable to more Christians, and mainstream Christianity rejected the one approach that would have sharply limited the scope of the Jewish-Christian debate.

It seems a bit strange to assert that the vigorous anti-Jewish position of the heretics would have minimized polemical activity, but this is indeed the case. Absolute rejection of the Hebrew Bible by Christians would have eliminated much of the wrangling over the meaning of verses which plays such a prominent role in medieval polemic. Moreover, the heretics' reading of the Bible was, in an ironic way, closer to that of the Jews than to that of orthodox Christians, because, like the Jews, they understood it literally. Total rejection eliminated the need for allegory entirely.[6]

In one area, however, such heretics enriched the Jewish-Christian argument. One of the central heretical methods of defending their pejorative evaluation of the Hebrew Bible was to show that it is replete with absurdities and contradictions. In discussions with heretics, orthodox

Christians tended to shrink from such arguments, but in debates with Jews they changed their tune. Of course, the arguments were rechanneled; they were no longer proof of the absurdity of the Hebrew Bible, only of the absurdity of literal interpretation. In effect, therefore, Jews found themselves defending their Bible against both heretical barbs and orthodox allegory.[7]

One of the sharpest points of contention in the early confrontation between Jews and Christians—one in which the Christian position was formed by both internal and external factors—was the famous assertion that Christians are the true (verus) Israel. Here again, acceptance of the Hebrew Bible led naturally to the need to transform it into a Christian document, and the process through which Israel came to refer to Christians was almost inevitable. In this case, however, powerful forces from the outside combined to make this an argument of extraordinary significance. The pagan accusation that Christianity was an innovation had to be answered because it could affect the very legitimacy of the new faith, and the only effective response was to don the mantle of antiquity through the identification of Christendom with Israel.

Jews could hardly have been expected to suffer such a claim with equanimity. The most succinct summary of the instinctive Jewish reaction to this assertion is the Greek quotation from the Dialogue with Trypho which Marcel Simon placed on the cover of his Verus Israel. "What?!" said Trypho. "You are Israel?!"[8] After the initial shock wore off, Jews realized that this was a direct assault against the fundamental underpinnings of Judaism, an effort to abscond with the Bible. They pointed with outrage to the arbitrariness of applying all favorable biblical statements about Israel to the church and all pejorative ones to the Jews, and by the high Middle Ages they had assembled passages from the Bible in which favorable and unfavorable references were inextricably intertwined. The same Israel would be exiled and redeemed, and since the church would not suffer the former fate it could hardly lay claim to the latter reward.[9] Whatever the Jewish response, the issue was critical, because it appeared that Christianity could lay claim to legitimacy only by denying it to Judaism. There was no room (at least according to the dominant view) for two spiritual Israels.

The corpus of early Christian works directed against Judaism is, as we have already noted, rather extensive. Anti-Christian works by Jews, on the other hand, are virtually nonexistent before the twelfth century.

One reason for this disparity is that Jews had no internal motivation for writing polemics against Christians; in times or places where Christianity was not a threat, we cannot expect Jews to be concerned with a refutation of its claims. Moreover, during much of the so-called Dark Ages, Jews in Christian lands produced no literature that has survived. Consequently, aside from some largely philosophical material in Arabic, our sources for the Jewish side of the discussion consist of scattered references in rabbinic literature,[10] the collections of folk polemic that go by the name *Toledot Yeshu*,[11] and quotations in Christian works.[12] The last group of sources is by far the richest, but determining the authenticity of Jewish arguments cited in some of the purely literary Christian dialogues is a risky procedure. The genuineness of such arguments can usually be tested by their appearance in later Jewish polemic or by their inherent plausibility, and despite the usefulness of these criteria it hardly needs to be said that they are far from foolproof. It is therefore not until the second half of the twelfth century that we can begin to speak with confidence about the details of the Jewish argument against Christianity.

An examination of Jewish-Christian polemic in the high Middle Ages reveals an arena in which most of the battles take place along well-charted lines but where certain new approaches are beginning to make themselves heard. The Christian side is usually on the offensive with respect to biblical verses, although, as I have indicated, there is a fundamentally defensive element in the entire enterprise of searching for biblical testimonies. Indeed, we find Jews arguing that Christianity is so inherently implausible that only the clearest biblical evidence could suffice to establish its validity.[13] Nevertheless, the structure of the Jewish-Christian debate was such that the initiative was taken by Christians in the area of scriptural evidence. On the other hand, Jews usually initiated the discussion of doctrinal questions, because they felt that the irrationality of Christianity could be established through such an approach. In each area, however, the initative could shift; Jews did not refrain from citing specific verses to refute Christian beliefs and Christians did not hesitate to attack Jewish doctrines on philosophical or moral grounds.

The bulk of polemical discussions continued to center around the time-honored issue of christological verses in the Hebrew Bible. Before such discussions could take place, ground rules had to be set up. What is the scope of the Hebrew Bible, and what text can legitimately be cited? Particularly in the early centuries, Christians would have liked very much to include the apocrypha in their arsenal, and they were even more anxious to quote certain Septuagint readings. The very nature of this issue, however, forced a resolution in favor of the Jews. It can be very frustrating and unprofitable to argue with someone who simply denies the legitimacy of your quotations, and it was nearly impossible to prove that the apocrypha should be canonical or that Septuagint variants are superior to the Masoretic text (especially when some of those variants were a result of the corruption of the Septuagint text itself). Jerome's respect for the Hebrew text accelerated the resolution of this matter in favor of the Jewish position, and despite the persistence of a handful of apocryphal quotations and a few Septuagint variants, Christians settled down to the task of demonstrating the christological nature of the biblical text accepted by Jews.[14]

This task was pursued on two levels, and it would be useful to draw a distinction between genuine polemic and what could be called exegetical polemic. Genuine polemic involved those verses whose christological interpretation provided a genuine challenge to a Jew. If *'almah* meant virgin, then Isaiah 7:14 really seemed to speak of a virgin birth. Jeremiah 31:31 really spoke of a new covenant that God would make with the house of Israel. What did that mean? Isaiah 53 really did refer to a servant of the Lord who would suffer, despite his innocence, as a result of the sins of others. Who was that servant, and how was such suffering to be explained? If *shiloh* somehow meant Messiah (and many Jews conceded that it did), then Genesis 49:10 could reasonably be taken to mean that Jewish kingship would last until the messianic age and then cease. If the Messiah had not yet come, why was there no Jewish king? Specific rejoinders were necessary to blunt the force of such arguments, and it is no accident that the verses which fall into this category constitute the *loci classici* of polemical literature.

Nevertheless, a great deal of that literature is devoted to a discussion of passages of such weak polemical force that specific refutation was hardly even necessary. Such passages multiplied as a result of Christian exegesis of the Bible, and their christological interpretation was probably not even intended to persuade the nonbeliever. As time passed, however, this type of material began to make its way into polemical works, and the refutation of such "exegetical polemic" became a major concern of some Jewish writers. Although they used many of the same techniques that were applied to more serious arguments, Jewish polemicists confronted a situation in which the most straightforward response was the observation that there was simply no evidence for the christological assertion. Why should Cyrus in Isaiah 45 be Jesus? On what basis are the heavens in Psalm 19 identified with the apostles? Who says that David in Psalm 17 is Jesus, and why should we assume that the speaker in Psalm 13 is the church?[15] The inclusion of such material blurred the already fuzzy line between polemic and exegesis, and biblical commentaries become a particularly important source of polemical material.

This is true not only of Christian commentaries, which are obviously a major source of exegetical polemic, but of Jewish commentaries as well. When a Jewish exegete reached a passage that was a crux of Christian polemic, he would frequently make an effort, whether implicitly or explicitly, to undermine the christological interpretation.[16] One exegetical tendency that was greatly encouraged by such polemical goals was the denial of the messianic nature of certain biblical passages and the assertion that they referred instead to historical figures. Such a tendency appears in nonpolemical contexts as well, and some scholars have argued that the polemical motivation has been overstated; it is, nevertheless, beyond question that the desire to refute Christian interpretation played some role in the development of this type of exegesis. This is especially clear when surprising historical interpretations appear in overtly polemical works. In the *Nizzahon Vetus,* the most striking use of such exegesis appears in the discussion of Isaiah 11. While the author himself apparently understood that chapter messianically, he made use of a long-standing but clearly radical Jewish interpretation by maintaining that it could be referred to Hezekiah and Sennacherib. This view eliminates any christological reference, but it also does away with one of the central messianic passages in the Bible. Polemic, then, was at least a factor in stimulating and legitimizing an important development in medieval Jewish exegesis.[17]

Christians were genuinely puzzled at the Jewish failure to accept the overwhelming array of scriptural arguments which they had marshaled. Every major Christian doctrine could be supported by several verses in the Hebrew Bible, and some of these appeared utterly irrefutable. Indeed, a few verses seemed so impressive that the persuasive force of any one of them should in itself have caused Jews to abandon their faith.[18] Only preternatural blindness or a conscious refusal to accept the truth could account for Jewish resistance, and both of these explanations played a major role in the medieval conception of the Jew.[19]

Jewish refutations of Christian interpretations of the Bible had to proceed on a verse-by-verse basis. There are, nevertheless, certain general principles that were applied time and again, and the most important of these was the argument from context. Jews argued that christological explanations of individual verses could rarely withstand scrutiny from the wider perspective of the passage as a whole, and they constantly cited adjoining verses to demonstrate this point. Perhaps the most important use of this argument was its application to the virgin birth explanation of Isaiah 7:14. This verse was by far the most significant evidence for the virgin birth in the Hebrew Bible, and its importance was enhanced by the fact that it was cited for this purpose in Matthew. Nevertheless, it was only with the greatest difficulty that Christians could respond to the Jewish argument that the birth was clearly expected to take place very shortly after Isaiah's announcement.[20] While the argument from context was not always as effective as it was here, it was the stock-in-trade of any medieval Jewish polemicist.

The Jewish posture with respect to the citation of biblical verses was not always defensive. Indeed, the very essence of the Jewish position rested upon certain monumental assertions built upon the straightforward reading of the Hebrew Bible as a whole; it is precisely because of this that Jews were less concerned with the citation of specific controversial verses. A reading of the Bible as a whole leaves the unmistakable impression that the Messiah would bring peace, that he would be a human being, that God is one, and that the ritual law means what it says. The burden of proof that any of these impressions should be modified, elaborated, or rejected was upon the Christians; this was recognized to some degree by the Christian side, and it was one of the fundamental assumptions of Jewish writers. Nevertheless, some Jewish polemicists did compile lists of verses to demonstrate the validity of certain basic Jewish beliefs.[21]

There was another Jewish approach that involved the citation of specific verses, but it is difficult to decide how seriously to take it. *The Nizzahon Vetus*, the earlier *Sefer Yosef HaMeqanne*, and some other Jewish polemics cite a series of verses which, they say, are aimed directly at Christianity. Several of these constitute clever responses to Christian assertions and are surely not to be taken seriously (e.g., the copper serpent does indeed represent Jesus and that is why Moses was commanded to hang it). I am inclined to think, however, that Jews were entirely serious about some of these quotations. One polemicist, in fact, cited such a verse immediately after a Christian question asking how the Torah could have omitted all reference to Jesus. Thus, the Bible explicitly warned against trusting in a man (Jer. 17:5; Ps. 146:3); it told Jews to punish a man who would claim to have a mother but not a father (Deut. 13:7); and it spoke of the humbling of anyone who pretended to be divine (Isa. 2:11). Such citations were hardly central to Jewish polemic, but they represent an effort by Jews to turn the tables on their opponents by finding "christological" verses of their own.[22]

With respect to doctrinal issues, it was the Jewish side that usually took the offensive. Jews were convinced that some of the central articles of faith professed by Christians were not only devoid of scriptural foundation but were without logical justification as well; to use Christian terminology, they lacked both *ratio* and *auctoritas*.

The trinity, which was an obvious target for logical questions, posed a peculiar problem for Jewish polemicists; they considered it so irrational that they had trouble in coming to grips with it. Although no Jewish writer formulates his difficulties in precisely this fashion, it seems clear that Jews, in effect, asked themselves the following questions: "What do they mean when they talk about a triune God? They say that there are three, and then they say that the three are one. But this is patent nonsense. What, then, do they really believe? Which of these contradictory assertions am I to take seriously and which shall I dismiss as meaningless double-talk? Since they talk about the separate incarnation of one of the three persons, it is apparently the assertion of multiplicity that they really mean. In that case, I shall have to demonstrate to them that there is only one God."

It is only some such line of reasoning that can explain the persistent Jewish efforts to persuade Christians to accept monotheism on both logical and scriptural grounds. Jacob ben Reuben cites philosophical evidence that the world was created by no more than one God. The author of the *Nizzaḥon Vetus* wants to know what will happen if one person of the trinity makes a decision and another person reverses it. Solomon de' Rossi compiles a list of biblical verses which say that there is one God. Writer after writer reminds Christians that God proclaimed,

"I, I am he, and there is no God beside me" (Deut. 32:39). To the Christian polemicist, of course, such arguments were virtually inexplicable and missed the point entirely. Christians, he would reply, believe in monotheism as much as Jews; the question is only the nature of that one God. On this issue, Jews and Christians were operating on different wavelengths, and the essence of the problem was the rationality of the Christian belief.[23]

Christians attempted to defend the plausibility of the trinitarian faith by analogies with physical phenomena or by the identification of the three persons of the trinity with major attributes of God. Such arguments raised complex philosophical questions about divine attributes which transcended the boundaries of the Jewish-Christian debate but did play a role in some of the more sophisticated polemical works. Some Jews tried to undermine this type of explanation by arguing that it could not coexist comfortably with the doctrine of the incarnation which implied the sort of separability among the persons of the trinity that could not be attributed to divine power, wisdom, and will.[24]

The incarnation itself was subjected to a Jewish critique that ranged from the questioning of its necessity to the contention that it is impossible even for an omnipotent God.[25] Christian works quote several Jewish polemicists who became so carried away with the tendency to maintain the impossibility of Christian dogmas that they made such an assertion even with respect to the virgin birth. Here they were on very shaky ground; Christians presented effective rebuttals, and the extant Jewish polemics which discuss the matter concede that God could theoretically have caused a virgin to conceive.[26]

One Christian doctrine that Jews attacked on moral rather than philosophical grounds was the belief in the universal damnation which came in the wake of original sin. They argued that such treatment is clearly unfair and inconsistent with the mercy of God, and at least one Jewish writer made the same argument with respect to the damnation of the unbaptized, especially unbaptized infants.[27] The terrible consequences of a failure to accept Christianity seemed particularly unjust in light of what Jews considered the unimpressive nature of the miracles associated with Jesus' career.[28] Moreover, some of the central assertions of the Christian faith appeared not only implausible but demeaning to God, and it did not seem right that someone who refused to believe such doctrines should be punished so severely.[29]

For their part, Christians were more than willing to engage in arguments appealing to reason, morality, or fairness. The ritual law, they said, was demonstrably unreasonable. Even where it did not contradict itself, no plausible reasons could be discovered for many of its precepts, and the contention that no reasons need to be given for the divine will is the refuge of desperate, unintelligent men.[30] The very fate of the Jewish people constitutes a rational argument against the validity of Judaism.[31] As for moral arguments, Jews believed that God revealed himself only to them,[32] they apparently thought that only they would be saved,[33] and they possessed a harsh and carnal Law.[34]

Each side, then, was well fortified with arguments from both Scripture and reason, and polemical activity in the twelfth and thirteenth centuries reached new heights. Among Christians, the outpouring of anti-Jewish polemic began in the late eleventh century and reached a crescendo in the twelfth. Peter Damian, Gilbert Crispin, Petrus Alfonsi, Rupert of Deutz, Peter the Venerable, "William of Champeaux," Peter of Blois, Walter of Châtillon, Alan of Lille—these and others made their contributions to the refutation of Judaism. Among Jews, the writing of polemic began in the late twelfth century and reached a peak (at least in France and Germany) in the thirteenth. Joseph Kimhi, Jacob ben Reuben, the author of the *Wikkuah LehaRadaq,* Meir of Narbonne, Joseph Official (Yosef HaMeqanne) and his father Nathan, Moses of Salerno, Mordecai of Avignon, Nahmanides, Jacob of Venice, Solomon de' Rossi and, finally, the anonymous author of the *Nizzahon Vetus* were the representatives of a concerted Jewish effort to present the case against Christianity. The renaissance of Christian polemic was as much a result of a general intellectual revival as of a new concern with Jews; the Jewish response, though somewhat delayed, was inevitable, and in two important instances, it was imposed in the form of forced disputations. Confrontations between Jews and Christians were on the increase, and their frequency, their tone, and even their content were being deeply influenced by the political, social, and economic changes of the twelfth and thirteenth centuries.

II. POLEMIC AND HISTORICAL REALITY

The *Nizzahon Vetus,* as we shall see, is a virtual anthology of Ashkenazic polemic in the twelfth and thirteenth centuries, and these centuries constitute a pivotal period in the history of the Jews of France and Germany. In France a major factor in the inexorable decline of the status of the Jews was the growing centralization of power in the hands of an unfriendly monarchy. The growing national unification, together with the increase in mass piety that had been stimulated as early as the eleventh century by the Gregorian reform and the Crusades, sharpened the awareness of the alien character of the Jew both nationally and religiously. The Christian piety of some of the French monarchs, particularly Louis IX, resulted in a major effort to bring about large-scale Jewish conversion, and considerable sums were expended for this purpose.[35] An investigation of the Talmud was pursued in 1240 by means of a Jewish-Christian debate that was really a trial, and the eventual burning of the Talmud shortly thereafter was a devastating psychological and cultural blow to French Jewry.[36] One Jewish source reports that the king of France encouraged the arrangement of public disputations in 1272–73 by a Jewish convert to Christianity who promised to show the Jews that they were without faith and that, like heretics, they deserved to be burned.[37] Thus, for at least some Jews in thirteenth-century France, religious polemic was simply unavoidable.

Religious motives, however, were not the only factors which undermined the position of the Jews. The French monarchy saw its Jewish subjects as a convenient target for fiscal exploitation, and the economic security of the Jews grew more and more precarious.[38] A feeling of economic insecurity had, in fact, been developing for some time and had even made its way into legal discussions by the twelfth century. The Talmud had recorded a view limiting the amount of interest that a Jew might collect from a Gentile to whatever the Jew needed for bare sustenance. In discussing this passage, some French Jewish commentators argued that such a ruling was of no practical effect under prevailing conditions; since "we do not know how much tax the king will demand," any sum must be regarded as bare sustenance.[39]

Similar evidence of such insecurity can be found in the application of another talmudic law. A Jew who was owed money by a Gentile was not supposed to collect the debt on a pagan holiday unless it was an oral debt; in the latter case, he could collect at any time because he had no assurance that he would be able to collect later. Here again Ashkenazic jurists maintained that under the conditions prevailing in medieval Europe, a debt for which the Jew had written proof (or even a pledge) could be collected on a Christian holiday because there was never any real assurance that even such a debt could be collected at a later date.[40]

It would, of course, be easy to argue that these rulings were rationalizations to justify widespread violations of the relevant talmudic regulations and that they do not therefore reflect genuine insecurity. The tosafists, however, did not manipulate talmudic law in quite so facile a manner. Whatever their motivations, they were convinced that they were describing their status accurately. It is clear, then, that considerable economic uncertainty was a genuine element in the Jewish psyche as early as the twelfth century, and in the thirteenth such uncertainty must have become more disturbing than ever. Legal attacks against Jewish moneylending were made by both Louis IX and Philip the Bold, while Philip the Fair resorted to outright extortion and eventual banishment in 1306. Even during those periods in the fourteenth century when the Jews were invited back, their security was tenuous. They were subjected to the indirect pressure of the Inquisition, they were vulnerable to the depredations of mobs like the Pastoureaux in 1320, and they were constantly aware of the possibility of another sudden expulsion.[41]

The status of German Jewry in the late thirteenth and early fourteenth centuries was also undergoing a precipitous decline. The most important change involved a new application of the old conception of Jewish servitude. As a theological concept, this doctrine goes back to the early Christian centuries, and it even gave rise to certain practical conclusions. Jews, for example, were not supposed to hold positions that would give them control over Christians, since that would constitute a violation of the biblical injunction (Gen. 25:23) that the older (i.e., the synagogue) must serve the younger (i.e., the church);[42] although honored more in the breach than the observance, this rule was not entirely without practical effect. Even the contention that Jews somehow belong to the royal treasury appears much earlier than the thirteenth century. Nevertheless, it was in that century that the fateful phrase *servi camerae* (serfs of the chamber) first appeared, and it was then that the potentially disastrous consequences of that phrase came to be applied in earnest.

Ironically, the immediate origins of this expression probably lie in a conflict that had no direct connection with the Jews and affected them at first in the form of an offer of protection. The Jewish question was a peripheral element in the struggle between pope and emperor concerning papal "fullness of power," and the assertion by Frederick II that the

Jews were the serfs of his chamber meant, at least initially, that he was their legitimate protector.[43] It did not take long, however, for this doctrine to be transformed into an instrument of severe economic exploitation that reflected an effort to deny to Jews the status of free men.[44] This development was aggravated by recurring blood libels, anti-Jewish riots, local expulsions, and "feudal anarchy";[45] consequently, although German Jews were spared the agony of a nationwide banishment, their legal and social status had sunk to an almost intolerable level.

Polemical works in general and the *Nizzahon Vetus* in particular both reflect and illuminate the historical epoch in which they appear. It is true that many aspects of polemic remained relatively static throughout the Middle Ages, particularly the various arguments and counterarguments regarding the exegesis of specific biblical verses. Nevertheless, the *realia* of any historical period quickly found expression in polemic, and the impact of various political, philosophical, and religious developments can be measured in part by the degree to which they are reflected in this literature. Examples of this can be cited from virtually every period in the development of polemic. The failure of the Bar-Kokhba revolt was reflected almost immediately in Justin's *Dialogue with Trypho;* the problems of "Judaizers" in the church were discussed in the diatribes of John Chrysostom; Agobard's works reflected the challenge of Jewish economic development and political influence; the relatively calm tone of the polemics of Peter Damian and Gilbert Crispin as compared with the vituperation in works of the later Middle Ages mirrored basic differences in Jewish-Christian relations; various philosophical developments had a major impact on the discussions of the trinity, incarnation, and virgin birth.[46]

In light of the deteriorating status of Ashkenazic Jewry described above, it is particularly interesting that one of the most striking characteristics of the *Nizzahon Vetus* and other Ashkenazic polemics of this period is their aggressiveness, vigor, and vituperation. The Jewish reader is instructed to press his arguments vigorously and not to permit the Christian to change the subject.[47] Christians are told that they will be condemned to hellfire.[48] A rabbi is said to have informed the king of Germany that "if one were to load a donkey with vomit and filth and lead him through the church, he would remain unharmed."[49] Sarcastic stories are told of conversations between Jesus and God,[50] while Jesus, Peter, Mary, and the holy spirit are all referred to in an insulting manner.[51] Some of these comments and witticisms are a reflection of what might be called folk polemic, since such arguments and anecdotes must have enjoyed wide circulation among Jews who were incapable of appreciating more complex and abstract discussions.[52]

Aggressiveness and vituperation were by no means universal among Jewish polemicists of this period and are characteristic primarily of *Sefer Yosef HaMeqanne* and the *Nizzahon Vetus,* which were written in northern France and Germany. Other writers were far more cautious and restrained. Jacob ben Reuben, for example, prefixed his pioneering critique of Matthew with a diffident, even fearful, introduction. He wrote that Jews should really keep silent on such matters, that he recorded only a few of the errors in Matthew, and that he did even this much only at the insistence of his friends. Moreover, he asked that his name not be mentioned in connection with the critique for fear that Christians would find out.[53] Solomon de' Rossi also counseled restraint at the beginning of his *'Edut ha-Shem Ne'emanah.* Indeed, he suggested that the Jewish polemicist avoid entirely such subjects as the trinity, incarnation, host, saints, priesthood—in short, anything that might be offensive. Discussion should be limited to "the coming of the Messiah, the signs of his time, the commandments of the Torah, and the words of the prophets." Moreover, Solomon's advice on the tactics of the Jewish polemicist provides a striking contrast with the above-mentioned instructions given by the author of the *Nizzahon Vetus.* "One who argues with them," says our author, "should be strong willed by asking questions and giving responses that deal with the specific issue at hand and not permitting his antagonist to extricate himself from that issue until it has been completed."[54] Solomon, on the other hand, suggests that if the Jew sees that he is winning the argument, he should not try to appear like the victor but should instead change the subject.[55]

Our author's practical advice to the Jewish polemicist is not the only evidence indicating that the aggressiveness reflected in the *Nizzahon Vetus* was at least partly expressed in actual debate. Agobard accused Jews of blaspheming Jesus in the presence of Christians.[56] In the twelfth century, Jews were said to have challenged Christians to battle in the manner of Goliath.[57] Walter of Châtillon asserted that Jews not only fail to accept the truth of Christianity but actively pose objections to it.[58] The oft-quoted remark of Louis IX that a Christian layman who is confronted by a Jewish polemicist should refute his adversary by stabbing him assumes that Jews were in the habit of initiating religious discussions.[59] Recent research has revealed that the unflattering explanation of Christian confession proposed in the *Nizzahon Vetus* was actually suggested to a Christian by a thirteenth-century French Jew; the priest, it was said, uses confession to obtain a list of adulterous women whom he can then seduce.[60] In light of this evidence, it appears that the assertiveness and self-confidence of Ashkenazic Jews were remarkable, and the view that most of the sarcastic comments in Jewish polemic were intended for internal consumption should probably be modified though not entirely discarded.[61]

Whether or not vituperative polemical remarks were intended for a Christian audience, such expressions of contempt toward the *sancta* of Christianity became known to the Inquisition. Bernard Gui, who directed the Inquisition in France in the early fourteenth century, referred to a *cematha* (= *shamta,* or curse) proclaimed by the Jews on the Day of Atonement which indicated through circumlocution that Jesus was the illegitimate son of a prostitute and Mary a woman of voluptuousness. In his study of Gui and the Jews of France, Y. Yerushalmi points to a liturgical poem quoted in *Endecktes Judenthum* that reads: "The nations link your holiness to the yoke of promiscuity, [but] your bethrothed revile the revelation to the promiscuous woman."[62]

This sort of expression appears in the *Nizzahon Vetus* several times, and Gui's attack points up the danger inherent in the use of such rhetoric even to a Jewish audience. Indeed, Gui was aware of a substantial number of Jewish works and expressions that he felt were directed against Christians or contained blasphemies. Among these were the *'Alenu* prayer, Rashi's commentaries, Maimonides' *Mishnèh Torah,* R. David Kimhi's commentary on Psalms, and the Talmud itself. Moreover, he was particularly sensitive to the Jewish practice of calling Christians "heretics" (*minim*), a practice that goes back to the Talmud and is reflected frequently in the *Nizzahon Vetus*.[63] Finally, it might be pointed out that a religious disputation actually became part of an inquisitorial proceeding in 1320; not surprisingly, the inquisitor emerged victorious in a debate whose ground rules left something to be desired.[64]

The increasing economic exploitation of Jews was reflected all too clearly in the polemical work of Meir of Narbonne. Here the satirical veneer that often concealed Jewish bitterness was dropped, and Meir allowed himself an undisguised outburst which reveals how deeply Jews were hurt by their growing insecurity. The unfair expropriation of property on such a scale "is worse for a man than being murdered. When a person is subjected to shame and disgrace, he would rather be dead; moreover, when he loses his money and he and his family remain 'in hunger, in nakedness, and in want of all things' [Deut. 28:48], then he will in fact die before his time." The culmination of this cry of anguish is Meir's anticipation of the day when the Gentiles will have to repay what they stole from the Jews.[65]

Many other aspects of the changing historical situation were also reflected in Jewish polemic. The growing importance of money-lending, for example, led to considerable discussion of its ethics and its biblical justification. Christians not only cited various time-honored verses to prove that usury is a moral offense of universal relevance, but were apparently willing to use Jewish typology to buttress their argument. Several Jewish works of this period cite the Christian contention that even if Christians are Edom (a Jewish stereotype), Jews should be forbidden to take interest from them in light of the verses which refer to Edom and Israel as brothers. Moreover, the Jewish response did not restrict itself solely to legalistic refutations; Christian polemicists were charged with hypocrisy on the grounds that Christians themselves were involved in extensive usurious activities.[66]

The truth is that this last accusation is but one expression of the more general contention that Christians behave immorally. Whatever the historical validity of such remarks may be, they are significant for what they reveal about the self-image of the Jews and the use of polemic to strengthen that image. One of the beliefs which sustained medieval Jewry through centuries of adversity was the firm conviction that Jews were clearly superior to their Gentile persecutors. No medieval Jew felt that he was subjected to other nations because they were morally, let alone religiously, superior to him. On the contrary, Ashkenazic Jewry in particular developed the theory that one reason for its suffering was that it was chosen because of its unique qualities to sanctify the divine name through martyrdom.[67] Consequently, martyrdom itself became evidence of the outstanding qualities of the Jews of France and Germany.

Indeed, Ashkenazic Jews were hardly able to discuss the issue of martyrdom, even in a halakhic context, without a passionate, emotional response. A remarkable *tosafot,* for example, points out that a certain talmudic passage seems to require a normative legal decision that a Jew is not obligated to resist to the death when forced to engage in a private idolatrous act. But, say the tosafists, "this is difficult," and one expects that this standard formula will be followed by the ordinary kind of legal or exegetical argumentation. Instead, we are confronted, at least initially, by an emotional outburst. "This is difficult, for God forbid that we should rule in a case of idolatry that one should transgress rather than die."[68] A similar reaction appears in a responsum of R. Meir of Rothenburg, who was asked whether atonement is necessary for a man who had killed his wife and children (with their consent) to prevent their capture by a mob demanding conversion to Christianity. Although he concedes the difficulty of finding justification for such an act in rabbinic sources, R. Meir will not even consider seriously the possibility that such behavior is illegal. "This is a matter," he says, "whose permissibility has been widely accepted, for we have heard of many great rabbis who slaughtered their sons and daughters. . . . And anyone who requires atonement for this is besmirching the name of the pious men of old."[69]

The *Nizzaḥon Vetus* supplies additional evidence of the centrality of martyrdom in the thought of Franco-German Jewry in this period. It contains a fascinating passage which illustrates how an Ashkenazic Jew transformed a story that contained no reference to martyrdom into one in which it emerges as the central theme; indeed, it becomes virtually a criterion of religious truth. In Judah Halevi's *Kuzari,* a pagan king calls in a philosopher, a Jew, a Muslim, and a Christian so that each can argue the merits of his position. The king is eventually persuaded of the truth of Judaism, partly because both the Muslim and the Christian grant it a certain degree of authenticity. The *Nizzaḥon Vetus,* on the other hand, tells an elaborate story in which a king threatens a Jew, a Christian, and a Muslim with death unless each one will convert to one of the other faiths. The Jew remains steadfast even at the very edge of the grave, while the other two ultimately lose their resolve and succumb to the king's threats. Both, however, choose Judaism, and "when the emperor heard that the Jew was willing to die for his Torah and would not move from his faith one bit, while the priest and the Muslim both denied their vain beliefs and accepted our faith, he himself chose our religion; he, the priest, and the Muslim were all converted and became true and genuine proselytes." The modification of the *Kuzari* story to

make the willingness to die a proof of the truth of Judaism is a truly
striking indication of the role martyrdom had come to play in the psyche
of the medieval Ashkenazic Jew.[70]

The one aspect of medieval Christian life that challenged the Jewish
image of moral superiority was the monastic ideal. At least some Christians, it appeared, were leading pure and ethical lives which could be
compared favorably with those of ordinary Jews and perhaps even of
rabbinic leaders. It is possible that it was the implicit challenge of
monasticism that provoked the vigorous attacks against both the monastic ideal and its practical implementation which are found in Jewish
polemic. The author of the *Nizzaḥon Vetus* argues that at best monks
and nuns are overcome with lustful desires that cannot be consummated,
and at worst, "they wallow in licentiousness in secret." Only marriage
can assure that a person will remain pious and God-fearing. Moreover,
monastic orders, some of which were expanding vigorously in the twelfth
and thirteenth centuries, were accused of unfair appropriation of land
and portrayed as depraved and unethical. Thus, the threat to the Jewish
self-image was negated, and Jews were even able to strengthen their
conviction of ethical superiority by a partisan examination of monasticism.[71]

It is significant that the relatively recent charge of ritual murder
appears in Ashkenazic polemic of the thirteenth century. Whatever the
roots of this accusation may be, official church doctrine never sanctioned
it. Indeed, at least the charge of ritual consumption of Christian blood
was vigorously condemned by the papacy, and it may even be appropriate to speak of a thirteenth-century rivalry between pope and emperor
over the right to protect the Jews against this libel.[72] It is consequently a
matter of particular interest to find Christians searching the Scriptures
to discover evidence, and rather complicated evidence at that, to prove
that Jews eat human beings and drink their blood.[73] This is one of the
earliest concrete indications of an attempt at a reasoned defense of the
blood libel.

The spread of heresy was one of the most important social and
religious developments in this period and had particularly sensitive implications with regard to Jewish-Christian relations. Christians had traditionally labeled members of any schismatic group "Jews," and had
occasionally attacked the latter as a means of getting at the former.[74]
Moreover, Jews were occasionally accused of harboring heretics, encour-

aging them, and even of leading orthodox Christians into heresy.[75] Nevertheless, despite considerable scholarly efforts, virtually no hard evidence concerning significant contacts between Jews and medieval heretics has been unearthed.[76]

Precisely such evidence, however, may be found in Jewish polemic. I have argued elsewhere that the *Nizzahon Vetus* contains a refutation of a heretical Christian doctrine, that a thirteenth-century French polemicist makes explicit reference to Albigensians and Bogomils in order to attack orthodox Christianity, and that Jacob ben Reuben's *Milhamot ha-Shem* may preserve evidence of an even more intriguing nature. Jacob's Christian disputant may have unwittingly quoted the arguments of a friend which were ostensibly aimed at Judaism but were really designed to undermine orthodox Christianity. Thus, Christian heretics may have used anti-Jewish polemics as a cover for attacks against the orthodox Christian faith.[77]

The twelfth and thirteenth centuries were also characterized by the broadening of the horizons of Europe that took place in the wake of the Crusades; indeed, the rise of heresy in Western Europe may have been stimulated by the new contacts between East and West.[78] These contacts with the Muslim world aided Jewish apologists in a very old and critical area of polemic, namely, the Christian argument that the success and wide diffusion of Christianity proved its superiority over a religion with a small number of adherents who were growing progressively weaker. Jews could now argue with genuine conviction and greater effectiveness that even by the numerical test alone, Christianity would not prevail; Muslims, they said, rule "half the world," and God's promise to Abraham that all nations of the world would be blessed in him and his seed was certainly not fulfilled through Christianity. Jews even attempted to make Christians feel isolated by arguing that the disgust at eating pork is really a *consensus omnium* with the sole exception of Christians. In fact, even the existence of Christian heresy could be cited as proof of the limited extent of orthodox Christianity. Finally, the failure of the Crusades was cited to show that the alleged success of Christianity was illusory; consequently, Christians would have to admit that temporal success is unrelated to religious truth. Once this admission was made, the old argument against Judaism would have to be abandoned.[79]

One of the most striking characteristics of the polemic reflected in the *Nizzahon Vetus* is the extensive use of the New Testament. The first extant critique of the New Testament by a European Jew is in the eleventh chapter of Jacob ben Reuben's *Milḥamot ha-Shem* (1170);[80] this work, however, deals only with Matthew. On the other hand, *Sefer Yosef HaMeqanne, Milḥemet Mizvah* of Meir b. Simon of Narbonne, and the *Nizzaḥon Vetus* reflect an intimate knowledge of all the Gospels and some awareness of the other books of the New Testament.[81]

There are certain instructive similarities between Jewish use of the New Testament in polemic and the Christian approach to the Talmud, which became important in the thirteenth century. Both religions had one sacred text—the Hebrew Scriptures—which they held in common, and another sacred body of teaching about whose authority they differed. Traditionally, polemical writings had largely restricted themselves to different interpretations of the text whose authority and divine origin both groups accepted. In our period, however, the usefulness of the New Testament for Jewish polemicists and of the Talmud for Christians began to become evident. There is, in fact, a clear parallelism between the approaches developed by each group to the sacred literature of its adversaries. On the one hand, that literature was subjected to a vigorous critique; on the other, it was exploited to disprove the beliefs of its own adherents.

Thus, beginning in the twelfth century a series of Christian authors attacked the Talmud as a work replete with absurdities, and in the 1230s, Nicholas Donin asserted that it contained blasphemies against Jesus which made it a candidate for destruction. The Jewish defense presented at the so-called disputation in Paris in 1240 did not succeed in thwarting Donin's wishes, and within a relatively short time a public burning of the Talmud took place. A few decades later in Spain the Talmud was again the focus of a disputation, but the approach was entirely different. Here, Pablo C(h)ristia(ni) maintained that the dogmas of Christianity could be demonstrated from the Talmud; the rabbis, for example, were said to have indicated that the Messiah had already come and that he is a preexistent being. Significant, though less spectacular, consequences resulted from this disputation as well, and the use of the Talmud to support Christianity became a central element of the Jewish-Christian debate in the centuries to come. Some later Christians even combined the two approaches, arguing that the Talmud contains both blasphemies and evidence of Christian truths.[82]

The Jewish critique of the Gospels had a similar twofold nature. Jews attacked the Christian Scriptures for their alleged absurdities and contradictions, and at the same time they tried to prove that later Christian dogmas are inconsistent with the Gospels themselves. It was, of course, much easier to maintain both Jewish attitudes at the same time than it was to do the same for both Christian arguments, and the dual approach is used without hesitation throughout the latter section of the *Nizzaḥon Vetus*.[83]

The knowledge of the New Testament displayed in *Yosef HaMeqanne* and the *Nizzaḥon Vetus* was at least partly firsthand since there are a substantial number of Latin quotations in both works.[84] Nevertheless, various citations of the opinions of proselytes leave no room for doubt that some of the familiarity with Christian texts and especially with Christian prayers, festivals, and rituals resulted from contact with these converts; indeed, the Rome manuscript passages that served as a source of the *Nizzaḥon Vetus* may well have been written by a student of a proselyte's son. Similarly, the Christian awareness of the Talmud stemmed largely from information supplied by Jewish converts. Petrus Alfonsi, for example, had proposed arguments against certain talmudic passages as early as the beginning of the twelfth century,[85] and both Nicholas Donin and Pablo C(h)ristia(ni) were recent converts to Christianity when they began their polemical activities.[86]

Jewish polemic, then, reflects some of the most important social, economic, and intellectual changes that were taking place in the twelfth and thirteenth centuries. Embittered relations, economic exploitation, usury, the expansion of monasticism, martyrdom, the blood libel, Christian heresy, the failure of the Crusades, wider familiarity with the New Testament and the Talmud—all these played a role in the Jewish-Christian debate, and polemical works can frequently supply insights into the impact of some of these momentous developments. Relations between Christians and Jews were indeed deteriorating, but the very symptoms of that deterioration lent greater variety and renewed interest to the vigorous religious discussions that persisted throughout this tragic age in the history of medieval Jewry.

NOTES

1. See M. D. Hooker, *Jesus and the Servant* (London, 1959); Y. Kaufmann, *Golah VeNekhar* (Tel Aviv, 1929/30), 1: 381–89.
2. The major anti-Jewish polemics through the twelfth century were summarized by A. L. Williams, *Adversus Judaeos* (Cambridge, 1935). See also B. Blumenkranz, *Les Auteurs Chrétiens Latins du Moyen Age sur les Juifs et le Judaisme* (Paris, La Haye, 1963). J. Pelikan has remarked that as Judaism became less of a threat to Christianity, Christian writers tended "to take their opponents less and less seriously" (*The Christian Tradition, vol. 1, The Emergence of Catholic Tradition [100–600]*, [Chicago and London, 1971], p. 21). There is some validity to this observation, but precisely this fact leads one to ask why Christians continue to write books refuting people that they do not take seriously.
3. See A. B. Hulen, "The Dialogue with the Jews as Source for the Early Jewish Argument against Christianity," *Journal of Biblical Literature* 51 (1932): 61.
4. On the polemical implications of *Cur Deus Homo?* see A. Funkenstein, "HaTemurot Be-Vikkuah HaDat Shebein Yehudim LeNoẓerim BaMe'ah HaYod-Bet," *Zion* 33 (1968): 129–32.
5. See my "St. Peter Damian: His Attitude toward the Jews and the Old Testament," *Yavneh Review* 4 (1965): 102–4. The issue of Christian sacrifices in the Middle Ages is raised in N.V. (pp. 207–09), but only in response to a Christian argument.
6. For a summary of Marcion's attitude toward the Hebrew Bible and his manipulation of the New Testament text, see E. C. Blackman, *Marcion and His Influence* (London, 1948), pp. 42–60, 113–24. Cf. also Pelikan, p. 77.
7. See David Berger, ed. and tr., *The Jewish-Christian Debate in the High Middle Ages* (Philadelphia, 1979), appendix 3.
8. *Dialogue with Trypho*, ch. 123.
9. On the subject of *verus Israel*, see Berger, *Debate*, pp. 169–71, and the notes to p. 126. On the typology of Jacob and Esau, see G. D. Cohen, "Esau as Symbol in Early Medieval Thought," in *Jewish Medieval and Renaissance Studies*, ed. A. Altmann, pp. 19–48, and cf. the notes to p. 55.
10. A list of such references appears in H. H. Ben Sasson's "Disputations and Polemics," *Encyclopaedia Judaica* (Jerusalem, 1971), 6: cols. 81–82.
11. See S. Krauss, *Das Leben Jesu nach Jüdischen Quellen* (Berlin, 1902).
12. See B. Blumenkranz's "Die Jüdischen Beweisgründe im Religionsgespräch mit den Christen," *Theologische Zeitschrift* 4 (1948): 119–47, and his *Juifs et Chrétiens dans le Monde Occidental, 430–1096* (Paris, 1960), pp. 213–89. It is likely that the brief *Sefer Nestor HaKomer* (Altona, 1875) also predates the high Middle Ages. For a short summary of some sporadic references to other early Jewish polemics, see J. Rosenthal, "Haganah Ve-

Hatqafah BeSifrut HaVikkuaḥ shel Yemei HaBeinayim," *Proceedings of the Fifth World Congress of Jewish Studies* (Jerusalem, 1969) 2: 354–55. On the degree to which early disputations reflect real encounters, see the summary in A. P. Hayman, *The Disputation of Sergius the Stylite against a Jew*, vol. 2 (Louvain, 1973), introd., pp. 64*–70*.

13. See J. Rosenthal's introduction to his edition of *Sefer Yosef HaMeqanne* (Jerusalem, 1970), p. 27.

14. See Berger, *Debate*, notes to p. 132.

15. Naturally, there are many scriptural arguments that resist neat classification, and not every weak argument should be labeled "exegetical." Nevertheless, these examples are illustrative of christological interpretations that hardly made any pretense of being demonstrably true. (Isaiah 45 was in a different category during the early stages of its polemical history; see Berger, *Debate*, the notes to p. 111.)

16. Some examples can be found in E. I. J. Rosenthal, "Anti-Christian Polemic in Medieval Bible Commentaries," *JJS* 11 (1960): 115–35. Jewish commentaries, of course, deal primarily with what I have called genuine polemic.

17. On Isaiah 11, see Berger, *Debate*, the notes to p. 108; cf. also p. 125 and the notes there. For a general treatment of medieval Ashkenazic exegesis, see S. Poznanski. *Mavo lePerush ʿal Yeḥezqel u-Terei ʿAsar leRabbi Eliezer miBalgenzi* (Warsaw, 1913; reprinted Jerusalem, 1965).

18. So Peter the Venerable with respect to Proverbs 30:4; see his *Tractatus adversus Judaeorum Inveteratam Duriitiem*, PL 189.519.

19. On blindness, see Berger, *Debate*, p. 68 and the notes there. For a possible Jewish reversal of the argument that Jews reject what they know to be the truth, see Berger, *Debate*, notes to pp. 216 and 219.

20. See Berger, *Debate*, the notes to p. 101.

21. The clearest instance of such an approach in pre–fourteenth-century Jewish polemic is Solomon de' Rossi's *ʿEdut HaShem Neʾemanah*, ed. J. Rosenthal, *Meḥqarim u-Meqorot* (Jerusalem 1967). 1:373–430. Jewish arguments based on the nonfulfillment of messianic prophecies of peace were very common; see Berger, *Debate*, notes to p. 107.

22. See Berger, *Debate*, pp. 46 and 147 and the notes there. The problem of determining how serious Jews were in their citations of such verses was pointed out briefly by Judah Rosenthal in connection with a sixteenth-century polemic; see his introduction to Ya'ir ben Shabbetai da Correggio's *Ḥerev Pifiyyot* (Jerusalem, 1958), p. 9. Cf. also his citation of several relevant verses in his "Haganah VeHatqafah . . . ," pp. 348–49. There is a non-polemical source which may contribute to the impression that there was some degree of seriousness in this enterprise. R. Jacob Tam, we are told, requested divine guidance in a dream to determine whether or not Jesus and Mary are alluded to in Scripture: see A. J. Heschel, " 'Al Ruaḥ HaQodesh Bimei HaBeinayim," *Alexander Marx Jubilee Volume*, New York, 1950, Heb. vol., p. 182, n27. See also Talmage's note in "HaPulmus Ha-Anti-Noẓri BaḤibbur Leqet Qaẓar." *Michael* 4 (1976): 71.

23. See Berger, *Debate,* the notes to pp. 42 (1. 12) and 75. The most sophisticated Jewish discussion of the trinity during our period is in Moses of
Salerno's *Ta'anot,* and not all Jewish polemicists based their arguments on
the undefended assumption that trinitarianism is simply a polytheism of
three. There was, nevertheless, a pervasive Jewish feeling that this is the
case. On this topic in general see D. Lasker, *Jewish Philosophical Polemics
against Christianity in the Middle Ages* (New York, 1977), pp. 48–104.
(Lasker's important work appeared too late to be utilized systematically in
this study; for an assessment, see my review in the *Association for Jewish
Studies Newsletter* 22 [March 1978]: 16–17, 19.)

24. See Berger, *Debate,* appendix 5, for a detailed discussion.

25. See ibid., appendix 2.

26. See ibid., p. 103 and the notes there.

27. See ibid., notes to p. 218.

28. See ibid., especially notes to p. 146.

29. See ibid., notes to p. 222.

30. See ibid., appendix 3.

31. See ibid., notes to p. 89.

32. See Tertullian, *Adversus Judaeos,* PL 2.599 = Tränkle, p. 4. On Jewish
selfishness, cf. also the citations from Bernard in my study, "The Attitude of
St. Bernard of Clairvaux toward the Jews," *Proceedings of the American
Academy for Jewish Research* 40 (1972): 100.

33. So a priest of Étampes quoted by Joseph Official; see the notes to Berger,
Debate, p. 89 for the full quotation and reference. There is, of course, a
well-known talmudic view that righteous Gentiles are admitted into the
world to come (*Tosefta Sanhedrin,* ch. 13; *B. Sanhedrin* 105a), but the
definition of righteousness was subject to several ambiguities. Moreover,
this priest can hardly be faulted in light of comments made by Joseph
Official's own father; see Berger, *Debate,* p. 68.

34. On the carnality of the Law, see Berger, *Debate,* p. 80 and the notes there.

35. See S. W. Baron, *A Social and Religious History of the Jews* (New York,
1965), 10: 60.

36. See Ch. Merchavia, *HaTalmud BiRe'i HaNazrut* (Jerusalem, 1970), pp.
227–48.

37. See A. Neubauer, "Literary Gleanings, IX," *JQR,* o.s. 5 (1893): 713–14; cf.
Baron, op. cit., 10: 63–64. See also R. Chazan, *Medieval Jewry in Northern
France* (Baltimore and London, 1973), pp. 149–153, for indications that
this convert was Pablo C(h)ristia(ni) and that the events may have taken
place in 1269.

38. See Baron, op. cit., 10: 57 ff. On the economic and political decline of
French Jewry in the twelfth and thirteenth centuries, see esp. Chazan, op.
cit., pp. 39–40, 63–96, 100–24, 133–41, 148, 154–86.

39. See S. Albeck, "Rabbenu Tam's Attitude to the Problems of His Time,"
(Hebrew), *Zion* 19 (1954): 107–08; cf. *Tosafot Bava Mezi'a,* 70b, s. v.
tashshikh.

40. *Tosafot 'Avodah Zarah,* 2a, s. v. *velifroa' mehen.* On Christian efforts to minimize the effectiveness of documents held by Jews which proved Christian indebtedness, see S. Grayzel, *The Church and the Jews in the Thirteenth Century* (Philadelphia, 1933), p. 57, note 78, and pp. 106–07, note 3. The Jewish feeling of economic insecurity is also reflected in the texts in B. Dinur, *Yisrael BaGolah* II.1 (Tel Aviv and Jerusalem, 1965), pp. 157–68.

41. On the early fourteenth century, see Y. Yerushalmi, "The Inquisition and the Jews of France in the Time of Bernard Gui," *HTR* 63 (1970): 317–77. See also R. Anchel, *Les Juifs de France* (1946), pp. 79–91, and Chazan, op. cit., pp. 191–205.

42. See Berger, *Debate,* notes to p. 55.

43. See Baron, op. cit., 9: 141–47. For a recent discussion of the doctrine of fullness of power, see W. D. McCready, "Papal *Plenitudo Potestatis* and the Source of Temporal Authority in Late Medieval Papal Hierocratic Theory," *Speculum* 48 (1973): 654–74.

44. See especially G. Kisch, *The Jews in Medieval Germany* (Chicago, 1949), pp. 159–68, and cf. Baron, op. cit., pp. 152 ff.

45. Baron, op. cit., pp. 193 ff.

46. There is no really good survey of Jewish-Christian polemic as a whole until the fourteenth century. A few studies, however, do give a picture of some of the areas of interaction between polemic and historical *realia.* See *Verus Israel; Auteurs; Juifs et Chrétiens;* J. Parkes, *The Conflict of the Church and the Synagogue* (London, 1934); I. Loeb, "La Controverse Religieuse entre les Chrétiens et les Juifs au Moyen Age," *Revue d'histoire des Religions* 17 (1888): 311–37; 18 (1888): 133–56 (also printed as a separate monograph); Baron, op. cit. 9:55–134, 266–307; Funkenstein, op. cit., pp. 125–44.

47. Berger, *Debate,* p. 169.

48. Ibid., p. 68.

49. Ibid., p. 69.

50. See Berger, *Debate,* pp. 43, 77.

51. See Berger, *Debate,* notes to p. 152.

52. Nevertheless, Rosenthal (*Jewish Social Studies* 27 [1965]: 121) justly rejects H. J. Schoeps's contention that N. V. stems from "the completely uneducated circles of German Jewry."

53. *Mil. HaShem,* p. 141. While Rosenthal is no doubt correct in suggesting that such factors as the higher philosophical level of *Mil. HaShem* were largely responsible for its less vituperative tone (introduction to *Sefer Yosef HaMeqanne,* p. 28), this passage shows that fear was also a factor. These observations by Rosenthal revise his earlier judgment that *Mil. HaShem* was the sharpest polemic written by a medieval Jew (introduction to *Mil. HaShem,* p. 19).

54. N. V., p. 169.

55. See Solomon de' Rossi, *'Edut HaShem Ne'emanah,* Rosenthal's *Meḥqarim,* 1:378–79. Cf. also the citations in Rosenthal's introduction to *Yosef Ha-*

Meqanne, p. 17. The contrast between Solomon and N. V. was noted briefly by E. Urbach, "Etudes sur la littérature polémique au moyen âge," *REJ* 100 (1935): 61.

56. PL 104.71, quoted in Williams, p. 355.

57. The *Tractatus* in TNA 5.1509 = PL 213.749; cf. M. Guedemann, *HaTorah VehaHayyim Bimei HaBeinayim* . . . (Tel Aviv, 1968; first printing, Warsaw, 1897), pp. 11–12.

58. Walter of Châtillon, *Tractatus* . . . PL 209.424.

59. See Anchel, op. cit., pp. 106–7. On "the Jewish mission" through the eleventh century, see also *Juifs et Chrétiens,* pp. 159–211.

60. See J. Shatzmiller, *Recherches sur la communauté juive de Manosque au moyen age* (Paris, La Haye, 1973), pp. 123–27; cf. Berger, *Debate,* p. 223. Although I find Shatzmiller's analysis quite persuasive, several cautionary remarks should be added. First of all, the text is fragmentary, and Shatzmiller's reconstruction is based in part on the existence of the parallel in N. V. Secondly, the Jew was subjected to a formal accusation as a result of his remarks, and this must obviously temper any conclusions to be drawn from this incident concerning Jewish aggressiveness and freedom of speech. Finally, the Jew denied the charges by presenting a significantly different version of what he had said, and this denial, as Shatzmiller indicates, cannot be dismissed with absolute certainty.

61. See Urbach, op. cit., pp. 60 ff., for a discussion of this problem. I. Levi had pointed to several sources which reflected Jewish initiation of vigorous religious debate, but he considered this a pre–thirteenth-century phenomenon; see his "Controverse entre un Juif et un Chrétien au XIe Siècle," *REJ* 5 (1882): 238. The view that Provençal Jews "took advantage of their freedom of speech" to a greater extent than other Jews was expressed by Grayzel. *The Church and the Jews in the Thirteenth Century,* p. 29. Baron has even suggested that outspoken polemical remarks may have been inspired by the Official family, and they themselves may have spoken as they did because of their roots in Narbonne, where Jews enjoyed exceptional privileges (op. cit., 9:277). Many remarks of this type, however, cannot be traced to the Officials, and quite a few are attributed to earlier Ashkenazic figures. The truth probably lies in the most straightforward reading of the evidence, which indicates that the Jews of northern France and Germany did not shrink from outspoken polemic, at least in private conversation, even in the dark days of the late thirteenth century. On the assertiveness that marked Ashkenazic Jewry in the pre-Crusade period, see I. Agus, *The Heroic Age of Franco-German Jewry* (New York, 1969), especially pp. 11–20; despite certain exaggerations, the main thrust of Agus's portrayal of this characteristic is valid. For an even earlier period, see Anchel, op. cit., pp. 31–32.

62. Yerushalmi, op. cit., pp. 362–63. The phrase is taken from Ezekiel 23:44. See also Merchavia, "HaShamta BeSifrut HaPulmus HaNoẓerit Bimei HaBeinayim," *Tarbiz* 41 (1971): 95–115; cf. especially pp. 97, 100.

63. See Yerushalmi, op. cit., pp. 350 ff. In the Talmud, *minim* probably referred primarily to Jewish Christians. For the charge that Jews curse Christians in prayer, cf. also Jerome and Agobard cited in Merchavia, *HaTalmud BiRe'i HaNaẓrut,* pp. 82–83. Cf. also the list of pejorative Jewish expressions about Christianity compiled by Christians in 1239 and summarized by Merchavia, p. 278.

64. See S. Grayzel, "The Confessions of a Medieval Jewish Convent," *Historia Judaica* 17 (1955): 89–120, and cf. Yerushalmi, op. cit., pp. 328–33.

65. *Milḥemet Miẓvah,* p. 23b. See also the quotation from Meir in Chazan, op. cit., p. 123.

66. See Berger, *Debate,* pp. 133–34 and the notes there. For a discussion of the Christian accusations that Jews engage in extensive usury, see Kisch, op. cit., pp. 327–9.

67. See H. H. Ben-Sasson, *Peraqim beToledot HaYehudim Bimei HaBeinayim* (Tel Aviv, 1958), pp. 174–84. Cf. Berger, *Debate,* p. 70, and the notes there.

68. *Tosafot 'Avodah Zarah,* 54a s. v. *ha beẓin'a.* See J. Katz, *Bein Yehudim LeGoyim* (Jerusalem, 1960), p. 90. (The equivalent passage in the English version [*Exclusiveness and Tolerance* (New York, 1961), pp. 83–84] presents such a bland paraphrase of the *Tosafot* that the emotional force of the argument is virtually lost.)

69. R. Meir of Rothenburg, *Teshuvot, Pesaqim, U-Minhagim,* ed. Y. Z. Kahane (Jerusalem, 1960), 2:54.

70. For further references, see Berger, *Debate,* notes to pp. 216–18.

71. See ibid., pp. 69–70, 98–99 223, and cf. the notes there. On the alleged immorality of priests, see also Guedemann, op. cit., pp. 42–43, 67–68. My feeling that monasticism posed a psychological threat to the Jewish self-image is almost impossible to substantiate definitively because no medieval Jew would say this openly. There is, however, interesting evidence that some Ashkenazic Jews in the early modern period felt insecure in the presence of genuine priestly celibacy; see the curious legend in *Shivḥei HaBesht* about the Baal Shem Tov's conversation with a priest (D. Ben-Amos and J. Mintz, *In Praise of the Baal Shem Tov* [Bloomington, 1970], p. 248).

72. Baron, op. cit., 9:144–45.

73. See Berger, *Debate,* pp. 54, 229 and the notes there.

74. So Cassiodorus, PL 70.74D ("Judaei vel Donatistae"); Hadrian I, PL 98.1255–56. Cf. *Juifs et Chrétiens,* pp. xvi–xvii and note 11 there. See also Damian's *De Sacramentis per Improbos Adminisratis,* PL 145.529, and his *Liber Qui Dicitur Gratissimus,* ch. 37, PL 145. 153, discussed in my "St. Peter Damian," pp. 86–87, 89–90. Cf. Humbert, PL 143.1093 C. On this practice in the Byzantine Empire, see Parkes, op. cit., pp. 300–03. Cf. also Baron, op. cit., 9:58–60.

75. Cf. Baron, op. cit., 59, 267–68.

76. See L. I. Newman, *Jewish Influence on Christian Reform Movements* (New York, 1925); G. Scholem, *Ursprung und Anfänge der Kabbala* (Berlin,

1962), pp. 206–210; F. Talmage, "An Hebrew Polemical Treatise: Anti-Cathar and Anti-Orthodox," *HTR* 60 (1967): 335–37.

77. See my "Christian Heresy and Jewish Polemic in the Twelfth and Thirteenth Centuries," *HTR* 68 (1975): 287–303. See also Berger, *Debate*, p. 153 and the notes there.

78. On the causes of the rise of heresy, see J. Russell's "Interpretations of the Origins of Medieval Heresy," *Medieval Studies* 25 (1963): 26–53, and his *Dissent and Reform in the Early Middle Ages* (Berkeley, 1965).

79. See Berger, *Debate*, p. 89 and the notes there for specific references and a fuller discussion.

80. For a discussion of this date, see J. Rosenthal's edition of *Mil. HaShem*, introduction, p. viii.

81. Cf. the reference to 1 Corinthians in Berger, *Debate*, p. 70. The impression of close familiarity with the New Testament is marred by the frequent attribution of a quotation to the wrong book of the Gospels. See e.g., ibid., pp. 180, 183, 188. These inaccurate ascriptions may offer a partial explanation for the lack of a systematic order in the section of N. V. that contains a critique of the Gospels. N. V. also contains some non-authentic quotations from Christian literature (e.g., pp. 160, 201) which J. Wakius complained about in a late seventeenth-century refutation. See his *Teshuvat HaDin 'al HaYehudim sive Recriminatio Actionis in nuperos Christi Accusatores cujus pars prima agit contra . . . librum Nizzachon Vetus* (Jenae, 1699), pp. 20–21, 28–29.

82. Both views were expressed in the Tortosa disputation in the early fifteenth century; cf. the citations in Baron, op. cit., 9: 90, 91. Baron, however, does not note that two originally disparate approaches are represented here. On medieval Christian use of the Talmud through the Donin episode, see Merchavia, *HaTalmud BiRe'i HaNazrut,* passim. Pablo's approach was adopted by Raymund Martini in his classic *Pugio Fidei* (Leipzig, 1687), which became a manual for Christian polemicists in late medieval Spain. For Donin's approach in thirteenth-century Italy, cf. C. Roth. *History of the Jews of Italy* (Philadelphia, 1946), pp. 99–100.

83. On the search for contradictions, see, for example, Berger, *Debate*, pp. 167–68, regarding the contradictory genealogies in Matthew and Luke. The argument against Christian dogma through Gospel citations is very common; see especially the notes to p. 183.

84. There is some discussion of Jacob ben Reuben's Hebrew translations of Matthew in Rosenthal's "Targum shel HaBesorah 'al pi Matti leYa'aqov ben Reuven," *Tarbiz* 32 (1962): 48–66. On Jacob's translation of selections from Gilbert Crispin's *Disputatio,* see my "Gilbert Crispin, Alan of Lille, and Jacob ben Reuben: A Study in the Transmission of Medieval Polemic," *Speculum* 49 (1974): 34–47. On Jewish knowledge of Latin see also the references in Merchavia, op. cit., p. 245. The author of the *Dialogus* attributed to William of Champeaux refers to his supposed Jewish disputant as a man expert in Jewish law and "not ignorant" of Christian literature

(PL 163.1045). Gilbert Crispin, after whose work "William" modelled this passage, had used an even stronger expression; the Jew "was well-versed (*bene sciens*) in our law and literature" (*Disputatio*, ed. Blumenkranz, p. 27). Solomon de' Rossi lists such knowledge as one of the requirements for a Jewish polemicist ('*Edut HaShem Ne'emanah*, in Rosenthal's *Meḥqarim*, 1:378).

85. See Merchavia, op. cit., pp. 93–127.

86. On the role of converts, see Blumenkranz, "Jüdische und Christliche Konvertiten im Jüdisch-Christlichen Religionsgespräch des Mittelalters," in Paul Wilpert's *Judentum im Mittelalter* (Berlin, 1966), pp. 264–82, and cf. Guedemann, op. cit., p. 11.

19

Champion of Jewish Economic Interests

David B. Ruderman

By the end of the fifteenth century and the beginning of the sixteenth, the small Jewish communities of Italy faced a formidable problem as mounting pressure from the Christian community attempted to remove their main source of livelihood, moneylending. Since the beginning of Jewish settlement in Italy, moneylenders had been the economic mainstay of the Italian Jewish communities and the chief source of communal leadership. Their concentrated and conspicuous presence soon evoked a noticeable reaction on the part of churchmen, especially those of the Franciscan order. The most vigorous attacks against Jewish usury in fifteenth-century Italy came from clergymen like Bernardino of Siena and Antonino of Florence, who openly deplored the economic basis of the Jewish community and its supposedly cancerous effect upon the local Christian populace. Others, like Bernardino of Feltre, launched the drive to establish *Monti di Pietà,* public lending establishments with the avowed purpose of eliminating Jewish usury in Italy altogether.[1]

The fate of the Jewish banking establishments in Ferrara was hardly different from that of the Jewish banks in the rest of Italy. The deterioration of their position in the early 1480s, especially in the case of the Norsa family, has been described above. Farissol had already left Ferrara when Bernardino of Feltre first arrived there in 1483, but he could not have been oblivious to the clergyman's powerful influence throughout Italy or to the special relationship he had cultivated with the Este house.[2]

Reprinted by the permission of Hebrew Union College Press from *The World of a Renaissance Jew: The Life and Thought of Abraham ben Mordecai Farissol,* by David B. Ruderman, Cincinnati, 1981, 85–97.

Bernardino visited Ferrara again in 1494 in order to convince the leaders of the city to open a local *Monte* for the poor of their community. This time Farissol may have personally observed the harrowing spectacle of the friar's mesmeric sermons and their electrifying effect upon the masses. While Bernardino's efforts were initially rebuffed in favor of the established economic policies of the Este government, the anti-Jewish propaganda stimulated by the movement continued unabated in Ferrara throughout the next decade. There was another outbreak of hostility in 1506 after the death of Ercole I and it continued through the following year. An entire regiment of soldiers was necessary to restore order in neighboring Modena when its populace, aroused by Franciscan preachers, physically assaulted members of the local Jewish community. In spite of the admonitions of Alfonso I and even Pope Julius II, the Franciscans and their following continued to pressure the Este government to undermine the influence of the Jews by initiating an alternative banking operation for the poor. One of the most effective friars was Jacob Ungarelli of Padua, who arrived in Ferrara in 1507. After a sermon delivered by Ungarelli on January 3, 1508 in the main cathedral of the city, Alfonso could no longer withstand public pressure to establish a *Monte;* in spite of his father's previous resistance to Bernardino's demands, he reluctantly acquiesced in the creation of the first *Monte di Pietà* in Ferrara in the heart of the major financial district of the city.[3]

The fact that Farissol's personal fate was identified with that of the Jewish bankers of Mantua, Ferrara, and other Italian Jewish communities during his long career has been emphasized throughout this study. Farissol was indebted to the banking élite not only for his economic livelihood but also for his social standing and leadership role in the Jewish community. When their position and economic power began to crumble, men such as Farissol were adversely affected, and ultimately the welfare of every member of the Jewish community was impaired. Under these circumstances so threatening to Jewish economic interests in Italy, Farissol devoted an entire chapter of his polemical work to a response to the Christian accusations. Written in full cognizance of the sophisticated Christian arguments against usury and with complete awareness of the economic realities, Farissol's defense of the Jewish position displays unusual insight and originality. Because of its novelty of ideological argumentation and as a response to a pressing and relevant concern of the Jewish-Christian relationship, it deserves special attention by the historian of Jewish-Christian polemics as well as the historian of economic thought.[4]

EARLIER AND CONTEMPORARY DEFENSES OF JEWISH USURY

The Christian attack against Jewish usury had long preceded Farissol's disputation in Ferrara. The argument was usually presented on two planes. Most common was the religious plane. Here the disputants justified their position in terms of biblical verses, and the Christians usually had the upper hand. They needed only to point to Deuteronomy 23:21 ("Unto a foreigner thou mayest lend upon interest; but unto thy brother thou shalt not lend upon interest . . .") and Psalm 15 ("O Lord, who shall dwell in thy tent . . . who does not put out his money at interest . . ."), as well as other biblical verses, to demonstrate that the Bible took a negative view of usury. The prohibition not to take interest from one's brother clearly included Christians, they maintained. The Christians were brothers of the Jews not only because all mankind are brothers but because Edom, traditionally synonymous with Christianity in medieval Jewish literature, once shared the status of brotherhood with the Israelites. Thus, to persist in usurious operations against Christians was to defy a biblical injunction. Since the biblical view was emphatic in prohibiting usury within the Jewish community, the Jews could not argue for the utility of usury. Their only recourse was to prove that Christians could not be considered brothers of the Jews. They argued that the Edomites were not regarded as brothers of the Israelites even in the biblical period; moreover, the identification of Edom with Christianity was inaccurate. In spite of their ingenious arguments to show that their usurious operations with Christians were licit, they were clearly at a disadvantage, for they were ignoring the literal meaning of the scriptural prohibition if not its spirit. The economic necessity of earning their livelihood through moneylending, however, scarcely allowed them any other interpretation.[5]

The second plane of the Christian argument was socio-economic. In this case, the Christians maintained that Jewish usury was injurious to the social fabric of society. Its operations exploited the poor by raising the interest rates beyond their reach and thus added misery to misfortune. Moreover, the Christians contended, it had a pernicious effect on the moral order of society. Instead of the initial natural order of human solidarity, helpfulness, and charity, Jewish usury created a new social climate which emphasized the ruthless, egotistical nature of humanity.[6] As a rebuttal to this argument, the Jews referred to the favorable economic conditions created by Jewish usury. Instead of injuring society, Jewish moneylending played a crucial and positive economic role in Christian society.

Two such responses had already been articulated in thirteenth-century France, where Jewish economic activity was quite active and conspicuous. The first response was contained in a compendium entitled *Milḥemet Miẓvah*, written in Narbonne:

Who could imagine that society might exist without usury? Even officers and kings must borrow—indeed even the great king, the King of France. His officers have not been able to pass two consecutive years without large loans. In fact, he almost lost some of his fortified cities during his war with the great baron, until his faithful Jewish official of Narbonne found him loans at high rates of interest. Why then don't the great leaders of the land consider that, if they need to borrow at interest, what of the vast majority?[7]

The writer clearly knew the economic and political realities of his environment. He pointed out that Jews provided a service not only to the poor but even to the monarch. A Provençal Jew named Jacob b. Elijah of Venice offered a similar answer in a polemical letter to the famous apostate Pablo Christiani written in the same century. Jacob also indicated that Jewish usury was indispensable for Christians in need of large amounts of capital. He cynically pointed out that the Christian leaders actually became rich through the assistance of Jewish moneylenders. The clergy were especially culpable of hypocrisy, for they condemned Jewish usury but lived in the lap of luxury through the efforts of the same usurers. Even the pope did not escape the author's stinging barbs. He too was portrayed as greedy for money gained at the expense of the Jews. Jacob maintained that the Christians themselves were guilty of forcing the Jews into so unpleasant an occupation by denying them the right to enter professions that were more socially acceptable. This condition, Jacob added, was in sharp contrast to the relative freedom and evenhandedness afforded to Jews living in Moslem lands.[8]

Although both of these writers forcefully describe the social and economic world of the time, they lacked the theoretical understanding of economics that would have provided a more effective basis for combating the formidable Christian arguments against Jewish moneylending.

Not until the end of the fifteenth century, at about the same time as Farissol's composition, did there appear a more theoretical presentation of the Jewish position. This presentation was written by Don Isaac Abravanel in his commentary on the Torah, composed in Monopoli at the end of the fifteenth century. After dealing with the conventional Christian religious arguments in his first three responses, Abravanel turned to the strictly economic side of the issue in his fourth response:

There is nothing unworthy about interest per se, because it is proper that people should make profit out of their money, their silver and gold, their wine and corn, and if someone wants money from someone else . . . why should the borrower not give the lender a certain amount of interest? Why should a farmer, for example, who was loaned 100 seah of wheat one year to sow his field . . . not give the lender 10 seah for the loan of 100? This is neither despicable nor contemptible. It is an ordinary business transaction and perfectly correct in itself.[9]

Abravanel's short answer reveals a precise theoretical understanding of the nature of interest. He defines interest as profit on money, in the same category as profit on wine and corn. In other words, Abravanel placed money in the category of fungible goods, whose use cannot be separated from the substance, or simply, that cannot be used without being consumed. Fungible goods include those goods that can be weighed (grain), measured (wine), or numbered (money). For the scholastics, a loan was defined only in relation to fungible goods, and profit on such a transaction was considered usury. For example, St. Thomas Aquinas, in his *Summa theologica,* wrote:

To take usury for money lent is unjust in itself, because this is to sell what does not exist, and this evidently leads to inequality which is contrary to justice. In order to make this evident, we must observe that there are certain things the use of which consists in their consumption; thus we consume wine when we use it for drink, and we consume wheat when we use it for food. Wherefore in such like things the use of the thing must not be reckoned apart from the thing itself and whosoever is granted the use of the thing, is granted the thing itself; and for this reason, to lend things of this kind is to transfer the ownership. Accordingly, if a man wanted to sell wine separately from the use of the wine, he would be selling the same thing twice, or he would be selling what does not exist, wherefore he would evidently commit a sin of injustice. In like manner, he commits an injustice who lends wine or wheat, and asks for double payment, viz.: one, the return of the thing in equal measure, the other, the price of the use, which is called usury.[10]

Abravanel, however, denied the distinction between profit on fungible goods and on nonfungible goods, maintaining that all profit was legitimate. His formulation of the issue leaves no doubt that he was well aware of this scholastic definition and emphatically rejected it.

CHRISTIAN CHARGES AND FARISSOL'S INITIAL RESPONSES

In his confrontation with his Christian opponents, Farissol was presented with the same two-pronged argument. The traditional biblical passages were presented in full, followed by the declaration that since Edom was the name given to the sons of Esau, who were brothers of the sons of Jacob (the Jews), it was forbidden for a Jew to take interest from a Christian. The argument that all mankind was descended from the same parents, Adam and Eve, and thus that all were brothers, was also presented. Moreover, the fact that interest could be taken from a stranger, according to Deuteronomy 23:21, was explained as a dispensation from Moses, who composed the law of Deuteronomy in full knowledge of the inclination of Israel to fatten itself with wealth.[11]

The second Christian charge was developed fully as well. Usury destroyed the natural political order, which had originally been established by divine wisdom. Initially the whole world represented a society of brothers where all men joined together to assist their fellow men. The Christians quoted Aristotle's *Ethics,* where this idyllic state is described. Usury, with its emphasis on the aggrandizement of wealth and profit-making, destroys this natural order.[12]

By Farissol's time, the second argument, the natural-law case against usury, had been highly developed by scholastic theologians. As Farissol himself indicates, the originator of this ethical-legal concept was Aristotle, who refers to natural law both in his *Ethics* and in his *Politics.* The concept was eventually passed down to the Roman jurists, who related the term *jus naturale* to a universal law of all mankind which they called *jus gentium.*[13] By the time the concept of natural law had reached the scholastics, it included an entire battery of arguments.[14] The most common of the natural-law arguments was that of Aquinas: since the use and ownership of consumptibles were one, interest on fungible goods was highly unjust.[15] A second argument was based on Aristotle, who claimed that money was essentially barren; it was unnatural for money to bear money. Since money bore no fruit and was essentially nonvendible, it was exempt from the laws of supply and demand and had to be exchanged gratuitously.[16] A third demonstration claimed that usury was unnatural since it is earned without any labor. A fourth demonstration was based on the concept of time. Since time is a common good, it belongs to no one in particular; thus interest cannot be charged on a free gift.[17]

The most prominent of the natural-law arguments was the social case against usury. Here, the scholastics demonstrated the corrosive influence of usury on the social and economic welfare of society and also contended that it destroyed the natural goodness of men. Thus Juan Garcia de Castojeriz wrote in 1320: "Usury is much to be reprehended and condemned because it is against the natural goodness of every creature; for every creature naturally lends as do light and fire and air and water and earth, which lend and give all their goodness to men and to all beasts and to all creatures."[18]

In Farissol's day, the natural-law arguments against usury had already received extended treatment in the writings of Antonino of Florence and Bernardino of Siena. Antonino repeated all of the arguments mentioned above.[19] Bernardino similarly reproduced the same arguments, placing special emphasis on the social one. In his sermons, he especially reiterated the distress the usurers caused to farmers and the urban poor, claiming that usury was responsible for the creation of a class of idle and socially parasitic rentiers who exploited all the other classes. He described the ideal community as a functioning human organism in which the stomach keeps only what it needs and equally distributes the remaining food to other members of the body: by not sharing his wealth with others, the usurer destroys the natural functioning of the social body, denies others their due share, and fattens himself at their expense.[20] While probably fully aware of all the strands of the natural-law argument, Farissol stressed the social argument in his description, the one most strongly emphasized by Bernardino.

Farissol's reply to the arguments from Scripture essentially follows that of his Jewish predecessors. He responded that the deuteronomic law on usury was not a prohibition by Moses but one by God Himself. This law, which permits taking interest from a Gentile, was enshrined in the Jewish tradition by its religious leaders, and the Jews, like the Christians, are commanded to obey their lawgivers. As for the "brother" arguments raised by the Christians, Edom and Esau are no longer recognizable as brothers since in the time of Moses, and again in the time of David, they had negated the covenant and their brotherhood with Israel by refusing the Israelites permission to cross their borders before entering Canaan. The Edomites are uncircumcised and thus disqualified from brotherhood. Moreover, one who negated his brother, as they did, could no longer be considered a brother. Finally, the Christians of Europe could not be considered the biblical Edom and Esau in the first place since the real Edom was situated to the south of Israel in the continent of Asia. There was no evidence that Edomites had ever come to live in Europe since, according to Josephus, it was Japhet, and not Edom, who came to Europe. Though Europe was traditionally called the exile of Edom, the Europeans themselves were descendants of Japhet, from whom the Jews are permitted to take interest.[21]

The original part of Farissol's response was related to the second Christian charge, the natural-law argument against usury. Farissol first contended that after the original natural order of society was destroyed, a new order, different from the first, had been created. This new economic order was based upon private property and upon profits. When one person needed a product or a service from another, he had to pay a sum of money for it. Except in the case of charity, the society functioned with a price system which provided rent on property, wages for workers, and fees for other borrowed objects. Similarly, one who damaged another man and his property has to pay a fixed price for it. To revert to the natural order of communal ownership and the free distribution of services would be to engender dissension and discord. Thus the custom of asking a fair and agreed price for goods and services has been established in society by both religious and secular authorities.[22]

In spite of the apparent contradictions between the scholastic natural-law analysis of usury and Farissol's arguments in favor of private property and profit, a scholastic would hardly have differed with anything stated in his first response. Farissol's answer was most ingenious, for every one of its conclusions rested on the economic assumptions of scholastic economic thought. Moreover, Farissol's real intention from the start seems to have been the construction of his case on precisely these same assumptions.

Farissol's seemingly bold statement of a new economic order based upon private property rather than communal sharing hardly represented a novel idea. The scholastics regarded the community of goods which had been a part of the natural order as merely utopian. In the present day, it could only be practiced on a small scale in monasteries and convents. Thomas Aquinas openly maintained that private property was not an institution of natural law but constituted a justifiable addition of human reason—justifiable, because common property is apt to be neglected and because public ownership only causes confusion and discord.[23] Similarly, Bernardino contended that private property was not based on divine or natural law but was regulated instead by positive or human convention, which could be modified and actually varied from country to country. It was instituted in order to prevent neglect, fraud, and discord.[24]

Not only private property but also the exchange of goods and services on the basis of profit was justified by scholastic thought. Thomas Aquinas maintained that merchants perform a useful function in providing society with indispensable commodities from abroad, provided they do not seek gain for the sake of gain but as a just reward for their efforts. He even stated that profit gained through trade cannot be considered a sin: ". . . gain which is the end of trading, though not implying, by its nature, anything virtuous or necessary, does not, in itself, connote anything sinful or contrary to virtue."[25] Bernardino appealed to the Augustinian dictum, also incorporated into canon law, which stated that "to trade is sometimes licit and sometimes illicit." Trade, for Bernardino, was not an evil in itself; it became a sin only when practiced deceitfully. He described three kinds of merchants whose services were useful to society: the importers-exporters, the storers of goods, and the transformers of raw materials into finished products. Thus business was perfectly legitimate if it performed a useful social function by transporting, distributing, or manufacturing goods. The accumulation of profits was permitted when it was incidental and not the primary purpose of business activity.[26] Antonino of Florence articulated similar views in regard to trade and the merchant. For him, the pursuit of profits as an end in itself was most reprehensible because the desire for profit knew no bounds. To be justified, profits had to be moderate and directed to a laudable end, such as the support of one's family, the relief of the poor, or the general welfare of the community.[27]

In his response, Farissol explicitly mentioned the licit practices of receiving rent for houses, providing wages for workmen, and taking fees for other lending of private property. Here, too, he was referring to practices fully acceptable to the churchmen. Regarding rent, the scholastics defined the exchange of nonfungible goods, such as a house or cattle, as a *commodatum* and not a *mutuum* (a money loan on fungible goods) as long as it was contracted gratuitously. When it ceased to be gratuitous, it did not become usurious but transformed itself into another kind of contract, a *locatio,* a lease or rental.[28]

Wages were regarded by the scholastics as not only a licit but a necessary means by which workers would support themselves and their families. Their analysis of the just wage was similar to that of the just price. The latter was determined by the forces operating in the market, namely, supply and demand. Thus in the case of labor, the wage was to be determined by the particular demand for labor in relation to the available supply. St. Antonino especially devoted much space in his *Summa theologica* to an explication of the just wage. He stated that the wage of the laborer represented a price, like any other price, which is determined by common estimation, in the absence of fraud or any other attempt to interfere with the freedom of the labor market. Elsewhere, he maintained that the purpose of wages was not only to compensate the worker for his labor but to enable him to provide for himself and his family according to his social situation.[29]

In short, in every detail, Farissol's first response represents an essential restatement of the scholastic position. Farissol knew as well as the churchmen that the concept of a natural society was a theoretical construct having no relationship to the economic reality the scholastics themselves had accepted both in theory and in practice. The real world of private property, trade, rents, and wages represented the world the scholastics had accepted as the norm of economic practice. Was not usury an inherent part of that real economic world?

Indeed, this was precisely the conclusion Farissol reached in his next response. If, in fact, the price system functioned in all markets of goods and services, should it not function as well in the money market? Was it not reasonable to expect a price for the use of money in the same manner as one expects a price for the use of nonfungible goods and wages? Farissol's statement represents a classic definition of the interest rate. Interest was defined as the price for the use of one's money. The clear assumption of this definition was that money was like every other commodity and was certainly not sterile; the command of it represented a condition for embarking on business ventures. Farissol added that a loan of money was often more valuable to a borrower than a loan of a specific good.[30]

Farissol reinforced his argument by pointing out examples of the open acceptance of interest by the Christians themselves in spite of their usury prohibition. He first mentions the 5 percent interest charge of the *Monti di Pietà,* the public institution for free loans to the Christian poor.[31] Here, Farissol clearly touched upon a sensitive issue that was heatedly debated in the Christian world. Since the founding of the first *Monte* in Perugia in 1462, the institution's interest rate had remained the central issue of a controversy between Franciscan and Dominican theologians. The founders of these public loan establishments soon found it necessary to exact a small fee of approximately 5 percent from the borrowers who received loans from them. This fee was explained not as a profit but as compensation for the cost of the services rendered. The Dominicans were highly suspicious of the fee and its supposed justification. They argued that the *Monti di Pietà* had no right to exist since the loans they furnished were provided by the taking of usury. By the end of the fifteenth century, the controversy between supporters and opponents of the *Monti* took the form of a major literary battle. In 1494, Nicholas Berianii composed the first written attack against the institution. He was answered by the Franciscan Bernardino de Busti, the chief disciple of Bernardino of Feltre. The debate continued until the Fifth Lateran Council of 1515, where the Franciscans emerged with a major victory in the official approval of the *Monti* and the 5 percent interest rate.[32]

Farissol also pointed out two other exceptions to the usury prohibition, those of interest on purchased rents and on dowries.[33] The practice of receiving revenue on purchased rents had been accepted as papal law since 1420 upon enactment by Martin V. At that time, the pope had declared that it was perfectly legal to authorize the seller of a deed of sale to redeem it at a fixed rate of interest. This was not to be considered a device to escape the usury law but a normal business transaction. Under such circumstances, a current rate of return upon investments in rent charges speedily grew up in each locality. Theologians and canonists had no serious difficulty in expressly allowing the practice as a respectable method of investment. By 1425, a large part of the revenues of ecclesiastical bodies consisted of these rent charges. In one instance, a number of persons in the diocese of Breslau, under the influence of the Hussite anti-clerical movement in Bohemia, refused to pay the clergy for their rents on the ground that they were usurious. Martin V's decision was in part an answer to their defiant action. He clearly stated that rent charges were not sinful as long as they fulfilled certain conditions: namely, that they were attached to *bona stabilia* (land or other fixed property), were redeemable by the person charged, and were not more than 7 percent to 10 percent of the purchase money. Farissol mentioned an interest rate of 8 percent on rents, a figure closely approximating the limits set by Martin. In 1455, Calixtus III reaffirmed Martin's decision. These two pronouncements ultimately became the basis of subsequent canon law.[34]

Similarly, revenue gained from dowries had become so completely a matter of course in normal economic affairs that Christian theologians and canonists hardly mentioned the practice. Ever since Innocent III's letter to the archbishop of Genoa in 1206, the income from a dowry was considered entirely licit. In his decision, the pope had advised that in certain cases a dowry "should be committed to some merchant so that an income might be derived by means of honest gain."[35] How, asked Farissol rhetorically, could the Church call such transactions as *Monti* fees, rent charges, and revenue from dowries nonusurious but term Jewish lending establishments, which provided much-needed capital to borrowers, usurious and consequently harmful to society?

FARISSOL'S FURTHER RESPONSE

Elsewhere in his discussion, Farissol considers the interest rate asked by Jewish moneylenders. He argues that the rate was agreed upon from the beginning of the transaction by the "communities" that required the loan. This rate was specifically determined by three factors: "The difference in locality and in particular customs, the abundance or scarcity of silver and gold in a particular place and demand for it, and the benefit to be derived from it."[36]

As before, Farissol's statement represents a precisely worded definition of an economic concept taken from scholastic economic thought. When he states that the interest rate was agreed upon by the "communities," he is merely offering the scholastic definition of a just price as it relates to nonfungible goods. The scholastics defined the just price of an article as the estimation made in common by all citizens of the community. Bernardino of Siena, for example, maintained that price was a social phenomenon and was not set by the arbitrary decision of individuals but by the community. The just price was defined as "the one which happens to prevail at a given time according to the estimation of the market, that is, what the commodities for sale are then commonly worth in a certain place." In short, the just price was equated with the market price reached on the basis of supply and demand.[37]

For the scholastics, however, the just price was merely a technical concept applying only to commodity sales, to nonfungible goods. It did not apply to loans. Usury was in no way a problem of just price; the two concepts were essentially different matters. The intention to profit on a sale was regarded as lawful, but the intention to profit on a loan was always regarded as unlawful. No scholastic theorist could claim that a moneylender might appeal to the theory of value suggested by just-price analysis.[38]

Yet it appears from Farissol's statement that this is precisely what he intended to do—to appeal to the just-price analysis of the scholastics to justify and to determine the interest rate. Thus he hoped to transfer usury to the area of just-price analysis. Instead of arguing his case on the justice of his own logic, Farissol sought to substantiate his position by appealing to the same logic articulated by the scholastics with regard to all commodities. In so doing, he was clearly pointing out the direct contradiction between the usury prohibition and the concept of just price. Theorists in the Christian world throughout the fifteenth and sixteenth centuries had attempted to transfer the jurisdiction of usury to just-price theory by all kinds of legal subtleties and exceptions to the rule.[39] In this regard the distinction made by the scholastics between a *mutuum* and a *cambium* (bill of exchange) was especially important in justifying the reality of sixteenth-century Italian banking operations. Without this legal distinction, a large percentage of European business transactions would have been considered usurious.[40] Only a Jew, unhampered by theological considerations, was in a position to so openly ignore these contradictions by defiantly stating their resolution rather than appealing to legal fictions and subterfuges.

The struggle to reconcile theological demands with economic reality continued to plague Christian theorists for centuries to come. The legal distinction between licit profit on bills of exchange and illicit profit on loans was upheld throughout the sixteenth century. Lessius (1554–1623) was the first who failed to distinguish between loans and exchanges by tacitly admitting a full-fledged market in loans.[41] Claude Saumaise or Salmalsius (1588–1653), a Calvinist, was the first Christian to openly accept an open market on loans when he wrote:

> It is licit to make money with things bought with money, why is it not licit to make money from money? The moneylender performs a highly useful service by meeting a great public need. He is licensed by the state; he has the state's approval if he is guilty of sin. These rates are set by supply and demand. If in commodities, there is no fraud in charging the highest market price, why not in regard to the usurer as well?[42]

For Salmalsius, all religious scruples against usury were brushed aside and the secular law set the only limit to profits.[43] Salmalsius' observations make it all the more remarkable that over one hundred years earlier, an Italian Jew, refusing to accept the blatant inconsistencies in scholastic economic thought, had already reached the same conclusion.

The second part of Farissol's statement is also worthy of further consideration. As mentioned, Farissol presented three factors which determined the just interest rate: the difference in locality and in particular customs, the abundance or scarcity of gold or silver in a particular place and the demand for it, and the benefit one may derive from it. Farissol's enumeration of these three distinct factors may also reveal his knowledge of another aspect of scholastic economic thought which he used to strengthen further his position. Raymond De Roover has pointed out that Bernardino of Siena made an important contribution to value and price determination theory by stating that the value of a good is composed of three elements: usefulness (*virtuositas*), scarcity (*raritas*), and pleasurableness or desirability (*complacibilitas*).[44] The distinction between *virtuositas* and *complacibilitas* is one between objective utility and a subjective factor depending upon the mood and preferences of the consumer. The latter could be called desirability or subjective utility. Bernardino's utility theory was adopted by Antonino of Florence and then disappeared from circulation. It was not retained by the sixteenth-century scholastics of the Salamanca school. De Roover tentatively suggests that Bernardino found the idea of subjective utility in the writings of an earlier theorist of Provençal origin, Pierre de Jean Olivi (1248–1298).

To argue that Farissol copied his three elements from what he had read of Bernardino may be too facile. Yet the fact remains that the three elements enumerated by the two men are quite similar. The abundance or scarcity of gold or silver could correspond with *raritas*. The benefit one derives from a loan could correspond with *virtuositas*. Finally, Farissol's first factor, the difference in locality and customs, may represent his description of the concept of *complacibilitas,* the subjective utility of a thing. It is quite possible that Farissol was not thinking at all of Bernardino's theory when he listed his three criteria to determine the price of a loan. On the other hand, in view of his familiarity with other aspects of scholastic thought, it is at least plausible that he had some idea of what fifteenth-century Italian scholastics had written about utility and price theory. If indeed he was relatively knowledgeable of the latter, this provides another example of how Farissol was able to use a theory conceived by the scholastics in order to demonstrate the inner contradiction of their position and the logic of his own.

Farissol also observed in his response how the papacy had traditionally tolerated the practice of Jewish usury.[45] This position, Farissol added, had been maintained despite the constant fluctuation of the interest rate. Even when the Third Lateran Council, in 1179, decreed that all Christian usurers would be liable to excommunication, the Jews were not prevented from taking money on interest since canon law did not apply to them. The same position was upheld at the Second Council of Lyons in 1274 and the Council of Vienne in 1311. The Fourth Lateran Council, in 1215, implicitly suggested that the Jew could take usury since only grave and excessive usury was explicitly forbidden him.[46]

Farissol later argued that Jewish usury ultimately benefited Christian society by supplying secular rulers with large revenues from the heavy taxes exacted from the Jews for the privilege of conducting loan transactions. By borrowing from the Jew, he observed, each citizen gained indirectly an additional sum through the taxes the Jew paid.[47] Of course, Farissol's argument here was somewhat specious since it is hardly possible to identify particular taxes with particular government programs, nor, as he well knew, is tax revenue ever shared equitably in a class-ordered society.[48]

Farissol's final remark is more perceptive and seems to reveal a knowledge of economics that was practical as well as theoretical. With or without the Jewish moneylender, he said, people would always be in need of money. The alternative to borrowing money at interest was to buy on credit at a high price or to barter for other goods. Either way, one stood to lose more by these means, he maintained, than by paying the agreed interest rate of the Jews:

For if they [people in need of money] do not find Jews or other moneylenders, they will lose more than by paying interest, since they will either buy what they need from someone else on credit and at a higher price, or they will exchange their garments and precious possessions, incurring a greater loss to their homes and property than that of the interest rate of the Jews. This fact is well known to them and to their merchants who, with an understanding of the times, sell their wares on credit at certain seasons thereby doing twice as much damage [to their buyers] as the fixed rate of interest known to be charged by the Jews.[49]

Farissol's statement indicates his clear understanding of the interest-rate market in Ferrara and northern Italy. Although the contours of the interest rates for Ferrara and its environs have not been reconstructed precisely, the basic levels charged have been established. Private usurers sometimes charged as much as 34.5 percent to 43.5 percent, while the private pawnshops of Florence never went below 20 percent for personal loans.[50] The *Monti di Pietà*, by contrast, charged only 5 percent on long-term loans in the fifteenth century. Figures on the sums exacted for credit or barter transactions are not available, but it seems obvious that Farissol would have made this observation only if it was in fact empirically verifiable.

Thus Farissol constructed his defense of Jewish economic interests on the basis of his theoretical knowledge of scholastic economic thought, his practical experience in the market, and his personal insights. He was well aware of the sophisticated economic concepts utilized by scholastic theologians such as Bernardino and Antonino and could exploit this knowledge to emphasize the inherent weakness in their theoretical framework. To Farissol, the scholastics, by stubbornly persisting in their case against usury, were constantly forced to contradict themselves. They argued in favor of a theoretical society based upon natural law when in reality they functioned in a real economic world based upon profits. They justified the legality of honest profit in the market of all goods and services but denied the same principle with regard to the market of money. They likewise defined the just price and explored the criteria for its precise determination but arbitrarily excluded interest on loans in their analysis. The Christian position was unsatisfactory not only because of theoretical deficiencies; it was also inadequate because it ignored obvious economic advantages of which every borrower, merchant, and ruler was cognizant. Jewish usury represented a major source of additional income to the state gained through taxing the Jews; for individual borrowers it also met a vital need since it afforded them access to money at a lower rate than any other means at their disposal. Intellectually, Farissol undoubtedly appeared an able advocate to his learned opponents. Yet the matter of Jewish usury represented more than an intellectual issue in Christian eyes. Religious faith was ultimately more pervasive in framing their stance. Perhaps that is why Farissol retreated somewhat at the end of his exposition and wrote: "However, one who flees from a bad name [of a usurer] and rightly chooses [a profession] in the worthy crafts or appropriate businesses while remembering the commandment of charity by freely giving to the poor, an infinite blessing will be bestowed upon him."[51]

NOTES

1. These developments are generally treated by Baron, S. W., *A Social and Religious History of the Jews*, 2d ed., 17 vols. to date (New York, 1952–), 12:159–69, and Shulvass, M. A. *Ḥayyei ha-Yehudim be-Italyah bi-Tekufat ha-Renesans* (New York, 1955), pp. 104–20. Additional material is found in the standard histories of C. Roth, *A History of the Jews in Italy* (Philadelphia, 1946), pp. 103–17, and A. Milano, *Storia degli ebrei in Italia* (Turin, 1963), pp. 109–50. Especially useful is A. Milano's "Considerazioni sulla lotta dei Monti di Pietà contro il prestito ebraico," in *Scritti in memoria di Sally Mayer* (Jerusalem, 1956), pp. 199–223, and L. Poliakov, *Les banchieri juifs et la Saint-Siège du XIIIᵉ au XVIIᵉ siècle* (Paris, 1965) (English trans. by M. Kochan, *Jewish Bankers and the Holy See* [London, Boston, 1977]). Specific events relating to Jewish usury in the northern Italian communities are treated fully in the standard communal histories by Cassuto, Simonsohn, and Carpi. Additional references are found throughout this study.
2. On Bernardino of Feltre's activity in Ferrara, see L. de Besse, *Le bienheureux Bernardin de Feltre et son ouevre*, 2 vols. (Tours, 1902), 1:466; F. Casolini, *Bernardino da Feltre, il martello degli usurai* (Milan, 1939), p. 132; P. Norsa, *Una famiglia di banchieri: La famiglia Norsa (1350–1950)*, 2 vols. (Naples, 1953–59), 1:38; A. Balletti, *Gli Ebrei e gli Estensi* (Modena, 1914), p. 63. See also A. Parsons, "Bernardine of Feltre and the Montes Pietatis," *Franciscan Studies* 22 (1941): 11–32; R. Segre, "Bernardino da Feltre, i Monti di Pietà e i banchi ebraici," *Rivista Storica Italiana* 90 (1978): 818–33.

3. These events are fully described by Norsa, *Una famiglia*, 2:12–13; Balletti, *Gli Ebrei*, p. 64; and Frizzi, *Memorie per la storia de Ferrara*, 4 vols. (Ferrara, 1796), 4:229.

4. This is chapter 73 of *Magen Avraham*. It was originally published by S. Lowinger, "Selections from *Sefer Magen Avraham* of Abraham Farissol" (Hebrew), *Ha-Zofeh le-Hokhmat Yisra'el* 12 (1928), pp. 290–97. The only scholars to treat this chapter, albeit in a cursory manner, were S. Stein, "Interest taken from Jews by Gentiles," *JJS*, 1 (1956): 141–64, and H. H. Ben Sasson, *Toledot Yisra'el bi-mei ha-Beinayim* (Tel Aviv, 1969), pp. 18–19 (English trans., *A History of the Jewish people*, ed. H. H. Ben Sasson [Cambridge, Mass., 1976], p. 391).

5. The Christian charge is fully discussed in B. Nelson, *The Idea of Usury* (Princeton, 1949). Earlier Jewish responses to this Christian argument are found in *Vikku'ah bein ha-Melekh Alfonzo mi-Sefarad im Tomas he-Hak-ham* (in J. D. Eisenstein, *Ozar ha-Vikkuhim* [New York, 1928] p. 146); Joseph and David Kimhi, *Sefer ha-Berit u-Vikkuhei Radak im ha-Nazrut*, ed. F. Talmage (Jerusalem, 1974), p. 27; and Joseph Albo; *Sefer ha-Ikkarim*, (Soncinco 1485), ed. I. Husik, 5 vols (Philadelphia, 1929–30), pp. 237–38. See also J. Rosenthal, "Interest from the Gentile" (Hebrew), *Talpiot* 5 (1951–52): 475–92 and 6 (1953): 139–152, who in his second article reproduces Albo's response in full as well as that of Abravanel and Farissol on Edom. See also Stein, "Interest," pp. 141–54. On Edom and Esau as symbols in medieval Jewish literature, see G. D. Cohen, "Esau as Symbol in Early Medieval Thought," *Jewish Medival and Renaissance Studies*, ed. A. Altmann (Cambridge, Mass., 1967), pp. 19–48.

6. This argument is mentioned, for example, by Albo in his disputation and by Abravanel in his commentary on Deuteronomy 23. It is more fully discussed in reference to Farissol's response below; consult also the additional Christian sources presented there.

7. Cited by R. Chazan, "Anti-Usury Efforts in Thirteenth-Century Narbonne and the Jewish Response," *PAAJR* 41–42 (1973–74): 61. Chazan identifies the war with the great baron as a probable reference to the abortive uprising of Raymond VII of Toulouse in mid-1242. The quotation was also partially cited earlier by Baron, *Social and Religious History*, 4:224, from "Rapport sur une mission scientifique dans le Midi de la France," ed. A. Neubauer, in *Archives des missions scientifiques et littéraires*, 3d ser., 1 (1873): 556–58. See also S. Stein, "A Disputation on Moneylending between Jews and Gentiles in Me'ir b. Simeon's *Milhemeth Miswah*," *JJS* 10 (1959): 45–63; idem, "The Development of the Jewish Law on Interest from the Biblical Period to the Expulsion from England," *HJ* 17 (1955): 33–34; and idem, *Jewish Christian Disputations in Thirteenth-Century Narbonne* (London, 1969); H. Gross, "Meir ben Simeon und seine Schrift *Milchemeth Mizwa*," *MGWJ* 30 (1881): 295–305, 442–52, 554–69; and *EJ*, 12:2156–57 and the additional bibliography there. R. Chazan has also treated the sections

on usury in the *Milḥemet Miẓvah* in his "A Jewish Plaint to Saint Louis," *HUCA* 45 (1974): 287–305.

8. J. Mann, "Une source de l'histoire juive au XIIIe siècle: La lettre polémique de Jacob b. Elie à Pablo Christiani," *REJ* 82 (1926): 363–77. The original letter was published by J. Kobak in *Jeschurun* 6 (1868): 1–34.

9. The passage is quoted in a rather free English translation by Stein, "Interest," pp. 153–54, where Stein adds: "It represents the first known Jewish attempt at an economic theory which foreshadows the general development towards capitalism so characteristic of the sixteenth century." The entire section is found in all editions of Abravanel's commentary to Deuteronomy, chap. 23; it is most accurately presented, however, in his *Mirkevet ha-Mishnah* (Sabbioneta, 1551), p. 77b, which I consulted. Whether Farissol made use of Abravanel's commentary is difficult to say. Farissol may have written the chapter either around the time of the debate (1487–90) or sometime after Abravanel had completed his commentary in 1496—perhaps as late as 1507, when the issue of Jewish usury was so prominent in Ferrara. That Farissol knew Abravanel's writings is proven by his extensive use of the latter's *Naḥalat Avot* in the writing of his own commentary to *Avot*. Cf. D. B. Ruderman, *The World of a Renaissance Jew: The Life and Thought of Abraham ben Mordecai Farissol* (Cincinnati, 1981), chapter 9, note 33.

10. St. Thomas Aquinas, *Summa Theologica*, English translation of the Fathers of the English Dominican Province, 20 vols. (London, 1911–35), vol. 2, q. 78, art. 1, pp. 330–31. The same definition of usury is articulated by Bernardino of Siena, *Opera omnia*, 7 vols. (Florence, 1950–59), *Quadragesimale De Evangelio aeterno*, vol. 4, sermo 36, cap. 2, p. 207: "Quod usura committitur solum in iis quae consistunt in numero, pondere et mensura." See also R. De Roover, *San Bernardino of Siena and Sant' Antonino of Florence* (Boston, 1967), p. 29.

11. Since the manuscript versions of this chapter are essentially the same, I will conveniently quote from Löwinger's text unless otherwise indicated. The argument above is found on pp. 291–92. It essentially follows the traditional Christian proofs. See especially Bernardino, *De Evangelio aeterno*, vol. 4, sermo 38, art. 2, pp. 254–58.

12. Löwinger, "Selections," pp. 290–91.

13. Aristotle *Ethics* 5. 7; *Politics* 1. 10; J. Schumpeter, *A History of Economic Analysis* (New York, 1954), p. 108.

14. What follows is essentially based on J. T. Noonan, Jr., *The Scholastic Analysis of Usury* (Cambridge, Mass., 1957), pp. 37–60.

15. Ibid., pp. 51, 81.

16. Ibid., pp. 51, 62, 81.

17. Ibid., pp. 62, 75. Noonan's comprehensive examination of these arguments makes it unnecessary to elaborate them here. See especially his presentation of Conrad Summenhart's twenty-two demonstrations of the unnaturalness of usury in his *Tractatus de contractibus* (Noonan, *The Scholastic Analysis,*

pp. 340–43). See also a similar analysis of the scholastic natural-law arguments in E. V. Bohm, *Capital and Interest: A Critical History of Economic Theory* (New York, 1957), pp. 21–24, and in R. H. Tawney, *Religion and the Rise of Capitalism* (New York, 1948), p. 41.

18. Quoted by Noonan, *The Scholastic Analysis*, p. 60.

19. Ibid., pp. 77–80. See B. Jarrett, S. *Antonino and Medieval Economics* (London, 1914), pp. 64–68.

20. Cf. Bernardino, *De Evangelio aeterno*, vol. 4, sermo 38, cap. 10, p. 252. The other natural-law arguments used by Bernardino can be found especially in this sermon, entitled: "Quod lege naturae, Scripturae et Sanctae Ecclesiae prohibetur usura," pp. 241–54. See Noonan's summary in *The Scholastic Analysis*, pp. 71–77.

21. This basically summarizes Farissol's third, fourth, fifth, and sixth arguments; cf. Löwinger, "Selections," pp. 293–96. For earlier versions of the same Jewish responses, see the references in note 5 above.

22. Löwinger, "Selections," p. 292.

23. Aquinas, *Summa theologica*, q. 66, art. 2, p. 224.

24. In this he followed Duns Scotus, who justified private property. Bernardino, *De Evangelio aeterno*, vol. 4, sermo 32, cap. 1, p. 120. See De Roover, *San Bernardino*, pp. 8–9, and R. Schlatter, *Private Property: The History of an Idea* (New Brunswick, N.J., 1954), p. 63.

25. Aquinas, *Summa theologica*, q. 77, art. 4, p. 327. See also E. Monroe, *Early Economic Thought* (Cambridge, Mass., 1954), p. 63.

26. Bernardino (*De Evangelio aeterno*, 4:140–49) discussed trade and profits in the first part of sermo 33, entitled: "De mercationibus et artificibus in generali et de conditionibus licitis et illicitis earumdem." Se also De Roover, *San Bernardino*, pp. 10–11.

27. Like Bernardino, Antonino quoted Augustine's dictum to justify the licitness of trade and moderate profit. Cf. S. Antonino, *Summa theologica*, 4 vols. (Verona, 1740), vol. 3, cap. 1, p. 293. See also De Roover, *San Bernardino*, pp. 14–16. On the general scholastic view of trade and the merchant, see J. W. Baldwin, "The Medieval Merchant before the Bar of Canon Law," *Michigan Academy of Science, Arts, and Letters* 44 (1959): 287–99, and R. De Roover, "The Scholastic Attitude toward Trade and Entrepreneurship," *Explorations in Entrepreneurial History*, 2d ser., 1 (1963–64): 76–87.

28. See Aquinas, *Summa theologica*, q. 78, art. 1, p. 331; Bernardino, *De Evangelio aeterno*, vol. 4, sermo 37, art. 1, pp. 223–24; De Roover, *San Bernardino*, p. 29.

29. Antonino, *Summa*, 3:293: "Finis mercedis suae debet esse, ut ex ea possit se & alios gubernare, & providere secundum statum suum; finis sustentationis sui & suorum debet esse, ut possint vivere virtuose." See also Bernardino, *De Evangelio aeterno*, vol. 4, sermo 25, art. 2, caps. 2 and 3, p. 198, and De Roover, *San Bernardino*, pp. 23–27.

30. Löwinger, "Selections," pp. 292–93.

31. Ibid., p. 293.
32. The entire bull of the Council is found in H. J. Schroeder, *Disciplinary Decrees of the General Councils* (St. Louis-London, 1937), pp. 639–41. The controversy over the *Monti di Pietà* is discussed by B. Nelson, *The Idea*, p. 19. On the *Monti* in general, see H. Holzapfel, *Die Anfänge des Montes Pietatis (1462–1515)* (Munich, 1903), and more recently, B. Pullan, *Rich and Poor in Renaissance Venice* (Cambridge, Mass., 1971), pp. 451–75, and the extensive bibliography found there. Whether Farissol was referring to the decision of the Lateran Council or simply to the general practice of the *Monti* long before 1515 is unclear. If the former is the case, it would suggest that he wrote this chapter as late as 1515.
33. Löwinger, "Selections," p. 293.
34. Cf. W. J. Ashley, *An Introduction to English Economic History and Theory*, 2 vols. (New York–London, 1906–9), 1:405–9.
35. Ibid., p. 419.
36. Löwinger, "Selections," p. 296. A later Italian Jewish writer, David de Pomi, utilized a similar argument when he wrote "that the moneylending of the Jews does not come under the name of usury, but rather of a contract agreed upon between an assembly of Christians and Jews publicly, and after mature considerations. . . . Moreover, one can only think that things which are allowed to spread by public consent must have been instituted to suit the convenience of all." Quoted in translation by H. Friedenwald, "Apologetic Works of Jewish Physicians," *JQR*, n.s. 32 (1941–42): 243 (reprinted in Friedenwald, *The Jews and Medicine*, 1:43). See also Stein, "Interest," p. 160.
37. Bernardino, *De Evangelio aeterno*, vol. 4, sermo 35, cap. 3, pp. 198–99. The scholastic concept of just price has been treated in De Roover, *San Bernardino*, pp. 16–23; "Scholastic Economics: Survival and Lasting Influence from the Sixteenth Century to Adam Smith," *Quarterly Journal of Economics* 69 (1955): 164; "The Concept of the Just Price: Theory and Economic Policy," *Journal of Economic History* 18 (1958): 418–34. See also Schumpeter, *A History of Economic Analysis*, p. 97; Noonan, *The Scholastic Analysis*, pp. 82–89; Tawney, *Religion and the Rise of Capitalism* (New York, 1948) pp. 42–43; and J. W. Baldwin, "The Medieval Theories of the Just Price," *Transactions of the American Philosophical Society*, n.s. 49 (1959): 3–92, reprinted in *Pre-Capitalist Economic Thought*.
38. See Noonan, *The Scholastic Analysis*, pp. 89–93.
39. See De Roover's discussion of *poena detentori, damnum emergens*, and *lucrum cessans* in his *San Bernardino*, pp. 30–33, and Noonan's more extensive treatment in *The Scholastic Analysis*, pp. 115–28, 249–68.
40. See Noonan, *The Scholastic Analysis*, pp. 171–92, 311–39, and De Roover, *San Bernardino*, pp. 33–38. See also by the latter, *The Rise and Decline of the Medici Bank* (Cambridge, Mass., 1963); *L'évolution de la lettre de change XIVe–XVIIIe siècles* (Paris, 1953); and F. C. Lane, "Investment and

Usury," *Explorations in Entrepreneurial History* 2 (1964): 3–15, reprinted in *Venice and History* (Baltimore, 1966), pp. 56–68.
41. Noonan, *The Scholastic Analysis*, p. 331.
42. Quoted in ibid., p. 371.
43. Ibid., pp. 371–76, and see there the other later theorists who held similar positions until Jeremy Bentham's famous defense of usury in 1818.
44. De Roover bases his discussion on Bernardino, *De Evangelio aeterno*, vol. 4, sermo 35, cap. 1, p. 191. De Roover's discussion is found in his *San Bernardino*, pp. 18–23, and in his article "Ancient and Medieval Economic Thought" in the *International Encyclopedia of the Social Sciences*, 17 vols. (New York, 1968), 4:432. See also Schumpeter, *A History of Economic Analysis*, p 98, who wrongly attributes the origin of this value theory to Antonino of Florence and not Bernardino; and Noonan, *The Scholastic Analysis*, pp. 83–84.
45. Löwinger, "Selections," p. 296.
46. See the *EJ*, 16:32; *New Catholic Encyclopedia*, 14:499; *Encyclopedia of Religion and Ethics*, ed. J. Hastings, 13 vols. (Edinburgh-New York, 1908–26), 12:551. On the decree of the Fourth Lateran Council, see S. Grayzel, *The Church and the Jews in the XIIIth Century* (New York, 1966), p. 306. Stein, "Interest," p. 157, identifies this passage with the position of Alexander VI Borgia (1492–1503). Yet papal acceptance of Jewish usury, if not always in theory at least in practice, certainly predated Alexander by centuries. Compare the view of Marquardus de Susannis, in his legal tract *De Iudaeis* (1558), summarized by K. Stow, *Catholic Thought and Papal Jewry Policy* pp. 87–89; and compare also L. Poliakov, *Les banchieri*, chap. 5.
47. Löwinger, "Selections," p. 296.
48. On this tax fallacy, see E. R. Rolph, "Taxation—general," in *International Encyclopedia of the Social Sciences*, 16:525.
49. Löwinger, "Selections," pp. 296–97.
50. The available knowledge on Italian interest rates in Farissol's lifetime is discussed by S. Homer, *A History of Interest Rates* (New Brunswick, N.J., 1963), pp. 106, 110. Pullan, *Rich and Poor*, p. 446, suggests that the rate of private usurers could be lowered to as little as 12 percent.
51. Löwinger, "Selections," p. 297.

Index

Claudius (Roman emperor), 141, 149, 164

Clement III (Guibert of Ravenna; anti-pope), 235

Clement III (pope), 237, 243, 253 n42

Clement IV (pope), 237, 243, 254 nn57, 60, 63, 258 n96

Clement V (pope), 412

Clement VI (pope), 242, 243, 253 n46, 255 n68

Clement VII (anti-pope), 243

Clement VIII (pope), 407

Clement XIII (pope), 257 n91

Clement XIV (pope), 257 n91

Clementine literature, 119
  First Epistle, 67

Clermont, Councils of, 195, 266, 268

Clichy, Council of (626/7), 195

Coelestine III (pope), 237, 243

Coelestine V (pope), 237, 243

Coimbra, 278. *See also* Spain

"Collection of Nine Books, The," 204

Cologne, 270, 283
  Jews expelled from, 349
  Jews slaughtered in, 283, 469, 480
  See also Germanic Empire/Germany

Colossians, Epistle to, 42, 67, 101
  on the Elect, 45, 66
  See also New Testament (NT); Paul

Commercial Revolution, 280, 282. *See also* economic conditions

Commodian (Christian Latin poet), 146

Concerning Heretics (Calvin), 392

confiscation of property. *See* property, Jewish

Conrad II (emperor), 215

Constant and Irene, papal letter to, 198

Constantine I (Roman emperor), 131, 160, 347
  conversion of, 11, 138
  period following rule of, 108, 155, 178, 181

Constantius (Roman emperor), 171 n102

Constitutio pro Judaeis (papal law), 285–286, 421 n24

Contra Judaeos (Isidore of Seville), 175

conversion to Christianity, 26, 136, 152, 315, 402
  and baptismal ritual, 184

canon law and, 194, 196, 203, 204, 225

eschatology and, 265, 266, 347

"falsification" of Bible to prevent, 217
  (*see also* Hebrew Bible)

forced, 23, 208–209, 300, 348
  Calvin on, 391
  canon law and, 194, 196, 269
  crusades and, 207, 233, 235, 249, 269, 470
  vs. exile or death, 200, 281, 501
  ritual murder libels and, 240–241
  Sicut Judeis and, 233–234, 243, 249

French monarchs and, 495

of Gentiles, 443, 449, 450

increase in numbers, 406

Jewish funds financing, 25

large-scale, 406, 495

in "last days," 265, 266

Luther and, 23, 352–353, 354, 357, 362, 368

miracles and, 201, 206, 304, 307

of Moses the Jew (Peter Alfonsi), 316

in nascent church, 443, 448, 458

papal policy centralized, 406

of polemicists, 505

prayers for, 206, 285

proselytization for, 205–209, 212, 249–250, 322 (*see also* Paul)

"purification" of Jew during, 288–289, 301

and reversion to Judaism, 201, 207, 208, 235, 240, 249, 348

of Saul (later Paul), 101, 119, 346

of slaves, Jewish fears of, 212

and Talmud, prohibition vs. use, 402–419

toleration linked with, 26, 403–404, 406

See also baptism; Marranos, the

conversion to Islam, *see* Moslems/Islam

conversion to Judaism, 15, 27, 433–434
  attraction to, 195, 199, 211
  as cause for expulsion, 281
  Christian agreement with OT and, 195
  circumcision in, 354, 355, 434, 442, 461
  forced (vs. death), 213
  heredity and, 434

(see also as "deliberate unbelievers,"
above)
as "subhuman" beings, 286, 298, 308
tannaitic view of, 434 *(see also* Tanna-
itic thought)
unity of, 134, 443, 444
violence against, *see* Christian anti-Sem-
itism
See also Judaism
Joannes Andreae, 339 n46
Joannes Teutonicus, 319
Joan of Arc, 114
Job, 145, 358
Book of, 477
Johannes Faventinus, 319
Johann Friedrich, elector of Saxony, 353–
354, 365, 370
Johann of Küstrin, Margrave of Neumark,
365
John (convert to Judaism; later Obadiah),
214
John (unknown author of Revelation),
263
John, Bishop of Speyer, 283
John, Epistles of. *See* Epistles
John, Gospel of. *See* John the Evangelist
and Johannine writings
John, king of England, 280
John XVIII (pope), 198, 200, 227 n10
John XXII (pope), 242, 258 n96
John Chrysostom, 139, 153, 161, 163,
179, 182, 497
and anti-Jewish laws, 158
the Christian theology, 11
and "deicide," 167 n24, 178
and Jews as "plague," 141, 154, 164
motivation of polemic of, 8
sermons against Jews, 13, 147–151,
175
sympathy of, 163
vilifies synagogue, 183
John of Capistrano, 256 n87, 259 n102
John of Damascene, 178
John the Baptist, 60, 62, 88 n163
John the Evangelist and Johannine writings, 42, 61, 65, 66, 446
and Church leadership, 118
Crucifixion as viewed by, 138–139
dualism of, 43, 44, 186

on flesh and Spirit, 63, 68, 70, 75
hostility predicted by, 90–91
Judaeans/Jews as viewed by, 90–98
paralleled by DSS, 39–40, 47
Paul compared to, 99
on predestination, 44
See also Fourth Gospel; Gospels; New
Testament (NT)
Jonathan b. Uzziel, 340 n52
R. Jose b. Judah, 440
R. Jose ha-Gelili, 448
Josel of Rosheim, 353–355, 364, 389–
390
Diary of, 389, 399 n24
Joseph (patriarch), 179, 376 n45, 397–
398 n20
Josephus, Flavius, 110 n19, 119, 166 n12,
170 n91, 309 n5, 521
on baptism, 60, 61
and Christianity as "sect of Judaism,"
89
on Daniel (Book of), 437
on the Essenes, 50–51, 79 n17
on miracles, 123, 302
on Pharisees and Sadducees, 89, 436,
437–438, 452 n20
repudiation of, 385
Joshua (Book of), Masius' commentary
on, 410
R. Joshua b. Levi, 309 n1
Jubilees (Book of), 52
Judaea, 96, 124, 383, 442
capitulation of Hasmonean, 4
destruction of, 450 *(see also*
Jerusalem)
Judaeans
Johannine view of, 8, 92–98
as known entity, 96
Roman view of, 99
use of term, 92
Judah, tribe of, 376 n45
Judah Halevi, 501
R. Judah the Prince, 440
Judaism
attractions of, 136 *(see also* conversion
to Judaism)
basic principles contradicted, 121–122
Christian need for, Christianity as "sect"
of, Christianity's similarity to,

paganism, 104, 108, 118 n91, 158, 177, 197, 299, 300, 356
  anti-Christianism of, 99, 135, 487
  anti-Semitism of, *see* Christian anti-Semitism (pagan roots of)
  Christian attacks on, 156, 161
  and Greco-Roman writings, 398 n20, 436
  Jewish rejection of, 163
  missionary activity against/conversion of, 205, 209, 265, 448
  protection of Jews under, 158, 159–160
  of slaves, 212, 468 n17
  temples of, 223–224, 265
Palestine, 121, 132, 263, 364
  anti-Roman messianism, 134
  anti-Semitism in, 157
  Jewish Christianity predominant in, 449, 450
  Jewish community in, 28, 29
  liturgical material from, 446
  pilgrimages to, 264 (*see also* crusade[s])
  as setting for Gospels, 95, 96, 97, 107
papacy and papal policy. *See* Roman Catholic Church; *Sicut Judeis* (papal bull); *entries for individual popes*
paradigms, 475–476
Paris
  Councils of (614/5, 829), 195, 202
  "disputation" in (1240), 504
  Jewish community in, 279 (*see also* France)
  Talmud burned in (1242), 324, 326
  University of, 20, 327
Parkes, James, 144, 158, 163, 170 n101
Paschasius Radbertus, 222
Passion narrative. Jewish acceptance of, 10. *See also* Gospels
Passion play, 398 n20
Passover, 197, 211, 305–306, 349, 459
Pastoureaux mobs (1320), 486
Paul, 76, 86–87 n141, 107, 224, 339 n49
  and anti-Semitism, 12, 137, 271, 387
  vs. concept of Jewish remnant, 162, 180
  attacked by Jews, disappears from history, 122
  on baptism, 62

central element of theology of, 100
as chief figure in missionary activity, 117
Christianity as developed by, 7, 98–101, 117, 119, 346, 450
  vs. Jerusalem Church, 118–122, 126
on circumcision, 358
compared to John and Matthew, 99, 106
conversion of, 101, 119, 346
death of Jesus as viewed by, *see* Crucifixion, the
dualism of, 58, 75, 186
and the Elect, 60, 66, 121
Epistles of, *see* Pauline Epistles
guilt of, 289
impact on Jews of message of, 265
rabbinic view of, 29
and relationship of "Israel" and community, 7, 55, 60
social setting of, 98–101
on Spirit/flesh and Spirit, 62, 63–64, 65, 68, 70, 73–75
and the two Covenants, 58, 59–60
Paul, "Brother." *See* Pablo Christiani
Paul III (pope), 247
Paul IV (pope), 404, 405–406
Pauline Epistles, 9, 44, 74, 80 nn35, 39, 81 n46
  on "another Gospel," 118–120
  and Christianity as "sect of Judaism," 90
  contrasted to Fourth Gospel, 98–101
  DSS paralleling, 39–44, 46–49
  dualism of, 41–44
  See also Colossians; Corinthians; Ephesians; Galatians; Hebrews; Paul; Philippians; Romans; Thessalonians
Paulo Alvaro of Cordova, 210, 215, 217, 219
Paul of Antioch ("Paul the Jew"), 383
Paul of Burgos, 353, 357, 358, 359
Paulus Christianus, 258 n97
Pavia, 216
  Council of (850), 202
pawnbroking. *See* moneylending
Peasants' Crusade. *See* crusade(s)
Pelikan, Jaroslav, 323
Pellican, Conrad, 396 n7

basic text of, 232
as *constitutio*, 231, 241, 244
crusades as impetus for, 235, 236, 238
decline of, 16, 242–247, 248–250
fees involved, 237
and forced conversions, 233–234, 243, 249
renewal discontinued, 237
rescinded, restored, 245–247
ritual murder charges prohibited by, 16, 239–241, 254 n64, 257 n91
as source of canon law, 231, 237, 241
Sifra quoted, 441
Sigismund, king of Germany, 256 nn75, 77
Simeon Ha-Faqoli, 445
R. Simeon the Great of Mainz, 201
Simeon Stylites, 157
Simon, Marcel, 3, 11, 12, 487
Simon Magus, 76
Simon (of *Altercatio*), 152
Simon of Gambs, 418
Simon of Trent, "Saint," 247, 306
Sinai, as formative event, 434, 436
Sirleto, Cardinal, 301, 406, 410, 418
Sixtus IV (pope), 247
Sixtus V (pope), 406
Sixtus of Siena, 408, 412, 416–417
slaves
    canon laws regarding, 195, 201, 202, 203, 204
    circumcision of, 358, 461
    Jewish ownership of, 202, 212
        and conversion of, to Judaism, 212, 214, 461–462
        prohibited, 195, 201, 203, 204
    Jews as, 133
        "of crown," 286, 349
        and *servi camerae*, 496–497
Smalley, Beryl, 15, 313, 314, 315, 320
social class, social dealings. *See* Jews; slaves; warrior class, medieval
Socrates, 114
Sodom, 178, 439
Solomon, builds Temple, 479. *See also* Temple(s)
Solomon b. Isaac. *See* Rashi
Solomon b. Samson, 470, 471, 476, 477, 481

Solomon b. Simon, 273 n13
Solomon de' Rossi, 492, 494, 498, 507 n21, 513 n84
Sombart, Werner, 25, 393
Southern, Richard W., 317
Spain, 243, 245, 386
    Christian Reconquest of, 234, 278, 282–283
    Church Councils in, 201 (*see also* Council[s])
    disputations in, 299, 504
    forced conversions in, 300
    Jewish communities in, 278, 364
        attacked, 156, 207, 282, 304
        ritual murder charges against, 287
    Jews expelled from, 16, 257 n94, 304, 360
    Moslem, 199, 201, 212–213, 269
    papal letters to, 197, 199, 200, 234, 247, 256 n79
    the Talmud in, 402, 504
    unification policy in, 194
    urban charters in, 286
    Visigothic, 194, 225, 234
    See also Inquisition, the
Speyer, 365
    Jews in, 277, 283, 482
        expelled, 349
        massacred, 469, 473, 475, 481
Spirit
    DSS and NT expression of, 63–76
    flesh and, 67–76
Stanton, Graham, 102
Stephen, 139, 146, 156, 168 n59, 177, 346
Stephen, king of England, 280
Stephen III (pope), 197, 200
Stow, Kenneth R., 25, 26
Strasbourg, 283, 354, 364, 365
    Calvin in, 381, 382, 389
Sturm, Jacob, 381
suicide, 30, 31, 281, 469, 472–481 *passim*
summa, the, 323
Summa theologica (Antonino), 523
Summa theologica (Thomas Aquinas), 518
Summa universae theologiae (Alexander of Hales), 326
Summenhart, Conrad, 532 n17

About the Editor

Jeremy Cohen is Samuel and Esther Melton Professor of Jewish History at The Ohio State University and Associate Professor in Jewish History at Tel Aviv University. He has written two books, *The Friars and the Jews: The Evolution of Medieval Anti-Judaism* (1982) and *"Be Fertile and Increase, Fill the Earth and Master It": The Ancient and Medieval Career of a Biblical Text* (1989), both of which received the National Jewish Book Award for scholarship.